Microsoft

MCSA/MCSE

Exam 70-290

Managing and
Maintaining a Microsoft

WINDOWS
SERVER™ 2003
ENVIRONMENT

Dan Holme and Orin Thomas

Self-Paced

Training Kit

PUBLISHED BY
Microsoft Press
A Division of Microsoft Corporation
One Microsoft Way
Redmond, Washington 98052-6399

Library of Congress Cataloging-in-Publication Data
Holme, Dan.
    MCSA/MCSE Self-Paced Training Kit (Exam 70-290): Managing and Maintaining a
  Microsoft Windows Server 2003 Environment / Dan Holme, Orin Thomas.
        p. cm.
    Includes index.
     ISBN 0-7356-1437-7
     ISBN 0-7356-1953-0 (Core Requirements)
     1. Electronic data processing personnel--Certification.   2. Microsoft
  software--Examinations--Study guides.   3. Microsoft Windows Server   I. Thomas, Orin.
  II. Title

   QA76.3.H668   2003
   005.7'13769--dc21   2003053990

Printed and bound in the United States of America.

1 2 3 4 5 6 7 8 9   QWT   8 7 6 5 4 3

Distributed in Canada by H.B. Fenn and Company Ltd.

A CIP catalogue record for this book is available from the British Library.

Microsoft Press books are available through booksellers and distributors worldwide. For further information about international editions, contact your local Microsoft Corporation office or contact Microsoft Press International directly at fax (425) 936-7329. Visit our Web site at www.microsoft.com/mspress. Send comments to *tkinput@microsoft.com*.

Active Directory, Microsoft, Microsoft Press, MS-DOS, Windows, the Windows logo, Windows NT, and Windows Server are either registered trademarks or trademarks of Microsoft Corporation in the United States and/or other countries. Other product and company names mentioned herein may be the trademarks of their respective owners.

The example companies, organizations, products, domain names, e-mail addresses, logos, people, places, and events depicted herein are fictitious. No association with any real company, organization, product, domain name, e-mail address, logo, person, place, or event is intended or should be inferred.

"Three Views of Share Permissions" reprinted by permission from Intelliem, Inc.

For Microsoft Press:
Acquisitions Editor: Kathy Harding
Project Editor: Karen Szall

SubAsy Part No. X09-72357
Body Part No. X08-16601

For nSight Publishing Services:
Project Manager: Susan H. McClung
Copyeditor: Peter Tietjen
Technical Editor: Bob Hogan
Desktop Publishing Specialist: Patty Fagan
Proofreaders: Jan Cocker, Jolene Lehr, Katie
    O'Connell, Robert Saley
Indexer: James Minkin

Dan Holme

A graduate of Yale University and Thunderbird, the American Graduate School of International Management, Dan has spent 10 years as a consultant and trainer, delivering solutions to tens of thousands of IT Professionals from the most prestigious organizations and corporations around the world. His clients have included AT&T, Compaq, HP, Boeing, Home Depot, and Intel, and he has recently been involved supporting the design and implementation of Active Directory at enterprises including Raytheon, ABN AMRO, Johnson & Johnson, Los Alamos National Laboratories and General Electric. Dan is the Director of Training Services for Intelliem, which specializes in boosting the productivity of IT professionals and end users by creating advanced, customized solutions that integrate clients' specific design and configuration into productivity-focused training and knowledge management services (info@intelliem.com). From his base in sunny Arizona, Dan travels to client sites around the world, and then unwinds on his favorite mode of transportation—his snowboard. It takes a village to raise a happy geek, and Dan sends undying thanks and love to those, without whom, sanity would be out of reach: Lyman, Barb & Dick, Bob & Joni, Stan & Marylyn & Sondra, Mark, Kirk, John, Beth, Dan & June, Lena and the entire crazy commando crew.

Orin Thomas

Orin is a writer, editor and systems administrator who works for the certification advice Web site Certtutor.net. His work in IT has been varied: he's done everything from providing first level networking support to acting in the role of systems administrator for one of Australia's largest companies. He has authored several articles for technical publications as well as contributing to The Insider's Guide to IT Certification. He holds the MCSE, CCNA, CCDA and Linux+ certifications. He holds a bachelor's degree in Science with honors from the University of Melbourne and is currently working toward the completion of a Ph.D in Philosophy of Science. Orin would like to thank his beautiful, amazing wife Oksana for being more wonderful and loving than he could ever have dreamed. Orin wants to thank their son Rooslan for making fatherhood so easy and fun. He would also like to thank the following friends and family: Ma, Mick, Lards, Gillian, Lee, Neil, Will, Jon, Alexander, Irina, Stas and Kasia as well as the entire Certtutor.net tutor team who offer great free advice to those who are interested in getting certified.

Contents at a Glance

Practices

Tables

Troubleshooting Labs

Case Scenario Exercises

Contents

Part II   Prepare for the Exam

14   Managing and Maintaining Physical and Logical Devices (1.0)   14-3

15   Managing Users, Computers, and Groups (2.0)   15-1

Part III   Appendix—Terminal Server

About This Book

Welcome to *MCSA/MCSE Self-Paced Training Kit (Exam 70-290): Managing and Maintaining a Microsoft Windows Server 2003 Environment.* We have designed this book to prepare you effectively for the MCSE examination, and, along the way, to share with you knowledge about what it takes to implement Windows Server 2003 in your enterprise network. We hope that by helping you understand the underlying technologies, the variety of options for configuring feature sets, and the complex interaction among components, you are better equipped to tackle the challenges that you face in the information technology (IT) trenches. We also hope to serve the community at large—to elevate the worth of the MCSE moniker—so that behind each certification is a knowledgeable, experienced, capable professional.

Note For more information about becoming a Microsoft Certified Professional, see the section titled "The Microsoft Certified Professional Program," later in this introduction.

Intended Audience

This book was developed for IT professionals who plan to take the related Microsoft Certified Professional exam 70-290, *Managing and Maintaining a Microsoft Windows Server 2003 Environment*, as well as IT professionals who administer computers running Microsoft Windows Server 2003.

Note Exam skills are subject to change without prior notice and at the sole discretion of Microsoft.

Prerequisites

This training kit requires that students meet the following prerequisites:

- A minimum of 12 to 18 months of experience administering Windows technologies in a network environment.
- An understanding of Microsoft Active Directory directory service and related technologies, including Group Policy.

About the CD-ROM

For your use, this book includes a Supplemental Course Materials CD-ROM, which contains a variety of informational aids to complement the book content:

- The Microsoft Press Readiness Review Suite Powered by MeasureUp. This suite of practice tests and objective reviews contains questions of varying degrees of complexity and offers multiple testing modes. You can assess your understanding of the concepts presented in this book and use the results to develop a learning plan that meets your needs.

- An electronic version of this book (eBook). For information about using the eBook, see the section "The eBook," later in this introduction.

- An eBook of the *Microsoft Encyclopedia of Networking, Second Editon*, and of the *Microsoft Encyclopedia of Security* provide complete and up-to-date reference materials for networking and security.

- Sample chapters from several Microsoft Press books give you additional information about Windows Server 2003 and introduce you to other resources that are available from Microsoft Press.

A second CD-ROM contains a 180-day evaluation edition of Microsoft Windows Server 2003, Enterprise Edition.

> **Note**   The 180-day Evaluation Edition provided with this training kit is not the full retail product and is provided only for the purposes of training and evaluation. Microsoft Technical Support does not support this evaluation edition.

For additional support information regarding this book and the CD-ROM (including answers to commonly asked questions about installation and use), visit the Microsoft Press Technical Support Web site at *http://www.microsoft.com/mspress/support/*. You can also e-mail *tkinput@microsoft.com* or send a letter to Microsoft Press, Attention: Microsoft Press Technical Support, One Microsoft Way, Redmond, WA 98052-6399.

Features of This Book

This book has two parts. Use Part 1 to learn at your own pace and practice what you've learned with practical exercises. Part 2 contains questions and answers that you can use to test yourself on what you've learned.

Part 1: Learn at Your Own Pace

Each chapter identifies the exam objectives that are covered within the chapter, provides an overview of why the topics matter by identifying how the information applies in the real world, and lists any prerequisites that must be met to complete the lessons presented in the chapter.

The chapters contain a set of lessons. Lessons contain practices that include one or more hands-on exercises. These exercises give you an opportunity to use the skills being presented or explore the part of the application being described. Each lesson also has a set of review questions to test your knowledge of the material covered in that lesson.

After the lessons, you are given an opportunity to apply what you've learned in a case-scenario exercise. In this exercise, you work through a multistep solution for a realistic case scenario. You are also given an opportunity to work through a troubleshooting lab that explores difficulties you might encounter when applying what you've learned on the job.

Each chapter ends with a summary of key concepts and a short section listing key topics and terms that you need to know before taking the exam, summarizing the key learnings with a focus on the exam.

> **Real World   Helpful Information**
>
> You will find sidebars like this one that contain related information you might find helpful. "Real World" sidebars contain specific information gained through the experience of IT professionals just like you.

Part 2: Prepare for the Exam

Part 2 helps to familiarize you with the types of questions that you will encounter on the MCP exam. By reviewing the objectives and the sample questions, you can focus on the specific skills that you need to improve before taking the exam.

> **See Also**   For a complete list of MCP exams and their related objectives, go to *http://www.microsoft.com/traincert/mcp*.

Part 2 is organized by the exam's objectives. Each chapter covers one of the primary groups of objectives, called *Objective Domains*. Each chapter lists the tested skills you must master to answer the exam questions and includes a list of further readings to help you improve your ability to perform the tasks or skills specified by the objectives.

Within each Objective Domain, you will find the related objectives that are covered on the exam. Each objective provides you with the several practice exam questions. The answers are accompanied by explanations of each correct and incorrect answer.

> **Note**   These questions are also available on the companion CD as a practice test.

Informational Notes

Several types of reader aids appear throughout the training kit:

- **Tip** contains methods of performing a task more quickly or in a not-so-obvious way.
- **Important** contains information that is essential to completing a task.
- **Note** contains supplemental information.
- **Caution** contains valuable information about possible loss of data; be sure to read this information carefully.
- **Warning** contains critical information about possible physical injury; be sure to read this information carefully.
- **See Also** contains references to other sources of information.
- **Planning** contains hints and useful information that should help you to plan the implementation.
- **Security Alert** highlights information you need to know to maximize security in your work environment.
- **Exam Tip** flags information you should know before taking the certification exam.
- **Off the Record** contains practical advice about the real-world implications of information presented in the lesson.

Notational Conventions

The following conventions are used throughout this book.

- Characters or commands that you type appear in **bold** type.
- *Italic* in syntax statements indicates placeholders for variable information. Italic is also used for book titles.
- Names of files and folders appear in Title caps, except when you are to type them directly. Unless otherwise indicated, you can use all lowercase letters when you type a file name in a dialog box or at a command prompt.
- File name extensions appear in all lowercase.

- Acronyms appear in all uppercase.

- `Monospace` type represents code samples, examples of screen text, or entries that you might type at a command prompt or in initialization files.

- Square brackets [ ] are used in syntax statements to enclose optional items. For example, [*filename*] in command syntax indicates that you can choose to type a file name with the command. Type only the information within the brackets, not the brackets themselves.

- Braces { } are used in syntax statements to enclose required items. Type only the information within the braces, not the braces themselves.

Keyboard Conventions

- A plus sign (+) between two key names means that you must press those keys at the same time. For example, "Press Alt+Tab" means that you hold down Alt while you press Tab.

- A comma (,) between two or more key names means that you must press each of the keys consecutively, not together. For example, "Press Alt, F, X" means that you press and release each key in sequence. "Press Alt+W, L" means that you first press Alt and W at the same time, and then release them and press L.

Getting Started

This training kit contains hands-on exercises to help you learn about implementing, supporting, and troubleshooting Windows Server 2003 technologies. Use this section to prepare your self-paced training environment. Most of the exercises can be completed on a single test computer in a lab environment. Several optional exercises require a second computer running Microsoft Windows XP, which must be connected to each other on a network.

 Caution Exercises, as well as the changes you make to your test computer, may have undesirable results if you are connected to a larger network. Check with your network administrator before attempting these exercises.

Hardware Requirements

The test computer must have the following minimum configuration. All hardware should be on the Microsoft Windows Server 2003 Hardware Compatibility List, and should meet the requirements listed at *http://www.microsoft.com/windowsserver2003 /evaluation/sysreqs/default.mspx*.

- Minimum CPU: 133 MHz for *x*86-based computers (733 MHz is recommended) and 733 MHz for Itanium-based computers

- Minimum RAM: 128 MB (256 MB is recommended)

- Disk space for setup: 1.5 GB for *x*86-based computers and 2.0 GB for Itanium-based computers

- Display monitor capable of 800 × 600 resolution or higher

- CD-ROM or DVD-ROM drive

- Microsoft Mouse or compatible pointing device

Software Requirements

The following software is required to complete the procedures in this training kit:

- Windows Server 2003, Enterprise Edition (A 180-day evaluation edition of Windows Server 2003, Enterprise Edition, is included on the CD-ROM.)

- Windows XP Professional (Not included on the CD-ROM. Required in optional hands-on exercises only.)

Caution   The 180-day Evaluation Edition provided with this training is not the full retail product and is provided only for the purposes of training and evaluation. Microsoft Technical Support does not support evaluation editions. For additional support information regarding this book and the CD-ROMs (including answers to commonly asked questions about installation and use), visit the Microsoft Press Technical Support Web site at *http://mspress.microsoft.com/mspress/support/*. You can also e-mail *tkinput@microsoft.com* or send a letter to Microsoft Press, Attn: Microsoft Press Technical Support, One Microsoft Way, Redmond, Wash. 98052-6399.

Setup Instructions

Set up your computer according to the manufacturer's instructions. The server should be configured as follows:

- Windows Server 2003, Enterprise Edition

- Computer name: Server01

- Domain controller in the domain *contoso.com*

- 1 GB of unpartitioned disk drive space

If you are very comfortable with the installation of Windows Server 2003, you may configure the server using the above guidelines. Otherwise, you may use the more comprehensive setup instructions that are provided in Chapter 1.

The second computer will act as a Windows XP client for the optional hands-on exercises in the course.

> **Caution**   If your computers are connected to a larger network, you must verify with your network administrator that the computer names, domain name, and other information used in setting up Windows Server 2003 as described above and in Chapter 1 do not conflict with network operations. If they conflict, ask your network administrator to provide alternative values and use those values throughout all the exercises in this book.

The Readiness Review Suite

The CD-ROM includes a practice test of 300 sample exam questions and an objective review with an additional 125 questions. Use these tools to reinforce your learning and to identify any areas in which you need to gain more experience before taking the exam.

To install the practice test and objective review

1. Insert the Supplemental Materials CD-ROM into your CD-ROM drive.

> **Note**   If AutoRun is disabled on your machine, refer to the Readme.txt file on the CD-ROM.

2. Click Readiness Review Suite on the user interface menu and follow the prompts.

The eBooks

The CD-ROM includes an electronic version of this training kit, as well as eBooks for both the *Microsoft Encyclopedia of Security* and the *Microsoft Encyclopedia of Networking, Second Edition*. The eBooks are in portable document format (PDF) and can be viewed using Adobe Acrobat Reader.

To use the eBooks

1. Insert the Supplemental Materials CD-ROM into your CD-ROM drive.

> **Note**   If AutoRun is disabled on your machine, refer to the Readme.txt file on the CD-ROM.

2. Click Training Kit eBook on the user interface menu. You can also review any of the other eBooks that are provided for your use.

The Microsoft Certified Professional Program

The Microsoft Certified Professional (MCP) program provides the best method to prove your command of current Microsoft products and technologies. The exams and corresponding certifications are developed to validate your mastery of critical competencies as you design and develop, or implement and support, solutions with Microsoft products and technologies. Computer professionals who become Microsoft certified are recognized as experts and are sought after industrywide. Certification brings a variety of benefits to the individual and to employers and organizations.

 See Also For a full list of MCP benefits, go to *http://www.Microsoft.com/traincert/start /itpro.asp*.

Certifications

The Microsoft Certified Professional program offers multiple certifications, based on specific areas of technical expertise:

- *Microsoft Certified Professional (MCP)*. Demonstrated in-depth knowledge of at least one Microsoft Windows operating system or architecturally significant platform. An MCP is qualified to implement a Microsoft product or technology as part of a business solution for an organization.

- *Microsoft Certified Solution Developer (MCSD)*. Professional developers qualified to analyze, design, and develop enterprise business solutions with Microsoft development tools and technologies including the Microsoft .NET Framework.

- *Microsoft Certified Application Developer (MCAD)*. Professional developers qualified to develop, test, deploy, and maintain powerful applications using Microsoft tools and technologies including Microsoft Visual Studio .NET and XML Web services.

- *Microsoft Certified Systems Engineer (MCSE)*. Qualified to effectively analyze the business requirements, and design and implement the infrastructure for business solutions based on the Microsoft Windows and Microsoft Server 2003 operating system.

- *Microsoft Certified Systems Administrator (MCSA)*. Individuals with the skills to manage and troubleshoot existing network and system environments based on the Microsoft Windows and Microsoft Server 2003 operating systems.

- *Microsoft Certified Database Administrator (MCDBA)*. Individuals who design, implement, and administer Microsoft SQL Server databases.

- *Microsoft Certified Trainer (MCT)*. Instructionally and technically qualified to deliver Microsoft Official Curriculum through a Microsoft Certified Technical Education Center (CTEC).

Requirements for Becoming a Microsoft Certified Professional

The certification requirements differ for each certification and are specific to the products and job functions addressed by the certification.

To become a Microsoft Certified Professional, you must pass rigorous certification exams that provide a valid and reliable measure of technical proficiency and expertise. These exams are designed to test your expertise and ability to perform a role or task with a product, and are developed with the input of professionals in the industry. Questions in the exams reflect how Microsoft products are used in actual organizations, giving them "real-world" relevance.

- Microsoft Certified Product (MCP) candidates are required to pass one current Microsoft certification exam. Candidates can pass additional Microsoft certification exams to further qualify their skills with other Microsoft products, development tools, or desktop applications.

- Microsoft Certified Solution Developers (MCSDs) are required to pass three core exams and one elective exam. (MCSD for Microsoft .NET candidates are required to pass four core exams and one elective.)

- Microsoft Certified Application Developers (MCADs) are required to pass two core exams and one elective exam in an area of specialization.

- Microsoft Certified Systems Engineers (MCSEs) are required to pass five core exams and two elective exams.

- Microsoft Certified Systems Administrators (MCSAs) are required to pass three core exams and one elective exam that provide a valid and reliable measure of technical proficiency and expertise.

- Microsoft Certified Database Administrators (MCDBAs) are required to pass three core exams and one elective exam that provide a valid and reliable measure of technical proficiency and expertise.

- Microsoft Certified Trainers (MCTs) are required to meet instructional and technical requirements specific to each Microsoft Official Curriculum course they are certified to deliver. The MCT program requires on-going training to meet the requirements for the annual renewal of certification. For more information about becoming a Microsoft Certified Trainer, visit *http://www.microsoft.com/traincert /mcp/mct/* or contact a regional service center near you.

Technical Support

Every effort has been made to ensure the accuracy of this book and the contents of the companion disc. If you have comments, questions, or ideas regarding this book or the companion disc, please send them to Microsoft Press using either of the following methods:

E-mail: *tkinput@microsoft.com*

Postal Mail: Microsoft Press
                     Attn: *MCSA/MCSE Self-Paced Training Kit (Exam 70-290):
                     Managing and Maintaining a Microsoft Windows Server
                     2003 Environment,* Editor
                     One Microsoft Way
                     Redmond, WA 98052-6399

For additional support information regarding this book and the CD-ROM (including answers to commonly asked questions about installation and use), visit the Microsoft Press Technical Support Web site at *http://www.microsoft.com/mspress/support/.* To connect directly to the Microsoft Press Knowledge Base and enter a query, visit *http://www.microsoft.com/mspress/support/search.asp.* For support information regarding Microsoft software, please connect to *http://support.microsoft.com/.*

Evaluation Edition Software Support

The 180-day Evaluation Edition provided with this training is not the full retail product and is provided only for the purposes of training and evaluation. Microsoft and Microsoft Technical Support do not support this evaluation edition.

> **Caution**   The Evaluation Edition of Windows Server 2003, Enterprise Edition, included with this book should not be used on a primary work computer. The evaluation edition is unsupported. For online support information relating to the full version of Windows Server 2003, Enterprise Edition, that *might* also apply to the Evaluation Edition, you can connect to *http://support.microsoft.com/.*

Information about any issues relating to the use of this evaluation edition with this training kit is posted to the Support section of the Microsoft Press Web site (*http://www.microsoft.com/mspress/support/*). For information about ordering the full version of any Microsoft software, please call Microsoft Sales at (800) 426-9400 or visit *http://www.microsoft.com.*

Part I
Learn at Your Own Pace

1 Introducing Microsoft Windows Server 2003

This chapter does not cover specific exam objectives. After introducing the Microsoft Windows Server 2003 family of products, this chapter covers some installation and configuration considerations with a focus on what you need to know for the 70-290 certification exam.

Why This Chapter Matters

The purpose of this book is to empower you to manage and maintain a Microsoft Windows Server 2003 environment, and to prepare you effectively for the 70-290 certification examination. Although it is assumed that you have experience with Microsoft Windows technologies, the Windows Server 2003 family and Microsoft Active Directory directory service itself may be new to you. The goal of this chapter, therefore, is to introduce you to the multiple versions and editions of Windows Server 2003, so that you can identify the key distinctions among them and determine the mix of versions that will most effectively meet the needs of your organization. You will then be guided through the process of installing and configuring a Windows Server 2003 computer that functions as a domain controller in an Active Directory domain.

Lessons in this Chapter:

Before You Begin

This chapter will guide you through the steps required to configure a computer running Windows Server 2003. You will be able to use that computer for the hands-on exercises throughout this training kit. The computer should have at least one disk drive that can be erased and used to install Windows Server 2003.

Lesson 1: The Windows Server 2003 Family

Windows Server 2003 is, of course, more secure, more reliable, more available, and easier to administer than any previous version of Windows. Let's take a close look at the platform and how it compares to Microsoft Windows 2000. This lesson provides a brief overview of the Windows Server 2003 family, focusing on the differences among the product editions: Web Edition, Standard Edition, Enterprise Edition, and Datacenter Edition.

After this lesson, you will be able to

- Identify the key differences among the Windows Server 2003 versions

Estimated lesson time: 5 minutes

Windows Server 2003 Editions

Windows Server 2003 is an incremental update to the platform and technologies introduced in Windows 2000. If you are coming to Windows Server 2003 with experience from Windows 2000 servers, you will find the transition a relatively easy one. If your experience is with Windows NT 4, welcome to the new world!

But don't let the incremental nature of the updates mislead you; behind the upgrades are significant and long-awaited improvements to the security and reliability of the operating system and to the administrative toolset. In many books, this would be the place where you would get a laundry list of new features. Actually, the Windows Server 2003 list is extensive and there are features that make upgrading to Windows Server 2003 an obvious choice for almost any administrator. However, the particular features that appeal to you may be different from those that appeal to another IT professional.

You may be drawn to the significant features and improvements added to Active Directory, the new tools to support popular but complex GPOs, the enhancements to enterprise security, the improvements to Terminal Services, or a number of other enhanced capabilities of the new operating system. If you are considering a move to Windows Server 2003, take a good look through the Microsoft Web site for the platform, at *http://www.microsoft.com/windowsserver2003* and judge for yourself which improvements are, in your environment, truly significant.

Although the list of new features is extensive, the evaluation of the operating system becomes more interesting because Windows Server 2003 is available in multiple flavors including the 32-bit, 64-bit, and embedded versions. But the most important distinctions are those among the four product editions, listed here in order of available features and functionality, as well as by price:

- Windows Server 2003, Web Edition
- Windows Server 2003, Standard Edition
- Windows Server 2003, Enterprise Edition
- Windows Server 2003, Datacenter Edition

Web Edition

To position Windows Server 2003 more competitively against other Web servers, Microsoft has released a stripped-down-yet-impressive edition of Windows Server 2003 designed specifically for Web services. The feature set and licensing allows customers easy deployment of Web pages, Web sites, Web applications, and Web services.

Web Edition supports 2 gigabytes (GB) of RAM and a two-way symmetric multiprocessor (SMP). It provides unlimited anonymous Web connections but only 10 inbound server message block (SMB) connections, which should be more than enough for content publishing. The server cannot be an Internet gateway, DHCP or fax server. Although you can remotely administer the server with Remote Desktop, the server cannot be a terminal server in the traditional sense. The server can belong to a domain, but cannot be a domain controller. The included version of the Microsoft SQL Server Database Engine can support as many as 25 concurrent connections.

Standard Edition

Windows Server 2003, Standard Edition, is a robust, multipurpose server capable of providing directory, file, print, application, multimedia, and Web services for small to medium-sized businesses. Its comprehensive feature set is expanded, compared to Windows 2000, with Microsoft SQL Server Database Engine (MSDE), a version of SQL Server that supports five concurrent connections to databases up to 2 GB in size; a free, out-of-the-box Post Office Protocol version 3 (POP3) service which, combined with the included Simple Mail Transfer Protocol (SMTP) service, allows a server to function as a small, stand-alone mail server; and Network Load Balancing (NLB), a useful tool that was only included with the Advanced Server edition of Windows 2000.

The Standard Edition of Windows Server 2003 supports up to 4 GB of RAM and four-way SMP.

Note   Through Release Candidate (RC) 1 of Windows Server 2003, the beta and prerelease code supported only two processors. That limitation was removed in RC2, and the Standard Edition supports four processors. Documentation and resources that were created prior to release may contain misleading information regarding SMP support.

Enterprise Edition

The Enterprise Edition of Windows Server 2003 is designed to be a powerful server platform for medium- to large-sized businesses. Its enterprise-class features include support for eight processors, 32 GB of RAM, eight-node clustering (including clustering based on a Storage Area Network (SAN) and geographically dispersed clustering) and availability for 64-bit Intel Itanium-based computers, on which scalability increases to 64 GB of RAM and 8-way SMP.

Other features that distinguish the Enterprise Edition from the Standard Edition include:

- Support for Microsoft Metadirectory Services (MMS), which enables the integration of multiple directories, databases, and files with Active Directory.

- Hot Add Memory, so that you can add memory to supported hardware systems without downtime or reboot.

- Windows System Resource Manager (WSRM), which supports the allocation of CPU and memory resources on a per-application basis.

Datacenter Edition

The Datacenter Edition, which is available only as an OEM version as part of a high-end server hardware package, provides almost unfathomable scalability, with support on 32-bit platforms for 32-way SMP with 64 GB of RAM and on 64-bit platforms for 64-way SMP with 512 GB of RAM. There is also a 128-way SMP version that supports two 64-way SMP partitions.

64-Bit Editions

The 64-bit editions of Windows Server 2003, which run on Intel Itanium-based computers, provide for higher CPU clock speeds and faster floating-point processor operations than the 32-bit editions of Windows. CPU coding improvements and processing enhancements yield significantly faster computational operations. Increased access speed to an enormous memory address space allows for smooth operation of complex, resource-intensive applications, such as massive database applications, scientific analysis applications, and heavily accessed Web servers.

Some features of the 32-bit editions are not available in the 64-bit editions. Most notably, the 64-bit editions do not support 16-bit Windows application, real-mode applications, POSIX applications, or print services for Apple Macintosh clients.

Lesson Review

The following questions are intended to reinforce key information presented in this lesson. If you are unable to answer a question, review the lesson materials and try the question again. You can find answers to the questions in the "Questions and Answers" section at the end of this chapter.

1. You are planning the deployment of Windows Server 2003 computers for a department of 250 employees. The server will host the home directories and shared folders for the department, and it will serve several printers to which departmental documents are sent. Which edition of Windows Server 2003 will provide the most cost-effective solution for the department?

_____

_____

2. You are planning the deployment of Windows Server 2003 computers for a new Active Directory domain in a large corporation that includes multiple separate Active Directories maintained by each of the corporation's subsidiaries. The company has decided to roll out Exchange Server 2003 as a unified messaging platform for all the subsidiaries, and plans to use Microsoft Metadirectory Services (MMS) to synchronize appropriate properties of objects throughout the organization. Which edition of Windows Server 2003 will provide the most cost-effective solution for this deployment?

_____

_____

3. You are rolling out servers to provide Internet access to your company's e-commerce application. You anticipate four servers dedicated to the front-end Web application and one server for a robust, active SQL database. Which editions will provide the most cost-effective solution?

_____

_____

Lesson Summary

- Windows Server 2003 is available in 64-bit as well as 32-bit versions.

- The primary distinctions among versions of Windows Server 2003 are the product editions: Web Edition, Standard Edition, Enterprise Edition, and Datacenter Edition, each of which supports a subset of features honed to a specific purpose.

- Taken as a whole, Windows Server 2003 is an upgrade to Windows 2000. However, the feature and security improvements are significant, and you are likely to find that particular upgrades provide critical enhancements for your particular environment.

Lesson 2: Installation and Configuration of Windows Server 2003 and Active Directory

The 70-290 examination focuses on the management and maintenance of a Windows Server 2003 environment. The objectives of the exam focus very little attention on Active Directory itself; some of the objectives, however, relate to the administration of Active Directory objects: users, groups, computers, printers, and shared folders in particular. The chapters that follow will explain the examination objectives in detail, and hands-on exercises will be an important component of your learning experience. Those exercises require you to have configured a domain controller running Windows Server 2003. If you are comfortable configuring a domain controller and creating basic user, group, and computer accounts, you can skip this lesson. If you are less familiar with Active Directory, this lesson will provide sufficient foundation for you to embark on a full exploration of Windows Server 2003.

After this lesson, you will be able to

- Install Windows Server 2003
- Identify the key structures and concepts of Active Directory
- Create a domain controller
- Create Active Directory objects including users, groups, and organizational units (OUs)

Estimated lesson time: 60 minutes

Installing and Configuring Windows Server 2003

As an experienced IT professional, you have no doubt spent considerable time installing Windows platforms. Some of the important and enhanced considerations when installing Windows Server 2003 are

- **Bootable CD-ROM installation**   Most administrators first became accustomed to installing an operating system by booting from the CD-ROM in the late 1990s. Windows Server 2003 continues the trend, and can be installed directly from the CD-ROM. But Windows Server 2003 adds a twist: there is *no* support for starting installation from floppy disks.

- **Improved graphical user interface (GUI) during setup**   Windows Server 2003 uses a GUI during setup that resembles that of Windows XP. It communicates more clearly the current state of the installation and the amount of time required to complete installation.

- **Product activation**   Retail and evaluation versions of Windows Server 2003 require that you activate the product. Volume licensing programs, such as Open License, Select License, or Enterprise Agreement, do not require activation.

The specific steps required to install Windows Server 2003 are outlined in Exercise 1.

After installing and activating Windows, you can configure the server using a well-thought-out Manage Your Server page, as shown in Figure 1-1, that launches automatically at logon. The page facilitates the installation of specific services, tools, and configurations based on server roles. Click Add Or Remove A Role and the Configure Your Server Wizard appears.

Figure 1-1   The Manage Your Server page

If you select Typical Configuration For A First Server, the Configure Your Server Wizard promotes the server to a domain controller in a new domain, installs Active Directory services, and, if needed, Domain Name Service (DNS), Dynamic Host Configuration Protocol (DHCP), and Routing And Remote Access (RRAS) service.

If you select Custom Configuration, the Configure Your Server Wizard can configure the following roles:

- **File Server** Provides convenient, centralized access to files and directories for individual users, departments, and entire organizations. Choosing this option allows you to manage user disk space by enabling and configuring disk quota management and to provide improved file system search performance by enabling the Indexing service.

- **Print Server** Provides centralized and managed access to printing devices by serving shared printers and printer drivers to client computers. Choosing this option starts the Add Printer Wizard to install printers and their associated Windows printer drivers. It also installs Internet Information Services (IIS 6.0) and configures Internet Printing Protocol (IPP) and installs the Web-based printer administration tools.

- **Application Server (IIS, ASP.NET)** Provides infrastructure components required to support the hosting of Web applications. This role installs and configures IIS 6.0 as well as ASP.NET and COM+.

- **Mail Server (POP3, SMTP)** Installs POP3 and SMTP so that the server can act as an e-mail server for POP3 clients.

- **Terminal Server** Provides applications and server resources, such as printers and storage, to multiple users as if those applications and resources were installed on their own computers. Users connect with the Terminal Services or Remote Desktop clients. Unlike Windows 2000, Windows Server 2003 provides Remote Desktop for Administration automatically. Terminal Server roles are required only when hosting applications for users on a terminal server.

- **Remote Access/VPN Server** Provides multiple-protocol routing and remote access services for dial-in, local area networks (LANs) and wide area networks (WANs). Virtual private network (VPN) connections allow remote sites and users to connect securely to the network using standard Internet connections.

- **Domain Controller (Active Directory)** Provides directory services to clients in the network. This option configures a domain controller for a new or existing domain and installs DNS. Choosing this option runs the Active Directory Installation Wizard.

- **DNS Server** Provides host name resolution by translating host names to IP addresses (forward lookups) and IP addresses to host names (reverse lookups). Choosing this option installs the DNS service, and then starts the Configure A DNS Server Wizard.

- **DHCP Server** Provides automatic IP addressing services to clients configured to use dynamic IP addressing. Choosing this option installs DHCP services and then starts the New Scope Wizard to define one or more IP address scopes in the network.

- **Streaming Media Server** Provides Windows Media Services (WMS). WMS enables the server to stream multimedia content over an intranet or the Internet. Content can be stored and delivered on demand or delivered in real time. Choosing this option installs WMS.

- **WINS Server** Provides computer name resolution by translating NetBIOS names to IP addresses. It is not necessary to install Windows Internet Name Service (WINS) unless you are supporting legacy operating systems, such as Windows 95 or Windows NT. Operating systems such as Windows 2000 and Windows XP do not require WINS, although legacy applications on those platforms may very well require NetBIOS name resolution. Choosing this option installs WINS.

To complete the hands-on exercises in this book, you will configure a computer as Server01, acting as a domain controller in the domain *contoso.com*. The steps for configuring the server as a domain controller using the Configure Your Server Wizard are listed in Exercise 2 at the end of this lesson.

Active Directory

Many books have been devoted to the planning, implementation, and support of Active Directory. If you're experienced with Active Directory, you will recognize that the following discussion has been simplified solely because it would take many books to discuss all the detail. The goal of this section is to distill that information to what you should know to approach the 70-290 exam.

Networks, Directory Services, and Domain Controllers

Networks were created on the day when the first user decided he or she didn't want to walk down the hall to get something from another user. In the end, networks are all about providing resources remotely. Those resources are often files, folders, and printers. Over time those resources have come to include many things, most significantly, e-mail, databases, and applications. There has to be some mechanism to keep track of these resources, providing, at a minimum, a directory of users and groups so that the resources can be secured against undesired access.

Microsoft Windows networks support two directory service models: the workgroup and the domain. The domain model is by far the more common in organizations implementing Windows Server 2003. The domain model is characterized by a single directory of enterprise resources—Active Directory—that is trusted by all secure systems that belong to the domain. Those systems can therefore use the security principals (user, group, and computer accounts) in the directory to secure their resources. Active Directory thus acts as an identity store, providing a single trusted list of Who's Who in the domain.

Active Directory itself is more than just a database, though. It is a collection of supporting files including transaction logs and the system volume, or Sysvol, that contains logon scripts and group policy information. It is the services that support and use the database, including Lightweight Directory Access Protocol (LDAP), Kerberos security protocol, replication processes, and the File Replication Service (FRS). The database and its services are installed on one or more domain controllers. A domain controller is a server that has been promoted by running the Active Directory Installation Wizard by running DCPROMO from the command line or, as you will do in Exercise 2, by running the Configure Your Server Wizard. Once a server has become a domain controller, it hosts a copy, or replica, of Active Directory and changes to the database on any domain controller are replicated to all domain controllers within the domain.

Domains, Trees and Forests

Active Directory cannot exist without at least one domain, and vice versa. A domain is the core administrative unit of the Windows Server 2003 directory service. However, an enterprise may have more than one domain in its Active Directory. Multiple domain models create logical structures called *trees* when they share contiguous DNS names. For example *contoso.com*, *us.contoso.com*, and *europe.contoso.com* share contiguous DNS namespace, and would therefore be referred to as a tree.

If domains in an Active Directory do not share a common root domain, they create multiple trees. That leads you to the largest structure in an Active Directory: the *forest*. An Active Directory forest includes all domains within that Active Directory. A forest may contain multiple domains in multiple trees, or just one domain. When more than one domain exists, a component of Active Directory called the Global Catalog becomes important because it provides information about objects that are located in other domains in the forest.

Objects and Organizational Units (OUs)

Enterprise resources are represented in Active Directory as objects, or records in the database. Each object has numerous attributes, or properties, that define it. For example, a user object includes the user name and password; a group object includes the group name and a list of its members.

To create an object in Active Directory, open the Active Directory Users And Computers console from the Administrative Tools program group. Expand the domain to reveal its containers and OUs. Right-click a container or OU and select New *object_type*.

Active Directory is capable of hosting millions of objects, including users, groups, computers, printers, shared folders, sites, site links, Group Policy Objects (GPOs), and even DNS zones and host records. You can imagine that without some kind of structure, accessing and administering the directory would be a nightmare.

Structure is the function of a specific object type called an organizational unit, or OU. OUs are containers within a domain that allow you to group objects that share common administration or configuration. But they do more than just organize Active Directory objects. They provide important administrative capabilities, as they provide a point at which administrative functions can be delegated and to which group policies can be linked.

Delegation

Administrative delegation relates to the simple idea that you might want a front-line administrator to be able to change the password for a certain subset of users. Each object in Active Directory (in this case, the user objects) includes an access control list (ACL) that defines permissions for that object, just as files on a disk volume have ACLs that define access for those files. So, for example, a user object's ACL will define what groups are allowed to reset its password. It would get complicated to assign the front-line administrator permissions to change each individual user's password, so instead you can put all of those users in a single OU and assign that administrator the reset password permission on the OU. That permission will be inherited by all user objects in the OU, thereby allowing that administrator to modify permissions for all users.

Resetting user passwords is just one example of administrative delegation. There are thousands of combinations of permissions that could be assigned to groups administering and supporting Active Directory. OUs allow an enterprise to create an active representation of its administrative model, and to specify who can do what to objects in the domain.

Group Policy

OUs are also used to collect objects—computers and users—that are configured similarly. Just about any configuration you can make to a system can be managed centrally through a feature of Active Directory called Group Policy. Group Policy allows you to specify security settings, deploy software, and configure operating system and application behavior without ever touching a machine. You simply implement your configuration within a GPO.

GPOs are collections of hundreds of possible configuration settings, from user logon rights and privileges to the software that is allowed to be run on a system. A GPO is linked to a container within Active Directory—typically to an OU, but can also be domains, or even sites—and all the users and computers beneath that container are affected by the settings contained in the GPO.

You will likely see Group Policy referred to on the 70-290 exam. The important things to remember about Group Policy are that it is a tool that can centrally implement configuration; that some settings apply to computers only and some settings apply to users only; and that the only computers or users that will be affected by a policy are those that are beneath the OU to which the policy is linked.

Learning More

As suggested earlier in this section, Active Directory is a large and complex topic that deserves significant examination if you are going to implement Windows Server 2003 as a domain controller. The following Microsoft Press titles are recommended reading:

- *Active Directory for Microsoft Windows Server 2003 Technical Reference*
- *MCSE Self-Paced Training Kit (Exam 70-294): Planning, Implementing, and Maintaining a Microsoft Windows Server 2003 Active Directory Infrastructure*

Practice: Installing Windows Server 2003

In this practice, you will configure a computer to run Windows Server 2003. You will then promote the server to become a domain controller in the *contoso.com* domain.

Exercise 1: Installing Windows Server 2003

This exercise should be performed on a computer compatible with Windows Server 2003. It assumes that the primary hard drive is completely empty. If your disk already has partitions configured, you can modify the exercise to match the configuration of your system.

1. Configure the computer's BIOS or the disk controller BIOS to boot from CD-ROM. If you are not sure how to configure your computer or disk controller to boot from CD-ROM, consult your hardware documentation.

2. Insert the Windows Server 2003 installation CD-ROM into the CD-ROM drive and restart the computer.

3. If the primary disk is not empty, a message appears prompting you to press any key to boot from CD. If you see this message, press any key.

   After the computer starts, a brief message appears explaining that your system configuration is being inspected, and then the Windows Setup screen appears.

4. If your computer requires special mass storage drivers that are not part of the Windows Server 2003 driver set, press F6 when prompted and provide the appropriate drivers.

5. The system prompts you to press F2 to perform an Automated System Recovery (ASR). Automated System Recovery is a new feature in Windows Server 2003 that replaces the Emergency Repair Disk feature of previous versions of Windows, and is described in Chapter 13. Do not press F2 at this time. Setup will continue.

   Notice that the gray status bar at the bottom of the screen indicates that the computer is being inspected and that files are loading. This is required to start a minimal version of the operating system.

6. If you are installing an evaluation version of Windows Server 2003, the Setup Notification screen appears informing you of this. Read the Setup Notification message, and then press Enter to continue.

   Setup displays the Welcome To Setup screen.

   Notice that, in addition to the initial installation of the operating system, you can use Windows Server 2003 Setup to repair a damaged Windows installation. The Recovery Console is described in Chapter 13.

7. Read the Welcome To Setup message, and then press Enter to continue. Setup displays the License Agreement screen.

8. Read the license agreement, pressing Page Down to scroll to the bottom of the screen.

9. Press F8 to accept the agreement.

   Setup displays the Windows Server 2003 Setup screen, prompting you to select an area of free space or an existing partition on which to install the operating system. This stage of setup provides a way for you to create and delete partitions on your hard disk.

   To complete the exercises in this book, you will need to configure a partition large enough to host the operating system installation (recommended minimum size is 3 GB) and unallocated space of at least 1 GB. The following steps assume your disk is at least 4 GB in size and is currently empty. You may make adjustments to accommodate your situation.

10. Press C to create a partition.

11. To create a 3 GB partition type **3072** in the Create Partition Of Size (In MB) box and press Enter.

12. Confirm that your partitioning is similar to that shown in Figure 1-2. Again, the recommendations for the hands-on exercises is a C: partition of at least 3 GB and 1 GB of unpartitioned space.

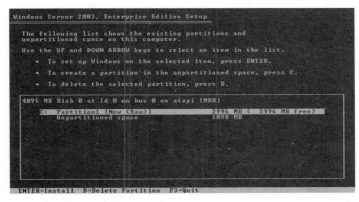

Figure 1-2   Partitioning the hard drive for setup

13. Select C: Partition1 [New (Raw)] and press Enter to install.

    You are prompted to select a file system for the partition.

14. Verify that the Format The Partition Using The NTFS File System option is selected, and press Enter to continue.

    Setup formats the partition with NTFS, examines the hard disk for physical errors that might cause the installation to fail, copies files to the hard disk, and initializes the installation. This process takes several minutes.

    Eventually, Setup displays a red status bar that counts down for 15 seconds before the computer restarts and enters the GUI mode of the setup process.

15. After the text mode of setup has completed, the system restarts. Do not, when prompted, press a key to boot to the CD-ROM.

Windows Setup launches and produces a graphical user interface that tracks the progress of installation in the left pane. Collecting Information, Dynamic Update, and Preparing Installation options are selected. Collecting Information was completed before the GUI appeared, and Dynamic Update is not used when starting from the CD-ROM. The system is now Preparing Installation by copying files to the local disk drive.

16. On the Regional And Language Options page, choose settings that are appropriate for your language and text input requirements, and then click Next.

> **Tip**   You can modify regional settings after you install the operating system using Regional And Language Options in Control Panel.

Setup displays the Personalize Your Software page, prompting you for your name and organization name.

17. In the Name text box, type your name; in the Organization text box, type the name of an organization, and then click Next.

Setup displays the Your Product Key page.

18. Enter the product key included with your Windows Server 2003 installation CD-ROM, and then click Next.

Setup displays the Licensing Modes dialog box, prompting you to select a licensing mode.

19. Verify that the Per Server Number Of Concurrent Connections option is 5, and then click Next.

> **Important**   Per Server Number Of Concurrent Connections and 5 concurrent connections are suggested values to be used to complete your self-study. You should use a legal number of concurrent connections based on the actual licenses that you own. You can also choose to use Per Device Or Per User option instead of Per Server.

Setup displays the Computer Name And Administrator Password page.

Notice that Setup uses your organization name to generate a suggested name for the computer. If you didn't enter an organization name earlier in the installation process, Setup uses your name to generate part of the computer name.

20. In the Computer Name text box, type **Server01**.

The computer name displays in all capital letters regardless of how it is entered. Throughout the rest of this self-paced training kit, the practices refer to Server01.

Caution   If your computer is on a network, check with the network administrator before assigning a name to your computer.

21. In the Administrator Password text box and the Confirm Password text box, type a complex password for the Administrator account (one that others cannot easily guess). *Remember this password* because you will be logging on as Administrator to perform most hands-on exercises.

Important   In a manual installation, Windows Server 2003 will not let you progress to subsequent steps until you enter an Administrator password that meets complexity requirements. You are allowed to enter a blank password, though this practice is strongly discouraged.

If the server has a modem installed, you will be presented with the Modem Dialing Information dialog box.

22. Type your area code, and then click Next. The Date And Time Settings page appears.

23. Type the correct Date & Time and Time Zone settings, and then click Next.

Important   Windows Server 2003 services depend on the computer's time and date settings. Be sure to enter the correct time and date, and to select the correct time zone for your location.

24. On the Networking Settings page, select Typical Settings, and then click Next.

The Workgroup Or Computer Domain page appears.

25. Verify that the first option is selected and that the workgroup name is Workgroup, and then click Next.

Setup installs and configures the remaining operating system components. When the installation is complete, the computer restarts automatically and the Welcome To Windows dialog box appears.

26. Press Ctrl+Alt+Delete to initiate logon, and type the password you configured for the Administrator account.

Note   Some editions of Windows Server 2003, including the Evaluation edition provided with this book, require that you activate the operating system after you install it. Activation must occur within 14 days of installation. The activation process is simple and can be completed over the Internet or by telephone. If you acquire your license to use Windows Server 2003 through one of the Microsoft volume licensing programs, you are not required to activate the license.

27. Click the balloon that appears in the System tray to initiate activation of Windows Server 2003. Follow the on-screen prompts.

Note   To activate by Internet, you will have to connect Server01 to the network and you may have to adjust the TCP/IP properties of your network interface card (NIC) to reflect an appropriate IP address, subnet mask, default gateway, and DNS server address.

Exercise 2: Configuring the Server

In this exercise, you will configure the server as the first domain controller in an Active Directory domain called *contoso.com*.

Note   When the Active Directory Installation Wizard is launched, the steps that it prompts you to follow will differ based on whether it detects another domain on the network. The steps presented below assume you are running the wizard on an isolated network. If you are connected to a network with another domain, the steps may vary, and you may either modify your choices appropriately or disconnect from the network prior to performing the exercise.

1. If it is not already open, open the Manage Your Server page from the Administrative Tools program group.

2. Click Add Or Remove A Role. The Configure Your Server Wizard appears.

3. Click Next and the Configure Your Server Wizard detects network settings.

4. Click Typical Configuration For A First Server, and then click Next.

5. In Active Directory Domain Name, type **contoso.com**.

6. Verify that NetBIOS Domain Name reads CONTOSO and click Next.

7. Verify that the Summary Of Selections matches that shown in Figure 1-3 and click Next.

   The Configure Your Server Wizard reminds you that the system will restart and asks you to close any open programs.

8. Click Yes.

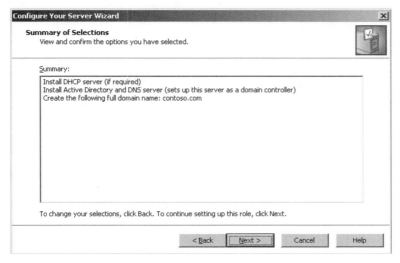

Figure 1-3   Summary Of Selections

9. After the system has restarted, log on as Administrator.

10. The Configure Your Server Wizard will summarize its final steps, as shown in Figure 1-4.

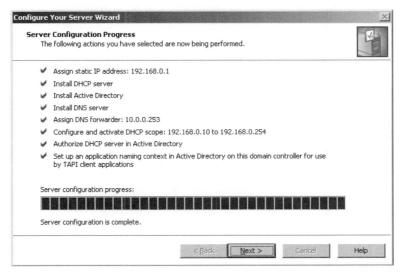

Figure 1-4   The Configure Your Server Wizard

11. Click Next and then click Finish.

12. Open Active Directory Users And Computers from the Administrative Tools group. Confirm that you now have a domain called *contoso.com* by expanding the domain and locating the computer account for Server01 in the Domain Controllers OU.

Lesson Review

1. Which of the following versions of Windows Server 2003 require product activation? (Select all that apply.)

    a. Windows Server 2003, Standard Edition, retail version

    b. Windows Server 2003, Enterprise Edition, evaluation version

    c. Windows Server 2003, Enterprise Edition, Open License version

    d. Windows Server 2003, Standard Edition, Volume License version

2. What are the distinctions among a domain, a tree, and a forest in Active Directory?

    _____

    _____

3. Which of the following is true about setup in Windows Server 2003? (Select all that apply.)

    a. Setup can be launched by booting to the CD-ROM.

    b. Setup can be launched by booting to setup floppies.

    c. Setup requires a non-blank password to meet complexity requirements.

    d. Setup will allow you to enter all 1's for the Product ID.

Lesson Summary

- Windows Server 2003 retail and evaluation versions require product activation.

- The Manage Your Server page and the Configure Your Server Wizard provide helpful guidance to the installation and configuration of additional services based on the desired server role.

- Active Directory—the Windows Server 2003 directory service—is installed on a server using the Active Directory Installation Wizard, which is launched using the Configure Your Server Wizard or by running DCPROMO from the command line.

Questions and Answers

Page
1-6

Lesson 1 Review

1. You are planning the deployment of Windows Server 2003 computers for a department of 250 employees. The server will host the home directories and shared folders for the department, and it will serve several printers to which departmental documents are sent. Which edition of Windows Server 2003 will provide the most cost-effective solution for the department?

Windows Server 2003, Standard Edition, is a robust platform for file and print services in a small- to medium-sized enterprise or department.

2. You are planning the deployment of Windows Server 2003 computers for a new Active Directory domain in a large corporation that includes multiple separate Active Directories maintained by each of the corporation's subsidiaries. The company has decided to roll out Exchange Server 2003 as a unified messaging platform for all the subsidiaries, and plans to use Microsoft Metadirectory Services (MMS) to synchronize appropriate properties of objects throughout the organization. Which edition of Windows Server 2003 will provide the most cost-effective solution for this deployment?

Windows Server 2003, Enterprise Edition, is the most cost-effective solution that supports MMS. Standard and Web editions do not support MMS.

3. You are rolling out servers to provide Internet access to your company's e-commerce application. You anticipate four servers dedicated to the front-end Web application and one server for a robust, active SQL database. Which editions will provide the most cost-effective solution?

Windows Server 2003, Web Edition, provides a cost-effective platform for the four Web application servers. However, Web Edition will not support enterprise applications like SQL Server; the edition of MSDE included with Web Edition allows only 25 concurrent connections. Therefore, Windows Server 2003, Standard Edition, provides the most cost-effective platform for a SQL Server.

Lesson 2 Review

1. Which of the following versions of Windows Server 2003 require product activation? (Select all that apply.)

   a. Windows Server 2003, Standard Edition, retail version

   b. Windows Server 2003, Enterprise Edition, evaluation version

   c. Windows Server 2003, Enterprise Edition, Open License version

   d. Windows Server 2003, Standard Edition, Volume License version

   The correct answers are a and b.

2. What are the distinctions among a domain, a tree, and a forest in Active Directory?

   A domain is the core administrative unit in Active Directory. A forest is the scope of Active Directory. A forest must contain at least one domain. If a forest contains more than one domain, domains that share a contiguous DNS namespace—meaning domains that have a common root domain—create a tree. Domains that do not share contiguous DNS namespace create distinct trees within the forest.

3. Which of the following is true about setup in Windows Server 2003? (Select all that apply.)

   a. Setup can be launched by booting to the CD-ROM.

   b. Setup can be launched by booting to setup floppies.

   c. Setup requires a non-blank password to meet complexity requirements.

   d. Setup will allow you to enter all 1's for the Product ID.

   The correct answers are a and c.

2 Administering Microsoft Windows Server 2003

Exam Objectives in this Chapter:

- Manage servers remotely
    - ❏ Manage a server by using Remote Assistance
    - ❏ Manage a server by using Terminal Services remote administration mode
    - ❏ Manage a server by using available support tools
- Troubleshoot Terminal Services
    - ❏ Diagnose and resolve issues related to Terminal Services security
    - ❏ Diagnose and resolve issues related to client access to Terminal Services

Why This Chapter Matters

In the daily work of a systems administrator, you frequently use tools to configure user accounts, modify computer software and service settings, install new hardware, and perform many other tasks. As the computing environment expands to include more computers, so expands the amount of work to be done. The Microsoft Management Console (MMC) allows for the consolidation and organization of some of the tools used most often. In addition, MMC consoles can be customized and tailored to fit the exact needs of the worker and the task at hand, so tasks can be delegated to more junior administrators with fewer chances for error.

When more global control of a remote computer is required, beyond what can be done remotely through the MMC, two key tools make administration of remote computers possible: Remote Desktop for Administration and Remote Assistance. Generally, you can regard Remote Desktop for Administration as a client-server application that allows for a window on your desktop computer to show the local console of a server computer, giving you the ability to control the keyboard and mouse functions as if you were logged on locally at the console of the server. Remote Assistance is similar in function, but is scoped for desktop computers running an operating system from the Microsoft Windows Server 2003 or Windows XP family. A user at that computer makes a request for assistance, and a remote connection can be established from a remote computer to that desktop.

Lessons in this Chapter:

Before You Begin

To perform the practices related to the objectives in this chapter, you must have

■ A computer that has Windows Server 2003 installed and operating. To follow the examples directly, your server should be named Server01 and function as a domain controller in the *contoso.com* domain.

■ Remote Desktop for Administration installed on Server01, with Remote Desktop and Remote Assistance enabled.

■ A configured and functioning Transmission Control Protocol/Internet Protocol (TCP/IP) network to which your console and remote administrative target computers can connect (for administration of remote computers).

Lesson 1: The Microsoft Management Console

The primary administrative tool for managing Windows Server 2003 is the MMC. The MMC provides a standardized, common interface for one or more of the applications, called *snap-ins*, that you use to configure the elements of your environment. These snap-ins are individualized to specific tasks, and can be ordered and grouped within the MMC to your administrative preference.

The primary administrative tools in Windows Server 2003 are MMC consoles with collections of snap-ins suited to a specific purpose. The Active Directory Users and Computers administrative tool, for example, is specifically designed to administer the security principals (Users, Groups, and Computers) in a domain. The snap-ins within the MMC—not the MMC itself—are the administrative tools that you use.

> **Note**   MMC consoles will run on Windows Server 2003, Windows 2000, Windows NT 4, Windows XP, and Windows 98.

After this lesson, you will be able to

- Configure an MMC with individual snap-ins
- Configure an MMC with multiple snap-ins
- Save an MMC in Author or User mode

Estimated lesson time: 15 minutes

The MMC

The MMC looks very much like a version of Windows Explorer, only with fewer buttons. The functional components of an MMC are contained within what are called snap-ins: Menus and a toolbar provide commands for manipulating the parent and child windows, and the console itself (which contains the snap-ins) allows targeted functionality. In addition, an MMC can be saved with and the various options and modes appropriate to the situation.

Navigating the MMC

An empty MMC is shown in Figure 2-1. Note that the console has a name, and that there is a Console Root. It is this Console Root that will contain any snap-ins that you choose to include.

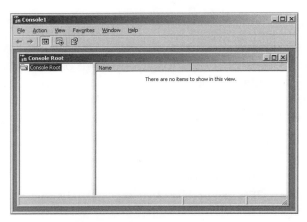

Figure 2-1   An empty MMC

Each console includes a console tree, console menu and toolbars, and the detail pane. The contents of these will vary, depending upon the design and features of the snap-in use. Figure 2-2 shows a populated MMC with two snap-ins loaded, and a child window of the Device Manager snap-in.

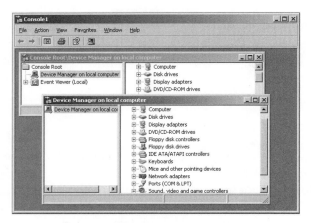

Figure 2-2   A populated MMC

Using the MMC Menus and Toolbar

Although each snap-in will add its unique menu and toolbar items, there are several key menus and commands that you will use in many situations that are common to most snap-ins, as shown in Table 2-1.

Table 2-1   Common MMC Menus and Commands

Menu	Commands
File	Create a new console, open an existing console, add or remove snap-ins from a console, set options for saving a console, the recent console file list, and an exit command
Action	Varies by snap-in, but generally includes export, output, configuration, and help features specific to the snap-in
View	Varies by snap-in, but includes a customize option to change general console characteristics
Favorites	Allows for adding and organizing saved consoles
Window	Open a new window, cascade, tile, and switch between open child windows in this console
Help	General help menu for the MMC as well as loaded snap-in help modules

Building a Customized MMC

Each MMC contains a collection of one or more tools called *snap-ins*. A snap-in extends the MMC by adding specific management capability and functionality. There are two types of snap-ins: stand-alone and extension.

You can combine one or more snap-ins or parts of snap-ins to create customized MMCs, which can then be used to centralize and combine administrative tasks. Although you can use many of the preconfigured consoles for administrative tasks, customized consoles allow for individualization to your needs and standardization within your environment.

Tip   By creating a custom MMC, you do not have to switch between different programs or individual consoles.

Stand-Alone Snap-Ins

Stand-alone snap-ins are provided by the developer of an application. All Administrative Tools for Windows Server 2003, for example, are either single snap-in consoles or preconfigured combinations of snap-ins useful to a particular category of tasks. The Computer Management snap-in, for example, is a collection of individual snap-ins useful to a unit.

Extension Snap-Ins

Extension snap-ins, or extensions, are designed to work with one or more stand-alone snap-ins, based on the functionality of the stand-alone. When you add an extension, Windows Server 2003 places the extension into the appropriate location within the stand-alone snap-in.

Many snap-ins offer stand-alone functionality and extend the functionality of other snap-ins. For example, the Event Viewer snap-in reads the event logs of computers. If the Computer Management object exists in the console, Event Viewer automatically extends each instance of a Computer Management object and provides the event logs for the computer. Alternatively, the Event Viewer can also operate in stand-alone mode, in which case it does not appear as a node below the Computer Management node.

Off the Record Spend a few minutes analyzing your daily tasks, and group them by type of function and frequency of use. Build two or three customized consoles that contain the tools that you use most often. You will save quite a bit of time not needing to open, switch among, and close tools as often.

Console Options

Console options determine how an MMC operates in terms of what nodes in the console tree may be opened, what snap-ins may be added, and what windows may be created.

Author Mode

When you save a console in Author mode, which is the default, you enable full access to all of the MMC functionality, including:

- Adding or removing snap-ins
- Creating windows
- Creating taskpad views and tasks
- Viewing portions of the console tree
- Changing the options on the console
- Saving the console

User Modes

If you plan to distribute an MMC with specific functions, you can set the desired user mode, then save the console. By default, consoles will be saved in the Administrative Tools folder in the users' profile. Table 2-2 describes the user modes that are available for saving the MMC.

Table 2-2   MMC User Modes

Type of User Mode	Description
Full Access	Allows users to navigate between snap-ins, open windows, and access all portions of the console tree.
Limited Access, Multiple Windows	Prevents users from opening new windows or accessing a portion of the console tree, but allows them to view multiple windows in the console.
Limited Access, Single Window	Prevents users from opening new windows or accessing a portion of the console tree, and allows them to view only one window in the console.

Note   MMCs, when saved, have an *.msc extension. Active Directory Users And Computers, for example, is named Dsa.msc (Directory Services Administrator.Microsoft Saved Console).

Practice: Building and Saving Consoles

In this practice you will create, configure, and save an MMC console.

Exercise 1: An Event Viewer Console

1. Click Start, and then click Run.

2. In the Open text box, type **mmc**, and then click OK.

3. Maximize the Console1 and Console Root windows.

4. From the File menu, choose Options to view the configured console mode.

   In what mode is the console running?

5. Verify that the Console Mode drop-down list box is in Author mode, and then click OK.

6. From the File menu, click Add/Remove Snap-In.

   The Add/Remove Snap-In dialog appears with the Standalone tab active. Notice that there are no snap-ins loaded.

7. In the Add/Remove Snap-In dialog box, click Add to display the Add Standalone Snap-In dialog box.

8. Locate the Event Viewer snap-in, and then click Add.

   The Select Computer dialog box appears, allowing you to specify the computer you want to administer. You can add the Event Viewer snap-in for the local computer on which you are working, or if your local computer is part of a network, you can add Event Viewer for a remote computer.

9. In the Select Computer dialog box, select Local Computer, and then click Finish.

10. In the Add Standalone Snap-In dialog box, click Close, and then in the Add/ Remove Snap-Ins dialog box, click OK.

   Event Viewer (Local) now appears in the console tree. You may adjust the width of the console tree pane and expand any nodes that you want to view.

11. On your own, add a snap-in for Device Manager (local).

12. Save the MMC as MyEvents.

Lesson Review

The following questions are intended to reinforce key information presented in this lesson. If you are unable to answer a question, review the lesson materials and try the question again. You can find answers to the questions in the "Questions and Answers" section at the end of this chapter.

1. What is the default mode when creating an MMC?

   _____

   _____

2. Can a snap-in have focus on both the local computer and a remote computer simultaneously?

   _____

   _____

3. If you want to limit the access of a snap-in, how do you construct the MMC that contains the snap-in?

   _____

   _____

Lesson Summary

The MMC is a useful tool for organizing and consolidating snap-ins, or small programs that are used for network and computer system administrative tasks. The hierarchical display, similar to that of Windows Explorer, offers a familiar view of snap-in features in a folder-based paradigm. There are two types of snap-ins, stand-alone and extension, with extensions appearing and behaving within the MMC based on the context of their placement. Any console can be configured to work in either of two modes, Author or User, with the User mode offering some restricted functionality in the saved console.

Lesson 2: Managing Computers Remotely with the MMC

Perhaps you work in a peer-to-peer network and need to help other users create user accounts or groups on their computers to share local folders. You can save yourself a trip to your coworkers' offices by connecting to the users' computers with your Computer Management console (as shown in Figure 2-3). Or perhaps you need to format drives or perform other tasks on a remote computer. You can perform almost any task on a remote computer that you can perform locally.

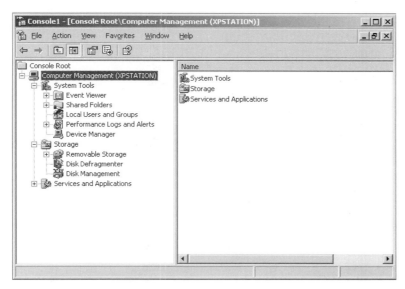

Figure 2-3   Connecting to a user's computer with the Computer Management console

---

After this lesson, you will be able to

■ Construct an MMC to manage a computer remotely

Estimated lesson time: 10 minutes

Setting Up the Snap-In for Remote Use

To connect to and manage another system using the Computer Management console, you must launch the console with an account that has administrative credentials on the remote computer. If your credentials do not have elevated privileges on the target computer, you will be able to load the snap-in, but will not be able to read information from the target computer.

> **Tip** You can use Run As, or secondary logon, to launch a console with credentials other than those with which you are currently logged on.

When you're ready to manage the remote system, you may open an existing console with the snap-in loaded, or configure a new MMC with a snap-in that you configure for remote connection when you build the console. If you configure an existing Computer Management console, for example, follow these steps:

1. Open the Computer Management console by right-clicking My Computer and choosing Manage from the shortcut menu.

2. Right-click Computer Management in the tree pane and choose Connect To Another Computer.

3. In the dialog box shown in Figure 2-4, type the name or IP address of the computer or browse the network for it, and then click OK to connect.

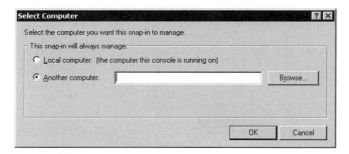

Figure 2-4   Setting the Local/Remote Context for a snap-in

Once connected, you can perform administrative tasks on the remote computer.

Practice: Adding a Remote Computer for Management (Optional)

> **Note** This practice requires that you have a computer available for remote connection, and that you have administrative privileges on that computer.

Exercise 1: Connecting Remotely with the MMC

In this exercise, you will modify an existing MMC to connect to a remote computer.

1. Open the saved MMC from the exercise in Lesson 1 (MyEvents).

2. From the File menu, click Add/Remove Snap-In.

3. In the Add/Remove Snap-In dialog box, click Add to display the Add Standalone Snap-In dialog box.

4. Locate the Computer Management snap-in, and then click Add.

5. In the Computer Management dialog box, select Another Computer.

6. Type the name or IP address of the computer, or browse the network for it, and then click Finish to connect.

7. Click Close in the Add Standalone Snap-In dialog box, then click OK to load the Computer Management snap-in to your MyEvents console.

   You can now use the management tools to administer the remote computer.

Lesson Review

The following questions are intended to reinforce key information presented in this lesson. If you are unable to answer a question, review the lesson materials and try the question again. You can find answers to the questions in the "Questions and Answers" section at the end of this chapter.

1. What credentials are required for administration of a remote computer using the MMC?

   _____

   _____

2. Can an existing MMC snap-in be changed from local to remote context, or must a snap-in of the same type be loaded into the MMC for remote connection?

   _____

   _____

3. Are all functions within a snap-in used on a local computer usable when connected remotely?

   _____

   _____

Lesson Summary

The MMC is able to load many different tools in the form of snap-ins. Some of these snap-ins are programmed with the ability to connect either to the local computer or to remote computers. The connection to a remote computer can be established when the snap-in is loaded, or after loading by right-clicking the snap-in and choosing Connect. You must have administrative privileges on the remote computer to use any tools affecting the configuration of the remote computer.

Lesson 3: Managing Servers with Remote Desktop for Administration

The Windows 2000 Server family introduced a tightly integrated suite of tools and technologies that enabled Terminal Services for both remote administration and application sharing. The evolution has continued: Terminal Services is now an integral, default component of the Windows Server 2003 family, and Remote Desktop has been improved and positioned as an out-of-the-box capability, so that with one click, a Windows Server 2003 computer will allow two concurrent connections for remote administration. By adding the Terminal Server component and configuring appropriate licensing, an administrator can further extend the technologies to allow multiple users to run applications on the server. In this lesson, you will learn how to enable Remote Desktop for Administration.

After this lesson, you will be able to

- Configure a server to enable Remote Desktop for Administration
- Assign users to the appropriate group to allow them to administer servers remotely
- Connect to a server using Remote Desktop for Administration Connection

Estimated lesson time: 15 minutes

Enabling and Configuring Remote Desktop for Administration

The Terminal Services service enables Remote Desktop, Remote Assistance, and Terminal Server for application sharing. The service is installed by default on Windows Server 2003, configured in Remote Desktop for remote administration mode. Remote Desktop mode allows only two concurrent remote connections, and does not include the application sharing components of Terminal Server. Therefore, Remote Desktop operates with very little overhead on the system, and with no additional licensing requirements.

Note   Because Terminal Services and its dependent Remote Desktop capability are default components of Windows Server 2003, every server has the capability to provide remote connections to its console. The term "terminal server" now therefore refers specifically to a Windows Server 2003 computer that provides application sharing to multiple users through addition of the Terminal Server component.

Other components—Terminal Server and the Terminal Server Licensing service—must be added using Add Or Remove Programs. However, all of the administrative tools required to configure and support client connections and to manage Terminal Server are installed by default on every Windows Server 2003 computer. Each of the tools and their functions are described in Table 2-3.

Table 2-3   Default Components of Terminal Server and Remote Desktop

Installed Software	Purpose
Terminal Services Configuration	Setting properties on the Terminal Server, including session, network, client desktop, and client remote control settings
Terminal Services Manager	Sending messages to connected Terminal Server clients, disconnecting or logging off sessions, and establishing remote control or shadowing of sessions
Remote Desktop Client Installation Files	Installation of the Windows Server 2003 or Windows XP Remote Desktop Client application. The 32-bit Remote Desktop client software is installed in %*Systemroot*%\System32\Clients\Tsclient\Win32 of the Terminal Server.
Terminal Services Licensing	Configuraiton of licenses for client connections to a terminal server. This tool is not applicable for environments which utilize only Remote Desktop for Administration.

To enable Remote Desktop connections on a Windows Server 2003 computer, open the System properties from Control Panel. On the Remote tab, select Allow Users To Connect Remotely To This Computer.

Note   If the Terminal Server is a Domain Controller, you must also configure the Group Policy on the Domain Controller to allow connection through Terminal Services to the Remote Desktop Users group. By default, Non-Domain Controller servers will allow Terminal Services connections by this group.

Remote Desktop Connection

Remote Desktop Connection is the client-side software used to connect to a server in the context of either Remote Desktop or Terminal Server modes. There is no functional difference from the client perspective between the two server configurations.

On Windows XP and Windows Server 2003 computers, Remote Desktop Connection is installed by default, though it is not easy to find in its default location in the All Programs\Accessories\Communications program group on the Start menu.

For other platforms, Remote Desktop Connection can be installed from the Windows Server 2003 CD or from the client installation folder (%*Systemroot*%\System32\Clients \Tsclient\Win32) on any Windows Server 2003 computer. The .msi-based Remote Desktop Connection installation package can be distributed to Windows 2000 systems using Group Policy or SMS.

> **Tip**   It is recommended to update previous versions of the Terminal Services client to the latest version of Remote Desktop Connection to provide the most efficient, secure and stable environment possible, through improvements such as a revised user interface, 128-bit encryption and alternate port selection.

Figure 2-5 shows the Remote Desktop client configured to connect to Server01 in the *contoso.com* domain.

Figure 2-5   Remote Desktop client

Configuring the Remote Desktop Client

You can control many aspects of the Remote Desktop connection from both the client and server sides. Table 2-4 lists configuration settings and their use.

Table 2-4   Remote Desktop Settings

Setting	Function
Client Settings	
General	Options for the selection of the computer to which connection should be made, the setting of static log on credentials, and the saving of settings for this connection.
Display	Controls the size of the Remote Desktop client window, color depth, and whether control-bar functions are available in full-screen mode.
Local Resources	Options to bring sound events to your local computer, in addition to standard mouse, keyboard, and screen output. How the Windows key combinations are to be interpreted by the remote computer (for example, ALT+TAB), and whether local disk, printer, and serial port connections should be available to the remote session.

Table 2-4   Remote Desktop Settings (Continued)

Setting	Function
Programs	Set the path and target folder for any program you want to start, once the connection is made.
Experience	Categories of display functions can be enabled or disabled based on available bandwith between the remote and local computers. Items include showing desktop background, showing the contents of the window while dragging, menu and window animation, themes, and whether bitmap caching should be enabled (this transmits only the changes in the screen rather than repainting the entire screen on each refresh period).
Server Settings	
Logon Settings	Static credentials can be set for the connection rather than using those provided by the client.
Sessions	Settings for ending a disconnected session, session limits and idle time-out, and reconnection allowance can be made here to override the client settings.
Environment	Overrides the settings from the user's profile for this connection for starting a program upon connection. Path and target settings set here override those set by the Remote Desktop Connection.
Permissions	Allows for additional permissions to be set on this connection.
Remote Control	Specifies whether remote control of a Remote Desktop Connection session is possible, and if it is, whether the user must grant permission at the initiation of the remote control session. Additional settings can restrict the remote control session to viewing only, or allow full interactivity with the Remote Desktop client session.
Client Settings	Override settings from the client configuration, control color depth, and disable various communication (I/O) ports.
Network Adapters	Specifies which network cards on the server will accept Remote Desktop for Administration connections.
General	Set the encryption level and authentication mechanism for connections to the server.

Terminal Services Troubleshooting

When using Remote Desktop for Administration, you are creating a connection to a server's console. There are several potential causes of failed connections or problematic sessions:

- **Network failures** Errors in standard TCP/IP networking can cause a Remote Desktop connection to fail or be interrupted. If DNS is not functioning, a client may not be able to locate the server by name. If routing is not functioning, or the Terminal Services port (by default, port 3389) misconfigured on either the client or the server, the connection will not be established.

- **Credentials**   Users must belong to the Administrators or Remote Desktop Users group to successfully connect to the server using Remote Desktop for Administration.

> **Exam Tip**   Watch for group membership if access is denied when establishing a Remote Desktop for Administration connection. In earlier versions of Terminal Server, you had to be a member of the Administrators group to connect to the server, although special permissions could be established manually. Having only two remote connections to the Terminal Server is a fixed limit, and cannot be increased.

- **Policy**   Domain controllers will only allow connections via Remote Desktop to administrators. You must configure the domain controller security policy to allow connections for all other remote user connections.
- **Too many concurrent connections**   If sessions have been disconnected without being logged off, the server may consider its concurrent connection limit reached even though there are not two human users connected at the time. An administrator might, for example, close a remote session without logging off. If two more administrators attempt to connect to the server, only one will be allowed to connect before the limit of two concurrent connections is reached.

> **See Also**   For more on Terminal Services and the latest developments in Remote Desktop client functionality, see *http://www.microsoft.com/technet/treeview/default.asp?url=/technet /prodtechnol/windowsserver2003/proddocs standard/sag_Server_Trouble_Topnode.asp*.

Practice: Installing Terminal Services and Running Remote Administration

In this practice, you will configure Server01 to enable Remote Desktop for Administration connections. You will then optimize Server01 to ensure availablity of the connection when the connection is not in use, and you will limit the number of simultaneous connections to one. You then run a remote administration session from Server02 (or another remote computer).

If you are limited to one computer for this practice, you can use the Remote Desktop client to connect to Terminal Services on the same computer. Adjust references to a remote computer in this practice to that of the local computer.

Exercise 1: Configure the Server for Remote Desktop

In this exercise, you will enable Remote Desktop connections, change the number of simultaneous connections allowed to the server, and configure the disconnection settings for the connection.

1. Logon to Server01 as Administrator.

2. Open the System properties from Control Panel.

3. On the Remote tab, enable Remote Desktop. Close System Properties.

4. Open the Terminal Services Configuration console from the Administrative Tools folder.

5. In the tscc (Terminal Services Configuration\Connections) MMC, right-click the RDP-tcp connection in the details pane, and then click Properties.

6. On the Network Adapter tab, change the Maximum Connections to 1.

7. On the Sessions tab, select both of the Override User Settings check boxes, and make setting changes so that any user session that is disconnected, by any means, or for any reason, will be closed in 15 minutes, that has no Active session time limit, and that will be disconnected after 15 minutes of inactivity.

   ❑ End a disconnected session: 15 minutes

   ❑ Active session limit: never

   ❑ Idle session limit: 15 minutes

   ❑ When session limit is reached or connection is broken: Disconnect from session

   This configuration will ensure that only one person at a time can be connected to the Terminal Server, that any disconnected session will be closed in 15 minutes, and that an idle session will be disconnected in 15 minutes. These settings are useful so as to not have a session that is disconnected or idle making the Remote Desktop for Administration connection unavailable.

Exercise 2: Connect to the Server with the Remote Desktop Client

1. On Server02 (or another remote computer, or from Server01 itself if a remote computer is not available), open Remote Desktop Connection (from the Accessories, Communications program group) and connect to and log to Server01.

2. On Server01, open the tscc (Terminal Services Configuration\Connections) MMC. You should see the remote session connected to Server01.

3. Leave the session idle for 15 minutes, or close the Remote Desktop client without logging off the Terminal Server session, and the session should be disconnected automatically in 15 minutes.

You have now logged on to Server01 remotely, and can perform any tasks on the Server01 computer that you could accomplish while logged on interactively at the console.

Lesson Review

The following questions are intended to reinforce key information presented in this lesson. If you are unable to answer a question, review the lesson materials and try the question again. You can find answers to the questions in the "Questions and Answers" section at the end of this chapter.

1. How many simultaneous connections are possible to a Terminal Server running in Remote Administration mode? Why?

   _____

   _____

2. What would be the best way to give administrators the ability to administer a server remotely through Terminal Services?

   a. Don't do anything; they already have access because they are administrators.

   b. Remove the Administrators from the permission list on the Terminal Server connection, and put their administrator account in the Remote Desktop for Administration Group.

   c. Create a separate, lower-authorization user account for Administrators to use daily, and place that account in the Remote Desktop for Administration Group.

3. What tool is used to enable Remote Desktop on a server?

   a. Terminal Services Manager

   b. Terminal Services Configuration

   c. System properties in Control Panel

   d. Terminal Services Licensing

Lesson Summary

Administrators and members of the Remote Desktop Users group have the ability to connect to a server using Remote Desktop Connection. Terminal Services are installed on Windows Server 2003 by default, and allow up to two Remote Desktop for Administration connections simultaneously. The Remote Desktop Connection client, a default component of Windows XP and Windows Server 2003, can be installed on any 32-bit Windows platform from the Windows Server 2003 installation CD or (after sharing the directory) from any Windows Server 2003 computer. Configuration of Remote Desktop for Administration connections is accomplished through settings on the client (Remote Desktop Connection) and server (Terminal Server Configuration). Key settings for the connections can be overridden by the server.

Lesson 4: Using Remote Assistance

Computer users, particularly users without much technical expertise, often have configuration problems or usage questions that are difficult for a support professional or even a friend or family member to diagnose and fix over the telephone. Remote Assistance provides a way for users to get the help they need and makes it easier and less costly for corporate help desks to assist their users.

> **After this lesson, you will be able to**
>
> - Enable a computer to accept requests for Remote Assistance
> - Use one of the available methods to request and establish a Remote Assistance session
>
> **Estimated lesson time: 30 minutes**

Making the Request for Assistance

In Windows Server 2003 Help, there is a wizard-driven section for Remote Assistance, the first page of which is shown in Figure 2-6.

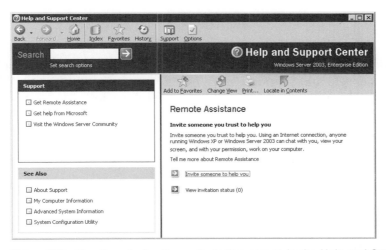

Figure 2-6   The Remote Assitance invitation screen in the Help and Support Center

The wizard-driven connection allows for a request to be sent either through a Microsoft .NET Passport account, through sending a saved file, or through a non-Passport e-mail account, along with allowing you to make a request using Windows Messenger. For a successful request through e-mail, both computers must be using a Messaging Application Programming Interface (MAPI)-compliant e-mail client.

To use the Windows Messenger service for your Remote Assistance connection, you must have the assistant's Windows Messenger user name in your contact list, and make the request from a Windows Messenger client. Windows Messenger will display their status as online or offline. Remote Assistance can only be requested directly when your assistant is online. Remote Assistant requires that both computers are running Windows XP or a product in the Windows Server 2003 family.

> **Note**   The indicator of online status in the Remote Assistance help window is not dynamic; you must therefore refresh the screen to see an accurate status update.

After receiving a request for Remote Assistance, the helper (expert) can remotely connect to the computer and view the screen directly to fix the problem. When you initiate a request for help, the Remote Assistance client sends an encrypted ticket based on Extensible Markup Language (XML) to the helper, who is prompted to accept the invitation.

> **Security Alert**   Remote Assistance, if enabled, allows for connection to a computer under relaxed security conditions. Make certain that you provide access only to trusted authorities for Remote Assistance sessions.

Using Remote Assistance

A user can request assistance from another Windows Messenger user by placing the request through the Help and Support Center application or directly through Windows Messenger. Both applications use the same mechanisms for determining if the expert is online, and then making a request for assistance. Figure 2-7 illustrates making a request for Remote Assistance using Windows Messenger.

Figure 2-7   Making a request for Remote Assistance

The Windows Messenger window opens, and the user selects the expert's Windows Messenger account. The expert receives the invitation as an Instant Message. When the expert clicks Accept, the Remote Assistance session is initiated. The requesting user confirms the session by clicking Yes.

When the remote connection is established, the Remote Assistance session begins on the expert's computer. The expert and user can share desktop control, file transfer capabilities, and a chat window through which they work together to solve the user's problem.

Security Alert   If the user chooses to send an e-mail or file request for Remote Assistance, a password will be required as a shared secret for the Remote Assistance session. The user should set a strong password, and let the expert know what the password is in a separate communication such as a telephone call or secure e-mail.

Offering Remote Assistance to a User

Remote Assistance is especially useful if you want to initiate troubleshooting on a user's computer. To do this, you must enable the Offer Remote Assistance Local Group Policy setting on the target (user's) local computer:

1. On the user's computer, click Start, Run, and then type **gpedit.msc**. The local Group Policy editor appears, enabling you to adjust policies that affect the local machine.

Note   A Domain Group Policy may prevent you from adjusting this policy.

2. Under the Computer Configuration node, expand Administrative Templates, then System, and then click Remote Assistance.

3. Double-click Offer Remote Assistance and then select Enabled.

4. Next, click Show, then specify the individual users that will be allowed to offer assistance by assigning helpers within the context of this policy. These "helper" additions to the list should be in the form of domain\username, and must be a member of the local administrators group on the local computer.

Initializing Remote Assistance

You can now initiate Remote Assistance from your computer, to a users computer, providing that the credentials that you supply match those of a helper defined in the target computer's local Group Policy:

1. Open the Help And Support Center, click Tools, and then click Help And Support Center Tools. Next click Offer Remote Assistance. Figure 2-8 illustrates the Help And Support Center Tools interface.

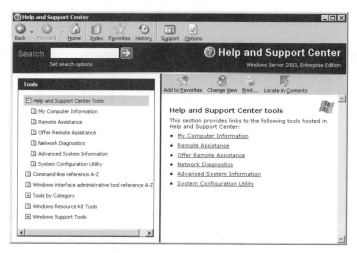

Figure 2-8   The Help And Support Center Tools

2. In the dialog box, type the name or IP address of the target computer, and then click Connect. (If prompted that several users are logged on, choose a user session.) Then click Start Remote Assistance.

    The user receives a pop-up box showing that the help-desk person is initiating a Remote Assistance session.

3. The user accepts, and Remote Assistance can proceed.

Security Alert   There are several issues to consider when managing and administering Remote Assistance in the corporate environment or large organization. You can specify an open environment in which employees can receive Remote Assistance from outside the corporate firewall, or you can restrict Remote Assistance by means of Group Policy and specify various levels of permissions such as only allowing Remote Assistance from within the corporate firewall. Connections from outside the firewall require port 3389 to be open.

Firewall Constraints to Remote Assistance

Remote Assistance runs on top of Terminal Services technology, which means it must use the same port used by Terminal Services: port 3389. Remote Assistance will not work when outbound traffic from port 3389 is blocked. In addition, there are several other firewall-related concerns, particularly in relation to Network Address Translation (NAT).

■ Remote Assistance supports Universal Plug and Play (UPnP) to Traverse Network Address Translation devices. This is helpful on smaller, home office networks, as Windows XP Internet Connection Sharing (ICS) supports UPnP. However, Windows 2000 ICS does *not* support UPnP.

> **Exam Tip** Watch for questions that use Windows 2000 ICS for remote assistance from a big, corporate help desk to a small satellite office. Because Windows 2000 ICS does not support UPnP, Remote Assistance problems will abound.

■ Remote Assistance will detect the Internet IP address and TCP port number on the UPnP NAT device and insert the address into the Remote Assistance encrypted ticket. The Internet IP address and TCP port number will be used to connect through the NAT device by the helper or requester workstation to establish a Remote Assistance session. The Remote Assistance connection request will then be forwarded to the client by the NAT device.

■ Remote Assistance will not connect when the requester is behind a non-UPnP NAT device when e-mail is used to send the invitation file. When sending an invitation using Windows Messenger, a non-UPnP NAT device will work if one client is behind a NAT device. If both the helper and requester computers are behind non-UPnP NAT devices, the Remote Assistance connection will fail.

If you are using a software-based personal firewall or NAT in a home environment, you can use Remote Assistance with no special configurations. However, if you are using a hardware-based firewall in a home environment, the same restrictions apply: you must open port 3389 to use Remote Assistance.

> **Note** The Instant Messenger Service itself relies upon port 1863 being open.

Practice: Using Remote Assistance through Windows Messenger

This practice requires either a partner, or a second computer for establishing the Remote Assistance session. Server01 and Server02 should have Windows Messenger installed and configured with two distinct accounts. If you are limited to a single computer for this practice, you may establish a Remote Assistance session using two separate Windows Messenger accounts configured on the same computer, but you will not be able to perform screen control.

1. From Server02 (or another computer) open Windows Messenger and log on to your Messenger Account #2.

2. From the Windows Messenger logged on as Messenger Account #1, choose Ask For Remote Assistance from the Actions menu.

3. In the Ask for Remote Assistance dialog box, choose the Messenger Account #2, and then click OK.

4. There will now be a sequence of requests and acknowledgments between the two Windows Messenger Applications. Choose Accept or OK in each query to establish the Remote Assistance session.

5. Initially, the Remote Assistance session is in Screen View Only mode. To take control of the novice's computer, you must select Take Control at the top of the Remote Assistance window. The novice user must Accept your attempt to take over the computer.

> **Note**   Either the novice or expert can end control or disconnect the session at any time.

Whether or not the expert takes over the novice's computer, screen view, file transfer, and live chat are enabled.

Lesson Review

The following questions are intended to reinforce key information presented in this lesson. If you are unable to answer a question, review the lesson materials and try the question again. You can find answers to the questions in the "Questions and Answers" section at the end of this chapter.

1. How is Remote Assistance like Remote Desktop for Administration? How is it different?

_____

_____

2. What are the benefits of Remote Assistance?

_____

_____

3. Which of the following are firewall-related constraints relating to Remote Assistance?

   a. Port 3389 must be open

   b. NAT cannot be used

   c. Internet Connection Sharing is not possible

   d. You cannot use Remote Assistance across a Virtual Private Network (VPN)

Lesson Summary

Remote Assistance is a mutual arrangement: the user can ask an expert for help or, if properly configured through Group Policy, the expert can initiate a help session. In either case, the user must actively agree to the establishment of the session and can always give to and remove control of the user's desktop from the expert. At no time can the expert take control of the user's desktop unannounced. Remote Assistance is built upon Terminal Services and uses the interface of the help system and Windows Messenger to allow for session initiation, chat, screen viewing, screen control, and file transfer. The technology of Terminal Services and Remote Assistance is so closely tied that both services use the same network port, 3389, which must be open through any firewall for the Remote Assistance session to succeed.

Case Scenario Exercise

As part of the Remote Administration of your enterprise, your company has enabled Remote Assistance on each computer. Your sales representatives travel frequently, and use laptops to perform their work while they travel.

On your internal network, you use Windows Messenger for spontaneous communication with your clients, and for Remote Assistance. You do not, however, allow for Instant Messenger traffic across the Internet by closing port 1863 at the firewall.

You want to perform Remote Assistance for your remote users, but cannot connect to them with Windows Messenger to determine whether they are online.

Is Remote Assistance possible for your remote users? If so, how would you accomplish it?

You must use one of the alternate methods of requesting Remote Assistance.

- **The E-Mail Method** Send an e-mail to the expert through Help and Support Tools. When the expert accesses the link in the e-mail, the expert will be able to establish a Remote Assistance session.

- **File Method** Create a Remote Assistance file through Help and Support Tools. E-mail the file to the expert, or have the expert access it through a file share point. When the expert accesses the link within the file, the expert will be able to establish a Remote Assistance session.

In both methods, it is highly recommended that you create a password for the Remote Assistance session, and give the expert the password in a secure fashion so that your Remote Assistance session cannot be accessed by an unauthorized person.

Troubleshooting Lab

You are trying to connect to a Windows Server 2003 server in your environment with a Remote Desktop Connection, but consistently get the message shown in Figure 2-9 when attempting to connect.

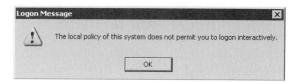

Figure 2-9 Error Logon Message when connecting to the Remote Desktop For Administration console

You have checked settings on the server, and confirmed the following:

- You are a member of the Remote Desktop Users group.

- You are not a member of the Administrators group.

- You are able to connect to share points on the Terminal Server computer, and the computer responds affirmatively to a ping.

What other settings will you check on the Terminal Server computer to troubleshoot this problem?

It is likely that the Terminal Server in question is a Domain Controller, and that the Default Domain Controller Group Policy has not been enabled to allow remote connections by the Remote Administrative Users group. The Local Group Policy on Domain Controllers forbids non-administrator remote connections, and must be changed. The easiest way to change the Local Policy is to override it with a change to the Default Domain Controller Group Policy.

Chapter Summary

- MMCs are the common, system tool interface in Windows Server 2003.

- Snap-ins are individual tools that can be loaded into an MMC.

- Some snap-ins can be used to configure remote computers; others are limited to local computer access.

- MMCs can be saved in either Author (full access) or User (limited access) modes. The mode of an MMC does not empower or disable a user from being able to do that which they have authorization and access to do via permission sets.

- Remote Desktop for Administration allows for the same administration of a server from a remote location as if logged on to the local console interactively.

- Remote Desktop for Administration, for desktop operating systems, is available only with Windows XP.

- Remote Assistance is like Remote Desktop for Administration for the desktop, allowing remote viewing and control of Windows XP desktop computers.

- Remote Assistance will also work on a Windows Server 2003 server.

- Two users are required for Remote Assistance to be viable: one user at the target desktop, and the expert helper at another computer. Both must agree on the control actions taken during the session, and the session can be ended by either party at any time.

Exam Highlights

Before taking the exam, review the key points and terms that are presented below to help you identify topics you need to review. Return to the lessons for additional practice and review the "Further Readings" sections in Part 2 for pointers to more information about topics covered by the exam objectives.

Key Points

- MMCs are the containers for snap-ins.

- Snap-ins can be used either in local or remote context, but cannot be connected to both the local and remote computers simultaneously.

- Snap-ins can be combined in a single console to suit administrative preference.

- MMCs can be saved in User mode to restrict their configuration, but the ability to perform tasks with the tool is governed by permissions, not by limitations placed on a particular MMC console. If a user has sufficient privilege to administer a computer, the user can create MMCs with any snap-in.

- Remote Desktop for Administration requires permissions to attach with the Remote Desktop client. By default, this permission is only granted to Administrators.

- Remote Assistance is a two-way, agreed session. At no time can an expert take unauthorized control of a user's computer.

- Port 3389, the same port used by Remote Desktop for Administration, must be open at the firewall for Remote Assistance sessions to be established.

Key Terms

Remote Assistance vs. Remote Desktop for Administration   Remote Assistance allows a remote control session to be established from an expert user as invited by a novice user. The credentials for authentication are supplied in the form of a shared secret password created within the invitation by the novice. Remote Desktop for Administration involves only one user connected remotely to a computer running the Terminal Server service and configured to allow Remote Desktop connections by the user.

Microsoft Management Console (MMC)   What functionality is possible through remote connection of a snap-in, and what credentials are required.

Remote Desktop for Administration   Credentials and server configuration required for Remote Desktop for Administration connections.

Questions and Answers

Page
2-8
Lesson 1 Review

1. What is the default mode when creating an MMC?

The default mode for an MMC is Author mode.

2. Can a snap-in have focus on both the local computer and a remote computer simultaneously?

No. Snap-ins can be configured to connect to the local computer, or a remote computer, but not both simultaneously.

3. If you want to limit the access of a snap-in, how do you construct the MMC that contains the snap-in?

Save the console in one of the User modes, depending on the level of limitation you want.

Page
2-11
Lesson 2 Review

1. What credentials are required for administration of a remote computer using the MMC?

You must have administrative credentials on the remote computer to perform remote administration.

2. Can an existing MMC snap-in be changed from local to remote context, or must a snap-in of the same type be loaded into the MMC for remote connection?

A snap-in's context might be changed by accessing the properties of the snap-in. A snap-in does not have to be reloaded to change its configuration.

3. Are all functions within a snap-in used on a local computer usable when connected remotely?

No, not all functionality is available. The Device Manager component in the Computer Management snap-in, for example, can only be used to view remote computer configurations: no changes can be made to the remote computer's device configuration.

Page
2-18
Lesson 3 Review

1. How many simultaneous connections are possible to a Terminal Server running in Remote Administration mode? Why?

Three; two remote connections and one at the console (but that's not fair, is it?). Technically, then, two is the limit because the application-sharing components are not installed with Terminal Server configured in Remote Desktop mode for remote administration.

2. What would be the best way to give administrators the ability to administer a server remotely through Terminal Services?

   a. Don't do anything; they already have access because they are administrators.

   b. Remove the Administrators from the permission list on the Terminal Server connection, and put their administrator account in the Remote Desktop for Administration Group.

   c. Create a separate, lower-authorization user account for Administrators to use daily, and place that account in the Remote Desktop for Administration Group.

   The correct answer is c. It is a best practice to log on using an account with minimal credentials, then to launch administrative tools with higher-level credentials using Run As.

3. What tool is used to enable Remote Desktop on a server?

   a. Terminal Services Manager

   b. Terminal Services Configuration

   c. System properties in Control Panel

   d. Terminal Services Licensing

   The correct answer is c.

Page 2-24 **Lesson 4 Review**

1. How is Remote Assistance like Remote Desktop for Administration? How is it different?

   Remote Assistance allows for remote control of a computer as if the user were physically at the console, as does a connection to a Terminal Server via Remote Desktop for Administration.

   Remote Desktop for Administration is controlled solely by the directory of accounts, either local or domain, that is configured for the Terminal Server connections on that computer. Remote Assistance requires a "handshake" of sorts between the user and the expert helper.

2. What are the benefits of Remote Assistance?

   The user does not have to have an expert on site to receive assistance. The difficulty of solving a problem over the telephone is removed.

3. Which of the following are firewall-related constraints relating to Remote Assistance?

   a. Port 3389 must be open.

   b. NAT cannot be used.

   c. Internet Connection Sharing is not possible.

   d. You cannot use Remote Assistance across a Virtual Private Network (VPN).

   The correct answer is a.

3 User Accounts

Exam Objectives in this Chapter:

- Create and manage user accounts
- Create and modify user accounts by using the Active Directory Users And Computers Microsoft Management Console (MMC) snap-in
- Create and modify user accounts by using automation
- Import user accounts
- Manage local, roaming, and mandatory user profiles
- Troubleshoot user accounts
- Diagnose and resolve account lockouts
- Diagnose and resolve issues related to user account properties
- Troubleshoot user authentication issues.

Why This Chapter Matters

Before individuals in your enterprise can access the resources they require, you must enable authentication of those individuals. Of course, the primary component of that authentication is the user's identity, maintained as an account in the Microsoft Active Directory directory service. In this chapter, you will review and enhance your knowledge related to the creation, maintenance, and troubleshooting of user accounts and authentication.

Each enterprise, and each day, brings with it a unique set of challenges related to user management. The properties you configure for a standard user account are likely to be different from those you apply to the account of a help desk team member, which are different still from those configured on the built-in Administrator account. Skills that are effective to create or modify a single user account become clumsy and inefficient when you are working with masses of accounts, such as when managing the accounts for new hires.

To address a diverse sampling of account management scenarios effectively, we will examine a variety of user management skills and tools including the Active Directory Users And Computers snap-in and powerful command-line utilities.

Lessons in this Chapter:

Before You Begin

This chapter presents the skills and concepts related to user accounts in Active Directory. This training kit presumes you have a minimum of 18 months' experience and a working knowledge of Active Directory, the MMC, and the Active Directory Users And Computers snap-in. If you desire hands-on practice, using the examples and lab exercises in the chapter, prepare the following:

- A Microsoft Windows Server 2003 (Standard or Enterprise) computer installed as Server01 and configured as a domain controller in the domain *contoso.com*

- First-level organizational units (OUs): Administrative Groups, Employees, and Security Groups

- Global groups, in the Security Groups OU, called Sales Representatives and Sales Managers

- The Active Directory Users And Computers MMC, or a customized console with the Active Directory Users And Computers snap-in

Lesson 1: Creating and Managing User Objects

Active Directory requires the verification of an individual's identity—a process called authentication—before that individual can access resources. The cornerstone of authentication is the user account, with its user logon name, password, and unique security identifier (SID). During logon, Active Directory authenticates the user name and password entered by the user. The security subsystem can then build the security access token that represents that user. The access token contains the user account's SID, as well as the SIDs of groups to which the user belongs. That token can then be used to verify user rights assignments, including the right to log on locally to the system, and to authorize access to resources secured by access control lists (ACLs).

The user account is integrated into the Active Directory user object. The user object includes not just the user's name, password, and SID, but also contact information, such as telephone numbers and addresses; organizational information including job title, direct reports and manager; group memberships; and configuration such as roaming profile, terminal services, remote access, and remote control settings. This lesson will review and enhance your understanding of user objects in Active Directory.

After this lesson, you will be able to

- Create user objects in Active Directory using the Active Directory Users and Computers snap-in
- Configure user object properties
- Understand important account options that are not self-explanatory based on their descriptions
- Modify properties of multiple users simultaneously

Estimated lesson time: 15 minutes

Creating User Objects with Active Directory Users and Computers

You can create a user object with the Active Directory Users and Computers snap-in. Although user objects can be created in the domain or any of the default containers, it is best to create a user in an organizational unit, so that administrative delegation and Group Policy Objects (GPOs) can be fully leveraged.

To create a user object, select the container in which you want to create the object, click the Action menu, then choose New and choose User. You must be a member of the Enterprise Admins, Domain Admins, or Account Operators groups, or you must have been delegated administrative permissions to create user objects in the container. If you do not have sufficient permissions to create user objects, the New User command will be unavailable to you.

The New Object–User dialog box appears, as shown in Figure 3-1. The first page of the New Object–User dialog box requests properties related to the user name. Table 3-1 describes the properties that appear on the first page of the dialog box.

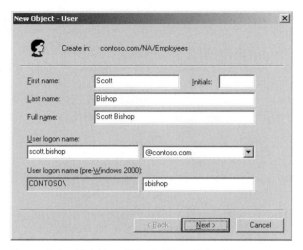

Figure 3-1   The New Object–User dialog box

Table 3-1   User Properties in the First Page of the New Object–User Dialog Box

Property	Description
First Name	The user's first name. Not required.
Initials	The middle initials of the user's name. Not required.
Last Name	The user's last name. Not required.
Full Name	The user's full name. If you enter values for the first or last name, the full name property is populated automatically. However, you can easily modify the suggested value. The field is required. The name entered here generates several user object properties, specifically CN (common name), DN (distinguished name), name, and displayName. Because CN must be unique within a container, the name entered here must be unique relative to all other objects in the OU (or other container) in which you create the user object.
User Logon Name	The user principal name (UPN) consists of a logon name and a UPN suffix which is, by default, the DNS name of the domain in which you create the object. The property is required and the entire UPN, in the format *logon-name@UPN-suffix*, must be unique within the Active Directory forest. A sample UPN would be *someone@contoso.com*. The UPN can be used to log on to any Microsoft Windows system running Windows 2000, Windows XP, or Windows Server 2003.

Table 3-1   User Properties in the First Page of the New Object–User Dialog Box (Continued)

Property	Description
User Logon Name (Pre–Windows 2000)	This logon name is used to log on from down-level clients, such as Microsoft Windows 95, Windows 98, Windows Millennium Edition (Windows Me), Windows NT 4, or Windows NT 3.51. This field is required and must be unique within the domain.

Once you have entered the values in the first page of the New Object–User dialog box, click Next. The second page of the dialog box, shown in Figure 3-2, allows you to enter the user password and to set account flags.

Figure 3-2   Second page of the New Object–User dialog box

Security Alert   The default account policies in a Windows Server 2003 domain, set in the Default Domain Policy GPO, requires complex passwords that have a minimum of seven characters. That means a password must contain three of four character types: uppercase, lowercase, numeric, and non-alphanumeric.

When you use Windows Server 2003 in a test or lab environment, you should implement the same best practices that are required in a production network. Therefore, in this book, you are encouraged to use complex passwords for the user accounts you create; it will be left to you to remember those passwords during exercises that require logging on as those users.

The properties available in the second page of the New Object–User dialog box are summarized in Table 3-2.

Table 3-2   User Properties in the Second Page of the New Object–User Dialog Box

Property	Description
Password	The password that is used to authenticate the user. For security reasons, you should always assign a password. The password is masked as you type it.
Confirm Password	Confirm the password by typing it a second time to make sure you typed it correctly.
User Must Change Password At Next Logon	Select this check box if you want the user to change the password you have entered the first time he or she logs on. You cannot select this option if you have selected Password Never Expires. Selecting this option will automatically clear the mutually exclusive option User Cannot Change Password.
User Cannot Change Password	Select this check box if you have more than one person using the same domain user account (such as Guest) or to maintain control over user account passwords. This option is commonly used to manage service account passwords. You cannot select this option if you have selected User Must Change Password At Next Logon.
Password Never Expires	Select this check box if you never want the password to expire. This option will automatically clear the User Must Change Password At Next Logon setting, as they are mutually exclusive. This option is commonly used to manage service account passwords.
Account Is Disabled	Select this check box to disable the user account, for example, when creating an object for a newly hired employee who does not yet need access to the network.

Off the Record   When creating objects for new users, choose a unique, complex password for each user that does not follow a predictable pattern. Select the option to enforce that the user must change password at next logon. If the user is not likely to log on to the network for a period, disable the account. When the user requires access to the network for the first time, ensure that the user's account is enabled. The user will be prompted to create a new, unique password that only the user knows.

Some of the account options listed in Table 3-2 have the potential to contradict policies set in the domain policies. For example, the default domain policy implements a best practice of disabling the storing of passwords using reversible encryption. However, in the rare circumstances that require reversible encryption, the user account property, Store Password Using Reversible Encryption, will take precedence for that specific user object. Similarly, the domain may specify a maximum password age, or that users must change password at next logon. If a user object is configured such that Password never expires, that configuration will override the domain's policies.

Managing User Objects with Active Directory Users And Computers

When creating a user, you are prompted to configure the most common user properties, including logon names and password. However, user objects support numerous additional properties that you can configure at any time using Active Directory Users And Computers. These properties facilitate the administration of, and the searching for, an object.

To configure the properties of a user object, select the object, click the Action menu, and then choose Properties. The user's Properties dialog box appears, as shown in Figure 3-3. An alternative way to view an object's properties would be to right-click the object and select Properties from the shortcut menu.

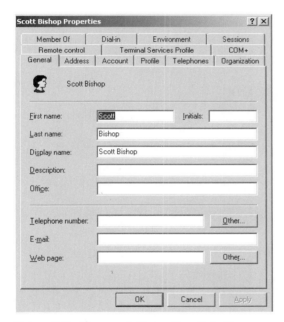

Figure 3-3   The user's Properties dialog box

The property pages in the Properties dialog box expose properties that fall into several broad categories:

- **Account properties: the Account tab**   These properties include those that are configured when you create a user object, including logon names, password and account flags.

- **Personal information: the General, Address, Telephones, and Organization tabs**   The General tab exposes the name properties that are configured when you create a user object.

- **User configuration management: the Profile tab**   Here you can configure the user's profile path, logon script, and home folder locations.

- **Group membership: the Member Of tab**   You can add and remove user groups, and set the user's primary group.

- **Terminal services: the Terminal Services Profile, Environment, Remote Control, and Sessions tabs**   These four tabs allow you to configure and manage the user's experience when they are connected to a Terminal Services session.

- **Remote access: the Dial-in tab**   Allows you to enable and configure remote access permission for a user.

- **Applications: the COM+ tab**   Assigns Active Directory COM+ partition sets to the user. This feature, new to Windows Server 2003, facilitates the management of distributed applications.

Account Properties

Of particular note are the user's account properties, on the Account tab of the user's Properties dialog box. An example appears in Figure 3-4.

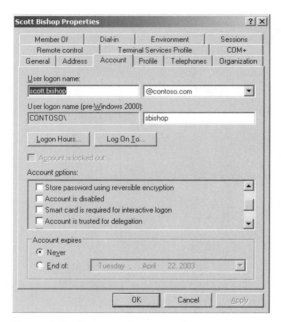

Figure 3-4   The user Account tab

Several of these properties were discussed in Table 3-2. Those properties were configured when creating the user object and can be modified, as can a larger set of account properties, using the Account tab. Several properties are not necessarily self-explanatory, and deserve definition in Table 3-3.

Table 3-3   User Account Properties

Property	Description
Logon Hours	Click Logon Hours to configure the hours during which a user is allowed to log on to the network.
Log On To	Click Log On To if you want to limit the workstations to which the user can log on. This is called Computer Restrictions in other parts of the user interface. You must have NetBIOS over TCP/IP enabled for this feature to restrict users because it uses the computer name, rather than the Media Access Control (MAC) address of its network card, to restrict logon.
Store Password Using Reversible Encryption	This option, which stores the password in Active Directory without using Active Directory's powerful, nonreversible encryption hashing algorithm, exists to support applications that require knowledge of the user password. If it is not absolutely required, do not enable this option because it weakens password security significantly. Passwords stored using reversible encryption are similar to those stored as plaintext. Macintosh clients using the AppleTalk protocol require knowledge of the user password. If a user logs on using a Macintosh client, you will need to select the option to Store password using reversible encryption.
Smart Card Is Required For Interactive Logon	Smart cards are portable, tamper-resistant hardware devices that store unique identification information for a user. They are attached to, or inserted into, a system and provide an additional, physical identification component to the authentication process.
Account Is Trusted For Delegation	This option enables a service account to impersonate a user to access network resources on behalf of a user. This option is not typically selected, certainly not for a user object representing a human being. It is used more often for service accounts in three-tier (or multi-tier) application infrastructures.
Account Expires	Use the Account Expires controls to specify when an account expires.

Managing Properties on Multiple Accounts Simultaneously

Windows Server 2003 allows you to modify the properties of multiple user accounts simultaneously. You simply select several user objects by holding the CTRL key as you click each user, or using any other multiselection options. Be certain that you select only objects of one class, such as users. Once you have multiselected, on the Action menu, choose Properties.

When you have multiselected user objects, a subset of properties is available for modification.

- **General tab** Description, Office, Telephone Number, Fax, Web Page, E-mail
- **Account tab** UPN Suffix, Logon Hours, Computer Restrictions (logon workstations), all Account Options, Account Expires
- **Address** Street, PO Box, City, State/Province, ZIP/Postal Code, Country/Region
- **Profile** Profile Path, Logon Script, and Home Folder
- **Organization** Title, Department, Company, Manager

Tip Be sure to know which properties can be modified for multiple users simultaneously. Exam scenarios that suggest a need to change many user objects' properties as quickly as possible are often testing your understanding of multiselect.

There are still many properties that must be set on a user-by-user basis. Also, certain administrative tasks, including the resetting of passwords and the renaming of accounts, can only be performed on one user object at a time.

Moving a User

If a user is transferred within an organization, it is possible that you might need to move his or her user object to reflect a change in the administration or configuration of the object. To move an object in Active Directory Users and Computers, select the object and, from the Action menu, choose Move. Alternatively, you can right-click the object and select Move from the shortcut menu.

Tip A new feature of Windows Server 2003 is that drag-and-drop operations are supported. You can move objects between OUs by dragging and dropping them in the Active Directory Users And Computers Snap-in.

Practice: Creating and Managing User Objects

In this practice, you will create three user objects. You will then modify properties of those objects.

Exercise 1: Create User Objects

1. Log on to Server01 as an administrator.
2. Open Active Directory Users And Computers.
3. Select the Employees OU.

4. Create a user account with the following information, ensuring that you use a strong password:

Text Box Name	Type
First Name	Dan
Last Name	Holme
User Logon Name	Dan.Holme
User Logon Name (Pre-Windows 2000)	Dholme

5. Create a second user object with the following properties:

Property	Type
First Name	Hank
Last Name	Carbeck
User Logon Name	Hank.Carbeck
User Logon Name (Pre-Windows 2000)	Hcarbeck

6. Create a user object for yourself, following the same conventions for user logon names as you did for the first two objects.

Exercise 2: Modify User Object Properties

1. Open the Properties dialog box for your user object.

2. Configure the appropriate properties for your user object on the General, Address, Profile, Telephones, and Organization tabs.

3. Examine the many properties associated with your user object, but do not change any other properties yet.

4. Click OK when finished.

Exercise 3: Modify Multiple User Objects' Properties

1. Open Active Directory Users And Computers and navigate to the Contoso.com Employees OU. Select the Employees OU in the tree pane, which will list the user objects you created in Exercise 1 in the details pane.

2. Click Dan Holme's user object.

3. Hold the CTRL key and click Hank Carbeck's user object.

4. Click the Action menu, and then click Properties.

5. Notice the difference between the Properties dialog box here, and the more extensive properties dialog box you explored in Exercise 2. Examine the properties that are available when multiple objects are selected, but do not modify any properties yet.

6. Configure the following properties for the two user objects:

Property Page	Property	Type
General	Description	Taught me everything I needed to know about Windows Server 2003
General	Telephone Number	(425) 555-0175
General	Web Page	*http://www.microsoft.com/mspress/*
Address	Street	One Microsoft Way
Address	City	Redmond
Address	State/Province	Washington
Address	ZIP/Postal Code	98052
Organization	Title	Author
Organization	Company	Microsoft Press

7. Click OK when you finish configuring the properties.

8. Open the properties of the object Dan Holme.

9. Confirm that the properties you configured in step 6 did, in fact, apply to the object. Click OK when you are finished.

10. Click Dan Holme's user object.

11. Hold the CTRL key and click Hank Carbeck's user object. Click the Action menu.

12. Notice that the Reset Password command is not available when you have selected more than one user object. What other commands are not available when multi-selecting? Experiment by selecting one user, opening the Action menu, then selecting two users and opening the Action menu.

Lesson Review

The following questions are intended to reinforce key information presented in this lesson. If you are unable to answer a question, review the lesson materials and try the question again. You can find answers to the questions in the "Questions and Answers" section at the end of this chapter.

1. You are using Active Directory Users And Computers to configure user objects in your domain, and you are able to change the address and telephone number properties of the user object representing yourself. However, the New User command is unavailable to you. What is the most likely explanation?

_____

_____

2. You are creating a number of user objects for a team of your organization's temporary workers. They will work daily from 9:00 A.M. to 5:00 P.M. on a contract that is scheduled to begin in one month and end two months later. They will not work outside of that schedule. Which of the following properties should you configure initially to ensure maximum security for the objects?

   a. Password

   b. Logon Hours

   c. Account expires

   d. Store password using reversible encryption

   e. Account is trusted for delegation

   f. User must change password at next logon

   g. Account is disabled

   h. Password never expires

3. Which of the following properties and administrative tasks can be configured or performed simultaneously on more than one user object?

   a. Last Name

   b. User Logon Name

   c. Disable Account

   d. Enable Account

   e. Reset Password

   f. Password Never Expires

   g. User Must Change Password At Next Logon

   h. Logon Hours

   i. Computer Restrictions (Logon Workstations)

   j. Title

   k. Direct Reports

Lesson Summary

- You must be a member of the Enterprise Admins, Domain Admins, or Account Operators groups, or you must have been delegated administrative permissions to create user objects.

- User objects include the properties typically associated with a user "account," including logon names and password, and the unique SID for the user.

- User objects also include properties related to the individuals they represent, including personal information, group membership, and administrative settings. Windows Server 2003 allows you to change some of these properties for multiple users, simultaneously.

Lesson 2: Creating Multiple User Objects

Occasionally, situations emerge that require you to create multiple user objects quickly, such as a new class of incoming students at a school or a group of new hires at an organization. In these situations you must know how to facilitate or automate user object creation effectively so that you do not approach the task on an account-by-account basis. In Lesson 1, you learned how to create and manage user objects with Active Directory Users and Computers. This lesson will extend those concepts, skills, and tools to include user object creation through template objects, imported objects, and command-line scripting of objects.

After this lesson, you will be able to

- Create and utilize user object templates
- Import user objects from comma-delimited files
- Leverage new command-line tools to create and manage user objects

Estimated lesson time: 15 minutes

Creating and Utilizing User Object Templates

It is common for objects to share similar properties. For example, all sales representatives may belong to the same security groups, are allowed to log on to the network during the same hours, and have home folders and roaming profiles on the same server. In such cases, it is helpful when creating a user object for that object to be pre-populated with common properties. This can be accomplished by creating a generic user object—often called a *template*—and then copying that object to create new users.

To generate a user template, create a user and populate its properties. Put the user into appropriate groups.

Security Alert   Be certain to *disable* the user, because it is just a template, to ensure that the account is not used for access to network resources.

To create a user based on the template, select the template and choose Copy from the Action menu. You will be prompted for properties similar to those when you created a new user: first and last name, initials, logon names, password, and account options. When the object is created, you will find that properties are copied from the template based on the following property-page-based description:

- **General**   No properties copied
- **Address**   All properties except Street address are copied

- **Account** All properties are copied, except for logon names, which you are prompted to enter when copying the template

- **Profile** All properties are copied, and the profile and home-folder paths are modified to reflect the new user's logon name

- **Telephones** No properties are copied

- **Organization** All properties are copied, except for Title

- **Member Of** All properties are copied

- **Dial-in, Environment, Sessions, Remote Control, Terminal Services Profile, COM+** No properties are copied

> **Tip** A user that has been generated by copying a template has, by default, the same group membership as the template. Permissions and rights that are assigned to those groups therefore apply to the new user. However, permissions or rights assigned directly to the template user object are *not* copied or adjusted, so the new user will not have those permissions or rights.

Importing User Objects Using CSVDE

CSVDE is a command-line utility that allows you to import or export objects in Active Directory from (or to) a comma-delimited text file (also known as a comma-separated value text file), which is, of course, a common format easily read in Notepad and Microsoft Excel. The command is a powerful way to generate objects quickly. The command's basic syntax is

csvde [-i] [-f *FileName*] [-k]

-i : Specifies import mode. If not specified, the default mode is export.

-f *FileName* : Identifies the import file name.

-k : Ignores errors including "object already exists," "constraint violation," and "attribute or value already exists" during the import operation and continues processing.

The import file itself is a comma-delimited text file (*.csv or *.txt), in which the first line is a list of Lightweight Directory Access Protocol (LDAP) attribute names for the attributes imported, followed by one line for each object. Each object must contain exactly the attributes listed on the first line. A sample file follows:

```
DN,objectClass,sAMAccountName,sn,givenName,userPrincipalName

"CN=Scott Bishop,OU=Employees, DC=contoso,DC=com",
user,sbishop,Bishop,Scott,scott.bishop@contoso.com
```

This file, when imported, would create a user object in the Employees OU called Scott Bishop. The logon names, first, and last name are configured by the file. The object will be disabled initially. Once you have reset the password, you can enable the object.

> **See Also**   For more information about the powerful CSVDE command, including details regarding its parameters and its usage to *export* directory objects, open the Windows Server 2003 Help and Support Center. The LDIFDE command, also covered in detail by the Help and Support Center, allows you to import and export accounts using LDAP formats. This command and its file structure is nowhere near as intuitive for administrators as the comma-delimited file supported by CSVDE.

Utilizing Active Directory Command-Line Tools

Windows Server 2003 supports a number of powerful command-line tools to facilitate the management of Active Directory. The following is a list, and brief description, of each tool:

- **DSADD**   Adds objects to the directory.
- **DSGET**   Displays ("gets") properties of objects in the directory.
- **DSMOD**   Modifies select attributes of an existing object in the directory.
- **DSMOVE**   Moves an object from its current container to a new location.
- **DSRM**   Removes an object, the complete subtree under an object, or both.
- **DSQUERY**   Queries Active Directory for objects that match a specified search criteria. This command is often used to create a list of objects, which are then piped to the other command-line tools for management or modification.

These tools use one or more of the following components in their command-line switches:

- **Target object type**   One of a predefined set of values that correlate with an object class in Active Directory. Common examples are: computer, user, OU, group, and server (meaning domain controller).
- **Target object identity**   The distinguished name (DN) of the object against which the command is running. The DN of an object is an attribute of each object that represents the object's name and location within an Active Directory forest. For example, in Lesson 1, Exercise 1, you created a user object with the distinguished name: CN=Dan Holme, OU=Employees, DC=Contoso, DC=com.

> **Note**   When using DNs in a command parameter, enclose the name in quotes when it includes spaces. If a subcomponent of the distinguished name includes a backslash or comma, see the online help topic listed below.

■ **Server**   You can specify the domain controller against which you want to run the command.

■ **User**   You can specify a user name and password with which to run the command. This is useful if you are logged in with non-administrative credentials and wish to launch the command with elevated credentials.

In addition, switches and parameters are case-insensitive, and can be prefixed with either a dash ("-") or a slash ("/").

> **See Also**   This lesson will focus on the most commonly used commands and parameters, and on the use of these commands for user objects. For more information regarding these utilities, including the full list of parameters they accept, open the Help and Support Center and search for the phrase, "directory service command-line tools" and be sure to surround the phrase in quotes. After clicking Search, you will see the Command Line Reference on the list of Help Topics, under Search Results.

DSQUERY

The DSQUERY command queries Active Directory for objects that match a specific criteria set. The command's basic syntax is:

```
dsquery object_type  [{StartNode | forestroot | domainroot}] [-o {dn | rdn | samid}]
[-scope {subtree | onelevel | base}] [-name Name] [-desc Description] [-upn UPN]
[-samid SAMName] [-inactive NumberOfWeeks] [-stalepwd NumberOfDays] [-disabled]
[{-s Server | -d Domain}] [-u UserName] [-p {Password | *}]
```

> **Tip**   Keep in mind, this command will often be used to generate a list of objects against which you will run other command-line utilities. This is accomplished by piping the output to the second command. For example, the following command line queries Active Directory for a user object with a name starting with "Dan," pipes the result set to DSMOD, which disables each object in the result set:
>
> dsquery user -name Dan* | dsmod user -disabled yes
>
> The other utilities accept DNs as their input, which is the default output type as well.

The basic parameters are summarized in Table 3-4.

Table 3-4   Parameters for th e   D S Q U E R Y   C o m m a n d

Parameter	Description
Query scope	
object_type	Required. The object type represents the object class(es) which will be searched. The object type can include computer, contact, group, OU, server, user, or the wildcard "*" to represent any object class. This lesson will focus on the command's use in querying for the user object type.
{*StartNode* forestroot | domainroot}	Optional. Specifies the node from which the search begins. You can specify the forest root (forestroot), domain root (domainroot), or a node's distinguished name (StartNode). If forestroot is specified, the search is performed using the global catalog. The default value is domainroot.
-scope {subtree | onelevel | base}	Specifies the scope of the search. A value of subtree indicates that the scope is a subtree rooted at start node. A value of onelevel indicates the immediate children of start node only. A value of base indicates the single object represented by start node. If forestroot is specified as StartNode, subtree is the only valid scope. By default, the subtree search scope is used.
How to display the result set	
-o {dn, rdn, samid}	Specifies the format in which the list of entries found by the search will be outputted or displayed. A dn value displays the distinguished name of each entry. A rdn value displays the relative distinguished name of each entry. A samid value displays the Security Accounts Manager (SAM) account name of each entry. By default, the dn format is used.
Query criteria	
-name *Name*	Searches for users whose name attributes (value of CN attribute) matches *Name*. You can use wildcards. For example, "jon*" or "*ith" or "j*th".
-desc *Description*	Searches for users whose description attribute matches *Description*. You can use wildcards.
-upn *UPN*	Searches for users whose UPN attribute matches *UPN*.
-samid *SAMName*	Searches for users whose SAM account name matches *SAMName*. You can use wildcards.
-inactive *NumberOfWeeks*	Searches for all users that have been inactive (stale) for the specified number of weeks.
-stalepwd *NumberOfDays*	Searches for all users who have not changed their passwords for the specified number of days.
-disabled	Searches for all users whose accounts are disabled.
Domain controller and credentials used for the command	
{-s *Server* | -d *Domain*}	Connects to a specified remote server or domain.

Table 3-4   Parameters for the DSQUERY Command (Continued)

Parameter	Description
-u *UserName*	Specifies the user name with which the user logs on to a remote server. By default, -u uses the user name with which the user logged on. You can use any of the following formats to specify a user name: ■ user name (for example, Linda) ■ domain\user name (for example, *widgets\Linda*) ■ UPN (for example, *Linda@widgets.microsoft.com*)
-p {*Password* | *}	Specifies to use either a password or a * to log on to a remote server. If you type *, you are prompted for a password.

> **Tip**   Inactivity is specified in weeks, but password changes are specified in days.

DSADD

The DSADD command enables you to create objects in Active Directory. When creating a user, utilize the DSADD USER command. DSADD parameters allow you to configure specific properties of an object. The parameters are self-explanatory, however the Windows Server 2003 Help And Support Center provides thorough descriptions of the DSADD command's parameters if you desire more explanation.

dsadd user *UserDN...*

The *UserDN...* parameter is one or more distinguished names for the new user object(s). If a DN includes a space, surround the entire DN with quotation marks. The *UserDN...* parameter can be entered one of the following ways:

■ By piping a list of DNs from another command, such as DSQUERY.

■ By typing each DN on the command line, separated by spaces.

■ By leaving the DN parameter empty, at which point you can type the DNs, one at a time, at the keyboard console of the command prompt. Press ENTER after each DN. Press CTRL+Z and ENTER after the last DN.

The DSADD USER command can take the following optional parameters after the DN parameter:

■ -samid *SAMName*

■ -upn *UPN*

■ -fn *FirstName*

■ -mi *Initial*

- -ln *LastName*
- -display *DisplayName*
- -empid *EmployeeID*
- -pwd {*Password* | *} where * will prompt you for a password
- -desc *Description*
- -memberof *GroupDN*;...
- -office *Office*
- -tel *PhoneNumber*
- -email *Email*
- -hometel *HomePhoneNumber*
- -pager *PagerNumber*
- -mobile *CellPhoneNumber*
- -fax *FaxNumber*
- -iptel *IPPhoneNumber*
- -webpg *WebPage*
- -title *Title*
- -dept *Department*
- -company *Company*
- -mgr *ManagerDN*
- -hmdir *HomeDirectory*
- -hmdrv *DriveLetter*:
- -profile *ProfilePath*
- -loscr *ScriptPath*
- -mustchpwd {yes | no}
- -canchpwd {yes | no}
- -reversiblepwd {yes | no}
- -pwdneverexpires {yes | no}
- -acctexpires *NumberOfDays*
- -disabled {yes | no}

As with DSQUERY, you can add -s, -u, and -p parameters to specify the domain controller against which DSADD will run, and the user name and password—the credentials—that will be used to execute the command.

- {-s *Server* | -d *Domain*}
- -u *UserName*
- -p {*Password* | *}

The special token $username$ (case-insensitive) may replace the SAM account name in the value of the -email, -hmdir, -profile, and -webpg parameters. For example, if a SAM account name is "Denise," the -hmdir parameter can be written in either of the following formats:

- -hmdir\users\Denise\home
- -hmdir\users\$username$\home

DSMOD

The DSMOD command modifies the properties of one or more existing objects.

```
dsmod user UserDN ... parameters
```

The command handles the *UserDN...* parameter exactly as the DSADD command, and takes the same parameters. Of course now, instead of adding an object with properties, you are modifying an existing object. Note that the exceptions are that you cannot modify the *SAMName* (-samid parameter) or group membership (-memberof parameter) of a user object using the DSMOD USER command. You can use the DSMOD GROUP command, discussed in Chapter 4, "Group Accounts," to change group membership from a command-line utility.

The DSMOD command also takes the -c parameter. This parameter puts DSMOD into continuous operation mode, in which it reports errors but continues to modify the objects. Without the -c parameter, DSMOD will stop operation at the first error.

DSGET

The DSGET command gets, and outputs, selected properties of one or more existing objects.

```
dsget user UserDN ... parameters
```

The command handles the *UserDN...* parameter exactly as the DSADD command does, and takes the same parameters except that DSGET takes *only* the parameter and not an associated value. For example, DSGET takes the -samid parameter, not the -samid *SAMName* parameter and value. The reason for this is clear: You are displaying, not adding or modifying, a property. In addition, DSGET does not support the -password parameter because it cannot display passwords. DSGET adds the -dn and -sid parameters, which display the user object's distinguished name and SID, respectively.

> **Exam Tip**   Keep track of the difference between DSQUERY and DSGET. DSQUERY finds and returns a result set of objects based on property-based search criteria. DSGET returns properties for one or more specified objects.

DSMOVE

The DSMOVE command allows you to move or rename an object within a domain. It cannot be used to move objects between domains. Its basic syntax is:

```
dsmove ObjectDN [-newname NewName] [-newparent ParentDN]
```

DSMOVE also supports the -s, -u, and -p parameters described in the section regarding DSQUERY.

The object is specified using its distinguished name in the parameter *ObjectDN*. To rename the object, specify its new common name in the *NewName* parameter. Specifying the distinguished name of a container in the *ParentDN* parameter will move the object to that container.

DSRM

DSRM is used to remove an object, its subtree, or both. The basic syntax is:

```
dsrm ObjectDN ... [-subtree [-exclude]] [-noprompt] [-c]
```

It supports the -s, -u, and -p parameters described in the section about DSQUERY.

The object is specified by its distinguished name in the *ObjectDN* parameter. The -subtree switch directs DSRM to remove the objects contents if the object is a container object. The -exclude switch excludes the object itself, and can be used only in conjunction with -subtree. Specifying -subtree and -exclude would, for example, delete an OU and its subtree, but leave the OU intact. By default, without the -subtree or -exclude switches, only the object is deleted.

You will be prompted to confirm the deletion of each object, unless you specify the -noprompt parameter. The -c switch puts DSRM into continuous operation mode, in which errors are reported but the command keeps processing additional objects. Without the -c switch, processing halts on the first error.

Practice: Creating Multiple User Objects

In this practice, you will create and manage user objects utilizing templates and command line tools.

Exercise 1: Create a User Template

1. Log on to Server01 as an administrator.

2. Open Active Directory Users And Computers.

3. Select the Employees OU in the tree pane.

4. Create a user account with the following information:

Text Box Name	Enter
First Name	Template
Last Name	Sales Representative
User Logon Name:	Template.sales.rep
User Logon Name (Pre–Windows 2000):	Templatesalesrep

5. Click Next.

6. Select Account Is Disabled. Click Next.

7. The summary page appears. Click Finish.

Note   As mentioned in the chapter's "Before You Begin" section, you should create a group in the Security Groups OU called Sales Representatives. If you have not created such a group, do so now. Configure a global security group with the name Sales Representative.

8. Open the properties of the Template Sales Representative object.

9. Configure the following properties for the template account:

Tab	Property	Value
Member Of	Member Of	Sales Representatives
Account	Logon Hours	Monday–Friday, 9:00 A.M.–5:00 P.M.
Account	Expires	Three months from the current date
Organization	Company	Contoso
Profile	Profile path	\\Server1\Profiles\%Username%

10. Click OK when you have finished configuring account properties.

Exercise 2: Create Users by Copying a User Template

1. Select the Employees OU in the tree pane.

2. Select the Template Sales Representative object.

3. Click the Action menu, and then click Copy.

4. Create a new user account with the following information:

Text Box Name	Enter
First Name	Scott
Last Name	Bishop
User Logon Name:	Scott.Bishop
User Logon Name (pre-Windows 2000):	Sbishop
Account Is Disabled	Clear the check box
Password/Confirm Password	Enter and confirm a complex password as described earlier in this chapter.

5. Click Next, and then click Finish.

6. Open the properties of the object Scott Bishop.

7. Confirm that the information configured for the template on the Member Of, Account, and Organization Property pages were applied to the new object.

8. Because you will use this account for other exercises in the chapter, reset two properties. On the Account tab, set the Account Expires option to Never, and set the Logon Hours so that logon is permitted at any time.

Exercise 3: Import User Objects Using CSVDE

1. Open Notepad.

2. Type the following information carefully, creating 3 lines of text:

   ```
   DN,objectClass,sAMAccountName,sn,givenName,userPrincipalName

   "CN=Danielle Tiedt,OU=Employees,
   DC=contoso,DC=com",user,dtiedt,Tiedt,Danielle,danielle.tiedt@contoso.com

   "CN=Lorrin Smith-Bates,OU=Employees, DC=contoso,DC=com",user,lsmithbates,Smith-
   Bates,Lorrin,lorrin.smithbates@contoso.com
   ```

3. Save the file as **"C:\USERS.CSV"** being certain to surround the filename with quote marks. Without quote marks, the file will be saved as C:\USERS.CSV.TXT.

4. Open the command prompt and type the following command:

   csvde –i -f c:\users.csv

5. If the command output confirms that the command completed successfully, open Active Directory Users and Computers to confirm that the objects were created. If the command output suggests that there were errors, open the USERS.CSV file in Notepad and correct the errors.

6. You will log on as these users later in this chapter. Because the users were imported without passwords, you must reset their passwords. Once the passwords have been configured, enable the accounts. Both the Reset Password and Enable Account commands can be found on either the Action or Objects shortcut menu.

7. If you have access to an application that can open comma-delimited text files, such as Microsoft Excel, open C:\USERS.CSV. You will be able to interpret its structure more easily in a columnar display than in Notepad's one-line, comma-delimited text file display.

Exercise 4: Utilize Active Directory Command-Line Tools

1. Open the command and type the following command:

   dsquery user "OU=Employees, DC=Contoso,DC=Com" -stalepwd 7

2. The command, which finds user objects that have not changed their password in seven days, should list, at a minimum, the objects you created in exercises 1 and 2. If not, create one or two new user objects and then perform step 1.

3. Type the following command and press ENTER:

   dsquery user "OU=Employees, DC=Contoso,DC=Com" -stalepwd 7 | dsmod user -mustchpwd yes

4. The command used the results of DSQUERY as the input for the DSMOD command. The DSMOD command configured the option "User must change password at next logon" for each object. Confirm your success by examining the Account tab of the affected objects.

Lesson Review

The following questions are intended to reinforce key information presented in this lesson. If you are unable to answer a question, review the lesson materials and try the question again. You can find answers to the questions in the "Questions and Answers" section at the end of this chapter.

1. What option will be most useful to generate 100 new user objects, each of which have identical profile path, home folder path, Title, Web Page, Company, Department, and Manager settings?

_____

_____

2. Which tool will allow you to identify accounts that have not been used for two months?

   a. DSADD

   b. DSGET

   c. DSMOD

   d. DSRM

   e. DSQUERY

3. What variable can be used with the DSMOD and DSADD commands to create user-specific home folders and profile folders?

   a. *%Username%*

   b. *$Username$*

   c. CN=*Username*

   d. *<Username>*

4. Which tools allow you to output the telephone numbers for all users in an OU?

   a. DSADD

   b. DSGET

   c. DSMOD

   d. DSRM

   e. DSQUERY

Lesson Summary

■ A user object template is an object that is copied to produce new users. If the template is not a "real" user, it should be disabled. Only a subset of user properties are copied from templates.

■ The CSVDE command enables you to import directory objects from a comma-delimited text file.

■ Windows Server 2003 supports powerful new command-line tools to create, manage, and delete directory objects: DSQUERY, DSGET, DSADD, DSMOVE, DSMOD, and DSRM. Frequently, DSQUERY will produce a result set of objects that are piped as input to other commands.

Lesson 3: Managing User Profiles

You probably wouldn't read this book if you weren't supporting users, and you know that there are elements of the user's system that cause the user pain when they are not present. For example, if a user logs on and does not have access to his or her Internet Explorer Favorites, or must reconfigure his or her custom dictionary, or does not see familiar shortcuts or documents on the desktop, the user's productivity takes an instant plunge, and the help desk gets a call. Each of these examples relate to components of the user profile. Profiles can be configured to enhance their availability, security, and reliability. In this lesson, you will learn how to manage local, roaming, group, and mandatory profiles.

After this lesson, you will be able to

- Understand the application of local and roaming user profiles
- Configure a roaming user profile
- Create a preconfigured roaming user or group profile
- Configure a mandatory profile

Estimated lesson time: 15 minutes

User Profiles

A user profile is a collection of folders and data files that contain the elements of your desktop environment that make it uniquely yours. Settings include:

- Shortcuts in your Start menu, on your desktop, and in your Quick Launch bar
- Documents on your desktop and, unless redirection is configured, in your My Documents folder

> **Tip**   The properties of the My Documents folder, and the Folder Redirection policies in group policy, enable you to redirect My Documents so that it targets a network folder. This best practice allows the contents of a user's My Documents folder to be stored on a server, where they can be backed up, scanned for viruses, and made available to users throughout the organization, should they utilize a system other than their normal desktop. My Documents can also be made available offline, so that users have access to their files even when users are not connected to the network.

- Internet Explorer favorites and cookies
- Certificates (if implemented)

- Application specific files, such as the Microsoft Office custom user dictionary, user templates, and autocomplete list

- My Network Places

- Desktop display settings, such as appearance, wallpaper, and screensaver

These important elements are specific to each user. It is desirable that they are consistent between logons, available should the user need to log on to another system, and resilient in the event that the user's system fails and must be reinstalled.

Local User Profiles

By default, user profiles are stored locally on the system in the %*Systemdrive*% \Documents and Settings\\%*Username*% folder. They operate in the following manner:

- When a user logs on to a system for the first time, the system creates a profile for the user by copying the Default User profile. The new profile folder is named based on the logon name specified in the user's initial logon.

- All changes made to the user's desktop and software environment are stored in the local user profile. Each user has their individual profiles, so settings are user-specific.

- The user environment is extended by the All Users profile, which can include shortcuts in the desktop or start menu, network places, and even application data. Elements of the All Users profile are combined with the user's profile to create the user environment. By default, only users of the Administrators group can modify the All Users profile.

- The profile is truly local. If a user logs on to another system, the documents and settings that are part of their profile do not follow the user. Instead, the new system behaves as outlined here, generating a new local profile for the user if it is the user's first time logging on to that system.

Roaming User Profiles

If users work at more than one computer, you can configure roaming user profiles (RUPs) to ensure that their documents and settings are consistent no matter where they log on. RUPs store the profile on a server, which also means that the profiles can be backed up, scanned for viruses, and controlled centrally. Even in environments where users do not roam, RUPs provide resiliency for the important information stored in the profile. If a user's system fails and must be reinstalled, an RUP will ensure that the user's environment is identical on the new system to the one on the previous system.

To configure an RUP, create a shared folder on a server. Ideally, the server should be a file server that is frequently backed up.

Note Be sure to configure share permissions allowing Everyone Full Control. The Windows Server 2003 default share permissions allow Read, which is not sufficient for a roaming profile share.

On the Profile tab of the user's Properties dialog box, type the Profile Path in the format: *<server >**<share>**%Username%*. The *%Username%* variable will automatically be replaced with the user's logon name.

It's that simple. The next time the user logs on, the system will identify the roaming profile location.

Exam Tip Roaming user profiles are nothing more than a shared folder and a path to the user's profile folder, within that share, entered into the user object's profile path property. Roaming profiles are not, in any way, a property of a computer object.

When the user logs *off*, the sytem will upload the profile to the profile server. The user can now log on to that system or any other system in the domain, and the documents and settings that are part of the RUP will be applied.

Note Windows Server 2003 introduces a new policy: Only Allow Local User Profiles. This policy, linked to an OU containing computer accounts, will prevent roaming profiles from being used on those computers. Instead, users will maintain local profiles.

When a user with an RUP logs on to a new system for the first time, the system does not copy its Default User profile. Instead, it downloads the RUP from the network location. When a user logs off, or when a user logs on to a system on which they've worked before, the system copies only files that have changed.

Roaming Profile Synchronization

Unlike previous versions of Microsoft Windows, Windows 2000, Windows XP, and Windows Server 2003 do not upload and download the entire user profile at logoff and logon. Instead, the user profile is *synchronized*. Only files that have changed are transferred between the local system and the network RUP folder. This means that logon and logoff with RUPs are significantly faster than with earlier Windows versions. Organizations that have not implemented RUPs for fear of their impact on logon and network traffic should reevaluate their configuration in this light.

Creating a Preconfigured User Profile

You can create a customized user profile to provide a planned, preconfigured desktop and software environment. This is helpful to achieve the following:

- Provide a productive work environment with easy access to needed network resources and applications

- Remove access to unnecessary resources and applications

- Simplify help desk troubleshooting by enforcing a more straightforward and consistent desktop

No special tools are required to create a preconfigured user profile. Simply log on to a system and modify the desktop and software settings appropriately. It's a good idea to do this as an account other than your actual user account so that you don't modify your own profile unnecessarily.

Once you've created the profile, log on to the system with administrative credentials. Open System from Control Panel, click the Advanced tab, and then click Settings in the User Profiles frame. Select the profile you created, and then click Copy To. Type the Universal Naming Convention (UNC) path to the profile in the format: **\\\<server>\\\<share>\\\<username>**. In the Permitted To Use section, click Change to select the user for whom you've configured the profile. This sets the ACL on the profile folder to allow access to that user. Figure 3-5 shows an example. Click OK and the profile is copied to the network location.

> **Note**   You must be a member of the Administrators group to copy a profile.

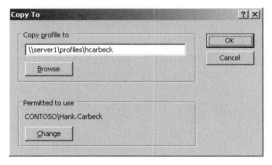

Figure 3-5   Copying a preconfigured user profile to the network

Finally, open the properties of the user object and, on the Profile tab, enter the same UNC Profile Path field. Voilà! The next time that user logs on to a domain computer, that profile will be downloaded and will determine his or her user environment.

Tip Be careful with preconfigured roaming profiles, or any roaming profiles, to pay attention to potential issues related to different hardware on systems to which a user logs on. For example, if desktop shortcuts are arranged assuming XGA (1024×768) resolution, and the user logs on to a system with a display adapter capable of only SVGA (800×600) resolution, some shortcuts may not be visible.

Profiles are also not fully cross-platform. A profile designed for Windows 98 will not function properly on a Windows Server 2003 system. You will even encounter inconsistencies when roaming between Windows Server 2003 systems and Windows XP or Windows 2000 Professional.

Creating a Preconfigured Group Profile

Roaming profiles enable you to create a standard desktop environment for multiple users with similar job responsibilities. The process is similar to creating a preconfigured user profile except that the resulting profile is made available to multiple users.

Create a profile using the steps outlined above. When copying the profile to the server, use a path such as: \\<server>\<share>\<group profile name>. You must grant access to all users who will utilize the profile, so, in the Permitted To Use frame, click Change and select a group that includes all the users, or the BUILTIN\USERS group, which includes all domain users. The only users to whom the profile will actually apply are those for which you configure the user object's profile path.

After copying the profile to the network, you must configure the profile path for the users to whom the profile will apply. Windows Server 2003 simplifies this task, in that you can multiselect users and change the profile path for all users simultaneously. Type the same UNC that you used to copy the profile to the network, for example, ***<server>\<share>\<group profile name>***.

Tip The profile path is configured as a property of one or more *user* objects. It is not assigned to a group object. Although the concept is that of a group profile, do not fall into the trap of associating the profile with a group object itself.

Finally, because more than one user will be accessing a group profile, you must make a group profile mandatory, as described in the following section.

Configuring a Mandatory Profile

A mandatory profile does not allow users to modify the profile's environment. More specifically, a mandatory profile does not maintain changes between sessions. Therefore, although a user can make changes, the next time the user logs on, the desktop will look the same as the last time he or she logged on. Changes do not persist.

Mandatory profiles can be helpful in situations in which you want to lock down the desktop. They are, in a practical sense, critical when you implement group profiles because you obviously don't want the changes one user makes to affect the environments of other users.

To configure a profile as mandatory, simply rename a file in the root folder of the profile. Interestingly, mandatory profiles are *not* configured through the application of permissions. The file you need to rename is Ntuser.dat. It is a hidden file, so you must ensure that you have specified to "Show hidden files and folders" in the Folder Options program in Control Panel, or use attrib from the command-line to remove the Hidden attribute. You may also need to configure Windows Explorer to display file extensions.

Locate the Ntuser.dat file in the profile you wish to make mandatory. Rename the file to Ntuser.man. The profile, whether roaming or local, is now mandatory.

Practice: Managing User Profiles

In this practice, you will create roaming and preconfigured roaming user profiles and mandatory group profiles. You will log on and log off a number of times. Because standard user accounts are not allowed to log on locally to a domain controller, you will begin by adding users to the Print Operators group, so that those users can log on successfully.

Exercise 1: Configure Users to Log On to the Domain Controller

In the real world, you would rarely want users to have permission to log on locally to a domain controller, however, in our one-system test environment, this capability is important. Although there are several ways to achieve this goal, the easiest is to add the Domain Users group to the Print Operators group. The Print Operators group has the right to log on locally.

1. Open Active Directory Users And Computers.
2. In the tree pane, select the Builtin container.
3. Open the Properties of the Print Operators group.
4. Use the Members tab to add Domain Users to the group.

Exercise 2: Create a Profiles Share

1. Create a Profiles folder on the C drive.
2. Right-click the Profiles folder and choose Sharing and Security.
3. Click the Sharing tab.
4. Share the folder with the default share name: Profiles.
5. Click the Permissions button.

6. Select the check box to allow Full Control.

7. Click OK.

> **Security Alert**   Windows Server 2003 applies a limited share permission by default when creating a share. Most organizations follow the best practice, which is to allow Full Control as a share permission, and to apply specific permissions to the folder using the Security tab of the folder's properties dialog box. However, in the event that an administrator has not locked down a resource before sharing it, Windows Server 2003 errs in favor of security, using a share permission that allows Read-Only access.

Exercise 3: Create a User Profile Template

1. Create a user account that will be used solely for creating profile templates. Use the following guidelines when creating the account:

Text Box Name	Enter
First Name	Profile
Last Name	Account
User Logon Name:	Profile
User Logon Name (Pre-Windows 2000):	Profile

2. Log off of Server01.

3. Log on as the Profile account.

4. Customize the desktop. You might create shortcuts to local or network resources, such as creating a shortcut to the C drive on the desktop.

5. Customize the desktop using the Display application in Control Panel. On the Desktop page of the Display Properties dialog box, you can configure the desktop background and, by clicking Customize Desktop, add the My Documents, My Computer, My Network Places, and Internet Explorer icons to the desktop.

6. Log off as the Profile account.

Exercise 4: Set Up a Preconfigured User Profile

1. Log on as Administrator.

2. Open System Properties from Control Panel, by double-clicking System.

3. Click the Advanced tab.

4. In the User Profiles frame, click Settings. This opens the Copy To dialog box.

5. Select the Profile account's user profile.

6. Click Copy To.

7. In the Copy Profile To frame, type **server01\profiles\hcarbeck**.

8. In the Permitted To Use section, click Change.

9. Type **Hank** and click OK.

10. Confirm the entries in the Copy To dialog box and click OK.

11. After the profile has copied to the network, click OK twice to close the User Profiles and System Properties dialog boxes.

12. Open the C:\Profiles folder to verify that the profile folder "Hcarbeck" was created.

13. Open Active Directory Users And Computers and, in the tree pane, select the Employees OU.

14. Open the properties of Hank Carbeck's user object.

15. Click the Profile tab.

16. In the Profile Path field, type **server01\profiles\%username%**.

17. Click Apply and confirm that the *%Username%* variable was replaced by hcarbeck. It is important that the profile path match the actual network path to the profile folder.

18. Click OK.

19. Test the success of the preconfigured roaming user profile by logging off and logging on with the user name *hank.carbeck@contoso.com*. You should see the desktop modifications that you made while logged on as the Profile account.

Exercise 5: Set Up a Preconfigured, Mandatory Group Profile

1. Log on as Administrator.

2. Open System Properties from Control Panel by double-clicking System.

3. Click the Advanced tab.

4. In the User Profiles frame, click Settings.

5. Select the Profile account's user profile.

6. Click Copy To.

7. In the Copy Profile To frame type **server01\profiles\sales**.

8. In the Permitted To Use frame, click Change.

9. Type **Users** and then click OK.

10. Confirm the entries in the Copy To dialog box and then click OK.

11. After the profile has copied to the network, click OK twice to close the User Profiles and System Properties dialog boxes.

12. Open the C:\Profiles folder to verify that the profile folder Sales was created.

13. Open Folder Options in Control Panel and, on the View tab, under Advanced Settings, ensure that the option, Show Hidden Files And Folders, is selected.

14. Open the C:\Profiles\Sales folder and rename the file Ntuser.dat to Ntuser.man. This makes the profile mandatory.

15. Open Active Directory Users And Computers and, in the tree pane, select the Employees OU.

16. In the details pane, select the following objects by clicking the first and pressing the CTRL key while selecting additional objects: Scott Bishop, Danielle Tiedt, Lorrin Smith-Bates.

17. Click the Action menu and choose Properties.

18. Click the Profile tab, and then select the Profile Path check box.

19. In the Profile Path field, type **server01****profiles****sales**.

20. Click OK.

21. Test the success of the preconfigured roaming user profile by logging off and logging on with the user name *danielle.tiedt@contoso.com*.

22. Test the mandatory nature of the profile by making a change to the desktop appearance. You will be able to make the change, but the change will not persist to future sessions.

23. Log of the computer, and then log on again as Danielle Tiedt. Because the profile is mandatory, the changes you made in the previous step should not appear.

24. Log off the computer, and log on again as Scott Bishop, with user name *scott.bishop@contoso.com*. The same desktop should appear.

Lesson Review

The following questions are intended to reinforce key information presented in this lesson. If you are unable to answer a question, review the lesson materials and try the question again. You can find answers to the questions in the "Questions and Answers" section at the end of this chapter.

1. Describe how a user's desktop is created when roaming user profiles are not implemented.

_____

_____

2. Arrange, in order, the steps that reflect the creation of a preconfigured roaming user profile. Use all steps provided.

   ❑ Customize the desktop and user environment.

   ❑ Log on as a user with sufficient permissions to modify user account properties.

   ❑ Copy the profile to the network.

   ❑ Create a user account so that the profile can be created without modifying any user's current profile.

   ❑ Log on as the profile account.

   ❑ Enter the UNC path to the profile in a user's Profile property sheet.

   ❑ Log on as a local or domain administrator.

3. How do you make a profile mandatory?

   a. Configure the permissions on the folder's Security property sheet to deny write permission.

   b. Configure the permissions on the folders Sharing property sheet to allow only read permission.

   c. Modify the attributes of the profile folder to specify the Read Only attribute.

   d. Rename Ntuser.dat to Ntuser.man.

Lesson Summary

- Windows Server 2003 provides individual profiles for each user who logs on to the system. Profiles are stored, by default, on the local system in %*Systemdrive*% \Documents and Settings\%*Username*%.

- Roaming profiles require only a shared folder, and the profile path configured in the user object's properties.

- Preconfigured profiles are simply profiles that are copied to the profile path before the profile path is configured in the user object.

- Group profiles must be made mandatory, by renaming Ntuser.dat to Ntuser.man, so that changes made by one user do not affect other users.

Lesson 4: Securing and Troubleshooting Authentication

Once you have configured user objects, and users are authenticating against those accounts, you expose yourself to two additional challenges: security vulnerabilities, which if unaddressed could compromise the integrity of your enterprise network; and social engineering challenges, as you work to make the network, and authentication in general, friendly and reliable for users. Unfortunately, these two dynamics are at odds with each other—the more secure a network, the less usable it becomes. In this lesson, we will address issues related to user authentication. You will learn the impact of domain account policies, including password policies and account lockout policies. You will also learn how to configure auditing for logon-related events, and to perform various authentication-related tasks on user objects.

After this lesson, you will be able to

■ Identify domain account policies and their impact on password requirements and authentication

■ Configure auditing for logon events

■ Modify authentication-related attributes of user objects

Estimated lesson time: 15 minutes

Securing Authentication with Policy

Active Directory on Windows Server 2003 supports security policies to strengthen passwords and their use within an enterprise. Of course, you must design a password policy that is sufficiently daunting to attackers while being sufficiently convenient for users, so that they do not forget passwords (resulting in increased calls to the help desk) or, worse, write down their passwords.

A system running Windows Server 2003 as a member server maintains a policy related to its local user accounts. The local security policy can be managed using the appropriately named snap-in: Local Security Policy.

You will more often be concerned with the policy that affects domain user objects. Domain account policy is managed by the Default Domain Policy. To examine and modify this policy, open Active Directory Users and Computers. Select the domain node and choose Properties from the Action menu. Click the Group Policy tab. The GPO listed as the first, or top object link is the policy object that will drive the domain account policies. It is typically, and in best practice, the Default Domain Policy. Select that policy and click Edit. The Group Policy Object Editor console opens, focused on the Default Domain policy. Navigate to Computer Configuration, Windows Settings, Security Settings, Account Policies.

Password Policy

The domain password policies enable you to protect your network against password compromise by enforcing best-practice password management techniques. The policies are described in Table 3-5.

Table 3-5   Password Policies

Policy	Description
Enforce Password History	When this policy is enabled, Active Directory maintains a list of recently used passwords, and will not allow a user to create a password that matches a password in that history. The result is that a user, when prompted to change his or her password, cannot use the same password again, and therefore cannot circumvent the password lifetime. The policy is enabled by default, with the maximum value of 24. Many IT organizations use a value of 6 to 12.
Maximum Password Age	This policy determines when users will be forced to change their passwords. Passwords that are unchanged or infrequently changed are more vulnerable to being cracked and utilized by attackers to impersonate a valid account. The default value is 42 days. IT organizations typically enforce password changes every 30 to 90 days.
Minimum Password Age	When users are required to change their passwords—even when a password history is enforced—they can simply change their passwords several times in a row to circumvent password requirements and return to their original passwords. The Minimum Password Age policy prevents this possibility by requiring that a specified number of days must pass between password changes. Of course, a password can be reset at any time in Active Directory by an administrator or support person with sufficient permissions. But the user cannot change their password more than once during the time period specified by this setting.
Minimum Password Length	This policy specifies the minimum number of characters required in a password. The default in Windows Server 2003 is seven.
Passwords Must Meet Complexity Requirements	This policy enforces rules, or filters, on new passwords. The default password filter in Windows Server 2003 (passfilt.dll) requires that a password: ■ Is not based on the user's account name. ■ Is at least six characters long. ■ Contains characters from three of the following four character types: ❑ Uppercase alphabet characters (A...Z) ❑ Lowercase alphabet characters (a...z) ❑ Arabic numerals (0...9) ❑ Nonalphanumeric characters (for example, !$#,%) Windows Server 2003 enables this policy, by default.

> **Note**   Configuring password length and complexity requirements does not affect existing passwords. These changes will affect new accounts and changed passwords after the policy is applied.

Account Lockout Policy

Account lockout refers, in its broadest sense, to the concept that after several failed logon attempts by a single user, the system should assume that an attacker is attempting to compromise the account by discovering its password and, in defense, should lock the account so no further logons may be attempted. Domain account lockout policies determine the limitations for invalid logons, expressed in a number of invalid logons in a period of time, and the requirements for an account to become unlocked, whether by simply waiting or contacting an administrator. Table 3-6 summarizes Account Lockout policies.

Table 3-6   Account Lockout Policies

Policy	Description
Account Lockout Threshold	This policy configures the number of invalid logon attempts that will trigger account lockout. The value can be in the range of 0 to 999. A value that is too low (as few as three, for example) may cause lockouts due to normal, human error at logon. A value of 0 will result in accounts never being locked out. The lockout counter is not affected by logons to locked workstations.
Account Lockout Duration	This policy determines the period of time that must pass after a lockout before Active Directory will automatically unlock a user's account. The policy is not set by default, as it is useful only in conjunction with the Account Lockout Threshold policy. Although the policy accepts values ranging from 0 to 99999 minutes, or about 10 weeks, a low setting (5 to 15 minutes) is sufficient to reduce attacks significantly without unreasonably affecting legitimate users who are mistakenly locked out. A value of 0 will require the user to contact appropriate administrators to unlock the account manually.
Reset Account Lockout Counter After	This setting specifies the time that must pass after an invalid logon attempt before the counter resets to zero. The range is 1 to 99999 minutes, and must be less than or equal to the account lockout duration.

Cross-Platform Issues

Organizations commonly implement a mix of directory service, server, and client platforms. In environments in which Windows 95, Windows 98, Windows Me, or Windows NT 4 participate in an Active Directory domain, administrators need to be aware of several issues.

- Passwords: While Windows 2000, Windows XP Professional, and Windows Server 2003 support 127-character passwords, Windows 95, Windows 98, and Windows ME support only 14-character passwords.

- Active Directory Client: The Active Directory Client can be downloaded from Microsoft's web site and installed on Windows 95, Windows 98, Windows Me, and Windows NT 4 systems. It enables those platforms running previous editions of Windows to participate in many Active Directory features available to Windows 2000 Professional or Windows XP Professional, including the following:

  - Site-awareness: a system with the Active Directory Client will attempt to log on to a domain controller in its site, rather than to any domain controller in the enterprise.

  - Active Directory Service Interfaces (ADSI): use scripting to manage Active Directory.

  - Distributed File System (Dfs): access Dfs shared resources on servers running Windows 2000 and Windows Server 2003.

  - NT LAN Manager (NTLM) version 2 authentication: use the improved authentication features in NTLM version 2.

  - Active Directory Windows Address Book (WAB): property pages

  - Active Directory search capability integrated into the Start–Find or Start–Search commands.

The following functionalites, supported on Windows 2000 Professional and Windows XP Professional, are *not* provided by the Active Directory client on Windows 95, Windows 98, and Windows NT 4:

- Kerberos V5 authentication

- Group Policy or Change and Configuration Management support

- Service principal name (SPN), or mutual authentication.

In addition, you should be aware of the following issues in mixed environments:

- Windows 98 supports passwords of up to 14 characters long. Windows 2000, Windows XP, and Windows Server 2003 can support 127-character passwords. Be aware of this difference when configuring passwords for users who log on using Windows 98.

- Without the Active Directory client, users on systems using versions of Windows earlier than Windows 2000 can change their password only if the system has access to the domain controller performing the single master operation called primary domain controller (PDC) emulator. To determine which system is the PDC emulator in a domain, open Active Directory Users And Computers, select the domain node, choose the Operations Masters command from the Action menu, and then click the PDC tab. If the PDC emulator is unavailable (that is, if it is offline or on the distant side of a downed network connection), the user cannot change his or her password.

- As you have learned in this chapter, user objects maintain two user logon name properties. The Pre-Windows 2000 logon name, or SAM name, is equivalent to the user name in Windows 95, Windows 98, or Windows NT 4. When users log on, they enter their user name and must select the domain from the Log On To box. In other situations, the user name may be entered in the format *<DomainName>\<UserLogonName>*.

- Users logging on using Windows 2000 or later platforms may log on the same way, or they may log on using the more efficient UPN. The UPN takes the format *<UserLogonName>@<UPN Suffix>*, where the UPN suffix is, by default, the DNS domain name in which the user object resides. It is not necessary to select the domain from the Log On To box when using UPN logon. In fact, the box becomes disabled as soon as you type the "@" symbol.

Auditing Authentication

If you are concerned that attacks may be taking place to discover user passwords, or to troubleshoot authentication problems, you can configure an auditing policy that will create entries in the Security log that may prove illuminating.

Audit Policies

The following policies are located in the Computer Configuration, Windows Settings, Security Settings, Local Policies, Audit Policy node of Group Policy Object Editor (or the Local Security Policy snap-in). You can configure auditing for successful or failed events.

- **Audit Account Logon Events** This policy audits each instance of user logon that involves domain controller authentication. For domain controllers, this policy is defined in the Default Domain Controllers GPO. Note, first, that this policy will create a Security log entry on a domain controller each time a user logs on inter-actively or over the network using a domain account. Second, remember that to evaluate fully the results of the auditing, you must examine the Security logs on all domain controllers, because user authentication is distributed among each domain controller in a site or domain.

- **Audit Account Management**   Configures auditing of activities including the creation, deletion, or modification of user, group, or computer accounts. Password resets are also logged when account management auditing is enabled.

- **Audit Logon Events**   Logon events include logon and logoff, interactively or through network connection. If you have enabled Audit Account Logon Events policy for successes on a domain controller, workstation logons will not generate logon audits. Only interactive and network logons to the domain controller itself generate logon events. Account logon events are generated on the local computer for local accounts and on the domain controller for network accounts. Logon events are generated wherever the logon occurs.

> **Tip**   Keep track of the distinction between Account Logon and Logon events. When a user logs on to their workstation using a domain account, the workstation registers a Logon event and the domain controller registers an Account Logon event. When the user connects to a network server's shared folder, the server registers a Logon event and the domain controller registers an Account Logon event.

Security Event Log

Once you have configured auditing, the security logs will begin to fill with event messages. You can view these messages by selecting Security from the Event Viewer snap-in, and then double-clicking the event.

> **Exam Tip**   Remember that Account Logon events will need to be monitored on each domain controller. Logon events must be monitored on all systems.

Administering User Authentication

When users forget their passwords, are transferred or terminated, you will have to manage their user objects appropriately. The most common administrative tasks related to user account security are unlocking an account, resetting a password, disabling, enabling, renaming, and deleting user objects.

Unlocking a User Account

The account lockout policy requires that when a user has exceeded the limit for invalid logon attempts, the account is locked and no further logons can be attempted for a specified period of time, or until an administrator has unlocked the account.

To unlock a user, select the user object and, from the Action menu, choose Properties. Click the Account tab and clear the check box: Account Is Locked Out.

Resetting User Passwords

If a user forgets his or her password, you must reset the password. You do not need to know the user's old password to do so. Simply select the user object and, from the Action menu, choose the Reset Password command. Enter the new password twice to confirm the change, and as a security best practice, select the User Must Change Password At Next Logon option.

Disabling, Enabling, Renaming, and Deleting User Objects

Personnel changes may require you to disable, enable, or rename a user object. The process for doing so is similar for each action. Select the user and, from the Action menu, choose the appropriate command, as follows:

- **Disabling And Enabling A User**   When a user does not require access to the network for an extended period of time, you should disable the account. Re-enable the account when the user needs to log on once again. Note that the only one of the commands to Disable or Enable will appear on the Action menu depending on the current status of the object.

- **Deleting A User**   When a user is no longer part of your organization, *and there will not soon be a replacement*, delete the user object. Remember that by deleting a user, you lose its group memberships and, by deleting the SID, its rights and permissions. If you recreate a user object with the same name, it will have a different SID, and you will have to reassign rights, permissions, and group memberships.

- **Renaming A User**   You will rename a user if a user changes their name, for example through marriage, or in the event that a user is no longer part of your organization, but you are replacing that user and you want to maintain the rights, permissions, group memberships, and most of the user properties of the previous user.

Tip   Be certain to understand the difference between disabling and deleting an object; and between enabling and unlocking a user.

Practice: Securing and Troubleshooting Authentication

In this practice, you will configure domain auditing policies. You will then generate logon events. Finally, you will examine and troubleshoot the results of those logons.

Exercise 1: Configure Policies

1. Open Active Directory Users And Computers.

2. Select the domain node, Contoso.com

3. From the Action menu, choose Properties.

4. On the Group Policy tab, select Default Domain Policy and then click Edit.

5. Navigate to Computer Configuration, Windows Settings, Security Settings, Account Policies, and finally Account Lockout Policy.

6. Double-click the Account Lockout Duration policy.

7. Select the Define This Policy Setting check box.

8. Type **0** for the duration, then click Apply.

   The system will prompt you that it will configure the account lockout threshold and reset counter policies. Click OK.

9. Click OK to confirm the settings, and then click OK to close the Policy dialog box.

10. Confirm that the Account Lockout Duration policy is zero, the threshold is 5, and the reset counter policy is 30 minutes.

11. Close the Group Policy Object Editor window.

12. Click OK to close the Properties dialog box for the *contoso.com* domain.

13. Select the Domain Controllers container, under the domain node.

14. From the Action menu, click Properties.

15. On the Group Policy tab, select Default Domain Controllers Policy and click Edit.

16. Navigate to Computer Configuration, Windows Settings, Security Settings, Local Policies, and finally Audit Policy.

17. Double-click the Audit Account Logon Events policy.

18. Select Define These Policy Settings, select both Success and Failure, and then click OK.

19. Double-click the Audit Logon Events policy.

20. Select Define These Policy Settings, select both Success and Failure, and then click OK.

21. Double-click the Audit Account Management policy.

22. Select Define These Policy Settings, select Success, and then click OK.

23. Close the Group Policy Object Editor window.

24. Click OK to close the Properties dialog box for the Domain Controllers Properties dialog box.

Exercise 2: Generate Logon Events

1. Log off of Server01.

2. Generate two logon failure events by attempting to log on twice with the username sbishop and an *invalid* password.

3. Log on correctly as sbishop.

4. Log off.

Exercise 3: Generate Account Management Events

1. Log on as Administrator.

2. Open Active Directory Users And Computers.

3. In the tree pane, navigate to and select the Employees OU.

4. In the details pane, select Scott Bishop's user object, and then click the Action menu.

5. Click the Reset Password command.

6. Enter and confirm a new password for Scott Bishop, and then click OK.

Exercise 4: Examine Authentication Security Event Messages

1. Open the Computer Management console from the Administrative Tools group.

2. Expand Event Viewer and select Security.

3. Make sure the Category column is wide enough that you can identify the types of events that are logged.

4. Explore the events that have been generated by recent activity. Note the failed logons, the successful logons, and the resetting of Scott Bishop's password.

Lesson Review

The following questions are intended to reinforce key information presented in this lesson. If you are unable to answer a question, review the lesson materials and try the question again. You can find answers to the questions in the "Questions and Answers" section at the end of this chapter.

1. You enable the password complexity policy for your domain. Describe the requirements for passwords, and when those requirements will take effect.

   _____

   _____

2. To monitor potential dictionary attacks against user passwords in your enterprise, what is the single best auditing policy to configure, and what log or logs will you evaluate?

   _____

   _____

3. A user has forgotten his or her password and attempts to log on several times with an incorrect password. Eventually, the user receives a logon message indicating that the account is either disabled or locked out. The message suggests that the user contact an administrator. What must you do?

   a. Delete the user object and recreate it.

   b. Enable the user object.

   c. Unlock the user object.

   d. Reset the password for the user object.

Lesson Summary

■ The Default Domain Policy drives account policies including the password and lockout policies.

■ The Default Domain Controllers Policy specifies key auditing policies for domain controllers.

■ Auditing for authentication generates events in each domain controller's security logs.

Case Scenario Exercise

One of Contoso's competitors recently made the news as a recent victim of a breach of password security, that exposed its sensitive data. You decide to audit Contoso's security configuration and you set forth the following requirements:

- Requirement 1: Because you upgraded your domain controllers from Windows 2000 Server to Windows Server 2003, the domain account policy remained that of Windows 2000 Server. The domain account policies shall require:
  - ❑ Password changes every 60 days
  - ❑ 8-character passwords
  - ❑ Password complexity
  - ❑ Minimum password duration of one week
  - ❑ Password history of 20 passwords
  - ❑ Account lockout after five invalid logon attempts in a 60-minute period
  - ❑ Administrator intervention to unlock locked out accounts
- Requirement 2: In addition, ensure that these policies take effect within 24 hours. Password policies are implemented when a user changes his or her password—the policies do not affect existing passwords. So you require that users change their passwords as quickly as possible. You do not want to affect accounts used by services. Service accounts are stored in Contoso's Service Accounts OU. User accounts are stored in the Employees OU and 15 OUs located under the Employees OU.
- Requirement 3: Lock down the desktops of the sales representatives so that they are less likely to install customized Web toolbars, weather watchers, wallpaper-of-the-day utilities, or other software that might connect to the Internet and expose the desktop to attack.

Requirement 1

The first requirement involves modifying password and account lockout settings.

1. What should be modified to achieve Requirement 1?
   a. The domain controller security template Hisecdc.inf
   b. The Default Domain policy
   c. The Default Domain Controller policy
   d. The domain controller security template Ssetup Security.inf

   The correct answer is b.

2. To configure account lockout so that users must contact the Help Desk to unlock their accounts, which policy should be specified?

   a. Account lockout duration: 999

   b. Account lockout threshold: 999

   c. Account lockout duration: 0

   d. Account lockout threshold: 0

   The correct answer is c.

Configure the appropriate domain policies. For guidance, refer to Lesson 4, Exercise 1.

Requirement 2

Requirement 2 indicates that you want to force users to change their password as quickly as possible. You know that user accounts include the flag User Must Change Password At Next Logon.

1. What will be the fastest and most effective means to configure user accounts to require a password change at the next logon?

   a. Select a user account. Open its properties and, on the Account page, select User Must Change Password At Next Logon. Repeat for each user account.

   b. Press CTRL+A to select all users in the Employees OU. Choose the Properties command and, on the Account page, select User Must Change Password At Next Logon. Repeat for each OU.

   c. Use the DSADD command.

   d. Use the DSRM command.

   e. Use the DSQUERY and DSMOD commands.

   The correct answer is e.

2. The DSQUERY command allows you to create a list of objects based on those objects' locations or properties, and pipe those objects to the DSMOD command, which then modifies the objects. Open a command prompt and type the following command:

   ```
   DSQUERY user "OU=Employees,DC=Contoso,DC=Com"
   ```

   The command will produce a list of all user objects in the Employees OU. An advantage of this command is that it would include users in sub-OUs of the Employees OU. The requirement indicates that you have 15 OUs under the Employees OU. All would be included in the objects generated by DSQUERY.

   Now, to meet the requirement, type the following command:

   ```
   DSQUERY user "OU=Employees,DC=Contoso,DC=Com" | DSMOD user -mustchpwd yes
   ```

Requirement 3

This requirement suggests that you modify the user profiles of the sales representatives.

1. What type of profile will be most useful to maintain a locked-down desktop common to all sales representatives?

    a. Local profile

    b. Local, mandatory profile

    c. The All Users profile

    d. Preconfigured roaming group profile

    e. Preconfigured roaming mandatory group profile

    The correct answer is b.

2. In Lesson 3, Exercise 5, you created a profile called Sales. You made it a mandatory profile by renaming Ntuser.dat to Ntuser.man. Finally, you assigned it to several users. How can you ensure that each new sales representative utilizes the same profile?

    Modify the Sales Representative template account you created in Lesson 2, Exercise 1. On the Profile tab, type the profile path: **\\server01\profiles\sales**. Confirm the success of your work by copying the template to create a new user account; then log on as that user. Make modifications to the desktop, log off, and log on again. The changes you made to the profile do not persist between sessions.

Troubleshooting Lab

In this lab, you will generate several types of logon and account-related failures. You will then identify the causes of those failures and correct them accordingly.

Before proceeding with this lab, you must have user accounts created. The user accounts mentioned in the lab are those generated in Lesson 2, Exercise 3. You must also have configured the domain account policies as in Lesson 4, Exercise 1.

Exercise 1: Generate Logon and Account Failures

1. Log off of Server01.

2. Generate an account lockout by logging on six times with the username lsmithbates and an *invalid* password. Notice the difference between the Logon Messages you receive after the attempts and the Logon Message you receive after the account has been locked out.

3. Log on as Danielle Tiedt, with username dtiedt.

4. Press CTRL+ALT+DELETE and change the password to a new password.

5. Press CTRL+ALT+DELETE and try to change the password to the original password. Is it possible? Why or why not?

6. Try to change the password to yet another new password. Is that possible? Why or why not?

7. Log off.

Exercise 2: Monitor and Identify Logon and Account Management Events

1. Log on as Administrator.

2. Open the Computer Management console from the Administrative Tools group.

3. Expand the Event Viewer and select Security.

4. Make sure the Category column is wide enough that you can identify the types of events that are logged.

5. Explore the events that have been generated by recent activity. Notice the failed logon attempts, the lockout, and the attempts to reset Danielle Tiedt's password.

Exercise 3: Correct Authentication and Account Problems

1. Open Active Directory Users And Computers

2. In the tree pane, navigate to and select the Employees OU.

3. In the details pane, select Danielle Tiedt's user object.

4. From the Action menu, click Reset Password.

5. Type Danielle Tiedt's original password as the new password. Why are you able to change the password when, while logged on as Danielle Tiedt, you could not?

6. Select Lorrin Smith-Bates's user object.

7. From the Action menu, click Properties.

8. On the Account tab, clear the Account Is Locked Out check box.

9. Click OK.

Chapter Summary

- You must be a member of the Enterprise Admins, Domain Admins, or Account Operators groups, or you must have been delegated administrative permissions to create user objects.

- User objects include the properties typically associated with a user "account," including logon names and password, and the unique SID for the user. They also include a number of properties related to the individuals they represent, including personal information, group membership, and administrative settings. Windows Server 2003 allows you to change some of these properties for multiple users, simultaneously.

- A user object template is an object which is copied to produce new users. If the template is not a "real" user, it should be disabled. Only a subset of user properties are copied from templates.

- The CSVDE command enables you to import directory objects from a comma-delimited text file.

- Windows Server 2003 supports powerful new command-line tools to create, manage, and delete directory objects: DSQUERY, DSGET, DSADD, DSMOVE, DSMOD, and DSRM. Frequently, DSQUERY will produce a result set of objects that can be piped as input to other commands.

- Windows Server 2003 provides individual profiles for each user who logs on to the system. Profiles are stored, by default, on the local system in *%Systemdrive%* \Documents and Settings\ *%Username%*.

- Roaming profiles require only a shared folder, and the profile path configured in the user object's properties.

- Preconfigured profiles are simply profiles that are copied to the profile path before the profile path is configured in the user object.

- Group profiles must be made mandatory, by renaming Ntuser.dat to Ntuser.man, so that changes made by one user do not affect other users.

- The Default Domain Policy drives account policies including the password and lockout policies, whereas the Default Domain Controllers Policy specifies key auditing policies for domain controllers.

- Auditing for authentication generates events in each domain controller's security logs.

Exam Highlights

Before taking the exam, review the key points and terms that are presented below to help you identify topics you need to review. Return to the lessons for additional practice and review the "Further Readings" sections in Part 2 for pointers to more information about topics covered by the exam objectives.

Key Points

- The group memberships or permissions, or both, required to create user accounts.

- The options at your disposal for creating or managing multiple user accounts: user templates, importing, and command-line utilities. Understand the differences among the options, and the relative strengths and weaknesses of each option.

- The properties that can be accessed or modified, or both, when creating a user, modifying a user in Active Directory Users and Computers, copying a template, querying with DSQUERY, or adding and modifying users with DSADD and DSMOD.

- The process for configuring a roaming user profile, a preconfigured roaming user profile, or a preconfigured, mandatory group profile.

- The impact of group policy on password and account lockout settings.

- How to audit authentication events.

Key Terms

User account template   You might hear this referred to by other terms, but the idea is the same. A template account is used as the basis for new accounts. It is *copied* to create a new user, and some of its properties, most notably its group memberships, are copied as well.

Disabled account versus locked account   An account is disabled if it has expired, or if it has been disabled by an administrator. An account is locked out if it has been subject to invalid logons beyond the threshold specified by the account lockout policy.

Mandatory profile   A user profile that does not maintain modifications between sessions. A user *can* modify a mandatory profile, but users' changes are not saved when they log off. Group profiles must be made mandatory, or a change made by one user will affect all users.

Questions and Answers

Page
3-13 **Lesson 1 Review**

1. You are using Active Directory Users And Computers to configure user objects in your domain, and you are able to change the address and telephone number properties of the user object representing yourself. However, the New User command is unavailable to you. What is the most likely explanation?

   You do not have sufficient privileges to create a user object in the container. The snap-in's commands will adjust to reflect your administrative capabilities. If you do not have the right to create an object, the appropriate New command will be unavailable.

2. You are creating a number of user objects for a team of your organization's temporary workers. They will work daily from 9:00 A.M. to 5:00 P.M. on a contract that is scheduled to begin in one month and end two months later. They will not work outside of that schedule. Which of the following properties should you configure initially to ensure maximum security for the objects?

   a. Password

   b. Logon Hours

   c. Account expires

   d. Store password using reversible encryption

   e. Account is trusted for delegation

   f. User must change password at next logon

   g. Account is disabled

   h. Password never expires

   The correct answers are a, b, c, f, g.

3. Which of the following properties and administrative tasks can be configured or performed simultaneously on more than one user object?

   a. Last Name

   b. User Logon Name

   c. Disable Account

   d. Enable Account

   e. Reset Password

   f. Password Never Expires

   g. User Must Change Password At Next Logon

h. Logon Hours

i. Computer Restrictions (Logon Workstations)

j. Title

k. Direct Reports

The correct answers are c, d, f, g, h, i, j.

Page
3-26

Lesson 2 Review

1. What option will be most useful to generate 100 new user objects, each of which have identical profile path, home folder path, Title, Web Page, Company, Department, and Manager settings?

DSADD will be the most useful option. You can enter one command line that includes all the parameters. By leaving the *UserDN* parameter empty, you can enter the users' distinguished names one at a time in the command console. A user object template does not allow you to configure options including Title, Telephone Number and Web Page. Generating a comma-delimited text file would be time-consuming, by comparison, and would be overkill, particularly when so many parameters are identical.

2. Which tool will allow you to identify accounts that have not been used for two months?

    a. DSADD

    b. DSGET

    c. DSMOD

    d. DSRM

    e. DSQUERY

The correct answer is e.

3. What variable can be used with the DSMOD and DSADD commands to create user-specific home folders and profile folders?

    a. *%Username%*

    b. *$Username$*

    c. CN=*Username*

    d. *<Username>*

The correct answer is b.

4. Which tools allow you to output the telephone numbers for all users in an OU?

   a. DSADD

   b. DSGET

   c. DSMOD

   d. DSRM

   e. DSQUERY

   The correct answers are b and e. DSQUERY will produce a list of user objects within an OU and can pipe that list to DSGET, which in turn can output particular properties, such as phone numbers.

Page
3-36

Lesson 3 Review

1. Describe how a user's desktop is created when roaming user profiles are not implemented.

   When a user logs on to a system for the first time, the system copies the Default User profile and creates a user-specific profile in a folder named, by default, *%Systemdrive%*\Documents and Settings*%Username%*. The environment that the user experiences is a combination of his or her user profile and the All Users profile.

2. Arrange, in order, the steps that reflect the creation of a preconfigured roaming user profile. Use all steps provided.

   ❑ Customize the desktop and user environment.

   ❑ Log on as a user with sufficient permissions to modify user account properties.

   ❑ Copy the profile to the network.

   ❑ Create a user account so that the profile can be created without modifying any user's current profile.

   ❑ Log on as the profile account.

   ❑ Enter the UNC path to the profile in a user's Profile property sheet.

   ❑ Log on as a local or domain administrator.

   1. Create a user account so that the profile can be created without modifying any user's current profile.

   2. Log on as the profile account.

   3. Customize the desktop and user environment.

   4. Log on as a local or domain administrator.

   5. Copy the profile to the network.

   6. Log on as a user with sufficient permissions to modify user account properties.

   7. Enter the UNC path to the profile in a user's Profile property sheet.

3. How do you make a profile mandatory?

    a. Configure the permissions on the folder's Security property sheet to deny write permission.

    b. Configure the permissions on the folders Sharing property sheet to allow only read permission.

    c. Modify the attributes of the profile folder to specify the Read Only attribute.

    d. Rename Ntuser.dat to Ntuser.man.

The correct answer is d.

Page
3-47
Lesson 4 Review

1. You enable the password complexity policy for your domain. Describe the requirements for passwords, and when those requirements will take effect.

The password must not be based on the user's account name; must contain at least six characters, with at least one character from three of the four categories: uppercase, lowercase, Arabic numerals, and nonalphanumeric characters. The requirements will take effect immediately for all new accounts. Existing accounts will be affected when they next change their password.

2. To monitor potential dictionary attacks against user passwords in your enterprise, what is the single best auditing policy to configure, and what log or logs will you evaluate?

The Audit Policy to audit Account Logon failures is the most effective policy to specify under these circumstances. Failed logons will generate events in the Security logs of all domain controllers.

3. A user has forgotten his or her password and attempts to log on several times with an incorrect password. Eventually, the user receives a logon message indicating that the account is either disabled or locked out. The message suggests that the user contact an administrator. What must you do?

    a. Delete the user object and recreate it.

    b. Rename the user object.

    c. Enable the user object.

    d. Unlock the user object.

    e. Reset the password for the user object.

The correct answers are d and e. Although the logon message text on Windows 2000 and other previous operating system versions indicates that the account is disabled, the account is actually locked. Windows Server 2003 displays an accurate message that the account is, in fact, locked out. However, you can recognize the problem by examining what caused the message: a user forgot his or her password. You must unlock the account and reset the password.

4 Group Accounts

Exam Objectives in this Chapter:

- Create and manage groups
    - Create and modify groups by using the Microsoft Active Directory Users And Computers MMC snap-in
    - Identify and modify the scope of a group
    - Manage group membership
    - Create and modify groups by using automation

Why This Chapter Matters

Users, groups, and computers are the key objects in the Active Directory directory service because they allow workers, their managers, system administrators—anyone using a computer on the network—to establish their identity on the network as a security principal. Without this identification, personnel cannot gain access to the computers, applications, and data needed to do their daily work. Although it is true that the minimal identification required is that of a user and computer, management of individual user security principals becomes needlessly complicated unless users are organized into groups. Assigning permissions to hundreds of users individually is not scalable; wise use of groups makes the process of creating and administering permissions much easier.

Microsoft Windows Server 2003 has two types of groups, each with three distinct scopes. Understanding the constructions of these groups within the correct scope ensures the best use of administrative resources when creating, assigning, and managing access to resources. The possibilities of group construction also depend on whether the domain or forest in which they are created is running in the Windows Server 2003 mixed, interim, or native domain functional level. Windows Server 2003 comes with several groups already created, or built-in. You can create as many additional groups as you need.

Lessons in this Chapter:

Before You Begin

To follow and perform the practices in this chapter, you need

■ A computer designated Server01 with Windows Server 2003 installed.

■ Server01 should be a domain controller in the *contoso.com* domain.

Lesson 1: Understanding Group Types and Scopes

Groups are containers that can contain user and computer objects within them as members. When security permissions are set for a group in the access control list (ACL) on a resource, all members of that group receive those permissions.

Windows Server 2003 has two group types: security and distribution. *Security groups* are used to assign permissions for access to network resources. *Distribution groups* are used to combine users for e-mail distribution lists. Security groups can be used as a distribution group, but distribution groups cannot be used as security groups. Proper planning of group structure affects maintenance and scalability, especially in the enterprise environment, in which multiple domains are involved.

Tip   Although settings for individual security principals—users and computers—can be set by ACLs, those settings are the exception rather than the rule of best administrative practices. If you find that you are setting an inordinate number of exceptions in ACLs for a user within a group, the user's membership in that group should be reexamined.

After this lesson, you will be able to
- Identify the two types of groups and their proper use
- Identify the three types of group scope and their proper use
- Understand the difference between groups and identities

Estimated lesson time: 15 minutes

Domain Functional Levels

In Windows Server 2003, four domain functional levels are available: Windows 2000 mixed (default), Windows 2000 native, Windows Server 2003 interim, and Windows Server 2003.

- **Windows 2000 mixed**   For supporting Windows NT 4, Windows 2000, and Windows Server 2003 domain controllers

- **Windows 2000 native**   For supporting Windows 2000 and Windows Server 2003 domain controllers

- **Windows Server 2003 interim**   For supporting Windows NT 4 and Windows Server 2003 domain controllers

- **Windows Server 2003**   For supporting Windows Server 2003 domain controllers

Limitations on group properties discussed in this chapter and elsewhere in this book will refer to these domain functional levels.

Group Scope

Group scope defines how permissions are assigned to the group members. Windows Server 2003 groups, both security and distribution groups, are classified into one of three group scopes: domain local, global, and universal.

> **Note**   Although local groups are not considered part of the group scope of Windows Server 2003, they are included for completeness.

Local Groups

Local groups (or machine local groups) are used primarily for backward compatibility with Windows NT 4. There are local users and groups on computers running Windows Server 2003 that are configured as member servers. Domain controllers do not use local groups.

- Local groups can include members from any domain within a forest, from trusted domains in other forests, and from trusted down-level domains.

- A local group has only machinewide scope; it can grant resource permissions only on the machine on which it exists.

Domain Local Groups

Domain local groups are used primarily to assign access permissions to global groups for local domain resources. Domain local groups:

- Exist in all mixed, interim and native functional level domains and forests.

- Are available domainwide only in Windows 2000 native or Windows Server 2003 domain functional level domains. Domain local groups function as a local group on the domain controllers while the domain is in mixed functional level.

- Can include members from any domain in the forest, from trusted domains in other forests, and from trusted down-level domains.

- Have domainwide scope in Windows 2000 native and Windows Server 2003 domain functional level domains, and can be used to grant resource permission on any Windows Server 2003 computer within, but not beyond, the domain in which the group exists.

Global Groups

Global groups are used primarily to provide categorized membership in domain local groups for individual security principals or for direct permission assignment (particularly in the case of a mixed or interim domain functional level domain). Often, global groups are used to collect users or computers in the same domain and share the same job, role, or function. Global groups:

- Exist in all mixed, interim, and native functional level domains and forests
- Can only include members from within their domain
- Can be made a member of machine local or domain local group
- Can be granted permission in any domain (including trusted domains in other forests and pre–Windows 2003 domains)
- Can contain other global groups (Windows 2000 native or Windows Server 2003 domain functional level only)

Universal Groups

Universal groups are used primarily to grant access to resources in all trusted domains, but universal groups can only be used as a security principal (security group type) in a Windows 2000 native or Windows Server 2003 domain functional level domain.

- Universal groups can include members from any domain in the forest.
- In Windows 2000 native or Windows Server 2003 domain functional level, universal groups can be granted permissions in any domain, including domains in other forests with which a trust exists.

Tip   Universal groups can help you represent and consolidate groups that span domains, and perform common functions across the enterprise. A useful guideline is to designate widely used groups that seldom change as universal groups.

Group Conversion

The scope of a group is determined at the time of its creation. However, in a Windows 2000 native or Windows Server 2003 domain functional level domain, domain local and global groups can be converted to universal groups if the groups are not members of other groups of the same scope. For example, a global group that is a member of another global group cannot be converted to a universal group. Table 4-1 summarizes the use of Windows Server 2003 domain groups as security principals (group type: security).

Table 4-1   Group Scope and Allowed Objects

Group Scope	Allowed Objects
Windows 2000 native or Windows Server 2003 functional level domain	
Domain Local	Computer accounts, users, global groups, and universal groups from any forest or trusted domain. Domain local groups from the same domain. Nested domain local groups in the same domain.
Global	Users, computers and global groups from same domain. Nested global (in same domain), domain local, or universal groups.
Universal	Universal groups, global groups, users and computers from any domain in the forest. Nested global, domain local, or universal groups.
Windows 2000 mixed or Windows Server 2003 interim functional level domain	
Domain Local	Computer accounts, users, global groups from any domain. Cannot be nested.
Global	Only users and computers from same domain. Cannot be nested.
Universal	Not available.

Special Identities

There are also some special groups called *special identities,* that are managed by the operating system. Special identities cannot be created or deleted; nor can their membership be modified by administrators. Special identities do not appear in the Active Directory Users And Computers snap-in or in any other computer management tool, but can be assigned permissions in an ACL. Table 4-2 details some of the special identities in Windows Server 2003.

Table 4-2   Special Identities and Their Representation

Identity	Representation
Everyone	Represents all current network users, including guests and users from other domains. Whenever a user logs on to the network, that user is automatically added to the Everyone group.
Network	Represents users currently accessing a given resource over the network (as opposed to users who access a resource by logging on locally at the computer where the resource is located). Whenever a user accesses a given resource over the network, the user is automatically added to the Network group.
Interactive	Represents all users currently logged on to a particular computer and accessing a given resource located on that computer (as opposed to users who access the resource over the network). Whenever a user accesses a given resource on the computer to which they are logged on, the user is automatically added to the Interactive group.

Table 4-2   Special Identities and Their Representation (Continued)

Identity	Representation
Anonymous Logon	The Anonymous Logon group refers to any user who is using network resources, but did not go through the authentication process.
Authenticated Users	The Authenticated Users group includes all users who are authenticated into the network by using a valid user account. When assigning permissions, you can use the Authenticated Users group in place of the Everyone group to prevent anonymous access to resources.
Creator Owner	The Creator Owner group refers to the user who created or took ownership of the resource. For example, if a user created a resource, but the Administrator took ownership of it, then the Creator Owner would be the Administrator.
Dialup	The Dialup group includes anyone who is connected to the network through a dialup connection.

Caution   These groups can be assigned permissions to network resources, although caution should be used when assigning some of these groups permissions. Members of these groups are not necessarily users who have been authenticated to the domain. For instance, if you assign full permissions to a share for the Everyone group, users connecting from other domains will have access to the share.

Practice: Changing the Group Type and Scope

In this practice, you get hands-on experience creating groups and modifying their scope.

Exercise 1: Creating and Modifying a Group

In this exercise, you will change the type of group and its scope.

1. In Active Directory Users And Computers, create a global distribution group in the Users container called Agents.

2. Right-click the Agents group, and then choose Properties.

   Can you change the scope and type of the group? If not, why not?

   If you cannot change the type and scope of the group, the domain in which you are operating is still in mixed or Windows Server 2003 interim domain functional level. You must raise the domain functional level to either Windows 2000 native or Windows Server 2003 to change group type or scope.

Lesson Review

The following questions are intended to reinforce key information presented in this lesson. If you are unable to answer a question, review the lesson materials and try the question again. You can find answers to the questions in the "Questions and Answers" section at the end of this chapter.

1. What type of domain group is most like the local group on a member server? How are they alike?

   _____

   _____

2. If you are using universal groups in your domain or forest, and you need to give permission-based access to the members of the universal group, what configuration must be true of the universal group?

   _____

   _____

3. In a domain running in Windows Server 2003 domain functional level, what security principals can be a member of a global group?

   _____

   _____

Lesson Summary

- There are two types of groups: security and distribution. Security groups can be assigned permissions, while distribution groups are used for query containers, such as e-mail distribution groups, and cannot be assigned permissions to a resource.

- Security permissions for a group are assigned in an ACL just as any other security principal, such as a user or computer.

- In Windows 2000 native or Windows Server 2003 domain functional level, groups of both security and distribution type can be constructed as domain local, global, or universal, each with a different scope as to which security principals they can contain.

Lesson 2: Managing Group Accounts

The Active Directory Users And Computers MMC is the primary tool you will use to administer security principals—users, groups, and computers—in the domain. In the creation of groups, you will configure the scope, type, and membership for each. You will also use the Active Directory Users And Computers MMC to modify membership of existing groups.

After this lesson, you will be able to

- Create a group
- Modify the membership of a group
- Find the domain groups to which a user belongs

Estimated lesson time: 10 minutes

Creating a Security Group

The tool that you will use most often in the creation of groups is the Active Directory Users And Computers MMC, which can be found in the Administrative Tools folder. From within the Active Directory Users And Computers MMC, right-click the details pane of the container within which you want to create the group, and choose New, Group. You then must select the type and scope of group that you want to create.

The primary type of group that you will likely create is a security group because this is the type of group used to set permissions in an ACL. In a mixed or interim domain functional level domain, you can only set a security group for the domain local and global scopes. As Figure 4-1 illustrates, you cannot create a security group that has universal scope in mixed or interim domain functional level domains.

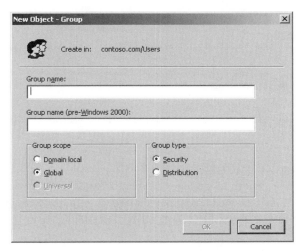

Figure 4-1   Security groups in mixed or interim functional level domains

Domain local, global, and universal groups can, however, be created as a distribution type in a mixed or interim domain functional level domain. In a mixed or interim domain functional level domain, security groups can be created in any scope.

Modifying Group Membership

Adding or deleting members from a group is also accomplished through Active Directory Users And Computers. Right-click any group, and choose Properties. Figure 4-2 illustrates the Properties dialog box of a global security group called Sales.

Figure 4-2   Properties page of the Sales security group

Table 4-3 explains the member configuration tabs of the Properties dialog box.

Table 4-3   **Membership Configuration**

Tab	Function
Members	Adding, removing, or listing the security principals that this container holds as members
Member Of	Adding, removing, or listing the containers that hold this container as a member

See Also   See Chapter 3, "User Accounts," for additional information on using Directory Service command-line tools for viewing and modifying group membership. These tools include DSQUERY, DSGET, DSMOD, and DSGROUP. DSGET is particularly useful for listing all group memberships for a user.

Finding the Domain Groups to Which a User Belongs

Active Directory allows for flexible and creative group nesting, where

- Global groups can nest into other global groups, universal groups, or domain local groups.

- Universal groups can be members of other universal groups or domain local groups.

- Domain local groups can belong to other domain local groups.

This flexibility brings with it the potential for complexity, and without the right tools, it would be difficult to know exactly which groups a user belongs to, whether directly or indirectly. Fortunately, Windows Server 2003 adds the DSGET command, which solves the problem. From a command prompt, type:

```
dsget user UserDN -memberof [-expand]
```

The -memberof switch returns the value of the MemberOf attribute, showing the groups to which the user directly belongs. By adding the -expand switch, those groups are searched recursively, producing an exhaustive list of all groups to which the user belongs in the domain.

Practice: Modifying Group Membership

In this practice, you will work with group memberships and nesting to identify which combinations of group memberships are possible.

Exercise 1: Nesting Group Memberships

1. If the domain functional level is not already set to Windows Server 2003, use the Active Directory Users And Computers MMC to raise the domain functional level to Windows Server 2003.

2. Create three global groups in the Users Organizational Unit (OU): Group 1, Group 2, and Group 3.

3. Create three user accounts: User 1, User 2, and User 3.

4. Make User 1, User 2, and User 3 members of Group 1.

5. Make Group 1 a member of Group 2.

   Which groups can now be converted to universal groups? Test your theory (you should be able to convert 2 of the 3 groups without error).

Lesson Review

The following questions are intended to reinforce key information presented in this lesson. If you are unable to answer a question, review the lesson materials and try the question again. You can find answers to the questions in the "Questions and Answers" section at the end of this chapter.

1. In the properties of a group, which tab will you access to add users to the group?

_____

_____

2. You want to nest the IT Administrators group responsible for the Sales group inside the Sales group so that its members will have access to the same resources (set by permissions in an ACL) as the Sales group. From the Properties page of the IT Administrators group, what tab will you access to make this setting?

_____

_____

3. If your environment consists of two domains, one Windows Server 2003 and one Windows NT 4, what group scopes can you use for assigning permissions on any resource on any domain-member computer?

_____

_____

Lesson Summary

- Modifying group memberships is accomplished through Active Directory Users And Computers.

- If you access the properties of a security principal that is to be a member of a group, you set the group membership in the Members Of tab of the Security principal's properties. If you access the container (group) that is to hold members, set the members of the container on the Members tab.

- Groups can be nested when the domain in which they reside is set to either the Windows 2000 native or Windows Server 2003 domain functional level. If the domain is in mixed or interim domain functional level, which means that you are still supporting Windows NT 4 domain controllers, no group nesting is possible.

- Changing the type or scope of a group is only possible when the domain functional level is Windows 2000 native or Windows Server 2003.

Lesson 3: Using Automation to Manage Group Accounts

Although the Active Directory Users And Computers MMC is a convenient way to create and modify groups individually, it is not the most efficient method for creating large numbers of security principals. A tool included with Windows Server 2003, Ldifde.exe, facilitates the importing and exporting of larger numbers of security principals, including groups.

After this lesson, you will be able to

- Import security principals with LDIFDE
- Export security principles with LDIFDE
- Use the DSADD and DSMOD commands to create and modify groups

Estimated lesson time: 30 minutes

Using LDIFDE

The Lightweight Directory Access Protocol (LDAP) Data Interchange Format (LDIF) is a draft Internet standard for a file format that may be used to perform batch operations against directories that conform to the LDAP standards. LDIF can be used to export and import data, allowing batch operations such as add, create, and modify to be performed against the Active Directory. A utility program called LDIFDE is included in Windows Server 2003 to support batch operations based on the LDIF file format standard.

LDIFDE is a command-line utility, available on all Windows Server 2003 editions. From a command prompt or command shell, you run the LDIFDE utility with the appropriate command switches. Figure 4-3 lists the primary commands used with LDIFDE displayed by typing **ldifde /?** at the command prompt.

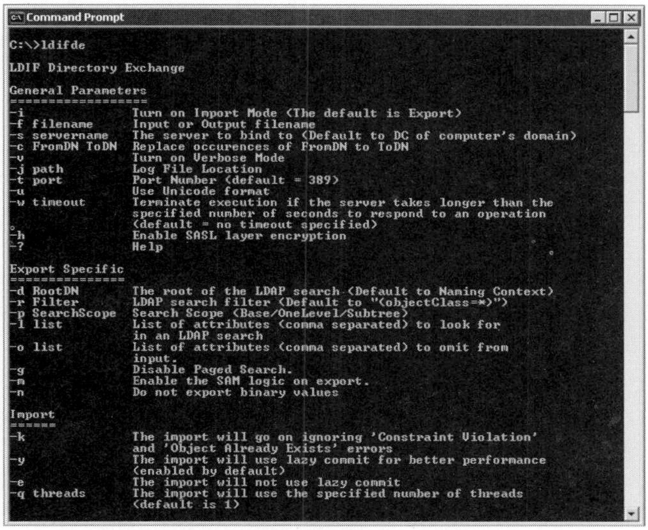

Figure 4-3   LDIFDE command-line help file

Table 4-4 details the primary LDIFDE commands.

Table 4-4   LDIFDE Commands (Primary)

Command	Usage
General parameters	
-i	Turn on Import mode (The default is Export)
-f *filename*	Input or Output *filename*
-s *servername*	The server to bind to
-c *FromDN ToDN*	Replace occurrences of FromDN to ToDN
-v	Turn on Verbose mode
-j *path*	Log File Location
-t *port*	Port Number (default = 389)
-?	Help
Export specific parameters	
-d *RootDN*	The root of the LDAP search (Default to Naming Context)
-r *Filter*	LDAP search filter (Default to "(objectClass=*)")
-p *SearchScope*	Search Scope (Base/OneLevel/Subtree)
-l *list*	List of attributes (comma-separated) to look for in an LDAP search
-o *list*	List of attributes (comma-separated) to omit from input
-g	Disable Paged Search
-m	Enable the Security Accounts Manager (SAM) logic on export
-n	Do not export binary values
Import specific parameters	
-k	The import will ignore "Constraint Violation" and "Object Already Exists" errors
Credentials parameters	
-a *UserDN*	Sets the command to run using the supplied user distinguished name and password. For example: "cn=administrator,dc=contoso,dc-com password"
-b *UserName Domain*	Sets the command to run as username domain password. The default is to run using the credentials of the currently logged on user.

> **Note**   The LDIFDE utility is included in Windows Server 2003, and can be copied to a computer running Windows 2000 Professional or Windows XP. It can then be bound and used remotely to the Windows Server 2003 Active Directory.

Creating Groups with DSADD

The DSADD command, introduced in Chapter 2, is used to add objects to Active Directory. To add a group, use the syntax

dsadd group *GroupDN...*

The *GroupDN...* parameter is one or more distinguished names for the new user objects. If a DN includes a space, surround the entire DN with quotation marks. The *GroupDN...* parameter can be entered one of the following ways:

- By piping a list of DNs from another command, such as dsquery.

- By typing each DN on the command line, separated by spaces.

- By leaving the DN parameter empty, at which point you can type the DNs, one at a time, at the keyboard console of the command prompt. Press ENTER after each DN. Press CTRL+Z and ENTER after the last DN.

The DSADD GROUP command can take the following optional parameters after the DN parameter:

- -secgrp {*yes* | *no*} determines whether the group is a security group (yes) or a distribution group (no). The default value is yes.

- -scope {*l* | *g* | *u*} determines whether the group is a domain local (l), global (g, the default), or universal (u).

- -samid *SAMName*

- desc *Description*

- -memberof *GroupDN...* specifies groups to which to add the new group.

- -members *MemberDN...* specifies members to add to the group.

As discussed in Chapter 3, you can add -s, -u, and -p parameters to specify the domain controller against which DSADD will run, and the user name and password—the credentials—that will be used to execute the command.

- {-s *Server* | -d *Domain*}

- -u *UserName*

- -p {*Password* | *}

Modifying Groups with DSMOD

The DSMOD command, introduced in Chapter 2, is used to modify objects in Active Directory. To modify a group, use the syntax

dsmod group *GroupDN...*

The command takes many of the same switches as DSADD, including -samid, -desc, -secgrp, and -scope. Typically, though, you won't be changing those attributes of an existing group. Rather, the most useful switches are those that let you modify the membership of a group, specifically

- **-addmbr *Member...***   adds members to the group specified in Group

- **-rmmbr *Member...***   removes members from the group specified in Group

where, as with all directory service commands, the DN is the full, distinguished name of another Active Directory object, surrounded by quotes if there are any spaces in the DN.

Note   On any one command line, you can use only -addmbr *or* -rmmbr. You cannot use both in a single DSMOD GROUP command.

Practice: Using LDIFDE to Manage Group Accounts

In the following exercises, you list the options available for LDIFDE, export users from the Active Directory, and create a group object in the directory.

Exercise 1: Starting LDIFDE

In this exercise, you list the command options available with LDIFDE.

1. Open a Command Prompt.
2. For a list of commands, at the command prompt, type: **ldifde /?**.

Exercise 2: Exporting the Users from an Organizational Unit

In this exercise, you will export the entire contents of an OU named Marketing, complete with all its users, from the *contoso.com* domain.

1. In the *contoso.com* domain (Server01 is a domain controller for *contoso.com*), create an OU named Marketing.
2. In the Marketing OU, add two or three users. These users may be named whatever you choose.
3. Open a command prompt and type the following LDIFDE command (the character **:** indicates continuation to the next line)

```
ldifde -f marketing.ldf -s server01 :
-d "ou=Marketing,dc=contoso,dc=com" :
-p subtree -r : "(objectCategory=CN=Person,CN=Schema,CN=Configuration,:
DC=contoso,DC=com)"
```

Figure 4-4 shows the code in action.

Figure 4-4   Output of LDIFDE export–Marketing OU

This creates a LDIF file named Marketing.ldf by connecting to the server named Server01 and executing a subtree search of the Marketing OU for all objects of the category Person.

Exercise 3: Using LDIFDE to Create a Group

In this exercise, you will use LDIFDE to add a group named Management to the Marketing OU of *contoso.com*.

1. Start a text editor, such as Notepad, and create a text file named Newgroup.ldf. (Save the file as an LDIF file, not as a text file.)

2. Edit the LDIF file Newgroup.ldf, and add the following text:

```
dn: CN=Management,OU=Marketing,DC=contoso,DC=com
changetype: add
cn: Management
objectClass: group
samAccountName: Marketing
```

3. Save and close the LDIF file.

4. Open a Command Prompt, type the following command and then press Enter:

   ldifde -i -f newgroup.ldf -s server01

> **Tip**   Watch for extra "white space" (tabs, spaces, carriage returns, line feeds) in the file. Extra white space in the file will cause the command to fail.

5. To confirm that the new group has been created, check the Active Directory Users And Computers snap-in.

Lesson Review

The following questions are intended to reinforce key information presented in this lesson. If you are unable to answer a question, review the lesson materials and try the question again. You can find answers to the questions in the "Questions and Answers" section at the end of this chapter.

1. Which of the following LDIFDE commands changes the function of LDIFDE from export to import?

   a. -i

   b. -t

   c. -f

   d. -s

2. What object classes are possible to export and import using LDIFDE?

   _____

   _____

3. You have a database of users that is capable of exporting CSV files. Can you use such a file, or must you create an *.ldf file manually for importing?

_____

_____

Lesson Summary

- LDIFDE is an included tool with Windows Server 2003 that allows for the importing and exporting of data into and out of Active Directory.

- If you have an existing directory of user data, you can use LDIFDE to export the desired data for importing into the Active Directory, which is, generally, a more efficient process than creating each element individually by hand. CSV files are usable, so long as the data is correctly formatted, with all required elements included and in their proper order.

- LDIFDE can be copied from a Windows Server 2003 to a Windows 2000 or Windows XP desktop for use with an Active Directory.

Case Scenario Exercise

You are in the process of building your Active Directory, and have some user data from the Human Resources department that includes first and last name, address, and telephone number. Company policy states that the user logon name should be the combination of first name or initial and last name (for example, Ben Smith would be bsmith).

You have 500 users, 30 groups, and 10 OUs. In practical terms, what is the best way to get your Active Directory set up as quickly and easily as possible?

Although there is no absolutely correct answer, there are different levels of complexity to consider. A blending of methods is probably best, given the following considerations:

- The user data can be edited as needed, but those edits are minimal, and the users can be brought into Active Directory using LDIFDE.

- The OU construction can be part of the user construction, all from the same file, with minimal editing. For the OUs, use LDIFDE as well.

- The groups might be another matter. Because group membership is a multivalued attribute in Active Directory, group membership must be listed, uniquely, for each group as it is created. It would be very confusing to do that within a single file, and errors would be likely. A better approach is to do the group memberships individually.

Troubleshooting Lab

Creating individual objects (users, groups, and computers) in your Active Directory is a straightforward process, but finding objects and their associations after many objects have been created can present challenges. In a large, multiple-domain environment (or in a complicated smaller one), solving resource access problems can be difficult. For example, if Sarah can access some but not all of the resources that are intended for her, she might not have membership in the groups that have been assigned permissions to the resources.

If you have multiple domains with multiple OUs in each domain, and multiple, nested groups in each of those OUs, it could take a great deal of time to examine the membership of these many groups to determine whether the user has the appropriate membership. Active Directory Users And Computers would not be the best tool choice.

You will use the DSGET command to get a comprehensive listing of all groups of which a user is a member. For the purposes of this lab, the user Ben Smith in the *contoso.com* domain, the Users OU will be used.

1. Choose a user in your Active Directory to use as a test case for the steps that follow. If you do not have a construction that is to your liking, create a number of nested groups across several OUs, making the user a member of only some of the groups.

2. Open a command prompt.

3. Type the following command (substituting your selected user name and OU for Ben Smith):

```
dsget user "CN=Ben Smith,CN=Users,DC=contoso,DC=com"
-memberof -expand
```

The complete listing of all groups of which the user is a member is displayed.

Chapter Summary

- Groups may be created within any OU within the Active Directory.

- There are two types of groups: security and distribution.

- There are three scopes of groups: domain local, global, and universal.

- Manual creation of groups is accomplished with the Active Directory Users And Computers MMC.

- Automated creation of groups is accomplished with the LDIFDE command-line tool.

- Directory Services Tools such as DSQUERY, DSGET, and DSMOD can be used to list, create, and modify groups and their membership.

- Group types can only be changed when the domain functional level is at least Windows 2000 native.

- Advanced group nesting is only possible when the domain functional level is at least Windows 2000 native.

Exam Highlights

Before taking the exam, review the key points and terms that are presented below to help you identify topics you need to review. Return to the lessons for additional practice and review the "Further Readings" sections in Part 2 for pointers to more information about topics covered by the exam objectives.

Key Points

- The types of groups and their available uses depending on the domain functional level

- The scope of groups and their various nesting constructions depending on the domain functional level

- The basic use of Active Directory Users And Computers in creating groups and modifying their membership

- The basic use of LDIFDE for exporting groups from one directory to another, and in creating groups

- The basic use of DSGET for listing complete group memberships for a user

Key Terms

Domain local group (scope)   In mixed or interim domain functional level, these local groups are available only on domain controllers, not domainwide.

Global group (scope)   A group that is available domainwide in any domain functional level.

Universal group (scope)   A group that can be available domainwide in any functional level, but limited to distribution scope in Windows 2000 mixed and Windows Server 2003 interim domain functional levels.

Security group (type)   Can have permissions assigned in an ACL.

Distribution group (type)   Cannot have permissions assigned in an ACL.

Page
4-8
Lesson 1 Review

1. What type of domain group is most like the local group on a member server? How are they alike?

   Domain local groups are very similar to local groups on a member server in that they are, in a mixed or Windows Server 2003 interim domain functional level domain, limited to the computers on which they reside; in the case of domain local groups, the domain controller. Until the domain functional level is raised to Windows 2000 native or Windows Server 2003, the domain local groups cannot be used for permission assignment on any servers in the domain other than the domain controllers.

2. If you are using universal groups in your domain or forest, and you need to give permission-based access to the members of the universal group, what configuration must be true of the universal group?

   For the universal group:

   - The domain functional level must be Windows 2000 native or Windows Server 2003.
   - The universal group must be of the type security (not distribution).

3. In a domain running in Windows Server 2003 domain functional level, what security principals can be a member of a global group?

   - Users
   - Computers
   - Universal groups
   - Global groups

Page
4-12
Lesson 2 Review

1. In the properties of a group, which tab will you access to add users to the group?

   The Members tab is used for adding members to the group.

2. You want to nest the IT Administrators group responsible for the Sales group inside the Sales group so that its members will have access to the same resources (set by permissions in an ACL) as the Sales group. From the Properties page of the IT Administrators group, what tab will you access to make this setting?

   The Members Of tab is used for adding the IT Administrators group to the Sales group.

3. If your environment consists of two domains, one Windows Server 2003 and one Windows NT 4, what group scopes can you use for assigning permissions on any resource on any domain-member computer?

In a Windows Server 2003 interim domain functional level domain, which is what you must be running to support a Windows NT 4 domain, you will only be able to use global groups as security principals. Domain local groups will only be useful on the domain controllers in the Windows Server 2003 domain, and universal groups cannot be used as security groups in a Windows Server 2003 interim domain functional level domain.

Page 4-18

Lesson 3 Review

1. Which of the following LDIFDE commands changes the function of LDIFDE from export to import?

   a. -i

   b. -t

   c. -f

   d. -s

The correct answer is a. The -i command changes the default function of LDIFDE from exporting to importing.

2. What object classes are possible to export and import using LDIFDE?

Any object in Active Directory can be exported or imported using LDIFDE, including users, groups, computers, or OUs. In addition, any property of these objects can be modified using LDIFDE.

3. You have a database of users that is capable of exporting CSV files. Can you use such a file, or must you create an *.ldf file manually for importing?

You can use a CSV file for importing user data into Active Directory. Windows Server 2003 will fill in missing values with default values where possible, but if a mandatory item is missing from the file, then errors will occur during importing and the object will not be created.

5 Computer Accounts

Exam Objectives in this Chapter:

- Create and manage computer accounts in a Microsoft Active Directory directory service environment

- Troubleshoot computer accounts

    - Diagnose and resolve issues related to computer accounts by using the Active Directory Users and Computers snap-in of the Microsoft Management Console (MMC)

    - Reset a computer account

Why This Chapter Matters

As an administrator, you are aware that, over time, hardware is added to your organization, computers are taken offline for repair, machines are exchanged between users or roles, and old equipment is retired or upgraded, leading to the acquisition of replacement systems. Each of these activities involves updating the computer accounts in Active Directory.

Just as a user is authenticated by the user object's user name and password, a computer maintains an account with a name and password that is used to create a secure relationship between the computer and the domain. A user can forget his or her password, requiring you to reset the password, or can take a leave of absence, requiring the disabling of the user object. Likewise, a computer's account can require reset or disabling.

In this chapter, you will learn how to create computer objects, which include the security properties required for the object to be an "account," and manage those objects using Active Directory Users And Computers' graphical user interface (GUI) as well as the powerful command-line tools of Microsoft Windows Server 2003. You will also review your understanding of the process through which a computer joins a domain, so that you can identify potential points of failure and more effectively troubleshoot computer accounts. Finally, you will master the key skills required to troubleshoot and repair computer accounts.

Lessons in this Chapter:

Before You Begin

This chapter presents the skills and concepts related to computer accounts in Active Directory. If you desire hands-on practice, using the examples and lab exercises in the chapter, you should have the following prepared:

■ A machine running Windows Server 2003 (Standard Edition or Enterprise Edition) installed as Server01 and configured as a domain controller in the domain *contoso.com*.

■ First-level organizational units (OUs): "Administrative Groups," "Desktops," and "Servers."

■ A global security group, in the Administrative Groups OU, called "Deployment."

■ The Active Directory Users And Computers console, or a customized console with the Active Directory Users And Computers snap-in.

■ One exercise, joining a computer to a domain, is possible only if you have a second computer running Microsoft Windows 2000 Professional, Windows XP, or Windows Server 2003, with connectivity to Server01. DNS services must be configured properly, on Server01 or elsewhere, and the second computer must be configured to use that DNS server, so that it can locate the domain controller (Server01) for *contoso.com*.

Lesson 1: Joining a Computer to a Domain

The default configuration of Windows Server 2003, and all Microsoft Windows operating systems, is that the computer belongs to a workgroup. In a workgroup, a Windows NT–based computer (which includes Windows NT 4, Windows 2000, Windows XP, and Windows Server 2003) can authenticate users only from its local Security Accounts Manager (SAM) database. It is a stand-alone system, for all intents and purposes. Its workgroup membership plays only a minor role, specifically in the browser service. Although a user at that computer can connect to shares on other machines in a workgroup or in a domain, the user is never actually logged on to the computer with a domain account.

Before you can log on to a computer with your domain user account, that computer must belong to a domain. The two steps necessary to join a computer to a domain are, first, to create an account for the computer and, second, to configure the computer to join the domain using that account. This lesson will focus on the skills related to the creation of computer accounts and joining computers to domains. The next lesson will explore, in more depth, the computer accounts themselves.

Computers maintain accounts, just as users do, that include a name, password, and security identifier (SID). Those properties are incorporated into the computer object class within Active Directory. Preparing for a computer to be part of your domain is therefore a process strikingly similar to preparing for a user to be part of your domain: you must create a computer object in Active Directory.

After this lesson, you will be able to

- Create computer accounts using Active Directory Users And Computers
- Create computer accounts using the DSADD command-line tool
- Create computer accounts using the NETDOM command-line tool
- Join a computer to a domain by changing the network identification properties
- Understand the importance of creating computer accounts prior to joining a domain

Estimated lesson time: 20 minutes

Creating Computer Accounts

You must be a member of the Administrators or Account Operators groups on the domain controllers to create a computer object in Active Directory. Domain Admins and Enterprise Admins are, by default, members of the Administrators group. Alternatively, it is possible to delegate administration so that other users or groups can create computer objects.

However, domain users can also create computer objects through an interesting, indirect process. When a computer is joined to the domain and an account does not exist, Active Directory creates a computer object automatically, by default, in the Computers OU. Each user in the Authenticated Users group (which is, in effect, all users) is allowed to join 10 computers to the domain, and can therefore create as many as 10 computer objects in this manner.

Creating Computer Objects Using Active Directory Users and Computers

To create a computer object, or "account," open Active Directory Users And Computers and select the container or OU in which you want to create the object. From the Action menu or the right-click shortcut menu, choose the New–Computer command. The New Object–Computer dialog box appears, as illustrated in Figure 5-1.

Figure 5-1   The New Object–Computer dialog box

In the New Object–Computer dialog box, type the computer name. Other properties in this dialog box will be discussed in the following lesson. Click Next. The following page of the dialog box requests a GUID. A GUID is used to prestage a computer account for Remote Installation Services (RIS) deployment, which is beyond the scope of this discussion. It is not necessary to enter a GUID when creating a computer account for a machine you will be joining to the domain using other methods. So just click Next and then click Finish.

Creating Computer Objects Using DSADD

Chances are, this is something you've done before. But before you decide there's nothing new under the sun, Windows Server 2003 provides a useful command-line tool, DSADD, which allows you to create computer objects from the command prompt or a batch file.

In Chapter 2, "Administering Microsoft Windows Server 2003," you used DSADD to create user objects. To create computer objects, simply type **dsadd computer ComputerDN**, where ComputerDN is the distinguished name (DN) of the computer, such as CN=Desktop123,OU=Desktops,DC=contoso,DC=com.

If the computer's DN includes a space, surround the entire DN with quotation marks. The *ComputerDN...* parameter can include more than one distinguished name for new computer objects, making DSADD Computer a handy way to generate multiple objects at once. The parameter can be entered in one of the following ways:

- By piping a list of DNs from another command, such as dsquery.

- By typing each DN on the command line, separated by spaces.

- By leaving the DN parameter empty, at which point you can type the DNs, one at a time, at the keyboard console of the command prompt. Press ENTER after each DN. Press CTRL+Z and ENTER after the last DN.

The DSADD Computer command can take the following optional parameters after the DN parameter:

- -samid *SAMName*

- -desc *Description*

- -loc *Location*

Creating a Computer Account with NETDOM

The NETDOM command is available as a component of the Support Tools, installable from the Support\Tools directory of the Windows Server 2003 CD. The command is also available on the Windows XP and Windows 2000 CDs. Use the version that is appropriate for the platform. NETDOM allows you to perform numerous domain account and security tasks from the command line.

To create a computer account in a domain, type the following command:

```
netdom add ComputerName /domain:DomainName /userd:User /PasswordD:UserPassword
[/ou:OUDN]
```

This command creates the computer account for *ComputerName* in the domain *DomainName* using the domain credentials *User* and *UserPassword*. The /ou parameter causes the object to be created in the OU specified by the *OUDN* distinguished name following the parameter. If no OUDN is supplied, the computer account is created in the Computers OU by default. The user credentials must, of course, have permissions to create computer objects.

Joining a Computer to a Domain

A computer account alone is not enough to create the secure relationship required between a domain and a machine. The machine must join the domain.

To join a computer to the domain, perform the following steps:

1. Right-click My Computer and choose Properties. Click the Computer Name tab.

    ❑ Open Control Panel, select System, and in the System Properties dialog box, click the Computer Name tab.

    ❑ Open the computer's Computer Name properties. These properties can be accessed in several ways:

> **Note**   The Computer Name tab is called Network Identification on Windows 2000 systems. The Change button is called Properties. The functionality is, however, identical.

2. Open the Network Connections folder from Control Panel and choose the Network Identification command from the Advanced menu.

3. On the Computer Name tab, click Change. The Computer Name Changes dialog box, shown in Figure 5-2 allows you to change the name and the domain and workgroup membership of the computer.

> **Exam Tip**   You will not be able to change a computer's name or membership if you are not logged on with administrative credentials on that system. Only users who belong to the local Administrators group will find the Change button enabled and functional.

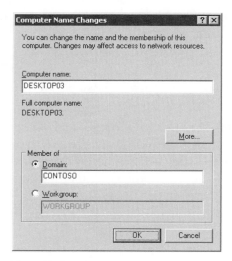

Figure 5-2   The Computer Name Changes dialog box

4. In the Computer Name Changes dialog box, click Domain and type the name of the domain.

> **Tip**   Although the NetBIOS (flat) domain name may succeed in locating the target domain, it is best practice to enter the DNS name of the target domain. DNS configuration is critical to a Windows 2000, Windows XP, or Windows Server 2003 computer. By using the DNS domain name, you leverage the preferred name resolution process and test the computer's DNS configuration. If the computer is unable to locate the domain you're attempting to join, ensure that the DNS server entries configured for the network connection are correct.

5. Click OK. The computer contacts the domain controller. If there is a problem connecting to the domain, examine network connectivity and configuration, as well as DNS configuration.

When the computer successfully contacts the domain, you will be prompted, as in Figure 5-3, for a user name and password with privileges to join the domain. Note that the credentials requested are your *domain* user name and password.

Figure 5-3   Prompt for credentials to join domain

If you have *not* created a domain computer account with a name that matches the computer's name, Active Directory creates an account automatically in the default Computers container. Once a domain computer account has been created or located, the computer establishes a trust relationship with the domain, alters its SID to match that of the account, and makes modifications to its group memberships. The computer must then be restarted to complete the process.

> **Note**   The NETDOM JOIN command can also be used to join a workstation or server to a domain. Its functionality is identical to the Computer Name Changes user interface, except that it also allows you to specify the OU in which to create an account if a computer object does not already exist in Active Directory.

The Computers Container vs. OUs

The Computers container is the default location for computer objects in Active Directory. After a domain is upgraded from Windows NT 4 to Windows 2000, all computer accounts are found, initially, in this container. Moreover, when a machine joins the domain and there is no existing account in the domain for that computer, a computer object is created automatically in the Computers container.

Tip   The *Microsoft Windows Server 2003 Resource Kit* includes the REDIRCOMP tool, which allows you to redirect the creation of automatic computer objects to an OU of your choice. The domain must be in Windows Server 2003 Domain functionality, meaning that all domain controllers must be running Windows Server 2003. Such a tool is useful to organizations in which computer account creation is less tightly controlled. Because automatically created computer objects are created in an OU, they can be managed by policies linked to that OU. See the *Windows Server 2003 Resource Kit* for more information on REDIRCOMP.

Although the Computers container is the default container for computer objects, it is not the ideal container for computer objects. Unlike OUs, containers such as Computers, Users and Builtin cannot be linked to policies, limiting the possible scope of computer-focused group policy. A best-practice Active Directory design will include at least one OU for computers. Often, there are multiple OUs for computers, based on administrative division, region, or for the separate administration of laptops, desktops, file and print servers, and application servers. As an example, there is a default OU for Domain Controllers in Active Directory, which is linked to the Default Domain Controller Policy. By creating one or more OUs for computers, an organization can delegate administration and manage computer configuration, through group policy, more flexibly.

If your organization has one or more OUs for computers, you must move any computer objects created automatically in the Computers container into the appropriate OU. To move a computer object, select the computer and choose Move from the Action menu. Alternatively, use the new drag-and-drop feature of the MMC to move the object.

Tip   Because a computer object in the Computers OU will not be governed by the group policies linked to the OUs your organization has created specifically for computers; and because it requires an extra step to move a computer object from the Computers OU into the appropriate OU, it is recommended to *create computer objects before joining the computer to the domain*. You can create the computer object in the correct OU initially, so that once the system joins the domain it is immediately governed by the policies linked to that OU.

You can also move a computer object, or any other object, with the DSMOVE command. The syntax of DSMOVE is:

```
dsmove ObjectDN [-newname NewName] [-newparent ParentDN]
```

The -newname parameter allows you to rename an object. The -newparent parameter allows you to move an object. To move a computer named DesktopABC from the Computers container to the Desktops OU, you would type the following:

```
dsmove ?CN=DesktopABC,CN=Computers,DC=Contoso,DC=com? -newparent
?OU=Desktops,DC=Contoso,DC=com?
```

In this command you again see the distinction between the Computers *container* (CN) and the Desktops *organizational unit* (OU).

You must have appropriate permissions to move an object in Active Directory. Default permissions allow Account Operators to move computer objects between containers including the Computers container and any OUs *except* into or out of the Domain Controllers OU. Administrators, which include Domain Admins and Enterprise Admins, can move computer objects between any containers, including the Computers container, the Domain Controllers OU, and any other OUs.

Practice: Joining a Computer to an Active Directory Domain

In this practice, you will create computer accounts using Active Directory Users and Computers and DSADD. You then can join a computer to the domain, if you have access to a second system.

Exercise 1: Creating Computer Accounts with Active Directory Users and Computers

1. Open Active Directory Users And Computers
2. In the Servers OU, create a computer object for a computer named "SERVER02." Configure only the computer name. Do not change any of the other default properties.

   Note that, like a user, a computer has two names—the computer name and the "Pre–Windows 2000" computer name. It is a best practice to keep the names the same.

Exercise 2: Creating Computer Accounts with DSADD

1. Open the command prompt.
2. Type the command:

   ```
   dsadd computer ?cn=desktop03,ou=servers,dc=contoso,dc=com?
   ```

Exercise 3: Moving a Computer Object

1. Open Active Directory Users And Computers.

2. Using the Move command, move the Desktop03 computer object from the Servers OU to the Desktops OU.

3. Drag Server02 from the Servers container to the Computers container.

4. Select the Computers container to confirm that Server02 arrived in the right place. Drag-and-drop is, of course, subject to user error.

> **Off the Record**   The MMC is notorious for causing mild panic attacks. It does *not* refresh automatically. You must use the Refresh command or shortcut key (F5) to refresh the console after making a change such as moving an object.

5. Open the properties of the Computers container. You will see that it does *not* have a Group Policy tab, unlike an OU such as Servers. This is among the reasons why organizations create one or more additional OUs for computer objects.

6. Open a command prompt.

7. Type the command:

```
dsmove ?CN=Server02,CN=Computers,DC=contoso,DC=com? -newparent
?OU=Servers,DC=contoso,DC=com?
```

This command, as you can deduce, will move the computer object back to the Servers OU.

8. Confirm that the computer is again in the Servers OU.

Exercise 4 (Optional): Join a Computer to a Domain

This exercise requires an additional system with network connectivity to Server01. In addition, DNS must be configured correctly so that Server01's service records (SRV) are created. The additional computer must have DNS configured so that it can locate Server01 as a domain controller for *contoso.com*.

1. If you have an additional system that you are able to join to the domain in the next exercise, create an account for it in the Desktops OU using either Active Directory Users And Computers or DSADD. Be certain that the name you use is the same name as the computer.

2. Log on to the computer. You must log on as an account with membership in the computer's local Administrators group to change its domain membership.

3. Locate the Computer Name tab by opening System from Control Panel, or the Network Identification command from the Advanced menu of the Network Connections folder.

4. Click Change.

5. Click Domain and type the DNS domain name, **contoso.com**.

6. Click OK.

7. When prompted, enter the credentials for the *contoso.com* domain's Administrator account.

8. Click OK.

9. The computer will prompt you that a reboot is necessary. Click OK to each message and to close each dialog box. Reboot the system.

Lesson Review

The following questions are intended to reinforce key information presented in this lesson. If you are unable to answer a question, review the lesson materials and try the question again. You can find answers to the questions in the "Questions and Answers" section at the end of this chapter.

1. What are the *minimum* credentials necessary to create a Windows Server 2003 computer account in an OU in a domain? Consider all steps of the process. Assume Active Directory does not yet have an account for the computer.

   a. Domain Admins

   b. Enterprise Admins

   c. Administrators on a domain controller

   d. Account Operators on a domain controller

   e. Server Operators on a domain controller

   f. Account Operators on the server

   g. Server Operators on the server

   h. Administrators on the server

2. Which locations allow you to change the domain membership of a Windows Server 2003 computer?

   a. The properties of My Computer

   b. Control Panel's System application

   c. Active Directory Users and Computers

   d. The Network Connections folder

   e. The Users application in Control Panel

3. What command-line tools will create a domain computer account in Active Directory?

   a. NETDOM

   b. DSADD

   c. DSGET

   d. NETSH

   e. NSLOOKUP

Lesson Summary

- Members of the Administrators and Account Operators groups have, by default, permission to create computer objects in Active Directory.

- Active Directory Users And Computers, DSADD, and NETDOM can be used to create computer accounts.

- You must be logged on as a member of the *local* Administrators group to change the domain membership of a machine.

Lesson 2: Managing Computer Accounts

In the previous lesson, you examined the fundamental components of a computer's relationship with a domain: the computer's account, and joining the computer to the domain. This lesson looks more closely at the computer object in Active Directory. You will learn about the other properties and permissions that make computer objects "tick," and how to manage those properties and permissions using GUI and command-line tools.

After this lesson, you will be able to

- Configure the permissions of a new Active Directory computer object
- Configure the properties of an Active Directory computer object
- Find and manage computer accounts using Active Directory Users And Computers

Estimated lesson time: 10 minutes

Managing Computer Object Permissions

In Lesson 1, you learned that you could join a computer to a domain by providing domain administrator credentials when prompted by the computer during the join process. Security concerns, however, require us to use the minimum necessary credentials to achieve a particular task, and it does seem like overkill to need a Domain Admins' account to add a desktop to the domain.

Fortunately, Active Directory allows you to control, with great specificity, the groups or users that can join a computer to a domain computer account. Although the default is Domain Admins, you can allow any group (for example, a group called "Installers") to join a machine to an account. This is most easily achieved while creating the computer object.

When you create a computer object, the first page of the New Object–Computer dialog box (previously shown in Figure 5-1) indicates The Following User Or Group Can Join This Computer To A Domain. Click Change and you can select any user or group. This change modifies a number of permissions on the computer object in Active Directory.

The following page of the New Object–Computer dialog box prompts you for the globally unique identifier (GUID) of the computer, which is necessary if you install a system using Remote Installation Services (RIS). For more information on RIS, see the Microsoft online Knowledge Base, *http://support.microsoft.com/*.

If the computer that is using the account that you are creating is running a version of Windows earlier than 2000, select the Assign This Computer Account As A Pre–Windows 2000 Computer check box. If the account is for a Windows NT backup domain controller, click Assign This Computer Account As A Backup Domain Controller.

> **Tip** Remember, only computers based on Windows NT technologies can belong to a domain, so Windows 95, Windows 98, and Windows Millennium Edition (Windows Me) cannot join or maintain computer accounts. Therefore, this check box really means Windows NT 4.

Configuring Computer Properties

Computer objects have several properties that are not visible when creating a computer account in the user interface. Open a computer object's Properties dialog box to set its location and description, configure its group memberships and dial-in permissions, and link it to a user object of the computer's manager. The Operating System properties page is read-only. The information is published automatically to Active Directory, and will be blank until a computer has joined the domain using that account.

Several object classes in Active Directory support the Manager property that is shown on the Managed By property page of a computer. This linked property creates a cross-reference to a user object. All other properties—the addresses and telephone numbers—are displayed directly from the user object. They are not stored as part of the computer object itself.

The DSMOD command, as discussed in Chapter 2, can also modify several of the properties of a computer object. You will see the DSMOD command in action in the following section regarding troubleshooting computer accounts.

Finding and Connecting to Objects in Active Directory

When a user calls you with a particular problem, you might want to know what operating system and service pack is installed on that user's system. You learned that this information is stored as properties of the computer object. The only challenge, then, is to locate the computer object, which may be more difficult in a complex Active Directory with one or more domains and multiple OUs.

The Active Directory Users and Computers snap-in provides easy access to a powerful, graphical search tool. This tool can be used to find a variety of object types. In this context, however, your search entails an object of the type Computer. Click the Find Objects In Active Directory button on the console toolbar. The resulting Find Computers dialog box is illustrated in Figure 5-4. You can select the type of object (Find), the scope of the search (In), and specify search criteria before clicking Find Now.

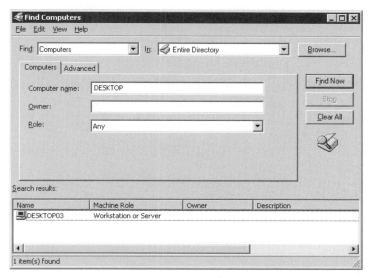

Figure 5-4   The Find Computers dialog box, as it appears after a successful search

The list of results allows you to select an object and, from the File menu or the shortcut menu, perform common tasks on the selected object. Many administrators appreciate learning that you can use the Manage command to open the Computer Management console and connect directly to that computer, allowing you to examine its event logs, device manager, system information, disk and service configuration, or local user or group accounts.

Practice: Managing Computer Accounts

In this practice, you will search for a computer object and modify its properties.

Exercise 1: Managing Computer Accounts

1. Open Active Directory Users And Computers.
2. Select the Security Groups OU and create a global security group called Deployment.
3. Select the Desktops OU.
4. Create a computer account for Desktop04. In the first page of the New Object–Computer dialog box, click Change below The Following User Or Group Can Join This Computer To A Domain. Type **deployment** in the Select User or Group dialog box, and then click OK.
5. Complete the creation of the Desktop04 computer object.

Exercise 2: Finding Objects in Active Directory

1. Open Active Directory Users And Computers.

2. On the toolbar, click the Find Objects in Active Directory icon.

3. By default, the Find dialog box is ready to search for Users, Contacts, and Groups. Choose Computers from the Find drop-down list, and select Entire Directory from the In drop-down list.

4. In the Computer Name field, type **server** and click Find Now.

   A result set appears that includes Server01.

Exercise 3: Changing Computer Properties

1. From the result set returned in Exercise 1, open Server01's properties dialog box.

2. Click the Location tab.

3. Type **Headquarters Server Room**.

4. Click the Managed By tab, and then click Change.

5. Type **Hank** and then click OK.

6. Note that the user's name and contact information appears.

7. Click the Operating System tab. Note the OS version and service pack level are displayed.

8. (Optional) If you joined a second computer to the domain in Exercise 4 of Lesson 1, open the properties of that computer object and note the Operating System properties of that computer.

Lesson Review

The following questions are intended to reinforce key information presented in this lesson. If you are unable to answer a question, review the lesson materials and try the question again. You can find answers to the questions in the "Questions and Answers" section at the end of this chapter.

1. What platforms are capable of joining a domain?

   a. Windows 95

   b. Windows NT 4

   c. Windows 98

   d. Windows 2000

   e. Windows Me

     f. Windows XP

     g. Windows Server 2003

2. You open a computer object and, on the Operating System tab, discover that no properties are displayed. What causes these properties to be absent?

_____

_____

3. An executive has a laptop running Windows XP, with a machine name of "TopDog." You want to allow the executive's laptop to join the domain, and you want to be sure that the computer is configured by the group policies linked to the Desktops OU immediately. How can you achieve this goal?

_____

_____

4. Why is it a best practice to create a computer account in the domain *prior* to joining a machine to the domain?

_____

_____

Lesson Summary

- You can allow any user or group to join a computer to a domain account by utilizing the property, The Following User Or Group Can Join This Computer To A Domain.

- The Find Objects In Active Directory button on the Active Directory Users And Computers snap-in toolbar allows you to search for, and then manage, computer and other Active Directory objects.

Lesson 3: Troubleshooting Computer Accounts

Active Directory domains treat computers as security principals. This means that a computer, just like a user, has an account—or, more specifically, properties within the computer object such as a name, a password, and a SID. Like user accounts, computer accounts require maintenance and, occasionally, troubleshooting. This lesson focuses on skills and concepts related to troubleshooting computer objects.

After this lesson, you will be able to

- Understand the important difference among deleting, disabling, and resetting computer accounts
- Recognize the symptoms of computer account problems
- Troubleshoot computer accounts by deleting, disabling, resetting, or rejoining, using both command-line and user-interface tools

Estimated lesson time: 20 minutes

Deleting and Disabling and Resetting Computer Accounts

Computer accounts, like user accounts, maintain a unique SID, which enables an administrator to grant permissions to computers. Also like user accounts, computers can belong to groups. Therefore, like user accounts, it is important to understand the effect of deleting a computer account. When a computer account is deleted, its group memberships and SID are lost. If the deletion is accidental, and another computer account is created with the same name, it is nonetheless a new account, with a new SID. Group memberships must be reestablished, and any permissions assigned to the deleted computer must be reassigned to the new account. Delete computer objects only when you are certain that you no longer require those security-related attributes of the object.

To delete a computer account using Active Directory Users And Computers, locate and select the computer object and, from the Action menu or the shortcut menu, select the Delete command. You will be prompted to confirm the deletion and, because deletion is not reversible, the default response to the prompt is No. Select Yes and the object is deleted.

The DSRM command-line tool introduced in Chapter 3 allows you to delete a computer object from the command prompt. To delete a computer with DSRM, type:

```
DSRM ObjectDN
```

Where *ObjectDN* is the distinguished name of the computer, such as "CN=Desktop15, OU=Desktops,DC=contoso,DC=com." Again, you will be prompted to confirm the deletion.

> **Tip**   When a computer is disjoined from a domain—when an administrator changes the membership of the computer to a workgroup or to another domain—the computer attempts to delete its computer account in the domain. If it is not possible to do so because of lack of connectivity, networking problems, or credentials and permissions, the account will remain in Active Directory. It may appear, immediately or eventually, as disabled. If that account is no longer necessary, it must be deleted manually.

If a computer is taken offline or is not to be used for an extended period of time, you may disable the account. Such an action reflects the security principle, that an identity store allow authentication only of the minimum number of accounts required to achieve the goals of an organization. Disabling the account does not modify the computer's SID or group membership, so when the computer is brought back online, the account can be enabled.

The context menu, or Action menu, of a selected computer object exposes the Disable Account command. A disabled account appears with a red "X" icon in the Active Directory Users And Computers snap-in, as shown in Figure 5-5.

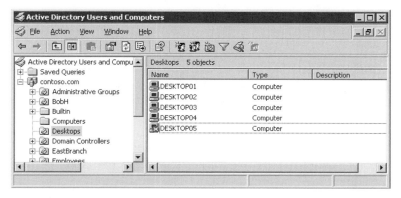

Figure 5-5   A disabled computer account

While an account is disabled, the computer cannot create a secure channel with the domain. The result is that users who have not previously logged on to the computer, and who therefore do not have cached credentials on the computer, will be unable to log on until the secure channel is reestablished by enabling the account.

To enable a computer account, simply select the computer and choose the Enable Account command from the Action or shortcut menus.

To disable or enable a computer from the command prompt, use the DSMOD command. The DSMOD command modifies Active Directory objects. The syntax used to disable or enable computers is:

```
DSMOD COMPUTER ComputerDN -DISABLED YES
```

```
DSMOD COMPUTER ComputerDN -DISABLED NO
```

If a computer account's group memberships and SID, and the permissions assigned to that SID, are important to the operations of a domain, you do not want to delete that account. So what would you do if a computer was replaced with a new system, with upgraded hardware? Such is one scenario in which you would *reset* a computer account.

Resetting a computer account resets its password, but maintains all of the computer object's properties. With a reset password, the account becomes in effect "available" for use. Any computer can then join the domain using that account, including the upgraded system.

In fact, the computer that had previously joined the domain with that account can use the reset account by simply rejoining the domain. This reality will be explored in more detail in the troubleshooting lesson.

The Reset Account command is available in the Action and context menus when a computer object is selected. The DSMOD command can also be used to reset a computer account, with the following syntax:

```
dsmod computer ComputerDN -reset
```

The NETDOM command, included with the Windows Server 2003 Support Tools in the CD-ROM's Support\Tools directory, also enables you to reset a computer account.

Recognizing Computer Account Problems

Computer accounts, and the secure relationships between computers and their domain are robust. In the rare circumstance that an account or secure channel breaks down, the symptoms of failure are generally obvious. The most common signs of computer account problems are:

Messages at logon indicate that a domain controller cannot be contacted; that the computer account may be missing; or that the trust (another way of saying "the secure relationship") between the computer and the domain has been lost. An example is shown in Figure 5-6.

Figure 5-6   Logon message from a Windows XP client indicating a possible computer account problem

- Error messages or events in the event log indicating similar problems or suggesting that passwords, trusts, secure channels, or relationships with the domain or a domain controller have failed.

- A computer account is missing in Active Directory.

If one of these situations occurs, you must troubleshoot the account. You learned earlier how to delete, disable, and reset a computer account and, at the beginning of the chapter, how to join a machine to the domain.

The rules that govern troubleshooting a computer account are:

A. If the computer account exists in Active Directory, it must be reset.

B. If the computer account is missing in Active Directory, you must create a computer account.

C. If the computer still belongs to the domain, it must be removed from the domain by changing its membership to a workgroup. The name of the workgroup is irrelevant. Best practice is to try and choose a workgroup name that you know is not in use.

D. Rejoin the computer to the domain. Alternatively, join another computer to the domain; but the new computer must have the same name as the computer account.

To troubleshoot any computer account problem, apply *all four rules*. These rules can be addressed in any order, except that Rule D, involving rejoining the computer to the domain, must as always be performed as the final step. Let's examine two scenarios.

In the first scenario, a user complains that when he or she attempts to log on, the system presents error messages indicating that the computer account might be missing. Applying Rule A, you open Active Directory Users And Computers and find that the computer account exists. You reset the account. Rule B does not apply—the account does exist. Then, using Rule C, you disjoin the system from the domain and, following Rule D, rejoin the domain.

In a second scenario, if a computer account is reset by accident, the first item that has occurred is Rule A. Although the reset is accidental, you must continue to recover by applying the remaining three rules. Rule B does not apply because the account exists in the domain. Rule C indicates that if the computer is still joined to the domain, it must be removed from the domain. Then, by Rule D, it can rejoin the domain.

With these four rules, you can make an informed decision, on the job or on the certification exams, about how to address any scenario in which a computer account has lost functionality.

Practice: Troubleshooting Computer Accounts

In this practice, you will troubleshoot a realistic scenario. A user in the *contoso.com* domain contacts you and complains that, when logging on to Desktop03, he or she receives the following error message:

"Windows cannot connect to the domain, either because the domain controller is down or otherwise unavailable, or because your computer account was not found. Please try again later. If this message continues to appear, contact your system administrator for assistance."

The user waited, attempted to log on, received the same message, waited again, and then received the same message a third time. The user has now spent 20 minutes trying to log on. In obvious frustration, the user contacts you for assistance.

Exercise 1: Troubleshooting Computer Accounts

1. Identify the most likely cause of the user's problem:
    a. The user entered an invalid user name.
    b. The user entered an invalid password.
    c. The user chose the incorrect domain from the Log On To list.
    d. The computer has lost its secure channel with the domain.
    e. The computer's registry is corrupted.
    f. The computer has a policy preventing the user from logging on interactively.

    The correct answer, as you can probably deduce, is d. The computer has lost its secure channel with the domain.

2. Identify the steps from the list below that you must take to troubleshoot the problem. Put the steps in order. You may not require all steps.
    a. Enable the computer account.
    b. Change Desktop03 to belong to *contoso.com*.
    c. Determine whether the computer account exists in Active Directory.
    d. Reset or re-create the computer account.

    e. Change Desktop03 to a workgroup.

    f. Delete the computer account.

    g. Disable the computer account.

The correct answer is steps e, c, d, and b. Step e does not have to occur first; it just has to be done anytime before step b. Steps c and d must occur, in that order, before step b, which must be the last step.

Exercise 2: Recover from Computer Account Problems

1. Open Active Directory Users And Computers.

2. Click Find Objects In Active Directory and search for Desktop03.

3. Desktop03 appears in the search results because you created it in Lesson 1.

4. Having identified that the account does exist, reset the account by right-clicking Desktop03 and choosing Reset Account.

Lesson Review

The following questions are intended to reinforce key information presented in this lesson. If you are unable to answer a question, review the lesson materials and try the question again. You can find answers to the questions in the "Questions and Answers" section at the end of this chapter.

1. After a period of expansion, your company created a second domain. Last weekend, a number of machines that had been in your domain were moved to the new domain. When you open Active Directory Users And Computers, the objects for those machines are still in your domain, and are displayed with a red "X" icon. What is the most appropriate course of action?

    a. Enable the accounts

    b. Disable the accounts

    c. Reset the accounts

    d. Delete the accounts

2. A user reports that during a logon attempt, a message indicated that the computer cannot contact the domain because the domain controller is down or the computer account may be missing. You open Active Directory Users And Computers and discover that the account for that computer is missing. What steps should you take?

_____

_____

3. A user reports that during a logon attempt, a message indicates that the computer cannot contact the domain because the domain controller is down or the computer account may be missing. You open Active Directory Users and Computers and that computer's account appears normal. What steps should you take?

_____

_____

Lesson Summary

■ Computers maintain accounts that, like users, include a SID and group memberships. Be careful about deleting computer objects. Disabling computer objects allows you to enable the objects again, when the computer needs to participate in the domain.

■ Problems with computer accounts are generally quite evident, with error messages and events logged that indicate problems in an account, a password, a secure channel or a trust relationship.

■ Using the four rules in Lesson 3, you can troubleshoot just about any computer account problem.

Case Scenario Exercise

Contoso decides to open two branch offices: East and West. Computers are purchased for 10 sales representatives in each office. The asset tags assigned to the computers are shown in the following table.

East Branch	West Branch
EB-2841	WB-3748
EB-2842	WB-3749
EB-2843	WB-3750
EB-2844	WB-3751
EB-2845	WB-3752
EB-2846	WB-3753
EB-2847	WB-3754
EB-2848	WB-3755
EB-2849	WB-3756
EB-2850	WB-3757

Your job is to prepare Active Directory for the deployment of these computers.

Exercise 1: Create OUs

Create two OUs in the *contoso.com* domain: EastBranch and WestBranch. Type the names as shown. Do not put a space between the words.

Exercise 2: Script the Creation of Computer Accounts

1. Open Notepad.

2. Type a line for each computer, following this example:

```
DSADD COMPUTER ?CN=EB-2841,OU=EastBranch,DC=Contoso,DC=COM? -desc ?Sales Rep
Computer? -loc ?East Branch Office?
```

   Be sure to modify the CN= parameter to match the asset tag of each computer, and the OU= and -loc parameters to reflect the name and location description of the branch office for each computer.

3. Save the file as "C:\ScriptComputers.bat" and be sure to surround the name with quotation marks, or Notepad will add a .txt extension automatically.

4. Open a command prompt and type **c:\scriptcomputers**.

5. Confirm the successful generation of the computer accounts by examining the EastBranch and WestBranch OUs. The MMC does not refresh automatically, so press F5 to refresh if you do not see the new computers initially.

Troubleshooting Lab

Following a weekend during which a consultant performed maintenance on the computers in the East Branch Office, users complain of trouble logging on. You examine the event log on one of the branch office computers and discover the following event:

There seems to be a problem with the computer account.

Which of the following steps must be performed to correct the problem?

1. Delete the computer accounts
2. Reset the user accounts
3. Join the computers to a workgroup
4. Disable the computer accounts
5. Reset the computer accounts
6. Enable the computer accounts
7. Create new computer accounts
8. Join the computers to the domain

> The correct answer is 5, 3, and 8. This is the most efficient solution; it involves resetting computer accounts and rejoining machines to the domain.

Exercise 1 (Optional): Simulation of the Problem

If you joined a second computer to the Contoso domain in Lesson 1, move the computer object for that computer into the EastBranch OU. Then, in Active Directory Users And Computers, reset the computer's account.

When you restart the computer, try logging on to the domain. Are you successful? Can you log on with Contoso domain accounts you have used in the past to log on to the computer? Why? (Hint: cached logons.)

Can you log on with new domain accounts, which have never logged on to the computer? When you attempt to do so, you will receive a typical error message indicating that the computer account may be missing.

Log on as the local Administrator and examine the event log. What error messages appear?

Exercise 2: Reset All East Branch Computer Accounts

The fastest way to reset the computer accounts, particularly because all the accounts are in the same OU, will be a command-line tool.

1. Open a command prompt.
2. Type the following command:

```
DSQUERY COMPUTER ?OU=EastBranch,DC=contoso,DC=com?
```

This command queries Active Directory for a list of computers in the EastBranch OU. The list should match the computer accounts created in the Case Scenario exercise.

3. Type the following command:

```
DSQUERY COMPUTER ?OU=EastBranch,DC=contoso,DC=com? | DSMOD COMPUTER -RESET
```

This time, we pipe the results of the DSQUERY command to the input of DSMOD. The DSMOD COMPUTER -RESET command will reset each of those accounts. Mission accomplished.

Exercise 3 (Optional): Rejoin the Domain

If you have a second system, just reset its computer account. You can now practice removing the machine from the domain by changing its membership to a workgroup. After restarting, join the domain again.

Chapter Summary

- You must have permissions to create a computer object in Active Directory. Administrators and Account Operators have sufficient permissions, and permissions can be delegated to other users or groups.

- When creating a computer object, you can specify what user or group can join the computer to the domain using that account.

- Active Directory Users And Computers allows you to create, modify, delete, disable, enable, and reset computer objects.

- From the command prompt, you can create a computer object with DSADD Computer and modify its properties using DSMOD Computer.

- DSMOD Computer is also used to reset, disable, and enable a computer object. DSRM will remove a computer object. The support tool, NETDOM, includes numerous switches to achieve similar tasks.

- A common troubleshooting recovery includes re-creating or resetting a computer account, removing the computer from the domain, and rejoining the domain.

Exam Highlights

Before taking the exam, review the key points and terms that are presented below to help you identify topics you need to review. Return to the lessons for additional practice and review the "Further Readings" sections in Part 2 for pointers to more information about topics covered by the exam objectives.

Key Points

- Identify the minimum permissions required to create a computer object in Active Directory, and the permissions required to change a machine's membership between workgroups and domains.

- Know the syntax of the DSADD, DSMOD, and DSRM commands. Remember that DSMOD and DSADD require one, or more, distinguished names as parameters. The DSQUERY command can be used to provide those names to DSMOD.

- Be very clear on the differences among disabling, resetting, and deleting a computer account. What is the impact of each on the computer object, its SID and group membership, and on the system itself?

- Know the four rules for troubleshooting computer account problems. Apply all four, every time, and you will be likely to nail every computer account troubleshooting question.

- Be comfortable with finding objects in Active Directory, and managing those objects from the search results. This skill set applies to many objects in Active Directory, and several objectives of the certification exam.

Key Terms

Computer account   An account created in Active Directory that uniquely identifies the computer in the domain.

Questions and Answers

Page
5-11

Lesson 1 Review

1. What are the *minimum* credentials necessary to create a Windows Server 2003 computer account in an OU in a domain? Consider all steps of the process. Assume Active Directory does not yet have an account for the computer.

   a. Domain Admins

   b. Enterprise Admins

   c. Administrators on a domain controller

   d. Account Operators on a domain controller

   e. Server Operators on a domain controller

   f. Account Operators on the server

   g. Server Operators on the server

   h. Administrators on the server

   The correct answers are d and h. Account Operators on a domain controller are assigned the minimum permissions necessary to create a computer object in the domain. You must be a member of the local Administrators group on the server to change its domain membership.

2. Which locations allow you to change the domain membership of a Windows Server 2003 computer?

   a. The properties of My Computer

   b. Control Panel's System application

   c. Active Directory Users and Computers

   d. The Network Connections folder

   e. The Users application in Control Panel

   The correct answers are a, b, and d.

3. What command-line tools will create a domain computer account in Active Directory?

   a. NETDOM

   b. DSADD

   c. DSGET

   d. NETSH

   e. NSLOOKUP

   The correct answers are a and b.

Lesson 2 Review

1. What platforms are capable of joining a domain?

    a. Windows 95

    b. Windows NT 4

    c. Windows 98

    d. Windows 2000

    e. Windows Me

    f. Windows XP

    g. Windows Server 2003

    The correct answers are b, d, f, and g.

2. You open a computer object and, on the Operating System tab, discover that no properties are displayed. What causes these properties to be absent?

    A computer has not joined the domain using that account. When a system joins the domain, by default it populates the properties shown on the Operating System tab.

3. An executive has a laptop running Windows XP, with a machine name of "TopDog." You want to allow the executive's laptop to join the domain, and you want to be sure that the computer is configured by the group policies linked to the Desktops OU immediately. How can you achieve this goal?

    Create a computer object in the Desktops OU for the TopDog computer. While creating the account, select the executive's user account for the property, The Following User Or Group Can Join This Computer To A Domain.

4. Why is it a best practice to create a computer account in the domain *prior* to joining a machine to the domain?

    There are several reasons why it is a best practice to create a computer account in the domain prior to joining a machine to the domain. The first reason relates to the fact that if an account is not created in advance, one will be generated automatically when the computer joins the domain, and that account will be located in the default Computers container. The result is that computer policies, which are typically linked to specific OUs, will not apply to the newly joined computer. And, because most organizations do have specific OUs for computers, you are left with an extra step to remember: moving the computer object to the correct OU after joining the domain. Finally, by creating a computer object in advance, you can specify which groups (or users) are allowed to join a system to the domain with that account. In short, you have more flexibility and control during deployment.

Lesson 3 Review

1. After a period of expansion, your company created a second domain. Last weekend, a number of machines that had been in your domain were moved to the new domain. When you open Active Directory Users And Computers, the objects for those machines are still in your domain, and are displayed with a red "X" icon. What is the most appropriate course of action?

   a. Enable the accounts

   b. Disable the accounts

   c. Reset the accounts

   d. Delete the accounts

   The correct answer is d. When the machines were removed from the domain, their accounts were not deleted, probably due to permissions settings. The machines now belong to another domain. These accounts are no longer necessary.

2. A user reports that during a logon attempt, a message indicated that the computer cannot contact the domain because the domain controller is down or the computer account may be missing. You open Active Directory Users And Computers and discover that the account for that computer is missing. What steps should you take?

   Create a computer account, disjoin the user's computer from the domain, and then rejoin it to the domain.

3. A user reports that during a logon attempt, a message indicates that the computer cannot contact the domain because the domain controller is down or the computer account may be missing. You open Active Directory Users and Computers and that computer's account appears normal. What steps should you take?

   Reset the computer account, disjoin the computer from the domain, then rejoin it to the domain.

6 Files and Folders

Exam Objectives in this Chapter:

- Configure access to shared folders
  - ❏ Manage shared folder permissions
- Configure file system permissions
  - ❏ Verify effective permissions when granting permissions
  - ❏ Change ownership of files or folders
- Troubleshoot issues related to access to files and shared folders
- Manage a Web server
  - ❏ Manage Internet Information Services (IIS)
  - ❏ Manage security for IIS

Why This Chapter Matters

Among the more common daily challenges facing you as an administrator are tasks related to the maintenance of network files and folders—resources that are required by users in your organization. When a user cannot access a resource that he or she needs to achieve a business task, the telephone at the help desk rings. As a result, you spend time and money modifying permissions or group memberships to correct the problem. When a sensitive resource is accessed by someone who should not be able to do so, the telephone on your desk rings—and as a result, you might have to spend time and money looking for a new job.

You have no doubt experienced the fundamental components of resource security in Windows technologies—the assigning of access permissions to users or groups. Microsoft Windows Server 2003 offers enhancements, nuances, tools, and capabilities beyond the feature set of Windows 2000 and Windows XP, and strikingly different than Windows NT 4. Each of these additions will affect the best practices for managing and troubleshooting files and folders.

In this chapter, you will review the concepts and skills related to managing shared folders, and examine the useful Shared Folders snap-in. You will explore the Access Control List Editor, or ACL editor, with its multiple dialog boxes, each of which supports important functionality. After examining a variety of permission configurations, you will evaluate *effective permissions*, the resulting set of permissions for a user based on user and group permissions, you will configure auditing to monitor for specific file access and operations. Finally, you will turn to IIS, which, like the File and Print Sharing service, offers another way to provide network access to files and folders.

Lessons in this Chapter:

Before You Begin

This chapter presents the skills and concepts related to computer accounts in the Microsoft Active Directory directory service.. If you want hands-on practice, using the examples and lab exercises in the chapter, prepare the following:

- A Windows Server 2003 (Standard or Enterprise Edition) installed as Server01 and configured as a domain controller in the *contoso.com* domain.

- First-level organizational units (OUs): Security Groups and Employees

- The Domain Users group must be a member of Print Operators so that, during lab exercises, "normal" users can log on to a domain controller.

- Five domain local security groups in the Security Groups OU: Project 101 Team, Project 102 Team, Engineers, Managers, and Project Contractors.

- User accounts in the Employees OU for Scott Bishop, Danielle Tiedt, and Lorrin Smith-Bates, with Scott Bishop belonging to the Engineers, Project Contractors and Project 101 Team groups, Danielle Tiedt belonging to the Engineers and Project 101 Team, and Lorrin Smith-Bates belonging to the Managers and Project 101 Team.

- Access to the Shared Folders snap-in through the Computer Management console, File Server Management console (available via Manage Your Server), or a custom MMC console.

Lesson 1: Setting Up Shared Folders

We would not have networks, or our jobs, if organizations did not find it valuable to provide access to information and resources stored on one computer to users of another computer. Creating a shared folder to provide such access is therefore among the most fundamental tasks for any network administrator. Windows Server 2003 shared folders are managed with the Shared Folders snap-in.

After this lesson, you will be able to

- Create a shared folder with Windows Explorer and the Shared Folders snap-in
- Configure permissions and other properties of shared folders
- Manage user sessions and open files

Estimated lesson time: 15 minutes

Sharing a Folder

Sharing a folder configures the File And Printer Sharing For Microsoft Networks service (also known as the Server service) to allow network connections to that folder and its subfolders by clients running the Client For Microsoft Networks (also known as the Workstation service). You certainly have shared a folder using Windows Explorer by right-clicking a folder, choosing Sharing And Security, and selecting Share This Folder.

However, the familiar Sharing tab of a folder's properties dialog box in Windows Explorer is available only when you configure a share while logged on to a computer interactively or through terminal services. You cannot share a folder on a *remote* system using Windows Explorer. Therefore, you will examine the creation, properties, configuration, and management of a shared folder using the Shared Folders snap-in, which can be used on both local and remote systems.

When you open the Shared Folders snap-in, either as a custom MMC console snap-in or as part of the Computer Management or File Server Management consoles, you will immediately notice that Windows Server 2003 has several default administrative shares already configured. These shares provide connection to the system directory (typically, C:\Windows) as well as to the root of each fixed hard disk drive. Each of these shares uses the dollar sign ($) in the share name. The dollar sign at the end of a share name configures the share as a *hidden share* that will not appear on browse lists, but that you may connect to with a Universal Naming Convention (UNC) in the form \\*servername**sharename*$. Only administrators can connect to the administrative shares.

To share a folder on a computer, connect to the computer using the Shared Folders snap-in by right-clicking the root Shared Folders node and choosing Connect To Another Computer. Once the snap-in is focused on the computer, click the Shares node and, from the shortcut or Action menu, choose New Share. The important pages and settings exposed by the wizard are

- **The Folder Path page** Type the path to the folder on the *local hard drives* so, for example, if the folder is located on the server's D drive, the folder path would be D:*foldername*.

- **The Name, Description, and Settings page** Type the share name. If your network has any down-level clients (those using DOS-based systems), be sure to adhere to the 8.3 naming convention to ensure their access to the shares. The share name will, with the server name, create the UNC to the resource, in the form *servername**sharename*. Add a dollar sign to the end of the share name to make the share a hidden share. Unlike the built-in hidden administrative shares, hidden shares that are created manually can be connected to by any user, restricted only by the share permissions on the folder.

- **The Permissions page** Select the appropriate share permissions.

Managing a Shared Folder

The Shares node in the Shared Folders snap-in lists all shares on a computer and provides a context menu for each share that enables you to stop sharing the folder, open the share in Windows Explorer, or configure the share's properties. All the properties that you are prompted to fill out by the Share A Folder Wizard can be modified in the share's Properties dialog box, illustrated in Figure 6-1.

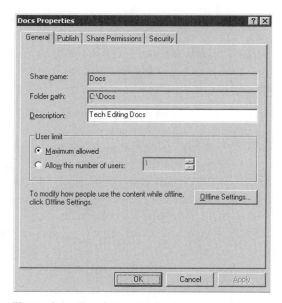

Figure 6-1 The General tab of a shared folder

The Properties tabs in the dialog box are

- **General**   The first tab provides access to the share name, folder path, description, the number of concurrent user connections, and offline files settings. The share name and folder path are read-only. To rename a share, you must first stop sharing the folder then create a share with the new name.

- **Publish**   If you select Publish This Share In Active Directory (as shown in Figure 6-2), an object is created in Active Directory to represent the shared folder.

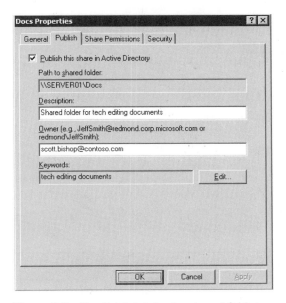

Figure 6-2   The Publish tab of a shared folder

The object's properties include a description and keywords. Administrators can then locate the shared folder based on its description or keywords, using the Find Users, Contacts and Groups dialog box. By selecting Shared Folders from the Find drop-down list, this dialog box becomes the Find Shared Folders dialog box shown in Figure 6-3.

- **Share Permissions**   The Share Permissions tab allows you to configure share permissions.

- **Security**   The Security tab allows you to configure NTFS permissions for the folder.

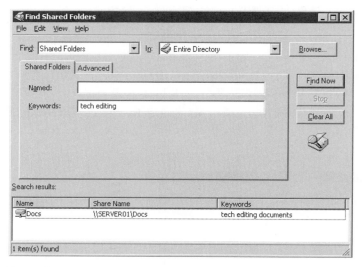

Figure 6-3   Searching for a shared folder

Configuring Share Permissions

Available share permissions are listed in Table 6-1. While share permissions are not as detailed as NTFS permissions, they allow you to configure a shared folder for fundamental access scenarios: Read, Change, and Full Control.

Table 6-1   Share Permissions

Permissions	Description
Read	Users can display folder names, file names, file data and attributes. Users can also run program files and access other folders within the shared folder.
Change	Users can create folders, add files to folders, change data in files, append data to files, change file attributes, delete folders and files, and perform actions permitted by the Read permission.
Full Control	Users can change file permissions, take ownership of files, and perform all tasks allowed by the Change permission.

Share permissions can be allowed or denied. The effective set of share permissions is the cumulative result of the Allow permissions granted to a user and all groups to which that user belongs. If, for example, you are a member of a group that has Read permission and a member of another group that has Change permission, your effective permissions are Change. However, a Deny permission will override an Allow permission. If, on the other hand, you are in one group that has been allowed Read access and in another group that has been denied Full Control, you will be unable to read the files or folders in that share.

Share permissions define the *maximum* effective permissions for all files and folders beneath the shared folder. Permissions can be further restricted, but cannot be broadened, by NTFS permissions on specific files and folders. Said another way, a user's access to a file or folder is the most restrictive set of effective permissions between share permissions and NTFS permissions on that resource. If you want a group to have full control of a folder and have granted full control through NTFS permissions, but the share permission is the default (Everyone: Allow Read) or even if the share permission allows Change, that group's NTFS full control access will be limited by the share permission. This dynamic means that share permissions add a layer of complexity to the management of resource access, and is one of several reasons that organizations cite for their directives to configure shares with open share permissions (Everyone: Allow Full Control), and to use only NTFS permissions to secure folders and files. See the "Three Views of Share Permissions" sidebar for more information about the variety of perspectives and drivers behind discussions of share permissions.

Three Views of Share Permissions

It is important to understand the perspectives from which share permissions are addressed in real-world implementations by Microsoft and by certification objectives and resources such as this book.

Share Permission Limitations

Share permissions have significant limitations, including the following:

- **Scope**   Share permissions apply only to network access through the Client for Microsoft Networks; they do not apply to local or terminal service access to files and folders, nor to other types of network access, such as Hypertext Transfer Protocol (HTTP), File Transfer Protocol (FTP), Telnet, and so on.

- **Replication**   Share permissions do not replicate through file replication service (FRS).

- **Resiliency**   Share permissions are not included in a backup or restore of a data volume.

- **Fragility**   Share permissions are lost if you move or rename the folder that is shared.

- **Lack of detailed control**   Share permissions are not granular; they provide a single permissions template that applies to every file and folder beneath the shared folder. You cannot enlarge access to any folder or file beneath the shared folder; and you cannot further restrict access without turning to NTFS permissions.

- **Auditing**   You cannot configure auditing based on share permissions.

- **The grass is truly greener** We have NTFS permissions, which are designed to provide solid, secure access control to files and folders. NTFS permissions do replicate, are included in a backup and restore of a data volume, can be audited, and provide extraordinary flexibility as well as ease of management. So organizations rely on NTFS permissions for resource access control.

- **Complexity** If both share permissions and NTFS permissions are applied, the most restrictive permission set will be effective, adding a layer of complexity to analyzing effective permissions and troubleshooting file access.

Real-World Use of Share Permissions

Because of these limitations, the use of share permissions does not occur except for the extraordinarily rare case in which a drive volume is FAT or FAT32, which then does not support NTFS permissions. Otherwise, the "real-world" rule is: Configure shares with Everyone: Allow Full Control share permissions, and lock down the shared folder, and any other files or folders beneath it, using NTFS permissions.

Microsoft's Tightening of Share Permissions

Before Windows XP, the default share permission was Everyone: Allow Full Control. Using such a default, adhering to "real-world" policies was simple: administrators didn't change the share permission, but went straight to configuring NTFS permissions. Windows Server 2003 sets Everyone: Allow Read and Administrators: Allow Full Control as the default share permission. This is problematic because, for all non-administrators, the entire shared folder tree is now restricted to read access.

Microsoft made this change with a noble goal: to increase security by restricting the extent to which resources are vulnerable by default when they are shared. Many administrators have shared a folder then forgotten to check NTFS permissions only to discover, too late, that a permission was too "open." By configuring the share with read permission, Microsoft helps administrators avoid this problem. Unfortunately, most organizations avoid share permissions, due to their limitations, and focus instead on providing security through NTFS permissions. Now administrators must remember to configure share permissions (to allow Everyone Full Control) to return to best practices laid out by their organizations.

Certification Objectives

There is a third perspective on share permissions: certification objectives. Although share permissions are typically implemented in accordance with strict enterprise policies (Everyone is allowed Full Control), the fact that share permissions might one day deviate from that setting, and the possibility that data might be stored on a FAT or FAT32 volume, for which share permissions are the only viable option for access control, means that you must understand share permissions to meet the objectives of the MCSA and MCSE exams. Of particular importance are scenarios in which both share permissions and NTFS permissions are applied to a resource, in which case the most restrictive effective permission set becomes the effective permissions set for the resource when it is accessed by a Client For Microsoft Networks service.

So pay attention to share permissions. Learn their nuances. Know how to evaluate effective permissions in combination with NTFS permissions. Then configure your shares according to your organization's guidelines, which will most likely be, unlike the new default share permission in Windows Server 2003, to allow Everyone Full Control.

Managing User Sessions and Open Files

Occasionally, a server must be taken offline for maintenance, backups must be run, or other tasks must be performed that require users to be disconnected and any open files to be closed and unlocked. Each of these scenarios will use the Shared Folders snap-in.

The Sessions node of the Shared Folders snap-in allows you to monitor the number of users connected to a particular server and, if necessary, to disconnect the user. The Open Files node enumerates a list of all open files and file locks for a single server, and allows you to close one open file or disconnect all open files.

Before you perform any of these actions, it is useful to notify the user that the user will be disconnected, so that the user has time to save any unsaved data. You can send a console message by right-clicking the Shares node. Messages are sent by the Messenger Service using the computer name, not the user name. The default state of the Messenger service in Windows Server 2003 is disabled. The Messenger service must be configured for Automatic or Manual startup and must be running before a computer can send console messages.

Practice: Setting Up Shared Folders

In this practice, you will configure a shared folder and modify the share permissions. You will then connect to the share and simulate the common procedures used before taking a server offline.

Exercise 1: Share a Folder

1. Create a folder on your C drive called Docs. Do *not* share the folder yet.

2. Open the Manage Your Server page from Administrative Tools.

3. In the File Server category, click Manage This File Server. If your server is not configured with the File Server role, you can add the role or launch the File Server Management console using the following Tip.

> **Tip**   The File Server Management console is a really nice console, so you might want to create a shortcut to it for easier access. The path to the console is %*SystemRoot*%\System32 \Filesvr.msc.

4. Select the Shares node.

5. Choose Add A Shared Folder from the task list in the details pane. There are equivalent commands for adding a shared folder in the Action and the shortcut menus as well.

6. The Share A Folder Wizard appears. Click Next.

7. Type the path **c:\docs** and then click Next.

8. Accept the default share name, docs, and then click Next.

9. On the Permissions page, click Use Custom Share And Folder Permissions and then click Customize.

10. Click the check box to Allow Full Control and then click OK.

11. Click Finish, and then click Close.

Exercise 2: Connect to a Shared Folder

1. In the File Server Management console, click the Sessions node. If the node shows any sessions, click Disconnect All Sessions, from the task list, and then click Yes to confirm.

2. Choose the Run command from the Start menu. Type the UNC to the shared folder **\\server01\docs**, and then click OK.

    By using a UNC rather than a physical path, such as c:\docs, you create a network connection to the shared folder, just as a user would.

3. In the File Server Management console, click the Sessions node. Notice you are now listed as maintaining a session with the server. You may need to refresh the console by pressing F5 to see the change.

4. Click the Open Files node. Notice that you are listed as having c:\docs open.

Exercise 3: Simulate Preparing to Take a Server Offline

1. Right-click the Shares node in the File Server Management console and, from the All Tasks menu, choose Send Console Message.

> **Tip**   The Messenger service must be running on the computers that are to receive the message. Because it is not expected that a human being will be interactively logged on to the console of a server, the Messenger service is disabled by default. To send a message to yourself in this exercise, you must use the Services console to configure the Messenger service to start automatically or manually, and then start the service.

2. Type a message indicating that the server is being taken offline and that users should save their work.

3. Click Send.

   If you have a second system available, you can simulate the scenario more realistically by connecting to the docs share and sending a message to that system.

4. Click the Open Files node.

5. Select the c:\docs file that is opened through your connection to the shared folder.

6. Close the open file. There are appropriate commands in the Action menu, the task list, and the shortcut menu.

7. Select the Sessions node.

8. Click Disconnect All Sessions in the task list. At this point, you can take the file server offline.

Lesson Review

The following questions are intended to reinforce key information presented in this lesson. If you are unable to answer a question, review the lesson materials and try the question again. You can find answers to the questions in the "Questions and Answers" section at the end of this chapter.

1. Which of the following tools allows you to administer a share on a remote server? Select all that apply.

   a. The Shared Folders snap-in.

   b. Windows Explorer running on the local machine, connected to the remote server's share or hidden drive share.

   c. Windows Explorer running on the remote machine in a Terminal Services or Remote Desktop session.

   d. The File Server Management console.

2. A folder is shared on a FAT32 volume. The Project Managers group is given Allow Full Control permission. The Project Engineers group is given Allow Read permission. Julie belongs to the Project Engineers group. She is promoted and is added to the Project Managers group. What are her effective permissions to the folder?

_____

_____

3. A folder is shared on a NTFS volume, with the default share permissions. The Project Managers group is given Allow Full Control NTFS permission. Julie, who belongs to the Project Managers group, calls to report problems creating files in the folder. Why can't Julie create files?

_____

_____

Lesson Summary

- Windows Explorer can only be used to configure shares on a local volume. This means you must be logged on locally (interactively) to the server, or using Remote Desktop (terminal services) to use Explorer to manage shares.

- The Shared Folders snap-in allows you to manage shares on a local or remote computer.

- You can create a hidden share that does not appear on browse lists by adding a dollar sign ($) to the end of the share name. Connections to the share use the UNC format: \\*servername**sharename*$.

- Share permissions define the maximum effective permissions for all files and folders accessed by the Client for Microsoft Networks connection to the shared folder.

- Share permissions do not apply to local (interactive), terminal services, IIS, or other types of access.

Lesson 2: Configuring File System Permissions

Windows servers support granular or detailed control of access to files and folders through NTFS. Resource access permissions are stored as access control entries (ACEs) on an ACL that is part of the security descriptor of each resource. When a user attempts to access a resource, the user's security access token, which contains the security identifiers (SIDs) of the user's account and group accounts, is compared to the SIDs in the ACEs of the ACL. This process of *authorization* has not changed fundamentally since Windows NT was introduced. However, the details of the implementation of authorization, the tools available to manage resource access, and the specificity with which you can configure access have changed with each release of Windows.

This lesson will explore the nuances and new features of Windows Server 2003's resource access control. You will learn how to use the ACL editor to manage permissions templates, inheritance, special permissions, and how to evaluate resulting effective permissions for a user or group.

After this lesson, you will be able to

- Configure permissions with the Windows Server 2003 ACL editor
- Manage ACL inheritance
- Evaluate resulting, or effective permissions
- Verify effective permissions
- Change ownership of files and folders
- Transfer ownership of files and folders

Estimated lesson time: 30 minutes

Configuring Permissions

Windows Explorer is the most common tool used to initiate management of resource access permissions, both on a local volume as well as on a remote server. Unlike shared folders, Windows Explorer can configure permissions locally and remotely.

The Access Control List Editor

As in earlier versions of Windows, security can be configured for files and folders on any NTFS volume by right-clicking the resource and choosing Properties (or Sharing And Security) then clicking the Security tab. The interface that appears has many aliases; it has been called the Permissions dialog box, the Security Settings dialog box, the Security tab or the Access Control List editor (ACL editor). Whatever you call it, it looks the same. An example can be seen in the Security tab of the Docs Properties dialog box, as shown in Figure 6-4.

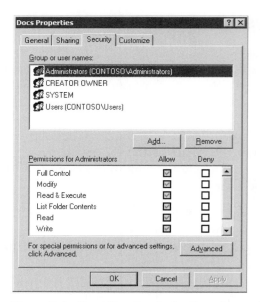

Figure 6-4   The ACL editor in the Docs Properties dialog box

Prior to Windows 2000, permissions were fairly simplistic, but with Windows 2000 and later versions, Microsoft enabled significantly more flexible and powerful control over resource access. With more power came more complexity, and now the ACL editor has three dialog boxes, each of which supports different and important functionality.

The first dialog box provides a "big picture" view of the resource's security settings or permissions, allowing you to select each account that has access defined and to see the permissions templates assigned to that user, group, or computer. Each template shown in this dialog box represents a bundle of permissions that together allow a commonly configured level of access. For example, to allow a user to read a file, several granular permissions are needed. To mask that complexity, you can simply apply the Allow:Read & Execute permissions template and, behind the scenes, Windows sets the correct file or folder permissions.

To view more details about the ACL, click Advanced, which exposes the second of the ACL editor's dialog boxes, the Advanced Security Settings For Docs dialog box, as shown in Figure 6-5. This dialog box lists the specific access control entries that have been assigned to the file or folder. The listing is the closest approximation in the user interface to the actual information stored in the ACL itself. The second dialog also enables you to configure auditing, manage ownership, and evaluate effective permissions.

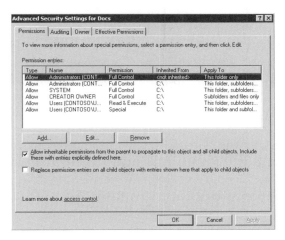

Figure 6-5   The ACL editor's Advanced Security Settings dialog box

If you select a permission in the Permission Entries list and click Edit, the ACL editor's third dialog box appears. This Permission Entry For Docs dialog box, shown in Figure 6-6, lists the detailed, most granular permissions that comprise the permissions entry in the second dialog box's Permissions Entries list and the first dialog box's Permissions For Users list.

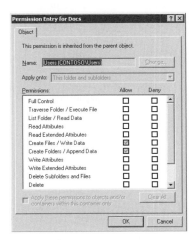

Figure 6-6   The ACL editor's Permission Entry dialog box

Exam Tip   The Shared Folders snap-in also allows you to access the ACL editor. Open the properties of a shared folder and click the Security tab.

Adding and Removing Permission Entries

Any security principal may be granted or denied resource access permissions. In Windows Server 2003, the valid security principals are: users, groups, computers, and the special InetOrgPerson object class (described in RFC 2798), which is used to represent users in certain cross-directory platform situations. To add a permission, click the Add button on either the first or second ACL editor dialog box. The Select User, Computer Or Group dialog box will help you identify the appropriate security principal. Then select appropriate permissions. The interface has changed slightly from previous versions of Windows, but not enough to prevent an experienced administrator from mastering the new user interface quickly. You can remove an explicit permission that you have added to an ACL by selecting the permission and clicking Remove.

Modifying Permissions

A permission may be modified in the dialog box by selecting or clearing the Allow or Deny check boxes on the Security tab to apply permissions templates.

For a finer degree of control, click Advanced, select a permission entry and click Edit. Only explicit permissions may be edited. Inherited permissions are discussed later in this lesson.

The Permission Entry For Docs dialog box, shown in Figure 6-6, will allow you to modify permissions and specify the scope of the permissions inheritance, through the Apply Onto drop-down list.

> **Caution**   Be certain that you understand the impact of changes you make in this dialog box. You can be grateful for the detailed control Microsoft has enabled, but with increased granularity comes increased complexity and increased potential for human error.

New Security Principals

Windows Server 2003, unlike Windows NT 4, allows you to add *computers* or groups of computers to an ACL, thereby adding flexibility to control resource access based on the client computer, regardless of the user who attempts access. For example, you may want to provide a public computer in the employee lounge, but prevent a manager from exposing sensitive data during his or her lunch break. By adding the computer to ACLs and denying access permission, the manager who can access sensitive data from his or her desktop is prevented from accessing it from the lounge.

Windows Server 2003 also allows you to manage resource access based on the type of logon. You can add the special accounts, Interactive, Network, and Terminal Server User to an ACL. Interactive represents any user logged on locally to the console. Terminal Server User includes any user connected via remote desktop or terminal services.

Network represents a connection from the network, for example a Windows system running Client for Microsoft Networks.

Permissions Templates and Special Permissions

Permissions templates, visible on the Security tab in the first dialog box are bundles of special permissions, which are fully enumerated in the third dialog box, Permissions Entry For Docs. Most of the templates and special permissions are self-explanatory, while others are beyond the scope of this book. However, the following points are worth noting:

- **Read & Execute**   This permissions template is sufficient to allow users to open and read files and folders. Read & Execute will also allow a user to copy a resource, assuming they have permission to write to a target folder or media. There is no permission in Windows to prevent copying. Such functionality will be possible with Digital Rights Management technologies as they are incorporated into Windows platforms.

- **Write and Modify**   The Write permissions template applied to a folder allows users to create a new file or folder (when applied to a folder) and, when applied to a file, to modify the contents of a file as well as its attributes (hidden, system, read-only) and extended attributes (defined by the application responsible for the document). The Modify template adds the permission to delete the object.

- **Change Permissions**   After modifying ACLs for a while, you might wonder who can modify permissions. The answer is, first, the owner of the resource. Ownership will be discussed later in this lesson. Second, any user who has an effective permission that allows Change Permission can modify the ACL on the resource. The Change Permission must be managed using the ACL editor's third dialog box, Permission Entry For Docs. It is also included in the Full Control permission template.

Inheritance

Windows Server 2003 supports permissions inheritance, which simply means that permissions applied to a folder will, by default, apply to the files and folders beneath that folder. Any change to the parent's ACL will similarly affect all contents of that folder. Inheritance enables you to create single points of administration, managing a single ACL on a branch or resources under a folder.

Understanding Inheritance

Inheritance is the result of two characteristics of a resource's security descriptor. First, permissions are, by default, inheritable. As previously shown in Figure 6-5, the permission Allow Users to Read & Execute is specified to Apply to: This folder, subfolders, and files. That alone, however, is not enough to make inheritance work. The other half of the story is that new objects, when created, are set by default to "Allow Inheritable Permissions From The Parent To Propagate To This Object..." the check box visible in the same figure.

So a newly created file or folder will inherit the inheritable permissions from its parent, and any changes to the parent will affect the child files and folders as well. It is helpful to understand this two-step implementation of inheritance because it gives us two ways to manage inheritance: from the parent and from the child.

Inherited permissions are displayed differently in each dialog box of the ACL editor. The first and third dialog boxes (Security tab and Permissions Entry For Docs) show inherited permissions as dimmed check marks, to distinguish them from permissions that are set directly on the resource, called explicit permissions, which are not dimmed. The second dialog box (Advanced Security Settings) shows, for each permission entry, from what folder the permission entry is inherited.

Overriding Inheritance

Inheritance allows you to configure permissions high in a folder tree. Such initial permissions, and any changes to those permissions, will propagate to all the files and folders in that tree that are, by default, configured to allow inheritance.

Occasionally, however, you might need to modify permissions on a subfolder or file, to provide additional access or restrict access to a user or group. You cannot remove inherited permissions from an ACL. You can override an inherited permission by assigning an explicit permission. Alternatively, you can block all inheritance and create an entirely explicit ACL.

To override an inherited permission by assigning an explicit permission, simply check the appropriate permissions box. For example, if a folder has an inherited Allow Read permission assigned to the Sales Reps group, and you do not want Sales Reps to access the folder, you can select the box to Deny Read.

To override all inheritance, open the resources Advanced Security Settings dialog box and clear Allow Inheritable Permissions From The Parent To Propagate To This Object... You will block all inheritance from the parent. You will then have to manage access to the resource by assigning sufficient explicit permissions.

To help you create an explicit permissions ACL, Windows gives you a choice when you choose to disallow inheritance. You are asked whether you want to Copy or Remove permissions entries, as shown in Figure 6-7.

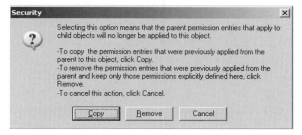

Figure 6-7   Copying or removing permissions entries

Copy will create explicit permissions identical to what was inherited. You can then remove individual permissions entries that you do not want to affect the resource. If you choose Remove, you will be presented with an empty ACL, to which you will add permissions entries. The result is the same either way; an ACL populated with explicit permissions. The question is whether it is easier to start with an empty ACL and build it from scratch or start with a copy of the inherited permissions and modify the list to the desired goal. If the new ACL is wildly different than the inherited permissions, choose Remove. If the new ACL is only slightly different than the result of inherited permissions, it is more efficient to choose Copy.

When you disallow inheritance by deselecting the Allow Inheritable Permissions option, you block inheritance. All access to the resource is managed by explicit permissions assigned to that file or folder. Any changes to the ACL of its parent folder will *not* affect the resource; although the parent permissions are inheritable, the child does not inherit. Block inheritance sparingly because it increases the complexity of managing, evaluating, and troubleshooting resource access.

Reinstating Inheritance

Inheritance can be reinstated in two ways: from the child resource or from the parent folder. The results differ slightly. You might reinstate inheritance on a resource if you disallowed inheritance accidentally or if business requirements have changed. Simply re-select the Allow Inheritable Permissions option in the Advanced Security Settings dialog box. Inheritable permissions from the parent will now apply to the resource. All explicit permissions you assigned to the resource remain, however. The resulting ACL is a combination of the explicit permissions, which you might choose to remove, and the inherited permissions. Because of this dynamic, you might not see some inherited permissions in the first or third ACL editor dialog boxes. For example, if a resource has an explicit permission, Allows Sales Reps Read & Execute, and the parent folder has the same permission, when you choose to allow inheritance on the child, the result will be that the child has both an inherited *and* an explicit permission. You will see a check mark in the first and third dialog boxes; the explicit permission obscures the inherited permission in the interface. But the inherited permission is actually present, which can be confirmed in the second dialog box, Advanced Security Settings.

The second method for reinstating inheritance is from the parent folder. In the Advanced Security Settings dialog box of a folder, you may select the check box, Replace Permission Entries On All Child Objects With Entries Shown Here That Apply To Child Objects. The result: all ACLs on subfolders and files are removed. The permissions on the parent are applied. You might see this as "blasting through" the parent's permissions. After applying this option, any explicit permission that had been applied to subfolders and files is removed, unlike the method used for reinstating inheritance on the child resources. Inheritance is restored, so any changes to the parent-folder ACL are propagated to its subfolders and files. At this point, you might set new, explicit permissions on subfolders or files. The Replace Permissions option does its job when you apply it, but does not continuously enforce parent permissions.

Effective Permissions

It is common for users to belong to more than one group, and for those groups to have varying levels of resource access. When an ACL contains multiple entries, you must be able to evaluate the permissions that apply to a user based on his or her group memberships. The resulting permissions are called *effective permissions*.

> **Exam Tip**   Effective permissions are a common exam objective on most of the Microsoft Windows Server 2003 core exams, as well as on design and client exams. Pay close attention to this information, and to any practice questions regarding effective permissions so you can be certain you have mastered the topic.

Understanding Effective Permissions

The rules that determine effective permissions are as follows:

- **File permissions override folder permissions.**   This isn't really a rule, but it is often presented that way in documentation, so it is worth addressing. Each resource maintains an ACL that is solely responsible for determining resource access. Although entries on that ACL may appear because they are inherited from a parent folder, they are nevertheless entries on that resource's ACL. The security subsystem does not consult the parent folder to determine access at all. So you may interpret this rule as: The only ACL that matters is the ACL on the resource.

- **Allow permissions are cumulative.**   Your level of resource access may be determined by permissions assigned to one or more groups to which you belong. The Allow permissions that are assigned to any of the user, group, or computer IDs in your security access token will apply to you, so your effective permissions are fundamentally the sum of those Allow permissions. If the Sales Reps group is allowed Read & Execute and Write permissions to a folder, and the Sales Managers group is allowed Read & Execute and Delete permissions, a user who belongs to both groups will have effective permissions equivalent to the Modify permissions template: Read & Execute, Write and Delete.

- **Deny permissions take precedence over Allow permissions.**   A permission that is denied will override a permission entry that allows the same access. Extending the example above, if the Temporary Employees group is denied Read permission, and a user is a temporary sales representative, belonging to both Sales Reps and Temporary Employees, that user will not be able to read the folder.

> **Note**   Best practice dictates that you minimize the use of Deny permissions and focus instead on allowing the minimal resources permissions required to achieve the business task. Deny permissions add a layer of complexity to the administration of ACLs, and should be used only where absolutely necessary to exclude access to a user who has been granted permissions to the resource through other group memberships.

> **Exam Tip**   If a user is unable to access a resource due to a Deny permission, but access is desired, you must either remove the Deny permission or remove the user from the group to which the Deny permission is applied. If the Deny permission is inherited, you may provide access by adding an explicit Allow permission.

- **Explicit permissions take precedence over inherited permissions.**   A permission entry that is explicitly defined for a resource will override a conflicting inherited permission entry. This follows common-sense design principles: A parent folder sets a "rule" through its inheritable permissions. A child object requires access that is an exception to the rule, and so an explicit permission is added to its ACL. The explicit permission takes precedence.

> **Exam Tip**   A result of this dynamic is that an *explicit Allow permission will override an inherited Deny permission*.

Evaluating Effective Permissions

Complexity is a possibility, given the extraordinary control over granular permissions and inheritance that NTFS supports. With all those permissions, users and groups, how can you know what access a user actually has?

Microsoft added a long-awaited tool to help answer that question. The Effective Permissions tab of the Advanced Security Settings dialog box, shown in Figure 6-8, provides a reliable approximation of a user's resulting resource access.

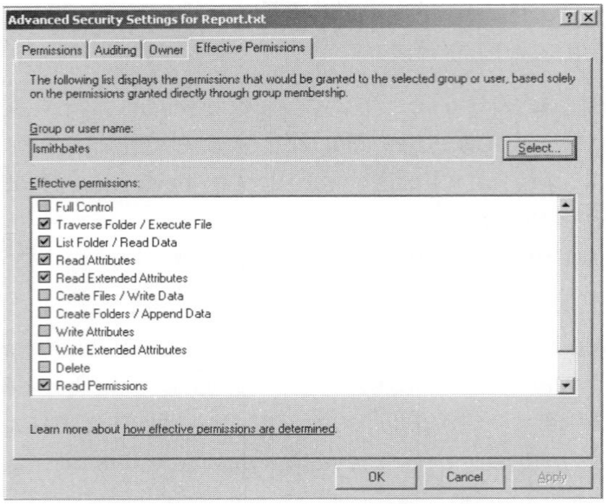

Figure 6-8   The Effective Permissions tab of the Advanced Security Settings dialog box

To use the Effective Permissions tool, click Select and identify the user, group, or built-in account to analyze. Windows Server 2003 then produces a list of effective permissions. This list is an approximation only. It does not take share permissions into account, nor does it evaluate the account's special memberships, such as the following:

- Anonymous Logon
- Batch
- Creator Group
- Dialup
- Enterprise Domain Controllers
- Interactive
- Network
- Proxy
- Restricted
- Remote Interactive Logon
- Service
- System
- Terminal Server User
- Other Organization
- This Organization

An ACL can contain entries for the Network or Interactive accounts, for example, which would provide the opportunity for a user to experience different levels of resource access depending on whether the user was logged on to the machine or using a network client. Because the user in question is not logged on, logon-specific permissions entries are ignored. However, as an extra step, you can evaluate effective permissions for a built-in or special account such as Interactive or Network.

Resource Ownership

Windows Server 2003 includes a special security principal called Creator Owner, and an entry in a resource's security descriptor that defines the object's owner. To fully manage and troubleshoot resource permissions, you must understand these two parts of the security picture.

Creator Owner

When a user creates a file or folder (which is possible if that user is allowed Create Files/Write Data or Create Folders/Append Data, respectively), the user is the creator and initial owner of that resource. Any permissions on the parent folder assigned to the special account Creator Owner are explicitly assigned to the user on the new resource.

As an example, assume that a folder allows users to create files (allow Create Files/ Write Data), and the folder's permissions allows users to Read & Execute, and Creator Owner Full Control. This permission set would allow Maria to create a file. Maria, as the creator of that file, would have full control of that file. Tia can also create a file, and would have full control of her file. However, Tia and Maria would only be able to read each other's files. Tia could, however, change the ACL on the file she created. Full Control includes the Change Permission.

Ownership

If for some reason Tia managed to modify the ACL and deny herself Full Control, she could nevertheless modify the ACL, because an object's owner can always modify its ACL, preventing users from permanently locking themselves out of their files and folders.

It is best practice to manage object ownership so that an object's owner is correctly defined. This is partly because owners can modify ACLs of their objects, and also because newer technologies, such as disk quotas, rely on the ownership attribute to calculate disk space used by a particular user. Prior to Windows Server 2003, managing ownership was awkward. Windows Server 2003 has added an important tool to simplify ownership transfer.

An object's owner is defined in its security descriptor. The user who creates a file or folder is its initial owner. Another user can take ownership, or be given ownership of the object using one of the following processes:

- **Administrators can take ownership.**   A user who belongs to the Administrators group of a system, or who has otherwise been granted the Take Ownership user right, can take ownership of any object on the system.

  To take ownership of a resource, click the Owner tab of the Advanced Security Settings dialog box, as shown in Figure 6-9. Select your user account from the list and click Apply. Select the Replace Owner On Subcontainers And Objects check box to take ownership of subfolders and files.

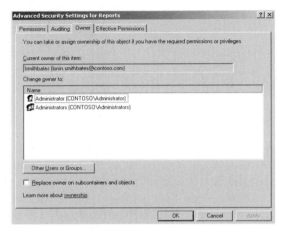

Figure 6-9   The Owner tab of the Advanced Security Settings dialog box

- **Users can take ownership if they are allowed Take Ownership permission.**   The special permission Take Ownership can be granted to any user or group. A user with an Allow Take Ownership permission can take ownership of the resource and then, as owner, modify the ACL to provide sufficient permissions.

- **Administrators can facilitate the transfer of ownership.**   An administrator can take ownership of any file or folder. Then, as owner, the administrator can change permissions on the resource to grant Allow Take Ownership permission to the new owner, who then can take ownership of the resource.

- **Restore Files And Directories user right enables the transfer of ownership.**   A user with the Restore Files And Directories rights may transfer ownership of a file from one user to another. If you have been assigned the Restore Files And Directories right, you can click Other Users Or Groups and select the new owner. This capability is new in Windows Server 2003, and makes it possible for administrators and backup operators to manage and transfer resource ownership without requiring user intervention.

Practice: Configuring File System Permissions

In this practice, you will use the ACL editor to secure resources, evaluate effective permissions and transfer ownership of files. Be certain that you have configured the user and group accounts outlined in this chapter's "Before You Begin" section.

Exercise 1: Configuring NTFS Permissions

1. Open the c:\docs folder that was shared in Lesson 1's practice.

2. Create a folder called Project 101.

3. Open the ACL editor by right-clicking Project 101, choosing Properties, and clicking the Security tab.

4. Configure the folder so that the folder allows the access outlined in the table below. This will require you to consider and configure, inheritance and permissions for groups.

Security Principal	Access
Administrators	Full Control
Users in the Project 101 Team	Can read data, add files and folders, and have full control of the files and folders they create.
Managers	Can read and modify all files, but cannot delete any files that they did not create. Managers should have full control of the files and folders they create.
System	Services running as the System account should have full control.

When you believe you have configured correct permissions, click Apply and click Advanced. Compare the Advanced Security Settings dialog box to the dialog box shown in Figure 6-10.

To configure these permissions, you must disallow inheritance. Otherwise, all users, not just those in the Project 101 group, will be able to read files in the Project 101 folder. The parent folder, c:\docs, is propagating the Users: Allow Read & Execute permission. The only way to prevent this access is to deselect the Allow Inheritable Permissions From The Parent… option. Notice that the requirements did not specify that you needed to prevent Users from reading, but it was also not indicated that Users required read access, and it is a security best practice to permit only the minimum required access.

After disallowing inheritance, the Advanced Security Settings dialog box should look like the dialog box in Figure 6-10.

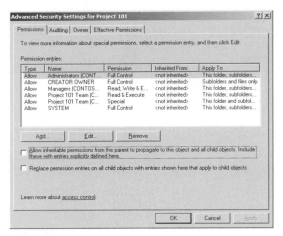

Figure 6-10   The Permissions tab of the Advanced Security Settings dialog box

The option to allow inheritance has been deselected and all permissions are shown as <not inherited>. Administrators, System, and Creator Owner have full control. Remember that when Creator Owner has full control, a user who creates a file or folder is given full control of that resource. The Project 101 group is listed as having a special permission entry. If you select that entry and click View/Edit, you will see the specific permissions assigned to the Project 101 group should match the dialog box shown in Figure 6-11.

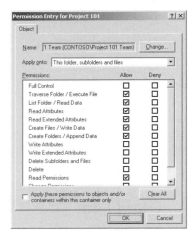

Figure 6-11   Special permissions for the Project 101 group

The Managers have Allow: Read, Write & Execute permission. This template includes the permissions to create files and folders and, like Project 101 team members, if a manager creates a resource, Managers are given the Creator Owner permissions for that resource. This permission set does *not* allow Managers to delete other users' files. Remember that the Modify permissions template, which you did not assign, *does* include the Delete permission.

Exercise 2: Working with Deny Permissions

1. Assume a group of contractors is hired. All user accounts for contractors are members of the Project Contractors group, and do not belong to any other group in the domain. What must you do to prevent contractors from accessing the Project 101 folder you secured in the previous exercise?

   Nothing. Because contractors do not belong to other groups in the domain, they do not have permissions given to them by the current ACL that would allow any resource access. It is therefore not necessary to deny permissions.

2. Assume that some user accounts, such as Scott Bishop's account, belong to both the Project Contractors and the Engineers groups. What must be done to prevent access by contractors?

   In this case, you must assign Deny permissions to the Project Contractors group. Because they will receive Allow permissions assigned to other groups, you must override those permissions with Deny permissions.

3. Configure the folder to Deny Project Contractors Full Control.

Exercise 3: Effective Permissions

1. Open the Advanced Security Settings dialog box for the Project 101 folder by opening the folder's properties, clicking Security, then clicking Advanced.

2. Click Effective Permissions.

3. Select each of the following users and verify their permissions.

User	Effective Permissions
Scott Bishop	No permissions
Danielle Tiedt	Traverse Folder / Execute File List Folder / Read Data Read Attributes Read Extended Attributes Create Files / Write Data Create Folders / Append Data Read Permissions

User	Effective Permissions
Lorrin Smith-Bates	Traverse Folder / Execute File List Folder / Read Data Read Attributes Read Extended Attributes Create Files / Write Data Create Folders / Append Data Write Attributes Write Extended Attributes Read Permissions

If these permissions do not match yours, there is either an error in the permission list (in which case, go back to Exercises 1 and 2) or in groups and group membership (in which case, see this chapter's "Before You Begin" section). Correct any errors and reverify effective permissions until they match these.

Exercise 4: Ownership

1. Log on as Danielle Tiedt.

2. Open the shared folder by connecting to \\Server01\Docs.

3. Open the Project 101 folder and create a text file called Report.

4. Open the Advanced Security Settings dialog box for Report.

5. Confirm that all permissions are inherited from the parent folder. What differences are there in the ACL between this object and the Project 101 folder?

   The Project 101 folder grants Full Control to Creator Owner. The Report file grants Full Control to Danielle. When she created the file, her SID was assigned the permissions granted to the special Creator Owner group. In addition, the Project 101 Team's permission to Create Files and Create Folders is a folder permission, so it does not appear on the ACL of Report.

6. Log on as Administrator.

7. Open the Advanced Security Settings dialog box for Report.

8. Click Owner.

9. Confirm that Danielle is listed as the current owner.

10. Select your user account and click Apply. You are now the owner of the object.

11. A user with the Restore Files And Directories user right is able to transfer ownership to another user. Click Other Users Or Group and select Lorrin Smith-Bates. Once Lorrin's account is displayed in the Change Owner To list, select it and click Apply.

12. Confirm that Lorrin is now the owner of the Report.

13. Do you think that Lorrin now has full control of the object? Why or why not? Do you think that Danielle will keep full control, or will her permissions change? Confirm using the Effective Permissions page.

Lorrin does not have full control—only Modify permission. Lorrin is a member of the Managers group, which has Modify permission. The Full Control permission assigned to Creator Owner is only applied to a user when the user creates an object.

Note   Once an object has been created, changing ownership does not modify the ACL in any way. However, the new owner (or any user with Allow Change Permissions) can modify the ACL, as an additional step, to provide himself or herself with sufficient resource access.

Lesson Review

The following questions are intended to reinforce key information presented in this lesson. If you are unable to answer a question, review the lesson materials and try the question again. You can find answers to the questions in the "Questions and Answers" section at the end of this chapter.

1. What are the minimum NTFS permissions required to allow users to open documents and run programs stored in a shared folder?

  a. Full Control

  b. Modify

  c. Write

  d. Read & Execute

  e. List Folder Contents

2. Bill complains that he is unable to access the department plan. You open the Security tab for the plan and you find that all permissions on the document are inherited from the plan's parent folder. There is a Deny Read permission assigned to a group to which Bill belongs. Which of the following methods would enable Bill to access the plan?

  a. Modify the permissions on the parent folder by adding the permission Bill:Allow Full Control.

  b. Modify the permissions on the parent folder by adding the permission Bill:Allow Read.

  c. Modify the permissions on the plan by adding the permission: Bill:Allow Read.

  d. Modify the permissions on the plan by deselecting Allow Inheritable Permissions, choosing Copy, and removing the Deny permission.

   e. Modify the permissions on the plan by deselecting Allow Inheritable Permissions, choosing Copy, and adding the permission Bill:Allow Full Control.

   f. Remove Bill from the group that is assigned the Deny permission.

3. Bill calls again to indicate that he still cannot access the departmental plan. You use the Effective Permissions tool, select Bill's account, and the tool indicates that Bill is, in fact, allowed sufficient permissions. What might explain the discrepancy between the results of the Effective Permissions tool and the issue Bill is reporting?

_____

_____

Lesson Summary

- NTFS permissions can be configured using the ACL editor, which itself has three dialog boxes: the Security tab, Advanced Security Settings, and Permission Entry For.

- Permissions can be allowed or denied; explicit or inherited. A Deny permission takes precedence over an Allow permission; and an explicit permission takes precedence over an inherited permission. The result is that an explicit Allow permission can override an inherited Deny permission.

- Inheritance allows an administrator to manage permissions from a single parent folder that contains files and folders that share common resource access requirements. A new object's ACL will, by default, include the inheritable permissions from the parent folder.

- It is possible to change the effect of inherited permissions on an object several ways. You can modify the original (parent's) permission and allow the new permission to be inherited by the object; you can set an explicit permission on the object, which will take precedence over the inherited permission; or you can disallow inheritance on the object and configure an ACL with explicit permissions that define resource access.

- The Effective Permissions tab of the Advanced Security Settings dialog box is a useful tool that provides an approximation of resource access for a user or a group by analyzing that account's permissions as well as the permissions of groups to which that account belongs.

- The owner of an object can modify the object's ACL at any time. A user that is allowed Take Ownership permission may take ownership of the object, and administrators may take ownership of any object on the system. Administrators, Backup Operators, and other accounts that have been given the Restore Files And Directories user right can transfer ownership of a file or folder from the current owner to any other user or group.

Lesson 3: Auditing File System Access

Many organizations elect to audit file system access to provide insight into resource utilization and potential security vulnerabilities. Windows Server 2003 supports granular auditing based on user or group accounts and the specific actions performed by those accounts. To configure auditing, you must complete three steps: specify auditing settings, enable audit policy, and evaluate events in the security log. This lesson will explore these three processes and provide guidance to effective auditing, so that you can leverage auditing to meet business requirements without being drowned in logged events.

After this lesson, you will be able to

- Configure audit settings on a file or folder
- Enable auditing on a standalone server or for a collection of servers
- Examine audited events in the Security log

Estimated lesson time: 20 minutes

Configuring Audit Settings

To specify the actions you wish to monitor and track, you must configure audit settings in the file's or folder's Advanced Security Settings dialog box. The Auditing tab, shown in Figure 6-12, looks strikingly similar to the Permissions tab before it. Instead of adding permissions entries, however, you add auditing entries.

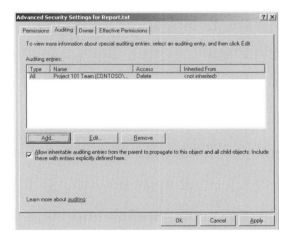

Figure 6-12   Auditing tab of the Advanced Security Settings dialog box

Click Add to select the user, group, or computer to audit. Then, in the Auditing Entry dialog box, as shown in Figure 6-13, indicate the permission uses to audit.

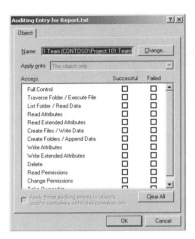

Figure 6-13 Auditing Entry dialog box

You are able to audit for successes, failures, or both as the account attempts to access the resource using each of the granular permissions assigned to the object.

Successes can be used to audit the following:

- To log resource access for reporting and billing.

- To monitor for access that would indicate that users are performing actions greater than what you had planned, indicating permissions are too generous.

- To identify access that is out of character for a particular account, which might be a sign that a user account has been breached by a hacker.

Auditing for failed access allows you:

- To monitor for malicious attempts to access a resource to which access has been denied.

- To identify failed attempts to access a file or folder to which a user does require access. This would indicate that permissions are not sufficient to achieve a business task.

Audit settings, like permissions, follow rules of inheritance. Inheritable auditing settings are applied to objects that allow inheritance.

Note Audit logs have the tendency to get quite large, quite rapidly, so a golden rule for auditing is to configure the bare minimum required to achieve the business task. Specifying to audit successes and failures on an active data folder for the Everyone group using Full Control (all permissions) would generate enormous audit logs that could affect the performance of the server and would make locating a specific audited event all but impossible.

Enabling Auditing

Configuring auditing entries in the security descriptor of a file or folder does not, in itself, enable auditing. Auditing must be enabled through policy. Once auditing is enabled, the security subsystem begins to pay attention to the audit settings, and to log access as directed by those settings.

Audit policy may be enabled on a stand-alone server using the Local Security Policy console, and on a domain controller using the Domain Controller Security Policy console. Select the Audit Policy node under the Local Policies node and double-click the policy, Audit Object Access. Select Define These Policy Settings and then select whether to enable auditing for successes, failures, or both.

> **Note**   Remember that the access that is audited and logged is the combination of the audit entries on specific files and folders, and the settings in Audit Policy. If you have configured audit entries to log failures, but the policy enables only logging for successes, your audit logs will remain empty.

You may also enable auditing for one or more computers using Active Directory Group Policy Objects (GPOs). The Audit Policy node is located under Computer Configuration, Windows Settings, Security Settings, Local Policies, Audit Policy. Like all group policies, the computers that are affected by the policy will be those contained within the scope of the policy. If you link a policy to the Servers OU and enable auditing, all computers objects in the Servers OU will begin to audit resource access according to audit entries on files and folders on those systems.

Examining the Security Log

Once audit entries have been configured on files or folders, and auditing object access has been enabled through local or group policy, the system will begin to log access according to the audit entries. You can view and examine the results using Event Viewer and selecting the Security log, as shown in Figure 6-14.

As you can see, the Security log can be quite busy, depending on the types of auditing being performed on the machine. You can sort the events to help you identify object access events by clicking the Category column header and locating the Object Access events.

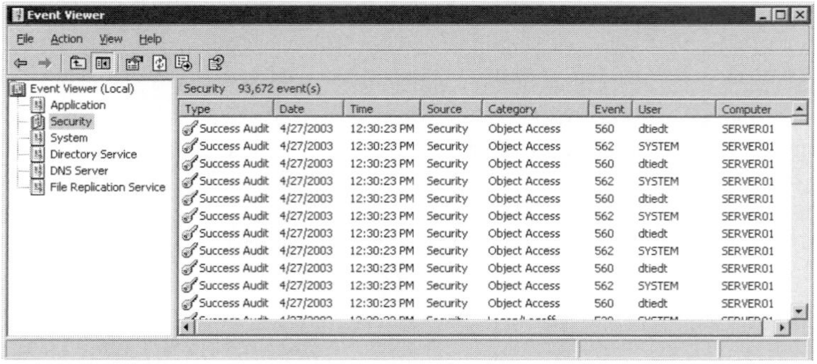

Figure 6-14   The Security log in Event Viewer

Sorting will, however, provide little assistance as you dig through the logged events. You will often be better served by filtering the event log, which can be done by choosing the Filter command from the View menu, or alternatively by selecting the Security log, then Properties from the Action or shortcut menus, and then clicking the Filter tab. The Filter tab enables you to specify criteria including the event type, category, source, date range, user, and computer. Figure 6-15 illustrates an example of a filter applied to identify object access audit events on a specific date.

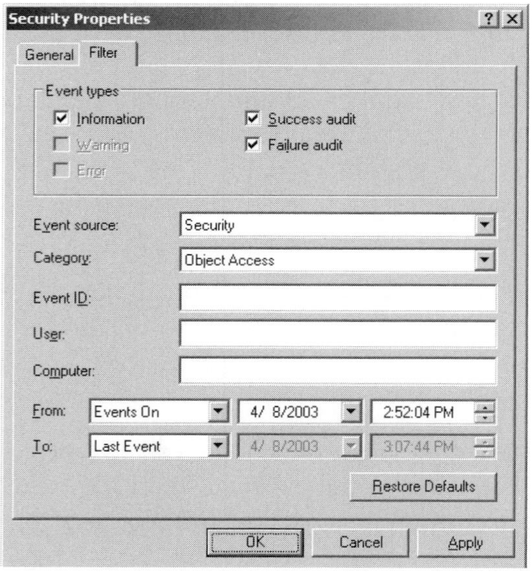

Figure 6-15   The Filter tab

Finally, you have the option to export the Security log by selecting the Save Log File As command from the log's context menu. The native event log file format takes a .evt extension. You can open that file with Event Viewer on another system. Alternatively, you can save the log to tab- or comma-delimited file formats, which can be read by a number of analysis tools including Microsoft Excel. In Excel, you can of course apply filters as well to search for more specific information, such as the contents of the event's Description field.

Practice: Auditing File System Access

In this practice, you will configure auditing settings, enable audit policies for object access, and filter for specific events in the security log. The business objective is to monitor the deletion of files from an important folder, to ensure that only appropriate users are deleting files.

Exercise 1: Configure Audit Settings

1. Log on as Administrator.
2. Open the Advanced Security Settings dialog box for the C:\Docs\Project 101 folder.
3. Click the Auditing tab.
4. Add an audit entry to track the Project 101 Team group. Specify that you wish to monitor Success and Failure of the Delete permission.

Exercise 2: Enable Audit Policy

Because you are logged on to a domain controller, you will use the Domain Controller Security Policy console to enable auditing. On a stand-alone server you would use Local Security Policy. You could also leverage GPOs to enable auditing.

1. Open Domain Controller Security Policy from the Administrative Tools folder.
2. Expand Local Policies and select Audit Policy.
3. Double-click Audit Object Access.
4. Select Define These Policy Settings.
5. Specify to enable auditing for both success and failure audit entries.
6. Click OK, and then close the console.
7. To refresh the policy, and to ensure that all settings have been applied, open a command prompt and type the command **gpupdate**.

Exercise 3: Generate Audit Events

1. Log on as Danielle Tiedt.
2. Connect to \\Server01\Docs\Project 101.
3. Delete the Report text file.

Exercise 4: Examine the Security Log

1. Log on as Administrator.

2. Open Event Viewer from the Administrative Tools folder.

3. Select the Security log.

4. What types of events do you see in the Security log? Only Object Access events? Other types of events? Remember that policies can enable auditing for numerous security-related actions, including directory service access, account management, logon, and more.

5. To filter the log and narrow the scope of your search, choose the Filter command from the View menu.

6. Configure the filter to be as narrow as possible. What do you know about the event you are trying to locate? You know it is a success or failure audit; that it is an Object Access event category; and that it occurred today. Check your work by referring to Figure 6-15.

7. Click Apply.

8. Can you more easily locate the event that marked Danielle's deletion of the Report file? Open the event and look at its contents. The description indicates the user and the file and the action. You could not filter for contents of the description in Event Viewer, but you could do so by exporting the file to a log analysis tool or to Microsoft Excel.

9. (Optional) If you have access to Microsoft Excel, right-click the Security log node and choose Save Log File As. Enter a name and select Comma-Delimited as the file type. Open the file in Excel.

Lesson Review

The following questions are intended to reinforce key information presented in this lesson. If you are unable to answer a question, review the lesson materials and try the question again. You can find answers to the questions in the "Questions and Answers" section at the end of this chapter.

1. Which of the following must be done to generate a log of resource access for a file or folder? Select all that apply.

   a. Configure NTFS permissions to allow the System account to audit resource access.

   b. Configure audit entries to specify the types of access to audit.

   c. Enable the Audit Privilege Use policy.

   d. Enable the Audit Object Access policy.

2. Which of the following are valid criteria for a security log filter to identify specific file and folder access events? Select all that apply.

    a. The date of the event

    b. The user that generated the event

    c. The type of object access that generated the event

    d. Success or failure audit

3. Users at Contoso Ltd. use Microsoft Office applications to access resources on Server01. Your job is to monitor Server01 to ensure that permissions are not too restrictive, so that users are not prevented from achieving their assignments. Which log, and which type of event, will provide the information you require?

    a. Application log; Success Event

    b. Application log; Failure Event

    c. Security log; Success Event

    d. Security log; Failure Event

    e. System log; Success Event

    f. System log; Failure Event

Lesson Summary

- Audit entries are contained in the security descriptor of files and folders on NTFS volumes. They are configured using Windows Explorer, from the properties of a file or folder, using the Advanced Security Settings dialog box.

- Audit entries alone do not generate audit logs. You must also enable the Audit Object Access policy from Local Security Policy, the Domain Controller Security Policy, or a GPO.

- The Security log, viewable with the Event Viewer snap-in, allows you to locate and examine object access events.

Lesson 4: Administering Internet Information Services

Lesson 1 discussed the issues related to sharing a folder so that users, with the Client For Microsoft Networks, can access resources on a server running the File And Print Sharing For Microsoft Networks service. That is, however, only one means by which users can access the files and folders they require. It is also possible to enable access through Internet technologies such as FTP and Web (HTTP) services.

In this lesson, you will learn how to configure and manage IIS. You will discover how to configure Web and FTP sites, virtual directories, and IIS security.

After this lesson, you will be able to

- Install IIS
- Set up a Web and FTP site
- Configure a Web default content page
- Create a Web virtual directory
- Modify IIS authentication and security settings

Estimated lesson time: 20 minutes

Installing IIS 6.0

To decrease the attack surface of a Windows Server 2003 system, IIS is not installed by default. It must be added using the Add/Remove Windows Components Wizard from Add Or Remove Programs, located in Control Panel. Select Application Server, click Details, and then select Internet Information Services (IIS). You can control the subcomponents of IIS that are installed, but unless you are very familiar with the role of subcomponents, do not remove any default components. You may, however, want to add components, such as ASP.NET, FTP or FrontPage Server Extensions.

Administering the Web Environment

When IIS is installed, a default Web site is created, allowing you to implement a Web environment quickly and easily. However, you can modify that Web environment to meet your needs. Windows Server 2003 provides the tools necessary to administer IIS and its sites.

After installation has completed, you may open the Internet Information Services (IIS) Manager console from the Administrative Tools group. By default, IIS is configured to serve only static content. To enable dynamic content, select the Web Service Extensions node. As shown in Figure 6-16, all the extensions are prohibited. Select the appropriate extension and click Allow.

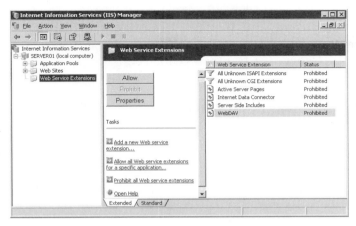

Figure 6-16   The Internet Information Services (IIS) Manager snap-in

The fundamental processes that take place as a client accesses a resource from IIS are

- The client enters a URL (Universal Resource Locator) in either of the following forms:

  ❑ *http://dns.domain.name/virtualdirectory/page.htm* or

  ❑ *ftp://dns.domain.name/virtualdirectory*

- Domain Name Service (DNS) resolves the name to an IP address and returns the address to the client

- The client connects to the server's IP address, using a port that is specific to the service (typically, port 80 for HTTP and port 21 for FTP)

- The URL does not represent the physical path to the resource on the server, but a virtualization of the path. The server translates the incoming request into the physical path and produces appropriate resources to the client. For example, the server might list files in the folder to an FTP client, or might deliver the home page to an HTTP client.

- The process can be secured with authentication (credentials, including a user name and password) and authorization (access control through permissions).

You can see this process in action by opening a browser and typing **http://server01**. The server produces the Under Construction page to the client browser.

Configuring and Managing Web and FTP Sites

IIS installation configures a single Web site, the Default Web Site. Although IIS, depending on your server's hardware configuration, can host thousands, or tens of thousands of sites, the Default Web Site is a fine place to explore the functionality and administration of Web sites on IIS. This Web site is accessible if you open a browser and type the URL: **http://server01.contoso.com**. The page that is fetched is the Under Construction page.

Remember that a browser's request to a Web server is directed at the server's IP address, which was resolved from the URL by DNS. The request includes the URL, and the URL often includes only the site name (*www.microsoft.com*, for example). How does the server produce the home page? If you examine the Web Site tab of the Default Web Site Properties, as shown in Figure 6-17, you see that the site is assigned to All Unassigned IP addresses on port 80. So the request from the browser hits port 80 on the server, which then identifies that it is the Default Web Site that should be served.

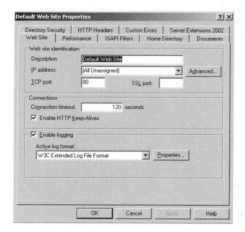

Figure 6-17   The Web Site tab of the Default Web Site Properties dialog box

The next question, then, is what information should be served. If the URL includes only the site name (for example, *www.microsoft.com* or *server01.contoso.com*), then the page that will be returned is fetched from the home directory. The Home Directory tab, as shown in Figure 6-18, displays the physical path to the home directory, typically *c:\inetpub\wwwroot*.

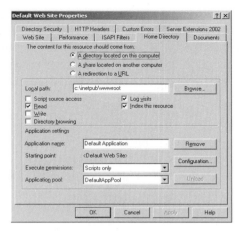

Figure 6-18   The Home Directory tab of the Default Web Site Properties dialog box

Which file, exactly, should be returned to the client? That is defined on the Documents tab, as shown in Figure 6-19. IIS searches for files in the order listed. As soon as it finds a file of that name in the local path of the home directory, that page is returned to the client and the server stops looking for other matches. If no match is found, the IIS returns an error (404–File Not Found) to the client indicating that the page could not be found.

Figure 6-19   The Documents tab of the Default Web Site Properties dialog box

A browser could, of course, refer to a specific page in the URL, for example *http:// server01.contoso.com/contactinfo.htm*. In that event, the specific page is fetched from the home directory. If it is not found, a File Not Found error (404) is returned.

To create a Web site, right-click the Web Sites node or an existing Web site in IIS Manager and choose New Web Site. To configure a Web site, open its Properties. You can configure the IP address of the site. If a server has multiple IP addresses, each IP address can represent a separate Web site. Multiple sites can also be hosted using different ports for each site, or using host headers. The specifics of these options are beyond the scope of this book. You can also configure the path to the directory that is used as the home directory. And you can modify the list or order of documents that can be fetched as the default content page.

A URL can also include more complex path information, such as *http:// www.microsoft.com/windowsserver2003*. This URL is not requesting a specific page; there is no extension such as .htm or .asp on the end of the URL. Instead, it is requesting information from the windowsserver2003 directory. The server evaluates this additional component of the URL as a virtual directory. The folder that contains the files referred to as windowsserver2003 can reside anywhere; they do not have to be located on the IIS server.

To create a virtual directory, right-click a Web site and choose New Virtual Directory. The wizard will prompt you for the alias, which becomes the folder name used in the URL, and the physical path to the resource, which can be on a local volume or remote server.

Exam Tip   You can also create a Web virtual directory on an NTFS drive by right-clicking a folder, choosing Properties, then clicking the Web Sharing tab.

FTP sites work, and are administered, similarly to Web sites. IIS installs one FTP site, the Default FTP Site, and configures it to respond to all incoming FTP requests (all unassigned addresses, port 21). The FTP site returns to the client a list of files from the folder specified in the Home Directory tab. FTP sites may also include virtual directories so that, for example, *ftp://server01.contoso.com/pub* may return resources from a different server than *ftp://server01.contoso.com/vendor-uploads*. FTP URLs and sites do not use default documents.

Complex IIS servers may host tens of thousands of sites, each with customized settings to make them tick. Losing all that configuration information could be painful, so although a normal file system backup might allow you to restore the data files after a failure, the configuration would be lost. To back up or restore IIS configuration, you must back up or restore the *metabase*, an Extensible Markup Language (XML) document that is used to store settings. Right-click the server node in IIS Manager and, from the All Tasks menu, choose Backup/Restore Configuration.

See Also   For more information about IIS, see the *Microsoft IIS 6.0 Administrator's Pocket Consultant* (Microsoft Press, 2003).

Securing Files on IIS

Security for files accessed by way of IIS falls into several categories: authentication, authorization through NTFS permissions, and IIS permissions. Authentication is, of course, the process of evaluating credentials in the form of a user name and password. By default, all requests to IIS are serviced by impersonating the user with the IUSR _computername_ account. Before you begin restricting access of resources to specific users, you must create domain or local user accounts and require something more than this default, Anonymous authentication.

Configuring Authentication Methods

You may configure the following authentication methods on the Directory Security tab of the server, a Web (or FTP) site, a virtual directory, or a file:

Web Authentication Options

- **Anonymous authentication** Users may access the public areas of your Web site without a user name or password.

- **Basic authentication** Requires that a user have a local or domain user account. Credentials are transmitted in clear text.

- **Digest authentication** Offers the same functionality as Basic authentication, while providing enhanced security in the way that a user's credentials are sent across the network. Digest authentication relies on the HTTP 1.1 protocol.

- **Advanced Digest authentication** Works only when the user account is part of an Active Directory. Collects user credentials and stores them on the domain controller. Advanced Digest authentication requires the user to be using Internet Explorer 5 or above and the HTTP 1.1 protocol.

- **Integrated Windows authentication** Collects information through a secure form of authentication (sometimes referred to as Windows NT Challenge/ Response authentication) where the user name and password are hashed before being sent across the network.

- **Certificate authentication** Adds Secure Sockets Layer (SSL) security through client or server certificates, or both. This option is available only if you have Certificate Services installed and configured.

- **.NET Passport authentication** Provides a single sign-in service through SSL, HTTP redirects, cookies, Microsoft JScript, and strong symmetric key encryption.

FTP Authentication Options

- **Anonymous FTP authentication** Gives users access to the public areas of your FTP site without prompting them for a user name or password.

- **Basic FTP authentication** Requires users to log on with a user name and password corresponding to a valid Windows user account.

Defining Resource Access with Permissions

Once authentication has been configured, permissions are assigned to files and folders. A common way to define resource access with IIS is through NTFS permissions. NTFS permissions, because they are attached to a file or folder, act to define access to that resource regardless of how the resource is accessed.

IIS also defines permissions on sites and virtual directories. Although NTFS permissions define a specific level of access to existing Windows user and group accounts, the directory security permissions configured for a site or virtual directory apply to *all* users and groups.

Table 6-2 details Web permission levels:

Table 6-2   IIS Directory Permissions

Permission	Explanation
Read (default)	Users can view file content and properties.
Write	Users can change file content and properties.
Script Source Access	Users can access the source code for files, such as the scripts in an Active Server Pages (ASP) application. This option is available only if either Read or Write permissions are assigned. Users can access source files. If Read permission is assigned, source code can be read. If Write permission is assigned, source code can be written to as well. Be aware that allowing users to have read and write access to source code can compromise the security of you server.
Directory browsing	Users can view file lists and collections.

The Execute permissions control the security level of script execution and are as described in Table 6-3.

Table 6-3   Application Execute Permissions

Permission	Explanation
None	Set permissions for an application to None to prevent any programs or scripts from running.
Scripts only	Set permissions for an application to Scripts only to enable applications mapped to a script engine to run in this directory without having permissions set for executables. Setting permissions to Scripts only is more secure than setting them to Scripts and Executables because you can limit the applications that can be run in the directory.
Scripts and Executables	Set permissions for an application to Scripts and Executables to allow any application to run in this directory, including applications mapped to script engines and Windows binaries (.dll and .exe files).

Exam Tip   If IIS permissions and NTFS permissions are both in place, the effective permissions will be the more restrictive of the two.

Practice: Administering IIS

In this practice, you will install IIS and configure a new Web site and virtual directory.

Exercise 1: Install IIS

1. Open Add Or Remove Programs from the Control Panel and click Add/Remove Windows Components.

2. Select Application Server and click Details.

3. Select Internet Information Services (IIS) and click Details.

4. Ensure that, at a minimum, Common Files, File Transfer Protocol (FTP) Service, World Wide Web Service, and Internet Information Services Manager are selected.

5. Complete the installation.

Exercise 2: Prepare Simulated Web Content

1. Create a folder on the C:\ drive called ContosoCorp.

2. Open Notepad and create a file with the text "Welcome to Contoso." Save the file as: **"C:\ContosoCorp\Default.htm"** being certain to surround the name with quotation marks.

3. Create a second file with the text "This is the site for Project 101." Save the file as: **"C:\Docs\Project 101\Default.htm"** being certain to surround the name with quotation marks.

Exercise 3: Create a Web Site

1. Open the Internet Information Services (IIS) Manager snap-in from the Administrative Tools group.

2. Right-click the Default Web Site and choose Stop.

3. Right-click the Web Sites node and choose New Web Site.

4. Give the site the name Contoso and the path C:\ContosoCorp. All other default settings are acceptable.

Exercise 4: Create a Secure Virtual Directory

1. Right-click the Contoso site and choose New Virtual Directory.

2. Enter the alias Project101 and the path C:\Docs\Project 101.

3. Open the properties of the Project101 virtual directory.

4. Click Directory Security.

5. In the Authentication and Access Control frame, click Edit.

6. Deselect the option to allow anonymous access. Permission to the files in the site will now require valid user accounts. Click OK twice.

7. Open Internet Explorer and type **http://server01.contoso.com**. The Welcome To Contoso page should appear.

8. Type the URL **http://server01.contoso.com/Project101**. You will be prompted for credentials. Log on as Scott Bishop and the Project101 home page appears.

9. Change the permissions on the C:\Docs\Project 101\Default.htm document so that only Administrators can read the document.

10. Close and reopen Internet Explorer. Connect to *http://server01.contoso.com/Project101* and authenticate as Administrator. The page should appear.

11. Close and reopen Internet Explorer again. Now, connect to the same URL as Scott Bishop. You should receive an Access Denied error (401–Unauthorized).

Lesson Review

The following questions are intended to reinforce key information presented in this lesson. If you are unable to answer a question, review the lesson materials and try the question again. You can find answers to the questions in the "Questions and Answers" section at the end of this chapter.

1. You're setting up a Web site in IIS on Server01. The site's Internet domain name is *adatum.com*, and the site's home directory is C:\Web\Adatum. Which URL should Internet users use to access files in the home directory of the site?

   a. *http://server01.web.adatum*

   b. *http://web.adatum.com/server01*

   c. *http://server01.adatum/home*

   d. *http://server01.adatum.com*

2. Data for your corporate intranet is currently stored on the D: drive of your IIS server. It is decided that the HR department will serve information about the company benefits and policies from its server, and that the URL to access the HR information should be *http://intranet.contoso.com/hr*. What do you need to configure?

   a. A new Web site

   b. A new FTP site

   c. A virtual directory from file

   d. A virtual directory

3. You want to ensure the highest level of security for your corporate intranet without the infrastructure of certificate services. The goal is to provide authentication that is transparent to users, and to allow you to secure intranet resources with the group accounts existing in Active Directory. All users are within the corporate firewall. What authentication method should you choose?

   a. Anonymous Access

   b. Basic Authentication

   c. Digest Authentication

   d. Integrated Windows Authentication

Lesson Summary

- IIS is not installed by default. You can install it using the Windows Components Wizard through Add Or Remove Programs.

- A Web or FTP site's home directory is the physical location of resources to be served by that site.

- A virtual directory is an alias and a path that points the IIS server to the location of resources. The URL takes the form *http://server.dns.name/virtualdirectory*. The resources can be located on a local volume or remote server.

- IIS supports multiple levels of authentication. By default, Anonymous Authentication allows any connecting user to access public areas of the site, and Integrated Windows Authentication allows you to assign NTFS permissions to resources that you wish to secure further.

- Access to IIS resources on NTFS volumes is controlled by ACLs, exactly as if the resource were being accessed by the Client For Microsoft Networks.

- IIS has directory and application permissions. If both IIS permissions and NTFS permissions are applied, the more restrictive permissions are effective.

Case Scenario Exercise

> **Note**   This Case Scenario exercise is designed to prepare for and to complement the follow-
> ing "Troubleshooting Lab" section. It is recommended that you complete both exercises to
> gain the maximum learning from these hands-on experiences with Windows Server 2003 file
> system security.
>
> You must have IIS installed (see Lesson 4, Exercise 1) and have created the group and user
> accounts as described in this chapter's "Before You Begin" section.

Contoso, Ltd. wants to configure an intranet site for company and departmental news. The specifications call for the site to be easy to use by both employees and the managers, who will be responsible for updating the news documents. All employees will use the latest version of Internet Explorer to browse the intranet. Managers will use other tools to create Web pages.

Exercise 1: Create Shared Folders and Sample Web Content

> **Note**   There are obviously many ways to create and share folders. In this situation, please
> use the methods described.

1. Open the command prompt.
2. Type the following commands:

   ```
   md c:\ContosoIntranetNews

   net share News=c:\ContosoIntranetNews
   ```

3. Open Notepad and create a file with the text "Contoso Company News." Save the file as **"C:\ ContosoIntranetNews\Default.htm"**, being certain to surround the name with quotation marks.
4. Add the following permission to the C:\ContosoIntranetNews folder:

   Managers: Allow Modify

5. In the C:\ContosoIntranetNews folder's Properties dialog box, click the Web Sharing tab.
6. From the Share On drop-down list, choose Contoso. If you did not complete the exercises in Lesson 4, you will not have the Contoso Web site; choose the Default Web Site instead. Click Share This Folder and type the alias **News**. The default permissions are adequate. Click OK.

Exercise 2: Optimize Intranet Access

In this exercise, you will confirm the functionality of the intranet and optimize its ease of use.

1. Open Internet Explorer and type the URL: **http://server01.contoso.com/News**.

2. You will be prompted for credentials. Authenticate as Administrator. The Contoso Company News page should appear.

3. Close Internet Explorer.

   You are being prompted for credentials because Company News is not allowing anonymous access. When you create a virtual directory by using the Web Sharing tab, anonymous access is disabled by default.

4. Using IIS manager, open the properties of the News virtual directory.

5. Click the Directory Security tab and click Edit in the Authentication and Access Control frame.

6. Enable anonymous access.

7. Repeat steps 1 through 3 to verify that the change was effective.

Exercise 3: Confirm That Managers Can Modify Intranet Contents

> **Note**   To simulate remote management of the intranet contents, it is important that you use the UNC path to the folders and files, as instructed. Do not use a local path.

1. Log off Server01 and log on again as the user Lorrin Smith-Bates, who is a member of the Managers group.

2. Open Notepad and create a document with the text "Good News Contoso!" Save the document as: **"\\server01\news\goodnews.htm"**, being certain to surround the name in quotation marks and to use the UNC path, not a local path, to the news folder.

3. Are you able to save the file?

   If you followed the instructions of this Case Scenario fully, you should not be able to do so. Continue with the Troubleshooting Lab to identify and solve the problem you just encountered.

Troubleshooting Lab

> **Note**   This troubleshooting lab is designed to complement the preceding Case Scenario Exercise. It is recommended that you complete both exercises to gain the maximum learning from these hands-on experiences with Windows Server 2003 file system security.
>
> You must have IIS installed (see Lesson 4, Exercise 1) and have created the group and user accounts as described in this chapter's "Before You Begin" section. You must also have completed at least Exercise 1 of the Case Scenario.

Lorrin Smith-Bates calls the help desk and reports that he is unable to save documents to the intranet news folder. He is creating a Web page in Notepad and saving it to "\\server01\News\goodnews.htm" when the error occurs.

The folder is located at C:\ContosoIntranetNews and is shared as News, and is configured as a virtual directory, News, for the Contoso Web site. The error message he receives is an Access Denied message. That indicates that his machine is likely able to connect to the server, but that a permission or privilege of some kind prevents him from saving the file.

Log on to Server01 as Administrator to perform these troubleshooting steps.

Step 1: Confirm Group Membership

You are fairly confident that you made Lorrin a member of the Managers group, and that the Managers group has Modify permission to the C:\ContosoIntranetNews folder. How can you confirm Lorrin's group membership?

The Dsget command, discussed in Chapter 3, can enumerate group memberships. Open a command prompt and type the command:

dsget user "CN=Lorrin Smith-Bates,OU=Employees,DC=Contoso,DC=com" -memberof -expand

You should see these groups listed, as well as other groups that may vary depending on which exercises from this book you have completed.

"CN=Managers,OU=Security Groups,DC=contoso,DC=com"

"CN=Project 101 Team,OU=Security Groups,DC=contoso,DC=com"

"CN=Domain Users,CN=Users,DC=contoso,DC=com"

"CN=Print Operators,CN=Builtin,DC=contoso,DC=com"

"CN=Users,CN=Builtin,DC=contoso,DC=com"

How else can you confirm Lorrin's group membership? Open Active Directory Users And Computers and examine the Member Of property page of Lorrin's Properties dialog box.

Step 2: Examine Effective Permissions

Explore the permission assigned to the C:\ContosoIntranetNews folder. You should see, in the Security tab and in the Advanced Security Settings dialog boxes, that Managers are granted Modify permission.

Click the Effective Permissions tab in the Advanced Security Settings dialog box and select Lorrin's user account. Examine his effective permissions. The permissions should suggest that he is allowed to create files and write data in the folder.

Step 3: Evaluate the Situation

If Lorrin does have effective permissions that allow him to create files and write data, why is he receiving an Access Denied message? If you haven't figured it out already, take a moment to review the Lesson Summaries after Lessons 1 and 4.

The problem might lie in other permissions assigned to the C:\ContosoIntranetNews folder. Share permissions, and Web site or virtual directory permissions define the maximum allowed access, so if one or more of those permissions were configured too restrictively, it could prevent Lorrin from fully using his NTFS Allow Modify permission.

When Lorrin was saving his Web page in Notepad, he was connecting to the server remotely. From the following list, identify the client and the service that were involved:

- FTP Publishing Service
- Worldwide Web Publishing Service
- Telnet Service
- File and Printer Sharing For Microsoft Networks
- Internet browser client
- FTP client
- Telnet client
- Client For Microsoft Networks

Lorrin is using the Client For Microsoft Networks service to connect to Server01's File and Printer Sharing service. You can identify that by examining the path Lorrin specified to save the file: "\\server01\News\goodnews.htm." It is a UNC path, which will connect using Microsoft networking.

Knowing that, you can eliminate as a cause of the problem any permissions assigned to the Web site or to the virtual directory; those permissions apply only to connections from Web clients to the Web service.

That leaves one possible cause for permission problems: the Share permissions. The default share permissions in Windows Server 2003 allow the Everyone group only Read permission. Because share permissions define the maximum allowed access, they are overriding the folder's NTFS Allow Modify permission.

Step 4: Solve the Problem

Modify the share permissions on C:\ContosoIntranetNews so that Everyone is allowed Full Control.

Now the business requirements for the intranet news site are that users should only be able to read documents. The default NTFS permission allows users to create files and folders and then, of course, as owners of those files and folders they can do whatever they please.

Lock down NTFS permissions on the folder so that Users have Read & Execute permission, without the special permissions (Create Files/Write Data; Create Folders/Append Data).

Confirm your actions by logging on as Scott Bishop. Scott should be able to see *http://server01.contoso.com/News*. If he connects to \\server01\News, he should *not* be able to create a new file or modify an existing file.

Then log on as Lorrin. Lorrin should also be able to see the intranet news site, but he should also be able to create and modify files in the \\server01\News share. You should be able to create the news document as described in Exercise 3 of the Case Scenario and then access that document at *http://server01.contoso.com/News/goodnews.htm*.

Chapter Summary

- Windows Server 2003 provides new consoles and snap-ins to manage shared folders, audit policy, and IIS. Windows Explorer is still used, as well as the Shared Folder snap-in, to manage NTFS ACLs, although the ACL editor is significantly more powerful.

- NTFS permissions can be allowed or denied; explicit or inherited. A Deny permission takes precedence over an Allow permission; and an explicit permission takes precedence over an inherited permission. The result is that an explicit Allow permission can override an inherited Deny permission.

- Access granted by NTFS permissions may be further restricted by share permissions and IIS permissions on FTP sites, Web sites, virtual directories and documents. Whenever two permission types are assigned to a resource, such as share permissions and NTFS permissions, you must evaluate each set of permissions, then determine which of the two sets is more restrictive. And that is the set that becomes effective.

- The security descriptor of a file or folder also includes information about the object's owner. The owner, as well as any user with Allow Change permissions, can modify the ACL. Ownership may be assumed by a user with the Allow Take Ownership permission; or may be transferred between users by anyone with the Restore Files And Directories user right.

- The security descriptor also contains auditing entries which, when audit policy is enabled, directs the system to log the specified types of access for the specified users or groups.

Exam Highlights

Before taking the exam, review the key topics and terms that are presented below to help you identify topics you need to review. Return to the lessons for additional practice and review the "Further Readings" sections in Part 2 for pointers to more information about topics covered by the exam objectives.

Key Points

- Familiarize yourself with the tools that are used to configure shared folders, NTFS permissions, auditing and IIS. Spend some time with each snap-in, examining the properties that can be configured, and the role those properties play in managing files and folders.

- Be fluent in the determination of effective permissions: the interaction of explicit, inherited, allowed, and denied permissions for multiple users, groups, computers, and logon types such as Interactive versus Network.

- Know the three steps required to configure auditing, and the strategies you can use to determine what kind of auditing (success or failure) to engage for a particular goal.

- Experience and understand the configuration of a Web site and virtual directory. If you are not experienced with IIS, be certain to implement the Practice in Lesson 4 as well as the Case Scenario and Troubleshooting Lab.

Key Terms

Hidden share   A shared folder can be hidden by appending a $ to its share name. Connections can be made to the share using the share's UNC (for example, \\server01\docs$), but the share will not appear on browse lists. Windows Server 2003 creates hidden administrative shares, such as Admin$, Print$, and a hidden share for the root of each disk volume. Only administrators can connect to the hidden administrative shares.

Inheritance   By default, permissions assigned to a folder apply to the folder, its subfolders and files. In addition, files and folders are configured by default to allow inheritable permissions from their parent folder or volume to propagate to their ACL. Through these two mechanisms, permissions assigned to a high-level folder are propagated to its contents.

Effective permissions   Permissions can be allowed or denied, inherited or explicitly assigned. They can be assigned to one or more users, groups, or computers. The effective permissions are the overall permissions that result and determine the actual access for a security principal.

Ownership   Each NTFS file or folder maintains a property that indicates the security principal that owns the resource. The owner is able to modify the ACL of the object at any time, meaning the owner cannot be locked out of the resource. Ownership can be taken and transferred based on the Take Ownership permission and the Restore Files And Directories user right, respectively.

The special accounts: Creator Owner, Network, and Interactive   These security principals are dynamic, and represent the relationship between a user and a resource. When a user creates a file or folder, they are the Creator Owner of that resource, and any inheritable permissions on the parent folder or volume assigned to Creator Owner will be explicitly assigned to the user on the new object. Network and Interactive represent the connection state of the user—whether the user is connected to the resource from a remote client, or is logged on interactively to the computer that is maintaining the resource.

Audit Object Access policy   This policy, available in the Local Security Policy of a standalone Windows Server 2003 computer, or in Group Policy Objects, determines whether access to files, folders, and printers is registered in the Security log. When this policy is enabled, the Auditing Entries for each object determine the types of activities that are logged.

Virtual directory   A virtual directory is an IIS object that allows a folder on any local or remote volume to appear as a subfolder of a Web site.

Questions and Answers

Page
6-11
Lesson 1 Review

1. Which of the following tools allows you to administer a share on a remote server? Select all that apply.

   a. The Shared Folders snap-in.

   b. Windows Explorer running on the local machine, connected to the remote server's share or hidden drive share.

   c. Windows Explorer running on the remote machine in a Terminal Services or Remote Desktop session.

   d. The File Server Management console.

   The correct answers are a, c, and d. Windows Explorer can be used only to administer a local share, so you would have to run a remote desktop session to the remote server, and run Windows Explorer in that session to manage that server's shares. A more common, and a better, practice is to use the Shared Folders snap-in, which is included in the File Server Management console.

2. A folder is shared on a FAT32 volume. The Project Managers group is given Allow Full Control permission. The Project Engineers group is given Allow Read permission. Julie belongs to the Project Engineers group. She is promoted and is added to the Project Managers group. What are her effective permissions to the folder?

   Full Control

3. A folder is shared on a NTFS volume, with the default share permissions. The Project Managers group is given Allow Full Control NTFS permission. Julie, who belongs to the Project Managers group, calls to report problems creating files in the folder. Why can't Julie create files?

   The default share permission in Windows Server 2003 is Everyone: Allow Read. Share permissions define the maximum effective permissions for files and folders in the share. The share permissions restrict the NTFS full control permission. To correct the problem, you would need to modify the share permissions to allow, at a minimum, the Project Managers group Change permission.

Page
6-29
Lesson 2 Review

1. What are the minimum NTFS permissions required to allow users to open documents and run programs stored in a shared folder?

   a. Full Control

   b. Modify

   c. Write

    d. Read & Execute

    e. List Folder Contents

The correct answer is d.

2. Bill complains that he is unable to access the department plan. You open the Security tab for the plan and you find that all permissions on the document are inherited from the plan's parent folder. There is a Deny Read permission assigned to a group to which Bill belongs. Which of the following methods would enable Bill to access the plan?

    a. Modify the permissions on the parent folder by adding the permission Bill:Allow Full Control.

    b. Modify the permissions on the parent folder by adding the permission Bill:Allow Read.

    c. Modify the permissions on the plan by adding the permission: Bill:Allow Read.

    d. Modify the permissions on the plan by deselecting Allow Inheritable Permissions, choosing Copy, and removing the Deny permission.

    e. Modify the permissions on the plan by deselecting Allow Inheritable Permissions, choosing Copy, and adding the permission Bill:Allow Full Control.

    f. Remove Bill from the group that is assigned the Deny permission.

The correct answers are c, d, and f.

3. Bill calls again to indicate that he still cannot access the departmental plan. You use the Effective Permissions tool, select Bill's account, and the tool indicates that Bill is, in fact, allowed sufficient permissions. What might explain the discrepancy between the results of the Effective Permissions tool and the issue Bill is reporting?

The Effective Permissions tool is only an approximation of a user's access. It is possible that a permission entry is assigned to a logon-related account, such as Interactive or Network, that could be denying access. Permissions for logon groups are not evaluated by the Effective Permissions tool. Or, if you are not logged on as a Domain Admin, you may not be able to read all group memberships, which might skew the resulting permissions report.

Page 6-36

Lesson 3 Review

1. Which of the following must be done to generate a log of resource access for a file or folder? Select all that apply.

    a. Configure NTFS permissions to allow the System account to audit resource access.

    b. Configure audit entries to specify the types of access to audit.

    c. Enable the Audit Privilege Use policy.

    d. Enable the Audit Object Access policy.

The correct answers are b and d.

2. Which of the following are valid criteria for a security log filter to identify specific file and folder access events? Select all that apply.

    a. The date of the event

    b. The user that generated the event

    c. The type of object access that generated the event

    d. Success or failure audit

The correct answers are a, b, and d.

3. Users at Contoso Ltd. use Microsoft Office applications to access resources on Server01. Your job is to monitor Server01 to ensure that permissions are not too restrictive, so that users are not prevented from achieving their assignments. Which log, and which type of event, will provide the information you require?

    a. Application log; Success Event

    b. Application log; Failure Event

    c. Security log; Success Event

    d. Security log; Failure Event

    e. System log; Success Event

    f. System log; Failure Event

The correct answer is d.

Page
6-46

Lesson 4 Review

1. You're setting up a Web site in IIS on Server01. The site's Internet domain name is *adatum.com*, and the site's home directory is C:\Web\Adatum. Which URL should Internet users use to access files in the home directory of the site?

    a. *http://server01.web.adatum*

    b. *http://web.adatum.com/server01*

    c. *http://server01.adatum/home*

    d. *http://server01.adatum.com*

The correct answer is d.

2. You want to ensure the highest level of security for your corporate intranet without the infrastructure of certificate services. The goal is to provide authentication that is transparent to users, and to allow you to secure intranet resources with the group accounts existing in Active Directory. All users are within the corporate firewall. What authentication method should you choose?

   a. Anonymous Access

   b. Basic Authentication

   c. Digest Authentication

   d. Integrated Windows Authentication

   The correct answer is d.

3. Data for your corporate intranet is currently stored on the D: drive of your IIS server. It is decided that the HR department will serve information about the company benefits and policies from its server, and that the URL to access the HR information should be *http://intranet.contoso.com/hr*. What do you need to configure?

   a. A new Web site

   b. A new FTP site

   c. A virtual directory from file

   d. A virtual directory

   The correct answer is d.

7 Backing Up Data

Exam Objectives in this Chapter:

- Manage backup procedures
  - Verify the successful completion of backup jobs
  - Manage backup storage media
- Configure security for backup operations
- Schedule backup jobs
- Restore backup data

Why This Chapter Matters

You've worked hard to configure and maintain a best practice server environment. You have outfitted the server with a sophisticated RAID subsystem, carefully managed file and share permissions, locked down the server with policy, and physically secured the server to prevent unauthorized interactive log on. But today, none of that matters, because the building's fire sprinklers went off last night, and today your servers are full of water. All that matters today is that you are able to restore your data from backup.

Among the many high priority tasks for any network administrator is the creation and management of a solid backup and restore procedure. Microsoft Windows Server 2003 offers powerful and flexible tools which will enable you to perform backups of local and remote data, including open and locked files, and to schedule those backups for periods of low utilization, such as during the night.

This chapter examines the Ntbackup utility's graphical user interface (GUI) and command-line functionality in the protection of data files. You will learn how to plan an effective backup and media management strategy, how to execute backups, and how to restore data correctly in a variety of scenarios. You will also leverage the new Volume Shadow Copy Service (VSS) to allow faster recovery of data lost by administrators and users alike. Later in the book, we will return to Ntbackup to focus on recovering the operating system during a system restore.

Lessons in this Chapter:

Before You Begin

For hands-on practice using the examples and lab exercises in the chapter, prepare the following:

- Active Directory Users And Computers snap-in
- A Windows Server 2003 (Standard or Enterprise) installed as Server01 and configured as a domain controller in the domain *contoso.com*

Lesson 1: Fundamentals of Backup

At the core of every backup procedure is a backup tool and a backup plan. Windows Server 2003 provides a robust, flexible utility called Ntbackup. Ntbackup supports much of the functionality found in third-party tools, including the ability to schedule backups, and interacts closely with VSS and the Removable Storage Management (RSM) system. In this lesson, you will examine the conceptual and procedural issues pivotal to the backing up of data, so that you understand the fundamentals of planning for and creating backup jobs with Ntbackup.

After this lesson, you will be able to

■ Back up data on local and remote computers

■ Understand backup job types

■ Create a backup strategy combining normal and incremental or differential backups

Estimated lesson time: 20 minutes

Introducing the Backup Utility

The backup utility in Windows Server 2003, commonly referred to by its executable name, Ntbackup, can be opened by clicking Backup in the Accessories–System Tools program group in the Start menu. Alternatively, it can be launched by typing **ntbackup.exe** in the Run dialog box.

The first time you launch the backup utility, it runs in Wizard mode, as shown in Figure 7-1. This chapter focuses on the more commonly used Backup Utility interface. If you agree with most administrators that it is easier to use the standard utility than the wizard, clear the Always Start In Wizard Mode check box, and then click Advanced Mode.

Figure 7-1   The Backup Or Restore Wizard

As you can see on the utility's Welcome tab in Figure 7-2, you can back up data manually (the Backup tab) or using the Backup Wizard. You can also schedule unattended backup jobs. The Backup Utility is also used to restore data manually (the Restore And Manage Media tab) or using the Restore Wizard. The Automated System Recovery (ASR) Wizard, which backs up critical operating system files, will be discussed later in this book.

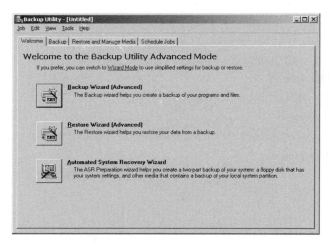

Figure 7-2   The Welcome tab of the Backup Utility

This lesson focuses on data backup planning and execution, and to explore the capability of the Backup Utility we will use the Backup tab, as shown in Figure 7-3, rather than the Backup Wizard.

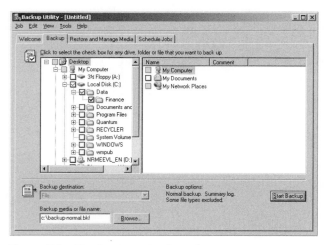

Figure 7-3   The Backup tab of the Backup Utility

Selecting Files to Back Up

You may use the Backup tab to select the files and folders to be backed up. Items may be on local volumes or in network folders. When you select an entire folder for backup, a blue check mark appears. If you select only certain items in a folder, the folder displays a dimmed check mark to indicate a partial backup.

To back up files or folders from remote machines, either select the items from a mapped drive or expand My Network Places. The latter is the equivalent of using a Universal Naming Convention (UNC), such as *Server01**Sharename**Path-to-resource*. Although selecting files and folders through My Network Places is more cumbersome (you must navigate more levels of the interface to locate the files), it has an advantage because drive mappings are more likely to change over time than UNCs.

> **Tip** You can save the set of selected files and folders using the Save Selections command in the Job menu. You can later load the selections using Load Selections from the Job menu, saving the time required to recreate your selection.

Selecting the Backup Destination

Windows Server 2003 allows you to create a backup job on a variety of media types: a tape drive, a removable drive such as the Iomega Jaz drive, and, most importantly, directly to file on a disk volume. If the destination is a tape, the name specified must match the name of a tape that is mounted in the tape device.

If backing up to a file, the Backup Utility creates a .bkf file in the specified location, which can be a local volume or remote folder. It is not uncommon for administrators using the Backup Utility to back up a file on each server and consolidate the resulting files on a central server, which then transfers the backups to removable media. To achieve such a consolidation, the backup destination is configured as either a UNC to a single location on a central server or a local file on each server, which is later copied to a central location.

There are two important limitations of the Backup Utility. First, it does not support writable DVD and CD formats. To work around this limitation, back up to a file, then transfer the file to CD or DVD. Second, backing up to any destination *except* a file requires that the target media be in a device physically attached to the system. This means, for example, that you cannot back up data to a tape drive attached to a remote server.

Determining a Backup Strategy

After selecting the files to back up and specifying the backup destination, there is at least one more critical choice to make. Click Start Backup, then click Advanced, and the Advanced Backup Options dialog box appears, allowing you to specify the backup type. The backup type determines which of your selected files is in fact transferred to the destination media.

Each backup type relates in one way or another to an attribute maintained by every file: archive. The archive (A) attribute is a flag that is set when a file has been created or changed. To reduce the size and duration of backup jobs, most backup types will only transfer to media the files that have their archive attribute set. The most common source of confusion regarding the archive attribute arises from terminology. You will frequently hear, "The file is marked as backed up," which really means that the archive attribute is *cleared* after a particular backup job. The next job will not transfer that file to media. If the file is modified, however, the archive attribute will again be set, and the file will be transferred at the next backup.

> **Exam Tip** As you explore each backup type, keep track of how the archive attribute is used and treated by the backup type. You will need to know the advantages and disadvantages of each backup type and how to fully restore a data structure based on the backup procedures that have been implemented.

Normal Backups

All selected files and folders are backed up. The archive attribute is cleared. A Normal backup does not use the archive attribute to determine which files to back up; all selected items are transferred to the destination media. Every backup strategy begins with a Normal backup that essentially creates a baseline, capturing all files in the backup job.

Normal backups are the most time-consuming and require the most storage capacity of any backup type. However, because they generate a complete backup, normal backups are the most efficient type from which to restore a system. You do not need to restore multiple jobs. Normal backups clear the archive attribute from all selected files.

Incremental Backups

Selected files with the archive attribute set are backed up. The archive attribute is cleared. Selected files with the archive flag are transferred to the destination media, and the flag is cleared. If you perform an incremental backup one day after a normal backup has been performed, the job will contain only the files that were created or changed during that day. Similarly, if you perform an incremental backup one day after another incremental backup, the job will contain only the files that were created or changed during that day.

Incremental backups are the fastest and smallest type of backup. However they are less efficient as a restore set, because you must restore the normal backup and then restore, in order of creation, each subsequent incremental backup.

Differential Backups

Selected files with the archive attribute set are backed up. The archive attribute is not cleared. Because a differential backup uses the archive attribute, the job includes only files that have been created or changed since the last normal or incremental backup. A differential backup does not clear the archive attribute; therefore, if you perform differential backups two days in a row, the second job will include all the files in the first backup, as well as any files that were created or changed during the second day. As a result, differential backups tend to be larger and more time-consuming than incremental backups, but less so than normal backups.

Differential backups are significantly more efficient than incremental backups as a restore set, however. To fully restore a system you would restore the normal backup and the most recent differential backup.

Copy Backups

All selected files and folders are backed up. Copy neither uses nor clears the archive attribute. Copy backups are not used for typical or scheduled backups. Instead, copy backups are useful to move data between systems or to create an archival copy of data at a point in time without disrupting standard backup procedures.

Daily Backups

All selected files and folders that have changed during the day are backed up, based on the files' modify date. The archive attribute is neither used nor cleared. If you want to back up all files and folders that change during the day without affecting a backup schedule, use a daily backup.

Combining Backup Types

Although creating a normal backup every night ensures that a server can be restored from a single job the next day, a normal backup may take too much time to create, perhaps causing the overnight job to last well into the morning, thus disrupting performance during working hours. To create an optimal backup strategy, you must take into account the time and size of the backup job, as well as the time required to restore a system in the event of failure. Two common solutions are:

- **Normal and differential backups** On Sunday a normal backup is performed, and on Monday through Friday nights, differential backups are performed. Differential backups do not clear the archive attribute, which means that each backup includes all changes since Sunday. If data becomes corrupt on Friday, you only need to restore the normal backup from Sunday and the differential backup from Thursday. This strategy takes more time to back up, particularly if data changes frequently, but is easier and faster to restore, because the backup set is on fewer disks or tapes.

■ **Normal and incremental backups**   On Sunday a normal backup is performed, and on Monday through Friday incremental backups are performed. Incremental backups clear the archive attribute, which means that each backup includes only the files that changed since the previous backup. If data becomes corrupt on Friday, you need to restore the normal backup from Sunday and each of the incremental backups, from Monday through Friday. This strategy takes less time to back up but more time to restore.

Practice: Performing Different Backup Types

In this practice, you will create several backup jobs, examining the role of the archive attribute.

Exercise 1: Create Sample Data

1. Open Notepad and create a text file with the following lines. Type each line carefully.

```
md c:\Data
net share data=C:\Data
md c:\Data\Finance
cd c:\data\Finance
echo Historical Financial Data > Historical.txt
echo Current Financials > Current.txt
echo Budget > Budget.txt
echo Financial Projections > Projections.txt
```

2. Save the file as "c:\createfiles.bat" including the quotation marks.

3. Open the command prompt and type **cd c:**.

4. Type the command **createfiles.bat**.

5. Open Windows Explorer and navigate to the c:\data\finance directory. You should see the following display:

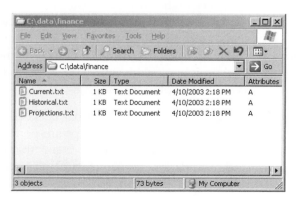

6. If the Attributes column is not visible, right-click the column headers Date Modified and select Attributes. The archive attribute is displayed.

> **Note**   Leave Windows Explorer open on C:\Data\Finance. You will refer to it throughout this practice.

Exercise 2: Perform a Normal Backup

1. Open the Backup Utility by running Ntbackup.exe from the command line, or selecting Backup from the Accessories–System Tools group on the Start menu.

2. Clear the Always Start In Wizard Mode check box.

3. Click Advanced Mode.

4. Select the Backup tab.

5. Expand My Computer, the C drive, and then the Data folder so that you can select the Finance folder.

   The Finance folder has a blue check mark, meaning a complete backup, whereas its parent folder has a dimmed check mark, indicating a partial backup. Any files *added* to the Finance folder will be included in the backup, but any files added to the Data folder will not.

6. On the Job menu, choose Save Selections.

7. Save the selections as **Finance Backup.bks**.

8. In the Backup Media Or Filename box, type **c:\backup-normal.bkf**.

> **Note**   In production environments you will be likely to use removable media for backups, but to keep hardware requirements to a minimum, practices in this lesson will back up and restore using local files. If you have access to a tape drive, feel free to use it during these practices.

9. Click Start Backup and then click Advanced.

10. Confirm that Normal is selected in the Backup Type drop-down box, and then click OK.

11. Select Replace The Data On The Media With This Backup and click Start Backup.

12. Observe the Backup Progress dialog box. When the backup is complete, click Report.

13. Examine the report. No errors should be reported.

14. Close the report and the Backup Utility.

    Note that in Windows Explorer, the Attributes column no longer shows the archive attribute.

Exercise 3: Perform Differential Backups

1. Open C:\Data\Finance\Current.txt and add some text. Save and close the file.

2. Examine C:\Data\Finance in Windows Explorer. What files are showing the archive attribute?

   Only the one you just changed.

3. Open the Backup Utility and click the Backup tab.

4. From the Job menu, choose Load Selections to load Finance Backup selections.

5. In the Backup Media Or Filename box, type **c:\backup-diff-day1.bkf**.

6. Click Start Backup.

7. Click Advanced and select Differential as the backup type.

8. Start the backup and, when complete, confirm that no errors occurred.

9. Close the Backup Utility.

10. Examine the folder in Windows Explorer. Which files have their archive attribute set?

    The file Current.txt is still flagged for archiving.

11. Open the Budget file and make some changes. Save and close the file. Confirm that its archive attribute is now set.

12. Repeat steps 3 through 9, creating a backup job in the location: **c:\backup-diff-day2.bkf**. Be sure to look at the resulting backup report. How many files were copied for the backup?

    Two.

Exercise 4: Perform Incremental Backups

1. Open the Backup Utility and click the Backup tab.

2. From the Job menu, choose Load Selections to load Finance Backup selections.

3. In the Backup Media Or Filename box, type **c:\backup-inc-day2.bkf**.

4. Click Start Backup.

5. Click Advanced and select Incremental as the backup type.

6. Start the backup and, when complete, confirm that no errors occurred.

7. Close the Backup Utility.

8. Examine the folder in Windows Explorer. Which files have their archive attribute set?

   None.

9. Open the Projections file and make some changes. Save and close the file. It should show the archive attribute in Windows Explorer.

10. Repeat steps 1 through 8, creating a backup job in the location: **c:\backup-inc-day3.bkf**.

Lesson Review

The following questions are intended to reinforce key information presented in this lesson. If you are unable to answer a question, review the lesson materials and try the question again. You can find answers to the questions in the "Questions and Answers" section at the end of this chapter.

1. Which of the following locations are *not* allowed to be used for a backup of a Windows Server 2003 system?

   a. Local tape drive

   b. Local CD-RW

   c. Local hard drive

   d. Shared folder on a remote server

   e. Local DVD+R

   f. Local removable drive

   g. Tape drive on a remote server

2. You are to back up a Windows Server 2003 file server every evening. You perform a manual, normal backup. You will then schedule a backup job to run every evening for the next two weeks. Which backup type will complete the fastest?

   a. Normal

   b. Differential

   c. Incremental

   d. Copy

3. You are to back up a Windows Server 2003 file server every evening. You perform a manual, normal backup. You will then schedule a backup job to run every evening for the next two weeks. Which backup type will provide the simplest recovery of lost data?

   a. Normal

   b. Differential

   c. Incremental

   d. Daily

4. You are to back up a Windows Server 2003 file server every evening. You perform a normal backup. On the second evening, you consider whether to use incremental or differential backup. Will there be any difference in the speed or size of those two backup jobs? If the server were to fail the following day, would there be any difference in the efficiency of recovery?

_____

_____

5. Review the steps taken during the Practice. Predict the contents of the following backup jobs:

   ❑ backup-normal.bkf

   ❑ backup-diff-day1.bkf

   ❑ backup-diff-day2.bkf

   ❑ backup-inc-day2.bkf

   ❑ backup-inc-day3.bkf

   Are there any differences between the contents of backup-diff-day2 and backup-inc-day2?

   _____

   _____

> **Note**   You can find the answers in the Questions and Answers section at the end of the lesson. However, you should test your predictions by performing the Practice in Lesson 2.

Lesson Summary

- The Backup Utility, Ntbackup, allows you to back up and restore data from local and remote folders.

- You may back up to local files, tape drives, and removable media or to shared folders on remote servers. You cannot back up to writable CD or DVD formats.

- A normal backup is a complete backup of all selected files and folders. It is always the starting point of any backup strategy.

- An incremental backup copies selected files that have changed since the most recent normal or incremental backup. Both normal and incremental backups clear the archive attribute.

- A differential backup copies all selected files that have changed since the last normal or incremental backup. Differential backups do *not* clear the archive attribute.

- Copy backups and daily backups are less frequently used. They back up all selected files, in the case of Copy backup, or files modified on a specific date, in the case of Daily backup. They do not reset the archive attribute, so they can be used to capture data for backup or transfer without interfering with the normal backup schedule.

Lesson 2: Restoring Data

In conjunction with the design of a backup strategy, you must create and verify restore procedures to ensure that appropriate personnel are knowledgeable in the concepts and skills that are critical to data recovery. This lesson will share the processes and options available for restoring data using the Backup Utility.

After this lesson, you will be able to

- Restore data to its original location or an alternate folder
- Configure restore options

Estimated lesson time: 10 minutes

Restoring with the Backup Utility

Restoring data is a straightforward procedure. After opening the Backup Utility and clicking the Restore And Manage Media tab as shown in Figure 7-4, you will be able to select the backup set from which to restore. Windows Server 2003 will then display the files and folders that the backup set contains by examining the backup set's catalog. You can then select the specific files or folders you wish to restore. As with the backup selection, a blue check mark indicates that a file or folder will be fully restored. A dimmed check mark on a folder means that some, but not all, of its contents will be restored.

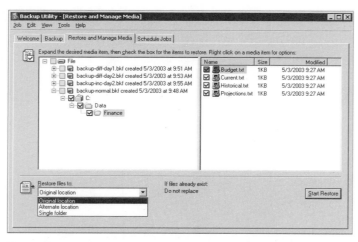

Figure 7-4   The Backup Utility's Restore And Manage Media tab

You are also asked to specify the restore location. For this option, you have three choices:

- **Original location**   Files and folders will be restored to the location from which they were backed up. The original folder structure will be maintained or, if folders were deleted, re-created.

- **Alternate location**   Files and folders will be restored to a folder you designate in the Alternate Location box. The original folder structure is preserved and created beneath that folder, where the designated alternate location is equivalent to the root (volume) of the backed up data. So, for example, if you backed up a folder C:\Data\Finance and you restored the folder to C:\Restore, you would find the Finance folder in C:\Restore\Data\Finance.

- **Single folder**   Files are restored to the folder you designate, but the folder structure is not maintained. All files are restored to a single folder.

After selecting the files to restore and the restore location, click Start Restore. Click OK and the restore process will begin. Confirm that no errors occurred.

Restore Options

Windows Server 2003 supports several options for how files in the restore location are handled during a restore. The following options are found in the Backup Utility's Tools–Options command, on the Restore tab shown in Figure 7-5:

- **Do Not Replace The File On My Computer.**   This option, the default, causes the Restore utility to skip files that are already in the target location. A common scenario leading to this choice is one in which some, but not all, files have been deleted from the restore location. This option will restore such missing files with the backed-up files.

- **Replace The File On Disk Only If The File On Disk Is Older.**   This option directs the restore process to overwrite existing files unless those files are more recent than the files in the backup set. The theory is that if a file in the target location is more recent than the backed-up copy, it is possible that the newer file contains information that you do not want to overwrite.

- **Always Replace The File On My Computer.**   Under this restore option, all files are overwritten by their backed-up versions, regardless of whether the file is more recent than the backup. You will lose data in files that were modified since the backup date. Any files in the target location that are *not* in the backup set will remain, however.

After selecting files to restore, restore options and a restore destination, click Start Restore, and then confirm the restore. The Start Restore dialog box appears.

Figure 7-5   Restore tab options

Before confirming the restore, you can configure how the restore operation will treat security settings on the backed-up files by clicking Advanced in the Confirm Restore dialog box and selecting the Restore Security option. If data was backed up from, and is being restored to, an NTFS volume, the default setting will restore permissions, audit settings, and ownership information. Deselecting this option will restore the data without its security descriptors, and all restored files will inherit the permissions of the target restore volume or folder.

Practice: Restoring Data

In this practice, you will verify your backup and restore procedures using a common method: restoring to a test location.

Exercise 1: Verify Backup and Restore Procedures

To verify backup and restore procedures, many administrators will perform a test restore of a backup set. So as not to damage production data, that test restore is targeted not at the original location of the data, but at another folder, which can then be discarded following the test. In a production environment, your verification should include restoring the backup to a "standby" server, which would entail making sure that the backup device (that is, the tape drive) is correctly installed on a server that can host data in the event that the primary server fails. To do this, perform the following steps:

1. Open the Backup Utility.

2. Click Restore And Manage Media.

3. Click the plus sign to expand the file.

4. Click the plus sign to expand Backup-normal.bkf.

5. Click the check box to select C:.

6. Expand C:, Data, and Finance. You will notice that your selection of the C: folder has selected its child folders and files.

7. In the Restore Files To drop-down box, select Alternate Location.

8. In the Alternate Location field, type **C:\TestRestore**.

9. Click Start Restore.

10. In the Confirm Restore dialog box, click OK.

11. When the restore job is complete, click Report and examine the log of the restore operation.

12. Open the C:\TestRestore folder and verify that the folder structure and files restored correctly.

13. Repeat steps 1 through 10, this time restoring the file backup-diff-day2.bkf. When the restore job is finished, continue to step 14 to examine its report.

14. When the restore job finishes, click Report to view the restore job log. If you accidentally close the job status window, choose the Report command from the Tools menu, select the most recent report and click View.

15. Examine the report for the job you just restored. How many files were restored?

    None.

    Why?

    The answer lies in the restore options.

16. Choose the Options command from the Tools menu and click the Restore tab. Now you can identify the problem. The default configuration of the backup utility is that it does not replace files on the computer. Therefore, the differential job, which contains files that were updated after the normal backup, was not successfully restored.

17. Choose Always Replace The File On My Computer.

18. Repeat the restore operation of backup-diff-day2.bkf. The report should confirm that two files were restored.

19. You have now verified your backup and restore procedures, including the need to modify restore options. Delete the C:\TestRestore folder.

Lesson Review

The following questions are intended to reinforce key information presented in this lesson. If you are unable to answer a question, review the lesson materials and try the question again. You can find answers to the questions in the "Questions and Answers" section at the end of this chapter.

1. A user has accidentally deleted the data in a Microsoft Word document and saved the document, thereby permanently altering the original file. A normal backup operation was performed on the server the previous evening. Which restore option should you select?

    a. Do Not Replace The File On My Computer.

    b. Replace The File On Disk Only If The File On Disk Is Older.

    c. Always Replace The File On My Computer.

2. An executive has returned from a business trip. Before the trip, she copied files from a network folder to her hard drive. The folder is shared with other executives, who modified their files in the folder while she was away. When she returned, she moved her copy of the files to the network share, thereby updating her files with the changes she made while away, but also overwriting all the files that had been changed by other executives. The other executives are unhappy that their files have been replaced with the versions that were active when she left for her trip. Luckily, you performed a normal backup operation on the folder the previous evening. What restore option should you choose?

    a. Do Not Replace The File On My Computer.

    b. Replace The File On Disk Only If The File On Disk Is Older.

    c. Always Replace The File On My Computer.

3. You would like to test the restore procedures on your server, but would also like to avoid affecting the production copies of the backed-up data. What is the best restore location to use?

    a. Original location

    b. Alternate location

    c. Single folder

Lesson Summary

- The Backup Utility will also allow you to restore backed-up data.

- When restoring a lost file or folder, it is common to select Original Location as the restore location.

- When testing restore procedures, it is common to select Alternate Location as the restore location so that you do not affect the original copies of the backed-up files and folders.

- When restoring a differential or incremental backup set after restoring the normal backup set, you will need to select the restore option Always Replace The File On My Computer.

- When restoring a folder in which files have been lost, but some files are intact, you should select the restore option Do Not Replace The File On My Computer or Replace The File On Disk Only If The File On Disk Is Older.

Lesson 3: Advanced Backup and Restore

Now that you have created a backup plan and verified your procedures for backup and restore, you will want to understand the process in more depth so that you can configure backup operations to be more flexible, more automated or perhaps even easier. This lesson will explore the technologies underlying data backup, such as VSC and RSM, and will lay out options for scripting and scheduling backup operations. You will then leverage the new Shadow Copies Of Shared Folders feature to enable users to recover from simple data loss scenarios without administrative intervention.

After this lesson, you will be able to

- Configure group membership to enable a user to perform backup and restore operations
- Manage tape backup media
- Catalog backup sets
- Configure backup options
- Execute a backup from the command prompt
- Schedule backup jobs
- Configure and utilize Shadow Copies Of Shared Folders

Estimated lesson time: 30 minutes

Understanding VSS

Windows Server 2003 offers VSS, also referred to as "snap backup." VSS allows the backing up of databases and other files that are held open or locked due to operator or system activity. Shadow copy backups allow applications to continue to write data to a volume during backup, and allow administrators to perform backups at any time without locking out users or risking skipped files.

Although VSS is an important enhancement to the backup functionality of Windows Server 2003, it is nevertheless best practice to perform backups when utilization is low. If you have applications that manage storage consistency differently while files are open, that can affect the consistency of the files in the backup of those open files. For critical applications, or for applications such as Microsoft SQL Server that offer native backup capabilities, consult the documentation for the application to determine the recommended backup procedure.

Backup Security

You must have the Backup Files And Directories user right, or NTFS Read permission, to back up a file. Similarly, you must have the Restore Files And Directories user right, or NTFS Write permission to the target destination, to restore a file. Privileges are assigned to both the Administrators and Backup Operators groups, so the minimum required privileges can be given to a user, a group, or a service account by nesting the account in the Backup Operators group on the server.

Users with the Restore Files And Directories user right can remove NTFS permissions from files during restore. In Windows Server 2003, they can additionally transfer ownership of files between users.

Therefore, it is important to control the membership of the Backup Operators group and to physically secure backup tapes. A "loose" backup tape makes it easy for any intelligent individual to restore and access sensitive data.

Managing Media

The Backup Utility of Windows Server 2003 works closely with the RSM service. RSM, which is designed to manage robotic tape libraries and CD-ROM libraries, accepts requests for media from other services or, in this case, applications, and ensures that the media is correctly mounted or loaded.

RSM is also used with single-media devices, such as a manually loaded backup tape drive, CD-ROM, or Iomega Jaz drive. In the case of single-media drives, RSM keeps track of media through their labels or serial numbers. The impact of RSM is that, even in a single-media drive backup system, each tape must have a unique label.

Media Pools

The Backup Utility of Windows Server 2003 manages tapes with RSM using *media pools*, as seen in Figure 7-6.

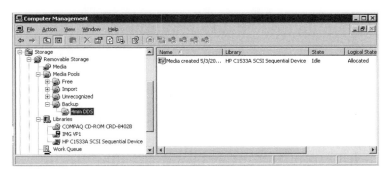

Figure 7-6   Media pools

There are four media pools related to backup:

- **Unrecognized**   Tape media that are completely blank or in a foreign format are contained in the Unrecognized pool until they are formatted.

- **Free**   This pool contains newly formatted tape media, as well as tapes that have been specifically marked as free by an administrator. Free media can be moved into the backup media pool by writing a backup set to them.

- **Backup**   This pool contains media that have been written to by the Backup Utility. The Backup Utility will only write to media in the Free media pool (and it will label the tape with the name you enter just before starting the backup) and to media, specified by name, in the Backup media pool.

- **Import**   This pool contains tape media that are not cataloged on the local disk drive. Cataloging such a tape will move the tape into the backup media pool.

Managing Tapes and Media Pools

In conjunction with backup procedures and tape rotation, you will need to manage your tapes in and out of these media pools. To that end, the following actions are available from the Restore And Manage Media page of the Backup Utility:

- **Format a tape**   Right-click a tape and choose Format. Formatting is not a secure way to erase tapes. If you need to erase tapes for legal or security reasons, use an appropriate third-party utility. Formatting does, however, prepare a tape and move it into the free media pool. Not all drives support formatting.

- **Retension a tape**   Right-click a tape and choose Retension. Not all drives support retensioning.

- **Mark a tape as free**   Right-click a tape and choose Mark As Free. This moves the tape into the free media pool. It does *not* erase the tape. If you need to erase tapes for legal reasons, use an appropriate third-party utility.

Catalogs

When the Backup Utility creates a backup set, it also creates a catalog listing files and folders included in the backup set. That catalog is stored on the disk of the server (the local or on-disk catalog) and in the backup set itself (the on-media catalog). The local catalog facilitates quick location of files and folders to restore. The Backup Utility can display the catalog immediately, rather than load the catalog from the typically slower backup media. The on-media catalog is critical if the drive containing the local catalog has failed, or if you transfer the files to another system. In those cases, Windows can recreate the local catalog from the on-media catalog.

The Restore And Manage Media page of the Backup Utility allows you to manage catalogs, as follows:

- **Delete Catalog**   Right-click a backup set and choose Delete Catalog if you have lost or damaged the backup media or if you are transferring files to another system and no longer require its local catalog. The on-media catalog is not affected by this command.

■ **Catalog**   A tape from a foreign system that is not cataloged on the local machine will appear in the import media pool. Right-click the media and choose the Catalog command. Windows will generate a local catalog from the tape or file. This does not create or modify the on-media catalog.

> **Tip**   If you have all the tapes in the backup set and the tapes are not damaged or corrupted, open the backup Options dialog box and, on the General tab, select Use The Catalogs On The Media To Speed Up Building Restore Catalogs On Disk. If you are missing a tape in the backup set or a tape is damaged or corrupted, clear that option. This will ensure that the catalog is complete and accurate; however, it might take a long time to create the catalog.

Backup Options

Backup options are configured by choosing the Options command from the Tools menu. Many of these options configure defaults that are used by the Backup Utility and the command-line backup tool, Ntbackup. Those settings can be overridden by options of a specific job.

General Options

The General tab of the Options dialog box includes the following settings:

■ **Compute Selection Information Before Backup And Restore Operations**   Backup estimates the number of files and bytes that will be backed up or restored before beginning the operation.

■ **Use The Catalogs On The Media To Speed Up Building Restore Catalogs On Disk**   If a system does not have an on-disk catalog for a tape, this option allows the system to create an on-disk catalog from the on-media catalog. However, if the tape with the on-media catalog is missing or if media in the set is damaged, you can deselect this option and the system will scan the entire backup set (or as much of it as you have) to build the on-disk catalog. Such an operation can take several hours if the backup set is large.

■ **Verify Data After The Backup Completes**   The system compares the contents of the backup media to the original files and logs any discrepancies. This option obviously adds a significant amount of time for completing the backup job. Discrepancies are likely if data changes frequently during backup or verification, and it is not recommended to verify system backups because of the number of changes that happen to system files on a continual basis. So long as you rotate tapes and discard tapes before they are worn, it should not be necessary to verify data.

- **Backup The Contents Of Mounted Drives** A mounted drive is a drive volume that is mapped to a folder on another volume's namespace, rather than, or in addition to, having a drive letter. If this option is deselected, only the path of the folder that is mounted to a volume is backed up; the contents are not. By selecting this option, the contents of the mounted volume is also backed up. There is no disadvantage in backing up a mount point, however if you back up the mount point and the mounted drive as well, your backup set will have duplication.

If you primarily back up to file and then save that file to another media, *clear* the following options. If you primarily back up to a tape or another media managed by Removable Storage, *select* the following options.

- Show Alert Message When I Start the Backup Utility And Removable Storage Is Not Running.

- Show Alert Message When I Start The Backup Utility And There Is Recognizable Media Available.

- Show Alert Message When New Media Is Inserted.

- Always Allow Use Of Recognizable Media Without Prompting.

> **Tip** The Always Allow Use Of Recognizable Media Without Prompting option can be selected if you are using local tape drives for backup only, not for Remote Storage or other functions. The option eliminates the need to allocate free media using the Removable Storage node in the Computer Management console.

Backup Logging

The Options dialog has a tab called Backup Log. Logging alerts you to problems that might threaten the viability of your backup, so consider your logging strategy as well as your overall backup plan. Although detailed logging will list every file and path that was backed up, the log is so verbose you are likely to overlook problems. Therefore, summary logging is recommended, and is the default. Summary logs report skipped files and errors.

The system will save 10 backup logs to the path *%UserProfile%*\Local Settings \Application Data\Microsoft\Windows NT\Ntbackup\Data. There is no way to change the path or the number of logs that are saved before the oldest log is replaced. You can, of course, include that path in your backup and thereby back up old logs.

File Exclusions

The Exclude Files tab of the Options dialog box also allows you to specify extensions and individual files that should be skipped during backup. Default settings result in the Backup Utility's skipping the page file, temporary files, client-side cache, debug folder, and the File Replication Service (FRS) database and folders, as well as other local logs and databases.

Files can be excluded based on ownership of the files. Click Add New under Files Excluded For All Users to exclude files owned by any user. Click Add New under Files Excluded For User *<username>* if you want to exclude only files that you own. You can specify files based on Registered File Type or based on an extension using the Custom File Mask. Finally, you can restrict excluded files to a specific folder or hard drive using the Applies To Path and the Applies To All Subfolders options.

Advanced Backup Options

After selecting files to back up, and clicking Start Backup, you can configure additional, job-specific options by clicking Advanced. Among the more important settings are the following:

- **Verify Data After Backup**   This setting overrides the default setting in the Backup Options dialog box.

- **If Possible, Compress The Backup Data To Save Space**   This setting compresses data to save space on the backup media, an option not available unless the tape drive supports compression.

- **Disable Volume Shadow Copy**   VSS allows the backup of locked and open files. If this option is selected, some files that are open or in use may be skipped.

The Ntbackup Command

The Ntbackup command provides the opportunity to script backup jobs on Windows Server 2003. Its syntax is

```
Ntbackup backup {"path to backup" or "@selectionfile.bks"} /j "Job Name" options
```

The command's first switch is *backup*, which sets its mode—you cannot restore from the command line. That switch is followed by a parameter that specifies what to back up. You can specify the actual path to the local folder, network share, or file that you want to back up. Alternatively, you can indicate the path to a backup selection file (.bks file) to be used with the syntax @*selectionfile*.bks. The at (@) symbol must precede the name of the backup selection file. A backup selection file contains information on the files and folders you have selected for backup. You have to create the file using the graphical user interface (GUI) version of the Backup Utility.

The third switch, /J "*JobName*", specifies the descriptive job name, which is used in the backup report.

You can then select from a staggering list of switches, which are grouped below based on the type of backup job you want to perform.

Backing Up to a File

Use the switch

/F "*FileName*"

where *FileName* is the logical disk path and file name. You must not use the following switches with this switch: /T /P /G.

The following example backs up the remote Data share on Server01 to a local file on the E drive:

```
ntbackup backup "\\server01\Data" /J "Backup of Server 01 Data folder" /F
"E:\Backup.bkf"
```

Appending to a File or Tape

Use the switch:

/A

to perform an append operation. If appending to a tape rather than a file, you must use either /G or /T in conjunction with this switch. Cannot be used with /N or /P.

The following example backs up the remote Profiles share on Server02 and appends the set to the job created in the first example:

```
ntbackup backup "\\server02\Profiles" /J "Backup of Server 02 Profiles folder" /F
"E:\Backup.bkf" /A
```

Backing Up to a New Tape or File, or Overwriting an Existing Tape

Use the switch:

/N "*MediaName*"

where *MediaName* specifies the new tape name. You must not use /A with this switch.

Backing Up to a New Tape

Use the switch

/P *"PoolName"*

where *PoolName* specifies the media pool that contains the backup media. This is usually a subpool of the backup media pool, such as 4mm DDS. You cannot use the /A, /G, /F, or /T options if you are using /P.

The following example backs up files and folders listed in the backup selection file c:\backup.bks to a tape drive:

```
ntbackup backup @c:\backup.bks /j "Backup Job 101" /n "Command Line Backup Job" /p
"4mm DDS"
```

Backing Up to an Existing Tape

To specify a tape for an append or overwrite operation, you must use either the /T or /G switch along with either /A (append) or /N (overwrite). Do not use the /P switch with either /T or /G.

To specify a tape by name, use the /T switch with the following syntax:

/T *"TapeName"*

where *TapeName* specifies a valid tape in the media pool.

To back up the selection file and append it to the tape created in the previous example, you would use this command line:

```
ntbackup backup @c:\backup.bks /j "Backup Job 102" /a /t "Command Line Backup Job"
```

To specify a tape by its GUID, rather than its name, use the /G switch with the following syntax:

/G *"GUIDName"*

where *GUIDName* specifies a valid tape in the media pool.

Job Options

For each of the job types described above, you can specify additional job options using these switches:

- **/M {*BackupType*}**   Specifies the backup type, which must be one of the following: normal, copy, differential, incremental, or daily.
- **/D {"*SetDescription*"}**   Specifies a label for the backup set.

- **/V:{yes | no}**   Verifies the data after the backup is complete.

- **/R:{yes | no}**   Restricts access to this tape to the owner or members of the Administrators group.

- **/L:{f | s | n}**   Specifies the type of log file: f=full, s=summary, n=none (no log file is created).

- **/RS:{yes | no}**   Backs up the migrated data files located in Remote Storage.

> **Tip**   The /RS command-line option is not required to back up the local Removable Storage database, which contains the Remote Storage placeholder files. When you backup the *%Systemroot%* folder, Backup automatically backs up the Removable Storage database as well.

- **/HC:{on | off}**   Uses hardware compression, if available, on the tape drive.

- **/SNAP:{on | off}**   Specifies whether the backup should use a Volume Shadow Copy.

Scheduling Backup Jobs

To schedule a backup job, create the job in the Backup Utility then click Start Backup and configure advanced backup options. After all options have been configured, click Schedule and, in the Set Account Information dialog box, type the user name and password of the account to be used by the backup job.

> **Security Alert**   Security best practices suggest that you create an account for each service, rather than run services under the System account. Do not configure a service to run using a User account, such as your User account or the Administrator account. When the password changes on a User account, you must modify the password setting on all services that run under the context of that account. The account for the backup job should belong to the Backup Operators group.

In the Scheduled Job Options dialog box, enter a job name and click Properties. The Schedule Job dialog box appears, as shown in Figure 7-7. Configure the job date, time, and frequency. The Advanced button will let you configure additional schedule settings including a date range for the job. The Settings tab of the Schedule Job dialog box allows you to refine the job, for example, by specifying that the job should only take place if the machine has been idle for a period of time.

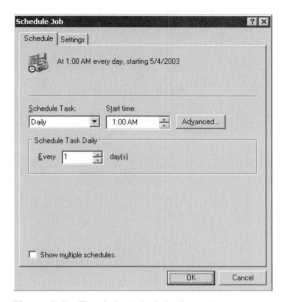

Figure 7-7   The Schedule Job dialog box

Once a job has been scheduled, you can edit the schedule by clicking the Schedule Jobs tab of the Backup Utility. Jobs are listed on a calendar. Click a job to open its schedule. Although you can also add a backup job by clicking Add Job on the Schedule Jobs tab, clicking Add Job will launch the backup wizard so that you can select the files to back up and some of the properties of the backup job. Most administrators find it more convenient to create a backup job on the Backup tab directly, then click Start Backup and Schedule, as described above.

Shadow Copies of Shared Folders

Windows Server 2003 supports another way for administrators and users alike to recover quickly from damage to files and folders. Using VSS, Windows Server 2003 automatically caches copies of files as they are modified. If a user deletes, overwrites, or makes unwanted changes to a file, you can simply restore a previous version of the file. This is a valuable feature, but is not intended to replace backups. Instead, it is designed to facilitate quick recovery from simple, day-to-day problems—not recovery from significant data loss.

Enabling and Configuring Shadow Copies

The Shadow Copies feature for shared folders is not enabled by default. To enable the feature, open the Properties dialog box of a drive volume from Windows Explorer or the Disk Management snap-in. On the Shadow Copies tab, as shown in Figure 7-8, select the volume and click Enable. Once enabled, all shared folders on the volume will be shadowed; specific shares on a volume cannot be selected. You can, however, manually initiate a shadow copy by clicking Create Now.

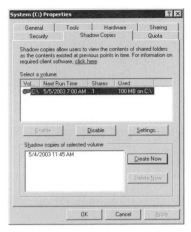

Figure 7-8   The Shadow Copies tab of a volume's Properties dialog box

Caution   If you click Disable, you delete all copies that were created by VSS. Consider carefully whether you want to disable VSS for a volume or whether you might be better served by modifying the schedule to prevent new shadow copies from being made.

The default settings configure the server to make copies of shared folders at 7:00 A.M. and noon, Monday through Friday; and 10 percent of the drive space, on the same drive as the shared folder, is used to cache shadow copies.

Each of the following settings can be modified by clicking Settings on the Shadow Copies tab:

■ **Storage volume**   To enhance performance (not redundancy), you can move the shadow storage to another volume. This must be done when no shadow copies are present. If shadow copies exist, and you want to change the storage volume, you must delete all shadow copies on the volume, then change the storage volume.

■ **Details**   The dialog box lists shadow copies that are stored and space utilization statistics.

■ **Storage limits**   This can be as low as 100 MB. When the shadow copy runs out of storage, it deletes older versions of files to make room for newer versions. The proper configuration of this setting depends on the total size of shared folders on a volume with shadowing enabled; the frequency with which files change, and the size of those files; and the number of previous versions you wish to retain. In any event, a maximum of 63 previous versions will be stored for any one file before the earliest version is removed from the shadow storage.

- **Schedule**   You can configure a schedule that reflects the work patterns of your users, ensuring that enough previous versions are available without prematurely filling the storage area and thereby forcing the removal of old versions. Remember that when a shadow copy is made, any files that have changed since the previous shadow copy are copied. If a file has been updated several times between shadow copies, those interim versions will not be available.

Using Shadow Copy

Shadow copies of shared folders allow you to access previous versions of files that the server has cached on the configured schedule. This will allow you to

- Recover files that were accidentally deleted
- Recover from accidentally overwriting a file
- Compare versions of files while working

To access previous versions, click the properties of a folder or file and click the Previous Versions tab, as shown in Figure 7-9.

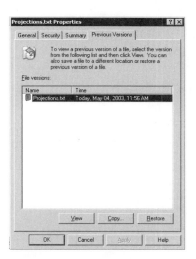

Figure 7-9   The Previous Versions tab of a shared resource

The Previous Versions page will not be available if Shadow Copies is not enabled on the server, or if there are no previous versions stored on the server. It will also be unavailable if the shadow copy client has not been installed on your system. This file is located in the *%Systemroot%*\System32\Clients\Twclient\x86 folder of a Windows Server 2003 system. The Windows Installer (.msi) file can be deployed using Group Policy, SMS, or an e-mail message. Finally, the Previous Versions page is only available when accessing a file's properties through a shared folder. If the file is stored on the local hard drive, you will not see the Previous Versions tab, even if the file is shared and VSS is enabled. See this lesson's Practice for an example.

You can then choose to Restore the file to its previous location or Copy the file to a specific location.

> **Exam Tip**   Unlike a true restore operation, when you restore a file with Previous Versions, the security settings of the previous version are not restored. If you restore the file to its original location, and the file exists in the original location, the restored previous version overwrites the current version and uses the permissions assigned to the current version. If you copy a previous version to another location, or restore the file to its original location but the file no longer exists in the original location, the restored previous version inherits permissions from the parent folder.

If a file has been deleted, you obviously cannot go to the file's Properties dialog box to locate the Previous Versions page. Instead, open the Properties of the parent folder, click the Previous Versions tab and locate a previous version of the folder that contains the file you want to recover. Click View and a folder window will open, as shown in Figure 7-10, that displays the contents of the folder as of the time at which the shadow copy was made. Right-click the file and choose Copy, then paste it into the folder where you want the file to be recreated.

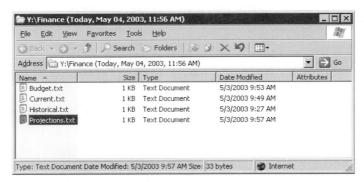

Figure 7-10   A folder's Previous Versions content list

Shadow copy, as you can see, is a useful addition to the toolset for managing file servers and shared data. With VSS, you can preserve data sets at scheduled points in time. Administrators or users can then restore deleted or corrupted files, or compare files to previous versions. As the VSS cache fills, old versions are purged and new shadow copies are added.

If a user requires data to be restored and that data is no longer available through Previous Versions, you can restore the data from backup. If the server becomes corrupted, you must restore the data from backup. Although VSS enhances the manageability and resiliency of shared files, there is no substitute for a carefully planned and verified backup procedure.

Practice: Advanced Backup and Restore

In this practice, you will schedule a backup job, execute a backup from a command prompt, and configure and use Shadow Copies of Shared Folders.

Exercise 1: Schedule a Backup Job

1. Open the Backup Utility and click the Backup tab.

2. From the Job menu, load the Finance Backup selections.

3. Configure the Backup Media Or File Name: C:\Backup-Everyday.bkf.

4. Click Start Backup.

5. Click Advanced and configure an Incremental backup type. Click OK.

6. Click Schedule.

7. In the Set Account Information dialog box, type your password and click OK.

8. Name the job Daily Incremental Backup.

9. Click Properties. Configure the job to run daily. Configure the time to be two minutes from the current time so that you can see the results of the job.

10. Complete configuration of the scheduled job. You will be prompted to enter your password again.

11. Close the Backup Utility.

12. Open the C drive in Windows Explorer and wait two minutes. You will see the backup job appear.

13. Open the Backup Utility, choose the Report command from the Tools menu and view the most recent backup log to confirm the status of the backup job. The number of files copied may be zero if you have not made changes to any of the files.

14. If the job did not run properly, open Event Viewer from the Administrative Tools folder. Examine the Application Log to identify the cause of the failure.

Exercise 2: Run a Backup from a Command Prompt

One of the easier ways to determine the correct switches to use for a command prompt backup is to schedule a backup, as you did in Exercise 1, and then examine the command that the scheduled task creates.

1. Open the Backup Utility and click the Schedule Jobs tab.

2. Click the icon, in the calendar, representing the scheduled job.

3. Click Properties.

4. Select the command in the Run box and press Ctrl+C to copy it.

5. Cancel to exit the Schedule Jobs dialog box and close the Backup Utility.

6. Open the command prompt.

7. Click the window menu (the icon of the command prompt in the upper-left corner of the command prompt window) and, from the Edit menu, choose Paste. The Ntbackup command with all of its switches is pasted into the command prompt. Press Enter. The backup job is executed.

> **Note**   It is recommended that you delete the scheduled backup job at this point in the Practice. You will schedule additional jobs in the Case Scenario, and it will be easier to work with those jobs if the current schedule is clear. In the Backup Utility, click the Schedule Jobs tab, then, in the calendar, click the icon representing the scheduled job. Click Delete.

Exercise 3: Enable Shadow Copies

1. Ensure that the C:\Data folder is shared and that the share permissions are configured to allow Everyone Full Control.

2. Open My Computer.

3. Right-click the C drive and choose Properties.

4. Click the Shadow Copies tab.

5. Select the C volume and click Enable.

6. A message will appear. Click Yes to continue.

Exercise 4: Simulate Changes to Network Files

1. Open the C:\Data\Finance folder and open Current.txt. Modify the file's contents, then save and close the file.

2. Delete the file C:\Data\Finance\Projections.txt.

Exercise 5: Recover Files Using Previous Versions

1. Open the data share by clicking Start, choosing Run, and then typing **\\server01\data**.

> **Note**   It is critical that you open the folder using its UNC, not its local path. The Previous Versions tab is only available when connected to a shared folder over the network.

2. Open the Finance folder.

3. Right-click the Current.txt file and choose Properties.

4. Select the Previous Versions tab.

5. Select the previous version of Current.txt.

6. Click Copy, select the Desktop as the destination, and then click Copy again.

7. Click OK to close the Properties dialog box.

8. Open Current.txt from your desktop. You will see that it is the version without the changes you made in Exercise 4.

9. Return to \\Server01\Data. This time, do not open the Finance folder.

10. To recover the deleted Projections.txt file, right-click the Finance folder and click Properties.

11. Select the Previous Versions tab.

12. Select the previous version of the Finance folder and click View.

    A window opens showing the contents of the folder as of the time that the shadow copy was made.

13. Right-click the Projections.txt file and choose Copy.

14. Switch to the folder that shows you the current \\server01\data folder.

15. Open the Finance folder.

16. Paste the Projections.txt file into the folder. You have now restored the previous version of Projections.txt.

Lesson Review

The following questions are intended to reinforce key information presented in this lesson. If you are unable to answer a question, review the lesson materials and try the question again. You can find answers to the questions in the "Questions and Answers" section at the end of this chapter.

1. Scott Bishop is a power user at a remote site that includes 20 users. The site has a Windows Server 2003 system providing file and print servers. There is a tape drive installed on the system. Because there is no local, full-time administrator at the site, you want to allow Scott to back up and restore the server. However, you want to minimize the power and the privileges that Scott obtains, limiting his capabilities strictly to backup and restore. What is the best practice to provide Scott the minimum necessary credentials to achieve his task?

    _____

    _____

2. Write the command that will allow you to fully back up the C:\Data\Finance folder to a file called Backup.bkf in a share called Backup on Server02, with the backup job name "Backup of Finance Folder." Then, write the command that will allow you to perform an incremental backup and append the backup set to the same file, with the same backup job name.

_____

_____

3. A user has deleted a file in a shared folder on a server. The user opens the properties of the folder and does not see a Previous Versions tab. Which of the following may be true? (Choose all that apply.)

   a. The folder is not enabled for Shadow Copy.

   b. The volume on the server is not enabled for Shadow Copy.

   c. The user doesn't have permission to view the Shadow Copy cache.

   d. The Shadow Copy client is not installed on the user's machine.

   e. The folder is on a FAT volume.

Lesson Summary

- You must have the right to backup and restore files to use the Backup Utility or any other backup tool. The right is assigned, by default, to the Backup Operators and Administrators groups.

- The Options dialog box allows you to configure General, Backup, and Restore settings, many of which become defaults that will drive the behavior of the Backup Utility and the Ntbackup command, unless overridden by job-specific options specified in the backup job's Advanced Backup Options dialog box, or in command-line switches.

- The Ntbackup command and its full complement of switches allows you to launch a backup job from a command prompt or batch file.

- Backup jobs can be scheduled to run regularly and automatically during periods of low utilization.

- Volume Shadow Copy Service (VSS) allows a user to access previous versions of files and folders in network shares. With those previous versions, users can restore deleted or damaged files or compare versions of files.

Case Scenario Exercise

You are asked to configure a backup strategy for the Finance Department's shared folder. The backup should occur automatically during the early-morning hours, as there are users working shifts from 4:00 A.M. to 12:00 midnight, Monday through Friday. Files in the folder change frequently—about half the files change once a week; the other half of the files change almost daily. You are told that if the server's hard drive ever fails, down time is extraordinarily costly to the company, so recovery should be as fast as possible.

1. With the knowledge that so many files change almost daily, and that recovery must be as quick as possible, what type of backup job should you consider running nightly?

   Consider normal backups. There is so much change happening to the shared folder, that you are receiving less than a 50 percent benefit using a differential or incremental backup versus a normal backup; and nothing is faster to restore than a normal backup, because the backup set contains all the files to restore.

2. You configure a normal daily backup job to run at 12:00 midnight, after the last shift has gone home for the evening. Unfortunately, you find that the backup job is not completed by 4:00 A.M. when the morning shift arrives. How should you modify your backup strategy?

   Create a normal backup once a week, perhaps on Sunday, and then create differential backups nightly during the week. While differential and incremental backups are both available, differential backups provide faster restore capability, as the most recent differential backup set includes all files that have been updated since the normal backup.

Exercise 1: Create Sample Data

1. Open My Computer and the C drive.

2. Delete the Data folder. You will be prompted to confirm the choice. You will also be informed that the folder is shared, and that deleting the folder will delete the shared folder. Confirm your understanding of the warning and continue.

3. Open the command prompt and type **cd c:**.

4. Type the command **createfiles.bat**.

> **Note**   If you did not create the createfiles.bat file in Lesson 1, Exercise 1, complete steps 1 through 3 of Exercise 1 to create the appropriate script.

Exercise 2: Schedule the Backup Job

Configure and schedule the following backup jobs. If you need guidance to achieve these tasks, refer to the instructions in the Practices in Lesson 1 and Lesson 3.

- Normal backup job to back up the C:\Data\Finance folder to a file called C:\BackupFinance.bkf (replacing the media), every Sunday at 9:00 P.M.

- Differential backup job to back up the same folder to the same file (appending to the media), at 12:15 A.M. on Tuesday through Saturday (that is, Monday night through Friday night).

Exercise 3: Simulate the Scheduled Jobs

Rather than waiting until Sunday night for the normal backup job to execute automatically, you will execute the backup job from the command prompt.

1. Open the Backup Utility.
2. Click the Schedule Jobs tab.
3. Click the icon in the calendar representing the Sunday night normal backup job.
4. Click Properties.
5. Select the command in the Run box and press Ctrl+C to copy it.
6. Cancel to exit the Schedule dialog box and close the Backup Utility.
7. Open the command prompt.
8. Click the window menu (the icon of the command prompt in the upper-left corner of the command prompt window) and, from the Edit menu, choose Paste. The Ntbackup command with all its switches is pasted into the command prompt. Press Enter. The backup job is executed.
9. Open C:\Data\Finance\Projections.txt and make changes to the file. Save and close the file.
10. Repeat steps 1-8, this time executing from the command prompt the *differential* backup job that is scheduled to run every night.

Exercise 4: Verify the Procedure

1. Open the Backup Utility.
2. From the Tools menu, click Report.
3. Open the two most recent backup reports and confirm that the jobs completed successfully. The normal job should have backed up four files. The differential job should have backed up one file.
4. Perform a test restore to a folder called C:\TestRestore. Restore the normal job and then the differential job. If you need guidance, refer to the Practice in Lesson 2.

> **Caution**   Remember, before restoring the differential job, that you must configure the Restore options (from the Tools menu, select Options) to always replace files. You may also need to catalog the file to see all the backup sets it contains.

Troubleshooting Lab

At 1:00 P.M. on Tuesday, a user in the Finance Department contacts you to let you know that he accidentally deleted some files from the Finance folder. You are confident that the backup procedure you established will help you recover the deleted files. However, you also want to ensure that you don't roll back any files that had been changed today, after the overnight backup job was executed.

In this lab, you will simulate the workflow that creates such a scenario, and then you will recover the missing data.

Exercise 1: Create a Data Loss

1. Open the C:\Data\Finance folder.

2. Open the file Current.txt. Make some changes to the file. Save and close the file.

3. Open the Budget file. Make some changes, save, and close the file.

4. Delete the Historical.txt and Projections.txt files.

Exercise 2: Plan the Recovery

Review the backup strategy you developed in the Case Scenario Exercise: a normal backup every Sunday night and a differential backup every weeknight.

1. How will you recover the missing data?

   A normal backup includes all selected files. It is the baseline from which you begin to recover from data loss. The differential backup includes all files that have changed since the normal backup. After you have restored the normal backup, you can restore the most recent differential backup. Keep in mind, however, that some of the files (Budget and Current) have been changed by users subsequent to the overnight differential backup.

2. How will you prevent those newer files from being overwritten by files in the backup set?

   The Options dialog box includes a Restore Options tab which allows you to specify how files in the backup set are written to the destination. You can direct the Backup Utility to overwrite files only if the files on the disk are older than the files in the backup set. Files that are newer will remain.

Exercise 3: Recover the Data

1. Open the Backup Utility.

2. Choose the Options command from the Tools menu.

3. Click the Restore tab.

4. Configure restore to leave newer files untouched by selecting Replace The File On Disk Only If The File On Disk Is Older, then close the Options dialog box.

5. Select the backup media that contains your normal and differential backup.

6. Restore the normal backup to its original location.

7. Restore the differential backup to its original location.

8. Open the Current and Budget files. Because these files were newer than those on the backup set, and because of the restore options you configured, they should include the changes you made in the Case Scenario exercise.

Chapter Summary

- You must have the right to back up and restore files to use the Backup Utility or any other backup tool. The right is assigned, by default, to the Backup Operators and Administrators groups.

- The Backup Utility, Ntbackup, allows you to back up and restore data from local and remote folders to local files, tape drives, removable media, or shared folders on remote servers. You cannot back up to writable CD or DVD formats.

- A backup strategy typically begins with a normal backup followed by regular incremental or differential backups. Incremental jobs create the backup more quickly; differential backups are faster to restore. Jobs can be scheduled to occur during periods of low utilization.

- Copy backups and daily backups can be used to capture files without interfering with the regular backup schedule.

- The Backup Utility will also allow you to restore backed up data to the original location or to an alternate location. The latter is useful to test and verify restore procedures. You can control, through the Options dialog box, Restore tab, which files are replaced during a restore.

- The Ntbackup command and its full complement of switches allows you to launch a backup job from a command prompt or batch file.

- Volume Shadow Copy Service (VSS) allows a user to access previous versions of files and folders in network shares. With those previous versions, users can restore deleted or damaged files or compare versions of files.

Exam Highlights

Before taking the exam, review the key points and terms that are presented below to help you identify topics you need to review. Return to the lessons for additional practice and review the "Further Readings" sections in Part 2 for pointers to more information about topics covered by the exam objectives.

Key Points

- Identify the group memberships or rights required to perform a backup or restore operation.

- Create a backup strategy based on requirements including the amount of time it takes to back up data, and the speed with which restores must be performed.

- Understand how to restore data under a variety of conditions, including complete and partial data loss. Compare the data loss to the backup schedule to identify the backup sets that must be restored. Integrate your knowledge of the order in which backup sets should be restored and how existing files on the hard drive should be replaced.

- Schedule a backup job and configure backup options.

- Enable shadow copies of shared folders and recover data using the Previous Versions tab of a file or folder's Properties dialog box.

Key Terms

Copy, daily, differential, incremental and normal backup   These five backup types select files to back up using specific criteria. *Copy* and *normal* back up all files; *daily* backs up files that have been modified on a specified date; *differential* and *incremental* back up files with their archive attribute set. *Normal* and *incremental* backups also reset the archive attribute.

Archive attribute   An attribute that is set when a file is created or modified. Incremental and differential backups will back up files with their Archive attribute set. Incremental backups also clear the Archive attribute.

Volume Shadow Copy Service (VSS)   A feature of Windows Server 2003 that allows you to back up files that are locked or open.

Media pools: unrecognized, import, free, backup   The four categories of removable media. Ntbackup will back up to media in the free and backup media pools only.

Shadow copies of shared folders   A feature of Windows Server 2003 that, once configured on the server and on clients, allows users to retrieve previous versions of files without administrator intervention.

Questions and Answers

Page
7-11

Lesson 1 Review

1. Which of the following locations are *not* allowed to be used for a backup of a Windows Server 2003 system?

   a. Local tape drive

   b. Local CD-RW

   c. Local hard drive

   d. Shared folder on a remote server

   e. Local DVD+R

   f. Local removable drive

   g. Tape drive on a remote server

   The correct answers are b, e, and g.

2. You are to back up a Windows Server 2003 file server every evening. You perform a manual, normal backup. You will then schedule a backup job to run every evening for the next two weeks. Which backup type will complete the fastest?

   a. Normal

   b. Differential

   c. Incremental

   d. Copy

   The correct answer is c.

3. You are to back up a Windows Server 2003 file server every evening. You perform a manual, normal backup. You will then schedule a backup job to run every evening for the next two weeks. Which backup type will provide the simplest recovery of lost data?

   a. Normal

   b. Differential

   c. Incremental

   d. Daily

   The correct answer is a.

4. You are to back up a Windows Server 2003 file server every evening. You perform a normal backup. On the second evening, you consider whether to use incremental or differential backup. Will there be any difference in the speed or size of those two backup jobs? If the server were to fail the following day, would there be any difference in the efficiency of recovery?

On the second evening, you could use either backup type. The normal backup cleared the archive attribute. Both incremental and differential backups will, on the second evening, transfer all files created or changed on the second day. There will be no difference in the contents of the two jobs. Therefore, there will be no difference in recovery on the third day: you would have to restore the normal backup, and then the backup from the second evening.

However, incremental and differential backups treat the archive attribute on backed up files differently: incremental turns off the attribute; differential leaves it on. So on the *next* backup, there starts to be a difference. A second incremental backup will transfer only files created or changed since the first incremental backup. However, a second differential backup will include all files created or changed since the normal backup; that is, it will include all files already copied by the first differential backup.

5. Review the steps taken during the Practice. Predict the contents of the following backup jobs:

   ❑ backup-normal.bkf

   ❑ backup-diff-day1.bkf

   ❑ backup-diff-day2.bkf

   ❑ backup-inc-day2.bkf

   ❑ backup-inc-day3.bkf

   Are there any differences between the contents of backup-diff-day2 and backup-inc-day2?

   ■ backup-normal.bkf: Historical, Current, Budget and Projections

   ■ backup-diff-day1.bkf: Current

   ■ backup-diff-day2.bkf: Current and Budget

   ■ backup-inc-day2.bkf: Current and Budget

   ■ backup-inc-day3.bkf: Projections

There are no differences between backup-diff-day2 and backup-inc-day2. Both backup types will back up data that has the archive attribute set. Because a normal backup was performed on the first day, all files that have changed since the first day will have the archive attribute set.

Lesson 2 Review

1. A user has accidentally deleted the data in a Microsoft Word document and saved the document, thereby permanently altering the original file. A normal backup operation was performed on the server the previous evening. Which restore option should you select?

    a. Do Not Replace The File On My Computer.

    b. Replace The File On Disk Only If The File On Disk Is Older.

    c. Always Replace The File On My Computer.

    The correct answer is c. The file does exist on the server, but the file has been corrupted. You should replace the file with the copy in the backup set.

2. An executive has returned from a business trip. Before the trip, she copied files from a network folder to her hard drive. The folder is shared with other executives, who modified their files in the folder while she was away. When she returned, she moved her copy of the files to the network share, thereby updating her files with the changes she made while away, but also overwriting all the files that had been changed by other executives. The other executives are unhappy that their files have been replaced with the versions that were active when she left for her trip. Luckily, you performed a normal backup operation on the folder the previous evening. What restore option should you choose?

    a. Do Not Replace The File On My Computer.

    b. Replace The File On Disk Only If The File On Disk Is Older.

    c. Always Replace The File On My Computer.

    The correct answer is b. This option will not overwrite files that were changed by the executive while she was away. Those files will have a date more recent than the backup. It will, however, restore the other executives' files over the older versions she uploaded to the network.

> **Tip**   Users should be trained to use the Offline Files feature, so that this kind of disaster, which is not uncommon, can be avoided. Offline Files synchronizes changed files only, so only the updates she made would have been uploaded to the network, leaving the other executives' changes intact.

3. You would like to test the restore procedures on your server, but would also like to avoid affecting the production copies of the backed-up data. What is the best restore location to use?

    a. Original location

b. Alternate location

c. Single folder

The correct answer is b. Restoring to an alternate location will restore the folder structure and files that were backed up. You can then compare the contents of the target location with the original backed-up files to verify the success of the restore procedure.

Page
7-35
Lesson 3 Review

1. Scott Bishop is a power user at a remote site that includes 20 users. The site has a Windows Server 2003 system providing file and print servers. There is a tape drive installed on the system. Because there is no local, full-time administrator at the site, you want to allow Scott to back up and restore the server. However, you want to minimize the power and the privileges that Scott obtains, limiting his capabilities strictly to backup and restore. What is the best practice to provide Scott the minimum necessary credentials to achieve his task?

   Make Scott a member of the Backup Operators group. The Backup Operators group is assigned, by default, the privilege to back up and restore files and folders.

2. Write the command that will allow you to fully back up the C:\Data\Finance folder to a file called Backup.bkf in a share called Backup on Server02, with the backup job name "Backup of Finance Folder." Then, write the command that will allow you to perform an incremental backup and append the backup set to the same file, with the same backup job name.

   ntbackup backup "c:\data\finance" /J "Backup of Finance Folder" /F "\\server02
   \backup\backup.bkf"

   ntbackup backup "c:\data\finance" /J "Backup of Finance Folder" /F "\\server01
   \backup\backup.bkf" /a /m incremental

3. A user has deleted a file in a shared folder on a server. The user opens the properties of the folder and does not see a Previous Versions tab. Which of the following may be true? (Choose all that apply.)

   a. The folder is not enabled for Shadow Copy.

   b. The volume on the server is not enabled for Shadow Copy.

   c. The user doesn't have permission to view the Shadow Copy cache.

   d. The Shadow Copy client is not installed on the user's machine.

   e. The folder is on a FAT volume.

   The correct answers are b and d. Shadow Copy is enabled per volume, not per folder. Once Shadow Copy is enabled, any user with the client installed will see a Previous Versions tab for a file or folder that has changed. Shadow Copy is supported on FAT and NTFS volumes.

8 Printers

Exam Objectives in this Chapter:

- Monitor print queues.
- Monitor file and print servers. Tools might include Task Manager, Event Viewer, and System Monitor.

Why This Chapter Matters

An administrator's to-do list usually teems with items relating to printers. Whether testing or deploying new printer hardware, troubleshooting print jobs, or securing and monitoring printer utilization, you are apt to be almost as busy with printers as with file and folder access.

Microsoft Windows Server 2003 provides a powerful feature set to support enterprise print services. This chapter introduces you to the setup and configuration of printers on Windows Server 2003, the interaction between printers and the Microsoft Active Directory directory service, connecting clients to network printers, and monitoring and troubleshooting print services. You will learn how to administer local, network, and Internet printers, and how to configure printers for maximum flexibility and security.

Lessons in this Chapter:

Before You Begin

This chapter presents the skills and concepts related to administering Windows Server 2003 printers. This training kit presumes you have a minimum of 18 months of experience and a working knowledge of Active Directory and the Microsoft Management Console (MMC). However, because many administrators come to Windows Server 2003 from other printer environments including Novell NetWare, and because printer terminology has changed slightly, this chapter's first lesson reviews fundamentals of printer configuration. Lesson 2 and Lesson 3 build on those fundamentals to prepare you for advanced, flexible administration, support, monitoring, and troubleshooting, of printers in a Windows Server 2003 environment.

Although it is advantageous to have a printer and two computers (a Windows Server 2003 computer and a client running Windows XP or Windows 2000 Professional), you can complete the exercises in this chapter without a printer, and with only one computer. Prepare the following:

- A Windows Server 2003 (Standard or Enterprise) installed as Server01 and configured as a domain controller in the domain *contoso.com*

- A first-level organizational unit (OU) called Security Groups

- The Active Directory Users And Computers console, or a customized console with the Active Directory Users And Computers snap-in

Lesson 1: Installing and Configuring Printers

Windows Server 2003 supports powerful, secure, and flexible print services. By using a Windows Server 2003 computer to manage printers attached locally to the computer or attached to the network, such printers can be made available to applications running locally on the Windows Server 2003 computer or to users on any client platform, including previous versions of Windows, as well as Netware, UNIX, or Apple Macintosh clients. This lesson will examine the basic concepts, terminology, and skills related to the setup of printers in Windows Server 2003.

After this lesson, you will be able to

- Understand the model and terminology used for Windows printing
- Install a logical printer on a print server for a network attached printer
- Prepare a print server to host clients including computers running previous versions of Windows
- Connect a printer client to a logical printer on a print server
- Manage print jobs

Estimated lesson time: 15 minutes

Understanding the Windows Server 2003 Printer Model

Windows Server 2003, and previous versions of Windows, support two types of printers:

- **Locally attached printers**   Printers that are connected to a physical port on a print server, typically a universal serial bus (USB) or parallel port.

- **Network-attached printers**   Printers connected to the network instead of a physical port. A network-attached printer is a node on the network; print servers can address the printer using a network protocol such as Transmission Control Protocol/Internet Protocol (TCP/IP).

Each type of printer is represented on the print server as a logical printer. The *logical printer* defines the characteristics and behavior of the printer. It contains the driver, printer settings, print setting defaults and other properties that control the manner in which a print job is processed and sent to the chosen printer. This virtualization of the printer by a logical printer allows you to exercise extraordinary creativity and flexibility in configuring your print services.

Note   In previous versions of Windows and in earlier versions of documentation, the printer was referred to as the "print device" and the logical printer was referred to as the "printer."

There are two ways to implement printing to network attached printers. One model is created by installing logical printers on all computers, and connecting those logical printers directly to the network-attached printer. In this model, there is no print server; each computer maintains its own settings, print processor, and queue. When users examine the print queue, they see only the jobs they have sent to the printer. There is no way for users to know what jobs have been sent to the printer by other users. In addition, error messages appear only on the computer that is printing the current job. Finally, all print job processing is performed locally on the user's computer, rather than being offloaded to a print server.

Because of these significant drawbacks, the most typical configuration of printers in an enterprise is a three-part model consisting of the physical printer itself, a logical printer hosted on a print server, and printer clients connecting to the server's logical printer. This lesson focuses exclusively on such a structure, although the concepts and skills discussed apply to other printer configurations.

Printing with a print server provides the following advantages:

- The logical printer on the print server defines the printer settings and manages printer drivers.

- The logical printer produces a single print queue that appears on all client computers, so users can see where their jobs are in relation to other users' jobs.

- Error messages, such as out-of-paper or printer-jam messages, are visible on all clients, so all users can know the state of the printer.

- Most applications and most print drivers will offload some, or a significant amount, of the print-job processing to the server, which increases the responsiveness of the client computers. In other words, when users click Print, their jobs are sent quickly to the print server and users can resume their work while the print server processes the jobs.

- Security, auditing, monitoring, and logging functions are centralized.

Installing a Printer on Windows Server 2003

Printers are managed most commonly through the Printers And Faxes folder, which integrates both printer and fax capabilities. The Add Printer Wizard guides you through the printer setup. The most critical choices you must make are the following:

- **Local Or Network Printer**   This page of the Add Printer Wizard is shown in Figure 8-1. When you set up a printer on a Windows Server 2003 computer, the terms local printer and network printer have slightly different meanings from what you might expect. A *local printer* is a logical printer that supports a printer attached directly to the server or a stand-alone, network-attached printer. When you direct the Add Printer Wizard to create a local printer by clicking Local Printer Attached

To This Computer, the server can share the printer to other clients on the network. A *network printer*, on the other hand, is a logical printer that that connects to a printer directly attached to another computer or to a printer managed by another print server. The user interface can be misleading, so remember that, in the common print server implementation, the print server will host local printers (whether the printer hardware is attached to the computer or network-attached), and workstations will create network printers connecting to the server's shared logical printer.

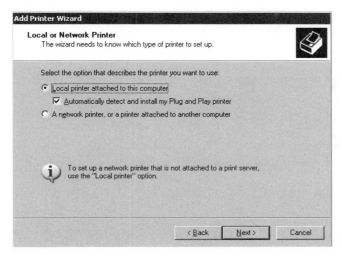

Figure 8-1   The Local Or Network Printer page of the Add Printer Wizard

- **Select A Printer Port**   When you create a local printer on a print server, the Add Printer Wizard asks you to specify the port to which the printer is attached. If the port already exists, whether a local port such as LPT1 or a network port specified by an IP address, select the port from the Use The Following Port drop-down list. When setting up a logical printer for a network attached printer for which a port has not been created, click Create A New Port, select Standard TCP/IP Port and click Next. The Add Standard TCP/IP Printer Port Wizard appears. Clicking Next prompts you for the IP address or DNS name of the printer. After the port has been added, you are returned to the Add Printer Wizard.

- **Install Printer Software**   If Plug and Play does not detect and install the correct printer automatically, you can select your printer from an extensive list that is categorized by manufacturer. If the printer does not appear on the list, you can click Have Disk and install the printer from drivers supplied by the manufacturer.

- **Printer Name and Share Name**   Although Windows Server 2003 supports long printer names and share names including spaces and special characters, it is best practice to keep names short and simple. The entire qualified name including the server name (for example, \\Server01\PSCRIPT) should be 32 characters or fewer.

The share name and the printer name appear, and are used in different places throughout the Windows user interface. Although the share name is independent of, and can be different from, the printer name, many enterprises unify the printer name and the share name to reduce confusion.

Configuring Printer Properties

After installing the logical printer, you can configure numerous properties by opening the printer's Properties dialog box, shown in Figure 8-2. The General tab allows you to configure the printer name, location, and comments, all of which were initially configured based on your responses to prompts in the Add Printer Wizard.

Figure 8-2   The General tab of a printer's Properties dialog box

The Sharing tab shown in Figure 8-3 allows you to specify whether the logical printer is shared, and is therefore available to other clients on the network, and whether the printer is listed in Active Directory, a default setting, for shared printers, that allows users to easily search for and connect to printers.

Note   You can use the Sharing tab to stop sharing a printer, if you take a printer offline and want to prevent users from accessing the printer.

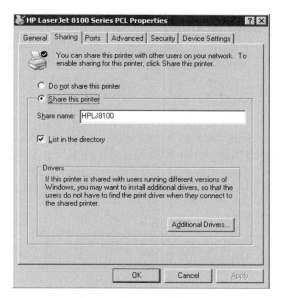

Figure 8-3   The Sharing tab of a printer's Properties dialog box

During printer setup, Windows Server 2003 loads drivers onto the print server that support that printer for clients running Windows Server 2003, Windows XP, and Windows 2000. Printer drivers are platform-specific. If other platforms will be connecting to the shared logical printer, install the appropriate drivers on the server, so that Windows clients will download the driver automatically when they connect. Otherwise, you will be prompted for the correct drivers on each individual client.

On the Sharing tab of the Properties dialog box, click Additional Drivers to configure the print server to host drivers for computers running versions of Windows prior to Windows 2000. When you select a previous version of Windows, the server will prompt you for the drivers for the appropriate platform and printer. Those drivers will be available from the printer's manufacturer, or sometimes on the original CD-ROM of the previous version of Windows.

By loading drivers on the server for all client platforms, you can centralize and facilitate driver distribution. Client computers running Windows NT, Windows 2000, Windows XP, and Windows Server 2003 download the driver when they first connect to the shared printer. They also verify that they have the current printer driver each time they print and, if they do not, they download the updated driver. For these client computers, you need only update printer drivers on the print server. Client computers running Windows 95 or Windows 98 do not check for updated printer drivers, once the driver is initially downloaded and installed. You must manually install updated printer drivers on these clients.

Other printer properties will be discussed later in this chapter.

Tip You can access other servers' printer folders by browsing the network or by choosing the Run command from the Start menu and typing **\\server_name**. You can drag those servers' Printer and Faxes folders to your own, giving you easy access to manage remote printers.

Connecting Clients to Printers

Printers that have been set up as logical printers on a print server can be shared to other systems on the network. Those systems will also require logical printers to represent the network printer.

Configuring a print client can be done in several ways, including the Add Printer Wizard, which can be started from the Printers And Faxes folder or from the common Windows Print dialog box in almost all Microsoft applications, including Internet Explorer and Notepad. On the Local or Network Printer page, select A Network Printer Or A Printer Attached To Another Computer. When prompted for the printer name, you can search Active Directory, enter the Universal Naming Convention (UNC) (for example, \\Server\Printersharename) or Uniform Resource Locator (URL) to the printer, or browse for the printer using the Browser service.

One of the more efficient ways to set up print clients is to search Active Directory for the printer. In the Specify A Printer page of the Add Printer Wizard, choose Find A Printer In The Directory and click Next. The Find Printers dialog box appears, as shown in Figure 8-4, and you can enter search criteria including printer name, location, model, and features. Wildcards can be used in many of the criteria. Click Find Now and a result set is displayed. Select the printer and click OK. The Add Printer Wizard then steps you through remaining configuration options.

Tip You can save a search by choosing Save Search from the File menu. As an administrator, you can create and save custom searches to users' desktops, allowing them to easily locate predefined subsets for the printers in your enterprise.

A logical printer includes the drivers, settings, and print queue for the printer on the selected port. When you double-click a printer in the Printers And Faxes folder, a window opens that displays the jobs in the printer's queue. By right-clicking any job, you can pause, resume, cancel, or restart the job. From the Printer menu, you can also pause or cancel all printing, access the printer properties, or set the printer as default or offline. Your ability to perform each of these actions depends, of course, upon the permissions on the printer's access control list.

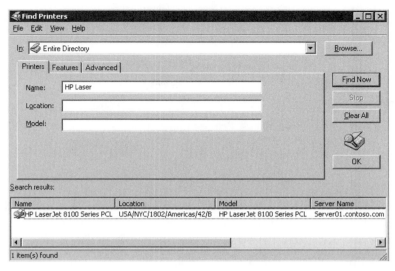

Figure 8-4   The Find Printers dialog box

As an alternative to using the Add Printer Wizard, if you are using Windows Server 2003 or Windows XP with the default Start menu, perform the following steps to configure a print client:

1. Click Start, and then select Search.

2. In the Search Companion pane, click Other Search Options, then Printers, Computers, Or People, and finally A Printer On The Network.

3. The Find Printers dialog box will be displayed, allowing you to search for the printer using various criteria.

4. After entering the desired criteria, click Find Now.

Practice: Installing and Configuring a Printer

In this practice, you will set up a logical printer on a print server and simulate connecting a client to the shared printer. You will then send a print job to the printer.

You do not need to have a print device connected to Server01 or to the network, nor are you required to have a second computer to act as a print client. However, if you have access to these additional components, you are encouraged to implement the exercises using that extra hardware.

Exercise 1: Add a Local Printer and Configure Print Sharing

In this exercise, you use the Add Printer Wizard to add a logical printer to Server01. The printer will connect to a network-attached HP LaserJet 8100 that is connected to the network at IP address 10.0.0.51. You do not need an actual printer to complete this exercise.

1. Log on to Server01 as Administrator.

2. Open the Printers And Faxes folder.

3. Double-click Add Printer. The Add Printer Wizard appears.

4. Click Next. The Local Or Network Printer page appears.

   You are prompted for the location of the printer. Although the printer is attached to the network, the logical printer serving that printer is being added to Server01, so the printer is referred to as a local printer.

5. Verify that the Local Printer option is selected and that the Automatically Detect And Install My Plug And Play Printer check box is cleared (because you are configuring a printer for a fictional device), and then click Next.

6. The Select A Printer Port page appears. Click Create A New Port.

7. Select Standard TCP/IP Port from the Type Of Port drop-down list.

   The port types that will be available, other than local port, depend on the installed network protocols. In this case, TCP/IP is installed, so this protocol-based port is available.

8. Click Next. The Add Standard TCP/IP Printer Port Wizard appears.

9. Click Next.

10. Enter the IP Address: 10.0.0.51 and accept the default port name, IP_10.0.0.51.

11. Click Next.

    Because a print device is not actually attached to the network at that address, there will be a delay while the Wizard attempts to locate and identify the printer. You will also be prompted to specify the type of network interface.

12. Select Hewlett Packard Jet Direct as the device type.

13. Click Next, and then click Finish. The Add Standard TCP/IP Printer Port Wizard closes, returning you to the Add Printer Wizard.

    The Wizard prompts you for the printer manufacturer and model. You will add an HP LaserJet 8100 Series PCL printer.

Tip The printers list is sorted in alphabetical order. If you cannot find a printer name, make sure that you are looking in the correct location.

14. From the Manufacturer list, click HP; from the Printers list, scroll down the list, click HP LaserJet 8100 Series PCL; and then click Next.

   The Name Your Printer page appears. The default name in the Printer Name field is the printer model, HP LaserJet 8100 Series PCL. The name you enter should conform to naming conventions in your enterprise. For this exercise, enter the name HPLJ8100.

15. Type **HPLJ8100** and Click Next.

   The Printer Sharing page appears, prompting you for printer-sharing information. The share name should also reflect naming conventions in your enterprise. As discussed earlier, the printer's UNC (that is, \\Servername\Printersharename) should not exceed 32 characters.

16. Verify that the Share Name option is selected.

17. In the Share Name text box, type **HPLJ8100**, and then click Next.

   The Location And Comment page appears.

> **Note**   The Add Printer Wizard displays the values you enter for the Location and Comment text boxes when a user searches the Active Directory for a printer. Entering this information is optional, but doing so helps users locate the printer.

18. In the Location text box, type **USA/NYC/1802Americas/42/B**.

19. In the Comment text box, type **Black and White Output Laser Printer-High Volume**.

20. Click Next.

   The Print Test Page screen appears. A test page that prints successfully would confirm that your printer is set up properly.

21. Choose No (because the printer doesn't exist) and click Next. The Completing The Add Printer Wizard page appears and summarizes your installation choices.

22. Confirm the summary of your installation choices, and then click Finish.

   An icon for the printer appears in the Printers And Faxes window. Notice that Windows Server 2003 displays an open hand beneath the printer icon. This indicates the printer is shared. Also notice the check mark next to the printer, which indicates the printer is the default printer for the print server.

23. Keep the Printers And Faxes window open because you will need it to complete the next exercise.

Exercise 2: Connect a Client to a Printer

If you have access to a second computer, you would install on each workstation a printer that connects to the shared printer on Server01. In this practice, you are required to have only one computer (Server01), but you can simulate connecting a printer client to the server's logical printer.

1. Open the Printers And Faxes folder.

2. Start the Add Printer Wizard and click Next.

3. In the Local Or Network Printer dialog box, select A Network Printer, Or A Printer Attached To Another Computer and click Next.

4. Confirm that Find A Printer In The Directory is selected and click Next. The Find Printers dialog box appears.

5. In the Location box, type ***NYC*** and then click Find Now.

6. Select the printer HPLJ8100 in the results list and click OK.

7. On the Add Printer Wizard's Default Printer page, select Yes and then click Next.

8. Click Finish.

   You will *not* see a new printer icon in the Printers And Faxes folder because it is not possible to create a printer client to a logical printer on the same computer. If you conduct this exercise on a second computer, you will see the icon for the new printer appear.

Exercise 3: Take a Printer Offline and Print a Test Document

In this exercise, you set the printer you created to offline status. Taking a printer offline causes documents you send to this printer to be held in the print queue while the print device is unavailable. Doing this will prevent error messages about unavailable print devices from occurring in later exercises. Otherwise, Windows Server 2003 will display error messages when it attempts to send documents to the fictional print device that is not actually available to the computer.

1. In the Printers And Faxes window, right-click the HPLJ8100 icon.

2. Choose Use Printer Offline. Notice that the icon appears dimmed to reflect that the printer is not available, and the status appears as Offline.

3. Double-click the HPLJ8100 icon. Notice that the list of documents to be sent to the print device is empty.

4. Click the Start menu, point to Programs, point to Accessories, and then click Notepad.

5. In Notepad, type any sample text that you want.

6. Arrange Notepad and the HPLJ8100 window so that you can see the contents of each.

7. From the File menu in Notepad, select Print. The Print dialog box appears, allowing you to select the printer and print options.

   The Print dialog box displays the location and comment information you entered when you created the printer, and it shows HPLJ8100 as the default and selected printer, and indicates that the printer is offline.

8. Click Print. Notepad briefly displays a message stating that the document is printing on your computer. On a fast computer, you might not see this message.

   In the HPLJ8100–Use Printer Offline window, you will see the document waiting to be sent to the print device. The document is held in the print queue because you took the printer offline. If the printer were online, the document would be sent to the print device.

9. Close Notepad, and click No when prompted to save changes to your document.

10. Select the document in the HPLJ8100 window and, from the Printer menu, select Cancel All Documents. A Printers message box appears, asking if you are sure you want to cancel all documents for HPLJ8100.

11. Click Yes. The document is removed.

12. Close the HPLJ8100–Use Printer Offline window.

13. Close the Printers And Faxes window.

Lesson Review

The following questions are intended to reinforce key information presented in this lesson. If you are unable to answer a question, review the lesson materials and try the question again. You can find answers to the questions in the "Questions and Answers" section at the end of this chapter.

1. You're setting up a printer on your Windows Server 2003 computer. The computer will be used as a print server on your network. You plan to use a print device that's currently connected to the network as a stand-alone print device. Which type of printer should you add to the print server? (Choose all that apply.)

   a. Network

   b. Shared

   c. Local

   d. Remote

2. You're installing a printer on a client computer. The printer will connect to a logical printer installed on a Windows Server 2003 print server. What type or types of information could you provide to set up the printer? (Choose all that apply.)

   a. TCP/IP printer port

   b. Model of the print device

   c. URL to printer on print server

   d. UNC path to print share

   e. Printer driver

3. One of your printers is not working properly, and you want to prevent users from sending print jobs to the logical printer serving that device. What should you do?

   a. Stop sharing the printer

   b. Remove the printer from the Active Directory

   c. Change the printer port

   d. Rename the share

4. You're administering a Windows Server 2003 computer configured as a print server. You want to perform maintenance on a print device connected to the print server. There are several documents in the print queue. You want to prevent the documents from being printed to the printer, but you don't want users to have to resubmit the documents to the printer. What is the best way to do this?

   a. Open the printer's Properties dialog box, select the Sharing tab, and then select the Do Not Share This Printer option.

   b. Open the printer's Properties dialog box and select a port that is not associated with a print device.

   c. Open the printer's queue window, select the first document, and then select Pause from the Document window. Repeat the process for each document.

   d. Open the printer's queue window, and select the Pause Printing option from the Printer menu.

Lesson Summary

- A printer client submits a print job to a print server, which in turn sends the job to the printer. The printer client and the print server each maintain a logical printer representing the printer.

- A local printer is one that supports a printer directly attached to the computer or attached to the network.

- A network printer connects to a logical printer maintained by another computer: a print server.

- Microsoft Windows clients will download the printer driver automatically from the logical printer on the print server. Printers can be added using the printer's Sharing property page.

Lesson 2: Advanced Printer Configuration and Management

In the previous lesson, you learned that the Windows printer model is best leveraged when a logical printer is created to support a physical device—either directly attached to the computer or attached to the network—and when that logical printer is shared to printer clients. That logical printer on the print server becomes a central point of configuration and management. The drivers that you install on the printer are downloaded automatically by Windows clients, and the settings you configure for the printer are distributed as the settings for each of the printer's clients.

This lesson takes this virtualization of printers as logical devices to the next level. After examining printer properties, including printer security, you will learn how to create printer pools to provide faster turnaround for client print jobs. You will also learn how to make better use of your printers by creating more than one logical printer for a device to configure, manage, or monitor print jobs or printer usage more effectively. Finally, you will learn how to manage Active Directory printer objects and Internet printing.

After this lesson, you will be able to

- Manage and configure printer properties
- Create a printer pool
- Configure multiple logical printers to support a single printer
- Manage and connect to printers using Active Directory and Internet Printing Protocol (IPP)

Estimated lesson time: 30 minutes

Managing Printer Properties

Printers and print jobs are managed from their properties dialog boxes. These properties dialog boxes can be accessed from the Printers And Faxes folder. Right-click a printer and select Properties to configure a printer. Double-click a printer and, in the print queue, right-click a print job and choose Properties to configure a print job. The initial properties of a print job are inherited from the properties of the printer itself. But a print job's default properties can be modified independently of the printer's.

Controlling Printer Security

Windows Server 2003 allows you to control printer usage and administration by assigning permissions through the Security tab of the printer's Properties dialog box. You can assign permissions to control who can use a printer and who can administer the printer or documents processed by the printer. A typical printer Security tab of a printer's Properties dialog box is shown in Figure 8-5.

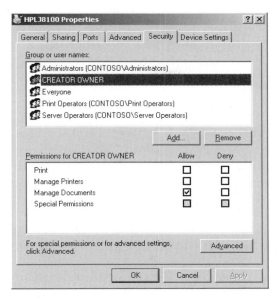

Figure 8-5   The Security tab of a printer's Properties dialog box

You can use a printer's access control list (ACL) to restrict usage of a printer and to delegate administration of a printer to users who are not otherwise administrators. Windows Server 2003 provides three levels of printer permissions: Print, Manage Printers, and Manage Documents.

By default, the Print permission is assigned to the Everyone group. Choosing this permission allows all users to send documents to the printer. To restrict printer usage, remove this permission and assign Allow Print permission to other groups or individual users. Alternatively, you can deny Print permission to groups or users. As with file system ACLs, denied permissions override allowed permissions. Also, like file system ACLs, it is best practice to restrict access by assigning allow permissions to a more restricted group of users rather than granting permissions to a broader group and then having to manage access by assigning additional deny permissions.

The Manage Documents permission provides the ability to cancel, pause, resume, or restart a print job. The Creator Owner group is allowed Manage Documents permission. Because a permission assigned to Creator Owner is inherited by the user that creates an object, this permission enables a user to cancel, pause, resume, or restart a print job that he or she has created. The Administrators, Print Operators and Server Operators groups are also allowed the Manage Documents permission, which means they can cancel, pause, resume, or restart *any* document in the print queue. Those three groups are also assigned the Allow Manage Printers permission, which enables them to modify printer settings and configuration, including the ACL itself.

> **Tip**   If a printer's security is not a major concern, you can delegate administration of the printer by assigning a group, such as the *<Printer>* Users group, Manage Documents, or even Manage Printers permission.

Assigning Forms to Paper Trays

If a print device has multiple trays that regularly hold different paper sizes, you can assign a form to a specific tray. A form defines a paper size. When users print a document of a particular paper size, Windows Server 2003 automatically routes the print job to the paper tray that holds the correct form. Examples of forms include Legal, Letter, A4, Envelope, and Executive.

To assign a form to a paper tray, select the Device Settings tab of the printer's Properties dialog box, as shown in Figure 8-6. The number of trays shown in the Form To Tray Assignment section obviously depends on the type of printer you have installed, and the number of trays it supports. Further down the Device Settings tree are settings to indicate the installation state of printer options, such as additional paper trays, paper handling units, fonts, and printer memory.

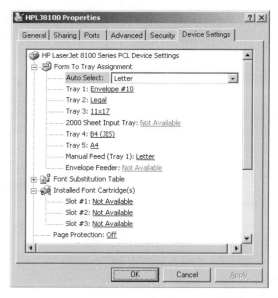

Figure 8-6   The Device Settings tab of a printer's Properties dialog box

Print Job Defaults

The General tab of the printer's Properties dialog box includes a Printing Preferences button, and the Advanced tab includes a Printing Defaults button. Both of these buttons display a dialog box that lets you control the manner in which jobs are printed by the logical printer, including page orientation (portrait or landscape), double-sided printing (if supported), paper source, resolution, and other document settings. These dialog boxes are identical to each other, and are also identical to the dialog box a user receives when clicking Properties in a Print dialog box.

Why are there three print job Properties dialog boxes? The Printing Defaults dialog box configures default settings for all users of the logical printer. If the printer is shared, its printing defaults become the default properties for all printers connected from clients to the shared printer. The Printing Preferences dialog box configures the user-specific, personal preferences for a printer. Any settings in the Printing Preferences dialog box override printing defaults. The Properties dialog box that can be accessed by clicking Properties in a Print dialog box configures the properties for the specific job that is printed. Those properties will override both printing defaults and printing preferences. This triad of print job property sets allows administrators to configure a printer centrally, by setting printing defaults on the shared logical printer, and allows flexibility and decentralized configuration by users or on a document-by-document basis.

Printer Schedule

The Advanced tab of a printer's Properties dialog box, as shown in Figure 8-7, allows you to configure numerous additional settings that drive the behavior of the logical printer, its print processor and spool. Among the more useful and interesting setting is printer's schedule.

Figure 8-7   The Advanced tab of a printer's Properties dialog box

The logical printer's schedule determines when a job is released from the spool, or queue, and sent to the printer itself. A user with Allow Print permission can send a job to the printer at any time, but the job will be held until the printer's schedule allows it to be directed to the printer's port. Such a configuration is not appropriate for normal, day-to-day printers. However a schedule is invaluable for situations in which users are printing large jobs, and you want those jobs to print after hours, or during periods of low use. By configuring a printer's schedule to be available during night hours, users can send the job to the printer during the day, the printer will complete the jobs overnight, and the users can pick up those printing jobs the next morning.

Tip   When you set up a printer pool, place the print devices in the same physical location so that users can easily locate their documents. When users print to a printer pool, there is no way to know which individual printer actually printed the job.

Setting Up a Printer Pool

A printer pool is one logical printer that supports multiple physical printers, either attached to the server, attached to the network, or a combination thereof. When you create a printer pool, users' documents are sent to the first available printer—the logical printer representing the pool automatically checks for an available port.

Printer pooling is configured from the Ports tab of the printer's Properties dialog box. To set up printer pooling, select the Enable Printer Pooling check box, and then select or add the ports containing print devices that will be part of the pool. Figure 8-8 shows a printer pool connected to three network-attached printers.

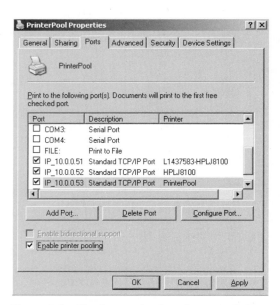

Figure 8-8   The Ports tab of a printer pool's Properties dialog box, showing a three-printer pool

> **Exam Tip**   The driver used by the printer pool must be compatible with all printers to which the pool directs print jobs.

Configuring Multiple Logical Printers for a Single Printer

Although a printer pool is a single logical printer that supports multiple ports, or printers, the reverse structure is more common and more powerful: multiple logical printers supporting a single port, or printer. By creating more than one logical printer directing jobs to the same physical printer, you can configure different properties, printing defaults, security settings, auditing, and monitoring for each logical printer.

For example, you might want to allow executives at Contoso Ltd. to print jobs immediately, bypassing documents that are being printed by other users. To do so, you can create a second logical printer directing to the same port (the same physical printer) as the other users, but with a higher priority.

Use the Add Printer Wizard to generate an additional logical printer. To achieve a multiple logical printer-single port structure, additional printers use the same port as an existing logical printer. The printer name and share name are unique. After the new printer has been added, open its properties and configure the drivers, ACL, printing defaults, and other settings of the new logical printer.

To configure high priority for the new logical printer, click the Advanced tab and set the priority, in the range of 1 (lowest) to 99 (highest). Assuming that you assigned 99 to the executives' logical printer, and 1 to the printer used by all users, documents sent to the executives' printer will print before documents queued in the users' printer. An executive's document will not interrupt a user's print job. However, when the printer is free, it will accept jobs from the higher-priority printer before accepting jobs from the lower-priority printer. To prevent users from printing to the executives' printer, configure its ACL and remove the print permission assigned to the Everyone group, and instead allow only the executives' security group print permission.

> **Exam Tip**   Remember that a printer pool is a single logical printer serving multiple ports; and all other variations on the standard print client—print server—printer structure are achieved by creating multiple logical printers serving a single port.

Windows Server 2003 Printer Integration with Active Directory

The print subsystem of Windows Server 2003 is tightly integrated with Active Directory, making it easy for users and administrators to search for and connect to printers throughout an enterprise. All required interaction between printers and Active Directory is configured, by default, to work without administrative intervention. You only need to make changes if the default behavior is not acceptable.

When a logical printer is added to a Windows Server 2003 print server, the printer is automatically published to Active Directory. The print server creates a printQueue object and populates its properties based on the driver and settings of the logical printer.

Off the Record   The printer objects are not easy to find in Active Directory Users and Computers. You must use the Find Objects In Active Directory button on the MMC toolbar or select View Users, Groups, And Computers As Containers from the View menu, at which point printer objects will become visible inside the print server. The printer is placed in the print server's computer object in the Active Directory service. The object can be moved to any OU.

When any change occurs in the printer's configuration, the Active Directory printer object is updated. All the configuration information is sent again to the Active Directory store even if some of it has remained unchanged.

Planning   Creation and updating of printer objects happens relatively quickly, but objects and attributes must be replicated before they affect the results of a Find Printers operation from a client. Replication latency depends on the size of your enterprise, and your replication topology.

If a print server disappears from the network, its printer object is removed from the Active Directory. The printer Pruner service confirms the existence of shared printers represented in Active Directory by contacting the shared printer every eight hours. A printer object will be pruned if the service is unable to contact the printer two times in a row. This might occur if a print server is taken offline. It will happen regularly if printers are shared on Windows 2000 or Windows XP workstations that are shut off overnight or on weekends. However, a print server will recreate the printer objects for its printers when the machine starts, or when the spooler service is restarted. So, again, administrative intervention is not required.

Publishing Windows Printers

Printers that are added by using the Add Printer Wizard are published by default. The Add Printer Wizard does not allow you to prevent the printer from being published to the Active Directory service when you install or add a printer.

If you want to re-publish a printer (for example, after updating its name or other properties), or if you do *not* want a shared printer published in Active Directory, open the printer's Properties dialog box, click the Sharing tab, and select or clear the List In The Directory check box.

Note   A printer connected to a local port is likely to be detected and installed automatically by Plug And Play. In this case, you must share and publish the printer manually using the Sharing tab.

Logical printers that are shared on computers running Windows NT 4 or Windows NT 3.51 are not published automatically, but can be manually published using the Active Directory Users And Computers MMC console. Simply right-click the OU or other container in which you want to create the printer and choose New Printer.

Planning   You should add only printer objects that map to printers on pre–Windows 2000 computers. Do not add printer objects for printers on computers running Windows 2000 or later; allow those printers to publish themselves automatically.

Manually Configuring Printer Publishing Behavior

All the default system behaviors described above can be modified using local or group policy. Printer policies are located in the Computer Configuration node, under Administrative Templates. For a description of each of these policies, open the Properties dialog box for a specific policy and click the Explain tab.

Printer Location Tracking

Printer location tracking is a feature, disabled by default, that significantly eases a user's search for a printer in a large enterprise by pre-populating the Location box of the Find Printers dialog box, so that the result set will automatically be filtered to list printers in geographic proximity to the user.

To prepare for printer location tracking, you must have one or more sites *or* one or more subnets. Site and subnet objects are created and maintained using the Active Directory Sites And Services MMC snap-in or console. You must also configure the Location tab of the site or subnet Properties dialog box using a naming convention that creates a hierarchy of locations, separated by slashes. For example, the location USA/NYC/1802Americas/42/B might refer to a building at 1802 Avenue of the Americas in Manhattan, on the 42nd floor in Area B. A location may span more than one subnet, or more than one site.

You must then enable printer location tracking using the Pre-Populate Printer Search Location Text policy.

Active Directory is able to identify a computer's site or subnet affiliation based on the computer's IP address. When the Find Printers dialog box is invoked, the computer's location, as defined in its corresponding site or subnet object, will be automatically placed in the Location box. A Browse button will also appear, enabling a user to browse the location hierarchy for printers in other locations.

This powerful feature simplifies printer administration and setup considerably. However, it obviously requires careful planning on the back end to ensure that all subnets are defined, and that a reasonable, hierarchical location naming convention has been applied consistently. More information about this feature is available in the online Help and Support Center.

Internet Printing

Windows Server 2003 supports an additional set of functionality through the Internet Printing Protocol (IPP), which enables users to connect to printers and send print jobs over encapsulated Hypertext Transfer Protocol (HTTP). Internet printing also gives administrators the option to manage and configure printers using any variety of Internet browsers and platforms.

Setting Up Internet Printing

Internet printing is not installed or enabled by default in Windows Server 2003. You must install Internet Information Services (IIS), as discussed in Chapter 6. Internet printing is available for installation when you install IIS. To install Internet printing, perform the following steps:

1. Open Add/Remove Programs in Control Panel and click Add/Remove Windows Components.

2. Select Application Server and click Details.

3. Select Internet Information Services (IIS) and click Details.

4. Select Internet Printing.

Once IIS and Internet printing are installed, you can disable or enable the feature using the IIS snap-in or console. Expand the server's node and click Web Service Extensions. In the details pane, select Internet Printing, and click Prohibit or Allow.

Internet printing creates a Printers virtual directory under the Default Web site. This virtual directory points to %*Systemroot*%\Web\Printers. The printer site is accessed using Microsoft Internet Explorer 4.01 and later by typing the address of the print server in the Address box followed by the Printers virtual directory name. For example, to access the Internet printing page for Server01, type **http://Server01/printers/**.

Note   You can configure authentication and access security for Internet printing using the virtual directory's Properties dialog box.

Using and Managing Internet Printers

You can connect to *http://printserver/printers* to view all printers on the print server. After locating the desired printer and clicking it, a Web page for that printer is displayed.

As a shortcut, if you know the exact name of the printer to which you want to connect, type the address of the printer using the following format:

http://printserver/printersharename/

Once the printer's Web page is displayed, you can connect to or manage the printer, assuming you have been allowed appropriate security permissions. When you click Connect on the printer's Web page, the server generates a .cab file that contains the appropriate printer driver files and downloads the .cab file to the client computer. The printer that is installed is displayed in the Printers folder on the client. The printer can then be used and managed from the Printers And Faxes folder like any other printer. Using a Web browser to manage printers has several advantages:

- It allows you to administer printers from any computer running a Web browser, regardless of whether the computer is running Windows Server 2003 or has the correct printer drivers installed.

- It allows you to customize the interface. For example, you can create your own Web page containing a floor plan with the locations of the printers and the links to the printers.

- It provides a summary page listing the status of all printers on a print server.

- Internet printing can report real-time print device data, such as whether the print device is in power-saving mode, if the printer driver makes such information available. This information is not available from the Printers And Faxes window.

Practice: Advanced Printer Configuration and Management

In this practice, you will configure printer pooling and configure a second logical printer to a single network-attached printer.

Exercise 1: Configure Printer Pooling

1. From the Printers And Faxes window, create a new printer. If you need guidance for how to create a printer, follow the steps in Lesson 1, Exercise 1. The printer should direct to the network address 10.0.0.52 (a new port). Configure the printer as an HP LaserJet 8100 Series PCL, and use PrinterPool as the printer name and the share name. All other properties, including location and comment, are the same as in Lesson 1, Exercise 1.

2. Open the properties of PrinterPool.

3. Click the Ports tab.

4. Select the Enable Printer Pooling check box, and then click the check box next to the port IP_10.0.0.51.

5. Click Apply. Both network ports are now selected.

   Will users sending print jobs to HPLJ8100 benefit from printer pooling?

   No. Printer pooling was configured for the shared printer named PrinterPool. Print jobs sent to PrinterPool can print to the printers at 10.0.0.51 and 10.0.0.52. Print jobs sent to HPLJ8100 can print only to the printer at 10.0.0.51.

Exercise 2: Configure Multiple Logical Printers for a Single Printer

1. From the Printers And Faxes window, create a new printer. If you need guidance for how to create a printer, follow the steps in Lesson 1, Exercise 1. The printer should direct to the network IP address 10.0.0.52 (note the port already exists). Configure the printer as an HP LaserJet 8100 Series PCL, and use PriorityPrinter as the printer name and the share name. All other properties, including location and comment, are the same as in Lesson 1, Exercise 1.

2. Open the properties of PriorityPrinter.

3. Click the Advanced tab.

4. Set the Priority to 99 (highest).

Exercise 3: Examine Active Directory Printer Objects

1. Open Active Directory Users And Computers.

2. From the View menu, select Users, Groups, And Computers As Containers.

3. Expand the Domain Controllers OU. Note that Server01 appears as a subcontainer.

4. Select Server01 in the tree.

   The printer objects appear in the details pane. If objects do not appear for the printers you created in Exercises 1 and 2, wait a few minutes. The print server may take a moment to publish its printers to Active Directory. You may need to press F5 (refresh) to see the printer objects once they are published.

5. Open the properties of the PriorityPrinter object.

   Note the differences between the properties that are published to Active Directory and the properties that you would see for the printer in the Printers And Faxes folder. Active Directory maintains a more limited number of properties—the properties that are most likely to be used in a search for a printer. Note also that changing a property in Active Directory does not change the property of the printer; but changing a property of the printer will, eventually, update the corresponding property in the Active Directory printer object.

Lesson Review

The following questions are intended to reinforce key information presented in this lesson. If you are unable to answer a question, review the lesson materials and try the question again. You can find answers to the questions in the "Questions and Answers" section at the end of this chapter.

1. You're administering a Windows Server 2003 computer configured as a print server. Users in the Marketing group complain that they cannot print documents using a printer on the server. You view the permissions in the printer's properties. The Marketing group is allowed Manage Documents permission. Why can't the users print to the printer?

    a. The Everyone group must be granted the Manage Documents permission.

    b. The Administrators group must be granted the Manage Printers permission.

    c. The Marketing group must be granted the Print permission.

    d. The Marketing group must be granted the Manage Printers permission.

2. You're setting up a printer pool on a Windows Server 2003 computer. The printer pool contains three print devices, all identical. You open the properties for the printer and select the Enable Printer Pooling option on the Ports tab. What must you do next?

    a. Configure the LPT1 port to support three printers.

    b. Select or create the ports mapped to the three printers.

    c. On the Device Settings tab, configure the installable options to support two additional print devices.

    d. On the Advanced tab, configure the priority for each print device so that printing is distributed among the three print devices.

3. You're the administrator of the Windows Server 2003 computer that is configured as a print server, and you want to administer the print services from a Web browser on a client computer. The server is named Mktg1, but you don't know the share name of the printer. Which URL should you use to connect to the printer?

    a. *http://mktg1/printers*

    b. *http://printers/mktg1*

    c. *http://windows/web/printers*

    d. *http://windows/mktg1*

4. You want to configure a logical printer so that large, low-priority documents will be printed overnight. Which of the following options will you configure in the printer's Properties dialog box?

   a. Priority

   b. Available From / To

   c. Start Printing After Last Page Is Spooled

   d. Print Directly To The Printer

   e. Keep Printed Documents

Lesson Summary

The Windows printer model supports the creative and flexible utilization of printers through logical printers. You can add one logical printer that sends jobs to multiple devices (a printer pool) or multiple logical printers that send jobs to one device, with each logical printer preconfigured with printer settings, print defaults, and permissions to support a particular type of printing task.

Printers are published to Active Directory, making it easy for users to find and connect to printers. Windows Server 2003 supports printer location tracking, which further simplifies printer searches. It is even possible to administer and print to printers over the intranet or Internet using IPP.

Lesson 3: Maintaining, Monitoring, and Troubleshooting Printers

Once logical printers have been set up, configured and shared on print servers, and once clients have been connected to those printers, you must begin to maintain and monitor those logical and physical printers. This lesson will give you guidance in the maintenance and troubleshooting of printers in a Windows Server 2003 environment. You will learn to support printer drivers, to redirect printers, to configure performance and utilization logs, and to methodically troubleshoot print errors.

After this lesson, you will be able to

- Manage printer drivers
- Redirect a printer
- Monitor printer performance
- Audit printer access
- Troubleshoot printer failures

Estimated lesson time: 20 minutes

Maintaining Printers

There are no regular maintenance tasks for the print service on a Windows Server 2003 computer. The maintenance tasks defined below are typically performed on a periodic, as-needed basis. Keep in mind that when managing printers, actions may affect an entire printer or all printers on the print server, not just individual print jobs.

Managing Printer Drivers

The first grouping of maintenance tasks relate to drivers on the print server. As mentioned earlier in the lesson, it is helpful to install drivers for all client platforms that will use a particular shared printer. Windows clients will download the driver automatically when they connect to the printer. Drivers for various platforms are installed by clicking Additional Drivers on the Sharing tab of a printer's Properties dialog box.

To update drivers for a single logical printer, select the Advanced tab of the Properties dialog box and click New Driver. You will then be able to select additional drivers by indicating the manufacturer and model, or by clicking Have Disk and providing the manufacturer's drivers.

You can also manage drivers for the print server as a whole. In the Printers And Faxes folder, select Server Properties from the File menu and click the Drivers tab. Here you can add, remove, reinstall, or access the properties of each of the drivers on the print server. Changes made to these drivers will affect all printers on the server.

If you want to list all of the files related to a particular printer driver, open the print server's Drivers tab select the driver, and click Properties. The names and descriptions of all the files that are part of the specific driver will appear. From this list, it is possible to view details regarding any of the files by selecting the file and then clicking Properties.

Redirecting Print Jobs

If a printer is malfunctioning, you can send documents in the queue for that printer to another printer connected to a local port on the computer, or attached to the network. This is called *redirecting* print jobs. It allows users to continue sending jobs to the logical printer, and prevents users with documents in the queue from having to resubmit the jobs.

To redirect a printer, open the printer's Properties dialog and click the Ports tab. Select an existing port or add a port. The check box of the port of the malfunctioning printer is immediately cleared unless printer pooling is enabled, in which case you must manually clear the check box.

Because print jobs have already been prepared for the former printer, the printer on the new port must be compatible with the driver used in the logical printer. All print jobs are now redirected to the new port. You cannot redirect individual documents. In addition, any documents currently printing cannot be redirected.

Monitoring Printers

Windows Server 2003 provides several methods to monitor printers and printing resources.

Using System Monitor and Performance Logs and Alerts

The System Monitor and Performance Logs And Alerts snap-ins, both of which are included in the Performance MMC, allow you to observe real-time performance of printers, log metrics for later analysis, or set alert levels and actions. System Monitor and Performance Logs And Alerts are discussed in detail in Chapter 12. To add a counter to System Monitor, right-click the graph area and choose Add Counters. Select the performance object (in this case Print Queue), the desired counters, and the instance representing the logical printer to monitor.

After selecting Print Queue as the performance object, a list of all available performance counters is provided. You can select any counter and click Explain to learn about that particular performance metric.

The most important performance counters for monitoring printing performance are the following:

- **Bytes Printed/Sec** The number of bytes of raw data per second that are sent to the printer. Low values for this counter can indicate that a printer is underutilized, either because there are no jobs, print queues are not evenly loaded, or the server is too busy. This value varies according to the type of printer. Consult printer documentation for acceptable printer throughput values.

- **Job Errors** Number of job errors. Job errors are typically caused by improper port configuration; check port configuration for invalid settings. A printing job instance will increment this counter only once, even if it happens multiple times. Also, some print monitors do not support job error counters, in which case the counter will remain at 0.

- **Jobs** The number of jobs being spooled.

- **Total Jobs Printed** The number of jobs sent to the printer since the spooler was started.

- **Total Pages Printed** The number of pages printed since the spooler was started. This counter provides a close approximation of printer volume, although it may not be perfect, depending on the type of jobs and the document properties for those jobs.

> **Exam Tip**   The Total Jobs Printed and Total Pages Printed counters are cumulative. They represent the number of jobs or pages printed since the system was started or since the spooler was restarted.

Using System Log

Using Event Viewer, you can examine the System log as a source of information regarding spooler and printer activity. By default, the spooler registers events regarding printer creation, deletion, and modification. You will also find events containing information about printer traffic, hard disk space, spooler errors, and other maintenance issues.

To control or modify spooler event logging, open the Printers And Faxes folder and choose Server Properties from the File menu. Click the Advanced tab to access the properties as shown in Figure 8-9. From this page, you can control printer event log entries and print job notifications. This is also the tab that enables you to move the print spooler folder—an important task when configuring an active print server, or when an existing print spool folder's disk volume becomes full.

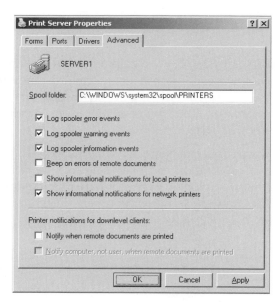

Figure 8-9   The Advanced tab of the Print Server Properties dialog box

Auditing Printer Access

Printer access, like file and folder access, can be audited. You can specify which groups or users and which actions to audit for a particular printer. After enabling object access auditing policy, you can view resulting audit entries using Event Viewer.

To configure auditing for a printer, open its Properties dialog box, click the Security tab, and then click Advanced. Click the Auditing tab and add entries for specific groups or users. For each security principal you add to the audit entry list, you can configure auditing for successful or failed access based on the standard printer permissions, including Print, Manage Documents, and Manage Printers.

You must then enable the Audit Object Access policy, which is located in group or local policy under Computer Configuration\Windows Settings\Security Settings\Local Policies\Audit Policy. After the policy has taken effect, you can examine the Security event log to see and analyze entries made based on printer auditing.

> **Tip**   Printer auditing creates dozens of entries for a single print job. It is therefore only useful when troubleshooting very specific problems. Printer auditing should not be used to monitor use or to bill for printer usage. Instead, performance counters such as Total Jobs Printed or Total Pages Printed should be analyzed.

Troubleshooting Printers

Troubleshooting is an important part of printer management. The following guidance will help you understand, identify, and address the types of incidents and problems that may occur in Windows Server 2003 printing.

Remember when troubleshooting that printing includes multiple components, typically:

- The application that is attempting to print.
- The logical printer on the computer on which the application is running.
- The network connection between the print client and the shared logical printer on the server.
- The logical printer on the server—its spool, drivers, security settings, and so on.
- The network connection between the print server and the printer.
- The printer itself—its hardware, configuration, and status.

An efficient way to solve most problems associated with printing is to troubleshoot each component logically and methodically.

Identify the Scope of Failure

If the user can print a job from another application on his or her computer, the error is most likely related to the failed job's application, rather than with the computer, the network, the print server, or the printer hardware. However, in some cases, using a different driver or data type can solve an application's print errors.

If the user cannot print to the printer from any application, identify whether the user can print to other printers on the same print server, or on other print servers. If all possibilities fail, and if other users can print to the printers on the network, the error is likely localized to the user's computer.

Try creating a local printer on the problematic system that points directly to the printer's port. In other words, bypass the printer server. If this process succeeds, there is a problem on the print server, with communication between the user's system and the print server, or with the printer connections on the client.

Verify That the Print Client Can Connect to the Print Server

You can confirm connectivity between the print client and the print server by opening the printer window from the Printers And Faxes folder on the client computer. If the printer window opens, showing any documents in the printer queue, the client is successfully connecting to the shared printer. An error opening the printer window would indicate a potential networking, authentication, or security permissions problem. Attempt to ping the print server's IP address. Click Start, choose Run, and type ***printserver***.

If the window opens showing the Printers And Faxes folder and any shared folders, the client is connecting to the server. Double-check security permissions on the logical printer.

Verify That the Printer Is Operational

Check the printer itself and ensure that it is in the ready state (ready to print). Print a test page from the printer console. Check the cable connecting the printer to the print server or the network. If the printer is network attached, confirm that the network interface card light is on, indicating network connectivity.

Verify That the Printer Can Be Accessed from the Print Server

Most printers can display their IP address on the printer console or by printing out a configuration page. Confirm that the printer's IP address matches the IP address of the logical printer's port. The port's IP address can be seen in the printer's Properties dialog box on the Ports tab. Ensure that it is possible to communicate with the printer over the network by pinging the printer's IP address.

Verify That the Print Server's Services Are Running

Using the Services MMC, check that services required for the printer are working properly. For example, confirm that the remote procedure call (RPC) service is running on the print server. RPC is required for standard network connections to shared printers. Confirm also that the print spooler service is running on the print server.

> **Tip**   The Net Stop Spooler command and Net Start Spooler command can be executed from the command prompt to restart the print spooler service. If you restart the spooler using command-line or user interface methods, all documents in all printer queues on the server are deleted.

You can also examine the volume on which the spool folder is stored to ensure that there is sufficient disk space for spooling. The spool folder location can be discovered and modified in the Server Properties dialog box, which you can access by choosing Server Properties from the File menu of the Printers And Faxes folder.

> **Note**   By default, the spool folder points to %*Systemroot*%\System32\Spool\Printers. For a high-volume print server, consider moving the spool folder to a partition other than the system or boot partition. If the partition where the spool folder resides fills to capacity with print jobs, printing will stop and, more importantly, the operating system might become unstable.

You should also look at the System log to see if the spooler has registered any error events, and, in the Printers And Faxes Folder, make sure that the printer is not in Offline mode.

Attempt to print a job from an application on the print server. If you can print to the printer from the print server, the problem is not with the printer. If you cannot print to the printer from an application on the print server, create a new printer directed at the same port and attempt to print to the new printer. If that job succeeds, there is a problem in the configuration of the original logical printer. If that job is unsuccessful, there is a problem communicating with the printer, or with the hardware itself.

Practice: Troubleshooting a Printer

In this practice, you will redirect a printer. Redirecting a printer is useful in both proactive and reactive troubleshooting. If you are going to take a printer offline, you can redirect its logical printer(s) to another device that is compatible with the logical printer's driver. If a printer fails due to a paper jam or other error, you can also redirect the jobs that have already been sent to, and spooled by, the logical printer, so that users do not have to wait for the failed printer to be repaired, and do not have to resubmit their jobs.

Note that additional troubleshooting practice is included in the "Case Scenario Exercise" and "Troubleshooting Lab" sections of this chapter.

Exercise 1: Redirect a Printer

If a printing device fails, you can redirect print jobs to another printer. Assume you are printing to HPLJ8100. While your job is in the queue, a job ahead of yours encounters a paper jam.

1. Open the Printers And Faxes folder and ensure that HPLJ8100 is offline. If it is not, right-click the printer and choose Use Printer Offline. This will prevent generating errors because the printer is directed to a non-existent network port.

2. Open Notepad and enter text into the blank document.

3. Choose the Print command from the File menu and select HPLJ8100 as the printer.

4. In the Printers And Faxes folder, double-click HPLJ8100 to open its printer window. Confirm that your print job is in the queue.

5. From the Printer menu, choose Properties.

6. Click the Ports tab.

7. As it was configured in Lesson 1, the printer should use the network port IP_10.0.0.51.

8. Select the check box next to the port IP_10.0.0.52.

9. Click OK. You have now redirected the printer. All jobs in the queue, except any in-progress jobs, will be directed to the new port. The printer attached to the new port must be compatible with the driver used by this logical printer, because jobs have already been processed and spooled based on the existing driver.

Lesson Review

The following questions are intended to reinforce key information presented in this lesson. If you are unable to answer a question, review the lesson materials and try the question again. You can find answers to the questions in the "Questions and Answers" section at the end of this chapter.

1. A Windows 2003 Server is configured as a print server. In the middle of the work-day, the printer fuse fails, and must be replaced. Users have already submitted jobs to the printer, which uses IP address 192.168.1.81. An identical printer uses address 192.168.1.217, and is supported by other logical printers on the server. What actions should you take so that users' jobs can be printed without resubmission?

    a. In the failed printer's Properties dialog box, select Enable Printer Pooling.

    b. At the command prompt, type **Net Stop Spooler**.

    c. At the command prompt, type **Net Start Spooler**.

    d. In the failed printer's Properties dialog box, select the port 192.168.1.217.

    e. In the failed printer's Properties dialog box, click Add Port.

    f. In the Printers And Faxes folder, right-click the failed printer and choose Use Offline.

2. You're setting up printing on a Windows Server 2003 computer. You attach a printer, configure a logical printer, and submit documents for printing, but the documents do not print completely and sometimes come out garbled. What is the most likely cause of the problem?

    a. There's insufficient hard disk space for spooling.

    b. You're using an incorrect printer driver.

    c. The selected port is not correct.

    d. The device settings for the printer are using an incorrect font substitution.

3. Which of the following options will give you the clearest picture of printer utilization—allowing you to understand the consumption of printer toner and paper?

    a. Configure auditing for a logical printer and audit for successful use of the Print permission by the Everyone system group.

    b. Export the System log to a comma-delimited text file and use Excel to analyze spooler events.

    c. Configure a performance log and monitor the Total Pages Printed counter for each logical printer.

    d. Configure a performance log and monitor the Jobs counter for each logical counter.

Lesson Summary

- The drivers for a logical printer can be updated or added using the properties of that printer. Drivers can be added, removed, or reinstalled for all printers on a print server using the Drivers tab of the Server Properties dialog box.

- If a printer is to be taken offline, or has already failed, you can redirect all its jobs, except those in progress, to another printer by adding or selecting the new printer's port in the properties of the original logical printer. The alternate port must represent a printer which is compatible with the driver in use by the original printer.

- The Total Jobs Printed and Total Pages Printed performance counters can help you monitor printer utilization. Bytes Printed/Sec and Errors counters will help you monitor potential problems with a printer.

- System events, logged by the spooler service, and security events, logged by enabling auditing on a printer and the Audit Object Access policy, can provide additional insight into printer functionality.

- Because the Windows Server 2003 printer model is modular, with the printer itself, the logical printer on a print server, and the printer on a client connected to the server's shared printer, you can methodically troubleshoot a printer failure by addressing each component and the links between those components.

Case Scenario Exercise

Printer usage is going through the roof at Contoso Ltd., and the chief operating officer has asked you to begin billing for printer usage by the Marketing and Sales departments, each of which are heavy users of printers.

Think Through Your Solution

1. What is the most effective way to monitor printer usage when you are billing for printer use?

   Windows Server 2003 adds a Printer Queue performance object, which allows you to monitor printer usage for each logical printer defined on the server. The Total Pages Printed counter provides important information about printer use. It is not perfect, because certain document properties and special printing features (such as a booklet printing or multiple-pages-per-page setting) will affect the printer hardware directly without the spool's being able to track their effects. However, it is the best approximation available. By configuring a performance log and capturing the counter, you can later analyze the log and bill for usage.

2. How can you monitor the Total Pages Printed counter for the Sales and the Marketing group separately?

   The Total Pages Printed counter captures performance data for a single, logical printer. To monitor the two groups separately, you must configure two separate logical printers. Each printer will address the same port—the same physical printer—but will allow only users from one group to print.

Set Up the Printers

If you are unsure how to install a logical printer, refer to Lesson 1, Exercise 1. Create two printers using the Add Printer Wizard. Use the settings described in the following tables to complete the Add Printer Wizard and the Add Standard TCP/IP Port Wizard.

Table 8-1   Sales Printer

Description	Setting
Local or Network Printer	Local printer attached to this computer. Do *not* use Plug and Play to detect the printer.
Select a Printer Port	Create a New Port: "Standard TCP/IP Port"
Printer Name or IP Address	10.0.0.53
Port Name	IP_10.0.0.53
Device Type	Hewlett Packard Jet Direct
Manufacturer	HP
Printer model	HP LaserJet 8100 Series PCL

Table 8-1   Sales Printer (Continued)

Description	Setting
Driver to use	Keep existing driver
Printer name	SalesPrinter
Default printer option	No
Share name	SalesPrinter
Location	NYC/US/1802Americas/42/B
Comment	Black and White Output Laser Printer–High Volume
Print a test page	No

Table 8-2   Marketing Printer

Description	Setting
Local or Network Printer	Local printer attached to this computer. Do *not* use Plug and Play to detect the printer.
Select a Printer Port	Use the following port: IP_10.0.0.53
Manufacturer	HP
Printer model	HP LaserJet 8100 Series PCL
Driver to use	Keep existing driver
Printer name	MarketingPrinter
Default printer option	No
Share name	MarketingPrinter
Location	NYC/US/1802Americas/42/B
Comment	Black and White Output Laser Printer–High Volume
Print a test page	No

Create Printer Users Groups

To assign permissions to the printers, you will need security groups. (If you are unsure how to create groups, refer to Chapter 4.) Create two security groups of Domain Local scope: Marketing Printer Users and Sales Printer Users.

Assign Permissions to the Printers

1. From the Printers And Faxes folder, open the Properties page of the SalesPrinter.
2. Click the Security tab.
3. Select the Everyone group and click Remove.
4. Click Add.
5. Type Sales Printer Users and click OK.

6. Assign Allow Print permission to the Sales Printer Users.

7. Repeat steps 1 through 6 to allow only the Marketing Printer Users group Print permission to the MarketingPrinter.

Configure a Performance Log

1. Open the Performance MMC from the Administrative Tools group.

2. Expand the Performance Logs And Alerts node and select Counter Logs.

3. Right-click Counter Logs and choose New Log Settings.

4. Enter the log name **Printer Utilization**.

5. Click OK. The Printer Utilization log's Properties dialog box appears.

6. Click Add Counters.

7. From the Performance Object drop-down list, select Print Queue.

8. In the Counters list, select Total Pages Printed.

9. In the Instances list, select SalesPrinter.

10. Click Add.

11. In the Instances list, select MarketingPrinter.

12. Click Add.

13. Click Close. The Printer Utilization dialog box indicates that the log will now track Total Pages Printed for each print queue.

14. Select 30 minutes as the sampling interval by typing **30** in the Interval box and selecting Minutes from the Units drop-down list.

Note   Because Total Pages Printed is cumulative, from the time a print server starts, or from the time the spooler service is restarted, it is unnecessary to maintain a short sampling interval. You could sample at very long intervals as long as the server or the spooler service is not restarted in the middle of those intervals.

15. Click OK to close the Printer Utilization dialog box.

16. If you have not configured another performance log on this computer, you will be prompted to create the "C:\Perflogs" folder, in which logs are saved by default. Click Yes to confirm.

17. In the Performance Logs detail pane, the Printer Utilization log is green, indicating that it is running.

18. Stop the log by right-clicking it and choosing Stop.

Once a performance log has been created, you can examine the log in System Monitor. Click the View Log Data button on the System Monitor toolbar and you can add the performance log you generated. This particular log will not be valid for two reasons. First, two samples must be saved in a performance log for System Monitor to make use of the log's data. Unless you wait 60 minutes, or decrease the sampling interval, you will not be able to load the log. Second, Total Pages Printed will not increment because the printer does not exist, so pages do not print.

Troubleshooting Lab

The Marketing department is complaining about print quality on the MarketingPrinter. When they print from their Windows XP desktops using Microsoft Office applications, documents print perfectly. But when they print from Adobe applications, the documents do not always reflect the desired results. The Sales department, which uses a mix of Windows 2000 and Windows XP workstations, Microsoft Office, and Microsoft Customer Relationship Management (CRM), does not report any problems with the SalesPrinter.

As you consider the problem, it occurs to you that some applications produce different results depending on whether the printer is using PostScript or a non-PostScript driver.

Analyze the Solution

Where should you consider adding PostScript drivers? (Choose all that apply.)

    a. The Server Properties dialog box of the print server.

    b. The printer Properties dialog box of the MarketingPrinter.

    c. The printer Properties dialog box of the SalesPrinter.

    d. The printers installed on the desktops of each marketing department user.

        The correct answer is b. Adding the PostScript driver for the MarketingPrinter will cause that printer to use the PostScript driver, without affecting the SalesPrinter. Although each client printer will require the PostScript driver as well, you do not need to add the driver manually. Windows 2000 and Windows XP clients will download the new driver automatically.

Change the Printer Driver

    1. Open the Printers And Faxes folder.

    2. Open the Properties dialog box of the MarketingPrinter.

    3. Click the Advanced tab.

    4. Click New Driver. The Add Printer Driver Wizard appears.

    5. Click Next.

6. Select the Manufacturer: HP.

7. Select the Printer: HP LaserJet 8100 Series PS.

8. Click Next, and then click Finish.

9. Notice that the PostScript driver is now the default driver.

10. Click the Driver drop-down list and you will find that the former, PCL driver is still listed. If changing the driver to PostScript does not solve the problem, you can easily switch back to the PCL driver.

Chapter Summary

- Printer implementation in Windows Server 2003 is modular, consisting of the printer hardware itself, a print server with a shared, logical printer representing the physical printer by indicating that printer's local or network attached port, and a logical printer on a client that connects to the shared printer on the print server. Understanding the structure and the terminology is critical because documentation and the user interface is inconsistent and sometimes misleading.

- Shared printers are published to Active Directory, which enables users to easily search for printers based on location or other printer properties.

- When a user finds a printer in the Find Printers dialog box, double-clicking the printer installs the printer to the user's computer. Computers running the Windows operating system download the driver from the server automatically if an administrator has loaded all appropriate drivers in the shared printer.

- A single logical printer can direct jobs to more than one port, creating a printer pool.

- A single physical printer (port) can be served by multiple logical printers, each of which can configure unique properties, drivers, settings, permissions, or monitoring characteristics. Such a structure enables you to leverage printer hardware with incredible flexibility.

- Printers can be managed, installed, and printed to via the Web if Internet Printing has been installed and enabled on the print server.

- Event logs and performance counters allow you to monitor printers for potential signals of trouble, and for utilization statistics.

Exam Highlights

Before taking the exam, review the key points and terms that are presented below to help you identify topics you need to review. Return to the lessons for additional practice and review the "Further Readings" sections in Part 2 for pointers to more information about topics covered by the exam objectives.

Key Points

- The important distinction between a printer—the hardware, also known as the print device or physical printer—and a logical printer—also known as a printer.

- The difference between a printer in the Printers And Faxes folder and an Active Directory printer object.

- How to manage printer ports. Understand the difference between, and how to configure, printer pooling and printer redirection.

- How to configure multiple logical printers to a single physical printer. Be familiar with the variety of properties that can be configured uniquely in each logical printer, including security permissions.

- How to monitor printer utilization and troubleshoot printer problems.

Key Terms

Logical printer   Represents a physical printer by serving the printer's port. The logical printer includes the queue, the drivers, settings, permissions, and printing defaults that manage the creation of a print job for a printer.

Network printer   In the context of the Microsoft Windows user interface, a logical printer that is a client of—that is connected to—a shared logical printer on another computer. Not to be confused with a network attached printer, which is served by a *local printer* on the print server.

Questions and Answers

Page
8-13

Lesson 1 Review

1. You're setting up a printer on your Windows Server 2003 computer. The computer will be used as a print server on your network. You plan to use a print device that's currently connected to the network as a stand-alone print device. Which type of printer should you add to the print server? (Choose all that apply.)

    a. Network

    b. Shared

    c. Local

    d. Remote

    The correct answers are b and c. A local printer is one that supports a printer directly attached to the computer or a stand-alone network attached printer. For the computer to act as a print server, the printer must be shared.

2. You're installing a printer on a client computer. The printer will connect to a logical printer installed on a Windows Server 2003 print server. What type or types of information could you provide to set up the printer? (Choose all that apply.)

    a. TCP/IP printer port

    b. Model of the print device

    c. URL to printer on print server

    d. UNC path to print share

    e. Printer driver

    The correct answers are c and d. When you add a network printer, you can search for the printer in Active Directory, enter the UNC or URL to the printer, or browse for the printer. When you connect to the printer, the model is specified by the shared logical printer, and the driver is downloaded automatically.

3. One of your printers is not working properly, and you want to prevent users from sending print jobs to the logical printer serving that device. What should you do?

    a. Stop sharing the printer

    b. Remove the printer from the Active Directory

    c. Change the printer port

    d. Rename the share

    The correct answer is a. If you stop sharing the printer, users will no longer be able to use the print device. You can use the Sharing tab in the printer's properties dialog box to stop sharing the printer.

4. You're administering a Windows Server 2003 computer configured as a print server. You want to perform maintenance on a print device connected to the print server. There are several documents in the print queue. You want to prevent the documents from being printed to the printer, but you don't want users to have to resubmit the documents to the printer. What is the best way to do this?

   a. Open the printer's Properties dialog box, select the Sharing tab, and then select the Do Not Share This Printer option.

   b. Open the printer's Properties dialog box and select a port that is not associated with a print device.

   c. Open the printer's queue window, select the first document, and then select Pause from the Document window. Repeat the process for each document.

   d. Open the printer's queue window, and select the Pause Printing option from the Printer menu.

   The correct answer is d. When you select the Pause Printing option, the documents will remain in the print queue until you resume printing. This option applies to all documents in the queue.

Lesson 2 Review

Page 8-27

1. You're administering a Windows Server 2003 computer configured as a print server. Users in the Marketing group complain that they cannot print documents using a printer on the server. You view the permissions in the printer's properties. The Marketing group is allowed Manage Documents permission. Why can't the users print to the printer?

   a. The Everyone group must be granted the Manage Documents permission.

   b. The Administrators group must be granted the Manage Printers permission.

   c. The Marketing group must be granted the Print permission.

   d. The Marketing group must be granted the Manage Printers permission.

   The correct answer is c. The Print permission allows users to send documents to the printer.

2. You're setting up a printer pool on a Windows Server 2003 computer. The printer pool contains three print devices, all identical. You open the properties for the printer and select the Enable Printer Pooling option on the Ports tab. What must you do next?

   a. Configure the LPT1 port to support three printers.

   b. Select or create the ports mapped to the three printers.

   c. On the Device Settings tab, configure the installable options to support two additional print devices.

    d. On the Advanced tab, configure the priority for each print device so that printing is distributed among the three print devices.

The correct answer is b. Printer pooling is configured from the Ports tab of the printer's properties dialog box. To set up printer pooling, select the Enable Printer Pooling check box, and then select or create the ports corresponding to printers that will be part of the pool.

3. You're the administrator of the Windows Server 2003 computer that is configured as a print server, and you want to administer the print services from a Web browser on a client computer. The server is named Mktg1, but you don't know the share name of the printer. Which URL should you use to connect to the printer?

    a. *http://mktg1/printers*

    b. *http://printers/mktg1*

    c. *http://windows/web/printers*

    d. *http://windows/mktg1*

The correct answer is a. To gain access to all printers on a print server by using a Web browser, open the Web browser and connect to *http://printserver/printers* to view a list of printers. From there you can access a specific printer. If you want to gain access to a specific printer without first viewing a list of all printers, use *http://printserver/printersharename*.

4. You want to configure a logical printer so that large, low-priority documents will be printed overnight. Which of the following options will you configure in the printer's Properties dialog box?

    a. Priority

    b. Available From / To

    c. Start Printing After Last Page Is Spooled

    d. Print Directly To The Printer

    e. Keep Printed Documents

The correct answer is b. The printer schedule allows a printer to receive jobs and hold them until the printer is available. The default setting, Always Available, sends a job to the printer when it is free. When you configure Available From / To, you specify the hours during which print jobs can be sent to the printer.

Lesson 3 Review

1. A Windows 2003 Server is configured as a print server. In the middle of the workday, the printer fuse fails, and must be replaced. Users have already submitted jobs to the printer, which uses IP address 192.168.1.81. An identical printer uses address 192.168.1.217, and is supported by other logical printers on the server. What actions should you take so that users' jobs can be printed without resubmission?

   a. In the failed printer's Properties dialog box, select Enable Printer Pooling.

   b. At the command prompt, type **Net Stop Spooler**.

   c. At the command prompt, type **Net Start Spooler**.

   d. In the failed printer's Properties dialog box, select the port 192.168.1.217.

   e. In the failed printer's Properties dialog box, click Add Port.

   f. In the Printers And Faxes folder, right-click the failed printer and choose Use Offline.

   The correct answer is d. Because the other printer is already supported by logical printers on the server, there is no need to add a new port. Simply select the existing port.

2. You're setting up printing on a Windows Server 2003 computer. You attach a printer, configure a logical printer, and submit documents for printing, but the documents do not print completely and sometimes come out garbled. What is the most likely cause of the problem?

   a. There's insufficient hard disk space for spooling.

   b. You're using an incorrect printer driver.

   c. The selected port is not correct.

   d. The device settings for the printer are using an incorrect font substitution.

   The correct answer is b. An incorrect printer driver can yield documents that are garbled or incompletely printed. Install the correct printer driver.

3. Which of the following options will give you the clearest picture of printer utilization—allowing you to understand the consumption of printer toner and paper?

   a. Configure auditing for a logical printer and audit for successful use of the Print permission by the Everyone system group.

   b. Export the System log to a comma-delimited text file and use Excel to analyze spooler events.

    c. Configure a performance log and monitor the Total Pages Printed counter for each logical printer.

    d. Configure a performance log and monitor the Jobs counter for each logical counter.

The correct answer is c. The Total Pages Printed counter gives the clearest picture of printer toner and paper consumption, as such consumption is most closely associated with the number of pages, not the number of jobs, printed. The spooler and object access events logged in the System and Security logs will be cumbersome at best and, most likely, completely unhelpful in this task.

9 Maintaining the Operating System

Exam Objectives in this Chapter:

- Manage software update infrastructure
- Manage software site licensing

Why This Chapter Matters

In 2002, the Code Red worm and its derivatives, Code Red v2 and Code Red II, tore through the Internet, exploiting a hole in Microsoft Index Server. Although the worms themselves did not cause tremendous damage, their astounding infection rate was a wake-up call to the tens of thousands of IT professionals who had spent hours upon hours securing and updating their systems. The wake-up call was particularly poignant because Microsoft had patched the Index Server vulnerability a month before the worms wreaked their havoc. It was clearer than ever that servers and workstations must be kept current with code updates. Nor was it a wise strategy to wait for Service Pack 3 before deploying Service Pack 2, as many enterprises had done in the past. Software updates now became part and parcel of the security strategies of an organization.

In this chapter, you will learn how to apply Microsoft Software Update Services (SUS) to keep servers and desktops up to date. SUS allows an enterprise to centralize the downloading, testing, approval, and distribution of Windows-critical updates and Windows security rollups. This service will play a significant role in maintaining the integrity of your enterprise network. You will also learn how to deploy Service Packs to one or more machines. Finally, you will examine the components of site software licensing.

Lessons in this Chapter:

Before You Begin

This chapter presents the skills and concepts related to administering Windows Software Update Services, service pack deployment, and licensing. Although it is advantageous to have two computers (a Microsoft Windows Server 2003 computer and a client running Windows XP or Windows 2000 Professional), you can complete the exercises in this chapter with only one computer. Prepare the following:

- A Windows Server 2003 (Standard Edition or Enterprise Edition) installed as Server01 and configured as a domain controller in the domain *contoso.com*

- A first-level organizational unit (OU) named Desktops

- Networking configured to provide Internet connectivity

Lesson 1: Software Update Services

To maintain a secure computing environment, it is critical to keep systems up to date with security patches. Since 1998, Microsoft has provided Windows Update as a Web-based source of information and downloads. With Windows XP and Windows 2000 service pack 3, Microsoft added Automatic Updates, whereby a system automatically connects to Windows Update and downloads any new, applicable patches or "hot-fixes." Although the Windows Update servers and Automatic Updates client achieve the goal of keeping systems current, many administrators are uncomfortable with either computers or users deciding which patches should be installed, because a patch might interfere with the normal functioning of a business-critical application.

The latest improvements to these technologies deliver Software Update Services (SUS). SUS is a client-server application that enables a server on your intranet to act as a point of administration for updates. You can approve updates for SUS clients, which then download and install the approved updates automatically without requiring local administrator account interaction.

In this lesson you will learn to install and administer SUS on a Windows Server 2003 computer. The following lesson will guide you through issues related to client configuration.

After this lesson, you will be able to

- Install SUS on a Windows Server 2003 computer
- Configure SUS
- Install or deploy Automatic Updates for SUS clients
- Administer SUS and Automatic Updates
- Monitor, troubleshoot, back up, and restore SUS

Estimated lesson time: 30 minutes

Understanding SUS

Since 1998, Microsoft Windows operating systems have supported Windows Update, a globally distributed source of updates. Windows Update servers interact with client-side software to identify critical updates, security rollups, and enhancements that are appropriate to the client platform, and then to download approved patches.

Administrators wanted a more centralized solution that would assure more direct control over updates that are installed on their clients. Software Update Services is a response to that need. SUS includes several major components:

- **Software Update Services, running on an Internet Information Services (IIS) server**   The server-side component is responsible for synchronizing information about available updates and, typically, downloading updates from the Microsoft Internet-based Windows Update servers or from other intranet servers running SUS.

- **The SUS administration Web site**   All SUS administration is Web-based. After installing and configuring SUS, administration typically consists of ensuring that the SUS server is synchronizing successfully, and approving updates for distribution to network clients.

- **Automatic Updates**   The Automatic Updates client is responsible for downloading updates from either Windows Update or an SUS server, and installing those updates based on a schedule or an administrator's initiation.

- **Group Policy settings**   Automatic Updates clients can be configured to synchronize from an SUS server rather than the Windows Update servers by modifying the clients' registries or, more efficiently, by configuring Windows Update policies in a Group Policy Object (GPO).

Installing SUS on a Windows Server 2003 Computer

SUS has both client and server components. The server component runs on a Windows 2000 Server (Service Pack 2 or later) or a Windows Server 2003 computer. Internet Information Services (IIS) must be installed before setting up SUS and, as you learned in Chapter 6, "Files and Folders," IIS is not installed by default on Windows Server 2003. For information about how to install IIS, see Chapter 6.

SUS is not included with the Windows Server 2003 media, but it is a free download from the Microsoft SUS Web site at *http://go.microsoft.com/fwlink/?LinkID=6930*.

Note   The SUS download is not available in every localized language. However, this download determines the installation and administrative interface for the server component only. Patches for *all* locales can be made available through SUS.

After downloading the latest version of SUS, double-click the file and the installation routine will start. After you agree to the license agreement, choose Custom setup and the Setup Wizard will prompt you for the following information:

- **Choose File Locations**   Each Windows Update patch consists of two components: the patch file itself and metadata that specifies the platforms and languages to which the patch applies. SUS always downloads metadata, which you will use to approve updates and which clients on your intranet will retrieve from SUS. You can choose whether to download the files themselves and, if so, where to save the updates.

> **Tip**   If you elect to maintain the update files on Microsoft Windows Update servers, Automatic Updates clients will connect to your SUS server to obtain the list of approved updates and will then connect to Microsoft Windows Update servers to download the files. You can thereby maintain control of client updating and take advantage of the globally dispersed hosting provided by Microsoft.

If you choose the Save The Updates To This Local Folder option, the Setup Wizard defaults to the drive with the most free space, and will create a folder called SUS on that drive. You can save the files to any NT file system (NTFS) partition; Microsoft recommends a minimum of 6 gigabytes (GB) of free space.

> **Note**   The SUS partition and the system partition must be formatted as NTFS.

- **Language Settings**   Although the SUS administrative interface is provided in English and a few additional languages, patches are released for all supported locales. This option specifies the localized versions of Windows servers or clients that you support in your environment.

- **Handling New Versions Of Previously Approved Updates**   Occasionally, an update itself is updated. You can direct SUS to approve automatically updates that are new versions of patches that you have already approved, or you can continue to approve each update manually.

- **Ready To Install**   Before installation begins, the Setup Wizard will remind you of the URL clients should point to, *http://SUS_servername*. Note this path because you will use it to configure network clients.

- **Installing Microsoft Software Update Services**   The Setup Wizard installs SUS.

- **Completing the Microsoft Software Update Services Setup Wizard**   The final page of the Setup Wizard indicates the URL for the SUS administration site, *http://SUS_servername/SUSAdmin*. Note this path as well, because you will administer SUS from that Web location. When you click Finish, your Web browser will start and you will be taken automatically to the SUS administration page.

Software Update Services installs the following three components on the server:

■ The Software Update Synchronization Service, which downloads content to the SUS server

■ An IIS Web site that services update requests from Automatic Updates clients

■ An SUS administration Web page, from which you can synchronize the SUS server and approve updates

---

IIS Lockdown

When run on a Windows 2000 server, the SUS Setup Wizard launches the IIS Lockdown Wizard to secure IIS 5.0. Windows Server 2003 is locked down by default, so IIS Lockdown is not necessary.

If you have Web applications running on an IIS server, those applications may not function properly after SUS has been installed. You can re-enable Internet Server Application Programming Interface (ISAPI) filters and open other components that are secured by IIS Lockdown. However, due to the sensitive nature of operating system updates, you should consider running SUS on a dedicated server without other IIS applications.

Configuring and Administering SUS

You will perform three administrative tasks related to SUS: configuring SUS settings, synchronizing content and approving content. These tasks are performed using the SUS Administration Web site, shown in Figure 9-1, which can be accessed by navigating to *http://SUS_servername/SUSAdmin* with Internet Explorer 5.5 or later, or by opening Microsoft Software Update Services from the Administrative Tools programs group. The administration of SUS is entirely Web-based.

Note   You may need to add Server01 to the Local Intranet trusted site list to access the site. Open Internet Explorer and choose Internet Options from the Tools menu. Click the Security tab. Select Trusted Sites and click Sites. Add Server01 and Server01.contoso.com to the trusted site list.

Note   You must be a local administrator on the SUS server to administer and configure Software Update Services. This is another consideration as you review dedicating the SUS server. With a dedicated SUS server, you can delegate administration of SUS without inadvertently delegating authority over other server roles or applications.

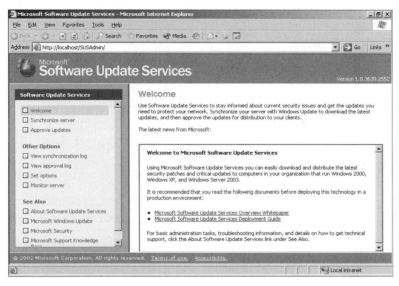

Figure 9-1   The SUS Administration Web site

Configuring Software Update Services

Although some of the configuration of SUS can be specified during a custom installation, all SUS settings are accessible from the SUS Administration Web page. From the Software Update Services administration page, click Set Options in the left navigation bar. The Set Options page is shown in Figure 9-2.

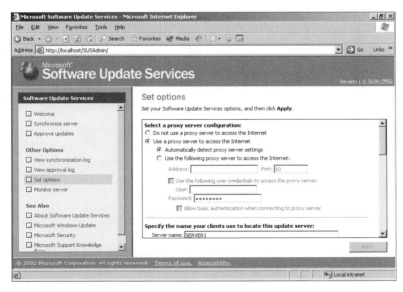

Figure 9-2   The SUS Set Options page

The configuration settings are as follows:

- **Proxy server configuration**   If the server running SUS connects to Windows Update using a proxy server, you must configure proxy settings.

> **Tip**   Although the SUS server can be configured to access Windows Update through a proxy server that requires authentication, the Automatic Updates client cannot access Windows Update if the proxy server requires authentication. If your proxy server requires authentication, you can configure SUS to authenticate, and you must store all update content—files as well as metadata—locally.

- **DNS name of the SUS server**   In the Server Name box, type the fully qualified domain name (FQDN) of the SUS server, for example, **sus1.contoso.com**.
- **Content source**   The first SUS servDer you install will synchronize its content from Microsoft Windows Update. Additional SUS servers can synchronize from Windows Update, from a "parent" SUS server, or from a manually created content distribution point. See the sidebar, "SUS Topology" for more information.
- **New versions of approved updates**   The Set Options page allows you to modify how SUS handles new versions of previously approved updates. This option is discussed earlier in the lesson.
- **File storage**   You can modify the storage of metadata and update files. This option is also discussed earlier in the lesson.

> **Tip**   If you change the storage location from a Windows Update server to a local server folder, you should immediately perform a synchronization to download the necessary packages to the selected location.

- **Languages**   This setting determines the locale specific updates that are synchronized. Select only languages for locales that you support in your environment.

> **Tip**   If you remove a locale, the packages that have been downloaded are not deleted; however, clients will no longer receive those packages. If you *add* a locale, perform a manual synchronization to download appropriate packages for the new locale.

SUS Topology

Software Update Services is all about enabling you to control the approval and distribution of updates from Microsoft Windows Update. In a small organization, SUS can be as simple as one server, synchronizing from Windows Update and providing a list of approved updates to clients.

In a larger organization, SUS topologies can be developed to make SUS more scalable and efficient. Although the 70-290 certification exam expects you only to administer existing topologies, it is helpful to understand some of the design possibilities:

- **Multiple server topology** Each SUS server synchronizes content from Windows Update, and manages its own list of approved updates. This would be a variation of a single-server model, and each SUS server administrator would have control over that server's list of approved updates. Such a configuration would also allow an organization to maintain a variety of patch and update configurations (one per SUS server). Clients can be directed to obtain updates from an SUS server with the appropriate list of approved updates.

- **Strict parent/child topology** A "parent" SUS server synchronizes content from Windows Update and stores updates in a local folder. The SUS administrator then approves updates. Other SUS servers in the enterprise synchronize from the parent, and are configured, on the Set Options page, to Synchronize List Of Approved Items Updated From This Location (Replace Mode). This setting causes the child SUS servers to synchronize both the update files and the list of approved updates. Network clients can then be configured to retrieve updates from the SUS server in or closest to their site. In this configuration (Synchronize List Of Approved Items), administrators of child SUS servers *cannot* approve or disapprove updates; that task is managed on the parent SUS server only.

- **Loose parent/child topology** A "parent" SUS server synchronizes content from Windows Update and stores updates in a local folder. Other SUS servers in the enterprise synchronize from the parent. Unlike the strict configuration, these additional SUS servers do not synchronize the list of approved updates, so administrators of those servers can approve or disapprove updates independently. Although this topology increases administrative overhead, it is helpful when an organization wants to minimize Internet exposure (only the parent SUS server needs to connect to the Internet), and requires (as in the multiple-server model) distributed power of update approval or a variety of client patch and update configurations.

> ■ **Test/production topology**   This model allows an organization to create a testing or staging of updates. The parent SUS server downloads updates from Windows Update and an administrator approves updates to be tested. One or more clients retrieve updates from the parent SUS server and act as test platforms. Once updates have been approved, tested, and verified, the contents of the parent SUS server are copied to a manually created content distribution point on a second IIS server. Production SUS servers synchronize both the updates and the list of approved updates from the manual content distribution point. The steps for configuring such a manual distribution point are detailed in the Software Update Service Deployment White Paper, available from the Microsoft SUS Web site.

Synchronizing SUS

On the SUS Administration Web page, click Synchronize Server. On the Synchronize Server page, as shown in Figure 9-3, you can start a manual synchronization or configure automatic, scheduled synchronization. Click Synchronize Now and, when synchronization is complete, you will be informed of its success or failure, and, if the synchronization was successful, you will be taken to the Approve Updates page.

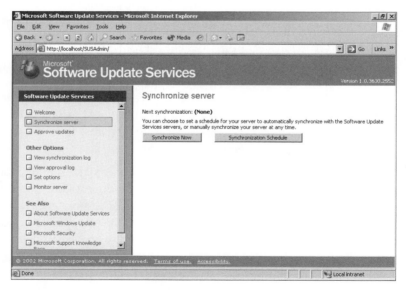

Figure 9-3   The Synchronize Server page

To schedule synchronization, click Synchronization Schedule. You can configure the time of day for synchronization, as shown in Figure 9-4, and whether synchronization occurs daily or weekly on a specified day. When a scheduled synchronization fails, SUS will try again for the Number Of Synchronization Retries To Attempt setting. Retries occur at 30-minute intervals.

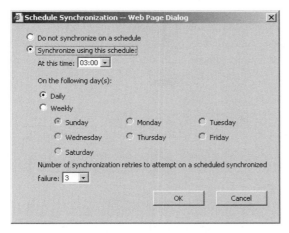

Figure 9-4   The Schedule Synchronization Web Page Dialog page

Approving Updates

To approve updates for distribution to client computers, click Approve Updates in the left navigation bar. The Approve Updates page, as shown in Figure 9-5, appears. Select the updates that you wish to approve, then click Approve. If you are unsure about the applicability of a particular update, click the Details link in the update summary. The Details page that opens will include a link to the actual *.cab file that is used to install the package, and a link to the Read More page about the update, which will open the Microsoft Knowledge Base article related to the update.

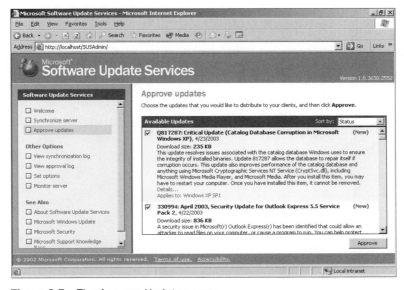

Figure 9-5   The Approve Updates page

> **Tip**   The first synchronization will download dozens of updates. It may be tedious to scroll and click each check box for approval. Instead, after clicking the first check box, press TAB twice to navigate to the next check box, and press the spacebar to select (or clear) the item.

The Automatic Updates Client

The client component of SUS is Windows Automatic Updates, which is supported on Windows 2000, Windows XP, and Windows Server 2003. The Automatic Updates client is included with Windows Server 2003, Windows 2000 Service Pack 3, and Windows XP Service Pack 1.

For clients running earlier releases of the supported platforms, you can download Automatic Updates as a stand-alone client from the Microsoft SUS Web site, at *http://go.microsoft.com/fwlink/?LinkID=6930*. The client, provided as an .msi file, can be installed on a stand-alone computer or by means of Group Policy (assign the package in the Computer Configuration\Software Settings policy), SMS, or even a logon script. If a localized version of the client is not available, install the English version on any locale.

The Automatic Updates client of Windows Server 2003 is configured to connect automatically to the Microsoft Windows Update server and download updates, then prompt the user to install them. This behavior can be modified by accessing the Automatic Updates tab in the System Properties dialog box, accessible by clicking System in Control Panel, in Windows XP and Windows Server2003. In Windows 2000 click Automatic Updates in Control Panel. The Automatic Updates tab is shown in Figure 9-6. Automatic Updates can also be configured using GPOs or registry values.

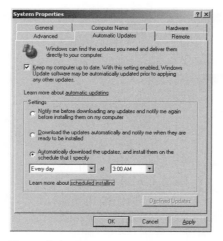

Figure 9-6   The Automatic Updates tab of the System Properties dialog box

Download Behavior

Automatic Updates supports two download behaviors:

- **Automatic**   Updates are downloaded without notification to the user.

- **Notification**   If Automatic Updates is configured to notify the user before down-loading updates, it registers the notification of an available update in the system event log and to a logged-on administrator of the computer. If an administrator is not logged on, Automatic Updates waits for a user with administrator credentials before offering notification by means of a balloon in the notification area of the system tray.

Once update downloading has begun, Automatic Updates uses the Background Intelligent Transfer Service (BITS) to perform the file transfer using idle network bandwidth. BITS ensures that network performance is not hindered due to file transfer. All patches are checked by the SUS server to determine if they have been correctly signed by Microsoft. Similarly, the Automatic Updates client confirms the Microsoft signature and also examines the cyclical redundancy check (CRC) on each package before installing it.

Installation Behavior

Automatic Updates provides two options for installation:

- **Notification**   Automatic Updates registers an event in the system log indicating that updates are ready for installation. Notification will wait until a local administrator is logged on before taking further action. When an administrative user is logged on, a balloon notification appears in the system tray. The administrator clicks the balloon or the notification icon, and then may select from available updates before clicking Install. If an update requires restarting the computer, Automatic Updates cannot detect additional updates that might be applicable until after the restart.

- **Automatic (Scheduled)**   When updates have been downloaded successfully, an event is logged to the system event log. If an administrator is logged on, a notification icon appears, and the administrator can manually launch installation at any time until the scheduled installation time.

   At the scheduled installation time, an administrator who is logged on will be notified with a countdown message prior to installation, and will have the option to cancel installation, in which case the installation is delayed until the next scheduled time. If a non-administrator is logged on, a warning dialog appears, but the user cannot delay installation. If no user is logged on, installation occurs automatically. If an update requires restart, a five-minute countdown notification appears informing users of the impending restart. Only an administrative user can cancel the restart.

> **Tip**   If a computer is not turned on at the scheduled Automatic Updates installation time, installation will wait to the next scheduled time. If the computer is never on at the scheduled time, installation will not occur. Ensure that systems remain turned on to be certain that Automatic Updates install successfully.

Configuring Automatic Updates Through Group Policy

The Automatic Updates client will, by default, connect to the Microsoft Windows Update server. Once you have installed SUS in your organization, you can direct Automatic Updates to connect to specific intranet servers by configuring the registry of clients manually or by using Windows Update group policies.

To configure Automatic Updates using GPOs, open a GPO and navigate to the Computer Configuration\Administrative Templates\Windows Components\Windows Update node. The Windows Update policies are shown in Figure 9-7.

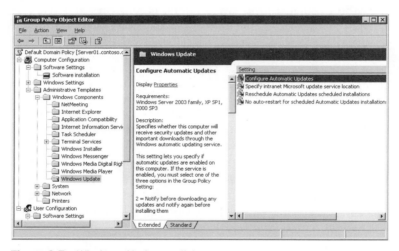

Figure 9-7   Windows Update policies

> **Note**   If you edit policy on a Windows 2000 Active Directory server, the policies may not appear. Automatic Updates policies are described by the *%Windir%*\Inf\Wuau.inf administrative template, which is installed by default when Automatic Updates is installed. If Automatic Updates has not been installed on the domain controller to which you are connected (typically, the PDC Emulator), you must right-click the AdministrativeTemplates node and choose Add/Remove Templates, click Add, then locate the Wuau.inf template, perhaps by copying it from a system that does have Automatic Updates installed.

The following policies are available, each playing an important role in configuring effective update distribution in your enterprise:

- **Configure Automatic Updates** The Configure Automatic Updates Behavior determines the behavior of the Automatic Updates client. There are three options: Notify For Download And Notify For Install, Auto Download And Notify For Install, and Auto Download And Schedule The Install. These options are combinations of the installation and download behaviors discussed earlier in the lesson.

- **Reschedule Automatic Updates Scheduled Installations** If installations are scheduled, and the client computer is turned off at the scheduled time, the default behavior is to wait for the next scheduled time. The Reschedule Automatic Updates Scheduled Installations policy, if set to a value between 1 and 60, causes Automatic Updates to reschedule installation for the specified number of minutes after system startup.

- **No Auto-Restart For Scheduled Automatic Updates Installations** This policy causes Automatic Updates to forego a restart required by an installed update when a user is logged on to the system. Instead, the user is notified that a restart is required for installation to complete, and can restart the computer at his or her discretion. Remember that Automatic Updates cannot detect new updates until restart has occurred.

- **Specify Intranet Microsoft Update Service Location** This policy allows you to redirect Automatic Updates to a server running SUS. By default, the client will log its interactions on the SUS server to which it connects. However, this policy allows you to point clients to another server running IIS for statistics logging. This dual policy provides the opportunity for clients to obtain updates from a local SUS server, but for all clients to log SUS statistics in a single location for easier retrieval and analysis of the log data, which is stored as part of the IIS log. IIS logs typically reside in *%Windir%*\System32\Logfiles\W3svc1.

Automatic Updates clients poll their SUS server every 22 hours, minus a random offset.

Any delay in patching should be treated as unacceptable when security vulnerabilities are being actively exploited. In such situations, install the patch manually so that systems do not have to wait to poll, download, and install patches.

After approved updates have been downloaded from the SUS server, they will be installed as configured—manually or automatically—at the scheduled time. If an approved update is later unapproved, that update is not uninstalled; but it will not be installed by additional clients. An installed update *can* be uninstalled manually, using the Add Or Remove Programs application in Control Panel.

SUS Troubleshooting

Although SUS works well, there are occasions that warrant monitoring and trouble-shooting.

Monitoring SUS

The Monitor Server page of the SUS Administration Web site displays statistics that reflect the number of updates available for each platform, and the date and time of the most recent update. The information is summarized from the Windows Update meta-data that is downloaded during each synchronization. Metadata information is written to disk and stored in memory to improve performance as systems request platform appropriate updates.

You can also monitor SUS and Automatic Updates using the following logs:

- **Synchronization Log**   You can retrieve information about current or past synchronizations, and the specific packages that were downloaded by clicking View Synchronization Log in the left navigation bar. You can also use any text editor to open the (Extensible Markup Language) XML–based database (History-Sync.xml) directly from the SUS Web site's \AutoUpdate\Administration directory in IIS.

- **Approval Log**   For information about packages that have been approved, click View Approval Log in the left navigation bar. Alternatively, you can open History-Approve.xml from the SUS Web site's \AutoUpdate\Administration directory in IIS.

- **Windows Update Log**   The Automatic Updates client logs activity in the *%Windir%*\Windows Update.log file on the client's local hard disk.

- **Wutrack.bin**   The client's interaction with SUS is logged to the specified statistics server's IIS logs, typically stored in the folder: *%Windir%*\System32\Logfiles \W3svc1. These logs, which are verbose and cryptic, are designed to be analyzed by programs, not by humans.

> **Exam Tip**   Although you should know what logs are available, and where they are located, you are not required for the 70-290 exam to be able to interpret cryptic messages or log entries. The SUS Deployment White Paper includes appendices with detailed information about event descriptions and log syntax.

SUS System Events

The synchronization service generates event log messages for each synchronization performed by the server, and when updates are approved. These messages can be viewed in the System log using Event Viewer. The events relate to the following scenarios:

- **Unable to connect**   Automatic Updates could not connect to the update service (Windows Update or the computer's assigned SUS server).

- **Install ready—no recurring schedule**   Updates listed in the event were downloaded and are pending installation. An administrator must click the notification icon and click Install.

- **Install ready—recurring schedule**   Updates listed in the event are downloaded and will be installed at the date and time specified in the event.

- **Installation success**   Updates listed in the event were installed successfully.

- **Installation failure**   Updates listed in the event failed to install properly.

- **Restart required—no recurring schedule**   An update requires a restart. If installation behavior is set for notification, restart must be performed manually. Windows cannot search for new updates until the restart has occurred.

- **Restart required—recurring schedule**   When Automatic Updates is configured to automatically install updates, an event is registered if an update requires restart. Restart will occur within five minutes. Windows cannot search for new updates until after the restart has occurred.

Troubleshooting SUS

Software Update Services on a Windows Server 2003 computer may require the following troubleshooting steps:

- **Reloading the memory cache**   If no new updates appear since the last time you synchronized the server, it is possible that no new updates are available. However, it is also possible that memory caches are not loading new updates properly. From the SUS administration site, click Monitor Server and then click Refresh.

- **Restarting the synchronization service**   If you receive a message that the synchronization service is not running properly, or if you cannot modify settings in the Set Options page of the administration Web site, open the Microsoft Management Console (MMC) Services snap-in, right-click Software Update Services Synchronization Service and choose Restart.

- **Restarting IIS**   If you cannot connect to the administration site, or if clients cannot connect to the SUS serve, restart the World Wide Web Publishing Service in the same manner.

If Automatic Updates clients do not appear to be receiving updates properly, open the registry of a client and ensure that the following values appear in HKEY_LOCAL_MACHINE\Software\Policies\Microsoft\Windows\WindowsUpdate:

- **WUServer**   Should have the URL of the SUS server, for example, *http://SUS_Servername*

- **WUStatusServer**   Should have the URL of the same SUS server or another IIS server on which synchronization statistics are logged

And, in the AU subkey:

- **UseWUServer**   Should be set to dword:00000001

SUS Backup and Recovery

As with any other server role or application, you must plan for recovery in the event of a server failure.

Backing Up SUS

To back up SUS, you must back up the folder that contains SUS content, the SUS Administration Web site, and the IIS metabase.

> **Exam Tip**   The process described to back up the IIS metabase is useful not only for backing up SUS, but for any other Web site or application running on Windows Server 2003 and IIS 6.0.

First, back up the metabase—an XML database containing the configuration of IIS. Using the MMC IIS snap-in, select the server to back up and, from the Action menu, select All Tasks, then Backup/Restore Configuration. Click Create Backup and enter a name for the backup. When you click OK, the metabase is backed up.

Then back up the following using Ntbackup or another backup utility:

- The default Web site, which is located unless otherwise configured in C:\Inetpub\Wwwroot.

- The SUS Administration Web site. SUSAdmin is, by default, a subfolder of C:\Inetpub\Wwwroot. In that event, it will be backed up when you back up the default Web site.

- The AutoUpdate virtual directory, also by default a subfolder of C:\Inetpub\Wwwroot.

- The SUS content location you specified in SUS setup or the SUS options. You can confirm the SUS content location in IIS manager by clicking Default Web Site and examining the path to the Content virtual root in the details pane.

- The metabase backup directory, *%Windir%*\System32\Inetsrv\Metaback, which contains the copy of the metabase made earlier.

See Also For more information about the Ntbackup utility, see Chapter 7.

This process of backing up the metabase, and then backing up the components of SUS, should be repeated regularly because updates will be added and approved with some frequency.

SUS Server Recovery

To restore a failed SUS server, perform the steps described below. If a certain step is unnecessary, you may skip it, but perform the remaining steps in sequence.

1. Disconnect the server from the network to prevent it from being infected with viruses.

2. Install Windows Server 2003, being sure to give the server the same name it had previously.

3. Install IIS with the same components it had previously.

4. Install the latest service pack and security fixes. If the server must be connected to the network to achieve this step, take all possible precautions to prevent unnecessary exposure.

5. Install SUS into the same folder it was previously installed.

6. Run Ntbackup to restore the most recent backup of SUS. This will include the SUS content folder, the Default Web Site, including the SUSAdmin and AutoUpdate virtual directories, and the IIS metabase backup.

7. Open the MMC IIS snap-in and select the server to restore. From the Action menu, select All Tasks, then Backup/Restore Configuration and select the backup that was just restored. Click Restore.

8. Confirm the success of your recovery by opening the SUS Administration Web site and clicking Set Options. Check that the previous settings are in place, and that the previously approved updates are still approved.

Note The preceding steps apply to Windows Server 2003 only. If you are recovering a Windows 2000-based SUS server, refer to SUS documentation for appropriate steps.

Lesson Review

The following questions are intended to reinforce key information presented in this lesson. If you are unable to answer a question, review the lesson materials and try the question again. You can find answers to the questions in the "Questions and Answers" section at the end of this chapter.

1. You are configuring a Software Update Services infrastructure. One server is synchronizing metadata and content from Windows Update. Other servers (one in each site) are synchronizing content from the parent SUS server. Which of the following steps is required to complete the SUS infrastructure?

   a. Configure Automatic Updates clients using Control Panel on each system

   b. Configure GPOs to direct clients to the SUS server in their sites

   c. Configure a manual content distribution point

   d. Approve updates using the SUS administration page

2. You are configuring SUS for a group of Web servers. You want the Web servers to update themselves nightly based on a list of approved updates on your SUS server. However, once in a while an administrator is logged on, performing late-night maintenance on a Web server, and you do not want update installation and potential restart to interfere with those tasks. What Windows Update policy configuration should you use in this scenario?

   a. Notify For Download And Notify For Install

   b. Auto Download And Notify For Install

   c. Auto Download And Schedule The Install

3. You want all network clients to download and install updates automatically during night hours, and you have configured scheduled installation behavior for Automatic Updates. However, you discover that some users are turning off their machines at night, and updates are not being applied. Which policy allows you to correct this situation without changing the installation schedule?

   a. Specify Intranet Microsoft Update Service Location

   b. No Auto-Restart For Scheduled Automatic Updates Installations

   c. Reschedule Automatic Updates Scheduled Installations

   d. Configure Automatic Update

Lesson Summary

- SUS is an intranet application that runs on IIS 6.0 (or on IIS 5.0 on a Windows 2000 Server) and is administered through a Web-based administration site: *http://SUS_Servername/SUSAdmin*.

- The SUS server synchronizes information about critical updates and security rollups and allows an administrator to configure approval centrally for each update. Typically, an enterprise configures SUS to download the actual update files as well.

- Automatic Updates, which runs on Windows 2000, Windows XP, and Windows Server 2003, is responsible for downloading and installing updates on the client.

- Group Policy can be used to configure Automatic Updates to retrieve patches from an SUS server rather than from the Windows Update servers. GPOs can also drive the download, installation and restart behavior of the client computers.

Lesson 2: Service Packs

Microsoft releases Service Packs to consolidate critical updates, security rollups, hotfixes, driver updates, and feature enhancements. As suggested at the beginning of this chapter, it is no longer feasible to wait until Service Pack 3 before installing Service Pack 2. You must stay current with Service Packs to maintain the security and integrity of your enterprise network. Software Update Services, discussed in the previous lesson, does not distribute service packs. To keep your network completely up to date with critical patches, you need to implement the skills covered in this lesson, which will allow you to deploy service packs by means of Group Policy.

After this lesson, you will be able to

- Download and extract a service pack
- Deploy a service pack with Group Policy–based software distribution

Estimated lesson time: 5 minutes

Downloading and Extracting Service Packs

When a service pack is released, Microsoft makes it available for installation and download from the Microsoft Web site. A service pack can be installed directly from a Microsoft server, in which case the client launches the service pack setup from the Microsoft site and a small setup utility is downloaded to the client. That setup utility reconnects to the Microsoft server and controls the download and installation of the entire service pack. Service packs are generally sizeable, so performing this task machine-by-machine is not an efficient deployment strategy in all but the smallest environments.

Service packs can also be obtained on CD from Microsoft and through many Microsoft resources, such as TechNet and MSDN. Service Pack CDs often include extras, such as updated administrative tools, new policy templates, and other value-added software. In an enterprise environment, it is therefore recommended to obtain the service pack media.

When you do not have access to a CD containing the service pack, and you want to deploy the service pack to more than one system, you can download the entire service pack as a single file, again from the Microsoft Web site. The service pack executable, if launched (by double-clicking, for example), triggers the installation of the service pack. This single-file version of the executable can also be *extracted* into the full folder and file structure of the service pack, just as it would be on the service pack CD, but without the value adds.

To extract a service pack, launch the executable from a command prompt with the -x switch. For example, to extract Windows XP Service Pack 1, type **xpsp1.exe -x**. You will then be prompted for a folder to which the service pack is extracted. Once the process is complete, you will see the full service pack folder structure contained in the target folder. You can then launch installation of the service pack, just as from the CD, by double-clicking I386\Update\Update.exe.

Deploying Service Packs with Group Policy

Service Pack installation requires administrative credentials on the local computer, unless the service pack is installed via Group Policy or Systems Management Server (SMS). Because service packs apply to systems, it is necessary to assign the service pack through computer-based, rather than user-based, group policy.

To distribute a service pack, create a shared folder and either extract the service pack to that folder or copy the contents of the service pack CD to the folder. Then, using the Active Directory Users And Computers snap-in, create or select an existing GPO. Click Edit and the Group Policy Object Editor console appears, focused on the selected GPO.

Expand the Computer Configuration\Software Settings node. Right-click Software Installation and choose New, then Package. Enter the path to the service pack's Update.msi file. Be certain to use a UNC format (for example, \\Server\Share) and *not* a local volume path, such as *Drive:\Path*. In the Deploy Software dialog box, select Assigned. Close the Group Policy Object Editor console. Computers within the scope of the GPO—in the site, domain, or OU branch to which the policy is linked—automatically deploy the service pack at the next startup.

 Tip   Windows XP systems with Logon Optimization configured may require two restarts. Logon Optimization can be disabled by enabling the policy Always Wait For The Network At Computer Startup And Logon, found in the policy path Computer Configuration\Administrative Templates\System\Logon.

Lesson Review

The following questions are intended to reinforce key information presented in this lesson. If you are unable to answer a question, review the lesson materials and try the question again. You can find answers to the questions in the "Questions and Answers" section at the end of this chapter.

1. What command should you use to unpack the single file download of a service pack?

   a. Setup.exe -u

   b. Update.exe -x

   c. Update.msi

   d. *<Servicepackname>*.exe -x

2. What type of Group Policy software deployment should be used to distribute a service pack?

   a. Published in the Computer Configuration Software Settings

   b. Assigned in the Computer Configuration Software Settings

   c. Published in the User Configuration Software Settings

   d. Assigned in the User Configuration Software Settings

Lesson Summary

- Service packs can be extracted using the -x switch.

- Group Policy can deploy service packs by assigning Update.msi through the computer configuration's software settings policy.

Lesson 3: Administering Software Licenses

The End User License Agreement (EULA) is more than just a nuisance that you must click through to begin installing a new operating system, update, or application. The EULA is a binding contract that gives you the legal right to use a piece of software. In an enterprise environment, managing software licenses is critically important. In this lesson, you will learn to use the licensing tools provided by Windows Server 2003 to register and monitor licenses and compliance.

After this lesson, you will be able to

- Understand Per Server and Per Device or Per User licensing modes
- Configure licenses using the Licensing properties in Control Panel, and the Licensing administrative tool
- Create license groups

Estimated lesson time: 20 minutes

Note   The Evaluation Edition of Windows Server 2003, Enterprise Edition, included on the Supplemental CD-ROM with this book, does not support licensing. You will not be able to follow along with the examples in this lesson without purchasing the full retail version of the product.

Obtaining a Client Access License

The server license for Windows Server 2003 enables you to install the operating system on a computer, but you need a Client Access License (CAL) before a user or device is legally authorized to connect to the server. CALs are obtained in bundles, and are often but not always included in the purchase of the operating system. Keep copies of the CAL certificates and your EULAs on file, in the event that your organization is audited for licensing compliance.

Tip   Remember that when upgrading a server from Windows NT 4 or Windows 2000 to Windows Server 2003, you must purchase CAL upgrades as well.

You must have a CAL for any connection to a Windows Server 2003 computer that uses server components, which include file and print services or authentication. Very few server applications run so independently that the client/server connection does not require a CAL. The most significant exception to the CAL requirement is unauthenticated access conducted through the Internet. Where there is no exchange of credentials during

Internet access, such as users browsing your public Web site, no CAL is required. CALs are therefore not required for Windows Server 2003 Web Edition.

There are two types of CALs: Windows Device CALs, which allow a device to connect to a server regardless of the number of users who may use that device; and Windows User CALs, which allow a user to connect to a server from a number of devices. Windows Device CALs are advantageous for an organization with multiple users per device, such as shift workers. Windows User CALs make most sense for an organization with employees that access the network from multiple or unknown devices.

> **Note**   The licensing tools and the user interface do not yet distinguish between Windows User or Windows Device CALs. A device CAL is registered indirectly, using license groups.

The number of CALs you require, and how you track those licenses, depends on which client access licensing mode you pursue.

Per-Server Licensing

Per-server licensing requires a User or Device CAL for each concurrent connection. If a server is configured with 1,000 CALs, the 1,001st concurrent connection is denied access. CALs are designated for use on a particular server, so if the same 1,000 users require concurrent connections to a second server, you must purchase another 1,000 CALs.

Per server licensing is advantageous only in limited access scenarios, such as when a subset of your user population accesses a server product on very few servers. Per server licensing is less cost-effective in a situation where multiple users access multiple resources on multiple servers. If you are unsure which licensing mode is appropriate, select Per Server. The license agreement allows a no-cost, one-time, one-way conversion from Per Server to Per Device or Per User licensing when it becomes appropriate to do so.

Per-Device or Per-User Licensing

The Per Device or Per User licensing mode varies from the Per Seat scheme of previous versions of Windows. In this new mode, each device or user that connects to a server requires a CAL, but with that license the device or user can connect to a number of servers in the enterprise. Per User or Per Device mode is generally the mode of choice for distributed computing environments in which multiple users access multiple servers.

For example, a developer who uses a laptop and two desktops would require only one Windows User CAL. A fleet of 10 Tablet PCs that are used by 30 shift workers would require only 10 Windows Device CALs.

The total number of CALs equals the number of devices or users, or a mixture thereof, that access servers. CALs can be reassigned under certain, understandable conditions—for example a Windows User CAL can be reassigned from a permanent employee to a temporary employee while the permanent employee is on leave. A Windows Device CAL can be reassigned to a loaner device while a device is being repaired.

Per Server and Per Device or Per User licensing modes are illustrated in Table 9-1.

Table 9-1   CAL Licensing Modes

Per Server	Per User or Per Device
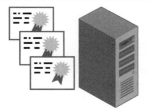	
■ Traditionally licensed in Per Server mode when there are few servers that require limited access. ■ The number of CALs needed is determined by the number of concurrent connections that are required.	■ Traditionally licensed in Per User or Per Device mode when there are many servers that require frequent and widespread access. ■ Usually more economical when the number of CALs needed is determined by the number of users or devices, or both, that require access to the servers.

Tip   Windows Server 2003 includes Terminal Services, also known as Remote Desktop. Remote Desktop includes a two (concurrent) connection license for administrators to connect to a remote server. For Terminal Services to perform as an application server, allowing non-administrative users to connect to hosted applications, you must acquire Terminal Services CALs, which are included in Windows XP Professional.

There are two utilities that will help you track and manage software licensing:

■ **Licensing in Control Panel**   The Control Panel Choose Licensing Mode tool, as shown in Figure 9-8, manages licensing requirements for a single computer running Windows Server 2003. You can use Licensing to add or remove CALs for a server running in per-server mode; to change the licensing mode from Per Server to Per Device or Per User; or to configure licensing replication.

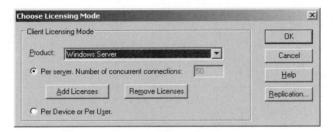

Figure 9-8   The Choose Licensing Mode tool in Control Panel

■ **Licensing in Administrative Tools**   The Licensing administrative tool, discussed in the next section, allows you to manage licensing for an enterprise by centralizing the control of licensing and license replication in a site-based model.

Administering Site Licensing

The License Logging service, which runs on each Windows Server 2003 computer, assigns and tracks licenses when server resources are accessed. To ensure compliance, licensing information is replicated to a centralized licensing database on a server in the site. This server is called the site license server. A site administrator, or an administrator for the site license server, can then use the Microsoft Licensing tool in Administrative Tools program group to view and manage licensing for the entire site. This new license tracking and management capability incorporates licenses not just for file and print services, but for IIS, for Terminal Services, and for BackOffice products such as Exchange or SQL Server.

The Site License Server

The site license server is typically the first domain controller created in a site. To find out what server is the license server for a site, open Active Directory Sites And Services, expand to select the Site node then right-click Licensing Site Settings and choose Properties. The current site license server is displayed, as shown in Figure 9-9.

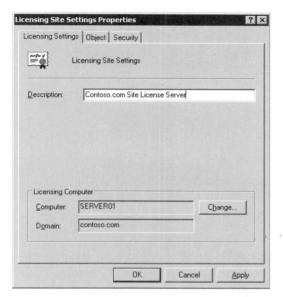

Figure 9-9   Identifying and changing the site license server

To assign the site license server role to another server or domain controller, click Change and select the desired computer. To retain the licensing history for your enterprise, you must immediately after transferring the role stop the License Logging service on the new license server, then copy the following files from the old to the new licensing server:

- *%Systemroot%*\System32\Cpl.cfg contains the purchase history for your organization.
- *%Systemroot%*\Lls\Llsuser.lls contains user information about the number of connections.
- *%Systemroot%*\Lls\Llsmap.lls contains license group information.

After all files have been copied, restart the License Logging service.

Administering Site Licenses

Once you have identified the site license server for a site, you can view the licensing information on that server opening Licensing from the Administrative Tools program group. The Server Browser tab in Licensing (as shown in Figure 9-10) enables you to manage licensing for an entire site or enterprise.

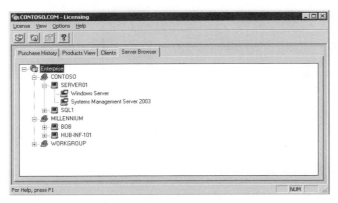

Figure 9-10   The Server Browser tab of the Microsoft Licensing administrative tool

The Server Browser page of Licensing allows you to manage any server in any site or domain for which you have administrative authority. You can locate a server and, by right-clicking it and choosing Properties, manage that server's licenses. For each server product installed on that server, you can add or remove per-server licenses. You can also, where appropriate, convert the licensing mode. Remember that per server licensing mode issues a license when a user connects to the server product. When a user disconnects from the server product, the License Logging service makes the license available to another user.

The server properties also allow you to configure license replication, which can be set on a server using its Licensing properties in Control Panel. By default, license information is replicated from a server's License Logging Service to the site license server every 24 hours, and the system automatically staggers replication to avoid burdening the site licensing server. If you want to control replication schedules or frequency, you must manually vary the Start At time and Start Every frequency of each server replicating to a particular site license server.

To manage Per Device or Per User licensing, click Licensing from the Administrative Tools program group, then choose the New License command from the License menu. In the New Client Access License dialog box, select the server product and the number of licenses purchased. Licenses are added to the pool of licenses. As devices or users connect to the product anywhere in the site, they are allocated licenses from the pool, with one license for each device or user. After a pool of licenses is depleted, license violations occur when additional devices or users access the product.

The Purchase History tab in Licensing (as shown in Figure 9-11) provides a historical overview of licenses purchased for a site, as well as the quantity, date, and administrator associated with the addition or removal of licenses.

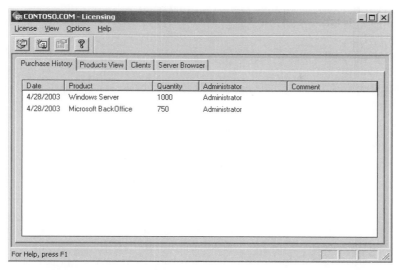

Figure 9-11   The Purchase History tab of the Microsoft Licensing administrative tool

To view cumulative information about licensing and compliance, click the Products View tab. This tab shows how many licenses have been purchased and allocated to users or devices (in Per Device or Per User mode) or the number of licenses purchased for all servers in the site and the peak connections reached to date (in Per Server mode). You can also determine compliance using the licensing status symbols shown in Table 9-2.

Table 9-2   Licensing Status Symbols

Symbol	Licensing Status
	The product is in compliance with legal licensing requirements. The number of connections is less than the number of licenses purchased.
	The product is not in compliance with legal licensing requirements. The number of connections exceeds the number of licenses purchased.
	The product has reached the legal limit. The number of connections equals the number of licenses purchased. If additional devices or users will connect to the server product, you must purchase and log new licenses.

License Groups

Per Device or Per User licensing requires one CAL for each device. However, the License Logging service assigns and tracks licenses by user name. When multiple users share one or more devices, you must create license groups, or else licenses will be consumed too rapidly.

A license group is a collection of users who collectively share one or more CALs. When a user connects to the server product, the License Logging service tracks the user by name, but assigns a CAL from the allocation assigned to the license group. The concept is easiest to understand with examples:

- **10 users share a single handheld device for taking inventory.**   A license group is created with the 10 users as members. The license group is assigned one CAL, representing the single device they share.

- **100 students occasionally use a computer lab with 10 computers.**   A license group is created with the 100 students as members, and is allocated 10 CALs.

To create a license group, click the Options menu and, from the Advanced menu, choose New License Group. Enter the group name and allocate one license for each client device used to access the server. The number of licenses allocated to a group should correspond to the number of devices used by members of the group.

Lesson Review

The following questions are intended to reinforce key information presented in this lesson. If you are unable to answer a question, review the lesson materials and try the question again. You can find answers to the questions in the "Questions and Answers" section at the end of this chapter.

1. What are the valid licensing modes in Windows Server 2003? Select all that apply.

    a. Per User

    b. Per Server

    c. Per Seat

    d. Per Device or Per User

2. You are hiring a team to tackle a software development project. There will be three shifts of programmers, and each shift will include six programmers. Each programmer uses four devices to develop and test the software, which authenticates against a Windows Server 2003 computer. What is the minimum number of CALs required if the servers involved are in Per Device or Per User licensing mode?

    a. 6

    b. 4

    c. 18

    d. 24

3. What tool will allow you to identify the site license server for your site?

    a. Active Directory Domains And Trusts

    b. The Licensing tool in Control Panel

    c. Active Directory Sites And Services

    d. DNS

4. You manage the network for a team of 500 telephone sales representatives. You have 550 licenses configured in Per Device or Per User licensing mode. A new campaign is launched and you will hire another shift of 500 reps. What do you need to do to most effectively manage license tracking and compliance?

    a. Revoke the licenses from the existing clients

    b. Delete the existing licenses, then add 500 licenses

    c. Create license groups

    d. Convert to Per Server licenses

Lesson Summary

- Windows Server 2003 provides a new mode of licensing, whereby a user can access a server product from multiple devices using one license, or a group of users can access a server product from a single device. This is called Per Device or Per User licensing.

- When more than one user accesses a server product from shared devices, add those users as a license group, and allocate licenses to that group equivalent to the number of devices.

- License information is replicated, by default every 24 hours, to the site license server.

- Licensing can be managed using the Licensing tool in Control Panel or, more centrally, using the Licensing administrative tool, from the Administrative Tools program group.

Case Scenario Exercise

You are configuring an update strategy for a network consisting of 1,000 clients running a mix of Windows XP and Windows 2000. Your goal is to prevent users from downloading updates directly from Windows Update, and to create a structure in which you can approve critical patches and security rollups for distribution.

You have recently purchased desktops and laptops, and you have applied the corporate standard image to those systems. Unfortunately, the image was created a while ago. The Windows XP image uses release-to-manufacture (RTM) code, and the Windows 2000 image has Service Pack 2 applied. So your first task is to update systems to the latest service pack level, so that the Automatic Updates client, as well as all patches and fixes, have been installed on the computers.

> **Note**   In this hands-on scenario, you may test the results using a second computer. To do so, join the computer to the domain and move its computer account to the Desktops OU. If the computer is running Windows 2000, modify the service pack deployment exercise accordingly.

Exercise 1: Download and Extract the Service Pack

1. Create a folder on the C drive and name the folder ServicePack.

2. From the Microsoft download site, *http://www.microsoft.com/downloads*, or from the Windows XP site, *http://www.microsoft.com/windowsxp*, download the latest service pack. Save it to the C:\ServicePack folder.

3. Open a command prompt and type **cd C:\ServicePack** to change to the Service-Pack folder.

4. Type ***xpsp1.exe* -x**. Substitute *xpsp1* with the filename for the most recent service pack you downloaded.

5. You will be prompted to indicate the location to which the service pack will be extracted. Type **C:\ServicePack**.

6. The service pack is extracted. Use Windows Explorer to navigate the folder structure that was created. Make note of the location of update.exe (in the Update folder), which is used to launch installation of the service pack on a single machine, and of update.msi (in the same folder), which will be used to deploy the service pack through group policy-based software distribution.

Exercise 2: Deploy the Service Pack with Group Policy

1. Share the C:\ServicePack folder with the share name ServicePack.

2. Open Active Directory Users And Computers.

3. Expand the domain and locate (or create) the Desktops OU.

4. Create a computer object in the Desktops OU called Desktop0569 to represent one of the new systems.

> **Note**   If you have a second system with which to perform this case scenario exercise, move that system's account into the Desktops OU.

5. Right-click the Desktops OU and choose Properties.

6. Click the Group Policy tab.

7. Click New to create a new GPO. Name the object SP-Deploy.

8. Select the SP-Deploy group policy link and click Edit. Group Policy Object Editor opens.

9. Navigate to Computer Configuration\Software Settings.

10. Right-click Software Installation and choose New, then Package.

11. Type the path **\\server01.contoso.com\servicepack** and press Enter. The browse dialog box will take you to the root of the extracted service pack.

12. Navigate to the Update.msi file you identified in the previous exercise. Select the Update.msi file and click Open.

13. Select Assigned and click OK. The package is created.

14. Close Group Policy Object Editor and the Desktop OU's Properties dialog box.

15. (Optional) If you have a second system, you can test the deployment of the service pack. Remember that Windows XP computers are configured by default to optimize logon, so it may take two restarts before the service pack is applied. You can confirm the service pack level on a machine by clicking Start, Run, and then typing **winver**.

Exercise 3: Install SUS

1. Navigate to *http://go.microsoft.com/fwlink/?LinkId=6930*. You will be prompted to add the site to your trusted sites list, which you should do.

2. Download the SUS installation package.

3. Start SUS installation by double-clicking the downloaded file.

4. On the Welcome screen, click Next.

5. Read and accept the End User License Agreement, and then click Next.

6. Choose a Custom installation and then click Next.

7. On the Choose File Locations page, choose Save The Updates To This Local Folder. The default, C:\SUS\Content, is fine. Click Next.

> **Note**   The updates might consist of several hundred megabytes of files. If you have a slow Internet connection, or if you want to save time during this exercise, choose the second option, Keep The Updates On A Microsoft Windows Update Server instead.

8. For Language Settings, choose English Only, then click Next.

9. On the following page, choose I Will Manually Approve New Versions Of Approved Updates, then click Next.

10. The following page should indicate that the client download location is *http://SERVER01*. Click Install.

11. When installation is complete, click Finish. Internet Explorer will be opened, and will take you to the SUS administration page. Continue with Exercise 4.

Exercise 4: Synchronize SUS

1. If you are not already viewing the SUS administration page, open Internet Explorer and navigate to *http://SERVER01/SUSAdmin*.

> **Note**   To view the SUS administration site, you may need to add Server01 to the Local Intranet trusted site list to access the site. Open Internet Explorer and choose Internet Options from the Tools menu. Click the Security Tab. Select Trusted Sites and click Sites. Add **Server01** and **Server01.contoso.com** to the trusted site list.

2. Click Synchronize Server on the left navigation bar.

3. Click Synchronization Schedule.

   You will manually synchronize for this exercise. However, you can examine synchronization options by clicking Synchronize Using This Schedule. When you are finished exploring settings, click Cancel.

4. On the Synchronize Server page, click Synchronize Now. If you have elected to download updates to the server, synchronization may take some time.

5. After synchronization has occurred, you will be redirected automatically to the Approve Updates page. You can also click Approve Updates on the left navigation bar.

6. Approve a small number of updates so that you can return later to experiment further with approval and automatic updates.

7. Examine other pages of the SUS administration site. After you have familiarized yourself with the site, close Internet Explorer.

Exercise 5: Configure Automatic Updates

1. Open Active Directory Sites and Services.

> **Note**   Most enterprises have found little reason to link GPOs to sites, rather than OUs or the domain. However, SUS-related policies lend themselves well to site application, since you are directing clients to the most site-appropriate SUS server.

2. Right-click the Default-First-Site-Name site and choose Properties.

3. Click the Group Policy tab.

4. Click New and name the new GPO **SUS-Site1**.

5. Click Edit. The Group Policy Object Editor opens.

6. Navigate to Computer Configuration\Administrative Templates\Windows Components\Windows Update.

7. Double-click the policy: Specify Intranet Microsoft Update Service Location.

8. Click Enabled.

9. In *both* text boxes, type **http://server01.contoso.com**.

10. Click OK.

11. Double-click the policy: Configure Automatic Updates.

12. Click Enabled.

13. In the Configure Automatic Updating drop-down list, choose 4-Auto Download And Schedule The Install.

14. Confirm the installation schedule: daily at 3:00 A.M.

15. Click OK.

16. Double-click the policy: Reschedule Automatic Updates Scheduled Installations.

17. Click Enabled.

18. In the Wait After System Startup (Minutes) box, type **1**.

> **Exam Tip**   The Wait After System Startup policy is used to reschedule a scheduled installation that was missed, typically when a machine was turned off at the scheduled date and time.

19. Click OK.

20. Close the Group Policy Object Editor and the Properties dialog box for Default-First-Site-Name.

21. To confirm the configuration, you can restart the server, which is also within the scope of the new policy. Open System from Control Panel and click the Automatic Updates tab. You will see that configuration options are disabled, as they are now being determined by policy.

Chapter Summary

- The Microsoft Software Update Services enable you to centralize and manage the approval and distribution of Windows critical updates and Windows security rollups. One or more SUS servers host lists of approved updates and, optionally but typically, the update files themselves. Automatic Updates clients are configured, usually through GPOs, to obtain updates from intranet SUS servers, rather than from Microsoft Windows Update.

- Software Update Services does not distribute service packs.

- Service packs can be obtained free of charge from Microsoft. If the service pack is a single file, it can be extracted from the command prompt by entering the service pack's filename followed by the -x switch.

- Service packs are deployed easily by assigning a software installation package to the computer configuration's software settings policies in a GPO.

- Tracking and managing licenses and compliance is an important part of an administrator's job. Windows Server 2003 gives you the ability to assign licenses based on concurrent connections to a specific server or to maintain a license for each device or user that connects to any number of servers in your enterprise.

- Licenses are replicated between servers' License Logging service and the site license server. The site license server can be identified using Active Directory Sites And Services, but site licensing is administered using the Licensing tool in the Administrative Tools programs group.

- A license group enables users to share one or more devices. The number of Windows Device CALs is assigned to the license group.

Exam Highlights

Before taking the exam, review the key points and terms that are presented below to help you identify topics you need to review. Return to the lessons for additional practice and review the "Further Readings" sections in Part 2 for pointers to more information about topics covered by the exam objectives.

Key Points

■ Have an understanding of SUS installation and configuration. Although the exam objectives will not address SUS setup directly, the way you configure SUS impacts the tasks you will perform to maintain the SUS infrastructure, so it is important to be comfortable with the "big picture" of SUS.

■ Focus on SUS administrative tasks, such as synchronizing, approving updates, viewing logs and events, and configuring Automatic Updates through System in Control Panel (on a stand-alone computer) or using Group Policy in a larger environment. Remember that you cannot direct a computer to an SUS server using the Automatic Updates properties on a client. You must use Group Policy, or a registry entry, to redirect the client to an intranet server rather than Microsoft Windows Update.

■ Be able to calculate license requirements in a variety of Per Server or Per Device or Per User scenarios. Remember that license groups allow multiple users to share one or more devices.

Key Terms

Client Access License   The license that allows a user or device to connect to a server product for any functionality, including file and print service or authentication.

Per Server license mode   Licenses are allocated when a user or device connects to the server or product. When the user disconnects, the license is returned to the available license pool. This mode requires sufficient licenses to support the maximum number of concurrent connections on each individual server.

Per Device or Per User mode   Licenses requirements allow a single CAL to authorize a user (who may use more than one device) or a device (which may be used by more than one user) to connect to any number of servers.

License group   Because the License Logging service allocates licenses based on user name and not device name, Windows Device CALs are given to a license group. A license group has one or more users, and is allocated licenses equivalent to the number of devices used by that group to connect to server products.

Questions and Answers

Page
9-20
Lesson 1 Review

1. You are configuring a Software Update Services infrastructure. One server is synchronizing metadata and content from Windows Update. Other servers (one in each site) are synchronizing content from the parent SUS server. Which of the following steps is required to complete the SUS infrastructure?

    a. Configure Automatic Updates clients using Control Panel on each system

    b. Configure GPOs to direct clients to the SUS server in their sites

    c. Configure a manual content distribution point

    d. Approve updates using the SUS administration page

    The correct answers are b and d.

2. You are configuring SUS for a group of Web servers. You want the Web servers to update themselves nightly based on a list of approved updates on your SUS server. However, once in a while an administrator is logged on, performing late-night maintenance on a Web server, and you do not want update installation and potential restart to interfere with those tasks. What Windows Update policy configuration should you use in this scenario?

    a. Notify For Download And Notify For Install

    b. Auto Download And Notify For Install

    c. Auto Download And Schedule The Install

    The correct answer is c. You want the Web servers to update themselves, so you must schedule the installation of updates. However, an administrator always has the option to cancel the installation.

3. You want all network clients to download and install updates automatically during night hours, and you have configured scheduled installation behavior for Automatic Updates. However, you discover that some users are turning off their machines at night, and updates are not being applied. Which policy allows you to correct this situation without changing the installation schedule?

    a. Specify Intranet Microsoft Update Service Location

    b. No Auto-Restart For Scheduled Automatic Updates Installations

    c. Reschedule Automatic Updates Scheduled Installations

    d. Configure Automatic Update

    The correct answer is c. Updates are automatically downloaded using background processes and idle bandwidth, but the installation is triggered by the specified schedule. If a computer is turned off at the installation time, it waits until the next scheduled date and time. The Reschedule Wait Time policy, if set between 1 and 60, causes Automatic Updates to start update installation 1 to 60 minutes after system startup.

Page
9-24
Lesson 2 Review

1. What command should you use to unpack the single file download of a service pack?

   a. Setup.exe -u

   b. Update.exe -x

   c. Update.msi

   d. *<Servicepackname>*.exe -x

   The correct answer is d.

2. What type of Group Policy software deployment should be used to distribute a service pack?

   a. Published in the Computer Configuration Software Settings

   b. Assigned in the Computer Configuration Software Settings

   c. Published in the User Configuration Software Settings

   d. Assigned in the User Configuration Software Settings

   The correct answer is b.

Page
9-32
Lesson 3 Review

1. What are the valid licensing modes in Windows Server 2003? Select all that apply.

   a. Per User

   b. Per Server

   c. Per Seat

   d. Per Device or Per User

   The correct answers are b and d.

2. You are hiring a team to tackle a software development project. There will be three shifts of programmers, and each shift will include six programmers. Each programmer uses four devices to develop and test the software, which authenticates against a Windows Server 2003 computer. What is the minimum number of CALs required if the servers involved are in Per Device or Per User licensing mode?

   a. 6

   b. 4

   c. 18

   d. 24

The correct answer is c. If you were to license based on devices, there are six times four devices, or 24 devices. It will be more cost-effective to license based on the number of users, which is 18.

3. What tool will allow you to identify the site license server for your site?

   a. Active Directory Domains And Trusts

   b. The Licensing tool in Control Panel

   c. Active Directory Sites And Services

   d. DNS

The correct answer is c.

4. You manage the network for a team of 500 telephone sales representatives. You have 550 licenses configured in Per Device or Per User licensing mode. A new campaign is launched and you will hire another shift of 500 reps. What do you need to do to most effectively manage license tracking and compliance?

   a. Revoke the licenses from the existing clients

   b. Delete the existing licenses, then add 500 licenses

   c. Create license groups

   d. Convert to Per Server licensing

The correct answer is c.

10 Managing Hardware Devices and Drivers

Exam Objectives in this Chapter:

- Install and configure server hardware devices
    - ❑ Configure driver signing options
    - ❑ Configure resource settings for a device
    - ❑ Configure device properties and settings
- Monitor server hardware. Tools might include Device Manager, the Hardware Troubleshooting Wizard, and appropriate Control Panel items.

Why This Chapter Matters

Hardware devices give us access to the information that is processed by a computer. From the monitor display to the keyboard, from mouse to multimedia, a computer without devices is virtually useless. Microsoft Windows Server 2003 categorizes devices, listing them for examination and configuration in Device Manager.

Devices and the software that the operating system uses to communicate with the device (a "driver") is a combination unique to the device being used and the version of the operating system on which it runs, and most drivers are not interchangeable between operating systems; that is, you cannot use a driver that is designed for use with the Windows 98 operating system with Windows XP or Windows Server 2003.

In addition to using the proper driver initially, ongoing maintenance of devices and driver configurations is necessary. Updates to drivers are common, as functional changes in operating systems and devices dictate corresponding changes in drivers. Changes must be installed in the form of a new driver, which is usually provided by the device vendor. Service Packs may also contain updated driver releases.

Given the precise match required among the device, driver, and operating system, faulty configurations quickly make for non-working devices. The correct driver for your device and the operating system for which it's designed should work properly, and as an administrator you can easily update these drivers through Device Manager.

In most environments, it is not desirable for an end-user to have the ability to install new drivers. However, administrators may not want (nor have the time) to work on each computer individually to configure all devices and their drivers properly. The configuration of driver signing options and the granting of selective privileges to the appropriate users will give the most flexibility for device configuration and installation of drivers.

Lessons in this Chapter:

Before You Begin

This chapter assumes that you have a fair, working knowledge of the most common types of computer devices such as printers, mouse devices, keyboards, network cards, and so on. Physical optimization, testing, and troubleshooting of physical devices is beyond the scope of this chapter.

Examples and practices involving the installation, configuration, and troubleshooting of devices and drivers will be performed in a Windows Server 2003 environment with standard devices. To emulate the exercises, you should have a Windows Server 2003 named Server01 as a domain controller in the *contoso.com* domain.

Lesson 1: Installing Hardware Devices and Drivers

Hardware devices communicate with the Windows Server 2003 operating system by means of a software driver. Devices and their drivers, if not installed automatically through Plug and Play, can be configured through the Device Manager.

After this lesson, you will be able to

- Understand the relationship between devices and drivers
- Use Device Manager to analyze detected devices
- Use Device Manager to install a device

Estimated lesson time: 20 minutes

Devices and Drivers

The easiest way to think about devices and their associated drivers is to divide the devices into two logical categories: Plug-and-Play (PnP) and non-Plug-and-Play (down-level) devices. Most devices manufactured since 1997 are PnP devices, and most PnP drivers for devices are included on the Windows Server 2003 installation CD. When a device is initially detected by Windows Server 2003, and if an acceptable driver is found for that device, the device will be installed and such resources as interrupt requests (IRQs) and direct memory access (DMA) will be allocated for use by the device. The device will then be listed in the categorized listing of devices in Device Manager.

If the PnP driver is not on the Windows Server 2003 Installation CD, you will need the vendor-supplied drivers available when the Windows Server 2003 initially detects, identifies and attempts to install the device. For devices that Windows Server 2003 can identify, you will be prompted for a driver. If the request for the driver is bypassed, Windows Server 2003 will indicate the identified, non-configured device with a yellow warning icon in Device Manager. This icon, as shown in Figure 10-1, is also used if there are duplicate devices on the system or if there are conflicts between the resource demands of drivers, which is extremely rare for newer computer systems and devices.

Figure 10-1   Device Manager warning icon

If a device cannot be identified by Windows Server 2003, no request for a driver will be issued, and the unknown device will be identified with a yellow question mark in Device Manager. For a non-configured or non-identified device, you must install the appropriate driver manually for the device to function properly.

Using Device Manager

Device Manager provides a view, similar to Windows Explorer, of the hardware that is installed on your computer. You can use Device Manager to update the drivers for hardware devices and modify settings related to devices. Device Manager is accessible through the Control Panel by selecting System, the Hardware tab on the Systems Properties dialog box, and then Device Manager to access the Device Manager Properties page, or as part of the Computer Management console, accessible from Administrative Tools. Table 10-1 describes the tasks for which Device Manager can be used.

Table 10-1   Device Manager Tasks

Task	Usage
Determine whether the hardware on your computer is working properly	Properly configured devices are listed by category. Detected devices that are not configurable, either because of a lack of an appropriate driver or an irresolvable resource conflict, are indicated by a yellow icon with an exclamation point. Devices that cannot be identified are indicated by a yellow question mark icon.
Print a summary of the devices that are installed on your computer	On the Action menu in Device Manager, select Print. Print options include System Summary, Selected Class or Device, and All Devices And System Summary.
Change hardware configuration settings	Right-clicking and choosing Properties (or double clicking) on any device will open the Properties page for the device.

Table 10-1   Device Manager Tasks (Continued)

Task	Usage
Device Properties Pages	
General tab	Identify the device type, manufacturer, location, and status of the device. The device can also be enabled or disabled from the Device Usage drop-down list.
Driver tab	View details of the device driver such as driver version, driver provider, and whether the driver has been digitally signed; install updated device drivers; update the device driver; roll back to a previously installed version of the driver.
Resources tab	Lists the resource usage by a device, including I/O ranges, memory addresses, and IRQ use. The ability to disable automatic configuration, which enables manual configuration, varies by device: Some devices do not allow for manual configuration of resources.

Exam Tip   You can use Device Manager to manage devices only on a local computer. On a remote computer, Device Manager will work only in read-only mode.

A list of devices, drivers, and system configuration can be printed through the Print command on the Action menu in Device Manager or output to a comma-separated-values (CSV) file using the Driverquery command-line utility, the parameters for which are listed in Table 10-2.

Table 10-2   Driverquery Command Parameters

Parameter	Output
/S system	Specifies the name or Internet Protocol (IP) address of a remote computer to connect to. The default is the local computer.
/U domain\user	Runs the command within the context of the user specified by User or Domain\User. The default is the permissions of the user who is logged on to the computer issuing the command.
/P password	Specifies the password of the user account that is specified in the /U parameter.
/FO format {TABLE | LIST | CSV}	Specifies the format to display the driver information. Valid values are TABLE, LIST, and CSV. The default format for output is TABLE.
/NH	Omits the header row from the displayed driver information. Valid when the /FO parameter is set to TABLE or CSV.
/V	Specifies that detailed driver information be displayed. Not a valid option for signed drivers.

Table 10-2   Driverquery Command Parameters (Continued)

Parameter	Output
/SI	Specifies to display the properties of signed drivers.
/?	Displays help at the command prompt.

Users, Administrators, and Device Installation

As with most installation tasks, administrators have the ability to install any device and its associated drivers. Users, on the other hand, have very limited ability to install devices on the computer. By default, users can install only PnP devices, with the following considerations:

- The device driver has a digital signature.

- No further action is required to install the device, requiring Windows to display a user interface.

- The device driver is already on the computer.

If any of these conditions is not met, the user cannot install the device unless delegated additional administrative authority.

> **Exam Tip**   If a PnP device requires no additional user interaction for installation, and the driver is already on the computer, a default user can connect and use the device. This applies to any universal serial bus (USB), parallel, IEEE 1394 device, especially printers. The Load And Unload Device Drivers user right, configurable through Group Policies, does not apply to PnP drivers, and need not be enabled for a user to install a PnP device.

Driver Signing Options

Device drivers and operating system files included with Windows 2000 or higher have a Microsoft digital signature. The *digital signature* indicates that a particular driver or file was not altered or overwritten by another program's installation process. Device drivers provided by vendors outside of Windows 2000 or higher may or may not be signed.

You can control how the computer responds to these unsigned driver files during their installation. These settings are configurable through Control Panel by selecting System, the Hardware tab on the Systems Properties dialog box, and then Driver Signing to access the Driver Signing Options Properties page on an individual computer. The options for unsigned driver installation behavior are:

- **Ignore**   To allow all device drivers to be installed on the computer, regardless of whether they have a digital signature. This option is available only if you are logged on as an administrator or as a member of the Administrators group.

- **Warn**   To display a warning message, allowing you to allow or deny driver installation, whenever an installation program or Windows attempts to install a device driver without a digital signature. This is the default behavior.

- **Block**   To prevent an installation program or Windows from installing device drivers without a digital signature.

Group Policy is an effective tool for simultaneously changing the Driver Signing Options setting on multiple computers. To prohibit a user from changing the setting on his or her computer, you must deny access to the Hardware Properties pages in Control Panel and disable the MMC snap-in for Device Manager in the Computer Management console. These settings will not change the user's ability to install PnP devices.

Practice: Installing Device Drivers

In this practice, you will install a network adapter, change the Driver Signing Options, and then return the computer to its default configuration.

Exercise 1: Install a Network Adapter

1. Open the System Properties page from Control Panel, and then on the Hardware tab, click Add Hardware Wizard.

2. Click Next and wait for the Hardware Wizard to scan your computer for new devices. If you have not added any devices, the wizard will ask whether the new device has been connected.

3. Select Yes, I Have Already Connected The Hardware, and then click Next.

4. From the Installed Hardware list, scroll to the bottom, select Add A New Hardware Device, and then click Next.

5. Select the Install The Hardware That I Manually Select From A List (Advanced) option, and then click Next.

6. From the Common Hardware Types list, select Network Adapters, and then click Next.

7. Select Microsoft as the Manufacturer, and Microsoft Loopback Adapter as the Network Adapter, and then click Next.

8. Click Next, and then Finish, to close the wizard.

Windows Server 2003 will now load the driver and install the device. The network adapter named Microsoft Loopback Adapter will appear in Device Manager under the Network Adapters category.

Exercise 2: Set Driver Signing Options

1. Open the System Properties page from Control Panel, and then on the Hardware tab, click Add Driver Signing.

2. Select the Block option.

3. Click OK.

You have now disallowed the installation of unsigned drivers.

Exercise 3: Return Computer to Default

1. Open Device Manager. Right-click Microsoft Loopback Adapter and choose Uninstall from the shortcut menu.

2. Click OK to confirm the device's removal.

3. Close Device Manager.

4. Open the Driver Signing Properties page again, and select Warn.

5. Select Make This Action The System Default.

6. Click OK twice.

You have returned your computer to its default configuration.

Lesson Review

The following questions are intended to reinforce key information presented in this lesson. If you are unable to answer a question, review the lesson materials and try the question again. You can find answers to the questions in the "Questions and Answers" section at the end of this chapter.

1. You want to make certain that no unsigned drivers are used on the desktop computers in your environment. What Driver Signing settings and related configuration will assure this condition?

   _____

   _____

2. A user wants to install a USB printer connected to their his or her computer. The drivers for the printer are included with Windows Server 2003. Can the user install the printer?

   _____

   _____

3. A user wants to install a USB printer connected to his or her local computer. The driver is provided by the vendor, and is not included with Windows Server 2003. The driver is digitally signed. Can the user install the printer?

_____

_____

Lesson Summary

- Device Manager lists all detected devices, and indicates problems with identification or driver configuration.

- Driver configuration can be output to a printed document using Device Manager, or to a CSV file using the Driverquery command.

- Users can connect and install any completely PnP device. If any user intervention is required, a user will not be able to install a device.

- Interface access points to device and driver configuration can be disabled through local and domain-based Group Policies.

- Unsigned Driver Installation behavior has three settings: Ignore, Warn, and Block.

Lesson 2: Configuring Hardware Devices and Drivers

Devices may require updated drivers due to changes in the Windows Server 2003 operating system or changes in the way that a vendor programs a device to function. Drivers can be updated through Device Manager.

To minimize the impact of possible problems with a new driver, a feature of Device Manager allows for a return to the previous driver. This rollback feature is accessible through the Properties page of the device.

Occasionally, the automatic resource configuration within Windows Server 2003 is insufficient to accommodate a unique pattern of device use on a particular computer. If a device needs to have static resources (IRQ, I/O Port, DMA, or Memory Range) set, Device Manager can be used to remove the Automatic Settings use in favor of a setting configured by the user/administrator.

After this lesson, you will be able to

- Use Device Manager to update, roll back, and uninstall drivers
- Use Device Manager to analyze and configure resource use by devices

Estimated lesson time: 15 minutes

Updating Drivers

In Device Manager, most devices can have their drivers updated. The driver update process is a manual one, whether the device is PnP or not, and must be accomplished by an administrator—assuming that the user has not been granted elevated privilege to do so—at the console of the local computer.

> **Note**   An exception to the requirement for local installation with administrative credentials exists if the driver is provided through Windows Update. See Chapter 9, "Maintaining the Operating System," for more information about the Software Update Services (SUS) and Windows Updates.

The process to update a driver is nearly the same as for a device that has been detected properly, but whose driver was not available at installation. After initiating the driver update process for a device from within Device Manager, the Add Hardware Wizard asks for the new driver's location and the driver is installed. Some core system drivers will require a restart of the computer after installation, but most peripheral devices will not. The Properties page where the update of a driver is started is shown in Figure 10-2.

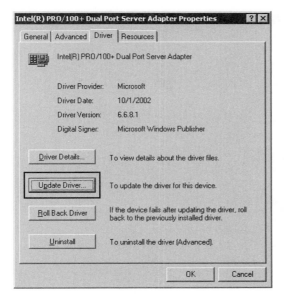

Figure 10-2   Driver update

Note   If you choose to uninstall a device that was configured through PnP, you must scan for hardware changes in Device Manager to have the device reinstalled because Windows Server 2003 removes the device from the configuration even if the device is still connected to the computer.

Rolling Back Drivers

Occasionally, a new driver will not function properly and cannot be kept in the configuration for the device. If the replaced driver was performing properly, then rolling back to the previous driver can be accomplished through Device Manager. Windows Server 2003 automatically backs up the driver that is being replaced through the update driver process, making it available through the Roll Back Driver option. The Properties page where the rollback of a driver can be initiated is shown in Figure 10-3. The contrast between this feature and the Last Known Good Configuration option is discussed in the next lesson.

Figure 10-3 The Roll Back Driver option

Uninstalling Drivers

Drivers may be uninstalled using Device Manager. The Uninstall Driver process is initiated from the Properties page, as shown in Figure 10-4.

Figure 10-4 Uninstall Driver

Uninstalling a driver has different effects depending on whether the device was detected and configured through the PnP process. If the device was configured through PnP, then removal of the driver will result in the removal of the device from Device Manager as well. If the driver for the device was added manually, the device will remain in Device Manager, but will not be configured with a driver.

Resource Configuration

Devices and their drivers require system resources to communicate with and process data through the operating system. These resources are configured automatically by Windows Server 2003, sometimes in a shared capacity with other devices within the system. In circumstances where resources must be statically configured, Device Manager allows for some control of the resources assigned for use by a device. If configuration is not available, the resources used by a device and its driver cannot be configured manually. The Resources tab of a device's Properties page of a manually configurable resource is shown in Figure 10-5.

Figure 10-5   The Resources tab of a device's configurable Properties

To configure a resource assignment manually, the Use Automatic Settings check box must first be cleared, then the resources can be set.

> **Caution**   Any resources set manually make both the resource and device unavailable for automatic configuration, limiting the ability of Windows Server 2003 to make adjustments. This may cause problems with other devices.

Control Panel and Device Configuration

Several devices have Control Panel applications associated with them that allow configuration of hardware devices. The same Device Manager limitations, which are based on user rights, for the installation, updating, or removal of device drivers exist within the Control Panel applications.

Such Properties pages are administered separately through Group Policies, and can be removed from user view and access. This setting is in the User Configuration section of a Group Policy.

Practice: Configuring Devices

In the following practice, you will temporarily change the configuration of a network card to remove it from service without uninstalling the device.

Exercise 1: Disable a Device

1. Open Device Manager, then select a network card configured for your computer.

2. In Device Manager, double-click the listing of the network card.

3. Select the Device Usage drop-down list and then select Do Not Use This Device (Disable).

   The device is now disabled from operation within this Hardware profile.

4. Open the Properties page for the network card, and choose Use This Device (Enable) to re-enable the network card for use in this Hardware profile. Alternatively, you can right-click the device and select Enable or Disable, depending on the current state of the device.

Lesson Review

The following questions are intended to reinforce key information presented in this lesson. If you are unable to answer a question, review the lesson materials and try the question again. You can find answers to the questions in the "Questions and Answers" section at the end of this chapter.

1. Under what circumstances would you adjust the resource settings for a device?

   _____

   _____

2. You need to remove a PnP device from a configuration temporarily, but want to leave it physically connected to the computer. You want to minimize the amount of work required to use the device later. Which of the following is the best option to accomplish your goal?

    a. From the Properties page of the device, choose Do Not Use this Device (Disable).

    b. From the Properties page of the device, choose Uninstall.

    c. Using the Safely Remove Hardware utility, choose to remove the device.

3. Greg's computer has an external USB Hard Disk connected to a USB hub on his computer. He is reporting that the disk is connected properly, but the drive (G) normally associated with the disk is not available. Upon investigation, you discover that the indicator light on the hub is not illuminated and the device does not appear in Device Manager. Disconnecting and re-connecting the device has no effect. What is likely the quickest way to return the disk to proper functionality?

    _____

    _____

Lesson Summary

- Device Manager can be used to Disable/Enable individual devices.

- Manual resource configuration is possible for some devices, but should be done only when there is a conflict with other resources on the computer. Manual configuration should be kept to a minimum so as to allow Windows Server 2003 the greatest amount of flexibility in automatically configuring resources for all devices.

- Driver Updating is done through Device Manager.

- Driver Roll Back is done through Device Manager, and allows for use of a driver that was previously configured for a device.

- Uninstalling a PnP device requires rescanning of the computer to re-enable the device. Uninstalling a non-PnP device requires reinstallation to enable the device.

Lesson 3: Troubleshooting Hardware Devices and Drivers

Problems with drivers will arise, particularly when driver configuration is not possible through PnP means, or when core system component drivers are updated. When a device configuration is not possible through strictly PnP means, the chance of mismatching devices and their drivers increases. With core system component driver updates, which require a computer restart, any problems with the driver will not be known until the computer restarts.

After this lesson, you will be able to

- Understand how to use Disaster Recovery Methods for Devices
- Understand and analyze driver-related problems

Estimated lesson time: 15 minutes

Recovering from Device Disaster

Occasionally, when you install or upgrade a driver for a device, there is a problem with the functioning of that device on your system. Depending on the importance of the device, the effect of the problem will range from annoying to catastrophic. Particularly for such core system components as video drivers, a faulty configuration can render the computer unusable. Rolling back the driver, after all, is difficult if you cannot see the screen.

Thankfully, there are multiple methods of recovery from faulty driver configuration. The tools available are specifically suited to different purposes, and have varying chances of success. Tools that can be used in the event of incorrect driver configuration are listed in Table 10-3.

Table 10-3   Driver Recovery Tools

Tool	Severity	Use
Driver Rollback (Device Manager)	Low. Most system functions remain intact.	Use the Property page for the device to go back to the last driver that was working properly. Contact the vendor to resolve the issue with the new driver.
Last Known Good Configuration	Medium/High. The device driver update requires a restart, and the computer will not resume to the point of allowing you to log on.	When you change drivers that require a restart, the Registry Key HKLM\System\CurrentControlSet can be restored with the old driver information. By pressing F8 as the system restarts, you can select the Last Known Good Configuration, which restores the key. If the problem does not surface until you have successfully logged on (which is often the case with an updated video driver), Last Known Good will be of little use because it is overwritten upon successful logon.

Table 10-3   Driver Recovery Tools   (Continued)

Tool	Severity	Use
Safe mode	Medium/High. System is unusable.	By pressing F8 as the system restarts, you can select Safe mode as a boot option. This mode uses only minimal system and device drivers—enough to start the computer and log on—which allows you to access Device Manager and disable the offending device.
Recovery Console	High. Last Known Good and Safe modes do not work.	The Recovery Console allows you to log on and access limited parts of the file system from a command prompt. From the Recovery Console, you can disable the device driver that is causing the problem, but you must know the correct name of the device or driver (or both), which can be cryptic.

Device Manager Status Codes

When a device fails, an error message is usually reported in Device Manager with an exclamation point in a yellow icon next to the device. If you double-click the device (or right-click the device and then click Properties), a dialog box is displayed and any error messages that Device Manager detects are listed. This Device Status has some friendly text with it, but troubleshooting may require that you understand more than the text message delivers. Often, there is a code listed with the text that gives a better idea of how to troubleshoot the problem. These codes and suggested troubleshooting strategies are listed in Table 10-4.

Table 10-4   Device Failure Troubleshooting

Code	Friendly Text	Troubleshooting Strategy
1	This device is not configured correctly. To update the drivers for this device, click Update Driver. If that doesn't work, see your hardware documentation for more information.	Use Update Driver to update the driver.
3	The driver for this device might be corrupted, or your system may be running low on memory or other resources.	The driver may be corrupted. If you attempt to load a file that is corrupted the system may think that it needs more memory. Use Task Manager to confirm that your system is not low on memory.

Table 10-4   Device Failure Troubleshooting (Continued)

Code	Friendly Text	Troubleshooting Strategy
10	The device cannot start. Try updating the device drivers for this device.	Run the Hardware Update Wizard using the Update Driver button, but do not let Windows Server 2003 automatically detect devices. Instead, select Install From A List Or Specific Location (Advanced), and manually point the wizard to the appropriate driver.
12	This device cannot find enough free resources that it can use. If you want to use this device, you will need to disable one of the other devices on this system.	Click the Resources tab on the Properties page containing the error. Windows Server 2003 will, likely, be able to enumerate the associated device that is in conflict with the device in question. Either disable or remove the device that is in conflict. You can then add the device you removed back into the system and see if the device can take new resources on its own, or if you will have to assign resources manually.
Most other codes	Various	Most other codes involve an inappropriate driver, which should be reinstalled.

Tip   Remember, if a driver is signed, it is verified to work with Windows Server 2003. You can get a list of signed drivers under Software Environment of the System Information utility. System Information is accessible through the System Tools program group, or by typing winmsd at the Run line.

Lesson Review

The following questions are intended to reinforce key information presented in this lesson. If you are unable to answer a question, review the lesson materials and try the question again. You can find answers to the questions in the "Questions and Answers" section at the end of this chapter.

1. You have finished configuring a new display driver, and are prompted to restart the computer for the changes to take effect. Shortly after logging on, the computer screen goes blank, making working on the computer impossible. Which troubleshooting techniques or tools will allow you to recover most easily from the problem with the display driver?

    a. Last Known Good Configuration

    b. Driver Rollback

    c. Safe mode

    d. Recovery Console

2. In Device Manager, you have a device that displays an error icon. On the Properties page for the device, you read that the Device Status is: "device could not start." What course of action will solve the problem?

_____

_____

3. The vendor for a wireless network card installed in your computer has released a new driver. You want to test the driver for proper functionality. Which Device Manager option will you select to test the new driver?

_____

_____

Lesson Summary

- The Last Known Good Configuration option is useful for reverting to a previously used, non-PnP driver, but only if you have not logged on to the system after restarting.

- Starting the computer in Safe mode loads a minimal set of drivers, allowing for access to Device Manager to either disable, uninstall, or roll back a driver that is prohibiting the system from functioning properly.

- Most driver problems occur during manual configuration of an inappropriate driver.

- Resource settings should only be adjusted manually when conflicting settings cannot be resolved by the operating system.

- All manually configured resource allocations must be unique.

Case Scenario Exercise

If a computer is experiencing hardware resource allocation conflicts, hardware profiles allow for the selection of devices to be enabled in different circumstances. As an alternative to manually attempting to configure which device should be assigned what resource, and perhaps never determining a working configuration, defining a hardware profile in which a device is not enabled allows for resources to be used for other devices.

Hardware profiles also allow for the optimization of performance and some control of power usage through the disabling of devices and services that are not used in a particular situation. A laptop computer, for example, can have its battery life extended through the creation of a "mobile" profile, which disables devices that are not needed when the computer is disconnected from the network.

In this exercise, you will disable the network card for use in a hardware profile on a laptop computer.

1. On the Hardware tab of System Properties, click Hardware Profiles.

2. Copy the current profile to a new profile. Name the profile "mobile" and leave the Hardware Profiles Selection setting at the default (selects the first profile in the list if a selection is not made within 30 seconds).

3. Restart the computer. When prompted for selection of a Hardware profile, choose Mobile as the hardware profile for the system to use.

4. Log on, and open Device Manager from the Hardware tab in System Properties.

5. Right-click the network card reported in Device Manager and choose Properties.

6. In the Device Usage drop-down list on the Properties page for the network card, select Do Not Use This Device In The Current Hardware Profile (disable).

You have now disabled the network card for use in a single profile. This technique can be used in many different situations, including troubleshooting devices, by creating Hardware profiles that enable or disable different devices whose combined interactions and resource usage you are testing.

Troubleshooting Lab

The distribution files for Windows Server 2003 include most of the drivers needed to configure the latest hardware devices, and misconfiguration is very rare. For configuration conflicts that must be resolved manually, however, misconfiguration is a more common occurrence.

When a device configuration change causes the computer to fail on restart, the Last Known Good Configuration allows for rollback to use of a driver that was last in use. Assuming that logon has not been accomplished since the problematic device driver was installed, the Last Known Good Configuration is a usable option.

If logon is accomplished, the Last Known Good Configuration is overwritten with the current configuration. If a driver fails, making the computer unusable after logon, then Safe mode is a boot option that loads only a minimal set of drivers to allow configuration of malfunctioning devices and drivers.

In this lab, you will activate the Last Known Good Configuration and Safe mode options during the startup of your computer.

1. Restart your computer.

2. As the computer is starting up, press F8.

3. Activate the Last Known Good Configuration (last configuration that worked).

   At this point, all non-PnP drivers installed since the last restart and logon will have reverted to their previous state.

4. Restart your computer.

5. As the computer is starting up, press F8.

6. Start the computer in Safe mode.

7. Log on to the computer, then start Device Manager.

   You can now configure devices and their drivers for booting in Normal mode.

Chapter Summary

- You must have administrative privileges on a computer to install non-PnP devices and their drivers.

- Users are able to install true PnP devices. If the drivers need to be added to the computer, or any additional configuration or input is necessary during the installation, the user will not be able to install the device.

- Device Manager will indicate, with one of several types of icons, any devices that cannot be configured due to driver identification or resource conflict problems.

- The Device Manager and any Control Panel applications that configure hardware can be made unavailable to the user through Group Policies.

- Updated drivers can be rolled back to the previously used driver with the Roll Back Driver function of Device Manager.

- Devices can be disabled or enabled through Device Manager.

- PnP devices that have signed drivers on the Windows Server 2003 distribution CD will configure automatically, requiring no user intervention.

Exam Highlights

Before taking the exam, review the key points and terms that are presented below to help you identify topics you need to review. Return to the lessons for additional practice and review the "Further Readings" sections in Part 2 for pointers to more information about topics covered by the exam objectives.

Key Points

- Review the use of Device Manager to install device drivers, update device drivers, roll back device drivers, and disable or enable devices in a hardware profile. Remember that Device Manager can change settings only on a local system—remote use of Device Manager is limited to read-only mode.

- Users can only install PnP devices.

- Administrative credentials are required to install non-PnP and vendor-supplied PnP drivers.

- Reinstallation of a driver is needed unless a resource conflict is being resolved.

- Resource conflicts are resolved by first clearing the Use Automatic Settings check box, then configuring the required resource settings.

- Last Known Good Configuration is only useful before a system restart /user logon cycle is complete.

- Safe mode will load a minimal set of drivers so that appropriate configuration can be made.

Key Terms

Roll Back Driver vs. Last Known Good Configuration A driver rollback requires logon, whereas a logon invalidates Last Known Good Configuration. Roll Back Driver and Last Known Good Configuration both revert to a previous configuration of a device driver.

Uninstalling vs. disabling a device Uninstalling a device will remove the device from all configurations. Depending on the type of device, a PnP detection might occur on the next system restart or Scan for Hardware changes. Configuration of the device on the next system restart or Scan for Hardware changes will treat the device as new.

Disabling a device maintains the driver as configured the next time that the device is enabled, but makes the device unavailable for use until enabled.

Safe Mode vs. Last Known Good Configuration Logging on in Safe mode loads a minimal set of drivers, but will not reset any drivers, whereas the Last Known Good Configuration will revert to the previous driver configuration.

Questions and Answers

Page
10-8
Lesson 1 Review

1. You want to make certain that no unsigned drivers are used on the desktop computers in your environment. What Driver Signing settings and related configuration will assure this condition?

In a Group Policy for the desktop computers, set the Security Option for Devices: Unsigned Driver Installation Behavior to Do Not Allow Installation. You can also use domain based Group Policies to deny access to hardware Properties pages and the MMC Device Manager snap-in for the users of the desktop computers.

2. A user wants to install a USB printer connected to their his or her computer. The drivers for the printer are included with Windows Server 2003. Can the user install the printer?

Yes. A USB printer with drivers included with Windows Server 2003 is a PnP printer, and the driver is signed, so installation should be possible with no intervention from the user. This assumes that there are no resource conflicts on that computer.

3. A user wants to install a USB printer connected to his or her local computer. The driver is provided by the vendor, and is not included with Windows Server 2003. The driver is digitally signed. Can the user install the printer?

No. The driver must be queried by the Add Hardware Wizard in Windows Server 2003, which requires user interaction through the interface, which (by default) is not permitted.

Page
10-14
Lesson 2 Review

1. Under what circumstances would you adjust the resource settings for a device?

Adjustments to a driver are usually necessary for resolution of device conflicts involving devices that cannot be completely configured automatically by the operating system, such as older Industry Standard Architecture (ISA) devices or devices bridged to Peripheral Component Interconnect (PCI).

2. You need to remove a PnP device from a configuration temporarily, but want to leave it physically connected to the computer. You want to minimize the amount of work required to use the device later. Which of the following is the best option to accomplish your goal?

    a. From the Properties page of the device, choose Do Not Use this Device (Disable).

    b. From the Properties page of the device, choose Uninstall.

    c. Using the Safely Remove Hardware utility, choose to remove the device.

The correct answer is a. This method will allow for the temporary disabling of the device. All that needs to be done for the device to be usable again is to Enable it. Other options require either a reinstallation or rescanning of the computer to reactivate the device.

3. Greg's computer has an external USB Hard Disk connected to a USB hub on his computer. He is reporting that the disk is connected properly, but the drive (G) normally associated with the disk is not available. Upon investigation, you discover that the indicator light on the hub is not illuminated and the device does not appear in Device Manager. Disconnecting and re-connecting the device has no effect. What is likely the quickest way to return the disk to proper functionality?

In Device Manager, right-click the USB Hub and choose Scan for Hardware Changes. This action will force a detection of the Hard Disk connected to the Hub as if it were a newly connected device.

Page
10-18

Lesson 3 Review

1. You have finished configuring a new display driver, and are prompted to restart the computer for the changes to take effect. Shortly after logging on, the computer screen goes blank, making working on the computer impossible. Which troubleshooting techniques or tools will allow you to recover most easily from the problem with the display driver?

   a. Last Known Good Configuration

   b. Driver Rollback

   c. Safe mode

   d. Recovery Console

   The correct answers are b and c. The Last Known Good Configuration option is useless because you have logged on to the computer, making the last changes permanent. Safe mode will allow you to roll back the driver by using Device Manager.

2. In Device Manager, you have a device that displays an error icon. On the Properties page for the device, you read that the Device Status is: "device could not start." What course of action will solve the problem?

   Install the appropriate driver for the device with the Update Driver function in Device Manager.

3. The vendor for a wireless network card installed in your computer has released a new driver. You want to test the driver for proper functionality. Which Device Manager option will you select to test the new driver?

   The Device Manager option you should select is Update Driver. Although the Reinstall Driver option would allow for the new driver to be used, selecting the Update Driver option will allow for the creation of a backup file containing the current driver, making driver rollback an option in the event that the driver does not perform properly.

11 Managing Microsoft Windows Server 2003 Disk Storage

Exam Objectives in this Chapter:

- Manage basic disks and dynamic disks
- Optimize server disk performance
- Implement a RAID solution
- Defragment volumes or partitions
- Monitor and optimize a server environment for application performance
- Monitor disk quotas
- Recover from server hardware failure

Why This Chapter Matters

If there's one truism about information technology, it's that no matter how much storage you have today, it will be full tomorrow. You probably remember when hard drives were measured in megabytes. Many organizations are now talking terabytes. And with all that data, and all those users needing all that information comes an enormous strain on the storage subsystems on your servers.

Large organizations are turning to storage area networks (SANs) made up of fiber-connected, fault-tolerant arrays of disk drives. But storage that is actually attached to your servers won't disappear quite yet, so you will want to make sure that you have configured server storage to provide the optimum balance of storage capacity, performance, and fault tolerance.

In this chapter, you will learn how to do just that: leverage one or more physical disks to address your storage requirements. You will learn about the storage options that Microsoft Windows Server 2003 provides, including flexible structures that make it easy to extend capacity, provide redundancy, and boost performance—usually without a restart! You'll also learn to configure and recover fault-tolerant disk sets created by Windows Server 2003's redundant array of independent disks (RAID) support. Finally, you will examine Check Disk, Disk Quotas and Disk Defragmenter, which will keep those drives working smoothly and perhaps delay the inevitable exhausting of their capacity.

Lessons in this Chapter:

Before You Begin

This chapter presents the skills and concepts related to disk storage. You are able to apply several concepts and skills using hands-on exercises that require the following configuration:

- A computer installed with Windows Server 2003, Standard Edition or Enterprise Edition.

- The server should have at least one disk drive with a minimum of 1 gigabyte (GB) of unallocated space.

- The computer should be named Server01 and should be a domain controller in the *contoso.com domain*.

Lesson 1: Understanding Disk Storage Options

Before you tackle the installation of a disk drive and the configuration of that drive, you must understand several important storage concepts. This lesson will introduce you to the concepts, technologies, features, and terminology related to disk storage in Windows Server 2003. You will learn about differences between basic and dynamic disk storage types, and the variety of logical volumes they support.

After this lesson, you will be able to

- Understand disk-storage concepts and terminology
- Distinguish between basic and dynamic storage
- Identify the strengths and limitations of basic and dynamic disks
- Identify the types of storage volumes supported on Windows Server 2003 managed disks

Estimated lesson time: 15 minutes

Physical Disks

Physical disks are the conglomeration of plastic, metal, and silicon that enable users to store enormous quantities of useless data and MP3s, and the occasional business document. Of course I'm being sarcastic here, but it is important to understand the difference between the physical disk, and its logical volume(s), which are discussed in the next paragraph. It is also helpful to remember that an advanced disk subsystem, such as hardware-based redundant array of independent disks (RAID) system, may consist of several physical disks, but its dedicated hardware controllers abstract the physical composition of the disk set so that Windows Server 2003 perceives and represents the disk system as a single physical disk.

Logical Volumes

A logical volume is the basic unit of disk storage that you configure and manage. A logical volume may include space on more than one physical disk. Logical volumes (also called logical disks in the context of performance monitoring) are physically distinct storage units, allowing the separation of different types of information, such as the operating system, applications, and user data. Logical volumes have traditionally been represented by a single drive letter.

As you dig into disk-related terminology, you will learn about partitions, logical drives, and volumes. Many resources will use all these terms interchangeably, which is possible because the technical distinctions between the terms are minuscule, and the user interface and command-line tools guide you clearly by exposing only the appropriate type of logical volume based on the task you are performing. Don't get too hung up on the distinctions between the terms; they will become clear through experience if not through analysis.

Mounted Volumes

You noticed that we said, "Logical volumes have traditionally been represented by a single drive letter." That structure severely limited (to 26, says my kindergarten teacher) the number of volumes you could create on a system, and the flexibility with which those volumes could be used. Windows Server 2003's NTFS file system allows you to assign one or no drive letter to a volume. In addition, you can mount a volume to one or more empty folders on existing NTFS volumes. For example, you might create an empty folder Docs, on an existing volume with the drive letter X:, and mount a new 120 GB logical volume to that folder. When users navigate to X:\Docs, the disk sub-system redirects the input/output (I/O) requests to the new volume. All of this is transparent to the user.

The possibilities using this powerful feature are, as they say, "limitless." By mounting a volume to a folder path, you can extend the available drive space on an existing volume. If the existing volume is not fault-tolerant, but the new volume is fault-tolerant, the folder to which the volume is mounted, X:\Docs, represents a fault-tolerant portion of the existing volume's namespace. You could, theoretically, mount all logical volumes on a server to folders on the server's C or D drive and thereby unify enormous storage capacity under the namespace of a single drive letter.

Fault Tolerance

Fault tolerance refers to a system's ability to continue functioning when a component—in this case, a disk drive—has failed. Windows Server 2003 allows you to create two types of fault-tolerant logical volumes: mirrored (RAID-1) and striped with parity (RAID-5). You will learn more about the details of these configurations later in the chapter, but it is important to remember several facts about Windows Server 2003 fault tolerance, often called software RAID:

- In fault-tolerant disk configurations, two or more disks are used, and space is allocated to store data that will enable the system to recover in the event of a single drive failure.

- The fault tolerance options supported by Windows Server 2003 do not provide a means for a disk volume to continue functioning if two or more disks fail.

- The operating system allows you to use any two or more disk drives to create fault-tolerant volumes. You do not have to purchase any additional hardware or software to benefit immediately from fault-tolerant server configurations. However, if you use Windows Server 2003 mirrored or RAID-5 volumes, it is best practice to use similar or identical disk drives on the same bus. Combining a variety of disk hardware, or using drives connected to a variety of small computer systems interface (SCSI) or Integrated Device Electronics (IDE) buses can affect performance significantly.

■ Speaking of performance, Windows Server 2003 fault tolerance is using processor cycles and other server resources to manage the volumes. RAID-5 can be particularly detrimental to server performance. It is possible, and affordable these days, to purchase hardware-based fault-tolerant disk arrays, known as *hardware RAID*. Hardware RAID uses dedicated controllers to manage fault tolerance, and such systems are generally faster and more flexible in both management and recovery than is Windows Server 2003 RAID.

■ Because hardware RAID controllers offload the management duties from the operating system, a hardware RAID array appears to Windows Server 2003 as a single disk.

Separation of Data

It is a good idea to analyze storage requirements carefully before configuring the disk subsystem of a server. Administrators typically elect to install the operating system on a logical volume separate from applications and data. By isolating the operating system, it is easier to secure the operating system volume and to manage disk space so that the volume does not run out of space. It is also usual to configure some kind of fault tolerance for the operating system.

Applications are generally stored in a separate volume, and user data and files in a third. Again, isolation of data types allows you to manage security, performance, and fault tolerance separately for each data type. If an application uses a transaction log to prepare entries into a database, as do Microsoft Active Directory directory service and Microsoft Exchange Server, it is typical to store those logs in volumes that reside on physical disks separate from the database itself, allowing the application to rebuild the database from the logs if the database fails.

Once you have thoroughly analyzed your storage requirements as they relate to the data type, security, performance, and fault tolerance, you can begin to determine how many disks you require and how those disks should be configured.

Basic and Dynamic Disks

An operating system must have a way to make sense of the physical space on a disk drive. There are two structures that Windows Server 2003 can apply to help it apportion and allocate drive space: basic and dynamic storage, also called basic and dynamic disks.

Basic Disks, Partitions, and Logical Drives

Basic disks maintain the structure with which you are probably most familiar. Each basic disk is partitioned, and each partition functions as a physically separate unit of storage. The information about the location and size of each partition is stored in the partition table of the Master Boot Record (MBR) on the drive. A basic disk can contain as many as four partitions, consisting of either four primary partitions or three primary partitions and one extended partition.

The logical volumes on a basic disk are primary partitions and logical drives. The logical volume, as mentioned, can be represented by zero or more drive letters and can be mounted to folders on an existing NTFS volume.

- **Primary partition**   Each primary partition maintains one logical volume on a basic disk. If a basic disk is used to start the operating system, one and only one primary partition on the disk must also be marked as active.

> **Tip**   The computer's basic input/output system (BIOS) looks to the active partition to locate the hardware-specific files required to load the operating system. That partition is technically referred to as the *system partition* and is usually assigned drive letter "C". Once the boot process has begun, the operating system is loaded. Most servers are configured with the operating system on the C drive as well. The partition on which the operating system is stored is called the *boot partition*. Yes, it can get confusing, particularly because the same volume is referred to by the variable *%Sysvol%*. Fortunately, it's not a distinction you're likely to need to know, since most installations are completely on drive C, making the C drive the system partition, the boot partition, and *%Sysvol%*.

- **Extended partition**   A basic disk may also contain an extended partition. Unlike primary partitions, extended partitions are not formatted or assigned drive letters. Instead, extended partitions are further divided into logical drives. Logical drives are logical volumes on a basic disk.

In earlier versions of Microsoft operating systems, including Windows 95, Windows 98, and MS-DOS, the operating system could only "see" the primary partition on which it was installed, plus the extended partition on the drive, if one existed. If you wanted additional storage segments on the drive, you had to configure an extended partition and apportion it into one or more logical drives. Because Windows NT, Windows 2000, Windows XP, and Windows Server 2003 can access all partitions on a disk, you only need an extended partition if you want more than four logical drives on a single disk.

Dynamic Disks and Volumes

Microsoft Windows 2000, Windows XP, and the Windows Server 2003 family also support dynamic storage. The storage units on dynamic disks are called volumes, and the first distinctions between basic and dynamic storage are that dynamic disks support an unlimited number of volumes, and that the configuration information about the volumes is stored in a database controlled by the Logical Disk Manager (LDM) service.

The logical volume of dynamic disks is the volume. Dynamic disks support simple volumes on a single disk. When a computer has more than one dynamic disk, you are provided more storage options from which to choose. Spanned, mirrored (RAID-1), striped (RAID-0), and striped with parity (RAID-5) volumes are logical volumes that utilize space on more than one physical disk. Each volume type uses disk space differently, and is characterized by a different level of fault tolerance. The list below summarizes the volume types, though each has nuances you will learn about as the chapter progresses.

- **Simple volume**   The equivalent to a basic disk partition is a dynamic disk simple volume. Simple volumes utilize space on a single physical disk, and correspond to a single logical volume. Simple volumes can be extended by appending unallocated space on other regions of the same disk, allowing you to adjust a volume's capacity with the growth of data stored in that volume. Because simple volumes exist on only one physical disk, they are not fault-tolerant.

- **Spanned volume**   A spanned volume includes space on more than one physical disk. Up to 32 physical disks can participate in a spanned volume, and the amount of space used on each disk can be different. Data is written to the volume beginning with the space on the first disk in the volume. When the space on the first disk fills, the second disk is written to, and so on. Spanned volumes provide an option for increasing drive capacity. If a simple or spanned volume is filling up, you can extend the volume onto additional new storage capacity.

   But spanned volumes are not fault-tolerant, and cannot participate in any fault-tolerant configurations. Because their size tends to be greater, and because multiple physical disks are involved, the risk for failure increases. If any one disk in a spanned volume is corrupted or lost, data on the entire volume is lost as well. For these reasons, Windows Server 2003 will not allow the installation of the operating system on a spanned volume, nor can you extend or span the system volume. Spanned volumes are recommended only as a stop-gap measure when an existing volume fills to capacity, or else in situations where tolerance for failure is high— for example, a large library of read-only data that can easily be restored from tape backup in the event of failure.

- **Striped volume**   A striped volume (RAID-0) combines areas of free space from multiple hard disks into one logical volume. Unlike a spanned volume, however, data is written to all physical disks in the volume at the same rate. Because multiple spindles are in use, read and write performance is increased almost geometrically as additional physical disks are added to the stripe. But like extended simple volumes and spanned volumes, if a disk in a striped volume fails, the data in the entire volume is lost.

■ **Mirrored volume**   A mirrored volume (also known as RAID Level 1, or RAID-1) consists of two identical copies of a simple volume, each on a separate hard disk. Mirrored volumes provide fault tolerance in the event that one physical disk fails.

■ **RAID-5 volume**   A RAID-5 volume is a fault-tolerant striped volume. Space on three or more physical disks is unified as a single volume. Data is written to all physical disks at the same rate, but unlike a striped volume, the data is interlaced with checksum information, called parity. Should a single disk in the volume fail, the data on that disk can be regenerated through calculations involving the remaining data and the checksum information. It is an interesting technical note that parity is distributed among all volumes in the RAID-5 set.

Basic vs. Dynamic Disks

So now that you know about basic and dynamic storage, and the types of partitions, logical drives, and volumes they support, which is better? The answer, as is frequently the case, is: "It depends."

Dynamic disks that store data are easily transferred between servers, allowing you to move a disk from a failed server to a functioning server with little downtime. Dynamic disks flex their muscle when there is more than one dynamic disk in a computer. Each Windows 2000, Windows XP, and Windows Server 2003 computer can support one disk group, which itself can contain multiple dynamic disks. The LDM database is replicated among all disks in the disk group, which increases the resiliency of disk configuration information for all the group's disks. In addition, disks can be configured to work together to create a variety of flexible and powerful volume types including spanned volumes, striped volumes (RAID-0), mirrored volumes (RAID-1), and striped-with-parity volumes (RAID-5).

Basic disks will continue to be used, however, for several reasons:

■ Basic storage is the default in Windows Server 2003, so all new disks are basic disks until you convert them to dynamic—a simple process you will learn in Lesson 2.

■ Dynamic disks do not offer advantages over basic disks in a computer that will have only one disk drive.

■ The behavior of the LDM database also makes it difficult to transfer a dynamic disk used for starting the operating system to another computer when the original computer fails.

■ Dynamic disks are not supported for removable media, and are not supported on laptops.

■ Basic storage is the industry standard, so basic drives are accessible from many operating systems, including MS-DOS, all versions of Microsoft Windows, and most non-Microsoft operating systems (there are a few). Therefore, dynamic disks cannot be used if you need to dual-boot an earlier operating system that requires access to the disks. Keep in mind that we are talking about *local* access only. When a client of any platform accesses files over the network, the underlying storage and volume type are transparent to the client.

> **Exam Tip**   Multiboot scenarios are less common these days with the advent of virtual machine technology (see *http://www.microsoft.com/windowsserver2003/techinfo/overview /virtualization.mspx*). However, if you implement a multibooted system with Windows Server 2003 as one of the operating systems, you should install each operating system on a separate, primary partition. Other configurations are risky at best. For more information on multi-booting, open the Help and Support Center and search using the keyword *multiboot*.

Lesson Review

The following questions are intended to reinforce key information presented in this lesson. If you are unable to answer a question, review the lesson materials and try the question again. You can find answers to the questions in the "Questions and Answers" section at the end of this chapter.

1. You are installing a new 200 GB disk drive. You want to divide the disk into five logical volumes for the operating system, applications, user home directories, shared data, and a software distribution point. The drive space should be distributed equally among the five logical volumes. You also want to leave 50 GB as unallocated space for future extension of a logical volume. Considering basic and dynamic disks and the types of logical volumes they support, what are your configuration options?

   _____

   _____

2. Which of the following provides the ability to recover from the failure of a single hard drive?

   a. Primary partition

   b. Extended partition

   c. Logical drive

   d. Simple volume

   e. Spanned volume

   f. Mirrored volume

   g. Striped volume

   h. RAID-5 volume

3. You are dual-booting a system in your test lab. The computer has Windows NT 4 installed on the first primary partition, and Windows Server 2003 installed on the second primary partition. The computer is running low on disk space, so you add a new disk drive. You boot to Windows Server 2003 and configure the drive as a dynamic disk. When you later restart to Windows NT 4, you are unable to see the disk. Why?

_____

_____

4. To provide fault tolerance, maximum performance, and the ability to hot-swap a failed drive, you purchase a seven-disk hardware RAID array. After installing the array, you see only one new disk on Windows Server 2003. Why?

_____

_____

Lesson Summary

■ Disk terminology can be confusing, but in the end a logical volume is almost synonymous with the terms *partition*, *logical drive*, or *volume*.

■ Windows Server 2003 supports basic and dynamic disks. Basic disks support as many as four partitions: four primary partitions or three primary partitions and one extended partition, which supports multiple logical drives. Dynamic disks support simple volumes or, when more than one dynamic disk is configured, spanned, mirrored, striped, and RAID-5 volumes.

■ Fault tolerance is provided by mirrored (RAID-1) volumes, which maintain a full copy of the volume's data on each of two disks, and striped-with-parity volumes (RAID-5), which stripe the data across multiple disks and use parity information to calculate data missing from any one failed disk.

■ Simple volumes, spanned volumes, striped volumes (RAID-0), and all basic disk logical drives are not fault-tolerant. All data is lost if any disk supporting such volumes fails. The larger those volumes, or the more physical disks supporting those volumes, the greater the likelihood of failure.

Lesson 2: Configuring Disks and Volumes

In this lesson, you will apply the concepts of disk storage covered in Lesson 1 to the actual skills needed to install, configure, and manage disk storage. You will learn how to use the Disk Management tool to direct the detection and initialization of newly installed disks, and to apportion that disk to partitions, logical drives, and volumes. In the event that a volume fills up, you will learn how to extend that volume's capacity. And you will explore the processes involved with moving disks between servers. Finally, you will uncover the powerful new DISKPART command, which allows you to manage storage from the command line.

After this lesson, you will be able to

- Install and initialize a physical disk
- Manage the configuration of logical volumes on basic and dynamic drives
- Mount a volume to a folder on an NTFS volume
- Extend a volume's capacity
- Move disks between servers
- Convert basic and dynamic disks
- Perform disk management tasks using DISKPART

Estimated lesson time: 25 minutes

Disk Management

Disk management activities are performed using the cleverly named Disk Management snap-in, which is part of the Computer Management console. Open the Disk Management snap-in in the Computer Management console, or add the snap-in to a custom console.

Tip   There is a stand-alone Disk Management console, but it is not visible in your Administrative Tools folder. Click Start, choose Run and type **diskmgmt.msc** to open the stand-alone console.

Disk Management can manage disk storage on local or remote systems. The snap-in does not manipulate disk configuration directly; rather, it works in concert with Dmadmin, the Logical Disk Manager Administrative Service that is started on the computer you are managing when you start the Disk Management snap-in.

The Disk Management interface is shown in Figure 11-1. The top frame—the list view—displays information about each partition, logical drive, or volume. The bottom frame—the graphical view—depicts disk space allocation per physical disk, as perceived by Windows Server 2003. You can right-click the volumes in either frame to access a shortcut menu to format, delete, or assign a drive letter to the volume. If you right-click an area of unallocated disk space, you can create a partition or volume. By right-clicking the disk drive's status box, on the left of the disk's graphical view, you can initialize a new disk, convert between basic and dynamic disks, and access the disk's hardware properties dialog box.

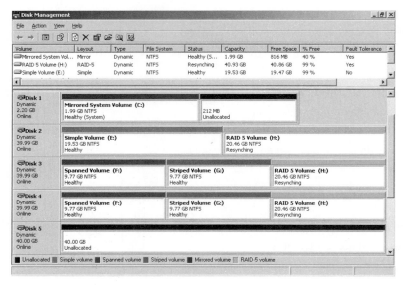

Figure 11-1   Disk Management console

Configuring Disks and Volumes

Configuring storage entails the following steps:

1. Physically installing the disk(s).

2. Initializing the disk.

3. On a basic disk, creating partitions and (if an extended partition) logical drives or, on a dynamic disk, creating volumes.

4. Formatting the volumes.

5. Assigning drive letters to the volumes, or mounting the volumes to empty folders on existing NTFS volumes.

You must be a member of the Administrators or Backup Operators group, or have been otherwise delegated authority, to perform these tasks, although only administrators can format a volume.

Installing the Disk

To add a new disk to a computer, install or attach the new physical disk (or disks). Open Disk Management and, if the drive has not been detected automatically, right click the Disk Management node and choose Rescan Disks. If a system must be taken offline to install a new disk, restart the computer, then open Disk Management. If the new disks are not automatically detected, rescan the disks.

Initializing the Disk

When you add a disk to a server, you will need to initialize that disk before you can begin to allocate its available space to partitions, logical drives, and volumes. Initializing a disk allows the operating system to write a disk signature, the end of sector marker (also called signature word), and an MBR or globally unique identifier (GUID) partition table to the disk.

If you start the Disk Management console after installing a new disk, the Initialize Disk Wizard will appear automatically. To initialize a disk manually using Disk Management, right-click the disk's status box and choose Initialize Disk.

> **Note**   On an Itanium computer, you will be prompted to select the partition style. Itanium computers containing multiple disks support two partition styles, GUID partition table (GPT) and MBR. The system partition on an Itanium computer uses the Extensible Firmware Interface (EFI) and the GPT partition style to support the 64-bit editions of the Windows Server 2003 family. More information about GPT partitions and EFI can be found in the Help And Support Center.

Creating Partitions and Volumes

After you have initialized the disk, you can begin to implement a storage structure of partitions, logical drives, or volumes.

A newly initialized disk is configured by default as a basic disk. If you wish to maintain the disk as a basic disk, you can divide the basic disk into primary and extended partitions by right-clicking unallocated space and choosing New Partition. If you choose to create a primary partition, the partition becomes a logical volume. After creating an extended partition, right-click the partition again and choose New Logical Drive. As you'll remember from earlier discussions, logical drives are logical volumes on an extended partition.

If you want to configure the disk as a dynamic disk, right-click the disk's status box in Disk Management and choose Convert To Dynamic Disk. You can then right-click the unallocated space on the disk and choose New Volume. The New Volume Wizard will step you through the creation of supported volume types. The Select Volume Type page of the wizard is shown in Figure 11-2.

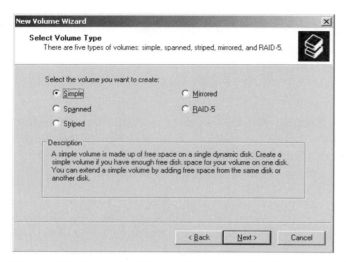

Figure 11-2 The Select Volume Type page of the New Volume Wizard

You can convert an existing basic disk to a dynamic disk—a solution that will be discussed later in this lesson.

Formatting Volumes

Windows Server 2003 supports three file systems: FAT, FAT32, and NTFS. Let's keep this discussion simple: use FAT or FAT32 only when you have very specific reasons for doing so. Only NTFS gives you the level of stability, resiliency, scalability, flexibility and security required by most organizations. Many core components of Windows Server 2003, such as file security, and services, including Active Directory and Remote Installation Services (RIS), require NTFS. All advanced storage management tasks, including multidisk volumes and disk quotas require NTFS. If you think you need FAT32, think again, then think again.

Assigning Drive Letters or Mounting Volumes

When you create a volume, it defaults to the next available drive letter. The New Volume Wizard and New Partition Wizard give you a chance to specify an alternative representation for the new logical volume. You can also right-click an existing volume and choose Change Drive Letter and Paths.

A volume can be represented by only one drive letter, though you can configure a volume to have no drive letter. However, you can mount a volume in one or more empty folders on local NTFS volumes. In the Change Drive Letter And Paths dialog box, you can click Remove or Change to delete or modify an existing drive letter or folder mounting for the volume.

> **Note**   You cannot change the drive letter of the volume that is a system partition or boot partition.

Click Add to add a drive letter or mount point. Figure 11-3 shows a server in which the Docs folder on the X drive is a mount point to another volume. Note that the folder appears in the Explorer namespace exactly where it should, but displays a drive volume icon. When a user navigates to that folder, the user is transparently redirected to the volume.

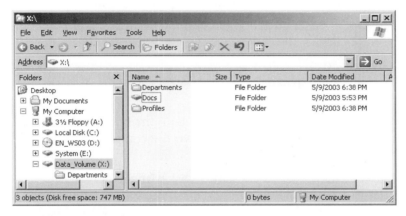

Figure 11-3   A volume mounted to a folder path

Mounting a volume in a folder on an existing volume effectively increases the target volume's size and free space. You can mount volumes regardless of whether the volumes involved are on basic or dynamic disks, and regardless of what type of volume they are. But the empty folder, the path of which becomes the path to the mounted volume, must reside on an NTFS volume. The mounted volume can, technically, be formatted as FAT or FAT32, but of course that is not the best practice.

Extending Volumes

Another way to increase a volume's capacity is to extend the volume. You can extend a simple or spanned volume on a dynamic disk so long as that volume is formatted as NTFS, and so long as the volume is not the system or boot volume. Right-click the volume and click Extend Volume. Follow the Extend Volume Wizard's instructions screen to select unallocated space on dynamic disks on which to extend the existing volume. If you extend a simple volume onto space on another physical disk, you create a spanned volume.

You can extend a partition on a basic disk using the DISKPART command. The basic partition must be formatted as NTFS, must not be the system or boot partition, and must be extended onto immediately contiguous space on the same physical disk that is either unallocated and unformatted, or formatted with NTFS.

Moving Disks Between Servers

It is possible to move disks between computers. If, for example, you plan to take a server offline, you might attach its physical disks to another server so that data can continue to be accessed. The process for doing so is the following:

1. Check the health of the disk while it is in the original server. It is recommended to open Disk Management and confirm that the disk status displays Healthy before moving the disk. If the disk is not healthy, repair the disk.

2. Uninstall the disk in the original computer. If the original server is online, uninstall the disk by right-clicking the disk in Device Manager and choosing Uninstall.

3. Remove a dynamic disk correctly. If the original server is online, open Disk Management, right-click the dynamic disk and choose Remove. This step is not necessary or possible with basic disks.

4. Physically detach the disk. If the computer supports hot-swapping the drive, you may remove the drive. Otherwise, shut down the computer to remove the physical disk.

5. Attach the disk to the target server. Open Disk Management and, if the drive has not been detected automatically, right click the Disk Management node and choose Rescan Disks. Otherwise, shut down the target server before adding the physical disk.

6. Follow instructions in the Found New Hardware Wizard. If the wizard does not appear, open Device Manager and see if the drive was detected and installed automatically. If not, open Add Hardware from Control Panel.

7. Open Disk Management. Right-click Disk Management and choose Rescan Disks.

8. Right-click any disk marked Foreign and choose Import Foreign Disks. Importing a disk reconciles the LDM databases on a new dynamic disk with the existing disks.

Some important notes about moving physical disks:

- If an imported disk contains volumes that span to other physical disks, you must attach and import all physical disks before the volumes can be accessed.

- If you move drives from several computers to a single computer, move all drives from one computer before beginning to move drives from the next computer.

- A basic volume that is moved to a new computer receives the next available drive letter. Dynamic volumes retain the drive letter they had on the original computer. If a dynamic volume did not have a drive letter on the previous computer, it does not receive a drive letter when moved to another computer. If the drive letter is already used on the computer where they are moved, the volume receives the next available drive letter.

- Use the Mountvol /n or the DISKPART automount commands to prevent new volumes from being automatically mounted and assigned a drive letter. If these commands have been used, when you add a new disk you must manually mount the volumes and assign drive letters or paths.

Converting Disk Storage

You can convert a basic disk to a dynamic disk. If the disk already contains partitions and logical drives, those units will be converted to the equivalent units for a dynamic disk: simple volumes. The structure of data on the disk is not modified, so it is possible to convert a basic disk that already contains data, although it is always best practice to back up volumes before performing disk management tasks.

To convert a basic disk to a dynamic disk, right-click the disk's status box and choose Convert To Dynamic Disk. It's that simple. If you convert a disk that contains a system or boot partition, the computer must restart.

> **Tip**   Do not convert basic disks to dynamic disks if they contain multiple operating systems (for example, the disk is set up to dual-boot with another operating system). After the disk is converted to dynamic, you can start the operating system that you used to convert the disk, but you will not be able to start the other operating systems on the disk.

Unfortunately, the reverse process is not as straightforward. Converting back to basic storage wipes out data on the drive. So you must first back up all data on the disk. Then you must delete all existing volumes on the dynamic disk before right-clicking the disk's status box in Disk Management and choosing Convert To Basic Disk. After recreating partitions and logical drives, restore the data onto the disk. Although you can convert from dynamic to basic from a technical perspective, you are actually wiping out the disk and starting over.

Performing Disk Management Tasks from the Command Prompt

Windows Server 2003 provides command-line alternatives for disk management, including the following:

- **Chkdsk**   Scan a disk for errors and, optionally, attempt to correct those errors.
- **Convert**   Convert a volume from FAT or FAT32 to NTFS.

- **Fsutil** Perform a variety of tasks related to managing FAT, FAT32, or NTFS volumes.

- **Mountvol** Manages mounted volumes and reparse points.

But the granddaddy of disk management command-line tools is DISKPART. Table 11-1 summarizes the DISKPART commands that achieve common disk management tasks. Diskpart can be used interactively or can call a script. To start Diskpart interactively, type **diskpart** at the command prompt. When the Diskpart command prompt (DISKPART >) appears, type **?** at any time for help. The command's built-in documentation will appear automatically when needed to help you achieve the tasks you perform. Diskpart is also well documented in the Help And Support Center.

Table 11-1   How to Complete Common Disk Management Tasks from the Command Prompt

Task	From DISKPART>	Description

List disk, partition, and volume information	`list disk`
	`list partition`
	`list volume`
		The first command lists disk information, the second command lists partition information for the current disk, and the third command lists volume and partition information for all disks.

Create a simple volume	`create volume simple` `size=500 disk=2`	Typed on one line, this taks creates a simple volume 500 MB in size on disk 2.
Assign a drive letter	`select volume 4` `assign letter j`	Assigns volume 4 as the J drive.
Extend a simple volume	`select volume 4` `extend size=250 disk=2`	Extends simple volume 4 (on disk 2) with an additional 250 MB on the same disk.
Create a spanned volume	`select volume 4` `extend size=250 disk=1`	Spans a simple volume 4 (on disk 2) with an additional 250 MB on disk 1.
Delete a spanned volume	`select volume 4` `delete volume`	Deletes spanned volume 4. If volume 4 was contained on disk 1 and disk 2, the space it occupied on the two disks becomes unallocated.
Create a volume mount point	`select volume 4` `assign mount=e:\Folder1`	Assigns a volume mount point to volume 4 that is accessed from E:\Folder1.
Create a striped volume	`create volume stripe` `size=500 disk=1,2`	Typed on one line, this task creates a striped volume which uses 500 MB on disks 1 and 2 for a total of 1 GB of storage space.
Create a mirrored volume	`create volume simple size=` `00 disk=1 add disk 2`	Typed on one line, this task creates a mirrored volume which uses 500 MB on disks 1 and 2 for a total of 500 MB of fault-tolerant storage space.

Table 11-1   How to Complete Common Disk Management Tasks from the Command Prompt (Continued)

Task	From DISKPART>	Description
Break a mirror	`select volume 5` `break disk 2`	Selects the mirror on volume 5 and break the mirror on disk 2.
Remove a mirror	`break disk 2 nokeep`	Deletes a mirror and remove the previously mirrored data on disk 2.
Create a RAID-5 stripe	`create volume raid` `size=500 disk=1,2,3`	Typed on one line, this task reates a RAID-5 volume which uses disks 1, 2, and 3 for a total of ~1 GB of fault-tolerant storage space.
Convert a disk from basic to dynamic storage	`select disk 2` `convert dynamic`	Converts disk 2 from basic storage to dynamic storage.
Convert a disk with unallocated space from dynamic to basic storage	`select disk 2` `convert basic`	Converts disk 2 from dynamic to basic.

Practice: Configuring Disks and Volumes

In this practice, you will use the Disk Management snap-in and Diskpart to perform a variety of disk-management tasks on Disk 0. Disk 0 must be configured as a basic disk and contain at least 1 GB of unallocated space to complete this exercise.

Exercise 1: Creating a Partition Using the Disk Management Snap-in

1. Log on to Server01 as Administrator and open the Disk Management snap-in in the Computer Management console.

   The Volume list appears in the upper pane and the graphical view appears in the lower pane.

2. In the graphical view, right-click the unallocated disk space on Disk 0 and choose New Partition. The New Partition Wizard appears.

3. Create a Primary Partition that is 250 MB. Accept the default drive letter assignment. Label the volume Data_Volume and perform a quick format using NTFS.

   After a few moments, a new drive named Data_Volume (*drive_letter:*) appears, where *drive_letter* is the letter that the New Partition Wizard assigned to the partition. When formatting is complete, the status of the partition displays Healthy.

Exercise 2: Converting a Disk from Basic to Dynamic Storage from the Disk Management Snap-In

1. In Disk Management, right-click Disk 0's status box in the graphical view and click Convert To Dynamic Disk. The Convert To Dynamic Disk dialog box appears and the Disk 0 check box is selected.

2. Follow the prompts to convert Disk 0 to a dynamic disk. Because Disk 0 is your system drive, the computer requires a restart.

Exercise 3: Using DiskPart

1. Open a command prompt.

2. Type **diskpart** and press Enter. The DISKPART> prompts appears.

3. Type **?** and press Enter. A list of Diskpart commands appear.

4. Type **list disk** and press Enter. A list of the disk or disks in Server01 appears.

5. Type **create volume simple size = 250 disk = 0** and press Enter.

6. Type **list volume** and press Enter.

   A new volume has been created. The new volume appears with an asterisk before its name. The asterisk denotes that the volume is selected. Notice that there is no drive letter assigned to the volume.

7. Type **assign letter z** and press Enter.

8. Type **list volume** and press Enter. The letter Z is assigned to the selected volume.

9. Type **extend size=250 disk=0** and press Enter.

10. Type **list volume** and press Enter. The selected volume (drive Z) is now 500 MB in size.

11. Type **exit** and press Enter. The command prompt reappears.

12. Type **format z: /fs:NTFS /v:Extended_Volume /q** and press Enter. A warning message appears stating that all data will be lost on drive Z.

13. Press Y and then press Enter. A quick format with NTFS is performed on drive Z.

14. Type **exit** to close the command window.

Exercise 4: Extending Volumes Using Disk Management

1. Open Disk Management.

2. Right-click Extended_Volume and choose Delete Volume.

3. Confirm the deletion of the volume by clicking Yes.

4. Right-click Data_Volume and choose Extend Volume. The Extend Volume Wizard appears.

5. Click Next.

6. Change the amount of space being used to extend the volume to 500 MB.

7. Click Next.

8. Read the summary information. Click Finish.

Exercise 5: Drive Letters and Mounted Volumes

1. Right-click Data_Volume and choose Change Drive Letter And Paths.

2. Change the drive letter to X.

3. Right-click Data_Volume (X:) and choose Open. Windows Explorer opens.

4. Create a folder called Docs.

5. Close Windows Explorer.

6. Right-click unallocated space on Disk 0 and choose New Volume.

7. Create a simple volume using all remaining space on the disk. Instead of assigning a drive letter, mount the volume in the path X:\Docs. Format the volume NTFS and label the volume More_Space.

8. Open Windows Explorer and make sure that Status Bar is selected in the View menu. Examine the X: volume. How much free space is shown? What free space is reported when you open the Docs folder?

Lesson Review

The following questions are intended to reinforce key information presented in this lesson. If you are unable to answer a question, review the lesson materials and try the question again. You can find answers to the questions in the "Questions and Answers" section at the end of this chapter.

1. This question continues the scenario that was presented in question 1 of the review in Lesson 1. You have installed a new 200 GB disk drive. You configured it as a basic disk and created three primary partitions of 30 GB each to host the operating system, user home directories, and shared data. You configured an extended partition and two logical drives of 30 GB each to host applications installed on the machine and a software distribution point. There remains 50 GB of unallocated space on the disk. Several months later, you notice that three of the volumes are nearing capacity. You want to prepare for the likely event that one or more partitions will need to be expanded. What action must you take?

   _____

   _____

2. What type of disk region supports logical drives?

   a. Primary partitions

   b. Simple volumes

   c. Spanned volumes

   d. Extended partitions

   e. Unallocated space

3. You recently added a disk to a computer. The disk had previously been used in a Windows 2000 Server. The disk appears in Device Manager, but is not appearing correctly in Disk Management. What task must you apply?

   a. Import Foreign Disk

   b. Format volume

   c. Rescan

   d. Change Drive Letter or Path

   e. Convert to Dynamic Disk

4. You attempt to convert an external FireWire disk from basic to dynamic, but the option to convert is not available. What is the most likely reason for this?

   _____

   _____

Lesson Summary

- Disk management tasks can be completed using the Disk Management snap-in or from the command prompt with tools such as Diskpart.

- Common disk management tasks include creating and deleting partitions and volumes and assigning drive letters and mount points.

- Windows Server 2003 allows you to assign one or no drive letter to a volume and, optionally, to mount the volume to one or more empty folders on NTFS volumes.

- Basic disks can be converted to dynamic disks, but all data and volumes must be deleted to convert a dynamic disk to a basic disk.

Lesson 3: Maintaining Disk Storage Volumes

Windows Server 2003 disk volumes are efficient and stable if formatted with NTFS, but somewhat less so when formatted with FAT or FAT32. The NTFS file system logs all file transactions, replaces bad clusters automatically, and stores copies of key information for all files on the NTFS volume. With these mechanisms, NTFS actively protects the integrity of the volume structure and the file system metadata (the data related to the file system itself). User data, however, can occasionally be corrupted, and can certainly become fragmented. Users also have the annoying habit of storing *enormous* amounts of archaic and non-business data on volumes to which they have access. In this lesson, you will learn how to maintain the integrity of disk volumes and to optimize those volumes by performing defragmentation and by setting storage limits through disk quotas.

After this lesson, you will be able to

- Monitor and maintain disk integrity using CHKDSK
- Monitor and improve disk performance using Disk Defragmenter
- Configure and monitor user disk storage using Disk Quotas

Estimated lesson time: 20 minutes

CHKDSK

CHKDSK, or "Check Disk", is a tool available in Windows Explorer or from the command-line that allows you to scan a disk volume for file system errors and, optionally, to test for and attempt to recover bad sectors on your hard disk.

To use Check Disk from Windows Explorer, open the properties dialog box for the volume you want to check. On the Tools tab, click Check Now. In the Check Disk dialog box, as shown in Figure 11-4, select the tasks you wish to launch.

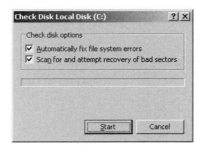

Figure 11-4   The Check Disk dialog box

When you select Automatically Fix File System Errors, Check Disk will attempt to fix inconsistencies in the file system catalog, such as files that appear in the catalog but don't appear in a directory on the volume. Check Disk makes three passes over the drive to examine the metadata, which is the data describing how files are organized on the disk. The passes attempt to ensure that all files on the volume are consistent with the master file table (MFT), that the directory structure is correct, and that the security descriptors are consistent.

If you select Scan For And Attempt Recovery Of Bad Sectors, Check Disk makes a fourth pass which tests the sectors in the volume reserved for user data (as opposed to file system metadata, which is always checked). If a bad sector is found, data is recovered and moved to a good sector if the volume is fault-tolerant; if the volume is not fault-tolerant, data cannot be recovered using Check Disk and must be restored from backup. The bad sector is then removed from active use and future data will not be written to the sector.

All files with open handles must be closed before Check Disk can run. If all handles cannot be released (which will be the case if you run Check Disk against a system volume), you will be prompted to schedule Check Disk to run when the system is restarted. When Check Disk is running, the volume will be inaccessible to other processes. Depending on the size of the volume, the check options you have selected, and the other processes running on the computer, Check Disk can take a significant amount of time to complete, and it is quite processor- and disk-intensive while it runs.

Check Disk can also be run from the command prompt using CHKDSK. Without switches, CHKDSK runs in read-only mode on the current drive. You'll see a report showing disk space usage. CHKDSK supports several switches allowing you to fix file system errors (/f) and bad sectors (/r), just like the Explorer version.

Disk Defragmenter

Files are stored on a volume in units called *clusters*. Cluster size is configured when formatting a drive; many NTFS volumes use a default cluster size of 4 KB. Each cluster can only contain one file, even if that file is smaller than the cluster size. If a file is larger than the cluster size, the file is saved to multiple clusters, with each cluster containing a pointer to the next segment of the file. When a drive is new, all clusters are free, so as files are written to the drive they tend to occupy physically adjacent clusters. But quickly, as files are deleted or expanded and contracted in size, free clusters are no longer completely contiguous, so a file may be saved to several clusters that are not physically close to each other on the disk drive. This fragmentation of a file results in slower read and write performance and, over time, fragmentation of multiple files on a server can degrade performance significantly.

Windows Server 2003 provides a defragmenter toolset—both a command-line and a graphical utility—with which volumes can be analyzed and defragmented. The tools are significantly improved over Windows 2000, as they can now defragment volumes with cluster sizes greater than 4 KB, and can defragment the master file table. You can use the tools to defragment any local disk volume. But to schedule defragmentation, or to defragment a remote volume, you must look for a third-party tool such as Diskeeper from Executive Software.

To use the built-in Disk Defragmenter, as shown in Figure 11-5, open the properties of a disk volume and, from the Tools tab, click Defragment Now. Alternatively, open the Disk Defragmenter snap-in in the Computer Management console or a custom Microsoft Management Console. Select a volume and click Analyze. The tool will display a recommendation. If the tool indicates that the volume is dirty, there may be corruption and CHKDSK should be run before defragmenting.

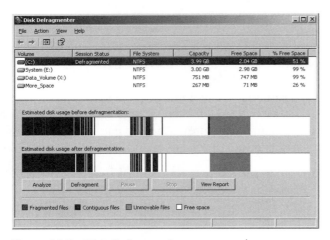

Figure 11-5   Disk Defragmenter

If the recommendation is to defragment, click Defragment. You can defragment any type of volume: FAT or NTFS, basic or dynamic. The volume can have open files, but open files may not be efficiently defragmented and may slow the process, so it is recommended to close all open files before defragmenting. Disk Defragmenter will move files around the drive in an attempt to collect all clusters of a file into contiguous clusters. The result will also consolidate free space, making it less likely that new files will be fragmented.

> **Note**   To completely defragment a volume, the volume must have at least 15 percent free space. This space is used to stage files as they are defragmented. If the volume contains numerous fragmented large files, the amount of free space required for effective defragmentation will be larger. If the volume contains less then 15 percent free space, then the volume will be only partially defragmented.

Disk Quotas

Windows 2000 introduced quota management as a built-in feature, allowing administrators to implement storage limits without an investment in third-party utilities. Windows Server 2003 supports the same functionality. When quotas are enabled, quota manager tracks the files on a volume that are owned by a user. It then compares the calculated total of disk usage by that user to limits that have been configured by an administrator and, when those limits are reached, notifies the user that the volume is near quota, or prevents the user from writing to the disk, or both.

Quota manager reports the amount of free space on a volume based on the user's quota, so if a user has a 50 MB quota on a 500 GB RAID volume, the user will see free space reported as 50 MB when the user first accesses the volume. When the user approaches the quota limit, the messages that appear are similar to a volume that is filling up or is full; the system warns that space is low and suggests deleting unneeded files.

> **Exam Tip**   Quotas are supported only on NTFS volumes.

Configure Quotas

Configuring quotas requires the following steps: enabling quotas on a volume, configuring default quota settings, and configuring quota entries for exceptions to the default.

Quotas are disabled by default in Windows Server 2003, and must be enabled on a volume-by-volume basis. To enable quotas, open the properties of the volume and click the Quota tab. The Quota properties of a volume are shown in Figure 11-6.

> **Tip**   Most documentation suggests opening the properties of the volume from Explorer, by right-clicking a drive and choosing Properties. Unfortunately, that process limits you to configuring quotas for lettered volumes only; Explorer cannot display the Quota tab for a volume mounted to a folder path. Therefore, it is recommended that you configure quotas from Disk Management. The Disk Management tool allows you to open the properties of any volume and access its Quota tab.

Select the Enable Quota Management check box. If you want to deny users who have exceeded their limit the ability to write additional files to the volume, select Deny Disk Space To Users Exceeding Quota Limit. If this box is not selected, users can continue to write to the volume.

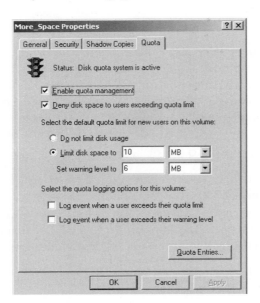

Figure 11-6   The Quota tab of a volume's Properties dialog box

Quotas are managed in two ways: first, by quota entries for specific users, setting a storage limit for each user (or setting "no limit" for a user), and second, by default quota settings that apply to all users for whom a quota entry does not exist. On the Quota tab, you can configure the default quota settings. Configure a default limit or "no limit" that will apply to as many users as possible, so that you can minimize the number of quota entries you must create for users whose limits are different from this default. Note that you can configure the disk space limit as well as a warning level, which should obviously be lower than the limit.

Finally, specify logging options. Quota manager registers events in the System log, identifying the user by name and specifying that they have exceeded their warning or quota limits.

After configuring the defaults for the volume on the Quota tab, click Quota Entries to open the Quota Entries dialog box, as shown in Figure 11-7.

Exam Tip   Administrators have No Limit configured as their quota entry. That enables administrators to install the operating system, services, applications, and data without exceeding a quota.

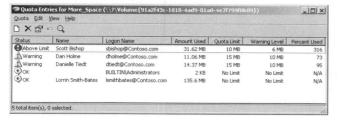

Figure 11-7   The Quota Entries dialog box

Click the New, Quota Entry button on the toolbar or choose New Quota Entry on the Quota menu, and you can select one or more users for which to create a quota entry. It is unfortunate that Windows Server 2003 does not allow you to assign quota entries based on groups (as most third-party quota management tools do), but in the Select Users dialog box you can at least select multiple users before clicking OK. The limits you configure in the Add New Quota Entry dialog box will apply to all selected users, individually.

Exporting Quota Entries

If you want to apply the same quota entries to another NTFS volume, you can export the entries and import them to the other volume. Select one or more quota entries and, on the Quota menu, click Export. On the other volume, choose Import.

Monitoring Quotas and Storage

The Quota Entries dialog box displays disk storage per user and whether that storage is at or above warning levels or limits. You can sort by column to identify users who have exceeded their quota levels or limits. There is no mechanism to alert you about quota limits, so you must monitor the Quota Entries dialog box or the System Log in Event Viewer.

> **Exam Tip**   Disk Quotas can be implemented per-volume and per-user only. You cannot implement quotas on a per-folder or per-group basis.

Practice: Implementing Disk Quotas

In this practice, you will configure default quota management settings to limit the amount of data users can store Server01. You will then configure custom quota settings to allow the users in the Marketing department to store more data, because their media files are generally larger than other users' business documents. And you allow developers to be exempt from quotas.

Exercise 1: Configuring Default Disk Quota Settings

1. Open Disk Management.

2. Right-click the More_Space volume and choose Properties.

3. Click the Quota tab.

4. Click the Enable Quota Management check box.

5. Select the Deny Disk Space To Users Exceeding Quota Limit check box.

6. Select Limit Disk Space To.

   Configure the limit as 10 MB and the warning level as 6 MB.

7. Select both Log check boxes.

8. Click Apply.

   A Disk Quota dialog box appears, warning you that the volume will be rescanned to update disk usage statistics if you enable quotas. Click OK to confirm.

9. Do not close the Volume Properties dialog box because you will use it in the next exercise.

Exercise 2: Creating Custom Quota Entries for Users

1. On the Quota tab of the More_Space Properties dialog box, click Quota Entries to open the Quota Entries dialog box.

> **Off the Record**   Notice that the Builtin\Administrators group is listed. If you created files while logged in as a non-administrator user, there would be a quota entry for that user as well because the user account owns files on the volume.

You will now create quota entries allowing your Marketing employees, Dan Holme and Danielle Tiedt, more disk storage than the default.

2. On the Quota menu, click New Quota Entry.

3. Click Advanced and click Find Now. All users in the domain are listed.

4. Select Dan Holme and Danielle Tiedt and click OK twice.

5. Set the quota entry to limit disk usage at 15 MB, and to warn the user at 10 MB. Click OK.

   You will now create quota entries allowing your developers, Lorrin Smith-Bates and Scott Bishop, to be exempt from quotas.

6. Repeat steps 2 through 5 to configure quota entries for Lorrin Smith-Bates and Scott Bishop. Set the entry so that their disk usage is not limited.

Exercise 3 (Optional): Test Disk Quotas

1. Log on as Danielle Tiedt.

2. Create a folder in the X:\Docs folder called Dtiedt.

3. Copy the Support folder from the Windows Server 2003 CD-ROM to the X:\Docs\Dtiedt folder. The Support folder is 11 MB, and is lower than Danielle Tiedt's quota. The copy completes successfully.

4. Log on as Dan Holme.

5. Create a folder in X:\Docs called Dholme.

6. Copy the Support folder from the Windows Server 2003 CD-ROM to the X:\Docs\Dholme folder. The folder is smaller than Dan Holme's quota limit, and completes successfully.

7. Copy the Valueadd folder from the Windows Server 2003 CD-ROM to the X:\Docs\Dholme folder. The folder is 6 MB, and therefore puts Dan Holme over his quota limit. The copy will be interrupted.

8. Log on as Administrator and open the Quota Entries dialog box for the More_Space volume. Notice the information presented about disk usage for each user.

Lesson Review

The following questions are intended to reinforce key information presented in this lesson. If you are unable to answer a question, review the lesson materials and try the question again. You can find answers to the questions in the "Questions and Answers" section at the end of this chapter.

1. You're the administrator of a Windows Server 2003 computer. You want to fix any file system errors and recover any bad sectors on your computer's hard disk. Which tool should you use?

   a. Check Disk

   b. Disk Defragmenter

   c. DISKPART

   d. Disk quotas

2. You're the administrator of a Windows Server 2003 computer. The computer's hard disk contains two data volumes: D and E. You enable disk quotas on volume D and E that limit all users to 20 MB of total storage. However, you want to limit storage in the users' home folders, stored in D:\Users, to 10 MB per user. Is this possible? Why or why not? Where can you implement quotas?

    a. On any server for all disks

    b. On any physical disk for all volumes

    c. On any volume for all folders

    d. On any folder

3. What is the required amount of free disk space on a volume in order to provide for complete defragmentation?

    a. 5 percent

    b. 10 percent

    c. 15 percent

    d. 25 percent

    e. 50 percent

Lesson Summary

- The Check Disk tool allows you to fix file systems errors and scan for and attempt to recover bad sectors on your hard disk.

- Disk Defragmenter improves performance by relocating files so that their clusters are contiguous.

- Disk Quotas allow you to set and monitor storage limits and, optionally, to deny write access to users exceeding those limits. Quotas are configured on a per-user, per-volume basis.

Lesson 4: Implementing RAID

A disk subsystem that includes a RAID configuration enables the disks in the system to work in concert to improve performance, fault tolerance, or both. In this lesson, you will learn about the three levels of RAID that can be created and managed by Windows Server 2003. You will learn the impact that each type of volume has on performance, volume capacity, and fault tolerance, and how to recover data in the event of a disk failure in a RAID configuration.

After this lesson, you will be able to

- Identify the best RAID implementation given a particular storage requirement regarding capacity utilization, fault tolerance, and performance
- Configure a striped volume (RAID-0)
- Configure a mirrored volume (RAID-1)
- Configure a RAID-5 volume (striped with parity)
- Recover from a single-disk failure in a fault-tolerant volume

Estimated lesson time: 25 minutes

Lesson 1 introduced the types of storage units available on a Windows Server 2003 computer. The types of volumes that reflect RAID configurations are striped volumes, mirrored volumes, and RAID-5 volumes.

Implementing Disk Fault Tolerance

As mentioned in Lesson 1, fault tolerance is the ability of a computer or operating system to respond to a catastrophic event, such as a power outage or hardware failure, so that no data is lost and that work in progress is not corrupted. Fully fault-tolerant systems using fault-tolerant disk arrays prevent the loss of data. You can implement RAID fault tolerance as either a hardware or software solution.

Hardware Implementations of RAID

In a hardware solution, the disk controller interface handles the creation and regeneration of redundant information. Some hardware vendors implement RAID data protection directly in their hardware, as with disk array controller cards. Because these methods are vendor specific and bypass the fault tolerance software drivers of the operating system, they offer performance improvements over software implementations of RAID.

Consider the following points when deciding whether to use a software or hardware implementation of RAID:

- Hardware fault tolerance is more expensive than software fault tolerance and might limit equipment options to a single vendor.

- Hardware fault tolerance generally provides faster disk I/O than software fault tolerance.

- Hardware fault tolerance solutions might implement hot swapping of hard disks to allow for replacement of a failed hard disk without shutting down the computer and hot sparing so that a failed disk is automatically replaced by an online spare.

Software Implementations of RAID

Windows Server 2003 supports one RAID implementation (striped, RAID-0) that is not fault-tolerant and two implementations that provide fault tolerance: mirrored volumes (RAID-1) and striped volumes with parity (RAID-5). You can create fault-tolerant RAID volumes only on dynamic disks formatted with NTFS.

With Windows Server 2003 implementations of RAID, there is no fault tolerance following a failure until the fault is repaired. If a second fault occurs before the data lost from the first fault is regenerated, you can recover the data only by restoring it from a backup.

Striped Volumes

A striped volume, which implements RAID Level 0, uses two or more disks and writes data to all disks at the same rate. By doing so, I/O requests are handled by multiple spindles, and read/write performance is the beneficiary. Striped volumes are popular for configurations in which performance and large storage area are critical, such as computer-aided design (CAD) and digital media applications.

 Note   You might not experience a performance improvement on IDE unless you use separate controllers. Separate controllers—ideally, one for each drive—will improve performance by distributing I/O requests among controllers as well as among drives.

Creating a Striped Volume

To create a striped volume, you must have unallocated space on at least two dynamic disks. Right-click one of the spaces and choose Create Volume. The New Volume Wizard will step you through the process of selecting a striped volume and choosing other disk space to include in the volume. Striped volumes can be assigned a drive letter and folder paths. They can be formatted only with NTFS.

Up to 32 disks can participate in a striped volume. The amount of space used on each disk in the volume will be equal to the smallest amount of space on any one disk. For example, if Disk 1 has 200 GB of unallocated space, and Disk 2 has 120 GB of space, the striped volume can contain, at most, 240 GB as the size of the stripe on Disk 1 can be no greater than the size of the stripe on Disk 2. All disk space in the volume is used for data; there is no space used for fault tolerance.

Recovering a Striped Volume

Because data is striped over more than one physical disk, performance is enhanced, but fault tolerance is decreased—there is more risk because if any one drive in the volume fails, all data on the volume is lost. It is important to have a backup of striped data. If one or more disks in a striped volume fails, you must delete the volume, replace the failed disk(s) and recreate the volume. Then you must restore data from the backup.

> **Exam Tip**   Striped volumes provide maximum storage and performance but support no fault tolerance. The only recovery potion is that of your regular backup routine.

Mirrored Volumes

A mirrored volume provides good performance along with excellent fault tolerance. Two disks participate in a mirrored volume, and all data is written to both volumes. As with all RAID configurations, use separate controllers (by adding a controller, you create a configuration called "duplexing") for maximum performance. Mirrored volumes relate to RAID-1 hardware configurations.

Create Mirrored Volumes

To create a mirrored volume, you must have unallocated space on two dynamic disks. Right-click one of the spaces and choose Create Volume. The New Volume Wizard will step you through the process of selecting a mirrored volume and choosing space on another disk to include in the volume. Mirrored volumes can be assigned a drive letter and folder paths. Both copies of the mirror share the same assignment.

You can also mirror an existing simple volume by right-clicking the volume and choosing Add Mirror and selecting a drive with sufficient unallocated space.

Once you have established the mirror, the system begins copying data, sector by sector. During that time, the volume status is reported as Resynching.

Recovering from Mirrored Disk Failures

The recovery process for a failed disk within a mirrored volume depends on the type of failure that occurs. If a disk has experienced transient I/O errors, both portions of the mirror will show a status of Failed Redundancy. The disk with the errors will report a status of Offline or Missing, as seen in Figure 11-8.

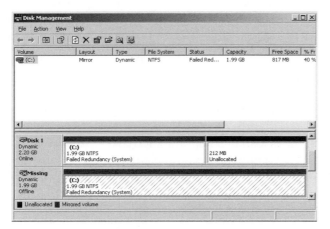

Figure 11-8   A mirrored volume with a failed disk

After correcting the cause of the I/O error—perhaps a bad cable connection or power supply—right-click the volume on the problematic disk and choose Reactivate Volume or right-click the disk and choose Reactivate Disk. Reactivating brings the disk or volume back online. The mirror will then resynchronize automatically.

If you want to stop mirroring, you have three choices, depending on what you want the outcome to be:

- **Delete the volume**   If you delete the volume, the volume and all the information it contains is removed. The resulting unallocated space is then available for new volumes.

- **Remove the mirror**   If you remove the mirror, the mirror is broken and the space on one of the disks becomes unallocated. The other disk maintains a copy of the data that had been mirrored, but that data is of course no longer fault-tolerant.

- **Break the mirror**   If you break the mirror, the mirror is broken but both disks maintain copies of the data. The portion of the mirror that you select when you choose Break Mirror maintains the original mirrored volume's drive letter, shared folders, paging file, and reparse points. The secondary drive is given the next available drive letter.

Knowing that information, how do you suppose you would replace a failed disk—a member of the mirrored volume that simply died? Well, after physically replacing the disk, you will need to open Disk Management to rescan, initialize the disk and convert it to dynamic. After all that work you will find that you can't remirror a mirrored volume, even though half of it doesn't exist. So far as the remaining disk is concerned, the mirrored volume still exists—its partner in redundancy is just out to lunch. You must remove the mirror to break the mirror. Right-click the mirror and choose Remove Mirror. In the Remove Mirror dialog box, it is important to select the half of the volume that is missing; the volume you select will be deleted when you click Remove Mirror. The volume you did not select will become a simple volume. Once the operation is complete, right-click the healthy, simple volume and choose Add Mirror. Select the new disk and the mirror will be created again.

Exam Tip   Mirrored volumes provide fault tolerance and better write performance than RAID-5 volumes. However, because each disk in the mirror contains a full copy of the data in the volume, it is the least efficient type of volume in terms of disk utilization.

RAID-5 Volumes

A RAID-5 volume uses three or more physical disks to provide fault tolerance and excellent read performance while reducing the cost of fault tolerance in terms of disk capacity. Data is written to all but one disk in a RAID-5. That volume receives a chunk of data, called parity, which acts as a checksum and provides fault tolerance for the stripe. The calculation of parity during a write operation means that RAID-5 is quite intensive on the server's processor for a volume that is not read-only. RAID-5 provides improved read performance, however, as data is retrieved from multiple spindles simultaneously.

As data in a file is written to the volume, the parity is distributed among each disk in the set. But from a storage capacity perspective, the amount of space used for fault tolerance is the equivalent of the space used by one disk in the volume.

From a storage capacity perspective, that makes RAID-5 more economical than mirroring. In a minimal, three disk RAID-5 volume, one-third of the capacity is used for parity, as opposed to one-half of a mirrored volume being used for fault tolerance. Because as many as 32 disks can participate in a RAID-5 volume, you can theoretically configure a fault-tolerant volume which uses only 1/32 of its capacity to provide fault tolerance for the entire volume.

Configure RAID-5 Volumes

You need to have space on at least three dynamic disks to be able to create a RAID-5 volume. Right-click one disk's unallocated space and choose New Volume. The New Volume Wizard will step you through selecting a RAID-5 volume type, and then selecting the disks that will participate in the volume.

The capacity of the volume is limited to the smallest section of unallocated space on any one of the volume's disks. If Disk 2 has 50 GB of unallocated space, but Disks 3 and 4 have 100 GB of unallocated space, the stripe can only use 50 GB of space on Disks 3 and 4—the space used on each disk in the volume is identical. The capacity, or Volume Size reported by the New Volume Wizard will represent the amount of space available for data after accounting for parity. To continue our example, the RAID-5 volume size would be 100 GB—the total capacity minus the equivalent of one disk's space for parity.

RAID-5 volumes can be assigned a drive letter or folder paths. They can be formatted only with NTFS.

Because RAID-5 volumes are created as native dynamic volumes from unallocated space, you cannot turn any other type of volume into a RAID-5 volume without backing up that volume's data and restoring into the new RAID-5 volume.

Recovering a Failed RAID-5 Volume

If a single disk fails in a RAID-5 volume, data can continue to be accessed. During read operations, any missing data is regenerated on the fly through a calculation involving remaining data and parity information. Performance will be degraded and, of course, if a second drive fails it's time to pull out the backup tapes. RAID-5 and mirrored volumes can only sustain a single drive failure.

If the drive is returned to service, you may need to rescan, and then you will need to right-click the volume and choose Reactivate Volume. The system will then rebuild missing data and the volume will be fully functional again.

If the drive does not offer a Reactivate option, or if you have had to replace the disk, you may need to rescan, initialize the disk, convert it to dynamic, then right-click the volume and choose Repair Volume. You will be asked to select the disk where the missing volume member should be recreated. Select the new disk and the system will regenerate the missing data.

Mirrored Volumes versus RAID-5 Volumes

Mirrored volumes (RAID-1) and RAID-5 volumes provide different levels of fault tolerance. Deciding which option to implement depends on the level of protection you require and the cost of hardware. The major differences between mirrored volumes and RAID-5 volumes are performance and cost. Table 11-2 describes some differences between software-level RAID-1 and RAID-5.

Table 11-2   RAID Performance and Costs

Mirrored Volumes (RAID-1)	Striped Volumes with Parity (RAID-5)
Can protect system or boot partition	Cannot protect system or boot partition
Requires two hard disks	Requires a minimum of three hard disks and allows a maximum of 32 hard disks

Table 11-2   RAID Performance and Costs (Continued)

Mirrored Volumes (RAID-1)	Striped Volumes with Parity (RAID-5)
Has a higher cost per MB	Has a lower cost per MB
50 percent redundancy[*]	33 percent maximum redundancy[*]
Has good read and write performance	Has excellent read and moderate write performance
Uses less system memory	Requires more system memory

* drive space dedicated or "lost" to provide fault tolerance

Creating Fault Tolerance for the System Volume

Because RAID-5 is a native dynamic volume, it is not possible to install or start the Windows Server 2003 operating system on a RAID-5 volume created by the Windows Server 2003 fault-tolerant disk technologies.

Tip   *Hardware RAID*, however, is invisible to Windows Server 2003, so the operating system can (and should, where available) be installed on hardware RAID arrays.

The only option for creating fault tolerance for the system, without buying hardware RAID, is thus to mirror the system volume. You can mirror the system volume by following the procedures described for creating a mirrored volume: right-click the system volume and choose Add Mirror. Unlike Windows 2000, you do not need to restart, and the BOOT.INI file is updated automatically so that you can start to the secondary drive if the primary drive fails.

If the drives are attached to IDE controllers, and the primary drive fails, you may have to remove that drive, change the secondary drive to the primary controller and set its jumpers or cable position so that it is the master. Otherwise, the system may not boot to the secondary drive.

Tip   If you are going to mirror the system volume, do so on one or two SCSI controllers. If you use two controllers, make sure they are of the same type. This configuration will be the most easily supported and recovered.

Upgrading Disks

There are two potential "gotchas" when you upgrade disks from previous versions of Windows, or attempt to move disks to a Windows Server 2003 computer from a computer running a previous version of Windows.

First, if a disk was configured in a Windows 2000 computer as a basic disk, then was converted to dynamic, you cannot extend that disk's simple volumes onto other disks using Windows Server 2003. In other words, if you move that disk to a Windows Server 2003 computer, or upgrade the operating system to Windows Server 2003, you cannot create spanned volumes out of the disk's simple volumes.

Second, Windows Server 2003 no longer supports multidisk arrays created in Windows NT 4. Windows NT 4 created mirrored, striped, and striped-with-parity (RAID-5) sets using basic disks. Windows 2000 permitted the use of those disk sets, although it was important to convert the sets to dynamic quickly in order to facilitate troubleshooting and recovery. Windows Server 2003 does not recognize the volumes. On the off chance that you upgrade a server from Windows NT 4 to Windows Server 2003, any RAID sets will no longer be visible. You must first back up all data prior to upgrading or moving those disks, and then, after recreating the fault-tolerant sets in Windows Server 2003, restore the data.

Practice: Planning RAID Configuration

In this practice, you will evaluate a server and its storage capacity against the requirements of *contoso.com* and determine an appropriate configuration.

You administer a server for Contoso, Ltd. The server has four disks on a SCSI subsystem:

- Disk 0: 80 GB
- Disk 1: 80 GB
- Disk 2: 40 GB
- Disk 3: 40 GB

You recently performed a clean installation of Windows Server 2003 by backing up all data on the disks, removing all partitions from those disks, and installing the operating system on a 20 GB partition on Disk 0.

You are now required to configure all the remaining drive space. User data will not be stored on the operating system volume. You want to maximize data storage and ensure uptime in the event of a single disk failure. What configuration do you implement, and what will the total storage capacity for user data be?

The answer is a combination of RAID-5 and mirrored volumes with a total capacity for user data of 140 GB.

To ensure uptime in the event of a single disk failure, you must provide fault tolerance for the operating system itself. Only a mirrored volume is capable of doing that; you cannot install or host the operating system on a RAID-5 volume. A minimum disk space of 20 GB is therefore required to mirror the operating system.

A RAID-5 configuration maximizes disk space without sacrificing single disk failure fault tolerance. You can configure a RAID-5 volume with three or more disks. In this scenario, configuring a RAID-5 volume with all four disks would maximize data storage. A RAID-5 volume's stripe can only be as wide as the smallest amount of unallocated space, so although disk 0 and 1 have 60 and 80 GB free, respectively, the smaller (40 GB) drives will determine the capacity of the volume. With a 40 GB space on four drives, the volume has a potential capacity of 160 GB, but RAID-5 uses the space equivalent to one disk for parity, meaning that the resulting capacity for data storage in this volume will be 120 GB.

That leaves disk 0 with 20 GB of unallocated space, and disk 1 with 40 GB of unallocated space. You can configure the mirror of the operating system volume on disk 1, leaving 20 GB on that drive. The remaining space (20 GB per disk on disks 0 and 1) can be configured as a mirrored volume for user data, with a storage capacity of 20 GB. A simple, spanned, or striped volume would not be fault-tolerant, and a RAID-5 volume requires a minimum of three physical disks, so a mirror is the most effective way to use remaining space for fault-tolerant data storage.

Lesson Review

The following questions are intended to reinforce key information presented in this lesson. If you are unable to answer a question, review the lesson materials and try the question again. You can find answers to the questions in the "Questions and Answers" section at the end of this chapter.

1. You're implementing software RAID on your Windows Server 2003 computer. You want to provide fault tolerance to the system and boot partitions. Which version of RAID should you use?

   a. RAID-0

   b. RAID-1

   c. RAID-5

   d. You cannot use software RAID to protect a boot partition.

2. You're setting up a Windows Server 2003 computer and you want to protect the data on the hard disk. You want to implement a solution that provides the fastest disk I/O possible and supports the hot swapping of hard disks. Which RAID solution should you use?

   a. RAID-0

   b. RAID-1

   c. RAID-5

   d. Hardware RAID

3. You're setting up RAID-5 on your Windows Server 2003 computer. You plan to use five hard disks, which are each 20 GB in size. What percentage of redundancy can you anticipate with this configuration?

   a. 20

   b. 25

   c. 33

   d. 50

4. You're setting up software RAID on your Windows Server 2003 computer to provide fault tolerance to the data stored on that system. The computer is used as a database server. The server performs many read operations but relatively few write operations. As a result, you want a fault-tolerant solution that provides excellent read performance. Which RAID solution should you use?

   a. RAID-0

   b. RAID-1

   c. RAID-5

5. A computer where you want to implement RAID-5 contains three disks, each with 2 GB of unallocated space. Using the Disk Management snap-in, you start the New Volume Wizard by right-clicking one of the regions of unallocated space. When you reach the Select Volume Type screen, the RAID-5 option is not available. What is the most likely reason for this behavior?

   a. RAID-5 is already implemented in hardware.

   b. One or two of the disks are configured with the basic storage type.

   c. All three disks are configured with the dynamic storage type.

   d. All three disks are configured with the basic storage type.

   e. RAID-5 is already implemented in software.

6. A disk in a mirrored volume is failing. You decide to replace the failing disk. How should you prepare the mirror for disk replacement?

_____

_____

Lesson Summary

- Some levels of RAID provide fault tolerance by implementing data redundancy. You can implement RAID fault tolerance as either a software or hardware solution.

- Hardware solutions offer better performance than software solutions, but they are generally more expensive.

- Windows Server 2003 supports three software implementations of RAID: striped volumes (RAID-0), mirrored volumes (RAID-1), and striped-with-parity volumes (RAID-5).

- A striped volume (RAID-0) distributes data across each disk in the volume, providing increased read and write performance, but no benefit to fault tolerance.

- In a RAID-5 volume, fault tolerance is achieved by adding a parity-information stripe to each disk partition in the volume.

- A mirrored volume uses the fault tolerance driver to write the same data to a volume on each of two physical disks simultaneously.

- The major differences between mirrored volumes and RAID-5 volumes are performance and cost. Mirrored volumes offer good read and write performance. RAID-5 volumes offer better read performance than mirrored volumes, but only moderate write performance.

- The only form of software RAID that can be used for the system volume is a mirrored volume.

Case Scenario Exercise

> **Note**   This case scenario requires Internet access.

You are a server administrator for Contoso, Ltd. The company's file servers are running out of disk capacity, and it is necessary to upgrade. In the past, the company has relied on tape backups for data redundancy. Due to recent growth, it is no longer acceptable to encounter more than a few minutes of downtime if a server disk drive fails. You have therefore been asked to evaluate disk storage options that provide fault tolerance.

Exercise 1: Consider Windows Server 2003 Fault-Tolerant Volumes

Review the information in Lesson 4 to consider how you could best configure fault-tolerant servers using Windows Server 2003 dynamic volumes. Use the Practice in Lesson 4 as a reminder of how various types of volumes can be configured to support fault tolerance.

Consider the challenges related to IDE drives. If the operating system is installed on a mirrored IDE drive and the primary drive fails, you must reconfigure the secondary drive's jumpers or cable position, and ensure it is attached to the primary IDE channel. With that in mind, you decide that a more robust configuration would utilize two SCSI controllers with one copy of the mirror as the first disk on each SCSI chain. That configuration would enable rapid recovery not only from a single drive failure, but from the failure of one of the SCSI controllers as well.

Now consider the performance and capacity effect of Windows Server 2003 RAID. Consider the amount of time that will be required to recover if a drive fails—downing the server, replacing the drive, restarting the server—and the amount of time it will take to regenerate a missing volume.

Exercise 2: Consider Hardware RAID

With all those thoughts in mind, you decide to examine hardware RAID as an option. What advantages does hardware RAID provide? See Lesson 4 for some of the answers.

Open Internet Explorer and browse to the Web site(s) of one or more computer hardware and supply vendors. Search their sites for RAID arrays. You will find RAID arrays, which include disk drives, and RAID controllers and RAID enclosures, to which you must add drives. Focus on the ready-to-go RAID arrays and answer the following questions:

- What options are available?
- What are some of the vendors of hardware RAID arrays?
- What types of storage capacities do hardware RAID arrays offer?
- What RAID configurations do the hardware RAID arrays implement? Are there configurations that Windows Server 2003 does not support?
- What is the price range for a hardware RAID array?
- What do some entry-level RAID arrays cost?

At the time of this writing, hardware RAID solutions offering 720 GB of storage—that's closer to a terabyte than to the size of any single drive in most servers—can be purchased for less than $3,000.

How would you position the value of hardware RAID to your manager? Would you recommend hardware RAID over Windows Server 2003 RAID? Why or why not?

Troubleshooting Lab

You are a server administrator for Contoso, Ltd. You inherited a server from a previous administrator that contains numerous internal SCSI disk drives. You open the Disk Management console to determine the configuration of those drives and their volumes. The configuration is shown below:

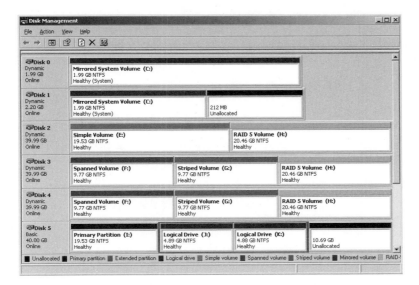

The weather forecast calls for a brutal storm to move into the city early tomorrow morning. To play it safe, you start a backup of your server on your way out the door. The storm is quite strong, forcing businesses, including yours, to be closed for several days. Electricity is lost to Contoso's building and, eventually, the batteries in your uninterruptible power supplies (UPSs) are drained, causing power to your servers to be completely lost. During the first few hours in which electricity is restored, several power fluctuations and surges are experienced.

When you return to the server room, you boot the servers. Your server indicates errors, and you open Disk Management to see the following, frightening graphical view of your disks and volumes:

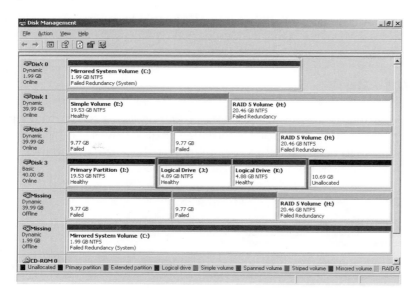

Two drives have failed in the server. One contained a mirror of the operating system volume. The other contained several volume types, including portions of a spanned, a striped, and a RAID-5 volume.

You have an 80 GB drive, still in its box. You shut down the server and remove the two failed drives. After inserting the new disk, you reboot the server.

Exercise

Take a moment, on a separate piece of paper, to plot the steps that will be required to recover the data on each volume that was lost. Be thorough. Include the steps required to clean up the missing disks and volumes as well as install, configure, and replace data on the new disk.

When you are confident that you have as comprehensive a list of steps as possible, compare your answer to the answer.

The components of recovery will include the following:

1. Log on to the system.

2. Finish installing the new disk drive. Follow any instructions presented by the Found New Hardware Wizard. If the Found New Hardware Wizard does not appear, check Device Manager to see if the disks installed automatically and silently. If the disks do not appear, use Add Hardware to install the disks.

3. Open Disk Management.

4. Detect and initialize the new disk. Disk Management will likely detect the new disk and present the Initialize Disk Wizard. If the wizard does not appear, check to see if the disk appears in Disk Management and, if not, right-click Disk Management and choose Rescan. Once the disk appears, right-click the disk and choose Initialize.

5. Recover the volumes (in any order).

Recover the RAID-5 volume

> **a.** Convert the new disk to a dynamic disk. Right-click the new disk and choose Convert to Dynamic.
>
> **b.** Right-click a functioning portion of the RAID-5 volume and choose Repair Volume. Select the new disk, which has ample space to support a member of the stripe. The RAID-5 volume will be created and synchronized.

Recover the mirrored volume

> **a.** Remove the mirror. Right-click the failed drive and choose Remove Mirror. Confirm that the portion marked Missing is selected and click Remove Mirror. The remaining portion of the mirror becomes a simple volume.
>
> **b.** Right-click the simple volume and choose Add Mirror. Select the new disk, which has ample space for the mirror, and click Add Mirror. The mirror will be created and synchronized.

Recover the striped volume

> **a.** Delete the volume. Striped volumes are not fault-tolerant. All data on the volume was lost.
>
> **b.** Re-create the volume. Right-click on unallocated space where the stripe had existed, and choose New Volume. Select a striped volume and add the new disk to the stripe. The striped volume will be created and formatted.
>
> **c.** Restore data from the backup to the striped volume.

Recover the spanned volume

> **a.** Delete the volume. Spanned volumes are not fault-tolerant. All data on the volume was lost.
>
> **b.** Re-create the volume. Right-click on unallocated space where the volume had existed, and choose New Volume. Select a spanned volume and add the new disk to the stripe. Select the appropriate amount of space to use on the new disk. The spanned volume will be created and formatted.
>
> **c.** Restore data from the backup to the spanned volume.

6. Remove the missing disks. Right-click the missing disks and choose Remove Volume. You cannot remove the disk with the missing mirror until after the mirror has been removed. You cannot remove the disk with the simple, spanned, and RAID-5 volumes until those volumes have been deleted and repaired.

7. Run CHKDSK after all volumes have been resynchronized and restored.

Chapter Summary

- Windows Server 2003 supports two types of storage, basic and dynamic, and several file systems, including FAT, FAT32, and NTFS. Most advanced storage management features are available only on dynamic disk volumes formatted as NTFS.

- Dynamic disks provide flexible and powerful options in configurations with more than one disk. You can implement spanned, mirrored, striped, and RAID-5 volumes to provide storage according to capacity, performance, and fault tolerance requirements.

- Disk volumes can be corrupted, can become fragmented, and often fill to capacity. Check Disk, Disk Defragmenter, and Disk Quotas are tools to help you manage existing volumes.

- Not all RAID configurations are fault-tolerant—mirrored and RAID-5 volumes are fault-tolerant, but striped volumes are not. None of the Windows Server 2003 volume types will provide fault tolerance if more than one disk fails in the volume.

Exam Highlights

Before taking the exam, review the key points and terms that are presented below to help you identify topics you need to review. Return to the lessons for additional practice and review the "Further Readings" sections in Part 2 for pointers to more information about topics covered by the exam objectives.

Key Points

- Understand the impact on capacity, performance, and fault tolerance for each type of disk volume. Be prepared to recommend disk configurations based on storage requirements.

- Know how to implement user disk quotas and the effect of both default quota settings and specific quota entries.

- Recognize and repair a volume that was temporarily offline but is now reconnected: Rescan and Reactivate Disk or Reactivate Volume, and CHKDSK.

- Know how to rebuild fault-tolerant volumes (mirrored and RAID-5 volumes) on a replaced disk and the appropriate commands that are used: Rescan, Initialize, Convert to Dynamic Disk, Break Mirror, Remove Mirror, and Repair Volume.

Key Terms

Simple volume   The equivalent to a basic disk partition is a dynamic disk simple volume. Because simple volumes exist on only one physical disk, they are not fault-tolerant.

Spanned volume   A spanned volume includes space on more than one physical disk. Because their size tends to be greater, and because multiple physical disks are involved, the risk for failure increases, and spanned volumes are not fault-tolerant.

Striped volume   Data is written to 2 to 32 physical disks at the same rate. Offers maximum performance and capacity but no fault tolerance.

Mirrored volume   Two disks contain identical copies of data. The only software RAID supported on the system volume. Good read and write performance; excellent fault tolerance; but costly in terms of disk utilization, because 50 percent of the volume's potential capacity is used for data redundancy.

RAID-5 volume   Data is written to 3 to 32 physical disks at the same rate, and is interlaced with parity to provide fault tolerance for a single disk failure. Good read performance; good utilization of disk capacity; expensive in terms of processor utilization and write performance as parity must be calculated during write operations.

Questions and Answers

Page
11-9
Lesson 1 Review

1. You are installing a new 200 GB disk drive. You want to divide the disk into five logical volumes for the operating system, applications, user home directories, shared data, and a software distribution point. The drive space should be distributed equally among the five logical volumes. You also want to leave 50 GB as unallocated space for future extension of a logical volume. Considering basic and dynamic disks and the types of logical volumes they support, what are your configuration options?

    Allocate 150 GB of disk space to leave 50 GB unallocated. That means that each of the five logical volumes will be 30 GB. You can configure the drive as a basic disk with zero to three primary partitions, each of which supports one logical drive (which is the logical volume for a basic disk). The remaining two to five logical volumes would be created as logical drives in an extended partition. If the disk is configured as a dynamic disk, all five logical volumes would be set up as simple volumes. Although these configurations are valid answers to the question, the best practice in this scenario would be to configure the disk as a dynamic disk, for reasons you will learn in the next lesson.

2. Which of the following provide the ability to recover from the failure of a single hard drive?

    a. Primary partition

    b. Extended partition

    c. Logical drive

    d. Simple volume

    e. Spanned volume

    f. Mirrored volume

    g. Striped volume

    h. RAID-5 volume

    The correct answers are f and h.

3. You are dual-booting a system in your test lab. The computer has Windows NT 4 installed on the first primary partition, and Windows Server 2003 installed on the second primary partition. The computer is running low on disk space, so you add a new disk drive. You boot to Windows Server 2003 and configure the drive as a dynamic disk. When you later restart to Windows NT 4, you are unable to see the disk. Why?

    Only Windows XP, Windows 2000, and the Windows Server 2003 family support dynamic disks.

4. To provide fault tolerance, maximum performance, and the ability to hot-swap a failed drive, you purchase a seven-disk hardware RAID array. After installing the array, you see only one new disk on Windows Server 2003. Why?

Once configured, hardware disk subsystems with an independent controller abstract, or mask, the physical disk structure from the operating system. They manage the operation and I/O to the disks in the array. Operating system performance is not affected by having to calculate parity or perform mirrored write operations.

Page
11-22

Lesson 2 Review

1. This question continues the scenario that was presented in question 1 of the review in Lesson 1. You have installed a new 200 GB disk drive. You configured it as a basic disk and created three primary partitions of 30 GB each to host the operating system, user home directories, and shared data. You configured an extended partition and two logical drives of 30 GB each to host applications installed on the machine and a software distribution point. There remains 50 GB of unallocated space on the disk. Several months later, you notice that three of the volumes are nearing capacity. You want to prepare for the likely event that one or more partitions will need to be expanded. What action must you take?

You must convert the disk to a dynamic disk. A partition on a basic disk can only be extended to immediately contiguous unallocated space. By converting the disk to a dynamic disk, you will convert each primary partition and logical drive to a simple volume. Simple volumes can be extended into any unallocated space.

2. What type of disk region supports logical drives?

   a. Primary partitions

   b. Simple volumes

   c. Spanned volumes

   d. Extended partitions

   e. Unallocated space

The correct answer is d.

3. You recently added a disk to a computer. The disk had previously been used in a Windows 2000 Server. The disk appears in Device Manager, but is not appearing correctly in Disk Management. What task must you apply?

   a. Import Foreign Disk

   b. Format volume

   c. Rescan

   d. Change Drive Letter or Path

   e. Convert to Dynamic Disk

The correct answer is c.

4. You attempt to convert an external FireWire disk from basic to dynamic, but the option to convert is not available. What is the most likely reason for this?

   A removable disk cannot be converted to a dynamic disk. External drives are considered removable.

Page
11-31 **Lesson 3 Review**

1. You're the administrator of a Windows Server 2003 computer. You want to fix any file system errors and recover any bad sectors on your computer's hard disk. Which tool should you use?

   a. Check Disk

   b. Disk Defragmenter

   c. DISKPART

   d. Disk quotas

   The correct answer is a.

2. You're the administrator of a Windows Server 2003 computer. The computer's hard disk contains two data volumes: D and E. You enable disk quotas on volume D and E that limit all users to 20 MB of total storage. However, you want to limit storage in the users' home folders, stored in D:\Users, to 10 MB per user. Is this possible? Why or why not? Where can you implement quotas?

   a. On any server for all disks

   b. On any physical disk for all volumes

   c. On any volume for all folders

   d. On any folder

   The correct answer is c. You can implement quotas per-volume only. You cannot configure a quota on the Users folder on volume D. The quota applies to the whole volume. You will also be unable to set a quota of 20 MB per user of combined storage on volumes D and E. You could, however, configure a limit of 15 MB on volume D and 5 MB on volume E, or some other combination that totals 20 MB.

3. What is the required amount of free disk space on a volume in order to provide for complete defragmentation?

   a. 5 percent

   b. 10 percent

   c. 15 percent

   d. 25 percent

   e. 50 percent

   The correct answer is c.

Lesson 4 Review

1. You're implementing software RAID on your Windows Server 2003 computer. You want to provide fault tolerance to the system and boot partitions. Which version of RAID should you use?

   a. RAID-0

   b. RAID-1

   c. RAID-5

   d. You cannot use software RAID to protect a boot partition.

   The correct answer is b. A mirrored volume can contain any partition, including the boot or system partition.

2. You're setting up a Windows Server 2003 computer and you want to protect the data on the hard disk. You want to implement a solution that provides the fastest disk I/O possible and supports the hot swapping of hard disks. Which RAID solution should you use?

   a. RAID-0

   b. RAID-1

   c. RAID-5

   d. Hardware RAID

   The correct answer is d. Although hardware RAID is more expensive than software fault tolerance, it provides faster disk I/O than software fault tolerance. In addition, hardware fault tolerance solutions might implement hot swapping of hard disks to allow for replacement of a failed hard disk without shutting down the computer and hot sparing so that a failed disk is automatically replaced by an online spare.

3. You're setting up RAID-5 on your Windows Server 2003 computer. You plan to use five hard disks, which are each 20 GB in size. What percentage of redundancy can you anticipate with this configuration?

   a. 20

   b. 25

   c. 33

   d. 50

   The correct answer is a. RAID-5 volumes have a cost advantage over mirrored volumes because disk usage is optimized. The more disks you have in the RAID-5 volume, the less the cost of the redundant data stripe. If you're using five disks in a RAID-5 configuration, you can anticipate 20 percent rate of redundancy.

4. You're setting up software RAID on your Windows Server 2003 computer to provide fault tolerance to the data stored on that system. The computer is used as a database server. The server performs many read operations but relatively few write operations. As a result, you want a fault-tolerant solution that provides excellent read performance. Which RAID solution should you use?

   a. RAID-0

   b. RAID-1

   c. RAID-5

The correct answer is c. Although RAID-5 has moderate write performance, it has excellent read performance. RAID-1 has good read and write performance, but the read performance is not as good as with RAID-5.

5. A computer where you want to implement RAID-5 contains three disks, each with 2 GB of unallocated space. Using the Disk Management snap-in, you start the New Volume Wizard by right-clicking one of the regions of unallocated space. When you reach the Select Volume Type screen, the RAID-5 option is not available. What is the most likely reason for this behavior?

   a. RAID-5 is already implemented in hardware.

   b. One or two of the disks are configured with the basic storage type.

   c. All three disks are configured with the dynamic storage type.

   d. All three disks are configured with the basic storage type.

   e. RAID-5 is already implemented in software.

The correct answer is b. To configure a RAID-5 volume, at least three disks must be configured for the dynamic storage type.

6. A disk in a mirrored volume is failing. You decide to replace the failing disk. How should you prepare the mirror for disk replacement?

Verify that no processes are accessing the mirrored volume. Verify that the mirror failure is due to a failed disk and not a failing disk controller. Then, using Diskpart or the Disk Management snap-in, select the failing drive and remove the mirror. After the mirror is removed, shut down the computer if necessary and replace the failing disk. Restart the computer and, from the remaining mirror drive, use Diskpart or the Disk Management snap-in to add the mirror. Adding the mirror will regenerate the mirror to the new disk.

12 Monitoring Microsoft Windows Server 2003

Exam Objectives in this Chapter:

- Monitor current system performance
- Monitor and analyze events
- Monitor and optimize a server for application performance
- Monitor memory performance objects
- Monitor network performance objects
- Monitor process performance objects
- Monitor disk performance objects
- Monitor server hardware for bottlenecks
- Monitor events

Why This Chapter Matters

When you first install a new computer, full of resources and uncomplicated by time and use, much is right with the world. However, as the newness of your server fades, and more demands are placed upon it by added applications and users, problems can develop. Without knowledge of the monitoring tools available and the best way to use them in your environment, you may watch your server performance degradation go from an annoyance to a significant problem.

The first monitoring steps for a new Microsoft Windows Server 2003 computer should include a thorough baselining of resource availability and performance data, which should be compared periodically with real-time data so that developing problems with applications or hardware can be solved or averted before they become serious. With the broad range of tools available in Windows Server 2003, no self-respecting system administrator should be caught unaware.

Lessons in this Chapter:

Before You Begin

To follow and perform the practices in this chapter, you need:

- A computer named Server01 with Windows Server 2003 installed.
- Server01 should be configured as a domain controller in the *contoso.com* domain.

Lesson 1: Using Event Viewer

Windows Server 2003 includes a set of log files that are configured and presented within the Event Viewer. By configuring the options on each of the logs to meet the requirements of your environment, you can collect data appropriate for troubleshooting hardware, application, system, and resource access.

After this lesson, you will be able to
- Identify the types of Event Viewer Logs
- Configure the appropriate recording of log data
- Display logged data in filtered form

Estimated lesson time: 20 minutes

Logs Available in Event Viewer

The Windows Server 2003 Event Log service, present and started automatically on all Windows Server 2003 computers, records events in one of three log files:

- **Application**   Developers of an application can program their software to report configuration changes, errors, or other events to this log.

- **System**   The Windows Server 2003 operating system will report events (service start or abnormal shutdown, device failures, and so on) to this log. The events reported to this log are preconfigured.

- **Security**   Logon and resource access events (audits) are reported to this log. Configuration for most of these events is at the discrimination of the system administrator.

Note   Although the Application and System log events are determined by the application developer and operating system, respectively, the Security log must first be configured for the type of events to record (Success or Failure for each). If File and Object Access events are selected, the security properties of each object must be configured to record auditing events to the Security log.

Windows Server 2003 computers filling the role of a Domain Controller contain two additional logs:

- **Directory Service**   This log contains events related to the Microsoft Active Directory directory service, such as irreconcilable object replication or significant events within the directory.

■ **File Replication Service** This log contains errors or significant events reported by the File Replication Service related to the copying of information between Domain Controllers during a replication cycle.

Lastly, a Windows Server 2003 computer filling the role of a Domain Name System (DNS) server will contain one additional log:

■ **DNS Server** This log contains errors or significant events reported by the DNS server.

Configuring Event Viewer Logs

When you first start Event Viewer, all events that are recorded in the selected log are displayed. Such a list may be lengthy, containing many entries of both informational and warning types. You can locate events by type using the Filter command on the shortcut menu's View menu for the log you want to view. The Filter properties page for the Security log is shown in Figure 12-1.

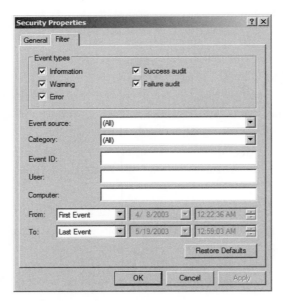

Figure 12-1 Filter settings for the Security log

Adjacent to the Filter tab in the properties of a log is the General tab, which provides access to the behaviors of the log, including

■ The display name for the view of the log.

■ The maximum size of the log.

■ Whether the oldest events in the log should be overwritten when the maximum log size is reached. There are three overwrite options:.

❑ **Overwrite Events As Needed (default)**   This behavior will overwrite the oldest entries in the log with newer ones when the log reaches the maximum size.

❑ **Overwrite Events Older Than *n* Days**   This configuration will overwrite events that exceed the age setting when the log reaches the maximum size.

❑ **Do Not Overwrite Events (Clear Log Manually)**   This configuration will halt event logging when the log reaches the maximum size.

Security Alert   Leaving the default setting of Overwrite Events As Needed on the Security log could overwrite important resource access or other security-related data if the log is not checked often. A regular schedule of analysis is recommended. Log files can be archived (that is, saved to disk) if needed for record-keeping or other administrative purposes.

For better assurance that no Security log entries have been lost, Windows Server 2003 Group Policy provides a setting in the Computer Configuration Policy: Security Settings that will force a computer to shutdown if it is unable to write to the Security log with audit information. This set-ting forces disciplined administrative practice if the Security log is set to be cleared manually.

The General tab for the Security log is shown in Figure 12-2.

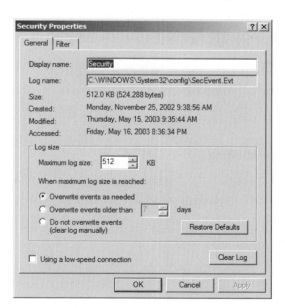

Figure 12-2   The General settings for the Security log

Practice: Event Monitor

In this practice, you will configure the Security log for File and Object Access, and filter the data displayed in the Security log.

Exercise 1: Configuring the Security Log

In this exercise, you will configure the auditing of File and Object Access.

1. Logged on to Server01 as an administrator, open Active Directory Users And Computers.

2. Right-click the Domain Controllers Organizational Unit (OU), and then choose Properties from the shortcut menu.

3. On the Group Policy tab, select the Default Domain Controllers Policy, and then click Edit.

4. Under the Computer Configuration node, expand Windows Settings, Security Settings, Local Policies, and then click Audit Policy.

5. In the details pane, right-click Audit Object Access, and then select Properties from the shortcut menu.

6. In the Audit Object Access Properties dialog box, select Audit These Attempts: Failure, and then click OK.

7. Close the Group Policy Object Editor, click OK to close the Domain Controllers Properties dialog box, and then close Active Directory Users And Computers.

8. Open a command window, type **gpupdate,** and then press Enter.

9. When the Computer Policy reports as refreshed, close the command window.

You have now enabled the auditing of failed Object Access attempts on Server01 (as part of the Domain Controllers OU), and refreshed Group Policy so that the settings take effect immediately.

Exercise 2: Setting File and Object Auditing

In this exercise, you will configure auditing on a folder that you will create. Permissions will be set so as to simulate a user attempting to gain unauthorized access to the resource.

1. On your desktop, create a folder called Data.

2. Right-click the folder and select Properties from the shortcut menu.

3. Select the Security tab, and then select your user account.

4. Select the check box indicating Deny:Full Control permissions for your user account, click Yes in the warning dialog box.

5. Click Advanced, and then select the Auditing tab. Add your user account to audit List Folder / Read Data: Failed, and then click OK to close all Property dialog boxes.

6. Double-click the Data folder to open it. You should receive an Access Denied warning message.

Exercise 3: Reading the Security Log

In this exercise, you will confirm the auditing of your failed access to the Data folder.

1. From Administratives Tools, open the Computer Management console.

2. Expand the Event Viewer node, and then click the Security log in the folder pane.

Near the top of the list of events, you should see several Failure Audit events (with ID 560) indicating your failed attempt to access the Data folder.

3. Right-click the Security log in the folder pane, select View from the shortcut menu, and then choose Filter.

4. In the Filter dialog box, select each of the following:

- ❑ Event Source: Security
- ❑ Category: Object Access
- ❑ Event Types: Failure selected, all others cleared

5. Click OK to apply the filter to the Security log.

You have now filtered the Security log data to display only the events that apply to failed object access.

Lesson Review

The following questions are intended to reinforce key information presented in this lesson. If you are unable to answer a question, review the lesson materials and try the question again. You can find answers to the questions in the "Questions and Answers" section at the end of this chapter.

1. On a domain controller running DNS, what logs will Event Viewer display by default? What are these logs, and what data do they collect?

_____

_____

2. You have configured your Windows Server 2003 computer to audit all failed object access, and all files and folders have auditing configured for List Folder / Read Data Failure. All other Event Viewer and Security log settings are at their default configurations. What will happen when the number of entries in the Security log reaches 512 KB?

_____

_____

3. You do not want data in the Security log to be overwritten, but also do not want your Windows Server 2003 computer to stop serving the network at any time. What settings will you configure on your server?

_____

_____

Lesson Summary

The Windows Server 2003 Event Viewer contains several logs which report errors and significant events during system operation. The System log contains data related to service and other internal operating system functioning. The Application log contains data written to it by software programs. The Security log contains data for successful and failed audits. Different from the other logs, the Security log is configurable by the administrator as to what data is written to it. Domain Controllers have additional logs for File Replication Services and the Active Directory. DNS servers have a log for DNS that is separate from other application logs.

In complex or lengthy logs, the display of data can be filtered by various criteria, including recording date and type of data, to make the data more readable. The data from the logs can be stored in a variety of file types, as follows:

- Performance Monitor Binary file (*.blg), with or without circular overwriting

- Text file (*.txt or *.csv)

- SQL Database

Once the settings for a log have been configured, the Performance Monitor settings can be saved (by selecting Save Settings As, from the log's context menu) as a hypertext markup language (HTML) file for later use (by selecting New Log Settings From, from the Counter Logs context menu).

All Event Viewer logs can be configured separately as to the maximum size of the log file, and how that log file should operate if the maximum size is reached. The choices when the maximum file size is reached is to overwrite older data immediately, only overwrite data that is of a certain age, or force a manual clearing of the log and never overwriting any data. In a related configuration, Group Policy can be enabled so as to force the immediate shutdown of a computer that is unable to write audit information to the Security log.

Lesson 2: Using the Performance Console

With the Performance Console, you can measure the activity of any computer on the network. System Monitor and the Performance Logs And Alerts snap-ins are built in as parts of the Performance console (perfmon.msc). The System Monitor snap-in allows for the viewing of real-time performance data as collected from configurable counters. The Performance Logs And Alerts snap-in allows for the recording of performance data (logs) and configurable actions when a threshold for a counter is breached (alerts). The Performance console allows you to perform multiple tasks, including the following:

- Collect and view real-time performance data

- View data collected in a log

- Present data in a graph, histogram, or report view

- Create HTML pages from views by importing of log file settings

- Save monitoring configurations that can be loaded into System Monitor on other computers

---

After this lesson, you will be able to

- Monitor real-time performance data
- Record performance data into a log file
- Configure system and performance data alerts

Estimated lesson time: 20 minutes

Configuring System Monitor

With System Monitor, you can collect and view data by configuring counters that report hardware, application, and service activity for any computer on your network. Three configurations must be made for the data you wish to collect.

- **Type of data**   You can specify one or more counter instances of performance monitor objects for which you want data to be reported.

- **Source of data**   Either local or remote computer data can be collected by a counter. You must be a local administrator or a member of the Performance Log Users group on the computer from which you wish to collect data.

- **Sampling intervals**   Data can be recorded manually in real time, or set to a periodic interval that you specify.

Viewing Data

When you first open System Monitor, three counters are loaded and begin to report real-time data:

- Memory: Pages/Second
- Physical Disk(_Total): Average Disk Queue Length
- Processor(_Total): % Processor Time

Figure 12-3 shows the System Monitor with the default counters loaded.

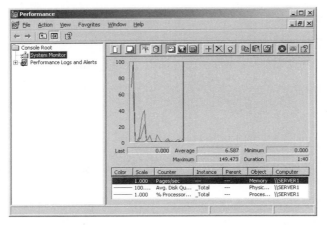

Figure 12-3   The System Monitor of the Performance console

Additional counters can be added or removed by choosing Add (Ctrl+I) on the toolbar, or right-clicking anywhere in the details pane and choosing Add Counters from the shortcut menu. In the Add Counters dialog box, you can select any of the available counters for either the local computer or any remote computer on your network. Counters are arranged and available for use based on the type of object, the counter in the object category, and the instance of the counter.

- **Object**   A logical collection of resource, service, or application counters.
- **Counter**   A data-reporting item. The data reported depends on the type of counter.
- **Instance**   Refers to one or more occurrences of a counter, indexed by the number available on the computer. For example, on a computer with two processors, Instance "0" would refer to the first processor, Instance "1" to the second, and "_Total" the aggregate of both instances. In the case of a single instance of a counter, Instance "0" and " _Total" will be available.

Figure 12-4 shows the %Processor Time counter for Server01, which is a single-processor computer.

Figure 12-4   %Processor Time Counter–Single Processor

> **Exam Tip**   Remember that "_Total" represents the combined data from multiple instances of a counter when multiple instances are available.

Logging and Alerts

With Performance Logs And Alerts, you can collect performance data automatically from local or remote computers. You can view logged counter data by using System Monitor, or you can export the data to spreadsheet programs or databases for analysis and report generation. You can configure any counters available within System Monitor for use in Performance Logs And Alerts, with the following options:

- Collect data in a CSV or tab-separated format for exporting.

- View Counter Log data during logging and post-collection.

- Set Trace Logs (event-driven) based on available providers.

- Define parameters for the log file including start and stop times and maximum file size.

- Set an alert on a counter with options to send an administrative message, an application is executed, or a log is started when the configured threshold on the counter is breached.

Figure 12-5 shows the configuration dialog box for an alert on Server01 when Free Disk Space drops below 20 percent.

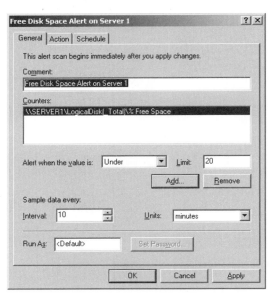

Figure 12-5   Alert Configuration for Disk Free Space

Real World   Monitoring Performance Data

When monitoring performance data for your server or network, start from the top down; that is, start with the broadest monitoring configurations of % Processor Time, Disk and Processor Queue Length, Memory Use, and Network I/O to determine where the bottleneck occurs. Once you have determined the problem area, then look at the particular services and applications using the resource, and at protocol and thread levels, if needed. Usually, there is either one device or application causing the problem, or a global lack of resources on the system. Single devices can be reconfigured or replaced, and global resources can be added (more memory, faster processor, and so on) as appropriate.

The results of this monitoring can be ambiguous; however, if you do not have a baseline of system performance by which to judge your monitoring results. As soon as is practical after configuring a new computer, perform a set of monitoring activities for the key Processor, Memory, Network, and Process (Application and Services) objects to determine how your computer performs under normal conditions—commonly called a *baseline*—in normal, idle, and peak performance states. When problems or bottlenecks occur during later monitoring, measurement against the baseline will help to find a solution.

Decisions About Objects and Counters

The object counters that you choose in monitoring a server, either for a baseline or ongoing performance evaluation, can be considered in one of two ways. One method of server monitoring examines the role that the server performs in the environment and the corresponding demands placed on that server by the user population. Another view of server monitoring involves examining object categories of counters such as Processor, Memory, Network Interface, and PhysicalDisk, with less emphasis on the role that the server fulfills and more on a consistent monitoring standard.

Server Roles

Monitoring by server role is useful when servers perform within a single role in the network environment. These roles are defined by the services or resources that the server provides to the users. Examples of server roles include domain controllers, file servers, and Web servers. A server's demand for resources can be matched, in a performance monitoring situation, with the appropriate object counters that measure the resources most heavily used by a server in that role. Ongoing performance monitoring data can be compared to baseline data for optimization within that role. Table 12-1 outlines the objects that are commonly used when analyzing a server by its role.

Table 12-1   Server Roles and Objects To Be Monitored

Server role	Resources used	Objects and counters
Application servers	Memory, network, and processor cache	Memory, Processor, Network Interface, and System
Backup servers	Processor and network	System, Server, Processor, and Network Interface
Database servers	Disks, network, and processor	PhysicalDisk, LogicalDisk, Processor, Network Interface, and System
Domain controllers	Memory, processor, network, and disk	Memory, Processor, System, Network Interface, protocol objects (network-dependent, but can include TCPv4, UDPv4, ICMP, IPv4, NBT Connection, NWLink IPX, NWLink NetBIOS, and NWLink SPX), PhysicalDisk, and LogicalDisk
File and print servers	Memory, disk, and network components	Memory, Network Interface, PhysicalDisk, LogicalDisk, and Print Queue
Mail/messaging servers	Processor, disk, network, and memory	Memory, Cache, Processor, System, PhysicalDisk, Network Interface, and LogicalDisk
Web servers	Disk, cache, and network components	Cache, Network Interface, PhysicalDisk, and LogicalDisk

For each server role, create a baseline using the counters within each object appropriate for the role, and periodically examine each of the servers for significant changes.

Object Categories

In a network environment where servers perform within multiple roles, role-based monitoring can leave important gaps in monitored data. In such cases, more complete data should be collected from each of the primary object categories.

Memory Counters   After you have established a baseline for memory use, periodic monitoring should be performed for deviations from that baseline. The following counters are useful in monitoring computer system memory:

- **Memory shortages: Memory\Available Bytes, Available Kbytes, or Available MBytes (to see the amount in megabytes); Process (All_processes)\Working Set; Memory\Pages/sec; Memory\Cache Bytes.**   These counters show how much memory is taken up by all processes, and how much memory is available.

- **Frequent hard page faults: Memory\Pages/sec; Process (All_processes)\Working Set; Memory\Pages Input/sec; Memory\Pages Output /sec.**   Hard page faults occur when a page of memory is needed but has been placed (swapped) into virtual memory. Excessive swapping degrades the performance of the computer, and can be addressed either by reducing the demands on the computer or increasing the amount of physical RAM.

Network Counters   Network counters report data from the network interface cards (NICs) installed in the computer, and from the segment on which the NICs communicate. The following counters are useful in measuring the performance of a computer on the network:

- **Network Interface\Output Queue Length; Bytes Total\sec.**   The Queue length should be low, and the total bytes high, which indicates a network card that is transferring packets quickly and without delay.

- **Network Interface: Bytes Sent/Sec; Current Bandwidth; Bytes Received/ Sec.**   High values in these counters consistently and over time indicate that a network is being expected to carry more traffic than is optimal. Segmenting the network into smaller pieces or increasing the bandwidth of the network will decrease the chances of bottlenecks due to excessive traffic.

Note   Different types of network configurations will allow for various levels of traffic efficiency and volume. When monitoring %Network Utilization, for example, 30 percent utilization is the maximum recommended for an unswitched Ethernet network. This means that a 10 megabyte (MB) Ethernet network becomes bottlenecked when its throughput exceeds 3 MB per second. If the value of the counter is above 40 percent, data collisions begin to hamper the performance of the network.

Process Counters   For each demand on a system resource, there is often a process that is the instrument of that demand. Using process counters allows for viewing the individual processes (including system services) that are using system resources. The following are important counters to use when gathering process-based performance data:

- **Memory leaks; memory-intensive applications: Memory\Pool Nonpaged Allocs; Memory\Pool Nonpaged Bytes; Memory\Pool Paged Bytes; Process(process_name)\Pool Nonpaged Bytes; Process(process_name)\Handle Count; Process(process_name)\Pool Paged Bytes; Process(process_name)\Virtual Bytes; Process(process_name)\Private Bytes.**   These counters show memory use by individual processes, allowing for redistribution of intensive applications (or isolation of applications with memory leaks) to other computers.

> **Note**   An application memory leak can be diagnosed by running that application on its own server, and monitoring for memory use that increases over time with no change in demand for services. This increase without a corresponding reason can indicate a memory leak.

Disk Counters   The PhysicalDisk object counters provide data on activity for each of the hard disk storage devices, and the LogicalDisk object counters provide data on defined volumes (C:\, D:\, and so on) in your system. Monitoring LogicalDisk free space and PhysicalDisk performance counters will provide useful data. The following are important counters for Physical and Logical Disk monitoring:

- **LogicalDisk\% Free Space.**   This counter reports the percentage of unallocated disk space to the total usable space on the logical volume. This counter is not available for a physical disk.

> **Note**   When calculating the _Total instance, the %Free Space counters recalculate the sum as a percentage for each disk.

- **PhysicalDisk\Avg. Disk Bytes/Transfer; \Avg. Disk sec/Transfer; \Avg. Disk Queue Length; \% Disk Time.**   These counters measure the size of input/output (I/O) operations over time, and how busy the drive is, performing the requested disk activity. The disk is efficient if it transfers large amounts of data relatively quickly, and has a queue length <2 over time for each disk spindle.

Practice: Using the Performance Console

In this practice, you will record Performance data, analyze the data in System Monitor, and export the data for import into an Excel spreadsheet.

Exercise 1: Recording Performance Data

In this exercise, you will create a log file with LogicalDisk, PhysicalDisk, and Server Work Queue data.

1. Log on to Server01 as an administrator, and start the Performance console.

2. Expand Performance Logs And Alerts in the folder pane, and then select Counter Logs.

3. In the detail pane, right-click and select New Log Settings from the shortcut menu.

4. Create a log file called Test, and add the LogicalDisk, PhysicalDisk, and Server Work Queues objects to the log, and set the data sampling interval to 8 seconds. Take note of the file name and location for the log, and then click OK to start the log.

5. As the log is recording, perform some activities with other applications on your computer. After approximately 30 seconds, return to Performance Logs And Alerts and stop the log recording.

6. In System Monitor, click View Log Data (Ctrl+L, or fourth button from the left), and load the log file from your test.

The graph in System Monitor now shows the recorded data from your logging session. You can now change the views between graph, histogram, and report to see the data in different ways. This log file that you have created is in the default format (Binary File), strictly for use in the Performance Console.

Exercise 2: Importing Logged Data

In this exercise, you will save the logged data from Exercise 1 for import into Microsoft Excel.

1. If needed, reopen the Performance console.

2. Right-click the Test log file setting, and then choose Properties.

3. In the Test Properties dialog box, click the Log Files tab, and then change the Log File Type from Binary File to Text File (Comma Delimited).

4. Click OK, and then start the log file recording. Perform some disk-related tasks on your computer for approximately 30 seconds, and then stop the log recording.

The log file you have created is in CSV format, and can be opened, viewed and analyzed in Excel.

Note   If you intend to load the CSV file into Excel, Performance Logs And Alerts cannot have the file open because Excel requires exclusive access to the file to open it.

Lesson Review

The following questions are intended to reinforce key information presented in this lesson. If you are unable to answer a question, review the lesson materials and try the question again. You can find answers to the questions in the "Questions and Answers" section at the end of this chapter.

1. Your goal is to monitor all your Windows Server 2003 servers so that they can be defragmented on a regular schedule, and as efficiently as possible. The disk defragmentation program that you use requires at least 20% free disk space on each volume in order to defragment properly. What should you do?

   _____

   _____

2. You have been monitoring one of your Windows Server 2003 servers due to poor performance on the network. The following data is representative of your findings:

   ❑ Processor: % Processor Time: High

   ❑ Physical Disk: % Disk Time: Low

   ❑ Memory: Pages/sec: Low

   ❑ Processor: Interrupts/sec: High

   ❑ Process: % Processor Time (for non-service processes):   Low

   ❑ Process: % Processor Time (for system services):   Low

   What is the most likely explanation for the problem?

   _____

   _____

3. The server that you are using to monitor the other servers on your network is overburdened with the task, so you must lighten its load of monitoring. To make the greatest impact for the monitoring computer's performance while maintaining as much monitored data as possible, what should you do?

   _____

   _____

Lesson Summary

The Performance console has two snap-ins configured: System Monitor and Performance Logs And Alerts. The System Monitor is designed for real-time reporting of data to a console interface, and can be reported in graph, histogram, or numeric form. The Performance Logs And Alerts snap-in is designed to write data to a file (log) and report counter values that breach a threshold (alert). Logs written by Performance Logs And Alerts can be loaded into System Monitor for analysis, and exported to various file types (such as CSV and HTML) for reporting purposes.

Lesson 3: Using Task Manager

Task Manager provides information about programs and processes running on your computer. It also displays several common process performance counters.

After this lesson, you will be able to

- Configure Task Manager to display performance data
- Use Task Manager to start and end applications and processes

Estimated lesson time: 15 minutes

Task Manager Overview

Task Manager can be opened by right-clicking an open area of the taskbar and then choosing Task Manager, or by pressing CTRL+ALT+DEL and then choosing Task Manager. The Windows Server 2003 Task Manager interface, by default, presents five tabs on which its data is categorized: Applications, Processes, Performance, Networking, and Users.

Applications Tab

The Applications tab shows the status of the user-level programs running on the computer. Services and system applications running in a context different from the logged on user are not displayed. On the Applications tab you can also start a new program with New Task, end a program with End Task, or switch to another program using Switch To. By right-clicking on an application, you can also select Go To Process from the shortcut menu, which will take you to the corresponding process on the Process tab. Figure 12-6 shows the Applications tab of Task Manager.

Figure 12-6   The Applications tab of Task Manager

Processes Tab

The Processes tab shows information about all processes running on your computer, including user-level applications, services, and other system processes. By choosing Select Columns from the View menu, you can add or remove columns of data including memory usage changes (deltas), process IDs, and processor use. You can sort by any column by clicking on the column header.

By right-clicking on any process, you can change the priority of processor time that the process receives, set the processor affinity on multiple processor computers, and end a process. For processes that have child or related processes, you can end all related processes by choosing End Process Tree. If you needed to end a mail application, for example, you might also need to end the MAPI spooler; appropriately, you would right-click on the mail application and choose to End Process Tree. The Processes tab is shown in Figure 12-7.

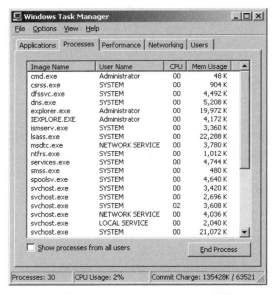

Figure 12-7   The Processes tab of Task Manager

Caution   Changing settings of a process such as priority or processor affinity can have an adverse effect on the performance of other applications running on your computer. Ending a process, especially a process tree, should be done only after normal termination procedures have failed. Windows Server 2003, thankfully, safeguards its processes from termination through Task Manager, but they are still susceptible to resource starvation through inappropriate priority adjustment of other processes.

Performance Tab

The Performance tab displays a real-time view of key elements of your computer's performance. Graphs are presented for each processor on the system and memory usage. Text displays show physical, kernel, and commit memory; also, the number of handles and threads in use by active processes are displayed. The Performance tab is shown in Figure 12-8.

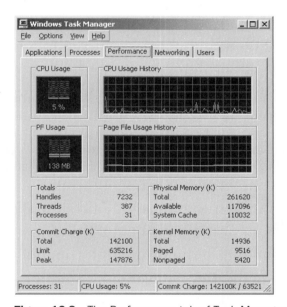

Figure 12-8   The Performance tab of Task Manager

Networking Tab

The Networking tab shows all active network connections by name, their connection speed, bandwidth usage, and status. The Networking tab is shown in Figure 12-9.

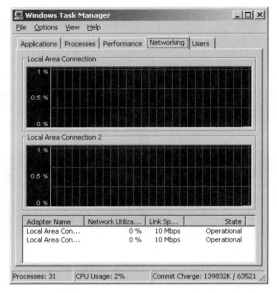

Figure 12-9 The Networking tab of Task Manager

Users Tab

The Users tab shows all users who are logged on, and allows for the logoff or forced disconnection of the user from the computer. Logged-on users may be local at the console, or remotely attached from the network. Network messages can be sent to remote users (it certainly is polite to tell them before you disconnect them) by selecting the users' session and then clicking Send Message. The Users tab is shown in Figure 12-10.

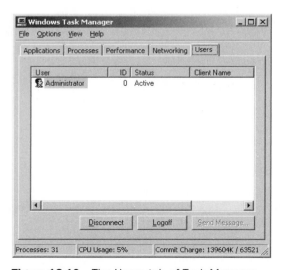

Figure 12-10 The Users tab of Task Manager

Practice: Task Manager

In this practice, you will use Task Manager to start an application and identify its process.

1. Right-click an open section of the taskbar, and choose Task Manager from the shortcut menu.

2. On the Applications tab, click New Task. Type **explorer**, and then click OK.

   Windows Explorer will open focused on its default window (typically My Documents), and the My Documents (or other focus window) application name will appear in the Application tab of Task Manager.

3. Right-click the newly-opened application name, and choose Go To Process.

The focus in Task Manager changes to the Processes tab, and the Explorer.exe process is highlighted. From this point, as a situation involving applications and Task Manager warrants, you can adjust the priority of the process or end it.

Lesson Review

The following questions are intended to reinforce key information presented in this lesson. If you are unable to answer a question, review the lesson materials and try the question again. You can find answers to the questions in the "Questions and Answers" section at the end of this chapter.

1. What information can Task Manager provide about the performance of applications?

   _____

   _____

2. Your computer crashes with almost clocklike predictability approximately one hour after each system startup. You suspect an application with a memory leak that is causing the system to run out of memory. How can you use Task Manager to determine which application is causing the problem?

   _____

   _____

3. You are running a database application on your computer. Your computer has two processors. You want the database application to run on the second processor. How can you use Task Manager to do this?

   _____

   _____

Lesson Summary

Task Manager provides dynamic views into current performance of your computer as it relates to running processes and applications. With configurable refresh intervals and selectable columns of data, the Task Manager shows the processor, memory, and I/O usage by processes. Applications can be started or ended from the Applications tab, and processes can be elevated in priority or terminated, including child processes, from the Processes tab. The Performance tab gives an aggregate view of processor and memory use on the computer. The Networking tab does the same for network utilization and basic configuration data. The Users tab, if available, will allow for logoff of a local session or disconnection of a remote session. Remote sessions can also have messages sent to the connected user.

Lesson 4: Using the WMI Event Logging Provider

Windows Management Instrumentation (WMI) is the Microsoft implementation of Web-Based Enterprise Management (WBEM), an initiative to establish standards for creating, reading, and modifying management information. WMI is WBEM-compliant and provides integrated support for the Common Information Model (CIM), the data model that describes the objects that exist in a management environment. The WMI repository is the database of object definitions, and the WMI Object Manager handles the objects as input from WMI providers. The WMI providers can receive a wide variety of input from services, applications, and system components.

After this lesson, you will be able to

- Use WMI and WMI command-line (WMIC) to monitor running services
- Use WMI and WMIC to identify installed programs
- Use WMI and WMIC to report Event data

Estimated lesson time: 30 minutes

How WMI Works

Described briefly, WMI sources of information ("providers") output information about their components (devices, services, applications, and so on) to the WMI Object Manager, which enters the information into the WMI database ("repository"). Depending on what is accepted as input and returned as output by each provider, administrators will be able to use methods to manipulate the components, set properties, and configure events that can alert administrators to changes in the components. The WMI Repository can be accessed by management tools supplied by a system, application, or device vendor; through Application Programming Interfaces (APIs) or scripting tools (Windows Scripting Host, for example), or from the command line using Windows Management Interface Command-line (WMIC).

Off the Record   You do not have to become a scripting expert to leverage WMI, and you have been using WMI even if you did not realize it. Many tools already leverage WMI to report and configure the object of the WMI provider. For example, several Windows Server 2003 tools that use WMI are System Information, System Properties, and Services.

Windows Management Interface Command-line (WMIC)

The WMIC provides a command-line interface to WMI, and can be used to manage, locally or remotely, any computer with WMI that can authenticate the user running WMIC. For WMIC to manage a remote computer, only WMI needs to be on the local computer from which the monitoring activity will be accomplished; WMIC does not have to be available on the remotely managed computer. You can use WMIC to accomplish various types of tasks:

- **Local management of a computer**   You are at the computer and use the WMIC command to manage it.

- **Remote management of a computer**   You are at the console of one computer and use WMIC to manage another computer.

- **Remote management of multiple computers**   You are at the console of one computer and use WMIC to manage multiple computers with a single command.

- **Administrative scripting**   You use WMIC to write a management script (batch file) to automate the management of a computer (local, remote, or multiple computers).

Administration with WMIC

Although a complete discussion of WMIC use with WMI is beyond the scope of this chapter (there are several good books devoted to the subject), a few points of reference are needed so that you can answer questions about monitoring with WMI and WMIC effectively. Unless otherwise noted, the remainder of discussion points in this chapter assumes that you are using WMIC in interactive mode, giving you the ability to issue single commands and view the results from within the WMIC environment.

> **Exam Tip**   Any references to WMIC in interactive mode versus non-interactive mode have no effect on the way commands are structured or used. The difference between interactive and non-interactive modes has to do with how many commands you intend to execute, and whether these commands are being entered manually or in a batch file. Enter the interactive mode of WMIC by typing **wmic** at a command line, pressing Enter, and then typing **exit** or **quit** to leave. Non-interactive mode consists of a single-line command beginning with WMIC either at a command line or in a batch file.

WMI works within the context of a namespace, the default being root\cli (MSFT_cli in the XSL stylesheet) that controls what properties, methods (verbs), and aliases are available in WMI. You can add aliases, methods, and properties if necessary (put on your programming hat), but the list is robust enough for most monitoring tasks.

Security for WMI is configured through the WMI Control snap-in (Wmimgmt.msc), in the WMI MMC. By default, users have permissions to read WMI provider information through WMIC on a local computer, but do not have permission to connect remotely or write information outside of the provider context. Administrators who want to grant additional permissions to a user or group must do so through the WMI Control snap-in.

WMIC Aliases The first parameter of a WMIC command line is the alias. The alias name must be unique in the WMI namespace schema, and provides access to WMI information without needing to remember more complex schema objects and properties. Table 12-2 lists the properties associated with each alias instance. The complete alias and namespace lists, and other detailed information about WMIC aliases, can be found in Windows Server 2003 Help and Support: Alias Namespaces and Classes.

Table 12-2 WMIC Aliases

Property	Description
FriendlyName	The name of the alias; it must be unique.
Description	A description of the alias. This is the descriptive text when /? is entered at the WMIC command line.
Formats	A list, each of which has a name and a list of properties (objects of the class MSFT_CliProperty) to be displayed for that format. All formats are objects of the class MSFT_CliFormat.
Verbs	A list, each of which are the various behaviors available through this alias. The behaviors come in two forms: Standard verbs, which are directly supported by the utility. User-defined verbs, which must map to some method defined for the target of the alias. All verbs are objects of the class MSFT_CliVerb.
Qualifiers	A list, similar to WMI qualifiers. All qualifiers are objects of the class MSFT_Qualifier.
Target	A list, similar to WMI qualifiers. All qualifiers are objects of the class MSFT_Qualifier.
PWhere clause	Optional WHERE clause that limits the Target. It has substitution values which are the parameters of the alias. The substitution values are marked with #. If multiple parameters are needed, they are matched with the # markers in sequence.
Connection	Details on which computers to connect to, the security details to be used, and so on. If a connection is not specified, the computers to be accessed are the value of /NODE, and the namespace is the value of /NAMESPACE. If a user name and password are not provided, then the value of /USER and /PASSWORD, if available, is used (otherwise the current account is used).
View an alias schema	Use a metaalias Alias to view an alias schema; example: ALIAS OS.

WMIC Verbs Most aliases have actions that they perform: these actions are initiated by issuing a verb along with the alias. In combination with parameters and switches, these alias-verb combinations control what configuration is set within the application or system, or what information is read from the WMI Repository. Table 12-3 lists the key verbs used in monitoring and their descriptions. The complete verbs list, and other detailed information about WMIC verbs, can be found in Windows Server 2003 Help and Support: WMIC Verbs.

Table 12-3   WMIC Verbs

Verb	Action	Parameters	Example
CALL	Executes methods	Method and parameter list if appropriate. Parameter lists are comma delimited. Use SERVICE CALL /? to get a list of available methods and their parameters for the current alias.	SERVICE WHERE CAPTION='TELNET' CALL STARTSERVICE
GET	Get specific properties	Property name or switch	PROCESS GET NAME
LIST	Show data	LIST is the default verb. There are many switches and adverbs that can be used with the LIST verb (example: BRIEF)	PROCESS LIST BRIEF

Using WMIC in Monitoring

With WMI running on a computer, and sufficient administrative credentials owned by the user running WMIC, local or remote monitoring of a computer is available at the command line. In non-interactive mode, multiple commands can be contained in a batch file that is run either manually or on an automated schedule. These WMIC commands can be output to a CSV file, text file, or HTML page to be viewed and analyzed. Following are examples of common monitoring scenarios and output that illustrate the use of WMIC for monitoring.

- PRODUCT

  This command will output to the console the results of a query for all installed software on the local computer.

- /OUTPUT:c:\applog.htm NTEVENT WHERE "eventtype<3 AND logfile='Application'" GET Logfile, SourceName, Eventtype, Message, TimeGenerated /FORMAT:htable:"sortby=EventType"

  This command will output to an HTML file (C:\applog.htm) any events with types 0, 1, or 2 from the Application Log of the local computer. The list will be formatted in an HTML table (using the XML stylesheet htable.xsl) and sorted by Event Type.

- /OUTPUT:c:\applog.csv /NODE:@"c:\serverlist.txt" NTEVENT WHERE "eventtype<3 AND logfile='Application'" GET Logfile, SourceName, Eventtype, Message, TimeGenerated /FORMAT:csv:"sortby=EventType"

  This command will output to a CSV file (c:\applog.csv) any events with types 0, 1, or 2 from the Application Logs of the computers in the file serverlist.txt. The list will be formatted in a comma-separated list (using the XML stylesheet csv.xsl) and sorted by Event Type.

■ OS ASSOC

This command displays information related to the operating system hotfixes and patches that have been installed.

Practice: WMI Data from Event Viewer

In this practice, you will extract data from the Event Viewer and publish it to a Web page.

1. Logged on as Administrator on Server01, open a command window, type **wmic** and press Enter. This enters WMIC in interactive mode.

2. At the WMIC prompt, type the following command to access the Security Log data from Lesson 1, Exercise 3:

   NTEVENT WHERE "EVENTTYPE=5 AND LOGFILE='SECURITY'" GET LOG-FILE, SOURCENAME, EVENTTYPE, MESSAGE, TIMEGENERATED

   This outputs the Failure Audit entries to the console.

3. At the WMIC prompt, type the following command to output the same information to a Web page called C:\seclog.htm.

   /OUTPUT:C:\seclog.htm NTEVENT WHERE "EVENTTYPE=5 AND LOG-FILE='SECURITY'" GET LOGFILE, SOURCENAME, EVENTTYPE, MESSAGE, TIMEGENERATED /FORMAT:htable

4. Double-click the file C:\Seclog.htm to open the file in Internet Explorer.

Lesson Review

The following questions are intended to reinforce key information presented in this lesson. If you are unable to answer a question, review the lesson materials and try the question again. You can find answers to the questions in the "Questions and Answers" section at the end of this chapter.

1. You need to get patch and hotfix information from a number of servers on your network. You would like to do this remotely. How can you use WMI to accomplish the task?

   _____

   _____

2. You want to get a list of all installed applications on 17 computers in the development department. You would like to do this remotely. How can you use WMI to accomplish this?

   _____

   _____

3. You want to give a small group of engineers the ability to use WMI to get information from some of the development servers, but you do not want to give them administrator privileges on the servers. What can you do to give the engineers access?

_____

_____

Lesson Summary

WMI is a WBEM-compliant utility that uses a CIM-compliant database of management information collected by running on each Windows Server 2003 computer. The command line interface for WMI is WMIC, which uses a series of aliases, verbs, switches and parameters to change configuration on or get information from a computer system. WMIC can connect to any computer remotely, so long as the user initiating the connection has sufficient privileges on the remote computer. The local administrator on a computer has permission to connect remotely, so Domain Administrators each have the ability to perform remote administration with WMI and WMIC. For archiving and reporting purposes, WMI data can be output through WMIC to CSV or HTML pages. Multiple computers can have commands issued to them either from the command line or from a text file. With the exception of needing to include the WMIC command at the beginning of each line, issuing commands from a batch file in non-interactive mode is no different from using WMIC in interactive mode.

Case Scenario Exercise

You have been placed in charge of the Information Technology department at your new company, and are trying to put better practices in place than your predecessor did. Server hardware failures are quite commonplace, and user satisfaction with network performance is very low. From your initial interviews with your administrative staff, there has been very little planning and very much fire-fighting over the past several years.

The mandate from the company's vice president is that you get things cleaned up quickly, and relieve his anxiety that important company data is walking out the door due to lax security practices. User productivity needs to improve, and that includes all the applications that the users have installed on their computer systems—against company policy.

Here, then, is the checklist you create for improving the technology environment:

■ Use WMI and other file utilities to get a complete list of all file-based resources that are located in servers on the network. Completely document the permission structure on those resources and cross-reference it with the department heads to be certain that you understand the file resource access needs clearly.

- Use Event Viewer and the Performance console to get an accurate picture of any immediate bottleneck problems due to device failure, service misconfiguration, or application incompatibilities. Replace hardware, properly configure services, and upgrade applications where necessary to improve the component parts of the running environment.

- Once the permissions are defined, put Failure Access Auditing in place to find anyone who is attempting to gain unauthorized resource access, and through what means.

- Use Performance Logs And Alerts to baseline the servers once clearly defined bottlenecks have been removed. Continue to monitor for changes in server performance against the baseline.

Troubleshooting Lab

Users in the Help Desk group have been creating their own Web pages to publish technical data for the rest of the group, and have many utilities that they use periodically in testing applications for functionality and stability. Recently, these users have been asking for some help in determining why their computers' performance has recently declined significantly.

Using the Performance console, take a baseline of the following counters:

- Cache\Data Map Hits %
- Cache\Fast Reads/sec
- Cache\Lazy Write Pages/sec
- Logical Disk\% Free Space
- Memory\Available Bytes
- Memory\ Pool Nonpaged Allocs
- Memory\ Pool Nonpaged Bytes
- Memory\ Pool Paged Allocs
- Memory\ Pool Paged Bytes
- Processor(_Total)\% Processor Time
- System\Context Switches/sec
- System\Processor Queue Length
- Processor(_Total)\Interrupts/sec

Monitor each of the suspect computers for one week of normal activity, recording the resulting output in a log file unique to each computer. Use a remote computer to collect the monitoring data so as not to skew the results of your baseline.

Analyze the data to determine if there are any obvious bottlenecks. This list of counters is particularly baselining memory, disk I/O, and processor performance on each of the computers. Once the bottleneck has been defined, the applications (processes) should be examined to determine which of them are the heaviest contributors to the problem. The applications can then be upgraded, if that helps; removed, or resources can be added to the computers sufficient to perform the required tasks.

Chapter Summary

- Event Viewer presents data in the form of logs. The Application, System, and Security logs are on every Windows Server 2003 server. Domain controllers have two additional logs relating to Active Directory, and other application servers (such as DNS) have their own set of log files.

- The Performance console (perfmon.msc) consists of two snap-ins: System Monitor and Performance Logs And Alerts. System Monitor shows real-time performance data based on Object counters, and can display the log data recorded by Performance Logs And Alerts either in the form of Counter (interval polling) logs, or Trace (event-driven) logs.

- Task Manager is used to view real-time performance data surrounding processes and applications. Processes can be initiated and ended using Task Manager. Processes can also be adjusted up or down in CPU priority, and can be assigned affinity to a particular processor on a multiprocessor computer.

- WMI is a management system that collects data from computer systems. The control interface of WMI Control snap-in allows for adjustment of permissions beyond the default of the local administrator to manage computers across the network. While WMI is capable of configuring many different types of system behavior including users, groups, and services, the focus of this chapter is on the ability to extract data from the WMI Repository using the command line interface to WMI, WMIC. WMIC is capable of reporting running services, installed applications, and publishing Event Viewer data to CSV or HTML files for ease of distribution and analysis.

Exam Highlights

Before taking the exam, review the key points and terms that are presented below to help you identify topics you need to review. Return to the lessons for additional practice and review the "Further Readings" sections in Part 2 for pointers to more information about topics covered by the exam objectives.

Key Points

- Event Viewer does not perform configuration, but collects data from different reporting providers. Data reported is organized into the appropriate log, and can be filtered, sorted, and exported for ease of analysis.

- Task Manager is a tool used only on the local computer, and does not allow configuration of memory, processor, or other settings. Task Manager is exclusively used to start, stop, prioritize, and set processor affinity for applications.

- The Performance Logs And Alerts snap-in can do no configuration, only reporting data through Counter Logs as reported by providers (object counters) on a configured interval, or through Trace Logs as reported by event-driven providers.

- WMI requires administrative credentials for access to the remote computer for configuration of settings.

- WMIC is not an Active Directory Schema Management Tool. WMI maintains its own schema.

Key Terms

Windows Management Instrumentation (WMI)   The Microsoft implementation of Web-Based Enterprise Management Initiative to establish standards of data in Enterprise Management

Windows Management Instrumentation Control (WMIC)   A command line utility that interfaces with the WMI Repository (database) for configuration and monitoring management

Task Manager   An interface tool for the manipulation of processes

System Monitor   A component of the Performance console, as is the Performance Logs And Alerts snap-in, and should not be confused with System Properties

Questions and Answers

Lesson 1 Review

Page
12-7

1. On a Domain Controller running DNS, what logs will Event Viewer display by default? What are these logs, and what data do they collect?

   - **Application**   Developers of an application can program their software to report configuration changes, errors, or other events to this log.

   - **System**   The Windows Server 2003 operating system will report events (service start or abnormal shutdown, device failures, and so on) to this log. The events reported to this log are preconfigured.

   - **Security**   Logon and resource access events (audits) are reported to this log. Configuration for most of these events is at the discrimination of the system administrator.

   - **Directory Service**   This log contains events related to the Active Directory, such as irreconcilable object replication or significant events within the directory.

   - **File Replication Service**   This log contains errors or significant events reported by the File Replication Service related to the copying of information between domain controllers during a replication cycle.

   - **DNS Server**   This log contains errors or significant events reported by the DNS server.

2. You have configured your Windows Server 2003 computer to audit all failed object access, and all files and folders have auditing configured for List Folder / Read Data Failure. All other Event Viewer and Security log settings are at their default configurations. What will happen when the number of entries in the Security log reaches 512 KB?

   The default configuration puts the maximum log file size at 512 KB, and allows for the file to overwrite, so once the file reaches 512 KB, the older data in the log will be overwritten.

3. You do not want data in the Security log to be overwritten, but also do not want your Windows Server 2003 computer to stop serving the network at any time. What settings will you configure on your server?

   In the properties for the Security log, configure the log to Do Not Overwrite Events (Clear Log Manually). You will *not* define the Group Policy that defines the Security Option: Audit: Shut Down System Immediately If Unable To Log Security Audits, as this will discontinue the server's availability to the network if the Security log fills. You will need to schedule a regular period of Security log analysis as good administrative practice, but you will not need to do so at such a frequency as to keep the server from shutting down because you did not clear the log soon enough.

Page
12-17

Lesson 2 Review

1. Your goal is to monitor all your Windows Server 2003 servers so that they can be defragmented on a regular schedule, and as efficiently as possible. The disk defragmentation program that you use requires at least 20% free disk space on each volume in order to defragment properly. What should you do?

Configure Performance Logs And Alerts on a workstation (or less-utilized server) to monitor all the remote servers' LogicalDisk object, % Free Space counter for each instance on that computer. In addition, configure each counter as an Alert with a threshold of Below 20% free space. Finally, configure each of the Alerts to send a message to the administrator (and any other user accounts that you want to receive the message).

2. You have been monitoring one of your Windows Server 2003 servers due to poor performance on the network. The following data is representative of your findings:

❑ Processor: % Processor Time:	High
❑ Physical Disk: % Disk Time:	Low
❑ Memory: Pages/sec:	Low
❑ Processor: Interrupts/sec:	High
❑ Process: % Processor Time (for non-service processes):	Low
❑ Process: % Processor Time (for system services):	Low

What is the most likely explanation for the problem?

It is likely that the Network Interface Card (or another device) is experiencing a problem at the device level. The high number of interrupts per second would cause the processor to be busy processing requests for service from the network interface. With all other counters being low, it is unlikely that an application or any System service is at fault.

3. The server that you are using to monitor the other servers on your network is overburdened with the task, so you must lighten its load of monitoring. To make the greatest impact for the monitoring computer's performance while maintaining as much monitored data as possible, what should you do?

Increase the polling interval for recording the data from the remote computers. By decreasing the frequency of the data poll, and perhaps staggering the logging times, the greatest amount of monitoring data can be maintained while reducing the load on the monitoring computer.

Page
12-23

Lesson 3 Review

1. What information can Task Manager provide about the performance of applications?

Task Manager can provide processor, memory usage (including the page file), and basic Input/Output on a process-by-process basis.

2. Your computer crashes with almost clocklike predictability approximately one hour after each system startup. You suspect an application with a memory leak

that is causing the system to run out of memory. How can you use Task Manager to determine which application is causing the problem?

Start all applications normally. In Task Manager, select the Memory Usage Delta column (View-Select Columns), and click on the column header. If you leave the system idle, then memory usage by any of the processes running on the computer should stabilize. If there is an application with a memory leak, it should stay at or near the top of the list of processes running on the computer, and its value for Memory Usage Delta should continue to increase even with no activity on the system.

3. You are running a database application on your computer. Your computer has two processors. You want the database application to run on the second processor. How can you use Task Manager to do this?

Right-click the database application in the Applications tab, and then choose Go To Process. Right-click the process, and set the processor affinity from the shortcut menu.

Page
12-29
Lesson 4 Review

1. You need to get patch and hotfix information from a number of servers on your network. You would like to do this remotely. How can you use WMI to accomplish the task?

Use the OS ASSOC alias with the /node: switch to run the WMIC command on any number of the computers remotely. Output to a CSV or HTML file for later use is possible as well using the /output alias and /format switch. For example, if Server01 and Server02 were the target computers for WMIC, the command would be /NODE:"SERVER01","SERVER02" OS ASSOC.

2. You want to get a list of all installed applications on 17 computers in the development department. You would like to do this remotely. How can you use WMI to accomplish this?

Type the computer names into a text file (computers.txt, for example). Use the WMIC PRODUCT alias with the node /node:@ switch to get the list of installed applications on each of the computers in the list. Output to a CSV or HTML file for later use is possible as well using the /output alias and /format switch. For example, /NODE:@c:\computers.txt PRODUCT would produce the desired results.

3. You want to give a small group of engineers the ability to use WMI to get information from some of the development servers, but you do not want to give them administrator privileges on the servers. What can you do to give the engineers access?

Give each engineer, or a group of all engineers, permission to the WMI namespace using WMI Control snap-in (Wmimgmt.msc), in the WMI MMC.

13 Recovering from System Failure

Exam Objectives in this Chapter:

- Perform Automated System Recovery (ASR)
- Perform server system recovery

Why This Chapter Matters

Although Microsoft Windows Server 2003 offers superior levels of stability and reliability, power supplies, cooling fans, chip sets and yes, even code, can cause a computer to fail. And when a server fails in the forest, everyone hears it fall. Throughout this training kit, you have learned how to implement and support best practices that will minimize the risk of failure. You have also learned how to recover from the failure of specific services, drivers, and hardware configurations. In this chapter, you will learn the remaining skills that are required to recover a server when the operating system itself is corrupted or inaccessible due to catastrophic failure.

Lessons in this Chapter:

Before You Begin

This chapter covers the concepts and skills related to recovering a failed server. To complete the exercises in this chapter, prepare the following:

- A computer running Windows Server 2003. The examples use the computer name Server01. It can be a member server or a domain controller. Backups that are created during the exercises will complete more quickly if the computer is a member server.

- A second physical disk is required to perform the exercise that demonstrates Automated System Recovery.

- If you complete the Automated System Recovery exercise, all data on the disk containing the system volume will be erased. Do not perform the Automated System Recovery if you want to maintain any data on that disk.

Lesson 1: Recovering from System Failure

In a worst-case scenario, server hardware fails and cannot be recovered. To return to operations, you must have a complete backup of the server that you can restore to a new piece of hardware. This complete backup will include data stored on the server, applications, and the operating system itself. In Chapter 7, you learned how to use the Backup Utility and the Ntbackup command-line tool to back up data. In this lesson, you will learn how to use the same utilities to back up the system so that you can return to operational status quickly in the event of such a worst-case scenario. You will also learn how to use the Recovery Console to perform surgical repairs of specific problems including service or driver failures.

After this lesson, you will be able to

- Back up the System State
- Prepare an ASR backup set and repair a computer using Automated System Recovery
- Install and use the Windows Server 2003 Recovery Console

Estimated lesson time: 60 minutes

A Review of Recovery Options

Throughout this book, we have addressed methods used to repair and recover from specific types of failures:

- Data loss or corruption: Chapter 7 discussed the backup and restore of data as well as the Volume Shadow Copy Service, the new feature in Windows Server 2003 that allows users to access or restore previous versions of files in shared folders on servers.

- Driver updates resulting in system instability: Chapter 10 introduced the new driver rollback capability of Windows Server 2003. If a driver has been updated and the system becomes unstable, that driver and any new settings that were configured can be rolled back to a previously installed version and state. Printer drivers cannot be rolled back. You also learned that it is easy, using Device Manager, to disable a device that causes instability. If an application or supporting software contributes to the instability, use Add Or Remove Programs to remove the offending component.

- Driver or service installation or update results in the inability to start the system: Chapter 10 covered the use of the Last Known Good Configuration, which rolls back the active ControlSet of the system's registry to the ControlSet that was used the last time a user successfully logged on to the system. If you install or update a service or driver and the system crashes or cannot reboot to the logon screen, the Last Known Good Configuration effectively takes you back to the version of the registry that was active before the driver or service was installed. You also learned about the variety of Safe mode options, which enable the system to start with specific drivers or services disabled. Safe mode can often allow you to start an otherwise unbootable computer and, using Device Manager, disable, uninstall, or roll back a troublesome driver or service.

- Failure of the disk subsystem: Chapter 11 discussed the steps required to configure disk redundancy through mirrored (RAID-1) or RAID-5 volumes, and how to recover from the failure of a single disk within a fault-tolerant volume.

Each of these recovery and repair processes makes the assumption that a system can be restarted to some extent. When a system cannot be restarted, the System State, Automated System Recovery, and the Recovery Console can return the system to operational status.

System State

Windows 2000 and Windows Server 2003 introduced the concept of *System State* to the backup process. System State data contains critical elements of a system's configuration including:

- The system's registry
- The COM+ Class Registration Database
- The boot files, which include boot.ini, ntdetect.com, ntldr, bootsect.dos, and ntbootdd.sys
- System files that are protected by the Windows File Protection service

In addition, the following are included in the System State when the corresponding services have been installed on the system:

- Certificate Services database on a certificate server
- Active Directory and the Sysvol folder on a domain controller
- Cluster service information on a cluster server
- Internet Information Services (IIS) metabase on a server with IIS installed

To back up the System State in the Backup Utility, include the System State node as part of the backup selection. The System State and its components are shown in Figure 13-1.

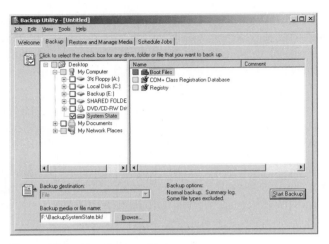

Figure 13-1   The System State

If you prefer to use the command line, use Ntbackup with the following syntax:

```
Ntbackup backup systemstate /J "backup job name" ...
```

Followed by the /F switch to indicate backing up to a file, or appropriate /T, /G, /N, /P switches to back up to a tape. The switches for the Ntbackup command are described fully in Chapter 7.

There are several important notes and considerations related to backing up the System State:

- You cannot back up individual components of the System State. For example, you cannot back up the COM+ Class Registration Database alone. Because of interdependencies among System State components, you can back up only the collection of System State components as a whole.

- You cannot use Ntbackup or the Backup Utility to back up the System State from a remote machine. You must run Ntbackup or the Backup Utility on the system that is being backed up. You can, however, direct the backup to a file on a remote server, which can then transfer the file onto another backup media. Or you can purchase a third-party backup utility that can remotely back up the System State.

- The System State contains most elements of a system's configuration, but may not include every element required to return the system to full operational capacity. It is therefore recommended to back up all boot, system, data, and application volumes when you back up the system state. The System State is a critical piece of a complete backup, but is only one piece.

- Performing a system state backup automatically forces the backup type to Copy, although the interface may not indicate that fact. Take that fact into consideration when planning whether to include other items in your backup selection.

To restore the System State on a computer that is operational, use the Backup Utility and, on the Restore And Manage Media tab, click the System State check box. If the computer is not operational, you will most likely turn to Automated System Recovery to regain operational status.

System State on a Domain Controller

The System State on a domain controller includes the Microsoft Active Directory directory service and the Sysvol folder. You can back up the System State on a domain controller just as on any other system, using the Backup Utility or Ntbackup command. As with all backup media, it is paramount to maintain physical security of the media to which the Active Directory is backed up.

To restore the System State on a domain controller, you must restart the computer, press F8 to select startup options, and select Directory Services Restore Mode. This mode is a variation of the Safe modes described in Chapter 10. In Directory Services Restore Mode, the domain controller boots but does not start Active Directory services. You can log on to the computer only as the local Administrator, using the Directory Services Restore Mode password that was specified when Dcpromo was used to promote the server to a domain controller.

When in Directory Services Restore Mode, the domain controller does not perform authentication or Active Directory replication, and the Active Directory database and supporting files are not subject to file locks. You can therefore restore the System State using the Backup Utility.

When restoring the System State on a domain controller, you must choose whether to perform a non-authoritative (normal) or authoritative restore of the Active Directory and Sysvol folder. After restoring the System State using the Backup Utility, you complete a non-authoritative restore by restarting the domain controller into normal operational status. Because older data was restored, the domain controller must update its replica of the Active Directory and Sysvol, which it does automatically through standard replication mechanisms from its replication partners.

There may be occasions, however, when you do not want the restored domain controller to become consistent with other functioning domain controllers and instead want all domain controllers to have the same state as the restored replica. If, for example, objects have been deleted from Active Directory, you can restore one domain controller with a backup set that was created prior to the deletion of the objects. You must then perform an authoritative restore, which marks selected objects as authoritative and causes those objects to be replicated *from* the restored domain controllers *to* its replication partners.

To perform an authoritative restore, you must first perform a non-authoritative restore by using the Backup Utility to restore the System State onto the domain controller. When the restore is completed and you click Close in the Backup Utility, you are prompted to restart the computer. When that occurs, you must select No. Do not allow the domain controller to restart. Then, open a command prompt and use Ntdsutil to mark the entire restored database or selected objects as authoritative. You can get more information about Ntdsutil and authoritative restore by typing **ntdsutil /?** at the command prompt or by using the online references in the Help And Support Center. The *MCSE Training Kit (Exam 70-294): Planning, Implementing, and Maintaining a Microsoft Windows Server 2003 Active Directory Infrastructure* (Microsoft Press, 2003) addresses domain controller recovery in detail.

> **Exam Tip**   What is most important to remember for the 70-290 exam is that the System State can only be restored on a domain controller by restarting the domain controller in Directory Services Restore Mode, and that Ntdsutil is used to recover deleted objects in Active Directory by marking those objects as authoritative, following a normal, or non-authoritative, restore of the System State with the Backup Utility.

Automated System Recovery

Recovering a failed server has traditionally been a tedious task, involving reinstallation of the operating system, mounting and cataloging the backup tape, then performing a full restore. Automated System Recovery makes that process significantly easier. Automated System Recovery requires you to create an ASR set, consisting of a backup of critical system files, including the registry, and a floppy disk listing the Windows system files that are installed on the computer. If the server ever fails, you simply restart with the Windows Server 2003 CD-ROM and select the option to perform an Automated System Recovery. The process uses the list of files on the ASR disk to restore standard drivers and files from the original Widows Server 2003 CD-ROM, and will restore remaining files from the ASR backup set.

To create an ASR set, open the Backup Utility from the Accessories program group, or by clicking Start, then Run, and typing **Ntbackup.exe**. If the Backup And Restore Wizard appears, click Advanced Mode. Then, from the Backup Utility's Welcome tab, or from the Tools menu, select ASR Wizard. Follow the instructions of the Automated

System Recovery Preparation Wizard. It will request a 1.44 megabyte (MB) floppy disk to create the ASR floppy. The ASR Wizard is shown in Figure 13-2.

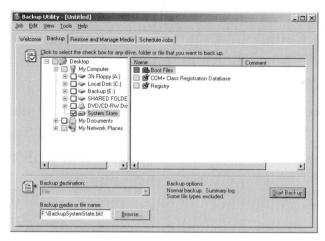

Figure 13-2   The Backup Destination page of the ASR Wizard

The backup created by the ASR Wizard includes disk configuration information for each disk in the computer, a System State backup, and a backup of files including the driver cache. The backup set is sizable. On a standard installation of Windows Server 2003, the ASR backup size will be more than 1 gigabyte (GB).

The ASR floppy disk is created by the Automated System Recovery Preparation Wizard, and is specific to the system and the time at which the ASR set was created. You should label the ASR backup set and floppy disk carefully and keep them together.

The ASR floppy disk contains two catalogs of files on the system: Asr.sif and Asrpnp.sif. If the system does not have a floppy drive when you create the ASR set, you can create the floppy disk after running the wizard by copying these two files from the *%Systemroot%*\repair folder on the system to another computer that does have a floppy drive, and copying the files to the floppy disk on that second system. If you lose the floppy disk, you can restore the two files from the *%Systemroot%*\repair folder in the ASR backup set. You *must* have the ASR floppy disk to perform an Automated System Recovery. If the system does not have a floppy drive you will need to connect one before performing the restore.

Tip The ASR set contains the files required to start the system. It is not a comprehensive backup of the entire system. Therefore it is highly recommended to create a complete backup, including the System State, system volume, applications and, perhaps, user data when you create your ASR set.

When you perform an Automated System Recovery, you will need

- The Windows Server 2003 setup CD-ROM
- The ASR backup set
- The ASR floppy disk created at the same time as the ASR backup set

Tip You will also need any mass storage device drivers that are not part of the standard Windows Server 2003 driver set. To facilitate recovery, you should consider copying those drivers to the ASR floppy disk.

To restore a system using Automated System Recovery, restart using the Windows Server 2003 CD-ROM, just as if you were installing the operating system on the computer. If the computer requires a mass storage device driver that is not included with Windows Server 2003, press F6 when prompted and provide the driver on a floppy disk. After loading initial drivers, the system will prompt you to press F2 to perform an Automated System Recovery. Press F2 and follow the instructions on your screen. Automated System Recover will prompt you for the system's ASR floppy, which contains two catalogs, or lists, of files required to start the system. Those files will be loaded from the CD-ROM. Automated System Recovery will restore remaining critical files, including the system's registry, from the system's ASR backup set. There is a restart during the process, and if the computer requires a vendor-specific mass storage device driver, you will need to press F6 during this second restart as well. Because there is a restart, you should either remove the floppy after the initial text-based portion of the restore, or set the restart order so that the system does not attempt to restart from the floppy drive.

Recovery Console

The Recovery Console is a text-mode command interpreter that allows you to access to the hard disk of a computer running Windows Server 2003 for basic troubleshooting and system maintenance. It is particularly useful when the operating system cannot be started, as the Recovery Console can be used to run diagnostics, disable drivers and services, replace files, and perform other targeted recovery procedures.

Installing the Recovery Console

You can start the Recovery Console by booting with the Windows Server 2003 CD-ROM and, when prompted, pressing R to choose the repair and recover option. However, when a system is down you will typically want to recover the system as quickly as possible, and you may not want to waste time hunting down a copy of the CD-ROM or waiting for the laboriously long restart process. Therefore, it is recommended to pro-actively install the Recovery Console.

To install the Recovery Console, insert the Windows Server 2003 CD-ROM and type **cd-drive:\i386\winnt32 /cmdcons** on the command line. The Setup Wizard will install the 8 MB console in a hidden folder called Cmdcons, and will modify the boot.ini file to provide the Recovery Console as a startup option during the boot process.

Removing the Recovery Console

If you ever decide to remove the Recovery Console, you must delete files and folders that are "super hidden." From Windows Explorer, choose the Folder Options command from the Tools menu. Click the View tab, select Show Hidden Files and Folders, clear Hide Protected Operating System Files, click OK and, if you are prompted with a warning about displaying protected system files, click Yes.

Then, delete the Cmdcons folder and the Cmldr file, each of which are located in the root of the system drive. You must next remove the Recovery Console startup option from Boot.ini. Open System from Control Panel, click the Advanced tab, click the Settings button in the Startup And Recovery frame, then, in the Startup And Recovery dialog box, under System startup, select Edit. Boot.ini will display in Notepad. Remove the entry for the Recovery Console, which will look something like this:

```
c:\cmdcons\bootsect.dat="Microsoft Windows Recovery Console" /cmdcons
```

Save the file and close Boot.ini.

Using the Recovery Console

After you have installed the Recovery Console, you can boot the system and select Microsoft Windows Recovery Console from the startup menu. If the console was not installed or cannot be launched successfully, you can restart using the Windows Server 2003 CD-ROM and, at the Welcome To Setup screen, press R to select Repair. The loading takes significantly longer from the CD-ROM, but the resulting Recovery Console is identical to that installed on the local system.

Once the Recovery Console has started, as shown in Figure 13-3, you will be prompted to select the installation of Windows to which you wish to log on. You will then be asked to enter the Administrator password. You must use the password assigned to the local Administrator account, which, on a domain controller, is the password configured on the Directory Services Restore Mode Password page of the Active Directory Installation Wizard.

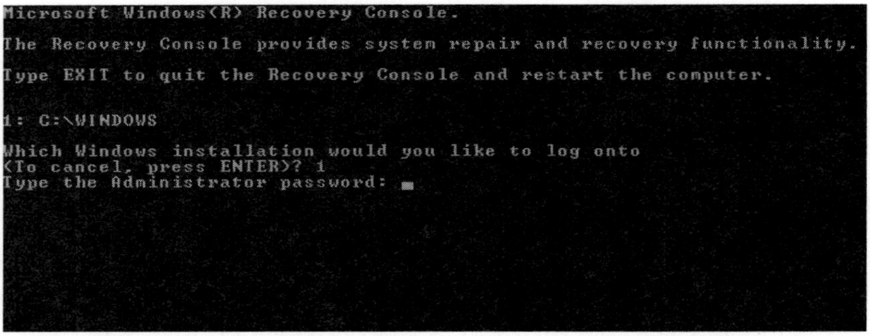

Figure 13-3   The Recovery Console

You can type **help** at the console prompt to list the commands available in the Recovery Console, and **help *command name*** for information about a specific command. Most are familiar commands from the standard command-line environment. Several of the commands deserve particular attention:

- **Listsvc**   Displays the services and drivers that are listed in the registry as well as their startup settings. This is a useful way to discover the short name for a service or driver before using the Enable and Disable commands.

- **Enable/Disable**   Controls the startup status of a service or driver. If a service or driver is preventing the operating system from starting successfully, use the Recovery Console's Disable command to disable the component, then restart the system and repair or uninstall the component.

- **Diskpart**   Provides the opportunity to create and delete partitions using an interface similar to that of the text-based portion of Setup. You can then use the Format command to configure a file system for a partition.

- **Bootcfg**   Enables you to manage the startup menu.

The Recovery Console has several limitations imposed for security purposes. These limitations can be modified using a combination of policies (located in the Computer Configuration, Windows Settings, Security Settings, Local Policies, Security Options node of the Local Computer Policy console) and Recovery Console environment variables.

- **Directory access**   You can only view files in the root directory, in %*Windir*% and in the \Cmdcons folder. Disable this limitation by setting the policy Allow Floppy Copy And Access To All Drives And All Folders, and using the command **set AllowAllPaths = true**. Be sure to include the space on either side of the equal sign when typing the set command.

- **File copy**   You can only copy files to the local hard disk, not from it. Use the policy mentioned above and the command **set AllowRemovableMedia = true**. Be sure to include the space on either side of the equal sign when typing the set command.

- **Wild cards**   You cannot use wildcards such as the asterisk to delete files. Implement the policy mentioned above then, in the Recovery Console, type the command **set AllowWildCards = true**. Be sure to include the space on either side of the equal sign when typing the set command.

Practice: Recovering from System Failure

In this practice, you will back up the System State and create an Automated System Recovery Set. You will also install and use the Recovery Console to troubleshoot driver or service failures. Finally, if you have access to a second physical disk drive, you will be able to perform Automated System Recovery to restore a failed server.

Exercise 1: Back Up the System State

1. Log on to Server01 as Administrator.
2. Open the Backup Utility.
3. If the Backup And Restore Wizard appears, click Advanced Mode.
4. Click the Backup tab and select the check box next to System State. Also click the System State label so that you can see the components of the System State listed in the other pane of the dialog box.
5. Type a file name for the backup file, such as **C:\SystemState.bkf**.
6. Start the backup.
7. When the backup is complete, examine the file size of the System State backup file. How big is the file?

Exercise 2: Create an ASR Set

This exercise requires a blank floppy disk and approximately 1.5 GB of free disk space. If you have a second physical disk in Server01, direct the backup to that disk so that you can perform an Automated System Recovery in Exercise 4.

1. Open the Backup Utility. If the Backup And Restore Wizard appears, click Advanced Mode.

2. Click Automated System Recovery Wizard, or choose ASR Wizard from the Tools menu.

3. Follow the prompts. Back up to a file called ASRBackup.bkf on the C drive or, if you have a second physical disk, on that volume.

4. When the backup is complete, examine the file size of ASRBackup.bkf. How big is it? How does its size compare to that of the System State backup?

Exercise 3: Installing and Using the Recovery Console

1. Insert the Windows Server 2003 CD-ROM.

2. Click Start, Run, and then type the following command in the Open box:

   ```
   D:\i386\winnt32.exe /cmdcons
   ```

   where *D:* is the drive letter for your CD-ROM. The Recovery Console will be installed on the local hard disk.

3. To simulate a service in need of troubleshooting, open the Services console from Administrative Tools. Locate the Messenger service. Double-click the service and choose Automatic as the Startup Type.

4. Restart the server.

5. When the server presents the startup boot menu, select Microsoft Windows Recovery Console.

6. When prompted, type **1** to select the installation of Windows Server 2003.

7. Type the password for the local Administrator account.

8. When the Recovery Console prompt appears (by default, C:\Windows>), type **help** to display a list of commands.

9. Type **listsvc** to display a list of services and drivers. Note that the short name of many services is not the same as the long name. However, the short name of the Messenger service is also Messenger. Confirm that its startup is set to Automatic.

10. Type **disable messenger** to disable the service. The output of the command indicates the success of the command and the original startup configuration for the service (in this case, SERVICE_AUTO_START). You should always make note of this setting, so that once troubleshooting has been completed you can return the service to its original state.

11. To quit the Recovery Console, type **exit** and press Enter.

Exercise 4: Restoring a System Using Automated System Recovery

> **Warning**   This exercise requires a second physical disk on which an ASR backup has been created in Lesson 2. This exercise will delete all data on the physical disk that contains the system and boot partition. Do not proceed if you have stored any data that you cannot afford to lose.

1. Power off your computer.

2. Restart the computer and open the computer's BIOS. Make sure the system is configured to start from the CD-ROM.

3. Insert the Windows Server 2003 installation CD-ROM.

4. Restart Server01. Watch carefully and, when prompted, press a key to start from the CD-ROM.

5. Early in the text-mode setup phase, setup prompts you to press F2 to run an Automatic System Recovery. Press F2.

6. You will then be prompted to insert the Windows Automated System Recovery disk into the floppy drive. Insert the floppy disk you created in Exercise 2 and press any key to continue.

7. Text-mode setup prepares for Automated System Recovery and a minimal version of the operating system is loaded. This step will take some time to complete.

8. Eventually, a Windows Server 2003 Setup screen will appear.

9. Windows Server 2003 Setup, partitions and formats the disk, copies files, initializes the Windows configuration and then prepares to restart.

10. Remove the floppy disk from the disk drive and allow the computer to restart.

    The installation will continue. When the installation completes, the computer should be restored to its previous state.

Lesson Review

The following questions are intended to reinforce key information presented in this lesson. If you are unable to answer a question, review the lesson materials and try the question again. You can find answers to the questions in the "Questions and Answers" section at the end of this chapter.

1. You're setting up a backup job on a computer running Windows Server 2003. You want to back up the registry, startup files, and the COM+ Class Registration database. Which backup option should you select?

   a. %*Windir*%

   b. %*Systemroot*%

   c. System State

   d. None of the above. You cannot back up the registry.

2. You install a scanner on a computer running Windows Server 2003. When you try to restart your computer, the operating system will not start. Which of the following would be the least invasive recovery method to try first to restore the system to operation?

   a. Automated System Recovery

   b. Recovery Console

   c. Safe mode

   d. Directory Services Restore mode

3. A hard disk on a server running Windows Server 2003 has failed. You replace the disk, boot the system, initialize the disk, and create an NTFS volume on the new disk. You now want to restore that data from the last backup job from the old disk. How should you restore the data?

   a. Use the Recovery Console to copy data to the disk.

   b. Use the Backup utility to launch the Restore Wizard.

   c. Use the ASR backup to restore the data.

   d. Use the Last Known Good Configuration option in Safe mode to set up the new disk.

4. A file server on your network will not start. After exhausting all other options, you have decided to use Automated System Recovery (ASR) to recover the system. You created an ASR backup immediately after you installed Microsoft Windows Server 2003 and another one two months ago after you installed a device driver. You perform a full backup of data files once a week. What will ASR restore? (Choose all that apply.)

   a. Data files two months ago

   b. Data files at the last full backup

   c. Disk configuration

   d. Operating system

   e. System State two months ago

   f. System State at the last full backup

Lesson Summary

- The System State includes the registry, startup files, COM+ Class Registration Database, and other service-specific critical system files. It is wise to plan a backup strategy that coordinates backing up the System State along with the system and boot volumes.

- Automated System Recovery uses a setup-like process to return a computer to operation, and then starts a restore operation to recover files from the ASR backup set. It is a recovery process that should be used to restore a system when other less invasive methods, such as Safe mode or the Recovery Console, have been ineffective.

- The Recovery Console is a text-mode command interpreter that allows you to access the hard disk of a computer running Windows Server 2003.

Exam Highlights

Before taking the exam, review the key points and terms that are presented below to help you identify topics you need to review. Return to the lessons for additional practice and review the "Further Readings" sections in Part 2 for pointers to more information about topics covered by the exam objectives.

Key Points

- The System State can be backed up using the Backup Utility or the command prompt, but must be backed up locally. You cannot back up the System State on a remote machine. However, you can back up the local System State to a file on a remote machine, which can then transfer that file to another backup medium.

- To restore the System State on a domain controller, you must restart the domain controller in Directory Services Restore Mode. The System State includes Active Directory. By restoring the domain controller's System State, you are performing a non-authoritative restore, and the domain controller will use standard replication mechanisms to bring itself back up to date. If you want to replicate objects from the restored data to other domain controllers, you must use Ntdsutil to perform an authoritative restore before restarting the domain controller to normal operation.

- Automated System Recovery relies on a catalog of system files stored on the ASR floppy disk to restore files from the Windows Server 2003 CD-ROM, and a comprehensive ASR backup. You prepare the ASR backup set and floppy using the ASR Wizard in the Backup Utility. To perform an Automated System Recovery, restart with the Windows Server 2003 CD and press F2 when prompted.

- The Recovery Console allows you to perform targeted repairs for certain causes of system failure. You can replace system files and disable problematic drivers or services. You can also perform a subset of other system maintenance tasks. The Recovery Console can be launched from the Windows Server 2003 CD or by installing the console on the server's hard drive using the **winnt32 /cmdcons** command.

Key Terms

System State   A collection of critical system components including the registry, COM+ Class Registration Database, and startup files. The System State components can be backed up using the Backup Utility or the Ntbackup command. You cannot back up the components separately.

Automated System Recovery (ASR)   A new feature that replaces the Emergency Repair process in earlier versions of Windows. Automated System Recovery returns a system to operation by reinstalling the operating system and restoring System State from an ASR backup set.

Recovery Console   A utility that provides command-line access to system files and a subset of commands to perform surgical repairs on a failed system.

Questions and Answers

Page
13-14

Lesson 1 Review

1. You're setting up a backup job on a computer running Windows Server 2003. You want to back up the registry, startup files, and the COM+ Class Registration database. Which backup option should you select?

    a. *%Windir%*

    b. *%Systemroot%*

    c. System State

    d. None of the above. You cannot back up the registry.

    The correct answer is c.

2. You install a scanner on a computer running Windows Server 2003. When you try to restart your computer, the operating system will not start. Which of the following would be the least invasive recovery method to try first to restore the system to operation?

    a. Automated System Recovery

    b. Recovery Console

    c. Safe mode

    d. Directory Services Restore mode

    The correct answer is c.

3. A hard disk on a server running Windows Server 2003 has failed. You replace the disk, boot the system, initialize the disk, and create an NTFS volume on the new disk. You now want to restore that data from the last backup job from the old disk. How should you restore the data?

    a. Use the Recovery Console to copy data to the disk.

    b. Use the Backup utility to launch the Restore Wizard.

    c. Use the ASR backup to restore the data.

    d. Use the Last Known Good Configuration option in Safe mode to set up the new disk.

    The correct answer is b.

4. A file server on your network will not start. After exhausting all other options, you have decided to use Automated System Recovery (ASR) to recover the system. You created an ASR backup immediately after you installed Microsoft Windows Server 2003 and another one two months ago after you installed a device driver. You perform a full backup of data files once a week. What will ASR restore? (Choose all that apply.)

   a. Data files two months ago

   b. Data files at the last full backup

   c. Disk configuration

   d. Operating system

   e. System State two months ago

   f. System State at the last full backup

   The correct answers are c, d, and e.

Part II
Prepare for the Exam

14 Managing and Maintaining Physical and Logical Devices (1.0)

One of the primary responsibilities of the systems administrator is to ensure that the physical and logical devices on the servers are correctly managed and maintained. A physical device is hardware that can be touched: a network card, a graphics adapter, or a SCSI hard disk drive. A logical device is one that has been created by the operating system. Partitions, volumes, and striped disks are examples of logical devices.

The disk management console provides the systems administrator with the ability to manage and maintain the physical and logical disks of a Microsoft Windows Server 2003 system. The disk management console can be found as a node in the Computer Management console or used as its own separate console by adding the appropriate snap-in to a custom-built Microsoft Management Console (MMC). The disk management console allows a systems administrator to convert disks from basic to dynamic and back, format them with the NTFS, FAT, or FAT32 file systems, extend volumes across multiple disks, configure disk mirroring as well as institute striped and RAID-5 volumes.

Over time, disk fragmentation can degrade the performance of even the quickest of hard disk drives. Fragmentation occurs as files are added and deleted from the hard disk drive. When a hard disk drive is new, files are laid down on the disk contiguously. As a disk sees more files added and deleted, files are laid down on the disk as space is available, quite often in a non-contiguous manner. A fragmented file is one that is stored on several different areas of the hard disk drive. It takes longer to read a fragmented file than a file that exists contiguously on the hard disk. The defragmentation process reorders files on the hard disk so that they are written contiguously as opposed to being stored in a fragmented manner. The disk defragmenter can be launched from a node in the Computer Management console, as a snap-in for a custom MMC or by the Defrag command-line utility.

The Device Manager allows a systems administrator to manage and configure other hardware device. A new and important feature to Windows Server 2003 is the ability to roll back a newly installed driver to a previously stable one. In the past if an unstable driver was installed on a server, the driver was very difficult to remove. It was also difficult to reinstall an older driver over the newer unstable one. The Device Manager can also be used to check which system resources particular devices use as well as resolving hardware conflicts between installed devices.

Testing Skills and Suggested Practices

The skills that you need to master the Managing and Maintaining Access to Resources objective domain on *Exam 70-290: Managing and Maintaining a Microsoft Window Server 2003 Environment* include

- Correctly convert basic disks to dynamic disks and mount volumes
    - ❑ Practice 1: Add a second physical hard disk drive to a Windows Server 2003 system. Convert this disk from basic to dynamic either by using the Disk Initialization and Configuration Wizard or by selecting the disk and using an option in the Action menu to convert it.
    - ❑ Practice 2: Create three empty folders on the System volume, Temp1, Temp2, and Temp3. Create three equal-sized volumes on the newly dynamic second physical hard disk drive. Format the volumes as NTFS and mount the first one off the Temp1 folder, the second off the Temp2 folder, and the third off the Temp3 folder.

- Monitor server hardware using the Device Manager and other tools
    - ❑ Practice 1: Locate Non-Plug and Play devices in the Device Manager by opening it, going to the view menu and selecting the Show Hidden Devices option. Note the different devices that are displayed when Show Hidden Devices is enabled and disabled.
    - ❑ Practice 2: Use the Device Manager to print a report first on a particular class of items on the system. Explore the report options and then print a report on all devices installed on a Windows Server 2003 system.

- Correctly optimize server disk performance
    - ❑ Practice 1: Add a second physical hard disk drive to a Window Server 2003 system, bringing the total installed on the system to two. Using the disk manager, create a mirror of the system volume. Once the mirrored volume has synchronized, break the mirror and examine the contents of the new physical disk.
    - ❑ Practice 2: Add three extra physical hard disk drives to a Windows Server 2003 system, bringing the total installed on the system to four. Use the new disks to create a RAID-5 volume.
    - ❑ Practice 3: Analyze and defragment each volume on the Windows Server 2003 system. Note which colors in the analysis display are used to represent each type of file. Perform a defragmentation of the volume and compare the difference between the colors on the initial analysis and that of the newly defragmented volume.

- Properly install and configure server hardware devices

  ❏ Practice 1: Locate a hardware device that can be installed on a Window Server 2003 system that is already configured. One suggestion might be a second network adapter. Shut down the system and install the card. Restart the system and go through the process of installing the drivers and configuring the card so that it works properly on the network.

  ❏ Practice 2: Use the Device Manager views to view a list of items installed on the system ordered by the resources that they use.

Further Reading

This section lists supplemental readings by objective. You should study these sources thoroughly before taking this exam.

Objective 1.1   Review Chapter 11, Lessons 1, 2, and 3: "Understanding Disk Storage Options," "Configuring Disks and Volumes," and "Maintaining Disk Storage Volumes." This chapter details the management and configuration of storage options on Windows Server 2003 systems.

Microsoft Corporation. Windows Server 2003 Help and Support Center. Review "Change a Basic Disk to a Dynamic Disk."

Microsoft Corporation. Windows Server 2003 Help and Support Center. Review "Initialize And Convert Disk Wizard."

Microsoft Corporation. Windows Server 2003 Help and Support Center. Review "Disk Management."

Objective 1.2   Review Chapter 12, "Monitoring Microsoft Windows Server 2003." This chapter reviews the different tools that can be used to monitor different aspects of the Windows Server 2003 operating system.

Microsoft Corporation. Windows Server 2003 Help and Support Center. Review "View Power Allocations for USB Hubs."

Microsoft Corporation. Windows Server 2003 Help and Support Center. Review "View Bandwidth Allocations for USB Host Controller."

Microsoft Corporation. Windows Server 2003 Help and Support Center. Review "Print Information About a Specific Device."

Microsoft Corporation. Windows Server 2003 Help and Support Center. Review "How to View Hidden Devices."

Microsoft Corporation. Windows Server 2003 Help and Support Center. Review "Device Manager."

Objective 1.3   Review Chapter 11, Lesson 4, "Implementing RAID." This section details how various methods of software RAID can be implemented on Windows Server 2003 systems.

Microsoft Corporation. Windows Server 2003 Help and Support Center. Review "Disk Defragmenter."

Microsoft Corporation. Windows Server 2003 Help and Support Center. Review "Disk Management."

Objective 1.4   Review Chapter 10, Lessons 1 and 2: "Installing Hardware Devices and Drivers" and "Configuring Hardware Devices and Drivers." These sections review some of the issues and processes an administrator should be aware of when they install and configure hardware devices.

Microsoft Corporation. Windows Server 2003 Help and Support Center. Review "Driver Signing."

Microsoft Corporation. Windows Server 2003 Help and Support Center. Review "Device Manager."

Manage Basic Disks and Dynamic Disks

The difference between basic and dynamic disks has a direct bearing on the options available to an administrator in managing the storage on a server. Dynamic disks provide more options than basic disks. Dynamic disks can be configured to use disk mirroring (RAID-1), disk spanning, striped volumes (RAID-0), and RAID-5 volumes. Basic disks do not have these options, they can be configured as simple or extended partitions only.

Disk management can be performed in two ways. The first is through the disk management console and the second is through the command-line interface. Both can be used to convert disks from basic to dynamic and back.

The Initialize And Convert Disk Wizard, which runs whenever a new disk is installed on a server, can be used to initialize a hard disk and convert it from basic to dynamic.

Only users with Administrator privileges, members of the Backup Operators group or users that have been especially delegated the appropriate authority are able to convert disks from basic to dynamic and back again.

All disks can be converted from basic to dynamic. However, if a basic disk has data on it when the conversion takes place, it cannot be extended to span other disks as a native dynamic disk can. A converted dynamic disk, however, can be mirrored, which means that the operating system volume can be provided with fault tolerance.

If a server has multiple operating systems installed the administrator should consider not converting the boot or system partitions to dynamic disks. A conversion to dynamic will mean that the server cannot boot into any other operating system than the one that performed this conversion.

Another important method of managing hard disks is using Hardware RAID. A hardware RAID controller connects to multiple hard disk drives and controls the RAID process. Hardware RAID controllers are usually much faster than a software RAID process like that of Windows Server 2003. Hardware RAID controllers also support more RAID types than are supported by Windows Server 2003.

Volume mounting involves mounting a volume off a folder located on another volume. This mounted volume can be hosted on a disk that is either basic or dynamic. This enables a volume to appear to store more information than its actual physical capacity. It has the advantage of meaning that folders that require a great deal of capacity can be mounted on separate larger hard disk drives as not to fill the entire original volume.

Objective 1.1 Questions

1. Rooslan is a systems administrator at a medium-sized organization that has a single Windows Server 2003 domain. His team is responsible for installing and maintaining six Windows Server 2003 systems. Each server has been configured as a stand-alone server and is not a member of the 2003 domain. Twelve new disk drives have arrived and two each are to be installed in each of these member servers. Rooslan delegates this task to an intern named Alex that is visiting the organization this month. Rooslan has configured Alex a simple user account that has been granted local logon rights on each of the servers via the local Group Policy Object (GPO). Organizational policy dictates that under no circumstances should Alex's user account be made a member of the Administrators group on any of the Windows Server 2003 servers. Rooslan then asks Alex to convert each of the newly installed disks from basic to dynamic. Alex tries this but finds that he is unable to perform this task. Which of the following can Rooslan do without making Alex's user account a member of the Administrators group on each of these Windows Server 2003 stand-alone servers?

    A. Rooslan should add Alex's account to the Backup Operators group on each server.

    B. Rooslan should add Alex's account to the Backup Operators group in the domain.

    C. Rooslan should add Alex's account to the Power Users group in the domain.

    D. Rooslan should modify the local GPO on each Windows Server 2003 to give Alex's account the Perform Volume Maintenance Tasks user right.

    E. Rooslan should modify the local GPO on each Windows Server 2003 to give Alex's account the Take Ownership Of Files And Other Objects user right.

2. Rooslan is the systems administrator of a Windows Server 2003 file server. The server currently has two disk drives. The first disk, which is 30 gigabytes (GB) in size, hosts all the operating system files. The second disk drive, which is 80 GB in size, hosts user data on five separate shares. Each share corresponds to a specific department at Rooslan's organization. Each share is distributed into three separate folders. The first folder is a departmental documents folder, the second is a collaboration folder, and the third is an individual user data folder.

    Users have read access to the departmental documents folder, read and write access to the collaboration folder, and each individual user has full control over his or her unique data folder. Only the individual user can access his or her data folder; other users cannot read or write to the contents of that folder. The five-share system works well and all employees in the organization understand where to store and find documents.

A problem has developed in that the user data sections of each of the five departmental shares are expanding so quickly that soon the disk that hosts the user data will be filled to capacity. It is important to the managers of the organization that any solution does not increase the number of shares that an employee must access.

Rooslan has the following goals:

Primary Goal: Add more space to each share so that the disk hosting the shared folders does not become full.

Secondary Goals:

Retain only five shares and keep the user data directory as a folder off each departmental share.

Provide fault tolerance for the file share.

Retain the security scheme currently in use so that individual users have full control over their own directories and other users cannot access them.

Rooslan performs the following actions. During a scheduled period after midnight when no users are connected to the server, Rooslan shuts down the server and installs five 100 GB hard disk drives on the server. He then formats each drive as a single volume with the NTFS file system. He then creates a new folder called Temp under each of the folders hosting each department's share. One by one, he then mounts the five disks to each of the Temp folders so that each Temp folder now points to its own individual mounted hard disk. Rooslan then copies the entire contents of the user data folder into the Temp folder under each share, and then deletes the original user data folder. Finally he renames the Temp folder with the name of the user data folder.

How many of his goals has Rooslan achieved?

A. Rooslan did not achieve any primary goals. All of Rooslan's secondary goals were achieved.

B. Rooslan has achieved the primary goal and one secondary goal.

C. Rooslan has achieved the primary goal and two secondary goals.

D. Rooslan has achieved all primary and secondary goals.

E. Rooslan has achieved none of the primary and secondary goals.

3. There are several folders on a Windows Server 2003 domain controller that take up a significant percentage of disk space on the system drive. These folders are as follows:

C:\Datastore\Compress

C:\Datastore\Encrypt

C:\Datastore\Indiperf

The Compress folder is compressed and all files and folders stored within it are also compressed. The Encrypt folder is encrypted and all files and folders within it are also encrypted. The Indiperf folder hosts user data. Each directory under the Indiperf directory has permissions individually tailored to each user.

You take the following steps: install a single 100 GB hard disk drive, create three 30 GB volumes on this drive, and, in the Datastore directory, you create the following folders:

C:\Datastore\Comptemp

C:\Datastore\Encrtemp

C:\Datastore\Inditemp

You then mount the first 30 GB volume to the Comptemp directory, the second 30 GB volume to the Encrtemp directory, and the third 30 GB volume to the Inditemp directory. You move the contents of the Compress directory to the Comptemp directory. You copy the contents of the Encrypt directory to the Encrtemp directory. You move the contents of the Datastore directory to the Inditemp directory.

You then delete the Compress, Encrypt, and Indiperf folders. Finally, you rename the Comptemp directory Compress, the Encrtemp directory Encrypt, and the Inditemp directory Indiperf.

Which of the following statements is true? (Select all that apply.)

A. The contents of the Compress directory will be compressed.

B. The contents of the Compress directory will be uncompressed.

C. The contents of the Encrypt directory will be encrypted.

D. The contents of the Encrypt directory will be unencrypted.

E. The contents of the Indiperf directory will retain their individually tailored NTFS permissions.

F. The contents of the Indiperf directory will not retain their individually tailored NTFS permissions.

4.   Lee has two 100 GB SCSI hard disk drives connected to a Windows Server 2003 server that he is responsible for administering. The server also has a single hardware RAID controller that supports RAID-0, RAID-1 and RAID-5. Currently 70 GB on the first drive is used and the second drive is empty. Lee is concerned that the hard disk drive of the server might fail and he would lose all the information on the first disk drive. Lee has considered regular backups but does not have the equipment with which to back up 70 GB on a regular basis. Lee would like to configure a solution that provides fault tolerance for the first drive. Which of the following should he consider, given the current configuration of his Windows Server 2003 server?

   A. Lee should configure Volume Shadow Copy services on the second hard disk drive by using disk properties.

   B. Lee should configure Volume Shadow Copy services on the first hard disk drive by using disk properties.

   C. Lee should configure the disks in a RAID-5 configuration using the hardware RAID controller's configuration utility.

   D. Lee should configure the disks in a RAID-0 configuration using the hardware RAID controller's configuration utility.

   E. Lee should configure the disks in a RAID-1 configuration using the hardware RAID controller's configuration utility.

5.   You have just installed a SCSI controller and three attached 100 GB SCSI disk drives to your Windows Server 2003 system. You start the server after installing the hardware, log on with an account that has administrative privileges and run the Disk Management console. As soon as the console comes up, you are confronted by the Initialize And Convert Disk Wizard. Which of the following can be done to the newly installed SCSI disks by using this wizard? (Select all that apply.)

   A. Initialize new disks.

   B. Convert dynamic disks to basic disks.

   C. Convert basic disks to dynamic disks.

   D. Create mirrored disk pairs.

   E. Create striped sets.

   F. Create RAID-5 volumes.

   G. Create spanned volumes.

   H. Create a primary partition.

   I. Create an extended partition.

Objective 1.1 Answers

1. **Correct Answers: A and D**

    A. **Correct:** The Backup Operators group has the right to perform the conversion task.

    B. **Incorrect:** This will not work because these are stand-alone servers and are not members of the domain.

    C. **Incorrect:** This will not work because these are stand-alone servers and are not members of the domain. There is also no Power Users group in the domain; the Power Users group exists only on stand-alone servers.

    D. **Correct:** This will work because users who have this right assigned through GPO can perform tasks such as defragmentation and conversion.

    E. **Incorrect:** Taking ownership of files and folders has nothing to do with basic-to-dynamic disk conversion.

2. **Correct Answers: B**

    A. **Incorrect:** Rooslan has achieved the primary goal by installing new 100 GB hard disks and, by copying the user data across, he has added space to each of the shares.

    B. **Correct:** Rooslan has achieved the primary goal by installing new 100 GB hard disks and, by copying the user data across, he has added space to each of the shares. Rooslan has achieved the first secondary goal by mounting the disks as the user data folder. Under the current shared folder hierarchy, there is no need to introduce extra shared folders. The files copied will not retain their NTFS permissions, so the third secondary goal will not be achieved. Nowhere has it been mentioned that any type of fault tolerance has been used; therefore, the second secondary goal has not been achieved.

    C. **Incorrect:** Rooslan has achieved the first secondary goal by mounting the disks as the user data folder under the current shared folder hierarchy. There is no need to introduce extra shared folders. The files copied will not retain their NTFS permissions, so the third secondary goal will not be achieved. Nowhere has it been mentioned that that any type of fault tolerance has been introduced, so the second secondary goal has not been achieved.

    D. **Incorrect:** Rooslan has achieved the first secondary goal by mounting the disks as the user data folder under the current shared folder hierarchy. There is no need to introduce extra shared folders. The files copied will not retain their NTFS permissions, so the third secondary goal will not be achieved. No type of fault tolerance has been introduced, so the second secondary goal has not been achieved.

E. **Incorrect:** Rooslan has achieved the primary goal by installing new 100 GB hard disks and, by copying the user data across, he has added space to each of the shares.

3. **Correct Answers: B, C, and F**

A. **Incorrect:** Files copied or moved between volumes, even if the volumes are mounted, will inherit the compression attribute of the target folder. In this example the compression attribute of the target folder was not set.

B. **Correct:** Files copied or moved between volumes, even if the volumes are mounted, will inherit the compression attribute of the target folder. In this example the compression attribute of the target folder was not set.

C. **Correct:** Encrypted files copied or moved between NTFS volumes will retain their encryption status regardless of the attributes set on the target folder.

D. **Incorrect:** Encrypted files copied or moved between NTFS volumes will retain their encryption status regardless of the attributes set on the target folder.

E. **Incorrect:** Files moved between volumes inherit the NTFS permissions of their target folder. All individual tailored NTFS permissions will be lost. The method of retaining the permissions is to back up the files and then restore them.

F. **Correct:** Files moved between volumes inherit the NTFS permissions of their target folder. All individual tailored NTFS permissions will be lost. The method of retaining the permissions is to back up the files and then restore them.

4. **Correct Answers: E**

A. **Incorrect:** Volume Shadow Copy services will not provide a fault-tolerant backup of all data on the first disk.

B. **Incorrect:** Volume Shadow Copy services will not provide a fault-tolerant backup of all data on the first disk.

C. **Incorrect:** RAID-5 is a fault-tolerant solution, but it is not an option in this scenario because there are only two disk drives. RAID-5 requires a minimum of three disk drives.

D. **Incorrect:** Although RAID-0 would provide better performance, it does not provide fault tolerance.

E. **Correct:** Lee should configure the disks in a RAID-1, also known as disk mirroring, configuration using the hardware RAID controller's configuration utility. The prior existence of data on the drives would also influence the options available. Although it is possible to mirror a drive with existing data, converting it to RAID-5 or RAID-0 without deleting the data is not an option.

5.   **Correct Answers: A and C**

A. **Correct:** The Initialize And Convert Disk Wizard runs each time a new disk is added to the system and the disk management console is run. Limited in scope it is only able to initialize a disk and convert it from basic to dynamic.

B. **Incorrect:** This function cannot be completed using the Initialize And Convert Disk Wizard.

C. **Correct:** The Initialize And Convert Disk Wizard runs each time a new disk is added to the system and the disk management console is run. Limited in scope, the wizard is only able to initialize a disk and convert it from basic to dynamic.

D. **Incorrect:** This function cannot be completed using the Initialize And Convert Disk Wizard.

E. **Incorrect:** This function cannot be completed using the Initialize And Convert Disk Wizard.

F. **Incorrect:** This function cannot be completed using the Initialize And Convert Disk Wizard.

G. **Incorrect:** This function cannot be completed using the Initialize And Convert Disk Wizard.

H. **Incorrect:** This function cannot be completed using the Initialize And Convert Disk Wizard.

I. **Incorrect:** This function cannot be completed using the Initialize And Convert Disk Wizard.

Objective 1.2

Monitor Server Hardware

Monitoring server hardware is generally done by using the Device Manager MMC. There are also other areas of the system, such as specific Control Panel add-ins or separate utilities such as WINMSD, which can be used to monitor and report on hardware attached to the server.

Device Manager, found in the Computer Management console or as its own MMC in the Administrative Tools program group is the first port of call for hardware management. It will display the operating status of all hardware connected to the system. Non-Plug and Play devices can be viewed by selecting the Show Hidden Devices option from the view menu.

The WINMSD utility, launched from the command line or Run menu, also provides an overview of the hardware that is installed on a particular Windows Server 2003 system.

Some devices, such as modems and display adapters, are best managed through their individual Control Panel application rather than with the Device Manager.

Objective 1.2 Questions

1. You are working on a Windows Server 2003 system that has been upgraded from Windows 2000 server. This server has a legacy SCSI RAID controller that is not Plug and Play. The device appears to be working perfectly but you cannot see it within the Device Manager. How can this device be viewed in the Device Manager?

    A. Only Plug and Play devices can be viewed in the Device Manager.

    B. You must upgrade the driver for this device to one that supports Plug and Play.

    C. Disk drive and RAID controllers are not visible in the Device Manager.

    D. You must go to the View menu in Device Manager and select Show Hidden Devices.

2. Rooslan is using several external universal serial bus (USB) hard disk drives as an extra storage option on a Windows Server 2003 system that he administers. He is also using an external USB CD-Writer and a Microsoft USB IntelliMouse and a USB keyboard. Recently, Rooslan has noticed that the performance of some of the USB hard disk drives has become erratic. He wants to generate a report on the current bandwidth and power consumptions of various USB devices attached to the Windows Server 2003 system. Which of the following will allow him to do this? (Select all that apply.)

    A. Rooslan needs to open the USB devices utility located in Control Panel. This utility lists the bandwidth and power consumptions of all USB devices attached to the system.

    B. Rooslan needs to open the Power utility located in Control Panel. From here he can navigate to the USB tab to discover the power consumption profiles of various devices attached to the system.

    C. Rooslan needs to open the Device Manager and navigate to the USB Root Hub, right-click and select Properties. He then needs to click the Power tab, which lists the power consumption by attached device.

    D. Rooslan needs to open the Device Manager and navigate to the USB Universal Host Controller, right-click and select Properties. He then needs to click the Advanced tab, which lists the bandwidth-consuming devices and the bandwidth they use.

    E. Rooslan needs to open the Bandwidth utility located in Control Panel. From here he can navigate to the USB tab to discover the bandwidth consumption profiles of various devices attached to the system.

    F. Rooslan needs to open the Task Manager and then select the USB Devices tab. This tab lists the bandwidth and power consumptions of all USB devices attached to the system.

3.   Orin's company is auditing all the devices that are attached to its Windows Server 2003 systems. The auditors have demanded that printouts be generated listing a summary of all devices that are installed on the system. This summary should include product version numbers, bus type, and resource information.

Orin has the following goals:

Primary Goal: Provide a printout that contains a summary of all devices installed on the system.

Secondary Goals:

Ensure that interrupt request (IRQ) resource information is included in this report.

Output the report to a file rather than a printer.

Orin proceeds as follows: From Computer Management in the Administrative Tools program group, he opens the Device Manager, selects the Windows Server 2003 system and, from the Action menu, selects Print. He then sets the report type to All Devices And System Summary and clicks Print.

Which of the following goals has Orin achieved?

A. Orin has achieved the primary goal and all secondary goals.

B. Orin has achieved the primary goal and one secondary goal.

C. Orin has achieved the primary goal and no secondary goals.

D. Orin has not achieved the primary goal and has achieved all secondary goals.

E. Orin has not achieved the primary goal and has achieved one secondary goal.

F. Orin has achieved none of the goals.

4. You are the systems administrator for a set of Windows Server 2003 systems that are used as Web servers for a medium-sized Internet service provider (ISP). You must prepare a report for your manager on the network adapters that are installed in each of the servers. This report should include the adapter type, and the hardware resources it uses such as IRQ. Because they experience sustained traffic load serving Web pages to the Internet, there are several network adapters in each server. To make matters more complex, these adapters have generally been added on an ad hoc basis so they are of various make and manufacture. Which of the following methods can you use to generate this report for your manager? (Select all that apply.)

A. Run the Device Manager on each Windows Server 2003 system. Select Network Adapters, and then from the Action menu, select Print. Choose Selected Class or Device and then click Print.

B. Select Network Connections in Control Panel on each Windows Server 2003 system. From the Advanced Tab select Network Hardware, and then click Generate Report.

C. Run WINMSD from the command prompt. From the Components node, select the Network node and then the Adapters node. From the File menu, select Print.

D. Run Winipcfg from the Run menu. From the Adapters tab, select Generate Hardware Report, and then click Print.

E. Run the Ipconfig/Adapter command from the command prompt. Copy the resulting information into a text file in Notepad and then print it.

5.   Rooslan is the senior systems administrator for a medium-sized organization. Several months ago he purchased and installed three Windows Server 2003 systems and configured them as domain controllers. After a week of successful testing in Rooslan's lab, each server was shipped to a remote location in the organizational network as part of the Windows Server 2003 rollout. Rooslan has just received a telephone call from a junior administrator at one of the sites to which these domain controllers was shipped. The junior administrator has noticed that when the domain controller starts an error report appears that states that a device driver was unable to load during the boot process. The junior administrator reports to Rooslan that he examined the Device Manager to see if there is anything that indicates that a device is experiencing a fault, but there is no indication that this is the case. Rooslan asks the junior administrator if he checked the hidden devices and the junior administrator replied that he was unaware of how to perform this task. Of the last 20 starts, the error has appeared three times. The error appeared again this morning prompting the phone call to Rooslan. Before telephoning, however, the junior administrator restarted the server and the error did not appear. Rooslan initiates a remote desktop connection to the server to examine it. Which of the following represents the path that Rooslan should follow to diagnose this fault?

   A. When connected to the remote domain controller, Rooslan should open the Device Manager and, on the View menu, select Show Hidden Devices.

   B. When connected to the remote domain controller Rooslan should examine the system log for any entries created by failing device drivers.

   C. When connected to the remote domain controller, Rooslan should examine the security log for any entries created by failing device drivers.

   D. When connected to the remote domain controller, Rooslan should examine the device log for any entries created by failing device drivers.

   E. When connected to the remote domain controller, Rooslan should examine the application log for any entries created by failing device drivers.

   F. When connected to the remote domain controller, Rooslan should run WINMSD and examine the driver list to see if any failures to start have been reported.

Objective 1.2 Answers

1. **Correct Answers: D**

  A. **Incorrect:** This is not true. Non–Plug and Play hardware can be viewed in the Device Manager by selecting Show Hidden Devices.

  B. **Incorrect:** Plug and Play is a hardware specification, not a software specification, so a driver upgrade will make no difference to the device's visibility in Device Manager.

  C. **Incorrect:** These devices can be viewed using Device Manager.

  D. **Correct:** By default, non–Plug and Play hardware is not displayed in Device Manager. To view such hardware in Device Manager, the Show Hidden Devices option must be set. This will then show all "hidden" devices, which include non–Plug and Play legacy devices such as the SCSI RAID controller described here.

2. **Correct Answers: C and D**

  A. **Incorrect:** There is no USB devices utility in Control Panel.

  B. **Incorrect:** The Power utility controls devices such as UPS and inactivity shutdown. It does not display information about the USB power consumption.

  C. **Correct:** The properties of the USB Root Hub located in Device Manager list the power consumption of USB devices.

  D. **Correct:** The USB Universal Host Controller lists the bandwidth usage by those devices that use bandwidth and report it back to the system. Not all USB devices use power from the system; many have their own independent power supply. Devices such as keyboards and mouse devices, however, are powered from the system. Similarly, not all devices consume USB bandwidth. If multiple bandwidth-consuming devices are installed on a system, it is important to monitor their usage lest they become sluggish.

  E. **Incorrect:** There is no Bandwidth utility in Control Panel.

  F. **Incorrect:** There is no USB Devices tab in the Task Manager.

3.   Correct Answers: B

A. Incorrect: Setting the report type to All Devices And System Summary will print an extensive report for each device installed on the system, including resource information, as well as generate a summary of the system. This achieves the primary goal and the first of the secondary goals. Because nothing was mentioned about checking Print To File, the second secondary goal was not achieved.

B. Correct: Setting the report type to All Devices And System Summary will print an extensive report for each device installed on the system, including resource information, as well as generate a summary of the system. This achieves the primary goal and the first of the secondary goals.

C. Incorrect: Setting the report type to All Devices And System Summary will print an extensive report for each device installed on the system, including resource information, as well as generate a summary of the system. This achieves the primary goal and the first of the secondary goals.

D. Incorrect: Setting the report type to All Devices And System Summary will print an extensive report for each device installed on the system, including resource information, as well as generate a summary of the system. This achieves the primary goal and the first of the secondary goals. Because nothing was mentioned about checking Print To File, the second secondary goal was not achieved.

E. Incorrect: Setting the report type to All Devices And System Summary will print an extensive report for each device installed on the system, including resource information, as well as generate a summary of the system. This achieves the primary goal and the first of the secondary goals.

F. Incorrect: Setting the report type to All Devices And System Summary will print an extensive report for each device installed on the system, including resource information, as well as generate a summary of the system. This achieves the primary goal and the first of the secondary goals.

4.   Correct Answers: A and C

A. Correct: Both the Device Manager and WINMSD can be used to generate this information into a report format that can be printed. In doing so, you will be able to quickly list all the relevant information that your manager requires.

B. Incorrect: The information you want cannot be generated in this manner.

C. Correct: Both the Device Manager and WINMSD can be used to generate this information into a report format that can be printed. In doing so, you will be able to quickly list all the relevant information that your manager requires.

D. Incorrect: The information you want cannot be generated in this manner.

E. Incorrect: The information you want cannot be generated in this manner.

5.   **Correct Answers: B**

A. **Incorrect:** The junior administrator reported that he had checked the device manager, although he did not know how to check hidden devices. It might be that the fault occurred in a hidden device but, because the system has started properly since the last fault, no evidence will be found in that location.

B. **Correct:** Because the system started without fault when the junior administrator called Rooslan, no fault will be evident in the Device Manager. Rooslan will be able to investigate further by looking at the system log, which has recorded the last few restarts, perhaps even more, and the problematic event will be recorded there.

C. **Incorrect:** This type of event will be written to the system log, not the security log.

D. **Incorrect:** There is no device log; these events will be written to the system log.

E. **Incorrect:** This event will be written to the system log, not the application log.

F. **Incorrect:** Because the system booted correctly on this occasion, WINMSD will not be able to shed any light on the problem.

Optimize Server Disk Performance

Having the disk subsystem of a server provide optimal performance is important for a systems administrator. Servers often have to carry out intensive read/write operations on their disks and even a fractional increase in speed can bring dramatic benefits.

There are three ways to increase the read/write performance of disks on a Windows Server 2003 system. The first is to implement disk striping (RAID-0). Disk striping uses 2 or more disks. In disk striping data is written to several disks at the same time. The start of a file may be written to one disk, while at the same time the middle of a file is written to a second disk and at the same time the end of the file is written to a third disk. Similarly the start, middle, and end of a file can be read simultaneously off all disks. Performing these operations in parallel brings a great performance benefit. The downside to RAID-0 is that if one of the disks that comprise the striped volume fails, all data on that volume is lost. Data should be hosted only on those volumes that need to be read and written quickly but that do not require fault tolerance.

The second way to increase the read/write speed of disks is to implement disk striping with parity, which is also known as RAID-5. The benefit of this method over disk striping is that the method is fault-tolerant. If one of the disks that comprise the RAID-5 volume is lost, the data can still be recovered by using the parity information stored on the other disks. RAID-5 is the safest way to increase the read/write performance of disks. The technique is easy to implement in the disk management console with three or more dynamic disks.

The final way of increasing the read/write speed of disks is to make sure that the files stored on them are relatively free of fragmentation. Fragmentation naturally occurs on hard disk drives as files are written and deleted. Because hard disks allocate free space as it becomes available, a newly written file may be stored at disparate locations across the hard disk drive. The less contiguous a file is on the hard disk drive, the longer it takes to be read or written. Defragmentation is the process by which files are rearranged on the hard disk so that they are contiguous rather than fragmented. This is performed either by using the Disk Defragmenter console or by using the DEFRAG command-line utility.

Objective 1.3 Questions

1. You have been documenting performance on several Windows Server 2003 systems. Specifically, you have been interested in the disk read and write speeds with various disk configurations including mirroring, striping, spanned, and RAID-5 all controlled by the Windows Server 2003 software. You run some tests on various configurations to understand which of them offer performance benefits over simple volumes and which do not. Which of the following statements about the various disk configurations and their performance is correct? (Select all that apply.)

   A. Disk mirroring offers approximately similar read/write performance to a simple volume.

   B. Disk striping offers better read/write performance than RAID-5.

   C. Disk striping (RAID-0) offers better read/write performance than disk spanning.

   D. Disk spanning offers better read/write performance than disk striping.

   E. Disk striping offers better read/write performance than a simple volume.

2. Rooslan is a consultant who has been approached by a medium-sized organization for his advice on the best way to optimize disk performance for three newly purchased Windows Server 2003 systems. There are three different systems in question, all with identical hardware. Each server has six 120 GB SCSI hard disk drives and no hardware RAID controller. Rooslan has been presented with the following specifications from the teams that will be using each Windows Server 2003 System.

The team that will use the first server has one goal. The team would like a second large volume of approximately 600 GB that will contain all the data. The first volume of 120 GB should contain the operating system files and the program files. Speed and fault tolerance are not important to this team.

The team that will use the second server has three goals. The first goal is that the primary volume be 120 GB in size, fault-tolerant, and host the operating system and program files. The second goal is that the secondary volume be 120 GB in size, fault-tolerant, and store program data. The third goal is that the tertiary volume be 240 GB in size and provide the fastest possible read/write speeds.

The team that will use the third server has two goals. The first goal is that the primary volume must be approximately 120 GB in size, host the operating system and the program files, and be fault-tolerant. The second goal is that the secondary volume must be approximately 480 GB in size and have the best read/write performance possible.

Rooslan installs Windows Server 2003 on the first team's server, using a full disk partition on which he installs the operating system and the program files. Once he is in Windows Server 2003 he converts the five other disks to dynamic and spans a single volume across all these disks.

On the second team's server, Rooslan installs Windows Server 2003 using the entire 120 GB available on the disk. When he has Windows Server 2003 configured, he mirrors this 120 GB disk onto the second 120 GB disk. He then installs the relevant program files onto this volume. He then creates two more mirrored pairs with the third and fourth and the fifth and sixth 120 GB disks.

On the third team's server, Rooslan installs Windows using the entire 120 GB available on the first disk. When he has Windows configured he mirrors the 120 GB disk onto the second 120 GB disk. He then installs the relevant program files onto this volume. Rooslan then creates a RAID-5 volume using the final four 120 GB disks.

Which of the following statements accurately summarizes the number of team goals that Rooslan accomplished?

A. Rooslan achieved the first team's goal, as well as all goals of the second team and all goals of the third team.

B. Rooslan achieved the first team's goal, two of the second team's goals, and all the third team's goals.

C. Rooslan achieved the first team's goal, all the second team's goals, and one of the third team's goals.

D. Rooslan did not achieve the first team's goal, achieved all the second team's goals, and achieved one of the third team's goals.

E. Rooslan did not achieve the first team's goal, achieved two of the second team's goals, and achieved one of the third team's goals.

F. Rooslan achieved the first team's goal, achieved two of the second team's goals, and achieved one of the third team's goals.

3. The following figure shows the disk management configuration of a Windows Server 2003 system. Given the information presented in this image, which of the following statements about the volumes on this Windows Server 2003 System is true? (Select all that apply.)

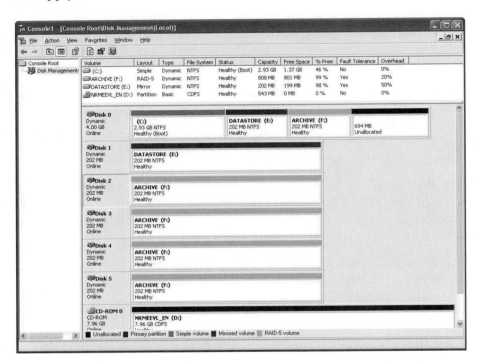

A. If disk 1 fails, no data will be lost.

B. If disk 0 fails, no data will be lost.

C. If disk 2 fails, no data will be lost.

D. Read/write speeds on the Datastore volume will be less than that on the Archive volume.

E. Read/write speeds on the Archive volume will be slower than that on the Datastore volume.

F. If disk 3 fails, data will be lost.

4.   Oksana is looking at a report generated by the disk defragmenter of her system. Her system contains two volumes. The first volume is 100 GB and is mirrored on a second 100 GB disk. The second volume is 400 GB and uses RAID-5 over five 100 GB disks. The report that Oksana is examining was an analysis performed on the second volume rather than the first.

Oksana is puzzled because there seems to be several sections on the second volume that are colored green. Green in a defragmenter analysis represents unmovable files. Oksana is puzzled because she believed that the only files that were unmovable for the disk defragmenter are located on the system or boot volumes. What is the cause of the unmovable files listed on the defragmenter analysis of the second volume? (Select all that apply.)

A. Oksana has mistakenly analyzed the first volume, which contains the boot and system files.

B. The page file has been located on the second volume.

C. Oksana has stored encrypted files on the second volume.

D. Oksana has stored compressed files on the second volume.

E. The NTFS change journal, stored on all NTFS volumes, is an unmovable file.

5.   Oksana has scheduled a command-line disk defragmentation job to take place at 2 A.M. every Sunday on all Windows Server 2003 systems at her site. This represents a perfect time to perform such a task because the amount of activity on any of the servers at this time is minimal. Checking through the logs on a Monday morning, Oksana finds that the Sunday morning defragmentation did not occur on one of the volumes on one of the Windows Server 2003 servers. Oksana logs onto the server from a remote desktop connection and checks the Disk Defragmenter in the Computer Management Console. Oksana decides to wait until the end of business that day and try to run the defragmentation process again on this volume. At 6:30 P.M. she logs on from the remote desktop again and attempts to initiate a defragmentation of the problematic volume. The process fails again. What could be causing the failure, and which of the following steps should Oksana take to defragment this volume?

A. The volume is failing to defragment because it is close to capacity. A volume must have at least 15 percent of space free for the defragmentation process to begin.

B. The volume has been marked as dirty. Oksana needs to run Chkdsk from the command line before she can defragment the volume successfully.

C. Oksana must take the volume offline manually to perform the defragmentation. Once this is done, the disk will defragment normally.

D. Oksana needs to dismount the disk hosting the volume to perform a defragmentation. Once this is done, the disk will defragment normally.

6. You are the systems administrator for several small businesses. One of the small businesses that you work for has reported that the performance of its server appears to be degrading. The server is configured as follows:

Volume	Type	File System	Fault Tolerance	Fragmentation
Drive C	Dynamic	NTFS	Mirrored	9%
Drive D	Basic	NTFS	None	13%
Drive E	Dynamic	NTFS	Striped	23%
Drive F	Dynamic	NTFS	RAID-5	32%
Drive G	Dynamic	NTFS	RAID-5	41%

On which of the Windows Server 2003 system volumes will Windows recommend that you run the defragmenter? (Select all that apply.)

A. Drive C

B. Drive D

C. Drive E

D. Drive F

E. Drive G

1.   **Correct Answers: A, B, C, and E**

    A. **Correct:** Disk mirroring provides no read/write benefit but does provide fault tolerance.

    B. **Correct:** RAID-5 must generate parity information while writing to the disks, something that disk striping (RAID-0) does not need to do. RAID-5 parity generation provides some latency, making this method slower than disk striping.

    C. **Correct:** Disk spanning has similar performance to a simple volume whereas disk striping is the quickest method of reading and writing to a volume.

    D. **Incorrect:** Disk spanning has similar performance to a simple volume, disk striping offers the best read/write performance.

    E. **Correct:** In disk striping, data can be written to or read from multiple disks making up the volume at one time. In a simple volume, only one disk can be written to or read simultaneously.

2.   Correct Answers: F

   A. Incorrect: Rooslan achieved all the goals of the first team. For the second team, he achieved the first and second goals. By choosing to mirror, rather than stripe, the third volume, he did not create a volume of 240 GB with the fastest read/write speed. The volume would have been 120 GB and would not have performed significantly better than a simple volume. Rooslan achieved one goal of the third team. He achieved the first goal, but by using RAID-5 instead of striping, he failed to achieve the second. The second volume would have been 360 GB rather than 480 GB as specified, the equivalent of one drive lost in storing parity information.

   B. Incorrect: Rooslan achieved all the goals of the first team. For the second team, he achieved the first and second goals. By choosing to mirror, rather than stripe, the third volume, he did not create a volume of 240 GB with the fastest read/write speed. The volume would have been 120 GB and would not have performed significantly better than a simple volume. Rooslan achieved one goal of the third team. He achieved the first goal, but by using RAID-5 instead of striping, he failed to achieve the second. The second volume would have been 360 GB rather than 480 GB as specified, the equivalent of one drive lost in storing parity information.

   C. Incorrect: Rooslan achieved all the goals of the first team. For the second team, he achieved the first and second goals. By choosing to mirror, rather than stripe, the third volume, he did not create a volume of 240 GB with the fastest read/write speed. The volume would have been 120 GB and would not have performed significantly better than a simple volume. Rooslan achieved one goal of the third team. He achieved the first goal, but by using RAID-5 instead of striping, he failed to achieve the second. The second volume would have been 360 GB rather than 480 GB as specified, the equivalent of one drive lost in storing parity information.

   D. Incorrect: Rooslan achieved all the goals of the first team. For the second team, he achieved the first and second goals. By choosing to mirror, rather than stripe, the third volume, he did not create a volume of 240 GB with the fastest read/write speed. The volume would have been 120 GB and would not have performed significantly better than a simple volume. Rooslan achieved one goal of the third team. He achieved the first goal, but by using RAID-5 instead of striping, he failed to achieve the second. The second volume would have been 360 GB rather than 480 GB as specified, the equivalent of one drive lost in storing parity information.

   E. Incorrect: Rooslan achieved all the goals of the first team. For the second team, he achieved the first and second goals. In choosing to mirror, rather than stripe, the third volume, he did not create a volume of 240 GB with the fastest read/write speed. The volume would have been 120 GB and would not have performed significantly better than a simple volume. Rooslan achieved one goal of the third team. He achieved the first goal, but by using RAID-5 instead of striping, he failed to achieve the second. The second volume would have been 360 GB rather than 480 GB as specified, the equivalent of one drive lost in storing parity information.

F. **Correct:** Rooslan achieved all the goals of the first team. For the second team, he achieved the first and second goals. In choosing to mirror, rather than stripe, the third volume, he did not create a volume of 240 GB with the fastest read/write speed. The volume would have been 120 GB and would not have performed significantly better than a simple volume. Rooslan achieved one goal of the third team. He achieved the first goal, but by using RAID-5 instead of striping, he failed to achieve the second. The second volume would have been 360 GB rather than 480 GB as specified, the equivalent of one drive lost in storing parity information.

3. **Correct Answers: A, C, and D**

   A. **Correct:** Disk 1 is a mirrored volume of a volume on Disk 0. No data will be lost if this disk fails.

   B. **Incorrect:** If disk 0 fails, data will be lost as any data that is not on the Datastore volume, such as the boot volume, is not protected.

   C. **Correct:** Disk 2 is part of a RAID-5 array, hence if disk 2 fails, parity information can be used to regenerate the data.

   D. **Correct:** Datastore is a mirrored volume compared to Archive on RAID-5, and RAID-5 is faster than RAID-1 (mirroring).

   E. **Incorrect:** Datastore is a mirrored volume compared to Archive on RAID-5. RAID-5 is faster than RAID-1 (mirroring).

   F. **Incorrect:** Disk 3 is also part of the RAID-5 array; therefore, if Disk 3 fails, data will not be lost.

4. **Correct Answers: B and E**

   A. **Incorrect:** The question states clearly that it is the second volume, so Oksana is not mistaken.

   B. **Correct:** Page files are unmovable files and therefore are reported in green by the disk defragmenter analyzer. Similarly, the NTFS change journal, on NTFS volumes, is also represented by the unmovable green.

   C. **Incorrect:** Encrypted and compressed files are not unmovable.

   D. **Incorrect:** Encrypted and compressed files are not unmovable.

   E. **Correct:** Page files are unmovable files and therefore are reported in green by the disk defragmenter analyzer. Similarly, the NTFS change journal, on NTFS volumes, is also represented by the unmovable green.

5. **Correct Answers: B**

   A. **Incorrect:** If a disk has less than 15 percent of space left, the defragmentation process will finish, but the disk will not be completely defragmented.

   B. **Correct:** Disk defragmentation will fail only when a disk has errors. If a disk has errors, it is classified as "dirty" by the operating system. The only way to change this state is to perform a Chkdsk operation on the disk and complete all required repairs.

   C. **Incorrect:** Disks cannot be defragmented if they are taken offline.

   D. **Incorrect:** Volumes cannot be defragmented if they are taken offline.

6. **Correct Answers: B, C, D, and E**

   A. **Incorrect:** This figure is below the 10% threshold, so Windows will not recommend a defragmentation.

   B. **Correct:** This figure is above the 10% threshold, so Windows will recommend a defragmentation.

   C. **Correct:** This figure is above the 10% threshold, so Windows will recommend a defragmentation.

   D. **Correct:** This figure is above the 10% threshold, so Windows will recommend a defragmentation.

   E. **Correct:** This figure is above the 10% threshold, so Windows will recommend a defragmentation.

Install and Configure Server Hardware Devices

A signed driver is one that has a digital certificate attached from Microsoft that guarantees that the driver has been tested on a wide variety of configurations and has been deemed reliable. Windows Server 2003 can be configured to look for this particular digital certificate and refuse to install drivers that have not met with Microsoft's approval.

An administrator may not wish to use only Microsoft-approved device drivers all the time. Administrators can override any signing settings by manually setting this option in the System Properties. The options include Block, Warn, and Ignore. Block disallows the installation of unsigned drivers, Warn allows the installation but produces a message that must be approved notifying the administrator that the user is about to install unsigned drivers, and Ignore produces no warning and simply installs the drives regardless of whether they have been digitally signed.

The resources that a hardware device uses can be configured in the Device Manager by selecting the device and, from the Action menu, selecting Properties. Newly installed hardware can sometimes conflict with other hardware on the system and these conflicts can best be resolved by adjusting resources such as I/O range and IRQ.

Objective 1.4 Questions

1. Oksana has recently replaced Rooslan as the systems administrator of six Windows Server 2003 systems. These six servers are stand-alone systems and not members of any domain. Several weeks into her tenure, Oksana receives the go-ahead to buy a Digital Audio Tape (DAT) backup drive for each of the Windows Server 2003 systems. At a prescheduled time she brings the servers down and installs the new hardware. When all the servers have been brought up, Oksana logs on to each and is confronted by the Add New Hardware Wizard. She begins the process of installing the software for the new hardware but finds that the process fails because the driver cannot be installed. Oksana then investigates the driver signing setting in the System Properties. The driver signing option is set to Block with the other options dimmed. Although the drivers have not been digitally signed by Microsoft, Oksana has decided that she wants to use them and that they will pose no problems to the stability of the servers that she administers. Which of the following actions can Oksana take to allow the installation of unsigned drivers on all six of these Windows Server 2003 systems? (Select all that apply.)

A. Oksana should reconfigure the domain GPO and set the Unsigned Driver Installation Behavior policy to Warn But Allow Installation.

B. Oksana should reconfigure the local GPO and set the Unsigned Driver Installation Behavior policy to Warn But Allow Installation.

C. Oksana should check the Administrator Option / Make This Action The System Default check box in the Driver Signing Options dialog box, accessible from the System Properties. This will enable her to switch the option from Block to Warn.

D. Oksana should reconfigure the GPO assigned to the site that the servers are set up in and set the Unsigned Driver Installation Behavior policy to Warn But Allow Installation.

E. Oksana should reconfigure the GPO applied to the OU that the servers are members of and set the Unsigned Driver Installation Behavior policy to Warn But Allow Installation.

2. You are a systems administrator at a medium-sized organization. You maintain a test lab of five Windows Server 2003 systems that are all members of your organization's single domain. Because the organization has had trouble in the past with some users with sufficient privileges installing unsigned drivers on the system the default domain GPO has been configured to block the installation of all unsigned drivers on computers that are members of the domain. The domain GPO also blocks access for all users to the System Properties and hides all icons on the desktop. Until recently this was unproblematic; however you have just received a new batch of high-performance network cards that you wish to test on your lab servers. These high performance network cards ship with drivers that have not been digitally signed by Microsoft. Because you cannot access the System Properties you cannot override the default domain GPO setting that blocks the installation of unsigned drivers. Which of the following methods allows you to override the default domain GPO and change the setting on your lab servers to Warn but not change the overall setting for other computers in your domain?

A. Edit the local GPO on each server and set the Unsigned Driver Installation Behavior policy to Warn But Allow Installation.

B. Edit the GPO applied to the site in which the servers in your lab reside and set the Unsigned Driver Installation Behavior policy to Warn But Allow Installation.

C. Create a new organizational unit called Mylab. Move the computer accounts for the Windows Server 2003 systems in to the Mylab OU. Create a GPO that sets the Unsigned Driver Installation Behavior policy to Warn But Allow Installation and apply it to the Mylab OU.

D. Edit the Domain GPO and set the Unsigned Driver Installation Behavior policy to Warn But Allow Installation.

E. Create a group and put your user account in this group. Create a GPO that sets the Unsigned Driver Installation Behavior policy to Warn But Allow Installation and apply this GPO to the newly created group.

3. You are the part-time systems administrator for a small desktop publishing business. There is a Windows Server 2003 stand alone at your office. You have recently come into possession of a legacy fax board, a device that allows multiple faxes to be sent and received at the same time. You install the board on the Windows Server 2003 system but discover that it does not work. You examine the Device Manager and notice that a yellow warning with a black exclamation mark sits beside the fax board icon. You suspect that there is an IRQ conflict with another device on this same system, a legacy RAID controller. Which of the following describes the correct method of altering the fax board's configuration so that there is no IRQ conflict between the legacy fax board and the legacy RAID controller?

A. Select the RAID controller in the Device Manager. From the Action menu, select Properties. Select the Resources Tab, and then clear the Use Automatic Settings check box. Select the IRQ and click Change Settings. Scroll through the IRQs until you find one that does not conflict with any others. Click OK and then restart the server.

B. Select the fax board in the Device Manager. From the Action menu, select Properties. Select the Resources tab, and then clear the Use Automatic Settings check box. Select the IRQ and click Change Settings Scroll through the IRQs until you find one that does not conflict with any others. Click OK and then restart the server.

C. Select the RAID controller in the Device Manager. From the Action menu, select Properties. Select the Resources tab, and then clear the Use Automatic Settings check box. Select the I/O Range and click Change Settings button. Scroll through the I/O Range until you find one that does not conflict with any others. Click OK and then restart the server.

D. Select the fax board in the Device Manager. From the Action menu, select Properties. Select the Resources tab, and then clear the Use Automatic Settings check box. Select the I/O Range and click Change Settings. Scroll through the I/O Range until you find one that does not conflict with any others. Click OK and then restart the server.

E. Select the RAID controller in the Device Manager. From the Action menu, select Properties. In the Device Usage drop-down list on the General tab, select Do Not Use This Device (Disable).

F. Select the fax board in the Device Manager. From the Action menu, select Properties. In the Device Usage drop-down list on the General tab, select Do Not Use This Device (Disable).

4.   You have recently installed three legacy network cards on a Windows Server 2003 member server. Two of the network cards are working properly, but a third appears to be conflicting with another device on your system. How can you determine which other device on the system is conflicting with the third network card?

   A. Run the Device Manager and look for another device with a yellow and black exclamation mark beside it.

   B. View the application log and look for an entry that describes the device with which the network card conflicts.

   C. Run the Device Manager and select the network card that has the yellow and black exclamation mark beside it. From the Action menu, select Properties. On the Resources tab, clear the Use Automatic Settings check box. A conflicting device list will be displayed with the resources that conflict.

   D. Run the Hardware Troubleshooting Wizard and select Resolve All Device Conflicts.

   E. Run the Hardware Troubleshooting Wizard and select Report On All Device Conflicts.

5.   You would like to view a list of devices connected to your Windows Server 2003 system listed numerically by IRQ. Which of the following methods could you use to do this? (Select all that apply.)

   A. Use the Device Manager and from the View menu, select Resources By Connection.

   B. Use the Device Manager and from the View menu, select Resources By Type.

   C. Use the Device Manager and from the View menu, select Devices By Connection

   D. Use the Device Manager and, from the View menu, select Devices By Type.

   E. This cannot be done.

6.   You have two modems connected to a Windows Server 2003 system that are used to create a multilink connection to a remote site using on-demand routing. You have found that the line quality to the remote site is not particularly high and you want to modify the port speed of both modems. Which of the following administrative tools would you use to do this?

   A. Use the Device Manager to find the modems and select their properties.

   B. Use the Phone And Modem Options in Control Panel to adjust the modem speeds.

   C. Use the Routing And Remote Access console to adjust the modem speed.

   D. Right-click on My Network Places and select Properties. Edit the properties of the multilink connection to the remote site and reduce the connection speed.

7. You are the systems administrator for a small agricultural college. One of the problems that you have encountered is students installing different devices on their Windows XP Professional workstations in their dormitory rooms. The college allows only Windows XP Professional workstations that it has leased to the students to join the dormitory network. This allows administration to restrict the students from engaging in undesirable activities such as peer-to-peer (P2P) file sharing.

Your group within the college is responsible for maintaining these workstations. After analyzing the amount of time that your group spends supporting the workstations, it has been found that 30 percent of the time goes to repairing faults caused by the installation of unsigned device drivers. You would like to prevent unsigned device drivers from being installed on the dormitory room workstations. Which of the following methods will achieve this goal without altering the settings on any other computers within the domain?

A. Move all computer accounts for dormitory room workstations into a newly created organizational unit named Dormwkstn. Create a GPO that sets the Unsigned Driver Installation Behavior policy to Warn But Allow Installation. Apply this GPO to the Dormwkstn OU.

B. Create a group named Dormwkstn and add all computer accounts for dormitory room workstations to this group. Create a GPO that sets the Unsigned Driver Installation Behavior policy to Warn But Allow Installation. Apply this GPO to the Dormwkstn group.

C. Create a group named Dormwkstn and add all dormitory room user accounts to this group. Create a GPO that sets the Unsigned Driver Installation Behavior policy to Warn But Allow Installation. Apply this GPO to the Dormwkstn group.

D. Move all computer accounts for dormitory room workstations into a newly created organizational unit named Dormwkstn. Create a GPO that sets the Unsigned Driver Installation Behavior policy to Do Not Allow Installation. Apply this GPO to the Dormwkstn OU.

E. Create a group named Dormwkstn and add all computer accounts for dormitory room workstations to this group. Create a GPO that sets the Unsigned Driver Installation Behavior policy to Do Not Allow Installation. Apply this GPO to the Dormwkstn group.

Objective 1.4 Answers

1.   Correct Answers: B and C

    A.   Incorrect: All six of the Windows Server 2003 server systems are stand-alones and not members of any domain. Editing GPOs applied to any domain has no influence on these servers because they are not affected by external GPOs.

    B.   Correct: The other options are dimmed because the Administrator Option / Make This Action The System Default check box is not selected. Selecting the check box means that any change is instantly reflected in the local GPO. The local GPO can also be edited without selecting this check box to obtain the same result.

    C.   Correct: The other options are dimmed because the Administrator Option / Make This Action The System Default check box is not selected. Selecting the check box means that any change is instantly reflected in the local GPO. The local GPO can also be edited without selecting this check box to obtain the same result.

    D.   Incorrect: All six of the Windows Server 2003 server systems are stand-alones and not members of any domain. Editing GPOs applied to any domain or site has no influence on these servers because they are not affected by external GPOs.

    E.   Incorrect: All six of the Windows Server 2003 server systems are stand-alones and not members of any domain. Editing GPOs applied to any domain has no influence on these servers because they are not affected by external GPOs.

2.   Correct Answers: C

    A.   Incorrect: Local GPOs are overridden by Site, Domain, and Organizational Unit GPOs. Because the GPO in question is applied at the Domain level, it will have precedence over the Local GPO settings.

    B.   Incorrect: Local GPOs are overridden by Site, Domain, and Organizational Unit GPOs. Because the GPO in question is applied at the Domain level it will have precedence over the Site GPO settings.

    C.   Correct: By creating an OU and moving the specific computer accounts in the test environment into the OU, a group policy can be applied that will influence only these specific systems. As Group Policy applied at the OU level overrides that applied at the Site or Domain level, a policy applied to the OU level on driver signing will override the default domain GPO for computers that are members of this OU.

    D.   Incorrect: This will change the settings for all computers in the domain, which was forbidden in the question setup.

    E.   Incorrect: GPO cannot be applied directly to groups; GPO can apply only to Sites, Domains, Organizational Units, and Locally. Groups can be used to modify which users in a Site, Domain, or OU the GPO applies do.

3. **Correct Answers: B**

    A. Incorrect: This alters the RAID controller configuration, not the fax board configuration. The question asked how the fax board configuration should be altered.

    B. Correct: The first thing to do is make sure that the IRQ, rather than the I/O on the fax board is adjusted. While the settings are adjusted, the dialog will display any other conflicts that might arise. Keep altering the IRQ setting until a free IRQ is found. There is no point stopping a conflict between a fax board and a RAID controller if it leads to a conflict between the fax board and another device.

    C. Incorrect: This answer configures the wrong hardware device and the wrong resource setting (I/O as opposed to IRQ).

    D. Incorrect: This answer configures the wrong resource setting (I/O as opposed to IRQ).

    E. Incorrect: This action merely disables the device; it does not resolve the conflict. Disabling the RAID controller will also not be helpful for maintaining a stable server.

    F. Incorrect: This action merely disables the device; it does not resolve the conflict.

4. **Correct Answers: C**

    A. Incorrect: Because the other device is working, it has taken precedence over the third network card. It will have no outward appearance of having any problems.

    B. Incorrect: If a conflict was logged, it would be logged in the system log rather than the application log.

    C. Correct: By examining the Resources tab on the Device Properties dialog box, you can generate a list of all devices that have resources that conflict with the particular device in which you are interested. From here you can decide also if you want to configure a device manually to use different resources or, if that is not possible, check the properties of the conflicting device to see if its resources can be changed.

    D. Incorrect: This option does not exist from the Hardware Troubleshooting Wizard.

    E. Incorrect: This option does not exist in the Hardware Troubleshooting Wizard.

5.   **Correct Answers: A and B**

A. **Correct:** A list of devices by IRQ can be generated by viewing resource by connection or by type in Device Manager. To locate the IRQ number for a particular device in other views, the specific device properties must be viewed.

B. **Correct:** A list of devices by IRQ can be generated by viewing resource by connection or by type in Device Manager. To locate the IRQ number for a particular device in other views, the specific device properties must be viewed.

C. **Incorrect:** This option does not sort by IRQ.

D. **Incorrect:** This option does not sort by IRQ.

E. **Incorrect:** A list of devices by IRQ can be generated by viewing resource by connection or by type in Device Manager. To locate the IRQ number for a particular device in other views, the specific device properties must be viewed.

6.   **Correct Answers: B**

A. **Incorrect:** Modem port speeds cannot be adjusted using the Device Manager.

B. **Correct:** Because the modem speeds need to be adjusted for several connections the best option is to edit the modem properties using Phone And Modem Options in Control Panel.

C. **Incorrect:** The Routing And Remote Access MMC cannot be used to adjust the modem port speed.

D. **Incorrect:** Network Connections (accessible through the My Network Places properties or Control Panel) cannot be used to adjust the modem port speed.

7.   **Correct Answers: D**

A. **Incorrect:** This option allows the installation of unsigned drivers rather than blocking it.

B. **Incorrect:** GPOs cannot be applied to distribution or security groups.

C. **Incorrect:** GPOs cannot be applied to distribution or security groups.

D. **Correct:** GPOs can be applied to sites, domains, and organizational units. There is also a GPO that can be edited and applied locally. The policy must be set to Do Not Allow Installation.

E. **Incorrect:** GPOs cannot be applied to distribution or security groups.

15 Managing Users, Computers, and Groups (2.0)

Users need access to resources on the network to do their daily work, but should not have access to unauthorized data. This access is gained by logging on to a computer that has access to the domain, and then being acknowledged as a member of assigned groups in the domain. Permissions to resources can only be set for users, groups, and computers that are recognized by the domain.

Creation of these user, group, and computer accounts can be done manually through tools provided in the Microsoft Windows Server 2003 interface, or automated through command-line tools or scripts. The methods of creating user, group, and computer accounts are important to success on the exam.

Related to the creation and management of user, group, and computer accounts are the granting of permissions appropriate to the level of access needed, and the management of data related to the account, such as logon scripts and user profiles.

Testing Skills and Suggested Practices

The skills that you need to master the Managing Users, Computers, and Groups objective domain on *Exam 70-290: Managing and Maintaining a Microsoft Window Server 2003 Environment* include

- Manage local, roaming, and mandatory user profiles.
  - ❏ Practice 1: Configure a roaming profile for secure access. Set the permissions on an individual profile folder for that user. Make sure that no other users have access to the data, and that users can log on and use their profile data successfully.
  - ❏ Practice 2: Change the configuration of the roaming profile to make it mandatory. Groups of users sharing a profile should not be able to change it. To do this rename the shared profile from Ntuser.dat to Ntuser.man. Using a mandatory profile does not limit the ability of users who share the profile from creating, modifying, or deleting application data files within the profile folder structure.

- Create and manage computer accounts in an active directory environment.

  - ❏ Practice 1: Use the Active Directory User And Computers MMC to create two new computer accounts within the domain.

  - ❏ Practice 2: Join a new Windows XP workstation to the Windows Server 2003 domain. Examine Active Directory Users And Computers and note that the new computer account is added to the directory.

- Create and manage groups.

  - ❏ Practice 1: Use manual methods to create user, group, and computer accounts. Use the Active Directory Users And Computers MMC snap-in, and the Directory Service command-line tools to create user, group, and computer accounts. Modify the properties of user accounts and test the effect of various property changes. Use the System Properties interface at a desktop computer to join computers to the domain.

  - ❏ Practice 2: Use automated methods to create user, group, and computer accounts.

  - ❏ Practice 3: Place users, groups, and computers as members of a group. Use both interface-based and command-line tools.

  - ❏ Practice 4: Identify group membership in a complex group hierarchy. Use the Directory Service command-line tools to do bulk analysis.

- Create and manage user accounts.

  - ❏ Practice 1: Create four different user accounts using the Active Directory Users And Computers MMC.

  - ❏ Practice 2: Create a single user account using the Active Directory Users and Computers MMC. Configure specific settings for the user's logon hours and group membership. Create three similar accounts using the copy command.

- Troubleshoot computer accounts.

  - ❏ Practice 1: Create a computer account in the Active Directory Users and Computers MMC. In the dialog box alter the group that can add the computer to the domain from the Domain Admins group to the Users group.

  - ❏ Practice 2: In the Active Directory Users and Computers MMC locate a test Windows XP computer account that has recently been joined to the domain. Using the Action menu, Disable the computer account. Try to use this computer to gain access to the domain.

- Troubleshoot user accounts

❏ Practice 1: Modify the Default Domain GPO and alter the Account Lockout threshold to three attempts. Log on with incorrect credentials to a Windows Server 2003 domain with a normal user account until the account is locked. Use the Active Directory Users and Computers MMC to re-enable the account.

❏ Practice 2: Reset the password on a user account and configure the account to force the user to change their password to one of their own the next time that they log on.

■ Troubleshoot user authentication issues.

❏ Practice 1: Edit the default domain policy GPO to change the password policies. Configure the Account Lockout Threshold policy to three invalid logon attempts. Set the Account Lockout Duration policy to 30 minutes.

❏ Practice 2: Edit the default domain policy GPO to change the password policies. Set the Enforce Password History policy to 10 passwords. Set the Minimum Password Age policy to 2 days. Set the Minimum Password Length policy to 10 characters.

Further Reading

This section contains a list of supplemental readings divided by objective. If you feel you need additional preparation before taking the exam, study these sources thoroughly.

Objective 2.1   Review Chapter 3, "User Accounts," which focuses on the creation and management of user accounts and user profiles.

Review Chapter 4, "Group Accounts," which contains additional information on automated creation of groups, group type and scope, and nesting groups.

Microsoft Corporation. *Microsoft Windows Server 2003 Deployment Kit*. Volume: *Designing a Managed Environment*. Redmond, Washington: Microsoft Press, 2003. This volume can be found on the Microsoft Web site at: *http://www.microsoft.com /windowsserver2003/techinfo/reskit/deploykit.mspx*.

Objective 2.2   Review Chapter 5, "Computer Accounts," which contains information about creating computer accounts through manual and automated means, various methods of joining the computer accounts to a domain, and resetting the password on a computer account.

Microsoft Corporation. Windows Server 2003 Help and Support Center. Review "Manage Computers."

Objective 2.3   Review Chapter 4, "Group Accounts," which focuses on the creation and management of user accounts and user profiles.

Microsoft Corporation. *Windows Server 2003 Help and Support Center.* "Managing Domain Users and Groups: Using Groups."

Objective 2.4   Review Chapter 3, "User Accounts," which focuses on the creation and management of user accounts and profiles.

Microsoft Corporation. *Windows Server 2003 Help and Support Center.* Managing Domain Users and Groups: User and Computer Accounts.

Objective 2.5   Review Chapter 5, "Computer Accounts," which contains information about creating computer accounts through manual and automated means, various methods of joining the computer accounts to a domain, and resetting the password on a computer account.

Microsoft Corporation. Windows Server 2003 Knowledge Base article 325850: "How to Use netdom.exe to Reset Machine Account Passwords of a Windows Server 2003 Domain Controller."

Objective 2.6   Review Chapter 3, "User Accounts," which describes some techniques for troubleshooting user of user accounts.

Microsoft Corporation. *Windows Server 2003 Help and Support Center.* Managing Domain Users and Groups: User and Computer Accounts.

Objective 2.7   Review Chapter 3, "User Accounts," which focuses on the creation and management of user accounts and profiles.

Microsoft Corporation. *Windows Server 2003 Help and Support*: Managing Domain Users and Groups: User and Computer Accounts.

Manage Local, Roaming, and Mandatory User Profiles

Upon logging on, a set of data is loaded for the user called the user's profile. This profile contains application settings, desktop configuration settings and files, and (by default) the My Documents, My Pictures, and other related folders for saving files. These folders can be redirected through group policy, or individually through settings on the user's account. Redirected profiles can be stored in any network location, and are considered roaming profiles when a network profile location is assigned to the user. Roaming profiles can be accessed from any computer to which the user can log on, and the profile will be loaded for use on the local computer. If a roaming profile is configured as mandatory, no changes to the profile made by the user can be saved. This makes practical use of the profile by more than one user possible.

Objective 2.1 Questions

1.   Your company has placed 35 computers in various locations throughout the building to allow access to company information when an employee is away from his or her desktop computer. These computers are used to check e-mail, to read corporate news and access policy information on the company's intranet.

You want to make it possible for a user at one of these shared computers to change his or her desktop settings, and to have these desktop settings apply to any of the other shared computers.

What should you do?

   A. Configure a mandatory profile and assign it to each user in the domain.

   B. Configure a mandatory profile and assign it to each shared computer.

   C. Configure a roaming profile and assign it to each user in the domain.

   D. Configure a roaming profile and assign it to each shared computer.

2.   You have been given the responsibility for maintaining user accounts, user profiles, and user access to resources on your network. Currently, all users share a single profile on the network, which allows for easy addition and deletion of objects to the users' desktops, but also allows for desktop changes to be made and saved by the users. You want to retain the ability to centrally manage user's desktops, but want to prohibit changes to desktop settings by the users.

What should you do?

   A. Configure the permissions on the profile folder's Security property sheet to deny write permission.

   B. Configure the permissions on the profile folder's Sharing property sheet to allow only read permission.

   C. Modify the attributes of the profile folder to specify the Read Only attribute.

   D. Modify the file name of Ntuser.dat in the profile folder to Ntuser.man.

3.   Your company has been using roaming profiles for members of the Sales and Information Technology departments for the last 10 months. The profile data is stored on a member-server running Microsoft Windows Server 2003. The file system in use on the volume on the server hosting the profiles is FAT32. The share hosting the profiles is called Profshare. Profile paths are correctly configured in each user's properties. Recently you have found that some users are able to access the data located in other's profiles. You want to secure the roaming user profiles on your network such that only the user logging on to the profile will have access to the data contained within it.

What should you do? (Choose two; each answer is part of the complete solution.)

A. Assign Read and Write permission on the folder where the profiles are stored to only those users who store roaming profiles.

B. Configure Server Message Block (SMB) signing on the server where the profiles are stored.

C. Configure Server Message Block (SMB) signing on each computer that uses roaming profiles.

D. Convert the volume where the profiles are stored to NTFS.

E. Configure Encrypting Files System (EFS) to encrypt the folder where the profiles are stored.

4.   You are the administrator of a company that has decided to place computers in the lobby for access to public company information. Members of the Sales department need to be able to log on to these computers with their Domain user credentials for client demonstrations, and public users will use the Guest account.

Members of the Sales department, whose desktop computers and user accounts are contained in the Sales Organizational Unit (OU), are configured to use roaming profiles. The shared computers in the lobby are contained in the Lobby OU.

You do not want the Sales users' desktop computer profiles to be used when they log on to one of the shared, lobby computers. All users of the lobby computers should have the same desktop without the ability to save changes.

What configuration changes must you make? (Choose three; each answer represents a partial solution.)

   A. Configure a local profile after logging on as Guest on one of the computers in the lobby. Copy it to the Default User folder. Repeat this process on each computer in the lobby.

   B. Configure a local profile on one of the computers in the lobby. Copy it to the Default User folder in the directory on the server that contains the roaming profiles.

   C. Create a Group Policy Object (GPO) linked to the Sales OU. Enable the Only Allow Local User Profiles Computer Configuration policy.

   D. Create a GPO linked to the Lobby OU. Enable the Only Allow Local User Profiles Computer Configuration policy.

   E. Change the file name of Ntuser.dat to Ntuser.man in the Default User folder on each computer in the lobby.

   F. Change the file name of Ntuser.dat to Ntuser.man in the Default User folder in the directory on the server that contains the roaming profiles.

   G. Instruct each salesperson to log on and log off of each lobby computer. Copy the contents of the Default User folder on each lobby computer to each user profile directory.

Objective 2.1 Answers

1.   **Correct Answers: C**

   A. Incorrect: Mandatory profiles do not allow any alterations to desktop settings made by the user to be retained.

   B. Incorrect: A mandatory profile does not allow for changed settings to be saved. Additionally, profiles are assigned to users, not computers.

   C. Correct: A roaming user profile allows for settings for any user configured with a roaming profile to have those settings applied at other computers on which they log on.

   D. Incorrect: Profiles are assigned to users, not computers.

2.   **Correct Answers: D**

   A. Incorrect: This action will cause the loading of the profile to fail, as read/write access to the profile is required when the profile is loaded.

   B. Incorrect: This action will cause the loading of the profile to fail, as read/write access to the profile is required when the profile is loaded.

   C. Incorrect: This action will cause the loading of the profile to fail, as read/write access to the profile is required when the profile is loaded.

   D. Correct: This action will allow for proper opening of the profile but will prohibit any changes made by the user from being saved upon logoff.

3.   **Correct Answers: A and D**

   A. Correct: This action will allow only users who are configured to have roaming profiles (the Sales and IT departments) to read data contained in a roaming user profile. All other users will be denied access. This can only be accomplished once the file system on the volume hosting the profile data is moved to NTFS. FAT32 cannot be configured for individual permissions.

   B. Incorrect: This action will, partially, ensure the integrity of any packet transmitted across the network, but will not prohibit access by unauthorized personnel when saved to disk.

   C. Incorrect: This action will, partially, ensure the integrity of any packet transmitted across the network, but will not prohibit access by unauthorized personnel when saved to disk.

   D. Correct: This action will allow for discretionary access control of the profiles as they are saved to disk on the server. The existing FAT32 file system would not allow such permissions to be set.

   E. Incorrect: Roaming profile data cannot be encrypted by the server.

4.   **Correct Answers: A, D, and E**

A. **Correct:** As you log on as Guest, a local profile is created. That profile can then be configured as desired. When the profile is copied to the Default User folder, it becomes the profile that will be used, initially, when any user logs on that will not be using a roaming profile.

B. **Incorrect:** The Default User folder data on the profile server is used to create new, roaming profiles, which will not be used here.

C. **Incorrect:** This GPO is a computer-based policy, and the object computers in this situation are those in the lobby, not in the sales department.

D. **Correct:** This GPO overrides the logging-on users' setting for use of a roaming profile by not allowing roaming profiles to be used on the computer. Computers in the lobby, as they have this GPO set, will not allow roaming profiles to be loaded, and will use only local profiles.

E. **Correct:** This configuration will prohibit any changes to the local profiles.

F. **Incorrect:** This will make all new, roaming profiles unchangeable, which is not the goal in this situation.

G. **Incorrect:** This overwrites the roaming user profile once, but the roaming behavior will resume the next time that the user logs on.

Create and Manage Computer Accounts in an Active Directory Environment

Computer accounts, one of the three types of security principals, have properties very similar to users and groups. Computers can have permissions set for access to resources, and can be placed as a member of a group. Computers can process Group Policy Objects, logon and logoff scripts, and perform tasks in coordination with other objects on the network.

Administration of these accounts involves the creation of the computer account, naming and configuration of the account, and permissions management. These functions can be performed through the Active Directory Users And Computers MMC snap-in, or through a variety of command-line tools.

Objective 2.2 Questions

1.   In your Windows Server 2003 domain *contoso.com*, in the Pservers (Print Servers) OU you have member server computer named Pserver01. This server has been offline for a lengthy period, and is not communicating with other computers in the domain to accept print jobs. You have determined that the password on this computer's account within the domain needs to be reset.

Which command can you issue to correctly reset the computer account?

    A. dsmod CN=pserver01,CN=PSERVERS,DC=contoso,DC=com -reset

    B. dsmod computer pserver01.contoso.com -reset

    C. dsmod contoso\pserver01 -reset

    D. dsmod computer CN=pserver01,CN=PSERVERS,DC=contoso,DC=com -reset

2.   A domain controller running Windows Server 2003 is failing to replicate with the other domain controllers in the *contoso.com* domain. In Event Viewer, you note messages that access has been denied to this domain controller. You suspect that the domain controller's password is not synchronized properly with the other domain controllers, and should be reset.

What should you do?

    A. In Active Directory Users And Computers, right-click the computer object and choose Reset Account.

    B. On the domain controller, use the Dsmod command-line tool to reset the computer password.

    C. On the domain controller, use the Netdom command-line tool to reset the computer password.

    D. Restart the server in the recovery console and use the console to reset the computer account.

3.   You are a network administrator managing a Windows Server 2003 domain, *contoso.com*. As part of a network restructuring, new child domains of *west.contoso.com* and *east.contoso.com* have been added to the forest. You need to move three computer accounts for file server computers from the *contoso.com* domain to the *west.contoso.com* domain. All servers to be moved are Windows Server 2003 member servers.

What should you do?

    A.   Use Active Directory Domains And Trusts to move the computer accounts.

    B.   Use Active Directory Users And Computers to move the computer accounts.

    C.   Use the Movetree command-line tool to move the computer accounts.

    D.   Use the Dsmove utility to move the computer accounts.

4.   You need to create a batch file to automate the setting of the attributes for computers within your Windows Server 2003 Active Directory domain, *contoso.com*. You want the batch file to modify all computers in a specific OU within the domain. Your manual input to the batch file will be the OU, the attribute, and the new value for the attribute. All other input and output from the batch file should be automated.

Which Windows Server 2003 commands will you need to include in the batch file? (Choose all that apply; each correct answer represents a partial solution.)

    A.   Dsget computer

    B.   Dsmod computer

    C.   Dsquery computer

    D.   Dsadd computer

    E.   Dsrm computer

Objective 2.2 Answers

1.   Correct Answers: D

   A. **Incorrect:** This command has the correct distinguished name syntax, but is missing the "computer" keyword.

   B. **Incorrect:** This command has the correct "computer" keyword, but does not list the computer to be reset with the correct distinguished name syntax.

   C. **Incorrect:** This command omits the "computer" keyword, and fails to use the correct distinguished name syntax.

   D. **Correct:** This command correctly uses the "computer" keyword, and distinguished name syntax.

2.   Correct Answers: C

   A. **Incorrect:** This action would be appropriate for a member server computer, but is not applicable to a domain controller. Domain controller passwords cannot be reset using Active Directory Users And Computers.

   B. **Incorrect:** The Dsmod command would be appropriate for a member server computer, but is not applicable to a domain controller. Domain controller passwords cannot be reset using the Dsmod command.

   C. **Correct:** This command, run with the syntax of Netdom /resetpwd at the console of the domain controller, will reset the password.

   D. **Incorrect:** The recovery console cannot be used to reset a computer's domain account.

3.   Correct Answers: C

   A. **Incorrect:** Active Directory Domains And Trusts is used to set properties for the domain such as the Domain Functional Level (and Forest Functional Levels), and to manage trusts between domains. It is not used to administer security principals within a domain or forest.

   B. **Incorrect:** Active Directory Users And Computers can be used to move objects within the same domain only.

   C. **Correct:** The Movetree command-line tool can be used to move objects between domains.

   D. **Incorrect:** The Dsmove utility can be used to move objects within the same domain only.

4.   **Correct Answers: B and C**

A. **Incorrect:** Dsget will return a value of all objects of a given type, and will accept input from the command Dsquery, but is not able to pipe input to another command. Dsget is not able to perform the modifications needed, nor pass information to one of the commands that is able to modify attributes.

B. **Correct:** Dsmod can receive input from the Dsquery command to make changes to attributes of objects in Active Directory.

C. **Correct:** Dsquery can pipe output to the Dsmod command, which can then modify attributes of objects in Active Directory.

D. **Incorrect:** The Dsadd command can add objects to Active Directory, but cannot modify attributes.

E. **Incorrect:** Dsrm can remove objects from Active Directory, but cannot modify attributes.

Objective 2.3
Create and Manage Groups

Grouping user accounts is an efficient way to organize individual users into logical units to which permissions can be assigned. Different from organizational units, groups are security principals, and can be added to the Discretionary Access Control List (DACL, or ACL) of a resource for permission assignment.

The types of groups that are available, their scope, and the combinations of nested groups that can be used depend on the Functional Level of the domain in which the groups reside; similarly, some groups can be converted to a different type or scope if the functional level of the domain is high enough. To support all group types, scopes, nesting and conversion possibilities, the functional level of the domain must be Windows 2000 Native or Windows Server 2003. At the lower functional level of Windows 2000 Mixed, group nesting is limited, and conversion is not possible.

Objective 2.3 Questions

1. You are administrator of a Windows Server 2003 domain that is, currently, at the domain functional level Windows 2000 Mixed. Your Windows 2003 domain, *contoso.com*, has an external trust established with a Windows NT 4 Domain, *contoso_north*. You are planning the use of groups in your domain, and need to determine what group scopes can be used in any domain in your forest.

   What group scope can be used in this context as a security principal?

   A. Domain Local

   B. Global

   C. Universal

   D. Domain Local with a nested global group

2. You have just raised the domain functional level of your single-domain forest, *contoso.com*, to Windows Server 2003. You want to take advantage of the security group nesting possibilities available to you.

   What Security group nesting is possible at this domain functional level? (Choose all that apply.)

   A. Domain Local in Domain Local

   B. Global in Domain Local

   C. Universal in Domain Local

   D. Domain Local in Global

   E. Global in Global

   F. Universal in Global

   G. Universal in Universal

   H. Global in Universal

   I. Domain Local in Universal

3.   You have just raised the domain functional level of your single-domain forest, *contoso.com*, to Windows Server 2003. You want to take advantage of the security group conversion possibilities available to you.

What security group conversion is possible at this domain functional level? (Choose all that apply.)

    A. Domain local with user members; convert to global

    B. Global with user members; convert to universal

    C. Global with global group members; convert to universal

    D. Universal group with universal group members; convert to domain local

    E. Universal group with universal group members; convert to global

    F. Global with user members; convert to domain local

    G. Domain local with user members; convert to universal

4.   You are the administrator of a Windows Server 2003 domain, *contoso.com*, that is set to domain functional Level Windows 2000 mixed during a migration of your network. You are planning your use of groups during this transitional period, and want to determine what group types you can create and what scopes those groups may have.

What group type and scope possibilities exist at this functional level? (Choose all that apply.)

    A. Domain Local Group: Security Type

    B. Domain Local Group: Distribution Type

    C. Global group: Security Type

    D. Global group: Distribution Type

    E. Universal group: Security Type

    F. Universal group: Distribution Type

Objective 2.3 Answers

1.   Correct Answers: B

A. **Incorrect:** Domain Local groups are only available for use as security principals on domain controllers in the Windows Server 2003 domain, contoso.com.

B. **Correct:** Global groups are available for permission assignment in any ACL in the forest.

C. **Incorrect:** Universal groups are only available as distribution groups, not security groups, in the Windows 2000 Mixed functional level.

D. **Incorrect:** Domain Local groups, at this functional level, are only available on domain controllers in the contoso.com domain, regardless of other groups that they may contain. The nested global group, however, is available for permission assignment.

2.   Correct Answers: A, B, C, E, G, and H

A. **Correct:** Domain local groups can contain other domain local groups from the same domain.

B. **Correct:** This nesting is possible regardless of the functional level.

C. **Correct:** Universal groups can be placed in domain local groups.

D. **Incorrect:** This nesting is not possible at any functional level.

E. **Correct:** Global groups can be placed in global groups.

F. **Incorrect:** This nesting is not possible at any functional level

G. **Correct:** Universal groups can be placed in universal groups.

H. **Correct:** Global groups can be placed in universal groups.

I. **Incorrect:** This nesting is not possible at any functional level.

3.   **Correct Answers: B, D, and G**

    A. Incorrect: Domain local groups cannot be converted to global groups, regardless of domain functional level.

    B. Correct: Global groups without other global groups as members can be converted to universal groups.

    C. Incorrect: The conversion of groups of this type could create a circular reference, and is not permitted.

    D. Correct: There is no restriction on this type of conversion, at this functional level, regardless of universal group memberships.

    E. Incorrect: The conversion of groups of this type could create a circular reference, and is not permitted.

    F. Incorrect: This type of conversion is not permitted.

    G. Correct: So long as a domain local group does not have any other domain local groups as members, conversion to a universal group is permitted.

4.   **Correct Answers: A, B, C, D, and F**

    A. Correct: Domain local groups can be created with a group type of security, but will be available only on the domain controllers in the domain in which they were created until the domain functional level is raised.

    B. Correct: Domain local groups can be created with a group type of distribution, but will be available only on the domain controllers in the domain in which they were created until the domain functional level is raised.

    C. Correct: Global groups can be created with a group type of security regardless of the domain functional level.

    D. Correct: Global groups can be created with a group type of distribution regardless of the domain functional level.

    E. Incorrect: Universal groups cannot be created with a group type of security until the domain functional level is raised.

    F. Correct: Universal groups can be created with a group type of distribution regardless of the domain functional level.

Create and Manage User Accounts

User accounts can be added individually through the Active Directory Users And Computers snap-in, or through the Directory Service command-line tool, Dsadd. These tools are preferred and sufficient for single accounts. Active Directory Users And Computers is also the easiest tool for managing the properties of user accounts, as it presents a common and usable interface to these properties. The Directory Service command-line tools are better suited for mass manipulation of the properties of existing collections of users such as groups, OUs, or the entire domain.

If you already have a directory or database of users, it may be more efficient to import these users into your Active Directory using Ldifde or Csvde.

Objective 2.4 Questions

1. Which of the following tools allow for the creation of Active Directory security principals (user, computer, and group accounts) based on user or file input? (Choose all that apply.)

     A. Active Directory Users And Computers

     B. Active Directory Domains And Trusts

     C. Ntdsutil

     D. Ldifde

     E. Csvde

     F. Dsadd

     G. Dsquery

     H. Dsmod

2. You are the administrator of the Windows Server 2003 domain *contoso.com*. Your company employs many temporary workers. Some of these workers are employed only once, others are employed periodically on a recurring basis.

Your goal is to automate a process that will determine which accounts have not been used within the last month and then disable them. If the accounts are needed again, you will re-enable them at that time.

Which Directory Service command-line tool is the appropriate one to achieve your goal?

     A. dsquery user domainroot -inactive 4 -disabled yes

     B. dsquery user domainroot -inactive 4|dsmod user -disabled yes

     C. dsquery user domainroot -inactive 4|dsrm -q

     D. dsquery user domainroot -inactive 4|dsmove –newparent OU=disabled,DC=contoso, DC=com -q

3. You have been given an administrative task related to user accounts in the *contoso.com* Active Directory. You need to move all accounts in the East group located in the Sales OU into the newly created East Sales OU.

Which procedure will accomplish this task?

A. Use Active Directory Users And Computers to move the East group to the East Sales OU.

B. Use Dsquery to get the members of the group, and then pipe (stdin) the output to the Dsmod command with the East Sales OU as the target.

C. Use Dsquery to get the members of the group, and then pipe (stdin) the output to the Dsmove command with the East Sales OU as the target.

D. Use Dsquery to get the members of the group, and then pipe (stdin) the output to the Dsadd command with the East Sales OU as the target.

4. You are configuring the properties of user accounts in the Sales OU of the *contoso.com* domain. You wish their home directories to be stored on the network server computer named Server01. The home directories are to be stored in a shared folder, named Home, on the server's D: drive. The share name is Homedir.

In the Home Folder property for each user, how will you set the home directories?

A. D:\Home*%Username%*

B. \\Server01\d$\Home*%Username%*

C. \\Server01*%Homedir%**%Username%*

D. \\Server01\Homedir*%Username%*

Objective 2.4 Answers

1.   Correct Answers: A, D, E, and F

    A. Correct: Active Directory Users And Computers is the primary interface tool for creating security principals.

    B. Incorrect: Active Directory Domains And Trusts is used for setting the functional level of the domain or forest, and for creating and managing trust relationships. Domain accounts are not created using this tool.

    C. Incorrect: Ntdsutil is used for data restoration, metadata manipulation, and other directory service functions. Ntdsutil is not used to create security objects within Active Directory.

    D. Correct: Ldifde can create objects within Active Directory using a data file or command-line parameters for input.

    E. Correct: Csvde can create objects within Active Directory using a comma-separated-values file for input.

    F. Correct: Dsadd is a command-line tool used to add objects to the Active Directory.

    G. Incorrect: Dsquery is used to output information from Active Directory. Its output may be used for other DS commands, but Dsquery cannot create objects within the directory.

    H. Incorrect: Dsmod is used to modify attributes of existing Active Directory objects.

2.   Correct Answers: B

    A. Incorrect: This command will return a list of user accounts that have been inactive for four weeks or more and are disabled. No action is taken by the Dsquery command.

    B. Correct: This command will return a list of user accounts that have been inactive for four weeks or more and then pipe that output into the Dsmod command, which will disable the accounts.

    C. Incorrect: This command will return a list of user accounts that have been inactive for four weeks or more, and pipe the output into the Dsrm command, which will remove the accounts.

    D. Incorrect: This command will move all accounts that have been inactive for four weeks or more into an OU named "disabled," but it will not disable the accounts.

3.   **Correct Answers: C**

    A. **Incorrect:** This action will move the group to the East Sales OU, but the user accounts will remain in the Sales OU.

    B. **Incorrect:** The Dsmod command can modify properties of a user account, but the OU is not a property of a user account.

    C. **Correct:** This action will appropriately move the accounts to an OU.

    D. **Incorrect:** This action would attempt to create new accounts in the East Sales OU and leave the old user accounts in the Sales OU. This will fail because although the OU and group are separate, they are all a part of the same domain, hence this process would fail with errors.

4.   **Correct Answers: D**

    A. **Incorrect:** This will set the home directory to the D drive on the user's computer.

    B. **Incorrect:** This setting would require explicit administrative permissions to access the root share of the D drive, which users do not have.

    C. **Incorrect:** The %Homedir% variable refers to the assigned home directory, which is being set by this property's value. The reference to the home directory will fail in this case.

    D. **Correct:** This will set the user's home directory to a folder within the Homedir share. The folder will be named with the user's logon name.

Objective 2.5

Troubleshoot Computer Accounts

Computer accounts are security principals in the Active Directory just as User and Group Accounts. Computer accounts, at creation, are assigned a security identifier (SID), relative identifier (RID), and globally unique Identifier (GUID). The RID is supplied by a domain controller in the Active Directory from a pool of RIDs distributed by the single domain controller that has been assigned the role of the RID Master. If the RID Master role is unavailable for an extended period of time, RID pools can be exhausted, making the creation of computer accounts in the domain impossible.

Computer accounts also have a password which is synchronized, internally, with the Active Directory. If these passwords become unsynchronized, they will need to be reset by the Administrator.

Objective 2.5 Questions

1. A user, returning from an extended leave of absence powers on his or her computer, Desk249, and attempts to log on to the domain but cannot do so. You attempt to log on to the user's computer, as a Domain Administrator, but cannot do so.

You return to your computer and search the Active Directory for the Desk249 computer, but find that no computer with that name exists in the directory. You log on with a local administrator account to the Desk249 computer and discover that the computer still believes it is a part of the domain. After consideration, you determine that you must re-create the computer account. You want to enable the user to log on at their computer as soon as possible, and with the least amount of administrative effort.

What should you do?

  A. Log on to the Desk249 computer with the local administrator account. In the System control panel, in the Computer Name tab click on the "To rename this computer or join a domain, Click change" change button. Join Desk249 to a workgroup named TEST and restart. Log on again with the local administrator account. Navigate back to the workgroup/domain membership page. Using an account with domain administrator privileges, rejoin the Desk249 computer to the Active Directory domain, and then restart Desk249.

  B. Use Active Directory Users And Computers to create a new computer account with the computer name Desk249 in the Computers container. Restart Desk249.

  C. Use Dsadd to create a new computer account with the computer name Desk249 in the Computers container. Restart Desk249.

  D. Use Ntdsutil to restore the computer account from a backup of Active Directory that contains the Desk249 account.

2. You are attempting to use the Computer Management snap-in to remotely manage a file server on your network. The file server is a member of the domain, and you are a member of the Domain Admins group.

You cannot connect the Computer Management snap-in to the file server from your computer, but are able to connect remotely to other servers on your network. You can access files on the file server, as can all other users on the network.

What could be the problem with the file server?

  A. The Browser service is not running.

  B. The Remote Registry service is not running.

  C. Routing and Remote Access is not installed on the file server.

  D. The computer account needs to be reset in Active Directory.

3.   You are deploying several Windows Server 2003 computers into your Windows NT 4 environment using the Sysprep utility. After deploying the image to all the servers, you test network connections to each to ensure that the deployment has gone properly.

When you try to log on to Server03 remotely, a message indicating that the "Trust relationship has failed" is displayed, and you are unable to connect.

What should you do to solve the problem? (Choose all that apply.)

A. Use the Dsmod command on Server03 to reset the password.

B. Use Active Directory Users And Computers to reset the password for Server03.

C. Join Server03 to a workgroup.

D. Join Server03 to the domain.

E. Delete the Server03 account from the domain.

F. Disable the Server03 account in the domain.

G. Create an account for Server03 in the domain.

H. Enable the Server03 account in the domain.

4.   You are in the process of adding users, computers, and groups to your new Windows Server 2003 domain. After several hundred objects have been added through batch importing, you begin to add the last 24 computers that must be entered manually. After entering three computer accounts successfully, you receive error messages and are unable to add more computers to the domain.

All other network connectivity and server functions appear to be functioning normally.

What is the most likely cause of the problem?

A. The RID Master role is unavailable.

B. The PDC Emulator role is unavailable.

C. The domain infrastructure role is unavailable.

D. The schema master role is unavailable.

Objective 2.5 Answers

1.   Correct Answers: A

A.   Correct: The relationship between a computer account in Active Directory and the local workstation, Desk249 in this case, is a synchronized relationship, which requires security settings on both components to be set within a single process. The Desk249 side of the relationship must be recreated as well as the account in Active Directory.

B.   Incorrect: This action creates a computer account that matches the Desk249 computer in name only. The two pieces of the object relationship, Active Directory object and local computer, will not be able to synchronize passwords or other security information in this situation.

C.   Incorrect: This action creates a computer account which matches the Desk249 computer in name only. The two pieces of the object relationship, Active Directory object and local computer, will not be able to synchronize passwords or other security information in this situation.

D.   Incorrect: Individual computer accounts cannot be restored from a backup, and the process of deleting the relationship from the client computer, then recreating the client and Active Directory computer account relationship is much simpler.

2.   Correct Answers: B

A.   Incorrect: The Browser service participates in location of named computers and services. You are able to locate the computer.

B.   Correct: The Remote Registry service is needed to determine whether sufficient privileges exist for remote connection. Starting this service will likely fix the problem.

C.   Incorrect: Routing and Remote Access is for governing dial-up and virtual private network (VPN) connections to, and routing through, a computer. It is not needed to connect to a computer for management.

D.   Incorrect: If the password were unsynchronized, file access would be problematic as well.

3.   **Correct Answers: C, D, E, and G**

A. **Incorrect:** The Dsmod command (and any other Directory Service command-line tool) is available only with Active Directory.

B. **Incorrect:** Active Directory Users And Computers is available only with an installation of Active Directory.

C. **Correct:** This step will eliminate the computer identification for the domain on the local computer.

D. **Correct:** This step will synchronize the computer account with its counterpart in the domain.

E. **Correct:** This step will eliminate the computer identification for the domain from the domain.

F. **Incorrect:** Disabling the account will not remove its identity. A mismatched identity is the problem.

G. **Correct:** This step will establish an account in the domain to which the computer can connect and synchronize.

H. **Incorrect:** If re-created, the computer account will already be enabled. If re-enabling after disabling, the same problem with the trust relationship will exist.

4.   **Correct Answers: A**

A. **Correct:** The RID Master is needed for the assignment of identifiers for new objects in the directory. Without these identifiers, no new objects can be created.

B. **Incorrect:** Objects can be written to any domain controller, so the PDC emulator role is not required.

C. **Incorrect:** This role is not involved with the creation of security principals within a domain.

D. **Incorrect:** This role is not suspect, as new objects have been created successfully to this point.

Objective 2.6
Troubleshoot User Accounts

User accounts provide the ability for users to authenticate and be granted access to resources both on the local computer and across the network. If properties of the user account are configured improperly, then one or more types of resource access will fail. Many problems of users not being able to accomplish their tasks on a computer are related to the settings within their user account.

The user properties for general access to the network include User Rights Assignments settings for local and network logon, Dial-in permissions, and Terminal Services access settings.

User preference configuration includes home directories and profile paths.

Logon configuration and restriction settings include password expiration, lockout policies, and the times that users are allowed to log on to selected workstations.

Objective 2.6 Questions

1.   A user reports that he or she cannot log on to the network from a laptop running Windows 98. The user can log on from a desktop computer that is running Windows XP.

Your environment is controlled by a Windows Server 2003 Active Directory domain.

The Windows 98 computer does not have the Active Directory Client installed.

What is the most likely cause of the problem?

   A. A computer account in the domain needs to be reset.

   B. The user's password is longer than 14 characters.

   C. The user's account needs to be configured to allow logon to all workstations.

   D. The user's home directory is corrupted.

2.   A user, John, reports that his profile settings are not roaming properly when he logs on to various computers on the network. John can log on to any computer in the environment successfully, but his desktop wallpaper, shortcuts, and other preferential settings are different on each computer.

You check the profile path in the user account properties, and see that it is set to "D:\profiles\John". You confirm that there is a folder named John in the profiles folder on the D: drive of Server01, which is the server that contains the user profiles for the network. The shared folder hosted off the profiles folder is also called Profiles.

Other users' profiles are roaming correctly.

What should you do to fix the problem?

   A. Reset John's password.

   B. Set the home directory for John to D:\Profiles*%Username%*.

   C. Set the profile path for John to \\Server01\Profiles*%Username%*.

   D. Copy the profile that John wants to use to D:\Profiles\John on the profile server.

3. A user reports that he or she cannot access the network by dialing in. The user can log on successfully to a local computer in the office.

You confirm that the default Remote Access policies are in place on the Routing and Remote Access Server computer. All modem devices pass diagnostic tests successfully.

What is likely the cause of the problem?

    A. The user does not have Terminal Server access enabled in his or her user account properties.

    B. The user does not have dial-in permission enabled in his or her user account properties.

    C. The user does not have a computer account in the domain for his or her remote computer.

    D. The user is not supplying the correct credentials when dialing in.

Objective 2.6 Answers

1. **Correct Answers: B**

   A. Incorrect: Windows 98 computers do not have a computer account in the domain.

   B. Correct: Windows 98 computers will not support user passwords longer than 14 characters. This can be remedied by installing the Active Directory Client.

   C. Incorrect: Windows 98 computers are not members of the domain, and cannot be controlled by this setting.

   D. Incorrect: The home directory is a repository for files, and would not prohibit logging on if corrupted.

2. **Correct Answers: C**

   A. Incorrect: John is able to log on, so the password is not the problem.

   B. Incorrect: Home directories and profiles are handled by different configurations, and none has to do with each other in this case.

   C. Correct: The profile path is set to a local drive letter, which corresponds to a drive on each local computer to which John logs on.

   D. Incorrect: Copying the profile will not solve the problem, as the configuration in the user properties is not set to a network location.

3. **Correct Answers: B**

   A. Incorrect: Terminal Server configuration settings are not used for dial-in permissions or access.

   B. Correct: The settings in the user account are likely prohibiting the user from accessing the network using a dial-in connection.

   C. Incorrect: This would not prohibit the user from dialing in to the network remotely.

   D. Incorrect: The user account is the same for both remote and local access, so confused credentials are unlikely.

Troubleshoot User Authentication

Without proper authentication, a user will be unable to access network resources, and, in some cases, will not be able to log on to his or her local computer. At the root of authentication is the combination of username and password which comprise the user's credentials. If there is a mismatch between what the user believes his or her credentials to be and what the authenticating system expects, the user will not be able to connect to that resource. If that resource is the local computer, the user will not be able to log on at all.

Objective 2.7 Questions

1. A traveling user has been away from the office for several months. The laptop computer with which the user travels is not configured for dial-in access to the corporate network because it is used mostly for presentations and client documentation.

    Upon returning to the office and connecting to the corporate network, the user is unable to log on to his or her computer using a local account, and is presented with the "Log on Failed" dialog box.

    What should you do?

    A. Reset the user's password in Active Directory.

    B. Reset the user's computer account in Active Directory.

    C. Use the password reset disk for that user to reset the password on the local computer.

    D. Disconnect the computer from the network, and then restart the computer.

2. A user has returned from an extended business trip, and reconnects his or her computer to the network. The user is able to log on, but is not able to connect to any network resources.

    You examine the accounts associated with the user in Active Directory Users And Computers, and note that the computer account for the user's laptop is marked with a red "X" icon.

    What should you do to solve the problem?

    A. Reset the user's password in Active Directory.

    B. Reset the laptop computer account in Active Directory.

    C. Delete the laptop computer account from the domain, join the laptop to a workgroup, then rejoin the laptop to the domain.

    D. Delete and recreate the laptop computer account.

3.   You are the systems administrator for a medium-sized organization that runs a single Windows Server 2003 domain. The Default Domain Group Policy object has the following password policy settings:

10 Passwords Remembered.

Maximum Password Age 10 days

Minimum Password Age 2 days

Minimum Password Length 10 characters

A group of 40 developers who work in a department in your organization has lobbied management for a separate set of password policies specific to its members. The developers want the minimum password age set to 0 days and the maximum password age set to 28 days. Which of the following methods will allow you to alter the password policy for this group of developers?

A. Create a child domain of the current domain and move the developers' accounts to this domain. Edit the Default Domain GPO of the child domain and implement the separate password policy requested by the developers.

B. Create a separate OU and move the 40 developers' user accounts into this OU. Create and edit a new GPO, implementing the separate password policy requested by the developers via this GPO. Apply the GPO to the newly created OU hosting the developers' accounts.

C. Resubnet the network and create a new site within Active Directory. Place all the 40 developers' workstations onto this new subnet. Create and edit a new GPO, implementing the separate password policy requested by the developers via this GPO. Apply the GPO to the newly created site hosting the developers' computer accounts.

D. Edit the Local GPO on each of the developer's workstations, implementing the separate password policy requested by the developers via this GPO.

Objective 2.7 Answers

1.   Correct Answers: C

A.   **Incorrect:** The "Logon Failed" dialog box appears only if a password reset disk has been created for an account on the local computer. The domain user account is not involved in this problem.

B.   **Incorrect:** The "Logon Failed" dialog box only appears if a password reset disk has been created for an account on the local computer. The domain computer account is not involved in this problem.

C.   **Correct:** The password reset disk is created for local user accounts, and can be used when a user is trying to access a local computer account with the incorrect credentials, as in this case.

D.   **Incorrect:** The computer's connection to the network or any network interaction does not cause the "Logon Failed" dialog box to appear.

2.   Correct Answers: B

A.   **Incorrect:** The user's password would not affect the computer account, as the icon indicates, in Active Directory.

B.   **Correct:** The password between the laptop and the domain computer account has become unsynchronized and must be reset.

C.   **Incorrect:** This would solve the problem, but might cause other problems if there are permissions set on resources for this laptop computer. Also, this process would take much more time than a computer password reset.

D.   **Incorrect:** This would compound the problem by not only having unsynchronized passwords, but mismatched SIDs as well.

3.   **Correct Answers: A**

A. **Correct:** Password policies apply domain-wide. The only method by which users can have separate password policies is if their user accounts reside in different domains. A child domain does not inherit the password policy of its parent domain.

B. **Incorrect:** Password policies apply domain-wide. Password policies applied at the OU level do not override the password policies set at the domain level. If this set of steps is taken, the password policies will remain as they did before at the domain level.

C. **Incorrect.:** Password policies apply domain-wide. Password policies applied at the site level do not override the password policies set at the domain level. If this set of steps is taken, the password policies will remain as they did before at the domain level.

D. **Incorrect:** Password policies apply domain-wide. Password policies applied at the local level do not override the password policies set at the domain level. If this set of steps is taken, the password policies will remain as they did before at the domain level.

16 Managing and Maintaining Access to Resources (3.0)

Access to resources requires proper identification and proper permissions. There is no additional configuration to be done to access files across a network than to make sure that the resource is accessible (shared) and that the user has appropriate permissions to accomplish the desired action (read, write, delete, and so on). This transactional process of analyzing the user's access token involves reading the entries on the access control list (ACL) of the resource, and comparing the list with the security identifiers (SIDs) on the token. If the security services governing the resource access process determine that the combination of SIDs and their permissions is sufficient to perform the requested task, permission and access is granted; if not, access to the resource is denied.

Such permission-based access is accomplished by the operating system based upon the file system that is installed on the storage device where the resource resides. On a FAT32 file system, for example, even if the operating system version is Windows Server 2003, permissions cannot be set at the file system level: NTFS permissions are required for this type of permission assignment.

Share permissions, however, can be set regardless of the file system on which the resources are stored. The operating system alone controls the share permissions, which are valid for any entity attempting to access the resource from across the network.

Terminal Services provides a different type of access to resources, in that it presents a local environment to the user over the network. The creation and use of this virtual local environment requires additional permissions and configuration, but the resource access to files and folders is still governed by network (share) and file system (NTFS) permissions. The understanding of these additional configuration needs and possibilities is key to the proper use of Terminal Services.

Testing Skills and Suggested Practices

The skills that you need to master the Managing and Maintaining Access to Resources objective domain on *Exam 70-290: Managing and Maintaining a Microsoft Window Server 2003 Environment* include

- Configure access to shared folders.
  - ❏ Practice 1: Set permissions for individual users and groups. Create increasingly complex sets of group memberships and permission assignments so as to make a 2–3 layer set of permissions using multiple group memberships for a user account, and nested memberships for groups.

❑ Practice 2: Configure sets of permissions on network share points. Configure NTFS permissions for the same resource, and analyze the effective resulting permissions for a user.

■ Troubleshoot terminal services.

❑ Practice 1: Configure Terminal Services in Remote Desktop for Administration mode such that various users are allowed or denied permissions. Set properties for allowed users to control their profile paths, home directories, and whether their sessions can be controlled remotely through another Terminal Services session.

❑ Practice 2: Configure Group Policy for Terminal Services users to redirect local printer and drive output to the Terminal Services session. Know the purposes and functionalities for each of these settings.

■ Configure file system permissions.

❑ Practice 1: Set permissions for individual users and groups. Create increasingly complex sets of group memberships and permission assignments so as to make a 2–3 layer set of permissions using multiple group memberships for a user account, and nested memberships for groups.

❑ Practice 2: Configure sets of NTFS permissions on file system objects. Configure share permissions for the same resource, and analyze the effective resulting permissions for a user.

■ Troubleshoot access to shared files and folders.

❑ Practice 1: Access the properties of a file for which you have set complex NTFS permissions for several groups of users. Select a user that is a member of more than one of the groups that you have assigned the permissions to for the file. Use the advanced button in the securities tab to access the "effective permissions" tab. Enter the user's name to discover his or her effective permissions to that file.

❑ Practice 2: Access the properties of a folder for which multiple groups have been given different NTFS permissions. Use the advanced button in the securities tab to access the "effective permissions" tab. Enter a group name to view the effective group permissions for that folder.

Further Reading

This section contains a list of supplemental readings divided by objective. Study these sources thoroughly before taking the exam.

Objective 3.1   Review Chapter 6, "Files and Folders." This chapter examines share permissions, NTFS permissions, and auditing of resource access.

Microsoft Corporation. *Frequently Asked Questions: Security Technologies.* This Web-based resource is free and can be accessed at the URL: *http://www.microsoft.com /windowsserver2003/community/centers/security/security_faq.asp.*

Objective 3.2   Review Chapter 2, Lesson 3, "Remote Administration with Terminal Services." This lesson discusses configuration and permission issues involved with Terminal Services, Remote Desktop, and Remote Assistance.

Microsoft Corporation. *Windows Server 2003, Help and Support Center: Remote Assistance.*

Objective 3.3   Review Chapter 6, "Files and Folders." This chapter explores share permissions, NTFS permissions, and auditing of resource access.

Microsoft Corporation. Technet; Script Center: Disks and File Systems. This Web-based resource is free, and can be accessed at the following URL: *http: //www.microsoft.com/technet/treeview/default.asp?url=/technet/scriptcenter/dfs /default.asp.*

Objective 3.4   Review Chapter 6, "Files and Folders." Examine the material on troubleshooting permissions, including how to view effective permissions.

Review the following article on Microsoft Technet: *http://www.microsoft.com /technet/prodtechnol/windowsserver2003/proddocs/standard/acl_view_effective _permissions.asp.*

Objective 3.1

Configure Access to Shared Folders

Share permissions are set within the Windows Server 2003 operating system on network access points—shares—within the file system. These share permissions are assigned in the folder properties interface (Sharing tab) in Windows Explorer. Individual files cannot be shared.

For multiple user entities, permissions are analyzed for each SID presented in the user's access token, and the most liberal permission is granted. The exception to this liberal permission assignment is when one (or more) of the SIDs presented in the token has a deny permission assigned in the resources' ACL; in that case, the deny permission takes precedence.

If NTFS permissions are in use on the file system, the effective share permission is compared to the effective NTFS permission, and the most restrictive permission is then assigned as the final, effective permission for the user on that resource.

Objective 3.1 Questions

1. Server01 is a file server running Microsoft Windows Server 2003 that is used by the accounting department to provide timesheet and expense report forms for employees. You are setting permissions on the share points for these folders, and must meet the following requirements:

- Employee-specific forms are stored in the Forms folder. These forms should be accessible by all employees.

- Only Authenticated Users should be able to access the forms.

- Employees can upload completed forms to a folder named Forms\Reports \<username>.

- Users should only be able to read their own forms, not forms submitted by other users.

- Supervisor-specific forms are stored in Forms\Supervisors. These forms should be accessible only by supervisors.

The Forms folder is shared as Forms, the Supervisors folder is shared as Supervisors, and each user's folder is shared as that user's username.

Supervisors are members of the Supervisors Global Group.

NTFS permissions are set on all folders to Authenticated Users–Modify.

Permissions are granted to the shared folders as follows:

Shared Folder	Share Permissions
Forms	Everyone, Allow Read
Supervisors	Supervisors, Allow Read
<username>	<username> Allow Change

Which of the following requirements is met? (Select all that apply.)

A. All employees can download their forms.

B. All employees can upload completed forms to their folders.

C. Employees can read only their own submitted forms.

D. Only Authenticated Users can download forms.

E. Only Supervisors can download Supervisor-specific forms.

2.   You are configuring share permissions for a shared folder on a file server. You want all Authenticated Users to be able to save files to the folder, read all files in the folder, and modify or delete files that they own.

What are the correct permissions that you need to set on the shared folder to achieve your objective? (Select all that apply.)

   A. Authenticated Users–Full Control

   B. Authenticated Users–Change

   C. Authenticated Users–Read

   D. Creator/Owner–Full Control

   E. Creator/Owner–Change

   F. Creator/Owner–Read

3.   You are configuring permissions for a shared folder on your network. You want all Authenticated Users to have read access to the files when attaching to the folder across the network from their computers, but only members of the Managers group should be able to read the files when logged on locally to the computer containing the files. Managers also need the ability to change the files when logged on locally.

All users are able to log on locally to the computer.

What permissions do you need to set on the shared folder? (Select all that apply.)

   A. NTFS–Interactive–Change

   B. NTFS–Interactive–Read

   C. NTFS–Authenticated Users–Change

   D. NTFS–Managers–Change

   E. Share Permission–Network–Read

   F. Share Permission–Interactive–Read

   G. Share Permission–Managers–Change

4. A folder, Documents, on Server01 is shared as Docs$. The permissions on the shared folder are set as follows:

- Docs$ Shared Folder Permissions: Everyone–Full Control
- Documents Folder NTFS Permissions: Authenticated Users–Read, Write; Managers–Modify; Administrators–Full Control

Which of the following statements regarding access to the resource are true? (Select all that apply.)

A. Only Administrators can access the shared folder from the network.

B. All Users can access the shared folder from the network.

C. Authenticated Users can delete files in the folder.

D. Managers can delete files in the folder.

E. Authenticated Users can write files in the folder.

F. Authenticated Users can change ownership of a file in the folder.

G. Managers can change ownership of a file in the folder.

1.   Correct Answers: A, B, and D

    A. Correct: All employees can access their forms through the Forms shared folder as part of the Everyone Group.

    B. Correct: All employees can access their user folders through the change permission assigned to them.

    C. Incorrect: Although the change permission on each username folder restricts access through that share point, any user can navigate to any individual folder through the Forms shared folder.

    D. Correct: In Windows Server 2003, by default, the Everyone group does not contain the identity Anonymous Logon.

    E. Incorrect: Although the users will not be able to access the Supervisors shared folder directly, they can navigate to it using the Forms shared folder.

2.   Correct Answers: C and E

    A. Incorrect: Giving Authenticated Users--Full Control permission will allow modification or deletion of any files in the folder, which gives more permission than required.

    B. Incorrect: Giving Authenticated Users--Change permission will allow modification of any files in the folder, which gives more permission that required.

    C. Correct: Giving Authenticated Users--Read permission will allow reading of any files in the folder, which fulfills the requirement.

    D. Incorrect: Giving permissions for Creator/Owner–Full Control will allow users to modify or delete their own files, but would also allow them to change permissions on the files. With the ability to change permissions, the Creator/Owner could set permissions that allow other users to modify or delete files.

    E. Correct: Giving permissions for Creator/Owner–Change will allow users who create the file to modify or delete it, which satisfies the requirements.

    F. Incorrect: Giving permissions for Creator/Owner–Read will not allow users to create or modify any files in the folder, which does not satisfy the requirements.

3.   Correct Answers: D and E

    A. Incorrect: This setting will allow any user logged on to the computer to change files. The NTFS permissions are the only permissions that apply to users logged on locally, which is what the Interactive entity group includes.

B. Incorrect: This setting will allow any user logged on to the computer to read files, which violates the requirements. The NTFS permissions are the only permissions which apply to users logged on locally, which is what the Interactive entity group includes.

C. Incorrect: This setting will allow any user logged on to the computer to read files, which violates the requirements. The NTFS permissions are the only permissions which apply to users logged on locally, which is what the Interactive entity group includes.

D. Correct: This setting will allow for the Managers to have change permission when logged on locally. They will also have the change permission when accessing the file from the network unless the share permissions are more restrictive.

E. Correct: This setting will allow all users who access the folder from across the network to have read access. With no other share permissions assigned, the Managers will not have any additional access to the files outside the context of their being in the Network entity group.

F. Incorrect: The interactive permission, although it can be set, does not have any effect for users attaching across the network. The Interactive entity group is for users who log on locally at the console of the computer.

G. Incorrect: This setting will allow the Managers to change the files from across the network, which violates the requirements: the Managers are only to be able to read and modify files when they are logged on locally to the computer.

4.   Correct Answers: B, D, and E

A. Incorrect: The $ in the share name hides the share from the browse list, but does not affect the permissions of the share available from the network. Although any shares created by the operating system as hidden shares to the root of a drive are configured with Administrator-only access permission, any hidden shares created manually do not have the Administrator-only access permissions set.

B. Correct: The combination of Full Control shared folder permissions and Read, Write NTFS permissions allow for access from the network by Authenticated Users.

C. Incorrect: Users do not have Delete or Modify permissions, which are required to delete files.

D. Correct: The NTFS Modify permission allows Managers to delete files.

E. Correct: The NTFS Write permission allows Authenticated Users to write files to the folder.

F. Incorrect: The NTFS Read, Write permissions are insufficient to allow modification of file ownership.

G. Incorrect: The NTFS Modify permission is insufficient to allow modification of file ownership.

Objective 3.2
Troubleshoot Terminal Services

Terminal Services has unique permission and configuration settings compared with share permissions on other resources. The use of Terminal Services requires User Rights (log on locally, for example) for the computer on which Terminal Services is running in addition to the explicit permission to use Terminal Services. In Windows Server 2003, all these rights and permission for the use of Terminal Services are given to the Remote Desktop Users group.

The settings in Terminal Services for Remote Control, home directory, application startup, and profile settings should not be confused with the permissions and User Rights needed to access Terminal Services.

Objective 3.2 Questions

1. You have configured several users to be able to connect to Server01 through Terminal Services, and have modified the default configuration with the Terminal Services Configuration console to allow for redirection of client printers. The goal is for all users of the Terminal Server to be able to print to print devices configured on their local computer from their Terminal Server session.

The users, however, report that they are unable to print to their locally configured print devices.

What should you do to correct the problem?

A. Enable the Client/Server data redirection setting in Group Policy for each Terminal Server client computer.

B. Enable the Client/Server data redirection setting in Group Policy for the Terminal Server computer.

C. Instruct the user to install the local printer from within their Terminal Server session.

D. Use a logon script for the users' Terminal Server session to add the printer.

2. You have configured several client computers with the Terminal Service client, Remote Desktop Connection, and have configured a Terminal Server in Remote Desktop for Administration (default) mode. When the users attempt to connect to the Terminal Server, they receive an error message stating that the local policy of this system does not permit them to log on interactively.

What should you do to correct the problem?

A. Add the users to the Remote Desktop Users group.

B. Configure the User Right to Log on locally on the Terminal Server for each user.

C. Enable the Group Policy setting for Client/Server data redirection.

D. Enable the Terminal Services Remote Control setting for each user.

3.   A user has sent you a request, by e-mail, for a Remote Assistance session. You attempt to connect to the user's computer to establish the Remote Desktop session, but cannot establish the network connection.

You are able to connect to the user's computer to access the file system through the C$ share.

What is the most likely cause of the problem?

  A. Your user account is not a member of the local Administrators group on the user's computer.

  B. You do not have the Terminal Services client installed on your computer.

  C. Port 3389 is not open on the firewall between your network segment and the network segment that the user's computer is on.

  D. The user's account in Active Directory is configured so as not to allow Remote Control.

4.   All computer users in your company access several applications through a single Terminal Server, Server01, located on the same Local Area Network segment. You are running a Windows Server 2003 Active Directory and DNS, and the Terminal Server is a Windows Server 2003 server.

At the end of business on the previous day, you renamed the Terminal Server to App1. You verified that the server was reachable using its new name through Terminal Services both as administrator and as a regular user, and through Windows Explorer.

This morning, all users report that they cannot connect to the Terminal Server. You verify that connection to the Terminal Server is possible through Windows Explorer, but that user connection through Terminal Services is not possible. You are able to connect to the Terminal Server as Administrator.

What is the most likely cause of the problem?

  A. The Terminal Server entry in DNS needs to be refreshed.

  B. The Terminal Server connection permissions need to be refreshed.

  C. A Terminal Services Licensing Server needs to be installed and configured.

  D. The Terminal Server needs to be restarted.

5.   You attempt to connect to Server01 through the Remote Desktop for Administration client, but receive a message that you cannot connect because the number of concurrent connections has been exceeded.

You can connect with the Remote Desktop for Administration client to Server02, Server03, and Server04, which are member servers in the same domain. You have administrator privileges on each of these servers.

Server01 is not physically accessible to you, as it is in a remote location.

What steps should you take to resolve the problem? (Select all that apply.)

   A. Connect to Server02 with the Remote Desktop for Administration client.

   B. Connect to Server01 from the Terminal Services session on Server02 with the Terminal Services Manager. Disconnect one of the Remote sessions.

   C. Connect to Server01 from the Terminal Services session on Server02 with the Remote Desktop for Administration client. Disconnect one of the Remote sessions.

   D. Open the Server01 Properties dialog box from Active Directory Users And Computers. Configure Server01 to deny Terminal Services connections, and then reconfigure Server01 to allow Terminal Services connections.

   E. Connect to Server01 from the Terminal Services session on Server02 with the Remote Desktop for Administration client. Open the System properties page for Server01 and configure Server01 to deny Remote Desktop Connections, and then reconfigure Server01 to allow Remote Desktop Connections.

Objective 3.2 Answers

1.   Correct Answers: A

A. Correct: Although set to Not Configured by default, if set to Disabled, this Group Policy setting will override the Terminal Server console settings for the property of data redirection. Changing this policy from Disabled to Enabled will correct the problem.

B. Incorrect: This Group Policy setting is for local computer behavior during a Terminal Services session from that computer. Enabling this setting for the Terminal Server computer would control outgoing Terminal Server sessions from that console, not incoming from the client computers as required here.

C. Incorrect: This would configure a network printer connection to the local computer, which is not what the circumstance requires. Additional steps to share and set permissions for the printer from the local computer would have to be taken.

D. Incorrect: This would configure a network printer connection to the local computer, which is not what the circumstance requires. Additional steps to share and set permissions for the printer from the local computer would have to be taken.

2.   Correct Answers: A

A. Correct: The Remote Desktop Users group has the appropriate configuration and rights to allow access to the Terminal Server.

B. Incorrect: This setting will remove one of the barriers to the user's connecting to the Terminal Server, but there are permissions for connection to the Terminal Server itself that still must be set. Additionally, this action would allow the user to log on locally to the console as well, which may not be desired.

C. Incorrect: This setting is for controlling how printer and drive redirection is accomplished within a user session, not for configuring logon access to the session itself.

D. Incorrect: This setting is for controlling how Remote Control can be used on an established Terminal Services session, not for the logon access to the session itself.

3.   Correct Answers: C

A. Incorrect: This is not the case, seeing as you are able to establish a connection to an administrative share point (C$) on the user's computer.

B. Incorrect: The Terminal Services client is not involved in a Remote Assistance session. The Windows Messenger Services are responsible for handling the establishment and usage of a Remote Assistance session.

C. Correct: The Remote Assistance services use port 3389 to communicate. If you are unable to establish a connection to the user's computer, this is likely the problem.

D. Incorrect: This setting controls whether or not Remote Control is allowed of a user's Terminal Server session, not Remote Assistance.

4.   Correct Answers: C

A. Incorrect: Because the computer is reachable through Windows Explorer, name resolution is not the problem.

B. Incorrect: The connection permissions were configured properly, as you verified after the name change on the Terminal Server, and there are no other refresh problems that would occur. These permissions are not affected by any DNS or Group Policy refreshing mechanism.

C. Correct: This is likely the cause of the problem. Terminal Services will install and run properly for 120 days. After this period has expired, the Terminal Server will refuse connections until a License Server is configured and available.

D. Incorrect: The service is not likely to be the problem because you can connect as Administrator, and the service was running properly when tested after the server name change.

5.   Correct Answers: A and B

A. Correct: By connecting to another Terminal Server (any of the others accessible to you would suffice), you will gain access to the Terminal Services Manager console, which is how you will disconnect one of the established Terminal Services sessions to Server01, allowing you to establish another under your credentials.

B. Correct: The Terminal Services Manager can connect to any server in the domain that is running Terminal Services. From the Terminal Services Manager, you are able to disconnect one of the remote sessions, allowing you to establish another under your credentials.

C. Incorrect: If you are unable to connect to Server01 using the Remote Desktop client on your computer, the same denial of connection will occur if you attempt to connect from any other computer, regardless of whether or not that other computer is a Terminal Server.

D. Incorrect: This is not a valid option. The Properties dialog box of a system in Active Directory Users And Computers does not allow the configuration of Terminal Services.

E. Incorrect: This disabling/enabling exercise will not change any configuration on the computer, nor will it disconnect any active sessions. Because the denial of your remote connection is due to the limit on the number of sessions, the problem persists.

Objective 3.3

Configure File System Permissions

To set permissions on objects (folders and files) within the file system, you must be able to add entries to the access control list (ACL) of the object. ACLs are part of the NTFS file system, so that file system must be installed on any computer on which there are resources that you wish to secure through the file system.

NTFS permissions function in the same way as share permissions in terms of blending to effective permissions. All the SIDs that are listed in your user token are compared with the entries in the ACL for a resource. All of the permissions for your various SIDs are sorted, and the most liberal permission is given.

Exceptions to this liberal blending are if any of the permissions associated with one of your SIDs is a deny permission: in that case, the deny permission overrides.

Objective 3.3 Questions

1. A user, Joe, has an account in the *contoso.com* domain, and is a member of the Sales global group. The permissions on the Documents folder on the file server, output using the Cacls command, are as follows:

```
C:\>cacls documents

C:\Documents CONTOSO\Joe:(OI)(CI)(DENY)(special access:)

                              READ_CONTROL

                              FILE_READ_DATA

                              FILE_READ_EA

                              FILE_READ_ATTRIBUTES


             CONTOSO\Sales:(OI)(CI)(DENY)(special access:)

                              FILE_WRITE_DATA

                              FILE_APPEND_DATA

                              FILE_WRITE_EA

                              FILE_WRITE_ATTRIBUTES


             BUILTIN\Administrators:F

             CONTOSO\Sales:(CI)R

             CONTOSO\Sales:(OI)(CI)(special access:)

                              READ_CONTROL

                              SYNCHRONIZE

                              FILE_GENERIC_READ

                              FILE_READ_DATA

                              FILE_READ_EA

                              FILE_READ_ATTRIBUTES
```

```
BUILTIN\Administrators:(OI)(CI)F

NT AUTHORITY\SYSTEM:(OI)(CI)F

CREATOR OWNER:(OI)(CI)(IO)F

BUILTIN\Users:(OI)(CI)R

BUILTIN\Users:(CI)(special access:)

            FILE_APPEND_DATA


BUILTIN\Users:(CI)(special access:)

            FILE_WRITE_DATA
```

What are Joe's effective permissions on the Documents folder?

A. Access Denied

B. Read

C. Change

D. Full Control

2.   You are configuring the permissions for a shared folder, Finance, on your file server, Server01. You need to configure permissions for the Accounting and AccountingExec groups on the folder to achieve the following objectives:

The Accounting group should have Read access to content in the Finance folder.

The AccountingExec group should have Change control over content in the Finance folder.

All users need Read access to a file named Summary.rpt in the Finance folder. Users should have access to no other files in the folder.

How will you configure share and NTFS permissions on the Finance folder?

A. Share: Accounting–Read; AccountingExec–Read; Users–Read
NTFS: Accounting–Read; AccountingExec–Modify; Users–Read

B. Share: Accounting–Full Control; AccountingExec–Full Control; Users–Read
NTFS: Accounting–Read; AccountingExec–Modify; Users–List, Read access on Summary.rpt

C. Share: Accounting–Read; AccountingExec–Modify; Users–Read
NTFS: Accounting–Read; AccountingExec–Full Control; Users–Read

D. Share: Accounting–Full Control; AccountingExec–Full Control; Users–Deny Read
NTFS: Accounting–Read; AccountingExec–Read; Users–List, Read access on Summary.rpt

3.   Current permissions set on the shared folder Documents are shown in the following graphic:

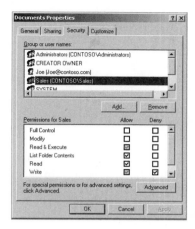

Which of the following statements is true of the permissions for the Sales Group? (Select all that apply.)

   A. Attributes of the folder can be read.

   B. Attributes of the folder can be written.

   C. Files can be written to the folder.

   D. Files cannot be written to the folder.

   E. Files can be read from the folder.

   F. Files cannot be read from the folder.

4.   A folder called Reports on Server01 resides in the Marketing\Summary folder. The Marketing folder is shared on the network with the name MKTG.

Users should not be able to read, modify, or add any files in the Marketing or Summary folders, but need to have access to the files in the Reports folder.

What is the minimum NTFS permission that these users need on the Marketing and Summary folders to access the files in the Reports folder from across the network?

   A. List Folder/Read Data

   B. Traverse Folder/Execute Files

   C. Read Extended Attributes

   D. Read Attributes

Objective 3.3 Answers

1.   Correct Answers: A

    A. Correct: The Deny–Read permission assigned to Joe's user account, processed at the top of the list of permissions, overrides all others, blocking his access to the folder.

    B. Incorrect: The Deny–Read permission assigned to Joe's user account, processed at the top of the list of permissions, overrides all others, blocking his access to the folder.

    C. Incorrect: The Deny–Read permission assigned to Joe's user account, processed at the top of the list of permissions, overrides all others, blocking his access to the folder.

    D. Incorrect: The Deny–Read permission assigned to Joe's user account, processed at the top of the list of permissions, overrides all others, blocking his access to the folder.

2.   Correct Answers: B

    A. Incorrect: These settings allow users full read access to all files in the Finance folder, which violates the requirements.

    B. Correct: These settings allow users read access through the share point, but with no permissions on the files through NTFS, except for the appropriate Read access to Summary.rpt, these settings meet the requirements.

    C. Incorrect: These settings allow users complete Read access to the Finance folder, which violates the requirements.

    D. Incorrect: These settings allow the Users appropriate access to the Summary.rpt file, but the NTFS settings restrict the AccountingExec users to Read access on all files in the Finance folder, which violates the requirements.

3.   Correct Answers: A, D, and E

    A. Correct: The Read permission, assigned both implicitly and explicitly, allows for the reading of attributes. Specific settings which restrict the reading of attributes can be made, but that would force the checkbox at this summary level of permission to be clear, not checked.

    B. Incorrect: Write permissions, granted to the Sales group implicitly but denied explicitly, mean that the Write permission is denied to the Sales group on this resource. Explicit Deny permissions override Inherited Allow permissions. The Write permissions include the writing of attributes.

C. Incorrect: Write permissions, granted to the Sales group implicitly but denied explicitly, mean that the Write permission is denied to the Sales group on this resource. Explicit Deny permissions override Inherited Allow permissions. The Write permissions include the creation of files.

D. Correct: Write permissions, granted to the Sales group implicitly but denied explicitly, mean that the Write permission is denied to the Sales group on this resource. Explicit Deny permissions override Inherited Allow permissions. The Write permissions include the writing of attributes.

E. Correct: The Read permission, assigned both implicitly and explicitly, allows for the reading of files within the folder.

F. Incorrect: The Read permission, assigned both implicitly and explicitly, allows for the reading of files within the folder.

4. **Correct Answers: B**

A. Incorrect: While this will allow users access to the Reports folder, it will also allow for the listing of files within the folder, and is not the minimally required permission.

B. Correct: This permission will allow the users to navigate through the Marketing and Summary folders to access the Reports folder. The users will not be able to access (or even list) any files in the Marketing or Summary folders.

C. Incorrect: Being able to read the extended attributes of the folders will not allow access to subfolders.

D. Incorrect: Being able to read the attributes of the folders will not allow access to subfolders.

Troubleshoot Access to Files and Shared Folders

When permissions are set for a resource, the rules of access are unbreakable. If a user attempts to gain access to a resource, and the effective permissions deny access, then access is denied. That is the expected part.

The unexpected part comes when resource access is thought to be configured properly, but is not. In these misconfigurations, either a user cannot access resources that they need to, or they can gain access to resources that they should not be able to. Either way, not a good situation.

The misconfiguration usually comes in one of two flavors: either the user is not a member of a group that has permission to the resource, or there is a precedence of share and NTFS permissions that you did not expect. Either way, a careful analysis of the configuration of group memberships and permission assignments should solve most resources access problems.

Objective 3.4 Questions

1. A user calls the help desk and states that he or she cannot log on to the network. Using Active Directory Users And Computers, you examine the Active Directory and determine that the user account does not exist. Further investigation into the Directory Service Event logs indicates that the account was deleted.

You re-create the user account in Active Directory Users And Computers. What else will you need to do to complete the restoration of the user's access to resources? (Select all that apply.)

   A. Place the user's account in the appropriate groups.

   B. Reset the computer account.

   C. Reassign and apply any appropriate Group Policies to the user account.

   D. Re-permission resources to which permission was given or denied based on the user account.

   E. Re-permission resources to which permission was given or denied based on group membership.

2. A user, Joe, is taking on additional network administrative responsibility for his department, Finance. From Joe's computer, logged on as Joe, you use the Run As command with your administrative credentials to load the Active Directory Users And Computers snap-in, and then you add Joe to the Department's Itadmin3 group, which has delegated administrative permissions for the user accounts in the Finance OU. You then close the Active Directory Users And Computers snap-in.

When Joe attempts to reset a user's password in the Finance OU, he is denied access.

What additional step do you need to take in order for the user to be able to perform the delegated administrative duties?

   A. Add Joe's user account to the Built-in Account Operators group for the domain.

   B. Add Joe's user account to the Itadmin3 OU.

   C. Reset Joe's computer account.

   D. Instruct Joe to log off, and then log on to his computer.

3. A user, Joe, has a user account that is a member of the Sales OU in the *contoso.com* domain. His user account is also a member of the Employees global group.

After Joe's departmental assignment to Finance, you make Joe's user account a member of the Finance global group. Joe then logs on to his computer and attempts to access a shared folder named Documents on Server01, but receives an Access Denied message when he tries to save any files to the folder.

The share Permissions on the Documents share are listed below.

Security Principal	Permissions
Joe (User Account)	Allow: Read
Finance (Global Group)	Allow: Read
Employees (Global Group)	Allow: Read

The NTFS permissions set on the Documents folder are listed below.

Security Principal	Permissions
Joe (User Account)	Allow: Read
Finance (Global Group)	Allow: Read, Write
Employees (Global Group)	Allow: Read
System	Allow: Full Control
Administrators	Allow: Full Control

Why can't Joe access the Documents folder?

A. Share permissions are overriding the NTFS permissions.

B. Joe's user account needs to be moved to the Finance OU.

C. The NTFS permissions for Joe's user account need to be removed, allowing the group NTFS permissions to take effect.

D. Joe's user account needs to be removed from the Employee global group.

Objective 3.4 Answers

1.   **Correct Answers: A and D**

> **A.** **Correct:** The user account will need to be made a member of the same group as the deleted user account. If the user account already exists in groups you're adding it to, it will need to be removed first, and then added again. The previous account, although using the same account name will have a different SID. Resource permissions for the group will not have to be reassigned because the only piece of information that is changing in this situation is the membership of the group.

> **B.** **Incorrect:** The computer account is not tied to a particular user account, so it need not be reset. Resetting the computer account is only necessary when the computer account becomes unsynchronized with the domain.

> **C.** **Incorrect:** Group policies are applied to Sites, Domains, and Organizational Units. Whatever Organizational Unit the new user account is placed within, the Group Policies for that OU, and the Group Policies at the domain level, will apply automatically and refresh automatically as soon as the user logs on.

> **D.** **Correct:** Any individual user account permission assignments that were made will have to be re-created. If the user account already exists in groups you're adding it to, it will need to be removed first, then added. The previous account, although using the same account name will have a different SID.

> **E.** **Incorrect:** The permissions for groups have not changed, just the membership, so no new permissions for the groups are needed based on the group taking on a new member. The user's token will add the list of all groups of which the user is a member to its list of SIDs when the user logs on.

2.   **Correct Answers: D**

   A. **Incorrect:** This action will extend Joe's authority far beyond the boundaries of the Finance OU to include the entire domain. There may also be additional capabilities and permissions that are associated with the Account Operators group that have not been delegated to the Itadmin3 group.

   B. **Incorrect:** The OU membership of Joe's account has nothing to do with his permission to administer the user accounts in the Finance OU. Group membership in the Itadmin3 group is what gives the delegated authority, not the user's account membership in an OU.

   C. **Incorrect:** Resetting of a computer account is necessary when a computer becomes unsynchronized from the domain, and is unrelated to the permissions of the user logged on to the computer at the time. As long as the computer can communicate with the domain, which it can as evidenced by Joe being logged on and able to attach to Active Directory, the user's permissions are what govern their ability to perform an administrative task such as this one.

   D. **Correct:** The group membership will not take effect until Joe's credentials are re-evaluated and a new token assigned that contains his new group membership. This token assignment occurs only at logon. Because Joe was logged on to his computer at the time of the group membership change, his token does not contain the SIDs associated with his new group membership.

3.   **Correct Answers: A**

   A. **Correct:** The share permissions of Read for Joe's user account and the Finance global group are limiting his access to Read permission. The most restrictive of the two effective permissions between NTFS and share permissions will take effect.

   B. **Incorrect:** The location of Joe's user account in the Active Directory has nothing to do with resource access. Users, Groups, and Computers are the only directory objects that are security principals, being able to have resource permissions assigned.

   C. **Incorrect:** Joe's effective NTFS permission is Read, Write because of his membership in the Finance global group. The restriction is coming from his effective share permission of read, not through a limitation of NTFS permissions.

   D. **Incorrect:** Removing Joe from the Employees global group will have no effect in this case, because the restriction of Write permission derives from the share permission, not an NTFS permission. Once either Joe's user account or Finance global group share permission is raised, Joe will be able to write files to the Documents folder.

17 Managing and Maintaining a Server Environment (4.0)

Managing a Microsoft Windows Server 2003 system requires an awareness of what is occurring on the system. The best place to find this information is in the event logs. The three main event logs that are on a Windows Server 2003 system are the System, Security, and Application logs. Event log views can be filtered so that only information in which the administrator is interested is displayed.

Another part of server management is ensuring that relevant updates are downloaded and applied to the system on a timely basis. Many of the largest system vulnerabilities of the last few years had already been patched by Microsoft, but systems administrators had not found the time to install those patches on servers. If administrators had found the time to install those patches, they would not have been vulnerable to such worms as Code Red and Slammer. Software Update Services (SUS) runs of Windows Server 2003 and allows an organization to use a Windows Server running on their network as the update server from which to download patches from Microsoft, rather than using Microsoft's Update servers located on the Internet.

Licensing is another area that requires attention. If the company is audited for license compliance and is found wanting, the punishment for infringement can be severe. Understanding clearly how licensing works can also save a company money because a company may find better licensing options than those it currently uses.

Several tools exist to manage servers remotely. These include Terminal Services, Remote Assistance, the Computer Management Console, and HTML remote administration tools. Each can be used in a specific situation to perform a specific set of tasks. Administrators should be aware of the benefits and limitations of each form of remote management.

The ability to maintain a reliable file and print server infrastructure is also important. System administrators must be able to diagnose and troubleshoot problems on file and print servers as well as monitor file and print server performance to determine if anything must be done to improve that performance.

Testing Skills and Suggested Practices

The skills that you need to master the Managing and Maintaining A Server Environment objective domain on *Exam 70-290: Managing and Maintaining a Microsoft Window Server 2003 Environment* include

- Monitor and analyze events.
    - ❑ Practice 1: Set up a filter on the Security log to look for all events that have been generated by the Administrator account.
    - ❑ Practice 2: Set up a filter on the System log to look for all failed device events that have occurred in the last week.

- Manage software update infrastructure.
    - ❑ Practice 1: Install and configure the SUS add-in to generate a list of updates that you have approved and to download those updates to the SUS server. Use Group Policy to configure a Windows XP Professional system to use the SUS server as its Automatic Updates server.
    - ❑ Practice 2: Deploy a service pack using Group Policy to a Windows XP Professional system.

- Manage software site licensing.
    - ❑ Practice 1: Run the Licensing console located in Control Panel and read the help menu about switching from Per Server to Per User/Per Device.
    - ❑ Practice 2: Install the License Logging Server on a Windows Server 2003 system.

- Manage servers remotely.
    - ❑ Practice 1: Install the Hypertext Markup Language (HTML) remote administration tools on a Windows Server 2003 member server and use the tools to change the server name.
    - ❑ Practice2: Log on to a remote Windows Server 2003 system using Terminal Services Remote Desktop for Administration mode.

- Troubleshoot issues related to print queues.
    - ❑ Practice 1: Create two shared printers that point to the same physical print device. Set the priority on one shared printer to 99 and the priority on the second shared printer to 1. Submit five print jobs to each and determine which shared printer completes its jobs first.
    - ❑ Practice 2: Send several print jobs to a printer. Pause one print job and rearrange the priority of the others to see how the order in which the jobs are printed changes.

- Monitor events.

  ❑ Practice 1: Configure auditing of account management events in the domain using Group Policy. Create five user accounts and two groups. Change the passwords on three of the new user accounts. View the Security log on the domain controller to see what events have been written there.

  ❑ Practice 2: Configure auditing of object access events in the domain. Edit the properties of a shared folder to allow auditing on the Everyone group. Use several different accounts to access the shared folder and then examine the Security log on the server that hosts the shared folder.

- Monitor current system performance.

  ❑ Practice 1: Create a Performance console view displaying the average values of the % Processor Time, Current Disk Queue Length and Available Memory in either kilobytes or megabytes.

  ❑ Practice 2: Create a Performance console view displaying the average % Processor Time values for several different applications running on the server.

- Monitor file and print servers.

  ❑ Practice 1: Enable a 10-megabyte (MB) quota for all users on a volume except the administrator. Create a shared folder on the volume. Open the shared volume on a Windows XP workstation with a non-administrator account. Try to copy more than 10 MB of data to the share.

  ❑ Practice 2: Set up a set of individual quotas on a volume on a Windows Server 2003 system. Set one user's quota to 10 MB, another user's quota to 15 MB, and a third user's quota to 20 MB. Export these quotas to a file and then import them to another volume.

- Manage a Web server.

  ❑ Practice 1: Configure a second IP address on the Ethernet adapter on a Windows Server 2003 system with Internet Information Services (IIS) installed. Configure one Web site to respond to HTTP requests on the first IP address and another Web site to respond to requests on the second IP address.

  ❑ Practice 2: Configure Web site security so that only hosts with particular IP addresses can access the Web site. Attempt to access the Web site from an allowed host and from a denied host IP address to check that the security works.

  ❑ Practice 3: Configure two Web sites to run off a single IP address, directing content using Host Header names.

Further Reading

This section lists supplemental readings by objective. We recommend that you study these sources thoroughly before taking this exam.

Objective 4.1   Review Chapter 12, "Monitoring Microsoft Windows Server 2003," which contains a lesson about using Event Viewer.

Microsoft Corporation. Windows Server 2003 Help And Support Center. Review "Event Viewer."

Objective 4.2   Review Chapter 9, "Maintaining the Operating System," which contains lessons about using Software Update Services and deploying service packs.

Microsoft Corporation. Windows Server 2003 Help And Support Center. Review "Deploying Software Updates."

Objective 4.3   Review Chapter 9, "Maintaining the Operating System," which contains a lesson about administering software licensing.

Microsoft Corporation. Windows Server 2003 Help And Support Center. Review "Licensing."

Objective 4.4   Review Chapter 2, "Administering Microsoft Windows Server 2003," which provides information about managing servers remotely with the MMC, Remote Administration with Remote Desktop for Administration, and using Remote Assistance.

Microsoft Corporation. Windows Server 2003 Help And Support Center. Review "Terminal Services," "HTML Remote Administration Tools," and "Remote Assistance."

Objective 4.5   Review Chapter 8, "Printers," which includes information about maintaining, monitoring, and troubleshooting printers.

Objective 4.6   Review Chapter 12, "Monitoring Microsoft Windows Server 2003," which includes a lesson about using Event Viewer.

Microsoft Corporation. Windows Server 2003 Help And Support Center. Review "Event Viewer."

Objective 4.7   Review Chapter 12, "Monitoring Microsoft Windows Server 2003," which includes a lesson about using System Monitor.

Microsoft Corporation. Windows Server 2003 Help And Support Center. Review "Performance."

Objective 4.8   Review Chapter 8, "Printers," which includes a lesson about advanced printer configuration and management.

Microsoft Corporation. Windows Server 2003 Help And Support Center. Review "Shared Printers."

Objective 4.9   Review Chapter 6, "Files and Folders," which includes a lesson about administering IIS.

Microsoft Corporation. Windows Server 2003 Help And Support Center. Review "Internet Information Services."

Objective 4.1

Monitor and Analyze Events

The Event log can be configured to record a vast amount of information about the system. Being able to sift that data to find a particular set of events can be difficult unless you know how to filter the logs to show only the type of information in which you are interested.

Events in the Event log can be filtered in several ways. The first is by specifying the event type, which can be Information, Warning, Error, Success Audit, or Failure Audit. The next type is the Event Source, the system or service on the Windows Server 2003 server that has generated the event. The category lists which subsystem of the server has generated the event. Events can also be filtered by Event ID, User name, Computer name, and can be limited to a specific set of dates. Efficiently filtering the Event log can quickly allow an administrator to view only the relevant data and not have to wade through events that are irrelevant to the task at hand.

Objective 4.1 Questions

1. You are interested in viewing Information and Warning events in the Application log generated by disk quotas. You only wish to view these types of events, not information and warning events from other sources. Which of the following steps should you take to do this?

    A. From the Event Viewer, edit the properties of the System log. In the Filter tab make sure that the Information and Warning events check boxes are selected and that the Error, Success Audit and Failure Audit check boxes are clear.

    B. From the Event Viewer, edit the properties of the Application log. In the Filter tab, make sure that the Information and Warning event check boxes are selected and that the Error, Success Audit and Failure Audit check boxes are clear.

    C. From the Event Viewer, edit the properties of the Application log. In the Filter tab, make sure that the Information and Warning Events check boxes are clear and that the Error, Success Audit and Failure Audit check boxes are selected. Set the Event Source to Disk Quota.

    D. From the Event Viewer, edit the properties of the Application log. In the Filter tab, make sure that the Information and Warning Events check boxes are selected and that the Error, Success Audit and Failure Audit check boxes are clear. Set the Event Source to Chkdsk.

    E. From the Event Viewer, edit the properties of the Application log. In the Filter tab, make sure that the Information and Warning Events check boxes are selected and that the Error, Success Audit and Failure Audit check boxes are unchecked. Set the Event Source to Disk Quota.

    F. From the Event Viewer, edit the properties of the System log. In the Filter tab, make sure that the Information and Warning Events check boxes are selected and that the Error, Success Audit and Failure Audit check boxes are clear. Set the Event Source to Disk Quota.

2. Rooslan is working with a Windows Server 2003 system that has been behaving erratically. The System log is set to a maximum log size of 50 MB and to overwrite events as needed. Rooslan wants to view Error events in the System log that have occurred over the last week. How can he do this?

    A. Run the Event Viewer Wizard and select the Display Errors check box. Set the display date to the last seven days.

    B. In the Event Viewer, Rooslan should edit the properties of the System log. In the Filters tab, he should make sure that only the Error check box is selected.

    C. In the Event Viewer, Rooslan should edit the properties if the Application log. In the Filters tab, he should make sure that only the Error check box is selected and that the first event date is set to the date seven days previously and the last event is set to today's date.

   D. In the Event Viewer, Rooslan should edit the properties of the System log. In the Filters tab, Rooslan should make sure that only the Error check box is selected and that the first event date is set to the date seven days previously and the last event is set to today's date.

   E. In the Event Viewer, Rooslan should edit the properties of the System log. In the Filters tab, Rooslan should make sure that only the Information check box is selected and that the first event date is set to the date seven days previously and the last event is set to today's date.

3. Rooslan has been instructed by senior management to generate a report on the logon activities of a particular user named Agim over the last two months. Management is trying to use Agim's logon activity to determine which days Agim came to work because his attendance has been erratic. Logon events have been audited within the Windows Server 2003 domain for the last six months. The size of all Event log files is set to 190,240 KB. No Event log has yet to be filled and data from the last six months is available. Which of the following represents the best way to display the data relevant to Rooslan's task?

   A. Create a filter on the System log. Look only for success audits and set the Event Source to Security. Set the First Event to a date two months ago and the Last Event to today.

   B. Create a filter on the System log. Look only for success audits and set the Event Source to Security. Set the User setting to Agim's account name. Set the First Event to a date two months ago and the Last Event to today.

   C. Create a filter on the System log. Look only for success audits and set the Event Source to Security Account Manager. Set the User setting to Agim's account name. Set the Event ID to 538. Set the First Event to a date two months ago and the Last Event to today.

   D. Create a filter on the Security log. Look only for success audits and set the Event Source to Security. Set the First Event to a date two months ago and the Last Event to today. Set the Event ID to 538.

   E. Create a filter on the Security log. Look only for success audits and set the Event Source to Security Account Manager. Set the User setting to Agim's account name. Set the Event ID to 538. Set the First Event to a date two months ago and the Last Event to today.

   F. Create a filter on the Security log. Look only for success audits and set the Event Source to Security. Set the User setting to Agim's account name. Set the Event ID to 538. Set the First Event to a date two months ago and the Last Event to today.

4.   Lee is concerned that another user in the office is attempting to log on to his workstation using his account. He does not believe that this has yet occurred, but he would like you to display a report of all the times that his account has experienced a logon failure in the past month. As a way of testing his hypothesis, Lee placed a note near his monitor with the words "Password = Gillian1948." Gillian1948 is not his password. He assumes that if someone had tried to log on to his workstation illicitly, then the dummy password has been tried. Only Logon Events are being audited for both success and failure in the domain. How can you generate a view in the Event Viewer to determine if there have been failed attempts to log on using Lee's user account?

A. Create a filter on the System log. Look only for failure audits and set the Event Source to Security. Set the User setting to Lee's account name. Set the First Event to a date one month ago and the Last Event to today.

B. Create a filter on the System log. Look only for success audits and set the Event Source to Security. Set the User setting to Lee's account name. Set the First Event to a date one month ago and the Last Event to today.

C. Create a filter on the System log. Look only for success audits and set the Event Source to Security Account Manager. Set the User setting to Lee's account name. Set the First Event to a date one month ago and the Last Event to today.

D. Create a filter on the Security log. Look only for success audits and set the Event Source to Security Account Manager. Set the User setting to Lee's account name. Set the First Event to a date one month ago and the last event to today.

E. Create a filter on the Security log. Look only for failure audits and set the Event Source to Security. Set the User setting to Lee's account name. Set the First Event to a date one month ago and the Last Event to today.

Objective 4.1 Answers

1.   **Correct Answers: E**

A. **Incorrect:** This will display all Information and Warning events from the System log rather than the Application log.

B. **Incorrect:** This will display all Information and Warning events from the Application log rather than those generated through disk quotas.

C. **Incorrect:** This will display the Error, Success Audit and Failure Audit events rather than the Information and Warning Events in which you are interested.

D. **Incorrect:** This will display the Information and Warning Events from the Checkdisk source rather than from the Disk Quota Source.

E. **Correct:** This will generate the correct output.

F. **Incorrect:** This will look at the System log rather than the Application log in which you are interested.

2.   **Correct Answers: D**

A. **Incorrect:** There is no Event Viewer Wizard.

B. **Incorrect:** This will not limit the display of error events to the last week.

C. **Incorrect:** The question asks for the System log rather than the Application log.

D. **Correct:** This filter will display only the error events in the System log that have occurred in the last seven days.

E. **Incorrect:** This will display only information events from the System log in the last seven days, not the Error events required.

3.   **Correct Answers: F**

   A. **Incorrect:** The Security log, not the System log, must be examined.

   B. **Incorrect:** The Security log, not the System log, must be examined.

   C. **Incorrect:** The Security log, not the System log, must be examined.

   D. **Incorrect:** This will list all user logon events over the last two months.

   E. **Incorrect:** The Event Source that should be used is Security, not Security Account Manager. Security Account Manager is used for Account Management events such as user additions and password changes.

   F. **Correct:** This will generate the requisite data display. Although all Event IDs listed in this question are 538, 538 is the logon event ID. If the User setting is not set to Agim's account name, then all user logon events will be displayed. Setting the correct dates will narrow the report to the specific period of interest.

4.   **Correct Answers: E**

   A. **Incorrect:** The Security log, not the System log, needs to be examined.

   B. **Incorrect:** The Security log, not the System log, needs to be examined.

   C. **Incorrect:** The Security log, not the System log, needs to be examined.

   D. **Incorrect:** The Event Source needs to be set to Security and the Audits need to be set to Failure.

   E. **Correct:** Because the only auditing that is being done pertains to logon events for both success and failure, and the filter is designed only to show failures for Lee's account over the last month, this will generate the required report.

Manage Software Update Infrastructure

Software Update Services (SUS) is an add-in to Windows Server 2003 and cannot be installed from the installation media. It must be downloaded from the Microsoft Web site. SUS enables Administrators to construct an approved list of updates that can be deployed throughout their organization.

SUS works in two parts. The first part is the SUS server, which hosts a list of approved updates. The SUS server can also be configured to store updates, saving clients the bother of downloading the approved updates from the Microsoft Windows Update servers. The second part is the clients that must be configured to use the SUS server rather than the Windows Update Server. This configuration can only be done through a setting change made in Group Policy; it cannot be done from the Automatic Updates tab of the System console in Control Panel. This can be done from a local Group Policy Object (GPO) as well as those applied to sites, domains, and organizational units.

Some updates, such as Service Packs, can also be deployed without SUS by simply using Group Policy software installation settings. The relevant area of Group Policy is in the Computer Configuration\Software Settings node. The service pack must be extracted to a file share that is accessible to all clients on the network. In some cases, with slow wide area network (WAN) links, administrators may wish to host the extracted service pack on a file share at each site and then use a site-linked GPO to point the computers at each site to their local update files rather than have all systems copy the service pack from a central location.

Objective 4.2 Questions

1. You are the systems administrator for a medium-sized organization and you are considering employing Software Update Services to manage updates provided by Microsoft for your Windows XP Professional systems. Your organization currently uses a proxy solution running on another platform that requires username and password authentication. The user and password database for the proxy is different from that used in your Windows Server 2003 domain. Given this situation, which of the following options is available to you in configuring a software update infrastructure?

    A. Because SUS cannot be configured to authenticate against a proxy, all updates must be manually downloaded by an administrator and placed on the SUS server. The Windows XP Professional machines should be configured using Group Policy to contact the SUS server for their software updates.

    B. Because SUS cannot be configured to authenticate against a proxy and Windows XP clients can, Windows XP clients should continue to contact Microsoft to download their updates.

    C. SUS can be configured to authenticate against a proxy to download a list of updates for your approval. Windows XP systems should be configured to check the SUS server to find which updates you have approved and then to automatically download those updates from the Microsoft Web site.

    D. SUS can be configured to authenticate against a proxy to download a list of updates for your approval as well as downloading the updates. Windows XP systems should be configured to check the SUS server to determine which updates are approved and then to retrieve them from the SUS server.

2. You are the systems administrator for a medium-sized organization that is considering implementing SUS on all Windows XP Professional workstations and Windows Server 2003 systems companywide. Before a companywide rollout is to go ahead, a pilot program is to be implemented. You have been assigned a lab with 10 Windows XP Professional workstations, a Windows Server 2003 member server running SUS, a Windows Server 2003 domain controller, and a stand-alone Windows Server 2003 system. You wish to configure all systems except the server running SUS to use the SUS server to automatically check for, download, and install updates at 7:00 A.M. each day. Which of the following steps should you take to do this? (Select all that apply.)

A. Use the Automatic Updates tab in the System console from Control Panel on every Windows XP Professional workstation computer to set the update server to the address of the SUS server. Set the Windows XP workstations to automatically download and install updates at 7:00 A.M. each day.

B. Use the Automatic Updates tab in the System console from Control Panel on each Windows Server 2003 system except the SUS server to set the update server to the address of the SUS server. Set these servers to automatically download and install updates at 7:00 A.M. each day.

C. Place the Windows XP Professional workstations and the Windows Server 2003 domain controller in a separate OU named Uptest. Edit a GPO's Windows Update properties for the Uptest OU, specifying the address of the update server as the SUS server in the Specify Intranet Microsoft Update Service Location policy. Set Configure Automatic Updates Policy to automatic download and install and set the scheduled install day to Every Day and the time to 7:00 A.M. Apply this GPO to the Uptest OU.

D. On the stand-alone Windows Server 2003 system, edit the local GPO's Windows Update properties specifying the address of the update server as the SUS server in the Specify Intranet Microsoft Update Service Location policy. Set Configure Automatic Updates Policy to automatic download and install and set the scheduled install day to Every Day and the time to 7:00 A.M. Apply this GPO to the Uptest OU.

E. On the SUS server, edit the local GPO's Windows Update properties specifying the address of the update server as the SUS server in the Specify Intranet Microsoft Update Service Location policy. Set Configure Automatic Updates Policy to automatic download and install and set the scheduled install day to Every Day and the time to 7:00 A.M. Apply this GPO to the Uptest OU.

3. Rooslan works for a company that has a single remote office connected by Integrated Services Digital Network Basic Rate Interface (ISDN BRI) to headquarters. The remote site has a 10 megabit connection to the Internet. Headquarters has a 20 megabit connection to the Internet. The ISDN BRI connections are mostly used to carry Active Directory and distributed file system (Dfs) replication traffic. The company has a single Windows Server 2003 domain. The remote office and the headquarters are each configured as a separate site in Active Directory for replication purposes. There are two Windows Server 2003 systems running SUS. One server is located at the headquarters location and is configured to host a list of approved updates and to store those approved updates locally. The other SUS server is located at the remote site.

Primary Goal:

Rooslan wants the Windows XP Professional workstations and the Windows Server 2003 systems download only updates that are on the approved list on the SUS server.

Secondary Goal:

Rooslan does not want to overburden the ISDN BRI connections with the transfer of updates from the SUS server located at headquarters.

Tertiary Goal:

Minimize the amount of updates downloaded to headquarters through the 20 megabit Internet connection.

Which of the following will allow Rooslan to accomplish his primary, secondary, and tertiary goals? (Select all that apply—the correct choices combine to form the right answer.)

A. Rooslan should edit a GPO and configure the Windows Update properties. The Specify Intranet Microsoft Update Service Location policy should have the settings of the second SUS server for the update detection and statistics fields. This Group Policy should be applied to the remote site.

B. Configure the second SUS server to retrieve a list of approved updates from the first SUS server. Also configure the second SUS server to maintain the update files on Microsoft Windows Update server.

C. Configure the first SUS server to host a list of approved updates and to download and store those approved updates.

D. Rooslan should edit a GPO and configure the Windows Update properties. The Specify Intranet Microsoft Update Service Location policy should have the settings of the first SUS server for the update detection and statistics fields. This Group Policy should be applied to the headquarters site.

E. Rooslan should edit a GPO and configure the Windows Update properties. The Specify Intranet Microsoft Update Service Location policy should have the settings of the first SUS server for the update detection and statistics fields. This Group Policy should be applied to the remote site.

F. Rooslan should edit a GPO and configure the Windows Update properties. The Specify Intranet Microsoft Update Service Location policy should have the settings of the second SUS server for the update detection and statistics fields. This Group Policy should be applied to the headquarters site.

4. Mick works as the network administrator for an organization that has five branch offices located across a city. The headquarters office has the only connection to the Internet and also hosts a proxy server. Headquarters has 200 Windows XP Professional workstations and several Windows Server 2003 systems. Each of the five branch offices has 150 Windows XP Professional workstations and several Windows Server 2003 systems. These branch offices are connected by ISDN BRI to the headquarters office. Currently none of the Windows systems is able to receive updates from Microsoft's Windows Update server because they are unable to authenticate against the proxy. Management has asked Mick to implement SUS throughout the organization so that approved updates can be installed on workstations and servers. Management also wants Mick to minimize the amount of update traffic running through the ISDN BRI lines. Which of the following methods will achieve this goal?

A. Configure a SUS server in the headquarters location to maintain a list of approved updates and to download and store those updates from the Microsoft Windows Update Servers. Configure a Group Policy that instructs clients to use the SUS server as their update server. Apply this GPO to the headquarters and branch-office sites.

B. Although this will allow updates to be rolled out to all clients within the organization it will also saturate the ISDN BRI lines with update traffic because each client workstation downloads its updates from the central SUS server.

Configure a SUS server in the headquarters location to maintain a list of approved updates but maintain those updates on the Microsoft Windows Update Servers. Configure a Group Policy that instructs clients to use the SUS server as their update server. Apply this GPO to the headquarters and branch-office sites.

C. Configure a SUS server in the headquarters location to maintain a list of approved updates but maintain those updates on the Microsoft Windows Update Servers. Configure a SUS server in each branch office location to maintain a list of approved updates but maintain those updates on the Microsoft Windows Update Servers. Create a GPO and apply it to each site. The GPO should have a policy that clients are to use their local SUS server as their update server.

D. Configure a SUS server in the headquarters location to maintain a list of approved updates and to download and store those approved updates. Configure SUS servers in each branch office to synchronize with the SUS server in the headquarters location. Configure a Group Policy that instructs clients to use the headquarters SUS server as their update server. Apply this GPO to the headquarters and branch-office sites.

E. Configure a SUS server in the headquarters location to maintain a list of approved updates and to download and store those approved updates. Configure SUS servers in each branch office to synchronize with the SUS server in the headquarters location. Create a GPO and apply it at each site. The GPO should have a policy that clients are to use their local SUS server as their update server.

5.   Orin is the systems administrator for an academic department at the local university. The department has 40 Windows XP Professional workstations and two Windows Server 2003 systems. One of these systems is configured as a Domain Controller, the other as a file and print server. All department computers are members of a single Windows Server 2003 domain. Microsoft has recently released a service pack for Windows XP and, after testing it, Orin feels confident enough to deploy it to the Windows XP Professional workstations in his department. Orin extracts the service pack to a directory on the file server called \\Fileshare\newsrvpk. Which of the following methods can Orin use to install the service pack on all Windows XP Professional workstations? (Select all that apply.)

   A.   Orin can visit each Windows XP Professional workstation and install the service pack from the file share.

   B.   Orin can create a group called Xpwkstn and put all the Windows XP Professional workstation computer accounts in this group. He can then create a GPO in which he sets up a new package in the Computer Configuration\Software Settings node using the location of the service pack .msi file on the \\Fileshare\newsrvpk share. In the Deploy Software dialog box, he should select Assign, then apply this GPO to the Xpwkstn group.

   C.   Orin can create a group called Xpusrs and put all who use Windows XP Professional workstations in this group. He can then create a GPO in which he sets up a new package in the Computer Configuration\Software Settings node using the location of the service pack .msi file on the \\Fileshare\newsrvpk share. In the Deploy Software dialog box he should select Assign, then apply this GPO to the Xpusrs group.

   D.   Orin can create an OU called Xpwkstn and put all the Windows XP Professional workstation computer accounts in this OU. He can then create a GPO in which he sets up a new package in the Computer Configuration\Software Settings node using the location of the service pack .msi file on the \\Fileshare\newsrvpk share. In the Deploy Software dialog box, he should select Assign, and then apply this GPO to the Xpwkstn OU.

Objective 4.2 Answers

1. **Correct Answers: D**

   A. **Incorrect:** SUS can be configured to authenticate against a proxy.

   B. **Incorrect:** SUS can be configured to authenticate against a proxy.

   C. **Incorrect:** Windows XP software update cannot be configured to authenticate against a proxy. In this situation, the SUS server should be configured to download the updates as well so that the Windows XP systems can in turn download and install relevant updates from the SUS server.

   D. **Correct:** Because Windows XP clients software update mechanism cannot authenticate against a proxy, they must retrieve the updates from the local SUS server. The list of updates that will be retrieved and installed will be based on the list of approved updates configured by the administrator of the SUS server.

2. **Correct Answers: C and D**

   A. **Incorrect:** Windows XP Professional computers cannot be configured to contact an alternate update server using the System console.

   B. **Incorrect:** Windows Server 2003 systems cannot be configured to contact an alternate update server using the System console.

   C. **Correct:** This is the correct way to do this for computers that are members of the domain: Add them all to an OU and then apply a Group Policy with the correct update settings.

   D. **Correct:** Because this server is not a member of the domain, this setting must be configured in the local GPO.

   E. **Incorrect:** The SUS server was not to be configured for updating from itself; it was still meant to update from Microsoft's site.

3. **Correct Answers: A, B, C, and D**

   A. **Correct:** This is the second part of the secondary goal and part of the primary goal. If the Group Policy pointed them at the first SUS server, the ISDN BRI link would be flooded by downloading updates from that server.

   B. **Correct:** This setting will mean that clients configured to contact this SUS server will use the approved list from this server but will download the updates themselves from Microsoft Windows Update servers. This is the first part of the secondary goal.

C. **Correct:** The first server will be able to provide update services to the headquarters site, including a list of approved updates as well as allowing those updates to be retrieved from the server. This is part of the tertiary and primary goals.

D. **Correct:** This will complete the tertiary goal and is part of the primary goal. By using the first SUS server rather than the second, the headquarters clients will retrieve their update list and the updates themselves from the first SUS server. If they were pointed at the second SUS server, they would download the approved updates from Microsoft, which would not be optimal use of the headquarters connection to the Internet.

E. **Incorrect:** This will mean that computers at the remote site will download their updates from the first SUS server rather than from the Microsoft update servers, flooding the bandwidth of the ISDN BRI line. This would violate the secondary goal.

F. **Incorrect:** This will result in clients at headquarters downloading approved updates from Microsoft instead of from the first SUS server, which would violate the tertiary goal.

4.   **Correct Answers: E**

A. **Incorrect:** Although this will allow updates to be rolled out to all clients within the organization, it will also saturate the ISDN BRI lines with update traffic because each client workstation downloads its updates from the central SUS server.

B. **Incorrect:** Although clients will have a list of updates, because they do not have the ability to authenticate against the proxy, they cannot download updates from the Microsoft Windows Update Servers.

C. **Incorrect:** Although clients will have a list of updates, because they do not have the ability to authenticate against the proxy, they cannot download updates from the Microsoft Windows Update Servers.

D. **Incorrect:** Although this will allow updates to be rolled out to all clients within the organization, it will also saturate the ISDN BRI lines with update traffic because each client workstation downloads its updates from the central SUS server. Branch office computers must use their local SUS server.

E. **Correct:** This solution will result in rolling out updates to each computer in the organization, but will also result in update traffic only being passed once across the ISDN BRI links. This solution meets management's criteria.

5.   Correct Answers: A and D

   A. Correct: This method will work although it is not the most efficient way of performing this operation.

   B. Incorrect: Group policies cannot be applied to groups, only to sites, domains, and organizational units.

   C. Incorrect: Group policies cannot be applied to groups, only to sites, domains, and organizational units.

   D. Correct: The group policy will apply only to those Windows XP Professional workstations that are in the Xpwkstn OU. Because all relevant Windows XP Professional workstations have been added to this OU, however, the service pack will be deployed the next time the computers restart.

Objective 4.3

Manage Software Site Licensing

Licensing is an issue that can confuse even the most technically adept systems administrator. There are two ways of licensing a Windows Server 2003 system, Per Server or Per User/Per Device modes. Per Server licensing authorizes concurrent connections to a single server. Per User/Per Device licenses connections from a single user or device to multiple servers. If you are unsure which mode to select at first, you should choose Per Server because the licensing model allows a no-cost conversion from this mode to Per User/Per Device licensing.

Per Server licensing works best when there are few servers that are accessed concurrently from any single workstation. Per User licensing works best when users work at multiple workstations to access a single or multiple servers. Per Device licensing works best when multiple users work at a single device to access multiple servers.

Terminal Server in application services mode requires Client Access Licenses (CALs) for the clients connecting to use the service. Terminal Services CALs are already included with Windows 2000 and Windows XP Professional, for connection to those client operating systems.

1. What is the difference between a Windows Device CAL and a Windows User CAL? (Select all that apply.)

  A. A Windows Device CAL allows a device, such as a workstation, to connect to a server regardless of how many users use that device.

  B. A Windows Device CAL allows a single user to connect to multiple servers so long as they use only a single workstation.

  C. A Windows User CAL allows a single user to access a server from multiple devices, such as workstations.

  D. A Windows User CAL allows a single user to access a server from a single workstation.

2. Rooslan is responsible for licensing at a medium-sized organization that has three Windows Server 2003 systems. These systems are named Server Alpha, Server Beta, and Server Gamma. Server Alpha is licensed in Per Server mode and is configured with 500 CALs. Server Beta is licensed in Per Server mode and is configured with 700 CALs. Server Gamma is licensed in Per Server mode and is configured with 600 CALs. If there are 550 Windows XP Professional workstations at Rooslan's company and 500 of those access Server Alpha, 525 of them access Server Beta and 540 access Server Gamma concurrently, how many per-server CALS are required at the organization?

  A. 500

  B. 540

  C. 1,565

  D. 1,800

3. You are in charge of licensing at a small organization. Your company has 17 developers and a sales force of 22. A total of 13 developers use two Windows XP Professional workstations on their desks. Four of the developers also use Tablet PCs in addition to their two Windows XP Professional workstations. The sales team works in pairs with one Tablet PC used between a two-member sales team. The file server at the organization is configured in Per Device or Per User mode. What is the minimum number of licenses required to comply with licensing responsibilities?

  A. 17 Per Device licenses and 11 Per User licenses.

  B. 22 Per Device licenses and 17 Per User licenses.

  C. 38 Per User licenses and 22 Per Device licenses.

  D. 17 Per User licenses and 11 Per Device licenses.

4.   Your organization has a single terminal server running in application server mode that allows multiple users to connect to the server to run a particular set of applications. Of the users who connect, 17 have Windows XP Professional workstations, 29 have Windows 2000 Professional workstations, 31 have Windows NT 4 workstations, and 15 have Apple Macintosh OSX workstations with the Microsoft RDP client installed. At any one time, a maximum of 70 concurrent connections are made to the Terminal Server in application mode. To retain compliance with licensing responsibilities, how many more Terminal Services CALs are required for this set of clients, assuming that 20 have currently been purchased?

   A. 92

   B. 70

   C. 56

   D. 53

   E. 20

5.   The License Logging service tracks Per Device or Per User licenses by user name. A company uses shift work with a total of 30 shift workers working 10 people to an 8-hour shift. Throughout a 24-hour period, three different users will use the same Windows XP Professional workstation. Each of the 30 shift workers has an individual logon account. What is the name of the method by which the usernames can be grouped into lots of three so that only one Per Device license is recorded on the License Logging server rather than 30 Per User devices?

   A. License Groups

   B. License Revocation

   C. License Clustering

   D. License Aggregation

Objective 4.3 Answers

1.   **Correct Answers: A and C**

   A. Correct: A Windows Device CAL allows a device, such as a workstation, to connect to a server regardless of how many users use that device. Windows Device CALs are useful for organizations that have multiple users using the same workstation, such as shift workers at call centers.

   B. Incorrect: A Windows Device CAL allows a device, such as a workstation, to connect to a server regardless of how many users use that device. Windows Device CALs are useful for organizations that have multiple users using the same workstation, such as shift workers at call centers.

   C. Correct: A Windows User CAL allows a single user to access a server from multiple devices, such as workstations. This is useful for users that use multiple workstations or devices at different times.

   D. Incorrect: A Windows User CAL allows a single user to access a server from multiple devices, such as workstations. This is appropriate for users accessing multiple workstations or devices at different times.

2.   **Correct Answers: C**

   A. Incorrect: A total of 500 per-server CALs will be required for Server Alpha, with 525 per-server CALs also required for Server Beta and 540 per-server CALS required for Server Gamma. The total of these CALs is 1,565.

   B. Incorrect: A total of 500 per-server CALs will be required for Server Alpha, with 525 per-server CALs required for Server Beta and 540 per-server CALs required for Server Gamma. The total of these numbers is 1,565.

   C. Correct: A total of 500 per-server CALs will be required for Server Alpha, with 525 per-server CALs required for Server Beta and 540 per-server CALs required for Server Gamma. The total of these numbers is 1,565.

   D. Incorrect: A total of 500 per-server CALs will be required for Server Alpha, with 525 per-server CALs required for Server Beta and 540 per-server CALs required for Server Gamma. The total of these numbers is 1,565. If 1,800 per-server CALs have been actually licensed, then only 1,565 of them are required to be in compliance.

3.   Correct Answers: D

A. Incorrect: Each developer can be assigned a Per User license and this will cover him or her for access using more than one system. Therefore, 17 developers equal 17 Per User licenses. Each Tablet PC used by the sales team can be allocated a Per Device license; therefore, 11 Tablet PCs equals 11 Per Device licenses.

B. Incorrect: Each developer can be assigned a Per User license and this will cover him or her for access using more than one system. Therefore, 17 developers equal 17 Per User licenses. Each Tablet PC used by the sales team can be allocated a Per Device license; therefore, 11 Tablet PCs equals 11 Per Device licenses. Solution B would be compliant, but is not the minimum required number.

C. Incorrect: Each developer can be assigned a Per User license and this will cover him or her for access using more than one system. Therefore, 17 developers equal 17 Per User licenses. Each Tablet PC used by the sales team can be allocated a Per Device license; therefore, 11 Tablet PCs equals 11 Per Device licenses. Solution B would be compliant, but is not the minimum required number.

D. Correct: Each developer can be assigned a Per User license and this will cover him or her for access using more than one system. Therefore, 17 developers equal 17 Per User licenses. Each Tablet PC used by the sales team can be allocated a Per Device license; therefore, 11 Tablet PCs equals 11 Per Device licenses.

4.   Correct Answers: D

    A.   Incorrect: Windows 2000 Professional workstations come with Terminal Services CALs built in, so extra licences are not required. 17 Windows XP Professional workstations do not come with Terminal Services CALs built in so extra licenses are required. The 31 Windows NT 4 and 15 Macintosh OSX workstations require Terminal Services CALs. A total of 20 have already been purchased, leaving 53 more to be purchased to achieve compliance.

    B.   Incorrect: Windows 2000 Professional workstations come with Terminal Services CALs built in, so extra licences are not required. 17 Windows XP Professional workstations do not come with Terminal Services CALs built in so extra licenses are required. The 31 Windows NT 4 and 15 Macintosh OSX workstations require Terminal Services CALs. A total of 20 have already been purchased, leaving 53 more to be purchased to achieve compliance.

    C.   Incorrect: Windows 2000 Professional workstations come with Terminal Services CALs built in, so extra licences are not required. 17 Windows XP Professional workstations do not come with Terminal Services CALs built in so extra licenses are required. The 31 Windows NT 4 and 15 Macintosh OSX workstations require Terminal Services CALs. A total of 20 have already been purchased, leaving 53 more to be purchased to achieve compliance.

    D.   Correct: Windows 2000 Professional workstations come with Terminal Services CALs built in, so extra licences are not required. 17 Windows XP Professional workstations do not come with Terminal Services CALs built in so extra licenses are required. The 31 Windows NT 4 and 15 Macintosh OSX workstations require Terminal Services CALs. A total of 20 have already been purchased, leaving 53 more to be purchased to achieve compliance.

    E.   Incorrect: Windows 2000 Professional workstations come with Terminal Services CALs built in, so extra licences are not required. 17 Windows XP Professional workstations do not come with Terminal Services CALs built in so extra licenses are required. The 31 Windows NT 4 and 15 Macintosh OSX workstations require Terminal Services CALs. A total of 20 have already been purchased, leaving 53 more to be purchased to achieve compliance.

5.   Correct Answers: A

    A.   Correct: A license group is a collection of users who collectively share one or more CALs. When a user connects to the server product, the License Logging service tracks the user by name, but assigns a CAL from the allocation assigned to the license group.

    B.   Incorrect: The correct name of the method is License Groups.

    C.   Incorrect: The correct name of the method is License Groups.

    D.   Incorrect: The correct name of the method is License Groups.

Manage Servers Remotely

Because server rooms are often loud and difficult sites from which to work, the majority of systems administrators manage their Windows Server 2003 systems remotely from their desks. Administrators may visit the server room from time to time to perform tasks such as swapping out backup tapes but very rarely do systems administrators spend the majority of their time in the same rooms as the servers they manage.

Windows Server 2003 offers several different methods for remote management. The first tool is the Computer Management Console, which can be configured to connect to a remote system and perform many of the same administration tasks that can be performed on a local system. Several servers can be added to a single Computer Management Console, meaning that the administrator can use the one tool to manage multiple systems.

The second form of remote management is to use Terminal Services to remotely control the server. This gives the administrator the appearance of actually sitting in front of the server console and allows administrators to perform all management tasks as though they were actually at the server.

Another form of remote management is the HTML remote administration tools. This allows an administrator to connect to a Web service running on the Windows Server 2003 system and perform a limited set of administrative tasks. It can provide an administrative option over low-bandwidth wide area network (WAN) lines, such as those that use modems, which would render a Terminal Services connection unusable.

Remote assistance is slightly different from connecting by Terminal Services to control a server. When a remote assistance invitation is issued, an administrator working on the server can issue an invitation so that another administrator can remotely watch, or contribute to, the steps that are taken.

Objective 4.4 Questions

1. Rooslan is the senior systems administrator at a medium-sized organization. His office is located at the company headquarters in Melbourne, Australia. He has just received a telephone call from Alex, who is responsible for maintaining a server at one of the organization's branch sites in Auckland, New Zealand. The two sites are connected by means of an ISDN PRI line. Alex is about to modify some registry settings on one of the servers in Auckland and wants Rooslan to watch him remotely so that he can check that Alex completes the procedure correctly. Which of the following technologies will allow Rooslan to watch Alex modify the Auckland server's registry and talk him through any parts of the procedure that he does not understand?

    A. Remote Assistance

    B. Terminal Services Remote Administration Mode

    C. HTML Remote Administration Tools

    D. Computer Management Console

    E. REGEDT32

2. Rooslan is working from home and is using a dial-up connection to his company's RRAS server, which allows him access to Windows Server 2003 systems on the corporate LAN. It is 2:15 A.M. and the building that hosts the servers is unoccupied. Rooslan would like to initiate a disk defragmentation on the hard disk drives of several of the servers located at his office. Rooslan's home Windows XP Professional workstation is not a member of the company's Windows Server 2003 domain. Which of the following tools can Rooslan use to initiate a remote disk defragmentation?

    A. He can use the Disk Defragmenter node in his Computer Management console in Windows XP Professional to connect to the remote systems to initiate disk defragmentation.

    B. Remote Assistance

    C. Terminal Services Remote Administration mode

    D. Using Defrag,exe from the command line of his Windows XP Professional Workstation.

3. You want to change the name of a stand-alone Windows Server 2003 system located at a remote site on your organization's network. The system works as an FTP and WWW server and does not have a local administrator available. This server is not a member of your organization's Windows Server 2003 domain and your Windows XP Professional workstation is. Which of the following tools can you use to accomplish this task? (Select all that apply.)

    A. Local Computer Management Console

    B. HTML Remote Administration Tools

    C. Terminal Services Remote Administration mode

    D. Active Directory Users And Computers Console

4. You are the systems administrator for a small organization that has recently bought out a rival company. Your organization has a Windows Server 2003 domain, of which all computers are members. The rival company has six stand-alone Windows Server 2003 systems. The two networks have been integrated and there are no firewalls between your Windows XP Professional workstation and the remote servers. Your Windows XP Professional system is a member of the domain and you have Domain Administrator privileges. You also have administrator credentials on each of the stand-alone servers. You also have the telephone numbers of staff at each site who currently have administrative privileges on each server and are logged on during business hours. Which of the following tools can be used to configure the remote stand-alone Windows Server 2003 systems to join your organization's domain? (Select any that apply.)

    A. The Computer Management Console on your Windows XP Professional System

    B. Active Directory Users and Computers

    C. HTML Remote Administration Tools

    D. Terminal Services Remote Administration mode

    E. Remote Assistance

5. Alex is the systems administrator of a remote satellite tracking facility located in Outback, Australia. The facility is connected by ISDN line to a central site in Sydney. Alex is having some trouble configuring tracking software on the server and is on a support call to an administrator at the central site who is attempting to talk him through it. The administrator asks if Alex would be able to send a remote assistance invitation to him so that he can better talk Alex through the procedure. Which of the following methods will allow the administrator to receive Alex's remote assistance invitation?

    A. Alex can send a remote invitation to the administrator by using Windows Messenger and the Remote Assistance Wizard.

    B. Alex can e-mail a remote assistance invitation to the administrator using the Remote Assistance Wizard.

    C. Alex can create the invitation as a file and place it on an FTP server where the administrator can download it and access it.

    D. Alex can run the Remote Desktop Connection client and set it to connect to the administrator's system.

    E. Alex can create the invitation as a file and place it on a file share where the administrator can access it.

Objective 4.4 Answers

1.   Correct Answers: A

  A. Correct: Alex can issue a Remote Assistance invitation to Rooslan, which will enable Rooslan to view the screen of the server as Alex makes the necessary registry modifications.

  B. Incorrect: Although this will allow Rooslan to view the server remotely, it will not enable him to view the changes that Alex makes to the registry as they happen.

  C. Incorrect: Although this technology allows Rooslan to administer the server remotely, it will not allow him to view the registry nor to watch Alex make the necessary modifications.

  D. Incorrect: Although this technology allows Rooslan to administer the server remotely, it will not allow him to view the registry nor to watch Alex make the necessary modifications.

  E. Incorrect: Although this technology allows Rooslan to view the registry on the remote server, it will not allow him to view the registry nor to watch Alex make the necessary modifications.

2.   Correct Answers: C

  A. Incorrect: The disk defragmenter that ships with Windows XP and Windows Server 2003 cannot be used to perform remote disk defragmentation.

  B. Incorrect: Because there is no one at the building that hosts the servers, Remote Assistance invitations cannot be sent.

  C. Correct: This tool will allow Rooslan to connect remotely to each server and to initiate a disk defragmentation.

  D. Incorrect: The Defrag.exe command cannot be used to defragment remote systems.

3.   Correct Answers: B and C

  A. Incorrect: Because the system is not a member of the domain, you will be unable to log on through the Local Computer Management Console to perform administrative tasks on this server.

  B. Correct: The HTML Remote Administration Tools can be used to rename a server as well as to join it to a domain. Certain servers, such as certificate servers, cannot be renamed.

   C. Correct: Terminal Services Remote Administration mode can be used to change the name of a stand-alone member server.

   D. Incorrect: This console cannot be used to change the name of a stand-alone server.

4.   **Correct Answers: C, D, and E**

   A. Incorrect: There is no way to authenticate the local Computer Management Console against the remote stand-alone servers, hence no way to alter their domain membership.

   B. Incorrect: Although this can be used to provide the stand-alone servers with computer accounts in the domain it will not change the domain membership of those servers remotely.

   C. Correct: The HTML remote administration tools can be used to alter a stand-alone Windows Server 2003 system's domain membership.

   D. Correct: You can connect to the server console in this manner and change the domain membership of the stand-alone servers.

   E. Correct: You can call one of the members of staff at each site and get them to issue you a remote assistance invitation when they are logged on to the server.

5.   **Correct Answers: A, B, C, and E**

   A. Correct: This method of delivering an invitation will work.

   B. Correct: This method of delivering an invitation will work.

   C. Correct: This method of delivering an invitation will work.

   D. Incorrect: This will not work because it does not transmit a remote administration invitation and Alex would be connecting to the administrator's system rather than the administrator connecting to the server on which Alex is working.

   E. Correct: This method of delivering an invitation will also work. Once the invitation has been copied to the administrator's local machine they will be able to initiate the remote administration session.

Objective 4.5

Troubleshooting Issues Related to Print Queues

Several types of problems can occur with print queues on print servers. The first can occur when there is insufficient enough disk space for larger print jobs to spool correctly. There are two ways to fix this: Increase the amount of disk space on the drive that hosts the spooler or move the print spooler to another volume that has more space.

Problems can also occur when certain users need to be able to print faster than other users. This can be fixed by altering the priority of print jobs. More than one shared printer can point to a particular print device and each shared printer can be assigned a different print priority. The higher the priority number, the quicker jobs submitted from that particular shared printer will reach the device.

Objective 4.5 Questions

1. Foley works as the systems administrator for a law firm. There is a group of 20 legal secretaries who provide administrative support to the lawyers. All the secretaries use a single high-speed laser printer shared on a Windows Server 2003 system. The secretaries must print large documents on a regular basis. Although the high-speed laser printer is fast, it is running almost constantly, printing documents. Some of the secretaries have found that when they submit a job to the high-speed laser printer, it can take almost 20 minutes for other jobs in the queue to be processed before their own job is output. None of the secretaries want to scroll through a list of available printers to check which one has the fewest jobs before submitting their documents. Which of the following options should Foley consider to minimize the amount of time that printers take to finish printing documents for all the secretaries?

A. Foley should order a second high-speed laser printer of the same make and model and institute a printer pool.

B. Foley should set different printer priorities for each legal secretary based on a list generated by the head of the group. The most important secretary should be set a priority of 1 and the least important a priority of 99.

C. Foley should set different printer priorities for each legal secretary based on a list generated by the head of the group. The most important secretary should be set a priority of 99 and the least important a priority of 1.

D. Foley should purchase three more high-speed laser printers and install them with their own individual printer shares on the print server. Secretaries can select the printer share that has the fewest jobs in the queue.

2. You are the systems administrator for a medium-sized organization. You have received several telephone calls from users at your company reporting that they are unable to print large 160-page print jobs to a departmental shared printer. If they send jobs to a printer shared on another server, they print with no trouble. If they break up the job into 10-page lots, they are also able to print, although they find this method cumbersome. The server that hosts the departmental shared printer also hosts a file share on the same volume. Which of the following actions should you take to resolve this problem?

A. Alter the shared printer properties and increase the size of the maximum print job to 200 pages.

B. Remove the quota set on the printer to allow larger jobs to be printed.

C. Create a new printer share on the same server and point it at the same print device.

D. Clean up the server's hard disk drive and remove unneeded files from the file share to increase the disk space.

3. You have received a telephone call from an irate senior manager named Gregory who informs you that he is trying to print a document to the printer but that it has not emerged. Gregory tells you that another job is printing and has been doing so for the last 20 minutes. Gregory is impatient to get the document printed because he is about to leave for an interstate flight. You examine the print queue and find it contains the following jobs. Each user on the printer has a default printing priority of 10.

2004Budget	Printing	Phillip	238/945
SalesDoc		Darren	24
Policies		James	45
Schematics		Lee	12
Takeoverbid		Gregory	5

Which of the following steps will make Gregory's print job output as soon as possible and leave Phillip's document to print only when other print jobs in the queue have been finished?

   A. Change the priority of Gregory's document to 99 and alter the priority of Phillip's, Darren's, James's, and Lee's documents to 1.

   B. Change the priority of Gregory's document to 1 and alter the priority of Phillip's, Darren's, James's, and Lee's documents to 99.

   C. Change the priority of Gregory's document to 99. Pause the printing of Phillip's document. Change the priority of Phillip's document to 1. After the other users' documents have printed, remove the pause from Phillip's document.

   D. Change the priority of Gregory's document to 1. Pause Phillip's document. Change the priority of Phillip's document to 99. After Gregory's document has started to print, remove the pause from Phillip's document.

4.   Foley works as the systems administrator for a law firm. There is a group of 20 legal secretaries who provide administrative support to the lawyers. All the secretaries use a single high-speed laser printer shared on a Windows Server 2003 system. The secretaries must print large documents on a regular basis. Although the high-speed laser printer is fast, it is printing documents almost constantly. Some of the legal secretaries have found that when they submit a job to the high-speed laser printer, it can take almost 20 minutes for other jobs in the queue to be processed before their own job is output. Five of the secretaries work for senior partners. Foley would like to configure it so that print jobs from those five legal secretaries who work for senior partners reach the printer more quickly than jobs from the 15 other secretaries. Which of the following methods will accomplish this?

   A.   Create a second shared printer called Snrprtnr and point it to the same high-speed laser printer device. Set the priority of this printer to 99. Create a security group and add the five legal secretaries that work for senior partners to this security group. Give only this group permission to print to the Snrprtnr shared printer. Ensure that the original shared printer retains the default printing priority of 1. Configure the workstations of the five legal secretaries that work for senior partners to print to the Snrprtnr shared printer rather than the original shared printer.

   B.   Create a second shared printer called Snrprtnr and point it to the same high-speed laser printer device. Set the priority of this printer to 1. Create a security group and add the five legal secretaries that work for senior partners to this security group. Only give this group permission to print to the Snrprtnr shared printer. Ensure that the original shared printer retains the default printing priority of 99. Configure the workstations of the five legal secretaries that work for senior partners to print to the Snrprtnr shared printer rather than the original shared printer.

   C.   Create a second shared printer called Snrprtnr and point it to the same high-speed laser printer device. Set the priority of this printer to 99. Create a security group and add the five legal secretaries that work for senior partners to this security group. Ensure that the original shared printer retains the default printing priority of 1. Configure the workstations of the 15 secretaries that do not work for senior partners to print to the Snrprtnr shared printer rather than the original shared printer.

   D.   Create a second shared printer called Snrprtnr and point it to the same high-speed laser printer device. Set the priority of this printer to 99. Create a security group and add the accounts of the 15 legal secretaries who do not work for senior partners to this security group. Only give this group permission to print to the Snrprtnr shared printer. Ensure that the original shared printer retains the default printing priority of 1. Configure the workstations of the five legal secretaries who work for senior partners to print to the Snrprtnr shared printer rather than the original shared printer.

Objective 4.5 Answers

1.   Correct Answers: A

    A. Correct: A printer pool will share jobs sent to the shared printer to two separate print devices.

    B. Incorrect: This will not work for several reasons. The first is that priorities are assigned to shared printers, not to users. Two shared printers print to the same print device, and the one with the higher priority gets to print first. Jobs sent to a printer with priority 99 will print more quickly than those sent with priority 1.

    C. Incorrect: This will not work because priorities are assigned to shared printers, not the users. Two shared printers print to the same print device, and the one with the higher priority gets to print first.

    D. Incorrect: The question states that the secretaries should not be forced to check which printers have longer queues than others.

2.   Correct Answers: D

    A. Incorrect: Shared printers do not block the printing of jobs based on the number of pages in the job.

    B. Incorrect: Quotas cannot be set on shared printers in Windows Server 2003.

    C. Incorrect: This will not solve this problem because the problem appears to be insufficient disk space to host a large spool file.

    D. Correct: The larger jobs are not printing because the print spool does not have enough disk space for large files. The smaller spools associated with smaller jobs are able to be created because their spool files are able to be created in the available space.

3.   **Correct Answers: C**

   A. Incorrect: In this case Gregory will still have to wait for Phillip's document to finish printing before his document will be output from the printer.

   B. Incorrect: This will give Gregory's document the lowest priority and it will mean that it prints after the rest of the documents in the queue. Further, if any other jobs are submitted, they will be queued above Gregory's.

   C. Correct: This will get Gregory's document printed quickly. Other users' documents will follow Gregory's. If you remove the pause after the other documents have printed, Phillip's document will continue printing.

   D. Incorrect: This will mean that Gregory has to wait for Darren's, James's, and Lee's documents to print, because they have a higher priority than his document.

4.   **Correct Answers: A**

   A. Correct: This will enable the documents of the five legal secretaries who work for senior partners to print with higher priority than those of the other 15 members of the secretary pool.

   B. Incorrect: A priority of 1 means that those secretaries that work for senior partners will have to wait until all other print jobs are finished before their print jobs will output on the high-speed laser printer.

   C. Incorrect: This will give the print jobs of the 15 legal secretaries who do not work for senior partners higher printing priority than the print jobs of the five legal secretaries who work for senior partners.

   D. Incorrect: The secretaries who work for senior partners will be unable to access the Snrprtnr shared printer because access has been given to the 15 other legal secretaries but not to them.

Objective 4.6

Monitor Events

The event monitor allows a systems administrator to view the activity that is occurring on the servers that they administer. The event monitor in conjunction with an efficient audit policy will allow the administrator to determine which users are using a particular right. Auditing is configured by means of Group Policy and should be configured at the Domain Level. In some cases, as with object access, further steps must be taken by adding particular groups whose activities the administrator wishes to audit.

Objective 4.6 Questions

1. You are the systems administrator for a medium-sized organization. You have been instructed by management to generate an audit log of all users who attempt to access a particular folder which stores confidential company financial information. Management is interested not only in those users that successfully access the folder in question but also those users who attempt to access the folder but are stopped because they have insufficient NTFS permissions. Which of the following types of auditing should you configure? (Select all that apply.)

   A. Successful Object Access

   B. Failed Object Access

   C. Successful Privilege Use

   D. Failed Privilege Use

   E. Successful Directory Service Access

   F. Failed Directory Service Access

2. Rooslan is the systems administrator for a small company that has fewer than 100 users. One Sunday when he was checking the backup tapes he noticed one of the color laser printers printing out inappropriate pictures in violation of company policy. No one else was in the office that day and he checked the remote access logs and found that 10 users were connected to the company network from home. He believes that the person who printed these pictures would come in later to collect them before they would be found when everyone returned to work on Monday morning. Of the 10 users who were logged on by remote access at the time, only five had the requisite permissions to print to that particular color laser printer. Rooslan configures a domain audit policy for a particular type of audit event and then uses the Shared Printer's advanced security features to audit use on the group that has access to the printer. Which type of audit event should Rooslan have configured in Group Policy to locate who has printed to this particular printer on Sunday afternoon?

   A. Audit Successful Privilege Use

   B. Audit Failed Privilege Use

   C. Audit Successful System Events

   D. Audit Failed System Events

   E. Audit Successful Object Access

   F. Audit Failed Object Access

3.   You are the administrator of a Windows Server 2003 IIS Web server. The Web site hosts a group of discussion forums. There is a secure Web site that can only be accessed by users entering a user name and password combination. One morning you have discovered that the name of one of the accounts that use the secure Web site has been posted maliciously to the forums. You delete the post, but you want to begin auditing to see if anyone has tried to guess the password of the account by attempting to log on to the secure site. The Windows Server 2003 system currently runs on a stand-alone server that is not a member of a domain. Which type of event should you audit?

     A.   Audit Successful Logon Events

     B.   Audit Failed Logon Events

     C.   Audit Successful Account Logon Events

     D.   Audit Failed Account Logon Events

     E.   Audit Successful Object Access

     F.   Audit Failed Object Access

4.   As a part of your company's policy, all actions by systems administrators related to accounts, such as account creation, deletion, renaming, as well as group creation, deletion, and renaming, and account disabling and password changes must be audited. These events are to be stored in the Security log. To comply with this policy you are currently editing the default domain GPO. Which audit event should you enable?

     A.   Audit Successful Privilege Use

     B.   Audit Failed Privilege Use

     C.   Audit Successful Account Management

     D.   Audit Failed Account Management

     E.   Audit Successful Account Logon Events

     F.   Audit Failed Account Logon Events

Objective 4.6 Answers

1. **Correct Answers: A and B**

    A. **Correct:** This is correct because you want to generate a list of people who have successfully accessed this folder.

    B. **Correct:** This is correct because you want to generate a list of people who have unsuccessfully attempted to access this folder.

    C. **Incorrect:** You are not interested in privilege use, only object access.

    D. **Incorrect:** You are not interested in privilege use, only object access.

    E. **Incorrect:** You are not interested in access to the directory service, only object access.

    F. **Incorrect:** You are not interested in access to the directory service, only object access.

2. **Correct Answers: E**

    A. **Incorrect:** Using a printer does not count as a privilege use; rather, it is an object access.

    B. **Incorrect:** Using a printer does not count as a privilege use; rather, it is an object access.

    C. **Incorrect:** Using a printer does not count as a system event; rather, it is an object access.

    D. **Incorrect:** Using a printer does not count as a system event; rather, it is an object access.

    E. **Correct:** This will generate a list in the Security log of all users who attempt to print to the printer. Rooslan can later look through the Security log to see if any other print jobs are sent to this printer on Sunday.

    F. **Incorrect:** As the user is able to print to this printer there is no point auditing failed object access, this will list users who have tried to print to the printer but cannot.

3.   **Correct Answers: D**

     A. Incorrect: This type of event occurs when an account authenticates against a domain controller. This is a stand-alone which is not a member of a domain.

     B. Incorrect: This type of event occurs when an account authenticates against a domain controller. This is a stand-alone which is not a member of a domain.

     C. Incorrect: This will list all successful logon events to the stand-alone server. This will not show unsuccessful attempts to log on to the stand-alone server.

     D. Correct: This will list all failed attempts to log on to the stand-alone server. This is the event type you should audit to check whether someone is trying to guess the password to the account name posted in the forums. As a security precaution, you should disable this account.

     E. Incorrect: Objects do not need to be audited to complete the task listed in the question; Account Logon events need to be audited.

     F. Incorrect: Objects do not need to be audited to complete the task listed in the question; Account Logon events need to be audited.

4.   **Correct Answers: C**

     A. Incorrect: The creation, deletion, and renaming of accounts is not a privilege use, but is listed under another type of auditing event, Audit Account Management.

     B. Incorrect: The creation, deletion, and renaming of accounts is not a privilege use, but is listed under another type of auditing event, Audit Account Management.

     C. Correct: Successful account management will write events to the system log each time an account is created, deleted, or renamed, or if groups are created, deleted, or renamed, or if accounts are disabled or passwords are changed.

     D. Incorrect: You are uninterested in failed account management events because the administrators have the correct security privileges to perform account management tasks.

     E. Incorrect: The creation, deletion, and renaming of accounts is not a privilege use, but is listed under another type of auditing event, Audit Account Management.

     F. Incorrect: The creation, deletion, and renaming of accounts is not a privilege use, but is listed under another type of auditing event, Audit Account Management.

Monitor Current System Performance

Maintaining a responsive server is very important for a systems administrator. A server that performs slowly will frustrate users who are likely to vent that frustration at the person responsible for managing those servers. A systems administrator should generate a baseline value for processor usage, network usage, disk usage, and memory usage soon after first configuring a server. The systems administrator should then regularly monitor the performance of the server to determine how current performance compares to the original base line. Performance statistics are generated by the Performance console. The Performance console can also collect performance statistics from remote servers allowing administrators, at a glance, to compare the performance of the servers under their control.

Objective 4.7 Questions

1. You are concerned that the CPU on a print server that hosts 10 shared printers is not able to process spool files quickly enough. Which of the following ways will you be able to check whether your supposition is correct?

    A. In the shared printer properties, check the spooler processor usage statistic.

    B. Configure the Performance console to track the processor usage of the print spool (Process\%Processor Time\spoolsv) on the Print Server over the period of a normal working day and configure the display to show the maximum value.

    C. Configure the Performance console to track the processor usage of the print spool (Process\%Processor Time\spoolsv) on the print server over the period of a normal working day and configure the display to show the average value.

    D. Configure the Performance console to the processor usage of the print spool (Process\%Processor Time\spoolsv) on his workstation over the period of a normal working day and configure the display to show the average value.

2. Rooslan wants to get an idea as to why a particular Windows Server 2003 system is performing poorly. He is unsure whether the problem is the disk drives, the processor, or the amount of available memory. Which of the following should he do to get a better idea about each system's performance over the course of a day? (Select all that apply.)

    A. He should use the Performance console to track the values of % Processor Time, Current Disk Queue Length, and Available MBytes. He should configure the view to display maximum values and run the console over the course of a normal operating day.

    B. He should use the Performance console to track the values of % Processor Time, Current Disk Queue Length, and Available MBytes. He should configure the view to display current values and run the console over the course of a normal operating day.

    C. He should use the Performance console to track the values of % Processor Time, Current Disk Queue Length, and Available MBytes. He should configure the view to display minimum values and run the console over the course of a normal operating day.

    D. He should use the Performance console to track the values of % Processor Time, Current Disk Queue Length, and Available MBytes. He should configure the view to display average values and run the console over the course of a normal operating day.

3. Rob is concerned that the network card on a file server he maintains needs to be upgraded from 10 megabits to 100 megabits. He monitors the average Output Queue Length on the network card over a period of a normal working day. Which values should be a cause for concern and indicate that Rob should upgrade the network card? (Select all that apply.)

A. 0

B. 1

C. 2

D. 3

E. 4

Objective 4.7 Answers

1.   Correct Answers: C

   A. Incorrect: No such statistic is available from the shared printer properties.

   B. Incorrect: The % Processor Time may reach peaks of 100% for a short period of time, which will give no indication of the average processor usage of the spooler.

   C. Correct: This will give a good indication of the amount of processor time the print spooler is taking up on the print server over the course of a normal working day.

   D. Incorrect: This will examine his workstation rather than the Print Server.

2.   Correct Answers: D

   A. Incorrect: Maximum values may be unusual peaks and are not indicative of average performance.

   B. Incorrect: Current values say nothing about the average performance over a day.

   C. Incorrect: Minimum values say nothing about average performance over a day.

   D. Correct: This will give a good indication of how each subsystem is performing over the course of the day, and Rooslan will be able to make a determination on his next course of action based upon these figures.

3.   Correct Answers: C, D, and E

   A. Incorrect: An average value of 0 is not a cause for concern.

   B. Incorrect: An average value of 1 is not a cause for concern; it means that the network card is operating with an occasional backlog of traffic.

   C. Correct: According to the explanation in the Performance console's counter statistics, values of 2 or over are cause for concern and might indicate that an upgrade is necessary.

   D. Correct: According to the explanation in the Performance console's counter statistics, values of 2 or over are cause for concern and might indicate that an upgrade is necessary.

   E. Correct: According to the explanation in the Performance console's counter statistics, values of 2 or over are cause for concern and might indicate that an upgrade is necessary.

Objective 4.8

Monitor File and Print Servers

The vast majority of servers used on local area networks perform either the function of print serving or hosting file shares. For an administrator it is vitally important that these servers function efficiently and reliably.

Administrators of file servers need to ensure that the volume hosting the file share does not fill with data. This can happen if old data is kept around long after it has served its use and new data is being written every day. Administrators also need to make sure that individual users do not store a disproportionate amount of data on the server compared to their colleagues. One way of ensuring that a volume does not fill up and that all users have limits placed on their ability to store data is to institute quotas on the partition. A quota blocks a user from using more than an allocated amount of disk space. The Quota tab can be accessed by editing the properties of an individual volume.

Print queues can be monitored on the server or remotely. They can also be monitored through the Performance console. The Performance console is able to be used to generate an "at-a-glance" report of the current number of print jobs assigned to any one particular print server. This will allow an administrator to decide if the printing load should be shared among other servers if things seem to be taking an inordinate amount of time.

1. Rooslan is the systems administrator of a medium-sized academic department at the local university. He is currently responsible for five Windows Server 2003 systems. One of these systems is used as the departmental file share with undergraduate, postgraduate, academic, and administrative staff all using the server to share files. The file server is configured with two disks. The first disk is separated into two volumes, one of which is 10 GB and hosts the operating system, the second of which is 30 GB and hosts the undergraduate file share. The second disk comprises a single 80 GB volume that hosts the postgraduate, academic, and administrative staff file shares. Rooslan is concerned that the volumes that host this data will become full and wishes to institute disk quotas. All departmental undergraduates are members of the Undergrad group, all postgraduates are members of the Postgrad group, all academics are members of the Academ group, and all members of administrative staff are members of the Secrat group. No user is a member of two or more of these groups. The share permissions are set so that only each individual group has access to the share. After consultation with various departmental representatives Rooslan has devised the following quota scheme:

Undergraduates will be allowed to store a maximum of 100 MB of data on the server.

Postgraduates will be allowed to store a maximum of 300 MB of data on the server.

Members of Administrative staff will be allowed to store a maximum of 500 MB of data on the server.

Members of Academic staff will be allowed to store a maximum of 800 MB of data on the server.

Which of the following methods will allow Rooslan to implement his quota scheme?

    A. Rooslan should edit the share properties of the undergraduate share, set the quota to 100 MB, and select the Deny More Disk Space To Users Over Quota check box. Next, he should edit the share properties of the postgraduate share and set the quota to 300 MB and select the Deny More Disk Space To Users Over Quota check box. He should then edit the share properties of the administrative staff share, set the quota to 500 MB, and select the Deny More Disk Space To Users Over Quota check box. Finally he should edit the share properties of the academic staff share, set the quota to 800 MB, and select the Deny More Disk Space To Users Over Quota check box.

    B. Rooslan should edit the properties of the folder that hosts the undergraduate share, set the quota to 100 MB, and select the Deny More Disk Space To Users Over Quota check box. Next, he should edit the properties of the folder that hosts the postgraduate share, set the quota to 300 MB, and select the Deny More Disk

Space To Users Over Quota check box. He should then edit the properties of the folder that hosts the administrative staff share, set the quota to 500 MB, and select the Deny More Disk Space To Users Over Quota check box. Finally he should edit the properties of the folder that hosts the academic staff share, set the quota to 800 MB, and select the Deny More Disk Space To Users Over Quota check box.

C. Rooslan should edit the properties of the volume that hosts the undergraduate share. He should navigate to the Quotas tab, select the Enable Quota Management and Deny Disk Space To Users Exceeding Quota Limit check boxes, and on the Quota Entries tab, add the Undergrad group and apply a 100 MB quota. Rooslan should then edit the properties of the volume that hosts the postgraduate, administrative, and academic staff shares. He should navigate to the Quotas tab, select the Enable Quota Management and Deny Disk Space To Users Exceeding Quota Limit check boxes. In the Quota Entries tab, he should add the Postgrad group and apply a 300 MB quota; he should then add the Secrat group and apply a 500 MB quota; and he should finally add the Academ group and apply an 800 MB quota.

D. Rooslan should edit the properties of the volume that hosts the undergraduate share. He should navigate to the Quotas tab, select the Enable Quota Management and Deny Disk Space To Users Exceeding Quota Limit check boxes, and limit the disk space to 100 MB. He should then back up the volume hosting the postgraduate, administrative, and academic staff shares to tape. Once this is done he should delete the volume and repartition the hard disk into three volumes of equal size. He should restore the postgraduate share to the first new volume, the administrative staff share to the second new volume, and restore the academic staff share to the third new volume. He should edit the properties of the volume that hosts the postgraduate share, navigate to the Quotas tab, select the Enable Quota Management and Deny Disk Space To Users Exceeding Quota Limit check boxes, and limit the disk space to 300 MB. He should edit the properties of the volume that hosts the administrative staff share, navigate to the Quotas tab, select Enable Quota Management and Deny Disk Space To Users Exceeding Quota Limit check boxes, and limit the disk space to 500 MB. He should edit the properties of the volume that hosts the academic staff share, navigate to the Quotas tab, select the Enable Quota Management and Deny Disk Space To Users Exceeding Quota Limit check boxes, and limit the disk space to 800 MB.

2. Rob has set up a set of individual quotas for 250 users on a partition of a Windows Server 2003 file server. Thirty of the users have a 10 MB quota, 45 have a 15 MB quota, 100 have a 30 MB quota, 25 have a 60 MB quota, and 50 have a 100 MB quota. There are four other Windows Server 2003 systems that require exactly the same quota scheme. Which of the following methods can Rob use to implement this quota scheme on the four other servers?

   A. Quotas are applied by Group Policy. Rob needs to add the four other servers to the same organizational unit.

   B. Rob needs to use the Active Directory Users And Computers console to add the four other systems to the quota security group that he created for the original server.

   C. This is not possible without using a third-party quota management product.

   D. Quota settings are stored in the registry. Rob needs to export the quota registry key on the initial server to disk and then import it into the registry of the other four servers.

   E. From the quota entries page Rob needs to select all 250 entries and export them to a file. He can then copy this file to the other server and import it to the quota entries page of each partition to which he wishes to apply this quota scheme.

3. Laherty is the IT consultant for a small graphic design business that has a single volume file server running Windows Server 2003. This file server also acts as a print server and is connected to a color laser printer that is used to print poster-sized advertising material as well as a normal black-and-white laser printer for letters and memos. Laherty has configured disk quotas on this server allowing each of the eight users at the office to store a maximum of 8 GB of files on the server. Laherty is the only one with access to change permissions on the file server. Laherty visits this small business once a week. When he is visiting this graphic design business on Friday, Rob, one of the users, informs him that he has been unable to print several posters since Wednesday. Rob also informs Laherty that he has been able to print documents to the black-and-white printer. Rob has not tried to print any other large files to the color laser printer. Laherty checks with other users at the business and finds that they have been able to print normally to both printers. Laherty gets one of the other users to try to print Rob's poster file. The file prints successfully. Rob tries to print it again but cannot. Laherty gets Rob to print a very small color picture to the printer and it completes successfully. Which of the following reasons best explains why Rob is unable to print?

   A. The permissions on the shared printer have been altered.

   B. The quotas applied to the printer have been set too low for Rob.

   C. There is a fault with the printer driver installed on Rob's Windows XP workstation.

   D. Rob is close to his allocated quota of disk space on the server.

   E. The file that Rob is trying to print is corrupted.

   F. The file that Rob is trying to print is too large for the printer's memory.

4.   Rooslan is the systems administrator for an organization that has four print servers. He is currently trying to determine which of the four servers prints the most jobs each day and which of the four servers prints the least jobs each day. He is considering creating three new shared printers and needs to select the print server with the lowest number of jobs printed. He also wants to check how many pages have been printed since the last restart. Which of the following will enable him to do this?

A. From the Printer Properties on each shared printer on each print server, check the Total Pages Printed Since Last Restart and Total Jobs Printed Since Last Restart statistics.

B. Run the Performance console on his Windows XP workstation. Add the Total Pages Printed counter object for each of the four print servers.

C. Run the Performance console on his Windows XP workstation. Add the Total Jobs Printed counter object for each of the four print servers.

D. Run the Performance console on his Windows XP workstation. Add the Total Jobs Printed counter object and the Total Pages Printed counter object for each of the four print servers that he wants to monitor.

Objective 4.8 Answers

1.   **Correct Answers: D**

    A. Incorrect: Quotas cannot be set by editing share properties. Quotas can only be set on a per-volume basis.

    B. Incorrect: Quotas cannot be set by editing folder properties. Quotas can only be set on a per-volume basis.

    C. Incorrect: Although quotas are added by the volume properties, they cannot be applied to groups—only to individual users and to the volume as a whole.

    D. Correct: Quotas can be set on a per-volume basis for individual users and applied to all users of the volume. Quotas cannot be set to specific user security groups. By backing up and repartitioning the disk each departmental share will have the correct quota applied to the users who use it.

2.   **Correct Answers: E**

    A. Incorrect: Quotas are not applied by Group Policy.

    B. Incorrect: Quotas are not applied by security groups.

    C. Incorrect: Quota settings can be exported to a file and then imported to function on another partition

    D. Incorrect: Quota settings are not applied by exporting and importing registry keys.

    E. Correct: This is the method used to place quotas on other partitions or on other servers. In the Quota Entries console select all entries that are to be exported, and from the quota menu select export. Copy the file to a place where it can be accessed by the other server and from its Quota Entries console, select Import from the Quota menu.

3.   **Correct Answers: D**

   A. **Incorrect:** No one except Laherty has access to these permissions and Laherty only visits on Fridays. Rob has only been unable to print his large file since Wednesday, indicating that this is not the problem.

   B. **Incorrect:** Windows Server 2003 does not natively support print quotas.

   C. **Incorrect:** This is unlikely because Rob was able to print a smaller color picture to the printer at a later time.

   D. **Correct:** Print jobs are spooled before being sent to the printer. In this situation the server has only a single volume, which has quotas applied. It is likely that Rob's job is unable to spool because the spool file surpasses his quota limit.

   E. **Incorrect:** This is unlikely because another user was able to print the same file to the printer.

   F. **Incorrect:** This is unlikely because another user was able to print the same file to the printer.

4.   **Correct Answers: D**

   A. **Incorrect:** These statistics do not exist.

   B. **Incorrect:** This will not generate the requisite information about number of jobs printed.

   C. **Incorrect:** This will not generate the requisite information about number of pages printed.

   D. **Correct:** This will generate the information that Rooslan wants. Rooslan may wish to leave this console running for some time to make sure that the figures are accurate. He may also wish to restart each of the servers at a similar time so that he doesn't have one server that has been operating for a significantly longer period of time skewing the results.

Objective 4.9

Manage a Web Server

Internet Information Services (IIS) version 6 ships with Windows Server 2003 but is not installed by default. A version of Windows Server 2003 that is built just for serving up Web pages is also available; it is called the Web Edition. The basic functionality of IIS is to serve up Web pages, whether that be to clients connecting remotely by the Internet or hosts connecting by the LAN. IIS can be used to do far more though. IIS can be used as a platform to support .NET Web services, Windows Media services, certificate services, and HTML remote administration of the Windows Server 2003 system. IIS also supports an FTP service, which can be used for file transfer between remote hosts and the server. IIS also supports a Network News Transfer Protocol (NNTP) service allowing newsgroups to be hosted off the server, which can be read by clients such as Outlook Express, as well as other newsgroup clients.

Access to IIS can be configured in several ways. Access can be restricted or granted based upon IP address, DNS name, or Network Address. Access can also be restricted to only those hosts that have the correct certificate or by Windows authentication, limiting access only to those users that have accounts on the system or within the domain. These forms of restriction and access are not mutually exclusive, for example: Clients can still be asked to provide authentication credentials even if they come from hosts that reside within an allowed network range.

The number of connections to a Web site can also be limited. This can be useful for several reasons: The first is to stop too many users from overloading the server and causing performance to suffer; the second is to reduce the Web server's impact on the Internet connection in case of a flood of traffic.

Objective 4.9 Questions

1.   Rooslan is the administrator of a Windows Server 2003 system that runs Internet Information Services. The server hosts a single Web site that contains confidential company information. This information should only be accessible by specific hosts from particular subnets within the corporate WAN. Rooslan would like to enable hosts to access the server only from the following IP address ranges:

10.10.10.1 through 10.10.10.126

10.10.10.129 through 10.10.10.190

10.10.20.225 through 10.10.20.238

10.10.30.193 through 10.10.30.254

Rooslan edits the default Web site properties, navigates to the Directory Security tab, and clicks Edit in the IP Address And Domain Name Restrictions frame. He selects Denied Access and then clicks Add to list the exceptions. Which of the following Network ID and Subnet Masks should he enter to limit access to the IP address ranges specified above? (Select all that apply.)

   A. Network ID: 10.10.10.0, Subnet mask: 255.255.255.128

   B. Network ID: 10.10.10.0, Subnet mask: 255.255.255.0

   C. Network ID: 10.10.10.128, Subnet mask: 255.255.255.64

   D. Network ID: 10.10.10.128, Subnet mask: 255.255.255.192

   E. Network ID: 10.10.20.224, Subnet mask: 255.255.255.224

   F. Network ID: 10.10.20.224, Subnet mask: 255.255.255.240

   G. Network ID: 10.10.30.192, Subnet mask: 255.255.255.192

2.   Oksana is concerned that a new Web site that she is about to launch will quickly overload her company's connection to the Internet. The Web site will be hosted on a Windows Server 2003 system running IIS 6.0 and contains streaming media as well as files for download. Oksana has talked to the network administrator and he has suggested that the Web site can use a maximum of 2 MB per second of the company's bandwidth without causing significant problems. Oksana would also like to limit the maximum number of users connecting to the Web site to 200 at a time. Which of the following should Oksana do to place these traffic restrictions on her Web site? (Select all that apply.)

A. Oksana should edit the network properties of the Windows Server 2003 system hosting the Web site and change the maximum outgoing speed to 2,048 kilobytes (KB) per second.

B. Oksana should edit the properties of the Web site. On the Performance tab, she should select the Bandwidth Throttling check box and set the Limit The Network Bandwidth Available To This Web Site: Maximum Bandwidth (in KB per second) to 2.

C. Oksana should edit the properties of the Web site. In the Performance Tab, she should select the Limit The Network Bandwidth Available To This Web Site check box and set the Maximum Bandwidth (in KB per second) to 2,000,000.

D. Oksana should edit the properties of the Web site. In the Performance Tab, she should select the Limit The Network Bandwidth Available To This Web Site check box and set the Limit The Network Bandwidth Available To This Web Site: Maximum Bandwidth (in KB per second) to 2,048.

E. Oksana should edit the properties of the Web site. On the Performance tab she should select the Web site connections option and set the Connections Limited To value at 100.

F. Oksana should edit the properties of the Web site. On the Performance tab, she should select and set the Connections Limited To value at 200.

3. You have cleared the Enable Anonymous Access check box in Authentication Methods of the Directory Security tab of the Default Web Site properties on a stand-alone Windows Server 2003 system running IIS. Which of the following methods of authentication are available to you? (Select all that apply.)

A. Integrated Windows Authentication

B. Digest Authentication

C. Basic Authentication

D. .NET Passport Authentication

4. You are the Web site administrator of a Windows Server 2003 system hosted by your ISP. You want to host several different Web sites off this server but your ISP is unable to allocate your hosted server more than a single public IP address. The public IP address you have been allocated is 207.46.248.234. The sites that you want to host are as follows:

www.adatum.com

www.alpineskihouse.com

www.proseware.com

www.tailspintoys.com

Each site is to contain completely unique content totally unrelated to the other sites. Which of the following steps should you take to resolve this problem? (Select two; each selection forms a part of the correct answer.)

A. Configure the DNS server hosting the records for *www.adatum.com, www.alpineskihouse.com, www.proseware.com,* and *www.tailspintoys.com* to point these hosts' records at IP address 207.46.248.234.

B. Configure the DNS server hosting the records for *www.adatum.com, www.alpineskihouse.com, www.proseware.com,* and *www.tailspintoys.com* to point these hosts records at IP address 207.46.234.248.

C. Create four separate Web sites, *www.adatum.com, www.alpineskihouse.com, www.proseware.com,* and *www.tailspintoys.com*. In the Web Site Creation Wizard, set the IP address of each Web site by entering **207.46.248.234**. For the host header of each Web site, enter the respective Web site name. In the path to the home directory for each Web site, type **c:\inetpub\wwwroot**. Disable the Default Web Site.

D. Create four separate Web sites, *www.adatum.com, www.alpineskihouse.com, www.proseware.com,* and *www.tailspintoys.com*. In the Web Site Creation Wizard, set the IP address of each Web site by entering **207.46.234.248**. For the host header of each Web site, enter the respective Web site name. In the path to the home directory for each Web site, enter the particular directory that hosts the corresponding Web site's unique content. Disable the Default Web Site.

E. Create four separate Web sites, *www.adatum.com, www.alpineskihouse.com, www.proseware.com,* and *www.tailspintoys.com*. In the Web Site Creation Wizard, set the IP address of each Web site by entering **207.46.248.234** For the host header of each Web site, enter the respective Web site name. In the path to the home directory for each Web site, enter the particular directory that hosts the corresponding Web site's unique content. Disable the Default Web Site.

Objective 4.9 Answers

1.   **Correct Answers: A, D, F, and G**

   A. **Correct:** This will allow the first set of hosts. 10.10.10.1 through 10.10.10.126 access to the Web site. 10.10.10.127 is the broadcast address for that subnet, hence not a host on the corporate WAN.

   B. **Incorrect:** This will allow access to hosts, specifically in the range of 10.10.10.224 through 10.10.10.254, that should not be granted access to the Web site.

   C. **Incorrect:** This is an invalid subnet mask. Subnet mask decimal quads can have the values 0, 128, 192, 224, 240, 248, 252, 254, and 255.

   D. **Correct:** This will allow the second set of hosts, 10.10.10.129 through to 10.10.10.190 to access the Web site. In this subnetting scheme, 10.10.10.128 is the network address and hence is not a host address. 10.10.10.190 is the broadcast address and therefore not an addressable host.

   E. **Incorrect:** This would allow hosts from 10.10.20.225 through to 10.10.20.255 to access the Web site.

   F. **Correct:** This will allow the third set of hosts, 10.10.20.225 through to 10.10.20.238 to access the Web site. 10.10.20.224 is the network address and 10.10.20.238 is the broadcast address in this particular subnetting scheme.

   G. **Correct:** This will allow the fourth set of hosts, 10.10.30.193 through 10.10.30.254 to access the Web site. 10.10.30.192 is the network address and 10.10.30.254 is the broadcast address in this particular subnetting scheme.

2.   **Correct Answers: D and F**

   A. **Incorrect:** The bandwidth usage of network cards cannot be controlled by network properties.

   B. **Incorrect:** This will limit the traffic to 2 KB rather than 2 MB.

   C. **Incorrect:** This will set the allowed bandwidth to approximately 1,953 MB per second.

   D. **Correct:** 2,048 KB is the same as 2 MB. This will limit the transfers from this server to 2 MB per second.

   E. **Incorrect:** This will limit connections to 100 at a time rather than 200.

   F. **Correct:** This will correctly set the maximum number of connections at any one time to 200.

3.   **Correct Answers: A, C, and D**

   A. **Correct:** This method is available to you and will use accounts created on the stand-alone Windows Server 2003 system.

   B. **Incorrect:** This option is only available if the Windows Server 2003 system is a member of an Active Directory environment. Because this is a stand-alone system, hence not a member of a domain, this option cannot be used.

   C. **Correct:** This option is available and will work with most browsers. The downside of this method is that it transmits authentication information in plaintext rather than encrypted format.

   D. **Correct:** This method of authentication is available although it will require some further configuration on the part of the administrator.

4.   **Correct Answers: A and E**

   A. **Correct:** This is the first part of the correct answer.

   B. **Incorrect:** This is the incorrect IP address (the last two octets have been switched around).

   C. **Incorrect:** This will point all the Web sites at the same content rather than the unique content.

   D. **Incorrect:** This will set the Web site to listen on the wrong IP address. The last two octets are switched around.

   E. **Correct:** This has both the correct IP address set and points to the corresponding directory hosting the unique Web site data.

18 Managing and Implementing Disaster Recovery (5.0)

Disasters will occur. Disks will fail, files will be lost, and power supplies will fuse with a puff of smoke, a few sparks, and an acrid smell. Systems administrators should not wait for a disaster to occur before deciding on a course of action. Before disaster strikes, administrators should have planned and put in place the procedures that will restore system functionality as soon as possible.

The first step in protecting data stored on Windows Server 2003 systems is to ensure that it is backed up correctly. Windows Server 2003 has a built-in backup application that enables the administrator to perform the vast majority of backup tasks. Critical systems should be backed up every 24 hours or more often in some cases. Backups can be written to several forms of media.

Windows Server 2003 also has a feature called Automated System Recovery (ASR) that is new to the server line of products. Automated System Recovery can be used to restore a completely non-functional system to working order. Automated System Recovery stores some configuration information on a special disk and other configuration information within the ASR backup set. Automated System Recovery only restores a system; it will not restore data that is stored on the system. Stored data must still be backed up in the normal manner.

It is also important for an administrator to understand how to repair a fault-tolerant volume set up within the Disk Management console if a disk happens to fail. The process for restoring a mirrored volume is different from that of restoring a RAID-5 volume. Administrators should test their fault-tolerant configurations, disabling disks to check that the server remains operational if a disk fails.

Finally, the ability to restore files and folders correctly from backup sets is also important. In general, if incremental or differential backups are used, restore first from the older backup set and then overwrite with data from the newer backup set.

Testing Skills and Suggested Practices

The skills that you need to successfully master the Managing and Implementing Disaster Recovery objective domain on *Exam 70-290: Managing and Maintaining a Microsoft Window Server 2003 Environment* include

- Perform system recovery for a server.
  - ❏ Practice 1: Perform an ASR backup on a server and then use the ASR process to perform a recovery of that server.
  - ❏ Practice 2: Backup the System State data on a server with Internet Information Services (IIS) installed. Change the IIS settings. Restore the System State data and notice what has changed in the IIS settings.

- Manage backup procedures.
  - ❏ Practice 1: Use different media such as tape drives, local hard disks and network storage to store backup sets.
  - ❏ Practice 2: Create several different backups and store them on a local hard disk drive. From the Restore and Manage Media tab, delete each of the catalogs associated with each particular file. Then right-click on the file box and select Catalog File. Browse to the different backups and allow them to be recataloged.

- Recover from server hardware failure.
  - ❏ Practice 1: Create a mirror of the boot/system volume. Restart the Windows Server 2003 system off the mirror.
  - ❏ Practice 2: Create a RAID-5 set within the Disk Management console. Store some data on the volume that is hosted on the RAID-5 set. Disable one of the disks in the RAID-5 set and then reactivate the set. Repair the RAID-5 set.

- Restore backup data.
  - ❏ Practice 1: From a full backup, practice restoring a particular set of files and folders to a separate location on the server.
  - ❏ Practice 2: Take a full backup and three incremental backups after the full backup. Restore them in the correct order to a different location in the folder, making sure that older files do not overwrite newer ones.

- Schedule backup jobs.
  - ❏ Practice 1: Create a backup job and schedule it to run each day.
  - ❏ Practice 2: Create a backup job that performs a full backup of a set of files and folders once a week. Create a second backup job that performs an incremental backup of the same set of files and folders every other day of the week.

Further Reading

This section lists supplemental readings by objective. We recommend that you study these sources thoroughly before taking this exam.

Objective 5.1   Review Chapter 13, "Recovering from System Failure."

Microsoft Corporation. Windows Server 2003 Help and Support Center. Review "System State Data."

Microsoft Corporation. Windows Server 2003 Help and Support Center. Review "Automated System Recovery Overview."

Microsoft Corporation. Windows Server 2003 Help and Support Center. Review "Volume Shadow Copy Overview."

Microsoft Corporation. Windows Server 2003 Help and Support Center. Review "Authoritative, Primary and Normal Restores."

Objective 5.2   Review Chapter 7, "Backing up Data."

Microsoft Corporation. Windows Server 2003 Help and Support Center. Review "Maintain Media."

Objective 5.3   Review Chapter 11, Lesson 4: "Implementing RAID."

Review Chapter 13, "Recovering from System Failure."

Microsoft Corporation. Windows Server 2003 Help and Support Center. Review "Replace a Failed Mirror with a New Mirror."

Objective 5.4   Review Chapter 7, Lesson 2: "Restoring Data"; and Lesson 3: "Advanced Backup and Restore."

Microsoft Corporation. Windows Server 2003 Help and Support Center. Review "Restore Data."

Objective 5.5   Review Chapter 7, Lesson 3: "Advanced Backup and Restore."

Microsoft Corporation. Windows Server 2003 Help and Support Center. Review "Schedule a Backup."

Perform Server System Recovery

When a Windows Server 2003 system crashes in a way that it cannot be fixed simply by performing a restart, other options must be explored. An option new to Windows Server 2003, Automated System Recovery, uses a combination of a Windows settings diskette, a special ASR backup set and the Windows Server 2003 installation media to restore a system. Automated System Recovery should be used as a measure of last resort as the operating system files will be reinstalled. It is also important to note that Automated System Recovery does not back up data stored on the server, only important Windows Server 2003 files.

When recovering a domain controller, systems administrators must decide about the type of active directory restoration, if any, they will perform. An authoritative restore allows the Microsoft Active Directory directory service database stored on the backup set to take precedence over the Active Directory database replicated in the domain. A non-authoritative restore allows the current Active Directory database to overwrite the database from the backup set.

In some cases, the restoration of the System State data will allow a server to return to operational status. The System State data includes the system's registry, COM+ class registration database. The boot files and system files protected by the Windows File Protection service. Depending on the services installed on the Windows Server 2003 system, System State data can also include the Certificate Services database, Active Directory and the Sysvol folder on a domain controller, cluster service information on a cluster server and the Internet Information Services (IIS) metabase. If one of these areas of the operating system has been corrupted, restoring the System State data may return the server to functionality.

Objective 5.1 Questions

1.   Rooslan is the systems administrator at a medium-sized organization that has 400 employees located at two sites. At 2 A.M. each day, a full backup, including System State data, is taken of the three Windows Server 2003 domain controllers on the network. One morning, Foley, a junior administrator who works for Rooslan, accidentally deleted three organizational units (OUs) from Active Directory. Foley did not discover his mistake until several hours later, by which time the mistake had replicated to the other domain controllers. No other changes have been made to the Active Directory database in the last 24 hours, so Rooslan decided to restore the System State data from the backup that was taken at 2 A.M. Which type of restore will return the three deleted OUs to the Active Directory database?

   A. Authoritative Restore

   B. Non-authoritative restore

   C. Primary Restore

   D. Diligent Restore

2.   Rooslan has just received a panicked telephone call from Foley, a junior administrator who works for Rooslan at a medium-sized organization. Foley has accidentally deleted the OU that contained the senior management team's user accounts from the Active Directory database. Before Foley was able to do anything about this mistake, the domain controller in the domain replicated and the deletion propagated across the network. Backups are taken of all domain controller System State data at 2:30 A.M. every day. No other changes have been made to the Active Directory database today, so Rooslan tells Foley that they should prepare to do an authoritative restore of the Active Directory database on one of the domain controllers. Rooslan goes to the server room, locates the previous night's backup media, and then shuts off one of the Windows Server 2003 domain controllers. In which of the following modes should Rooslan start the Windows Server 2003 domain controller?

   A. Start the Windows Server 2003 domain controller in Last Known Good Configuration.

   B. Start the Windows Server 2003 domain controller in Safe mode.

   C. Start the Windows Server 2003 domain controller in the Recovery Console.

   D. Start the Windows Server 2003 domain controller normally.

   E. Start the Windows Server 2003 domain controller in Directory Services Restore mode.

3. You are the systems administrator of five Windows Server 2003 systems that are members of the domain. These five servers host a variety of Web sites using Internet Information Services (IIS). Each of these servers has two hard disk drives. The first disk hosts the volume that contains the operating system and program files. The second disk hosts a volume that stores all the Web site data. The Web site data and System State is backed up every 24 hours to a network file server. All the Web site settings, such as security permissions and domain access restrictions, are unique to each Web site.

This morning the hard disk drive hosting the operating system failed on one of the IIS servers. The second hard disk drive hosting the Web site data is fully operational. You get a replacement hard disk drive from the storeroom, install it into the server and install Windows Server 2003 and the program files that had been on the server. Which of the following methods can you use to restore the functionality that existed before the crash to the Web server? (Select all that apply.)

A. All functionality has already been restored to the server, and nothing more needs to be done.

B. Use the Backup Utility to restore the files that comprise the Web sites from the network file share to the second hard disk drive for the IIS server you are trying to restore.

C. Use Directory Services Restore mode on the IIS server to restore the System State data from the network share.

D. While logged on to the IIS server you are trying to restore, copy the most recent backup across from the network file server to the local hard disk drive. Restore the System State data from this backup and restart the server if required.

E. While logged on to the IIS server you are trying to restore, use the Backup Utility to restore the System State data from the backup stored on the network location and restart the server if required.

4. Which of the following statements is true about restoring a stand-alone root certificate authority (CA) that has suffered a hard disk failure on the volume that hosts the operating system and the certificate database?

A. The certificate database can only be restored using the Certification Authority snap-in.

B. When restoring a CA, the IIS metabase must also be restored if it has been damaged or lost.

    C. A password must be entered when restoring System State data on a server that has a stand-alone CA installed.

    D. A password must be entered when restoring Private Key, CA Certificate, Certificate Database, and Certificate Database Log which has been backed up by using the Certification Authority snap-in of the Microsoft Management Console (MMC).

    E. The certificate database is restored when Automated System Recover is performed.

5. A hacker has gained access to your Web server and deleted or corrupted many of the important system files on a Windows Server 2003 system that you are responsible for administering. After spending some time using the recovery console you conclude that the damage is so extensive that you must use Automated System Recovery to restore the server to its former working state. You last prepared the server for automated system recovery four days ago. Which of the following methods presents the correct way of starting automated system recovery?

    A. Restart in Directory Services Restore mode using the ASR disk that was created during the ASR preparation process four days ago.

    B. Restart using the Windows Server 2003 installation CD-ROM and, when prompted, insert the ASR disk that was created during the ASR preparation process four days ago.

    C. Restart in Safe mode and, when prompted, insert the ASR disk that was created during the ASR preparation process four days ago.

    D. Start in Directory Services Restore mode and, when prompted, insert the ASR disk that was created during the ASR preparation process four days ago.

    E. Start in the Recovery console and, when prompted, insert the ASR disk that was created during the ASR preparation process four days ago.

6.   Oksana is a junior systems administrator at your organization. She is responsible for administering two Windows Server 2003 systems that host Internet Information Services. Each server hosts a single Web site and each Web site has unique configuration information. This unique configuration includes individual lists of allowed and disallowed hosts as well as account access lists. Both Windows Server 2003 systems have IIS installed in its default location. Oksana telephones to inform you that a virus appears to have infiltrated one of the IIS servers. The virus has caused the deletion of 95 percent of the Web content stored on the server as well as the corruption of the IIS metabase. The system has now been cleaned with an updated virus scanner removing all traces of infected files. However several other areas of the system have become corrupted by the virus, rendering it highly unstable. Major updates to different areas of the Web site have been occurring throughout the week. Today is Friday. Oksana has performed the following disaster recovery tasks on the server in the past week.

Thursday: Automated system recovery backup.

Wednesday: Incremental backup of Web site data.

Tuesday: Incremental backup of Web site data.

Monday: System State data backup.

Sunday: Full backup of Web site data.

All relevant backup media is available. Which of the following methods should Oksana use to restore the IIS metabase and the Web site data that was lost?

   A.   Oksana needs to perform only an Automated System Recovery.

   B.   Oksana must perform an Automated System Recovery. Once that is complete, she needs to restore the backup data from Wednesday.

   C.   Oksana needs to perform an Automated System Recovery. Once that is complete, she needs to restore Sunday's, Tuesday's, and Wednesday's backup data.

   D.   Oksana needs to restore Monday's backup of the System State data, Sunday's full backup, and Wednesday's incremental backup.

   E.   Oksana must restore Monday's backup of the System State data, Sunday's full backup, as well as Tuesday's and Wednesday's incremental backup data.

7.   There has been a fire in the server room. You have lost the box that contains all the ASR disks, but the storage unit that contains the backup tapes is intact. Three of your Windows Server 2003 systems have been damaged, rendering them inoperable, and two more seem to have emerged from the fire unscathed. Each Windows Server 2003 system had its own 40 gigabyte (GB) digital audio tape (DAT) drive. A complete ASR backup on each server was performed several days ago. Each of the five Windows Server 2003 systems had a unique configuration that was different from all the others.

Which of the following statements about recovering the three damaged servers using Automated System Recovery is true?

A. Once the hardware has been repaired, these servers cannot be recovered. Special files, located on an ASR disk, are unique to the server being recovered. If that disk is lost, the corresponding ASR set for that server is rendered useless.

B. Once the hardware has been repaired, these servers can be recovered. You should perform an ASR backup on one of the functional servers creating a new disk. You can then use this ASR disk to perform the ASR process on the damaged servers.

C. Once the hardware has been repaired, these servers can be recovered. You should run the Backup Utility on one of the functional servers and use it to restore the Asr.sif and Asrpnp.sif from the functional server's ASR backup set to floppy disk. You can then use this ASR disk to perform the ASR process on the servers that had suffered damage.

D. Once the hardware has been repaired, these servers can be recovered. You should run the Backup Utility on one of the functional servers and use it to restore the Asr.sif and Asrpnp.sif from each of the damaged server's ASR backup sets to floppy disks. You can then use each formerly damaged server's corresponding ASR disk during in the ASR process on that server.

8. Rooslan would like to make sure that only members of the Administrators group can restore System State data from a particular Windows Server 2003 system that contains a certificate authority database. Which of the following ways correctly describes how this can be done without removing the right of the Backup Operators group to restore other backup sets?

A. When starting the backup, ensure that the Allow Only The Owner And The Administrator Access To The Backup Data option, in the Backup Job Information dialog box, is selected.

B. From the Restore And Manage Media tab, select the media properties to which the System State data is being written. Change the permissions so that only the Administrators group has access to this media.

C. Restoration of backup sets can always be done by members of the Administrators group as well as members of the Backup Operators group. Access cannot be restricted to one group or the other.

D. Edit the local Group Policy object and change the Backup Files And Directories policy located in the Computer Configuration\Windows Settings\Security Settings\Local Policies\User Rights Assignment container and remove the Backup Operators group.

E. Edit the local Group Policy object and change the Restore Files And Directories policy located in the Computer Configuration\Windows Settings\Security Settings\Local Policies\User Rights Assignment container and remove the Backup Operators group.

Objective 5.1 Answers

1. **Correct Answers: A**

  A. **Correct:** An authoritative restore means that Active Directory objects that had originally been deleted from the Active Directory database will not be overwritten the next time the restored server replicates with other domain controllers in the domain. If an authoritative restore is not used, the deleted items will simply be removed the next time the other domain controllers in the domain replicate.

  B. **Incorrect:** Any Active Directory objects restored using a non-authoritative restore that have since been deleted from the directory will be removed the next time the server replicates with other domain controllers in the domain.

  C. **Incorrect:** Any Active Directory objects restored using a primary restore that have since been deleted from the directory will be removed the next time the server replicates with other domain controllers in the domain.

  D. **Incorrect:** There is no such method as a diligent restore.

2. **Correct Answers: E**

  A. **Incorrect:** Starting the domain controller in Last Known Good Configuration will not allow the Active Directory database to be restored in a way that the OU containing the senior management team's account will be recoverable.

  B. **Incorrect:** Starting the domain controller in Safe mode will not allow the Active Directory database to be restored in a way that the OU containing the senior management team's account will be recoverable.

  C. **Incorrect:** The Active Directory database cannot be recovered from the Recovery Console.

  D. **Incorrect:** Starting the domain controller normally will not allow the Active Directory database to be restored in a way that the OU containing the senior management team's account will be recoverable.

  E. **Correct:** Directory Services Restore mode is a special mode that can be used to recover the Active Directory database. From Directory Services Restore mode the administrator can choose whether to do an authoritative or non-authoritative restore of the Active Directory database.

3.   Correct Answers: D and E

A. Incorrect: Although the data exists, none of the Web site settings will exist. These are stored in the System State data that has to be restored.

B. Incorrect: Because the Web site files are unaffected, using the Backup Utility will not make any difference. It will simply overwrite the files that are already stored on the second disk drive with exact duplicates.

C. Incorrect: Because these servers are not domain controllers but are members of the domain they will not have an Active Directory database, nor will the option exist to start them into Directory Services Restore mode.

D. Correct: The IIS metabase, which contains all the IIS settings, is backed up when the System State data is backed up. Although it can be restored from the network location, this will also work if the backup is copied to the local hard disk drive.

E. Correct: The IIS metabase, which contains all the IIS settings, is backed up when the System State data is backed up. So long as you are logged on to the server on which you are doing the restoration, you can use backup data stored on remote servers.

4.   Correct Answers: B, D, and E

A. Incorrect: The certificate database can be restored using the Backup Utility because the certificate database is also part of the System State data.

B. Correct: Without IIS working correctly and configured to support the CA, the certificate services Web pages will fail to load. When a CA is installed, the appropriate modifications are made to the IIS metabase

C. Incorrect: No password is required to restore System State data. Backups and restorations can, however, be restricted to the Administrators group.

D. Correct: This is to provide a level of security so that an intruder who may have acquired the backup tapes cannot use the backup data to create his or her version of the same CA. If the database has been backed up using the System State, no password is required to access this data.

E. Correct: Automated System Recovery stores the System State data and the certificate database is part of that data.

5.   **Correct Answers: B**

   A. **Incorrect:** The ASR disk cannot be used as a boot disk. It contains information about the system but does not contain the necessary files to start Windows Server 2003.

   B. **Correct:** This is the correct method of performing Automated System Recovery on a Windows Server 2003 system. The disk created in Automated System Recovery is not a boot disk, it merely stores important system configuration files, such as the disk layout, which are needed at the beginning of the recovery process. Other files are either copied from the installation media or from the ASR backup set.

   C. **Incorrect:** Starting in Safe mode will not initiate the ASR process.

   D. **Incorrect:** The ASR process cannot be initiated from Directory Services Restore mode.

   E. **Incorrect:** The recovery console cannot be used to initiate the ASR process.

6.   **Correct Answers: C**

   A. **Incorrect:** Automated System Recovery does not restore data, although it will restore the IIS metabase and fix the files that are causing the system instability.

   B. **Incorrect:** Automated System Recovery does not restore data, although it will restore the IIS metabase and fix the files that are causing system instability.

   C. **Correct:** The Automated System Recovery will restore the files that are causing instability as well as the IIS metabase. Because the backups are incremental, each incremental backup as well as the original full backup must be restored to reproduce all the missing files.

   D. **Incorrect:** This will not fix the instability that is caused by files other than those backed up by the System State. Also any files that were backed up in Tuesday's incremental backup will not be restored.

   E. **Incorrect:** Although this will restore the metabase and all the Web site data, it will do nothing about other files that are causing system instability.

7. **Correct Answers: D**

    A. Incorrect: This is not true. A new ASR disk can be generated from the corresponding ASR set on the DAT tapes for that server.

    B. Incorrect: Each server was said to have a unique configuration, which means that the information written to one server's ASR disk will be different from that written to another server's ASR disk.

    C. Incorrect: Although this process is almost correct, restoring Aas.sif and Asr-pnp.sif from the functional server's ASR backup set, rather than those files from the damaged server's ASR backup set, will mean that the ASR disk contains the wrong information to restore the damaged servers correctly.

    D. Correct: When an ASR backup set is written the files that are written to the ASR disk are also written to the ASR backup set stored on the backup media. This means that even if the ASR disk is lost, it can be recovered from information stored in the ASR backup set.

8. **Correct Answers: A**

    A. Correct: This is the only method of limiting which users or groups can perform a restoration of a particular backup set.

    B. Incorrect: This functionality does not exist from the Restore And Manage Media tab.

    C. Incorrect: Access can be restricted to the Administrators group by following the procedure outlined in answer A.

    D. Incorrect: This will not change the right of the Backup Operators group to restore backup sets, but will prevent them from backing up files and folders.

    E. Incorrect: This will stop the Backup Operators group from restoring all data, not just the System State data.

Manage Backup Procedures

When the System State data is backed up, the following items are written to the backup set: System's Registry, COM+ Class Registration database, boot files, and system files that are protected by the Windows File Protection service. Depending on which services have been installed on the Windows Server 2003 system, System State data can also include the Certificate Services database, Active Directory and the Sysvol folder on a domain controller, cluster service information on a cluster server and the IIS metabase.

If an administrator wants to verify that a backup job has completed successfully, the verification must be configured before the backup job is run. Verification of backup jobs cannot be done separately after the job has completed. Verification checks that the files and folders that have been written to the backup match the files and folders that were backed up. Although checking the backup logs can alert an administrator that an error has occurred, it will not inform the administrator if the backed-up file does not match the original unless verification has been enabled.

Certain types of media such as tape drives, hard disks, and some forms of removable storage can hold backup sets. Backup sets can also be written to network file shares. Some media, such as CD-ROM writers, are not supported by the Windows Server 2003 Backup Utility.

Objective 5.2 Questions

1.   Rooslan is the systems administrator of a Windows Server 2003 system running Internet Information Services. This server is used to issue digital certificates to third parties on the Internet. These certificates enable subscribers to access specially restricted portions of the Web site that are not available to other users that visit the site. Rooslan wants the IIS configuration and the certificate database backed up once a week. Rooslan also wants to make sure that once a week every file and folder in the C:\Inetpub folder is backed up. Finally Rooslan wants any changes made to files or folders in this directory after the weekly backup to be backed up each day, but in a method that uses the smallest amount of space on the backup media. Which of the following backups should Rooslan perform? (Select all that apply.)

   A.   A full backup each day of the week

   B.   A full backup once a week

   C.   A full backup, including System State data, once a week

   D.   A differential backup each day of the week

   E.   An incremental backup each day of the week

2.   Which of the following methods will allow automatic verification that a backup has successfully completed?

   A.   When starting the backup job, click Advanced and select Verify Data After Backup.

   B.   Use the Backup Wizard to run a verification job.

   C.   From the Restore And Manage Media tab of the Backup Utility, select the Properties backup that has been performed and then select Verify.

   D.   There is no way to verify that a job has successfully completed in the Windows Server 2003 Backup Utility.

3.   To which of the following devices can backups be written by the Windows Server 2003 Backup Utility? (Select all that apply.)

   A.   CD-ROM burner

   B.   Network share

   C.   DAT tape drive

   D.   DVD-ROM burner

4. You have been administering several Windows Server 2003 file servers. Your department has recently purchased a file server that has significantly more storage capacity than any other server on your LAN. You are in the process of moving several file shares off the other server and onto this new server. As each file server contains unique NTFS permissions, you are using the Windows Server 2003 Backup And Restore utility to ensure that the permissions that were on the original files and folders are retained once they are moved to their new server host. The backup sets are now located on one of the volumes of the new server. Their locations are as follows:

E:\Fileshbak1.bkf

E:\Fileshbak2.bkf

E:\Fileshbak3.bkf

You run the Windows Server 2003 Backup Utility. You want to have each of the backup sets imported into the Backup Utility's Restore And Manage Media tab so that you can restore all the files and folders to new directories on the new server. Which of the following methods will enable you to do this?

A. Double-click each of the files. This will import them into the Restore And Manage Media tab.

B. Drag each of the backup files from Windows Explorer to the Restore And Manage Media tab of the Backup Utility.

C. On the Tools menu, from the Backup Wizard select Catalog A Backup File. Browse to each file separately and then catalog them.

D. Media not created by the Backup Utility cannot be imported for restoration.

Objective 5.2 Answers

1. **Correct Answers: C and E**

   A. **Incorrect:** This will not back up the IIS configuration or certificate database. It will also not use the smallest amount of space on the backup media.

   B. **Incorrect:** This will not back up the IIS configuration or certificate database.

   C. **Correct:** This will back up the IIS configuration and the certificate database as well as perform the full backup required.

   D. **Incorrect:** Differential backups use more space on the backup media than incremental backups do. Differential backups store all information created or modified since the last full backup.

   E. **Correct:** Incremental backups use the least amount of space. They back up only data that has been created or modified since the last incremental backup.

2. **Correct Answers: A**

   A. **Correct:** This is the way to ensure that the backup has correctly stored the selected data.

   B. **Incorrect:** There is no such thing as a verification job in the Windows Server 2003 Backup Utility.

   C. **Incorrect:** This option does not exist.

   D. **Incorrect:** This is incorrect. A job must be verified immediately after it has completed by setting the Verify Data After Backup.option when running the backup job.

3. **Correct Answers: B and C**

   A. **Incorrect:** CD-ROM burners are not recognized as devices to which backups can be written by the Windows Server 2003 Backup Utility.

   B. **Correct:** Backups can be written from the Windows Server 2003 Backup Utility to network shares.

   C. **Correct:** Tape drives are the traditional method of backing up data and as such are recognized by the Windows Server 2003 Backup Utility.

   D. **Incorrect:** CD-ROM and DVD-ROM burners are not recognized as devices to which backups can be written by the Windows Server 2003 Backup Utility.

4.   **Correct Answers: C**

    A. **Incorrect:** Although this will open the Backup Utility, it will not automatically set up the selected file for import or restoration.

    B. **Incorrect:** This method will not work.

    C. **Correct:** This is one method by which the contents of these files can be added to the Restore And Manage Media tab.

    D. **Incorrect:** This is not true. The Catalog A Backup File command on the Tools menu allows backup files to be imported to the utility.

Recover from Server Hardware Failure

If a server has been configured with fault tolerance in mind, the process of recovering from the failure of a disk drive is not as frightening as it may initially sound. Windows Server 2003 can be configured through the Disk Management console to use either disk mirroring or RAID-5 sets, both of which will allow the server to function after the loss of a hard disk drive.

Mirrored volumes (RAID-1) are generally used for the boot/system volume of a Windows Server 2003 system. This is in part because the boot/system volume cannot be configured to function within a software RAID-5 array by the Windows Server 2003 disk management utilities. The server can be booted from either disk in a mirrored set and, once a mirrored set is created, a new option is added to the operating system selection menu (boot.ini) at startup.

RAID-5 volumes are generally used to store data and program files. Requiring three or more disks, though never more than 32, a RAID-5 volume can continue to function after the loss of one of its component disk drives. Performance will be reduced but the volume will still function. At a later time, the administrator will be able to power off the server, install a replacement disk, and then regenerate the volume. Once the volume is regenerated, original performance will be restored.

1. Rooslan is the systems administrator of a Windows Server 2003 system that has four Small Computer System Interface (SCSI) hard disk drives. The server contains two volumes, each of which takes up an entire SCSI hard disk drive. The first disk drive hosts the first volume, which contains the operating system and the program files. The second disk drive hosts the second volume, which contains program data and several file shares. Disk Mirroring has been configured within the Disk Management console. The first volume is mirrored on the third disk and the second volume is mirrored on the fourth disk.

The fourth disk fails. Which of the following must Rooslan do to restore the fault tolerance on this server? (Select all that apply.)

   A. Rooslan must remove the mirror between the first and third disks before installing a replacement disk.

   B. Rooslan must break the failed mirror between the second and fourth disks before installing a replacement disk.

   C. Rooslan must create a new mirror between the second and the fourth disks after the replacement disk has been installed.

   D. Rooslan must remove the failed disk, install the new disk and then break the mirror between the first and third disks.

2. Oksana is the systems administrator of a Windows Server 2003 system that has the system volume mirrored on a second physical hard disk drive through the Disk Management console. The first hard disk, which hosts the system volume, fails and the system halts. A replacement disk is available. Which of the following things should Oksana do to restore fault tolerance to the Windows Server 2003 system?

   A. Use the Windows Server 2003 installation media to launch a Recovery Console. From the Recovery Console, remove the mirror. Shut down the server and install the replacement disk. Use the Windows Server 2003 installation media to launch the Recovery Console. Use the Recovery Console to create a new mirror set.

   B. Remove the failed hard disk drive and boot off the mirrored volume. Run the Disk Management console and remove the mirror to the failed hard disk. Shut down the system and install the replacement disk. Boot the server from the mirrored volume. Run the Disk Management console. Initialize the newly installed disk and convert it to dynamic. Create a mirrored pair between the original mirror and this new disk.

C. Remove the failed disk. Install the replacement disk. Boot the server from the Windows Server 2003 installation media and select repair installation.

D. Remove the failed disk. Install the replacement disk. Start the server into Last Known Good Configuration. Run the System Repair Wizard.

3. Rooslan is the systems administrator of a Windows Server 2003 system that runs SQL Server 2000. The server has six SCSI hard disk drives attached. The first two form a mirrored pair and host the volume that contains the operating system and the program files. The other four SCSI disks are configured in RAID-5 and host a single volume that contains all the database data. Currently, 40 percent of the volume is used. One of the four disks in the RAID-5 volume fails. Which of the following statements about this situation is true?

A. The server will continue operating and no data has been lost.

B. The server will halt. The server will be operational once the failed disk has been replaced.

C. Once the volume is reactivated the server will continue operating. New data cannot be written to the RAID-5 volume, but current data can be read and backed up.

D. All data will be lost. A striped set, rather than RAID-5, is required for fault tolerance.

4. There are nine SCSI hard disk drives installed on a Windows Server 2003 system. Disk 1 hosts the volume that contains the operating system. Disks 2, 5, and 8 comprise a single RAID-5 volume. Disks 3, 4, and 6 host a single RAID-5 volume. Disk 1 is mirrored by Disk 7. Disk 9 hosts a single volume.

Which of the disks can fail at the same time but leave the server fully operational after a restart?

A. Disks 1, 2, and 5 fail at the same time.

B. Disks 6, 7, and 8 fail at the same time.

C. Disks 1, 7, and 8 fail at the same time.

D. Disks 1, 6, and 9 fail at the same time.

E. Disks 1, 2, and 3 fail at the same time.

Objective 5.3 Answers

1.   Correct Answers: B and C

A. **Incorrect:** Neither the first nor the third disk has failed, so breaking the mirror will do nothing to restore fault tolerance, merely reduce the current level of fault tolerance.

B. **Correct:** Until this mirror is removed a new mirror cannot be created

C. **Correct:** Doing this will restore fault tolerance by recreating the mirror set with a new disk.

D. **Incorrect:** Breaking the mirror between the first and the third disks will not improve fault tolerance. It is the pairing of the second and fourth disks that is problematic.

2.   Correct Answers: B

A. **Incorrect:** The Recovery Console cannot be used to remove or create mirrored sets.

B. **Correct:** This is one way to restore the fault tolerance of this server. Once a mirrored volume is created the server can use the mirrored volume as it would the original.

C. **Incorrect:** This process will not restore the fault tolerance of the original setup.

D. **Incorrect:** This process will not restore the fault tolerance of the original setup.

3.   Correct Answers: A

A. **Correct:** The server will keep operating and no data will be lost. The read and write performance will be worse than normal as parity information will need to be converted into readable data. At some stage in the future the failed disk also must be replaced.

B. **Incorrect:** The volume can be reactivated from within the Disk Management console, hence this answer is incorrect.

C. **Incorrect:** Because only 40 percent of the volume was currently being used, data can be written and read from the disk. It will be done with degraded performance, however.

D. **Incorrect:** Striped sets are not fault tolerant, hence this answer is incorrect. The data will not be lost if one of the members of the RAID-5 volume fails.

4.   **Correct Answers: B and E**

  A. **Incorrect:** Disk one is mirrored by Disk 7, so it is fault-tolerant. However, Disk 2 is a member of the same RAID-5 volume as Disk 5. RAID-5 cannot recover from two disks failing at the same time.

  B. **Correct:** Disk 6 is not in a RAID-5 set with Disk 7 or 8. Disk 7 is paired with Disk 1 and Disk 8 is not in a RAID-5 set with Disk 6 or Disk 7.

  C. **Incorrect:** Disks 1 and 7 form a mirrored set of the system volume.

  D. **Incorrect:** Disk 9 has no fault tolerance.

  E. **Correct:** Disk 1 is paired with Disk 7, so it can fail. Disk 2 is not in a RAID-5 volume with Disk 3, so it can fail, and Disk 3 is not in a RAID-5 volume with Disk 2, so it also can fail and the server will remain operational after a restart.

Restore Backup Data

The aim of any restoration procedure is to ensure that all the data that has been backed up is restored correctly. Unless a full backup is taken every day onto separate backup media, understanding which tapes to use in a backup and in what order to restore them becomes a complex task.

Pivotal to understanding how to restore files is understanding how the different backup methods work. A systems administrator should understand why all the tapes including the last full backup must be restored when incremental backups have been taken. Similarly a system administrator must understand why only the last full and the most recent differential backup need to be restored when the differential method is used.

Although systems administrators back up data fearing that the backups will be required for a complete server rebuild, the most likely time that restorations will occur will be when a user has lost or deleted a file. Being able to quickly identify the backup set that contains the missing file saves an administrator time. An administrator does not wish to restore a week's worth of backup sets trying to locate a single file when going through one backup set would suffice.

Objective 5.4 Questions

1. You are the systems administrator responsible for several Windows Server 2003 systems at a medium-sized industrial plant. One of the servers is a file and print server. The server comprises three disks, one of which hosts the volume containing the operating system. The other two are configured as a striped set and host several file shares. Backups are written to a DAT drive on the server and backup tapes are stored off site. The backed-up data includes every file and folder on the striped volume hosting the file shares as well as the System State data. The rest of the operating system volume is not backed up, though an Automated System Recovery set is generated once a month. The backup regime is as follows:

2:00 A.M. Sunday. Full Backup and System State Data.

2:00 A.M. Monday through Saturday. Incremental Backup and System State Data.

On Thursday at 2:00 P.M., the second disk in the striped set suffers a failure. You have an identical replacement on site and are able to retrieve the last seven days of backup tapes, including the ASR set and disk, from the off-site location. Which of the following is required to restore the lost data?

    A. Remove the failed disk and replace it with the duplicate. Use the Disk Management console to regenerate the striped volume.

    B. Remove the failed disk and replace it with the duplicate. Restart the server from the installation CD-ROM and insert the ASR disk to perform the ASR process.

    C. Remove the failed disk and replace it with the duplicate. Restore the System State data. Use the Disk Management console to regenerate the striped volume.

    D. Remove the failed disk and replace it with the duplicate. Use the Disk Management console to recreate the striped volume across the original disk and the replacement. Use the Backup Utility to restore the data to the striped volume from the backup sets made on Sunday and Thursday.

    E. Remove the failed disk and replace it with the duplicate. Use the Disk Management console to recreate the striped volume across the original disk and the replacement. Use the Backup Utility to restore the data to the striped volume from the backup sets made on Sunday, Monday, Tuesday, Wednesday, and Thursday.

2.   You are the systems administrator responsible for managing four Windows Server 2003 file servers in a university's department. You receive a telephone call from the secretary of the department head telling you that she has accidentally deleted an important file from the file server. It was a research paper that the department head is presenting to a symposium tomorrow and it is urgent that the file be recovered. A differential backup is performed every evening except for Friday at 10:00 P.M., when a full backup is performed. Each day's backup is written to a separate tape, which is labeled with the day the backup is performed. Today is Thursday. The secretary believes that she deleted the file yesterday morning. The file was last modified Monday and was not accessed over the weekend. Assuming that she is correct, which of the following backup tapes will contain a copy of the file? (Select all that apply.)

  A. Friday's tape

  B. Saturday's tape

  C. Sunday's tape

  D. Monday's tape

  E. Tuesday's tape

  F. Wednesday's tape

3.   You are responsible for managing a Windows Server 2003 file server for an accounting firm. One of the accountants informs you that she has deleted several important spreadsheets accidentally from the file server. A differential backup is performed every morning except for Monday, when a full backup is performed at 2:00 A.M. Each day's backup is written to a separate tape, which is labeled with the day the backup is taken. Today is Friday. The accountant believes that she accidentally deleted the spreadsheets yesterday evening. There are five missing spreadsheets. Only two have been worked on in the last week. The first was last modified Monday afternoon and the second has not been edited except for a minor change on Wednesday. Which of the following statements about the backup tapes is correct? (Select all that apply.)

  A. The three files that have not been modified in the last week will be present only on the Monday backup tape.

  B. That all five files will be present on the Thursday backup tape.

  C. That two of the five deleted spreadsheet files will be present on the Thursday backup tape.

  D. Two of the five deleted spreadsheet files will be present on the Wednesday backup tape.

  E. None of the five deleted spreadsheet files will be present on the Tuesday backup tape.

4.   Rooslan is responsible for the backups of a Windows Server 2003 system that hosts several Web sites. These Web sites are full of content that is updated on a daily basis by individual site administrators. All the Web site files are located on a separate disk and volume from the one that hosts the operating system and the program files. A full backup, including System State data, is taken of the Web site to a network location every Tuesday at 3:00 A.M. This backup takes approximately two hours to complete. A differential backup is taken of the Web site to a network location every other morning at 3:30 A.M. and this takes approximately one-and-a-half hours to complete. On Saturday at 4:30 A.M., the disk that hosts the volume storing the Web site data fails completely. You receive a message on your pager and are in the server room by 5:30 A.M. You have a replacement hard disk that has identical properties to the one that has failed. You replace the failed disk and are about to begin the restoration process. Which of the following backup sets will you use to restore the most complete version possible of the Web site data? (Select all that apply.)

    A. Tuesday's backup set

    B. Wednesday's backup set

    C. Thursday's backup set

    D. Friday's backup set

    E. Saturday's backup set

5.   Rooslan is responsible for backing up the departmental intranet server. This server runs IIS on Windows Server 2003. The server has a single physical disk that contains a single volume formatted with the NTFS file system. A share has been created on the Wwwroot folder. Only administrators and the member of staff responsible for maintaining the intranet server have access to this share. The member of staff that maintains the intranet server pages has this share mapped as a separate drive by a login script. Rooslan performs an ASR backup of the server on the first of each month. Every Monday at 7 A.M., he performs a full backup of the Wwwroot folder and all its subfolders as well as backing up the System State data. On Tuesday, Wednesday, Thursday, and Friday at 8:00 A.M., he performs an incremental backup on the Wwwroot folder and all its subfolders. No backups are performed over the weekend on this server. All backups are written to DAT and are labeled with the day that the backup was taken. Rooslan receives a visit at his cubicle after lunch on Thursday. The member of staff responsible for maintaining the intranet server was infected this morning with a virus. It has wiped out all the documents on her hard drive as well as all the files and folders in the mapped Wwwroot folder. Rooslan goes down to the server room and locates the backup tapes from the last seven days. Which of the backup tapes will he need to use to create the most complete restoration of the Web site files? (Select all that apply.)

   A. Monday's tape

   B. Tuesday's tape

   C. Wednesday's tape

   D. Thursday's tape

   E. Friday's tape

6.   Oksana is responsible for the administration of several departmental file servers at the local community college. Each file server is configured with three hard disk drives. The first hard disk drive contains a single volume hosting the operating system and program files. The other two hard drives host a single spanned volume. All the shared folders are located on the spanned volume. Backups are performed every 24 hours to DAT. A full backup of all files and folders on the spanned volume, including a backup of the System State data, occurs every Sunday at 5 A.M. Incremental backups occur on Monday, Wednesday, and Friday at 6 A.M. Each tape is labeled with the day the backup it stores is taken. One of the disks hosting the spanned volume fails early Friday afternoon. Oksana replaces the disk and recreates the spanned volume. Which of the following correctly describes the order in which Oksana should restore the backup tapes to the spanned volume?

   A. Sunday's tape, followed by Friday's tape

   B. Friday's tape, followed by Sunday's tape

    C. Sunday's tape, followed by Monday's, Wednesday's, and Friday's tapes

    D. Friday's tape, followed by Wednesday's, Monday's, and finally Sunday's tapes

    E. Sunday's tape, followed by Monday's and Friday's tapes

7. Rooslan is the administrator responsible for managing a Windows Server 2003 system that is used to analyze experimental scientific data. The server has four SCSI hard disk drives. One hosts a single volume that holds the operating system and the data analysis program. The other three SCSI hard disk drives are configured in a single volume stripe set. The stripe set volume stores both the raw and processed data. A full backup is taken of the stripe set volume once a day at 6:00 A.M. Differential backups of the stripe set volume are taken every four hours, the first at 10:00 A.M., the second at 2:00 P.M., the third at 6:00 P.M., and the final at 10:00 P.M. Five DATs are used for backup each day, one for each backup taken. They are labeled with the day and time of the backup. At 7:08 P.M. on Tuesday, one of the SCSI hard disk drives that comprise the stripe set volume fails. Rooslan has replaced it by 7:30 P.M. and has recreated a new stripe set volume. He has access to the last 10 DATs used to take backups on this server. Which of the following represents the way that Rooslan should restore the data to the stripe set volume in the minimum amount of time?

    A. The Tuesday 6:00 A.M. full backup, followed by the Tuesday 6:00 P.M differential backup.

    B. Tuesday 6:00 P.M., followed by Tuesday 6:00 A.M.

    C. Tuesday 6:00 P.M., followed by Tuesday 2:00 P.M., Tuesday 10:00 A.M., and finally Tuesday 6:00 A.M.

    D. Tuesday 6:00 A.M., followed by Tuesday 10:00 A.M., then Tuesday 2:00 P.M., and finally Tuesday 6:00 P.M.

    E. Tuesday 6:00 P.M. only.

8. Mick is the systems administrator of a Windows Server 2003 system that is used as a departmental file share at a local airport. The server has two SCSI hard disks. Each disk hosts a single volume. The first volume hosts the operating system and program files. The second volume hosts the file shares. The server is backed up every day to an individual DAT, which is labeled with the day that the backup is taken. The backup regime is as follows:

Saturday 4:00 A.M. full backup

Sunday 4:00 A.M. differential backup

Monday 5:30 A.M. incremental backup

Tuesday 4:00 A.M. differential backup

Wednesday 5:30 A.M. incremental backup

Thursday 4:00 A.M. differential backup

Friday 5:40 A.M. incremental backup

The disk hosting the volume that contains the file shares fails at 1:34 P.M. on Thursday. Mick is able to replace the disk and recreate the volume within 30 minutes. He has full access to the last 10 days of backup tapes. Which of the following represents the order of restoration that Mick should use to achieve the most complete restoration of the file shares?

  A. Saturday's tape

  B. Thursday's tape, followed by Wednesday's tape, followed by Monday's tape, with Saturday's tape being restored to the volume last

  C. Thursday's tape, followed by Tuesday's tape, followed by Sunday's tape, with Saturday's tape being restore to the volume last

  D. Saturday's tape, followed by Sunday's tape, then Tuesday's tape, with Thursday's tape being used to restore the volume last

  E. Saturday's tape, followed by Monday's tape, with Wednesday's tape being restored to the volume last

  F. Saturday's tape, followed by Monday's tape, then Wednesday's tape, with Thursday's tape being restored to the volume last

9. Laherty is the systems administrator of a Windows Server 2003 system running IIS hosting several Web sites. The server has four SCSI hard disk drives installed. The first SCSI hard disk drive hosts a single volume that contains the operating system and program files. The other three SCSI hard disk drives are configured in RAID-5 and contain a single volume that hosts all the Web site data. The RAID-5 volume is backed up every 24 hours to an individual DAT. The backup schedule is as follows:

Friday 6:00 A.M. full backup, including System State data.

Saturday 6:00 A.M. differential backup

Sunday 6:00 A.M. incremental backup

Monday 6:00 A.M. differential backup

Tuesday 6:00 A.M. incremental backup

Wednesday 6:00 A.M. differential backup

Thursday 6:00 A.M. incremental backup

The following files are written or modified at the corresponding times:

FileA.htm	Created Friday 1 P.M.
FileB.htm	Modified Saturday 2 P.M.
FileC.htm	Modified Sunday 10 A.M.
FileD.htm	Created Monday 9 A.M.
FileE.htm	Modified Tuesday 11 A.M.
FileF.htm	Modified Wednesday 4 P.M.

On Thursday at 5:12 P.M., a virus on the network infects the Windows Server 2003 system and deletes all the content hosted on the RAID-5 volume. Laherty disinfects the server and begins the restoration process. He starts by restoring all files on the Friday backup, and then restores all files on the Saturday backup, followed by the Monday backup, Wednesday backup, and finally the Thursday backup. When Laherty has finished this procedure, which restored files will be missing or not be of the latest version?

- **A.** FileA.htm
- **B.** FileB.htm
- **C.** FileC.htm
- **D.** FileD.htm
- **E.** FileE.htm
- **F.** FileF.htm

1.   Correct Answers: E

A. Incorrect: Striped volumes are not striped volumes with parity, hence when one of the set fails, all data on the volume is lost and must be restored from backup tape.

B. Incorrect: The ASR process recovers the system files; it does not recover data. Data must be backed up independently of the ASR process.

C. Incorrect: Striped volumes are not striped volumes with parity, hence when one of the set fails, all data on the volume is lost and must be restored from backup tape. The System State data will not be helpful in this case because all that was lost was file-share data.

D. Incorrect: This process would be correct if the Monday through Saturday back-ups were differential, rather than incremental, backups. Any files altered after the 2 A.M. Sunday backup finishes and after the 2 A.M. Wednesday backup finishes would not be recovered.

E. Correct: This is the correct process. Recreating the striped volume will mean that it has no data on it. Restoring the data from the backup tapes, being sure to use both the full backup and all the incremental backups will mean that as much information as possible will be salvaged.

2.   Correct Answers: A, D, and E

A. Correct: Friday's tape contains a full backup. It will contain a copy of the file as it existed last Friday at 10:00 P.M.

B. Incorrect: Because the file was not accessed on the weekend, it will not have changed. No change means that it will not be picked up by a differential backup.

C. Incorrect: Because the file was not accessed on the weekend, it will not have changed. No change means that it will not be picked up by a differential backup.

D. Correct: The file was changed on Monday, hence it will be written to Monday's tape. Because this is a differential backup, the archive bit will not be set.

E. Correct: Although the file was changed on Monday, the archive bit will not have been set by a differential backup. This means that Tuesday's tape will also contain a copy of the file.

F. Incorrect: The file was deleted on Wednesday, so it will not be present on the Wednesday backup tape.

3.   **Correct Answers: A and C**

A. Correct: All five files will be present on the Monday backup tape; however, two of those files will not be in their most recent form as they have been edited later in the week.

B. Incorrect: Only the two files that have been modified this week will be present on the Thursday backup tape.

C. Correct: Because the Thursday backup tape is generated at 2 A.M., these files will be present. They were deleted on Thursday evening. The minor change on Wednesday afternoon means that the first time that the second file will be backed up after the change is on Thursday morning.

D. Incorrect: The spreadsheet that was only modified on Wednesday afternoon will not be present on the Wednesday backup tape because that differential backup was taken at 2 A.M. Wednesday.

E. Incorrect: The spreadsheet that was modified Monday afternoon will be present on the Tuesday backup tape.

4.   **Correct Answers: A and D**

A. Correct: This backup set contains the System State data, which in turn contains the IIS metabase, as well as all the files on the Web sites as of Tuesday morning.

B. Incorrect: Wednesday's backup set is not needed because all the files that it contains will be included in Friday's backup set. This backup set would be required, however, if the backup type were incremental, not differential.

C. Incorrect: Thursday's backup set is not needed because all the files that it contains will be included in Friday's backup set. This backup set would be required, however, if the backup type were incremental, not differential.

D. Correct: This will contain all the files that were modified between the full backup taken on Tuesday morning and the beginning of the Friday backup. All files modified during the day on Friday will be lost as the Saturday backup would not have had time to complete before the hard disk drive failed.

E. Incorrect: This backup set will not have completed and will be unable to be restored because the backup file that holds the set on the server will not have been fully written at the time the crash occurred.

5. **Correct Answers: A, B, C, and D**

A. **Correct:** Monday's tape contains all the files in their original form. Any files that have been modified can be overwritten by restorations of tapes made later in the week.

B. **Correct:** Any files that were modified between the Monday and Tuesday backups will be located on this tape.

C. **Correct:** Any files that were modified between the Tuesday and Wednesday backups will be located on this tape.

D. **Correct:** Any files that were modified between the Wednesday and Thursday backups will be located on this tape.

E. **Incorrect:** The Friday tape has not been written yet.

6. **Correct Answers: C**

A. **Incorrect:** This leaves out the Monday and Wednesday incremental backups.

B. **Incorrect:** This leaves out the Monday and Wednesday incremental backups as well as overwriting the more recent files (Friday's tape) with older ones (Monday's tape).

C. **Correct:** This is the correct way to restore the volume. The most complete set is written first with newer files overwriting older ones until the newest set, Friday's, overwrites those previously restored to the volume.

D. **Incorrect:** This is the opposite order and will achieve the same result as if only Sunday's tape were restored to the volume.

E. **Incorrect:** This leaves out files that were modified between the time of Monday's backup and Wednesday's backup.

7. **Correct Answers: A**

A. **Correct:** The first will restore all data that exists on the volume at 6:00 A.M. on Tuesday. The Tuesday 6:00 P.M. tape will overwrite those files that have been altered and add any new ones that have been created since the Tuesday 6:00 A.M. full backup.

B. **Incorrect:** This will first restore all the files created or altered since the Tuesday 6:00 A.M. backup. All modified files will then be overwritten by the Tuesday 6:00 A.M. files. Any files modified since the morning full backup will be lost because they are overwritten by the older files.

C. **Incorrect:** This will first restore all the files created or altered since the Tuesday 6:00 A.M. backup. All modified files will then be overwritten by the Tuesday 6:00 A.M. files. Any files modified since the morning full backup will be lost as they are overwritten by the older files.

D. **Incorrect:** Although this will restore the files correctly, it will not do it in the minimum amount of time. This will produce exactly the same result as simply restoring the Tuesday 6:00 A.M. tape followed by the Tuesday 6:00 P.M. tape. However, in using this method, two extra tapes will be restored unnecessarily.

    E. Incorrect: This will only restore those files created or changed since the Tuesday 6:00 A.M. backup. All files that exist on the server that have not been created or altered in the last 13 hours will not be restored.

8. Correct Answers: F

    A. Incorrect: This will restore the file share to the point it was six days before the failure.

    B. Incorrect: This is the correct set of tapes; the order of restoration is back-to-front, though, with every file that has been modified in the last six days being overwritten by the version that existed the previous Saturday morning.

    C. Incorrect: This will not restore all the files and it will mean that older files overwrite newer versions of the same file.

    D. Incorrect: Understanding why this answer is wrong is a little complicated. Because of the nature of the backups, any file that is written between Sunday 4:00 A.M. and Monday 5:30 A.M. will not be restored using the procedure outlined above. This is because the Monday 4:00 A.M. backup will reset the archive bit, so when the Tuesday differential backup comes along it will only back up files altered since the Monday backup. The same applies for files written between Tuesday and Wednesday mornings.

    E. Incorrect: This sequence will miss any files that were written between Wednesday 5:30 A.M. and Thursday 4:00 A.M.

    F. Correct: This sequence will achieve the most complete restoration of the file shares, restoring all files that existed on the file share up until 4:00 A.M. Thursday.

9. Correct Answers: B and D

    A. Incorrect: FileA.htm will be restored when Laherty restores the Saturday backup.

    B. Correct: The most recent version of FileB.htm will not be restored. The archive bit will be set during the Sunday backup which means that the Monday differential will not pick it up.

    C. Incorrect: FileC.htm will be restored when Laherty restores the Monday backup.

    D. Correct: FileD.htm will not be restored. The archive bit will be set during the Tuesday incremental backup meaning that the Wednesday differential backup will miss it.

    E. Incorrect: FileE.htm will be restored when Laherty restores the Wednesday differential backup.

    F. Incorrect: FileF.html will be restored when Laherty restores the Thursday incremental backup.

Schedule Backup Jobs

Backup jobs are best run at a time when there is minimal use of the server that is to be backed up. This tends to be at times in the middle of the night rather than during the normal hours that a systems administrator is in the office. Rather than having to come back to work each night at 2:00 A.M., or having to wake up to initiate an early morning Terminal Services connection, the Windows Server 2003 Backup Utility allows the scheduling of backup jobs.

A wide variety of scheduling options is available. Jobs can be configured to run when the system starts, when it is idle, when a user logs on, daily, weekly or monthly. Jobs can be configured to run every week, every second week or every 100th week, just as they can be configured to run every day, every second day, or every 100th day.

Systems administrators are likely to configure multiple schedules on a server, performing a full backup certain days of the week and performing incremental or differential backups other days of the week. The type of schedule they configure depends on the type of media they use to store the backup sets. Six days of incremental backups after a full backup is going to take less time and less space than six days of differential backups after a full backup.

Objective 5.5 Questions

1. You are designing a backup strategy for a Windows Server 2003 system that runs IIS. The server has a single hard disk drive that contains a single volume. You have the following goals:

Primary Goal: To write a full backup to tape once a week.

Secondary Goals: To back up the IIS metabase on Monday, Wednesday, and Friday. To ensure that all files modified or created since the last full backup are backed up on Tuesday and Thursday.

Which of the following sets of scheduled backups will fulfill these goals? (Select all that apply.)

A. Full backup every Sunday at 2:00 A.M. Daily backup with System State every Monday, Wednesday, and Friday at 3:00 A.M.

B. Full backup with System State on Monday at 2:00 A.M. Daily backup with System State on Wednesday, Friday, and Sunday at 3:00 A.M. Differential backup on Tuesday and Thursday at 3:30 A.M.

C. Full backup with System State on Friday at 11:00 P.M. Incremental backup with System State data on Wednesday and Monday at 11:30 P.M. Differential backup on Tuesday and Thursday at 11:30 P.M.

D. Full backup with System State on Wednesday at 11:00 P.M. Daily backup with System State on Monday and Friday at 11:00 P.M., differential backup with System State on Tuesday and Thursday at 11:00 P.M.

E. Incremental backup with System State data on Monday, Wednesday, and Friday at 2:00 A.M. Differential backup with System State data on Tuesday and Thursday at 2:00 A.M. Copy backup Sunday at 2:00 A.M.

2. Rooslan is designing a backup strategy for four Windows Server 2003 systems that are used as file shares for a university's department. The hardware on each Windows Server 2003 system is rigorously fault-tolerant, hence the backup strategy focuses around the recovery of deleted and lost files as well as file rollback rather than strict disaster recovery. It is also departmental policy to keep a weekly snapshot of the state of the file servers in an archived location for 20 years. Rooslan's backup strategy should take into account the following conditions:

Condition 1: At least one backup of all files and folders on each Windows Server 2003 system per week.

Condition 2: A maximum of two backup sets to be used in any single file-recovery operation, including a full restore of all files and folders on the server.

Condition 3: Files need to be able to be retrieved on a daily basis. If a file is changed on Tuesday, Wednesday, and Thursday during a week, three different versions of that file must be able to be recovered from the backup sets. Multiple copies of the same file do not need to adhere to condition two.

Which of the following backup strategies meets Rooslan's needs? (Select all that apply.)

   A. Full backup on each server at 1:30 A.M. every Monday. Copy backup every day of the week except Monday at 2:00 A.M. on each server.

   B. Full backup on each server at 10:00 P.M. every Thursday. Incremental backup each day of the week except Monday at 11:00 P.M. on each server.

   C. Full backup of all the files and folders on each server at 9:00 P.M. every day.

   D. Full backup of all the files and folders on each server at 11:00 P.M. Monday, Wednesday, Friday, and Saturday. Incremental backup of all servers on Tuesday, Thursday, and Sunday at 11:00 P.M.

3. Oksana is designing a backup strategy for a Windows Server 2003 system that runs IIS. The server hosts a high-traffic Web site where content is updated on an almost hourly basis. Several aspects of the IIS configuration change during the week. The configuration has become so complicated that it is important that it be regularly backed up as well. Oksana's backup strategy should take into account the following conditions:

Condition 1: All the Web site data must be backed up completely at least once every two weeks.

Condition 2: The System State data must be backed up at least twice a week.

Condition 3: Any backup set except a full backup should not include files and folders that have not been altered or created in the last 24 hours. System State data is exempt from this condition.

Which of the following schedules would take into account all three of Oksana's conditions?

A. Full backup of selected files and folders every Monday at 11:50 P.M. Incremental backup of selected files and folders all weekdays except Monday at 11:55 P.M.

B. Full backup of selected files and folders every second Monday at 11:50 P.M. Differential backup of selected files and folders all days of the week except Monday at 11:55 P.M. System State backup every Monday, Wednesday, and Friday at 2:00 P.M.

C. Full backup of selected files and folders every second Monday at 12:05 A.M. Incremental backup of selected files and folders including System State data every day of the week at 11:55 P.M.

D. Full backup of selected files and folders every second Monday at 12:05 A.M. Daily backup of selected files and folders, including System State data, every day of the week at 11:59 P.M.

E. Full backup of selected files and folders every second Monday at 12:05 A.M. Copy backup of selected files and folders including System State data every day of the week at 11:59 P.M.

4.   The following users have accounts that are members of the corresponding groups on a stand-alone Windows Server 2003 system.

Orin–Administrators

Oksana–Backup Operators

Rooslan–Power Users

Mick–Replicator

Laherty–Network Configuration Operators

None of these users or groups has been altered using local group policy. A full backup of all files and folders on the server, including System State data, is to be scheduled to run once a day at 2:00 A.M. In the schedule configuration, the Backup Utility requests that an account with the appropriate credentials be entered to run this backup. Which of the above listed user accounts have the necessary permissions to correctly execute this scheduled backup job?

A. Orin

B. Oksana

C. Rooslan

D. Mick

E. Laherty

Objective 5.5 Answers

1.   Correct Answers: B and D

   A. **Incorrect:** This will achieve the primary goal and the first of the secondary goals. It will not achieve the second secondary goal.

   B. **Correct:** This will achieve the primary goal and both secondary goals. The meta-base is backed up when the System State data is backed up. This means that the metabase will be backed up under this scheme on Monday, Wednesday, Friday, and Sunday. Sunday isn't necessary for the primary goal, but it does not invalidate it. The differential backup on Tuesday and Thursday meets the second part of the secondary goals.

   C. **Incorrect:** This meets the primary goal and the first secondary goal. It does not meet the second secondary goal because the incremental backups will mean that the differential backups on Tuesday and Thursday will back up only files changed since the last incremental rather than the last full backup.

   D. **Correct:** The primary goal is achieved as well as both secondary goals. The key is to remember that like differential backups, daily backups do not reset the archive bit. The next backup taken after a daily or differential assumes that the file has not been backed up yet if it has been altered or is new since the time of the last backup.

   E. **Incorrect:** Although the Incremental backup does reset the archive bit, it does not count as a full backup of the server once a week. The copy backup does not reset the archive bit and hence is functionally similar to the differential backup.

2.   Correct Answers: A, C, and D

   A. **Correct:** The full backup on each server at 1:30 A.M. every Monday meets the first condition. Using copy backups meets the second condition. Performing copy backups every day meets the third condition.

   B. **Incorrect:** Although the first and third conditions are met, the second condition is not met because with incremental backups, more than one backup set may be required to restore the server completely.

   C. **Correct:** This will meet all three conditions. It will take up more space than other options, but it does meet the outlined requirements.

   D. **Correct:** This will meet all three conditions. There is never more than one consecutive incremental backup, hence the second condition will not be violated. If there were more than one incremental backup consecutively, the second condition would not hold.

3.   **Correct Answers: C and D**

    A. Incorrect: This backup schedule does not meet the second condition.

    B. Incorrect: Using differential backup will not conform to the third condition.

    C. Correct: This option meets all three criteria.

    D. Correct: This option meets all three criteria. Although a daily backup does not reset the archive bit, it will only back up files or folders within the selection that have been modified that day; hence, it will meet the third condition.

    E. Incorrect: Copy backup works similar to a differential backup in that it does not reset the archive bit, but it also copies all files, including those that have not been modified.

4.   **Correct Answers: A and B**

    A. Correct: Members of the Administrators and Backup Operators groups have the necessary permissions to allow scheduled backup jobs to run.

    B. Correct: Members of the Administrators and Backup Operators groups have the necessary permissions to allow scheduled backup jobs to run.

    C. Incorrect: Members of the Power Users group do not have sufficient permissions to allow scheduled backup jobs to run.

    D. Incorrect: Members of the Replicator group do not have sufficient permissions to allow scheduled backup jobs to run.

    E. Incorrect: Members of the Network Configuration Operators group do not have sufficient permissions to allow scheduled backup jobs to run.

Part III
Appendix

Appendix
Terminal Server

Exam Objectives in this Chapter:

- Troubleshoot Terminal Services
- Diagnose and resolve issues related to Terminal Services security
- Diagnose and resolve issues related to client access to Terminal Services

In Chapter 2, you learned how to use Terminal Services, specifically Remote Desktop for Administration, to connect to a server session from a remote client. You learned that Remote Desktop for Administration is installed on every Microsoft Windows Server 2003 by default and, once it is enabled using the System application in Control Panel, a server will support two concurrent connections from users who belong to the Remote Desktop Users group.

Windows Server 2003 Terminal Services also supports applications to multiple users running concurrent sessions. This feature, similar to the Terminal Services Application Server mode of Windows 2000, is now called Terminal Server. This appendix discusses Terminal Server and the unique issues related to supporting and troubleshooting a Terminal Server environment.

Installing and Configuring a Terminal Server Environment

There are several key considerations related to the deployment of a Terminal Server environment.

The Terminal Server Component

Terminal Server can be installed by using the Add/Remove Windows Components Wizard, which is found in Add/Remove Programs, or by choosing the Configure Your Server Wizard from the Manage Your Server page. It is best practice to configure standalone member servers as terminal servers, not domain controllers. Hardware recommendations can be found in the Help and Support Center.

Applications

Because applications on a terminal server will be provided to multiple users, perhaps concurrently, certain registry keys, files and folders must be installed on a terminal server differently from installation on a non-terminal server. Always use the Add/Remove Programs tool in Control Panel to install an application on a terminal server. Add/Remove Programs will automatically switch the terminal server into installation mode prior to starting the application's setup routine. While in installation mode, the terminal server manages the configuration of the application appropriately so that the application can run in multiuser mode.

Occasionally, an application, patch, or other installation-related process cannot be initiated by using Add/Remove Programs. For example, a vendor might provide an online update capability for its application and such a capability cannot be started from Add/ Remove Programs. In such cases, open the command shell and use the Change User/ Install command prior to invoking the installation or patch process. Once the process has completed, use the Change User/Execute command. Also note that some applications require compatibility scripts to modify their installation behavior on a terminal server.

It is best practice to install Terminal Server prior to installing any applications that will be run in multiuser mode. Similarly, prior to removing Terminal Server from a server, you should uninstall all applications that were installed in multiuser mode. If you must install additional applications on an existing terminal server, be sure to reset (log off) any current user sessions using Terminal Server Connections and to disable new connections by typing **change logon /disable** on the command line. Once applications have been installed, type **change logon /enable** on the command line to allow new connections once again. The Remote tab of System Properties will also allow you to enable and disable Terminal Services connections.

When installing Terminal Server, you will be given the choice of Full Security and Relaxed Security. Full Security, the default, protects certain operating system files and shared program files. Older applications may not function in this more secure configuration, at which point you may choose Relaxed Security. The setting can be changed at any time using the Server Settings in the Terminal Server Configuration console.

Many administrators misunderstand the use of the Terminal Services Home Folder. This setting, which can be configured as part of the user account, as shown in Figure A-1, or through Group Policy, determines the location of a folder that is used by Terminal Services to store user-specific files for multiuser applications. It does not affect the storage location for user data files. By default, the Terminal Services Home Folder is created as a folder called Windows in the user's profile. To manage where user data is stored, configure the user's standard Home Folder setting on the Profile tab of the user account, or use the best practice of redirecting the My Documents folder.

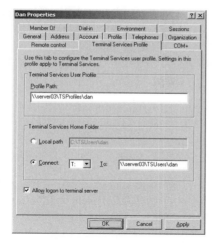

Figure A-1   The Terminal Services Home Folder setting of a user account

Installation of the Remote Desktop Client

The Remote Desktop client (Mstsc.exe) is installed by default on all Windows Server 2003 and Microsoft Windows XP computers. The client supports all 32-bit Windows platforms, and can be installed with Group Policy on Windows 2000 systems, or with other software deployment methods on earlier platforms. Once installed, the client can be tricky to locate in the Start menu. Look in the Accessories program group under Accessories, and then create a shortcut to the client in a more accessible location.

Licensing

After a 120-day evaluation period, connections to a computer running Terminal Server will not be successful unless the terminal server cannot obtain a client license from a Terminal Server License Server. Therefore, as part of your Terminal Server deployment, you must install a Terminal Server License Server, preferably on a server that is not a terminal server.

Use Add/Remove Programs to install Terminal Server Licensing. You will be asked whether the server should be an Enterprise License Server or a Domain License Server. An Enterprise License Server is the most common configuration, and the server can provide licenses to terminal servers in any Windows 2000 or Windows Server 2003 domain within the forest. Use a Domain License Server when you want to maintain a separate license database for each domain, or when terminal servers are running in a workgroup or a Windows NT 4 domain.

Once installed, Terminal Server Licensing is managed with the Terminal Server Licensing console in Administrative Tools. The first task you will perform is activating the Terminal Server License Server by right-clicking the Terminal Server License Server and choosing Activate Server. Once the server has been activated, client license packs must be installed. The Help and Support Center includes detailed instructions for this process. Terminal Server Licensing supports two types of client access licenses (CALs): Per Device and Per Session. Both types of CALs can be managed by the same Terminal Server License Server.

Terminal Server Licensing is maintained separately from server and client access licenses (CALs) for Windows Server 2003. See Chapter 9 for a discussion of managing licenses for non-Terminal Server servers and clients.

Exam Tip   Terminal Server CALs are licenses for the connection to a user session on a terminal server; you must still consider licensing requirements for applications that users access within their session. Consult the applications' End User License Agreements (EULAs) to determine appropriate licensing for applications hosted on a terminal server.

Managing and Troubleshooting Terminal Server

Several tools exist that can configure terminal servers, Terminal Services user settings, Terminal Services connections, and Terminal Services sessions. These include Group Policy Editor, Terminal Services Configuration, Active Directory Users and Computers and the Remote Desktop client itself. This section will help you understand the use of each tool, and the most important configuration settings, by examining the creation, use, and deletion of a user session.

Points of Administration

There are several processes that occur as a user connects to a terminal server; and at each step, there are opportunities to configure the behavior of the connection.

The Remote Desktop client allows 32-bit Windows platforms to connect to a terminal server using the Remote Desktop Protocol (RDP). The client has been greatly improved over earlier versions of the Terminal Services client, and now a wider variety of data redirection types (including file system, serial port, printer, audio, and time zone) and supports connections in up to 24-bit color. The client includes numerous settings that configure the connection and the user's experience. Some of those settings are shown in Figure A-2. Settings are saved Remote Desktop Connection (.rdp) files that can easily be opened for future connections, or distributed to other users as a connection profile. Settings in the .rdp file or the Remote Desktop client affect the current user's connection to the specified terminal server.

Figure A-2   The Remote Desktop client

When a user connects to a terminal server, the server will examine the Terminal Services properties of the user's account to determine certain settings. If Terminal Services user accounts are stored on the terminal server, the Local Users and Groups snap-in will expose Terminal Services settings in the Properties of user accounts. More commonly, user accounts are in Active Directory, in which case the Active Directory Users and Computers snap-in exposes Terminal Services settings on the Environment, Remote Control, and Terminal Services Profile tabs within the user properties dialog box, as shown previously in Figure A-1. Settings in the user account will override settings in the Remote Desktop client.

A client connects to the terminal server by specifying the server's name or Internet Protocol (IP) address. The Terminal Server receives the connection request through the specified network adapter. This connection is represented by a connection object, which is visible in the Terminal Services Configuration console, as shown in Figure A-3. The connection object's properties configure settings that affect all user connections through the network adapter. Settings in the connection will override client requested settings and settings in the user account.

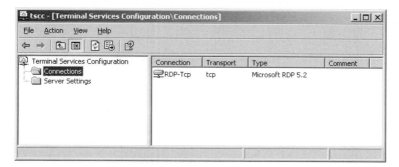

Figure A-3   Terminal Services Configuration

> **Exam Tip**   A terminal server's RDP-Tcp connection properties, accessible through Terminal Services Configuration, will override client and user account settings for all user sessions through the connection on that individual terminal server.

Windows Server 2003 Group Policy includes numerous computer-based and user-based policies to control Terminal Services. Configurations specified by Group Policy Objects (GPOs) will override settings in the Remote Desktop client, in the user account, or on the RDP-Tcp connections of terminal servers. Of course, those settings will apply only to the users or computers within the scope of the organizational unit (OU) to which the GPO is linked. In an environment consisting only of terminal servers running one of the Windows Server 2003 family operating systems, Group Policy will enable Terminal Services Configuration with the least administrative effort. Terminal Services group policies do not apply to terminal servers running earlier versions of Windows.

Once a user session has been enabled, the Terminal Services Manager administrative tool can be used to monitor users, sessions, and applications on each terminal server. Terminal Services Manager can also be used to manage the server and to connect to, disconnect, or reset user sessions or processes.

Before continuing the examination of Terminal Server Configuration options and tools, take a moment to memorize the order of precedence for configuration settings:

1. Computer-level group policies. Most Terminal Services Configuration can be set by GPOs linked to an OU in which terminal server computer objects are created. These policies override settings made with any other tool.

2. User-level group policies.

3. Configuration of the terminal server or the RDP-Tcp connection using the Terminal Services Configuration tool. Although this tool is server- and connection-specific, and therefore cannot specify a single configuration as Group Policy can, this tool can configure Windows 2000 terminal servers. In addition, there are times when a configuration between terminal servers or between connections should be different. Terminal Services Configuration is the tool to manage such a scenario.

4. User account properties configured with the Active Directory Users And Computers snap-in.

5. Remote Desktop client configuration.

Connection Configuration

A user's ability to connect and log on to a terminal server is determined by a number of factors, each of which, if not functioning properly, produces a unique error message:

- The connection on the terminal server must be accessible. If the client cannot reach the server using TCP/IP, or if the terminal server's RDP-Tcp connection is disabled, a particularly uninformative error message appears that indicates that the client cannot connect to the server.

- Remote Desktop must be enabled. The ability of a terminal server to accept new connections can be controlled on the Remote tab of the System properties dialog box or by using the **change logon /disable** and **change logon /enable** commands. If logon has been disabled, an error message appears indicating that terminal server sessions are disabled or that remote logons are disabled.

- The server must have available connections. The properties of the connection—the default RDP-Tcp connection, for example—determine the number of available connections on the Network Adapter tab, as shown in Figure A-4. If sufficient connections are not available, an error message appears that indicates that a network error is preventing connection.

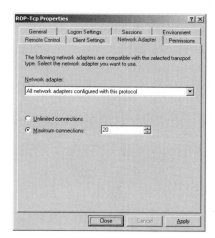

Figure A-4   The Network Adapter tab of the RDP-Tcp Properties dialog box

- Encryption must be compatible. The default allows any client to connect to a terminal server without regard to its encryption capability. If you modify the encryption requirements for a connection by using the Encryption list on the General tab of the connection properties, as shown in Figure A-5, clients that are not capable of that encryption mode will not be allowed to connect.

Figure A-5   The General tab of the RDP-Tcp Properties dialog box

- The user must have sufficient connection permissions. As shown in Figure A-6, the Remote Desktop Users group has User Access permissions, which gives the group sufficient permissions to log on to the server. The access control list (ACL) of the connection can be modified to control access in configurations that differ from the default. Refer to the Help and Support Center for more information. If a user does not have sufficient permission to the connection, an error message will appear that indicates that the user does not have access to the session.

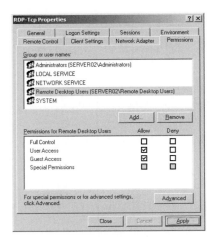

Figure A-6   The Permissions tab of the RDP-Tcp Properties dialog box

- The user must have the user logon right to log on to the terminal server. Windows Server 2003 separates the right required to log on *locally* to a server from the right required to log on to a server using a remote desktop connection. The user rights Allow Log On Through Terminal Services, as shown in Figure A-7, and Deny Log On Through Terminal Services can be used to manage this right, using either local policy or Group Policy. On member servers, the local Administrators and Remote Desktop Users groups have the right to log on through Terminal Services. On domain controllers, only Administrators have the right by default. If a user does not have sufficient logon rights, an error message will appear that indicates that the policy of the Terminal Server does not allow logon.

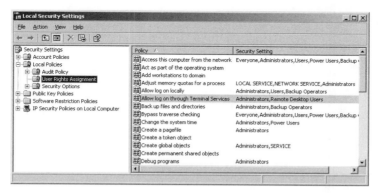

Figure A-7   The Allow Log On Through Terminal Services user right

- The user must belong to the correct group or groups. Assuming you have managed connection permissions and the right to log on through Terminal Services by assigning rights and permissions to a group, the user attempting to connect to the terminal server must be in that group. With the default configuration of Terminal Server on a member server, users must be members of the Remote Desktop Users group to connect to a terminal server.

- Allow logon to terminal server enabled. The user account's Terminal Services Profile tab, as shown in Figure A-1, indicates that the user is allowed to log on to a terminal server. If this setting is disabled, the user will receive an error message indicating that the interactive logon privilege has been disabled. This error message is easy to confuse with insufficient user logon rights; however, in that case, the error message indicates that the local policy of the server is not allowing logon.

A terminal server has one RDP-Tcp connection by default, and can have only one connection object per network adapter, but if a terminal server has multiple adapters, you can create connections for those adapters. Each connection maintains properties that affect all user sessions connected to that server connection.

Device Redirection

Once a user has successfully connected, Windows Server 2003 and the Remote Desktop client provide a wide array of device redirection options including:

- Audio redirection, which allows audio files played within the Terminal Server session to be played by the user's PC. This feature is specified on the Local Resources tab of the Remote Desktop client, as shown in Figure A-2. However, audio redirection is disabled by default on the Client Settings tab of the RDP-Tcp Properties dialog box, as shown in Figure A-8. Audio redirection can be specified by a GPO.

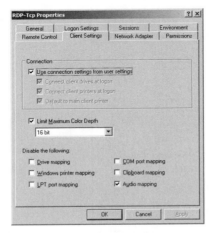

Figure A-8   The RDP-Tcp Properties dialog box Client Settings tab

- Drive redirection, which allows the user to access drives that are local to the user's PC from within the Terminal Server session. Local drives are visible in My Computer under the Other group, as shown in Figure A-9. This option is disabled by default, and can be enabled on the Local Resources tab of the Remote Desktop client. Terminal Server Configuration can override the client setting and disable drive redirection from the properties of the connection. These settings can also be specified by Group Policy. The user account's Connect Client Drives At Logon setting does *not* affect drive redirection using the Remote Desktop client; it is meant to manage drive redirection for Citrix's Integrated Computing Architecture (ICA) clients.

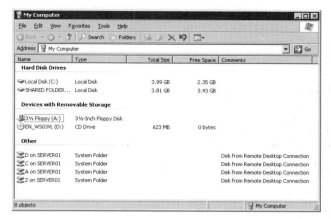

Figure A-9   My Computer in a Terminal Server session showing redirected client drives

■ Printer redirection, which allows the user to access printers that are local to the user's workstation, as well as network printers that are installed on the user's workstation, from within the Terminal Server session. The Printers And Faxes folder will display printers that are installed on the terminal server as well as the client's redirected printers, as shown in Figure A-10.

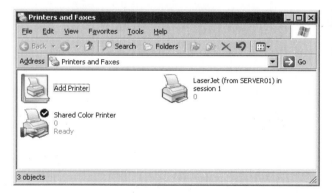

Figure A-10   The Printers And Faxes folder shows a client's redirected printer

Like drive redirection, printer redirection is specified on the Local Settings tab of the Remote Desktop client. Printer redirection can be disabled by properties of the RDP-Tcp connection. Printer redirection will also be disabled if the Connect Client Printers At Logon setting is not enabled in the user account properties, as shown in Figure A-11. Selecting this option in the user account does *not* cause printer redirection; the client must specify redirection on the Local Resources tab. But if disabled, the user account setting will override the client setting. The user account properties also provides a Default To Main Client Printer setting which, if enabled while printer redirection is in effect, will set the default printer in the Terminal Server session to the same printer set as default on the user's workstation. If the

Default To Main Client Printer setting is disabled, the Terminal Server session will use the default printer of the Terminal Server computer. Printer redirection settings can be specified by a GPO.

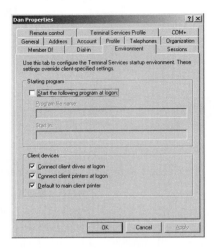

Figure A-11   The Environment tab of a user's properties dialog box

■   Serial Port redirection, which allows a user to launch an application within a terminal server session that uses a device, such as a barcode reader, attached to the serial port of the user's workstation. This feature is also on the Local Resources tab of the client, and can be disabled in the properties of the RDP-Tcp connection. Serial port redirection can be specified by a GPO.

■   LPT and COM port mapping, which allows a user to install a printer within the Terminal Server session that maps to a printer attached to an LPT or COM port on the user's workstation. This method of printer redirection is not necessary with Windows Server 2003 and the Remote Desktop client, which support printer redirection in a much simpler way as described above. LPT and COM port mapping is, however, still done by default. The RDP-Tcp connection properties can disable port mapping, as can a GPO.

■   Clipboard mapping, which allows the user to copy and paste information between a Terminal Server session and the desktop. This feature is enabled by default in the Remote Desktop client and cannot be changed within the client's user interface (UI). The RDP-Tcp connection properties can disable clipboard mapping, as can a GPO.

Managing Sessions and Processes

The Terminal Services Manager console provides the capability to monitor and control sessions and processes on a terminal server. You can disconnect, log off, or reset a user or session, send a message to a user, or end a process launched by any user. Task Manager can also be used to monitor and end processes; just be certain to select the Show Processes From All Users check box. If a terminal server's performance is lethargic, use Terminal Server Manager or Task Manager to look at the processes being run by all users to determine if one process has stopped responding and is consuming more than its fair share of processor time.

Managing User Sessions

There are a variety of settings that determine the behavior of a user session that has been active, idle, or disconnected for a time. These settings can be configured on the Sessions tab of the Terminal Server Connection properties dialog box, as shown in Figure A-12. The settings can also be configured with Group Policy.

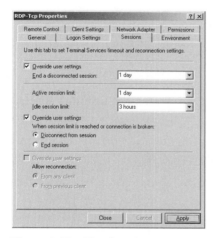

Figure A-12   The Sessions tab of the RDP-Tcp Properties dialog box

Load-Balancing Terminal Servers

In previous implementations of terminal services, it was difficult to load-balance terminal servers. Windows Server 2003 Enterprise and Datacenter Editions introduce the ability to create server clusters, which are logical groupings of terminal servers. When a user connects to the cluster, the user is directed to one server. If the user's session is disconnected and the user attempts to reconnect, the terminal server receiving the connection will check with the Session Directory to identify which terminal server is hosting the disconnected session, and will redirect the client to the appropriate server.

To configure a terminal server cluster, you need

- A load-balancing technology such as Network Load Balancing (NLB) or DNS round-robin. The load-balancing solution will distribute client connections to each of the terminal servers.

- A Terminal Services Session Directory. You must enable the Terminal Services Session Directory, which is installed by default on Windows Server 2003 Enterprise and Datacenter Editions, using the Services console in Administrative Tools. It is best practice to enable the session directory on a server that is not running Terminal Server. The Terminal Services Session Directory maintains a database that tracks each user session on servers in the cluster. The computer running the session directory creates a Session Directory Computers local group, to which you must add the computer accounts of all servers in the cluster.

- Terminal server connection configuration. Finally, you must direct the cluster's servers to the session directory. This process involves specifying that the server is part of a directory, the name of the session directory server, and the name for the cluster, which can be any name you wish as long as the same name is specified for each server in the cluster. These settings can be specified in the Server Settings node of Terminal Server Configuration, or they can be set using a GPO applied to an OU that contains the computer objects for the cluster's terminal servers.

When a user connects to the cluster, the following process occurs:

1. When the user logs on to the terminal server cluster, the terminal server receiving the initial client logon request sends a query to the session directory server.

2. The session directory server checks the username against its database and sends the result to the requesting server as follows:

   - If the user has no disconnected sessions, logon continues at the server hosting the initial connection.

   - If the user has a disconnected session on another server, the client session is passed to that server and logon continues.

3. When the user logs on to a new or disconnected session, the session directory is updated.

Exam Tip   Be sure to know the pieces that are required to establish a terminal server cluster. Should you decide to implement a terminal server cluster within your enterprise, you can refer to the Help And Support Center for detailed instructions for doing so.

Remote Control

Terminal Server allows an administrator to view or take control of a user's session. This feature not only allows administrators to monitor user actions on a terminal server, but also acts like Remote Assistance, allowing a help desk employee to control a user's session and perform actions that the user is able to see as well.

To establish remote control, both the user and the administrator must be connected to terminal server sessions. The administrator must open the Terminal Server Manager console from the Administrative tools group, right-click the user's session, and choose Control. By default, the user will be notified that the administrator wishes to connect to the session, and can accept or deny the request.

> **Important**   Remote Control is available only when using Terminal Server Manager *within* a terminal server session. You cannot establish remote control by opening Terminal Server Manager on your PC.

Remote control settings include the ability to remotely view and remotely control a session, as well as whether the user should be prompted to accept or deny the administrator's access. These settings can be configured in the user account properties on the Remote Control tab, as shown in Figure A-13, and can be configured by the properties of the RDP-Tcp connection, which will override user account settings. Group Policy can also be used to specify remote control configuration.

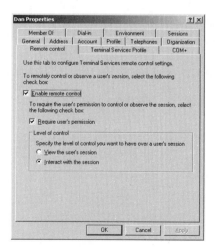

Figure A-13   The Remote Control tab of a user's properties dialog box

In addition to enabling remote control settings, an administrator must have permissions to establish remote control over the terminal server connection. Using the Permissions tab of the RDP-Tcp Properties dialog box, you can assign the Full Control permission template or, by clicking Advanced, assign the Remote Control permission to a group, as shown in Figure A-14.

Figure A-14   The Remote Control permission

Review

This appendix provides an overview of Terminal Server and the tools, technologies, and processes used to configure and, ultimately, troubleshoot the feature. The aim of this appendix, like the rest of this training kit, is to prepare you for the 70-290 certification exam. If you plan to deploy or support Terminal Server in your production network, be sure to refer to online help and the Microsoft Knowledge Base for additional detail.

Glossary

Numbers

802.11   Refers to a family of Institute of Electrical and Electronics Engineers (IEEE) specifications for wireless networking.

802.11a   An extension to 802.11 that applies to wireless local area networks (WLANs) and provides up to 54 Mbps in the 5 GHz band.

802.11b   An extension to 802.11 that applies to wirelessLANs and provides 11 Mbps transmission (with a fallback to 5.5, 2, and 1 Mbps) in the 2.4 GHz band. 802.11b is a 1999 ratification to the original 802.11 standard, allowing wireless functionality comparable to Ethernet. Also called Wi-Fi.

802.11g   An extension to 802.11 that applies to wireless LANs and provides 54 Mbps transmission in the 2.4 GHz band. 802.11g is backward compatible with 802.11b, allowing the two to work together.

A

access control entry (ACE)   An entry in an access control list (ACL) that defines the level of access for a user or group.

access control list (ACL)   A set of data associated with a file, directory, or other resource that defines the permissions users or groups have for accessing it. In Active Directory, the ACL is a list of access control entries (ACEs) stored with the object it protects. In Microsoft Windows NT, an ACL is stored as a binary value called a security descriptor.

access token or security access token   A collection of security identifiers (SIDs) that represent a user and that user's group memberships. The security subsystem compares SIDs in the token to SIDs in an access control list (ACL) to determine resource access.

account lockout   A security feature that disables a user account if failed logons exceed a specified number in a specified period of time. Locked accounts cannot log on and must be unlocked by an administrator.

Active Directory   Beginning in Microsoft Windows 2000 Server and continuing in Windows Server 2003, Active Directory replaces the Windows NT collection of directory functions with functionality that integrates with and relies upon standards including Domain Name System (DNS), Lightweight Directory Access Protocol (LDAP), and Kerberos security protocol.

Active Directory–integrated zone   A DNS (Domain Name System) zone stored in Active Directory so it has Active Directory security features and can be used for multimaster replication.

Active Directory Service Interface (ADSI)   A programming interface that provides access to Active Directory.

ActiveX   A loosely defined set of technologies that allows software components to interact with each other in a networked environment.

ActiveX component   Reusable software component that adheres to the ActiveX specification and can operate in an ActiveX–compliant environment.

address   A precise location where a piece of information is stored in memory or on disk. Also, the unique identifier for a node on a network. On the Internet, the code by which an individual user is identified. The format is *username@hostname*, where *username* is your user name, logon name, or account number, and *hostname* is the name of the computer or Internet provider you use. The host name might be a few words strung together with periods.

Address Resolution Protocol (ARP)   A Transmission Control Protocol/Internet Protocol (TCP/IP) and AppleTalk protocol that provides IP-address-to-MAC (media access control) address resolution for IP packets.

Advanced Configuration Power Interface (ACPI)   An industry specification, defining power management on a range of computer devices. ACPI compliance is necessary for devices to take advantage of Plug and Play and power management capabilities.

allocation unit   The smallest unit of managed space on a hard disk or logical volume. Also called a *cluster*.

anonymous FTP   A way to use an FTP program to log on to another computer to copy files when you do not have an account on that computer. When you log on, enter anonymous as the user name and your e-mail address as the password. This gives you access to publicly available files. See also *File Transfer Protocol (FTP)*.

AppleTalk   Local area network architecture built into Macintosh computers to connect them with printers. A network with a Windows Server 2003 server and Macintosh clients can function as an AppleTalk network with the use of AppleTalk network integration (formerly Services for Macintosh).

Archive (A) attribute   An attribute of each file that is used by backup utilities to determine whether or not to back up that file. The Archive attribute is set to TRUE whenever a file is created or modified. Differential and incremental backup jobs will back up files only if their archive attribute is TRUE.

Associate   To connect files having a particular extension to a specific program. When you double-click a file with the extension, the associated program is launched and the file you clicked is opened. In Windows, associated file extensions are usually called registered file types.

Asynchronous Transfer Mode (ATM)   A network technology based on sending data in cells or packets of a fixed size. It is asynchronous in that the transmission of cells containing information from a particular user is not necessarily periodic.

attribute   A characteristic. In Windows file management, it is information that shows whether a file is read-only, hidden, compressed, encrypted, ready to be backed up (archived), or should be indexed.

audit policy   Defines the type of security events to be logged. It can be defined on a server or an individual computer.

authentication   Verification of the identity of a user or computer process. In Windows Server 2003, Windows 2000, and Windows NT, authentication involves comparing the user's security identifier (SID) and password to a list of authorized users on a domain controller.

authoritative restore   Specifies a type of recovery of Active Directory. When an authoritative restore is performed using the Backup Utility and Ntdsutil in the Directory Services Restore Mode, the directory or the specific object(s) in the directory that have been authoritatively restored are replicated to other domain controllers in the forest. See also *non-authoritative restore*.

Automated System Recovery (ASR)   A feature of Windows Server 2003 that allows an administrator to return a failed server to operation efficiently. Using the ASR Wizard of the Backup Utility, you create an ASR set which includes a floppy disk with a catalog of system files, and a comprehensive backup. When a server fails, boot with the Windows Server 2003 CD-ROM and press F2 when prompted to start Automated System Recovery.

Automatic Updates   A client-side component that can be used to keep a system up to date with security rollups, patches, and drivers. Automatic Updates is also the client component of a Software Update Services (SUS) infrastructure, which allows an enterprise to provide centralized and managed updates.

B

Background Intelligent Transfer Service (BITS)   A service used to transfer files between a client and a Hypertext Transfer Protocol (HTTP) server. BITS intelligently uses idle network bandwidth, and will decrease transfer requests when other network traffic increases.

backup domain controller (BDC)   In a Windows NT domain, a computer that stores a backup of the database that contains all the security and account information from the primary domain controller (PDC). The database is regularly and automatically synchronized with the copy on the PDC. A BDC also authenticates logons and can be promoted to a PDC when necessary. In a Windows Server 2003 or Windows 2000 domain, BDCs are not required; all domain controllers are peers, and all can perform maintenance on the directory.

backup media pool   A logical set of backup storage media used by Windows Server 2003 and Windows 2000 Server Backup.

bandwidth   On a network, the transmission capacity of a communications channel stated in megabits per second (Mbps). For example, Ethernet has a bandwidth of 10 Mbps. Fast Ethernet has a bandwidth of 100 Mbps.

basic disk   A physical disk that is configured with partitions. The disk's structure is compatible with previous versions of Windows and with several non-Windows operating systems.

Basic Input/Output System (BIOS)   The program used by a personal computer's microprocessor to start the system and manage data flow between the operating system and the computer's devices, such as its hard disks, CD-ROM, video adapter, keyboard, and mouse.

binding   A software connection between a network card and a network transport protocol such as Transmission Control Protocol/Internet Protocol (TCP/IP).

BOOTP   Used on Transmission Control Protocol/Internet Protocol (TCP/IP) networks to enable a diskless workstation to learn its own IP address, the location of a BOOTP server on the network, and the location of a file to be loaded into memory to boot the machine. This allows a computer to boot without a hard disk or a floppy disk. Stands for "Boot Protocol."

bottleneck   Refers to the point of resource insufficiency when demand for computer system resources and services becomes extreme enough to cause performance degradation.

broadcasting   To send a message to all computers on a network simultaneously. See also *multicasting*.

Browser service   The service that maintains a current list of computers and provides the list to applications when needed. When a user attempts to connect to a resource in the domain, the Browser service is contacted to provide a list of available resources. The lists displayed in My Network Places and Active Directory Users and Computers (among others) are provided by the Browser service. Also called the *Computer Browser service*.

C

Caching   A process used to enhance performance by retaining previously-accessed information in a location that provides faster response than the original location. Hard disk caching is used by the File and Print Sharing for Microsoft Networks service, which stores recently accessed disk information in memory for faster retrieval. The Remote Desktop Connection client can cache previously viewed screen shots from the terminal server on its local hard disk to improve performance of the Remote Desktop Protocol (RDP) connection.

catalog   An index of files in a backup set.

certificate   A credential used to prove the origin, authenticity, and purpose of a public key to the entity that holds the corresponding private key.

certificate authority (CA)   The service that accepts and fulfills certificate requests and revocation requests and that can also manage the policy-directed registration process a user completes to get a certificate.

certificate revocation list (CRL)   A digitally signed list (published by a certificate authority) of certificates that are no longer valid.

child domain   A domain located directly beneath another domain name (which is known as a *parent domain*). For example, Engineering.scribes.com is a child domain of scribes.com, the parent domain. Also called a *subdomain*.

child object   An object inside another object. For example, a file is a child object inside a folder, which is the parent object.

Client Access License (CAL)   The legal right to connect to a service or application. CALs can be configured per server or per device/per user.

cluster   A set of computers joined together in such a way that they behave as a single system. Clustering is used for network load balancing as well as fault tolerance. In data storage, a cluster is the smallest amount of disk space that can be allocated for a file.

Cluster service   The collection of software on each node that manages all cluster-specific activity.

codec   Technology that *com*presses and *de*compresses data, particularly audio or video. Codecs can be implemented in software, hardware, or a combination of both.

common name (CN)   The primary name of an object in a Lightweight Directory Access Protocol (LDAP) directory such as Active Directory. The CN must be unique within the container or organizational unit (OU) in which the object exists.

concurrent   Simultaneous.

console tree   The default left pane in a Microsoft Management Console (MMC) that shows the items contained in a console.

container   An Active Directory object that has attributes and is part of the Active Directory namespace. Unlike other objects, it does not usually represent something concrete. It is a package for a group of objects and other containers.

D

delegate   Assign administrative rights over a portion of the namespace to another user or group.

Device Driver   A program that enables a specific device, such as a modem, network adapter, or printer, to communicate with the operating system. Although a device might be installed on your system, Windows cannot use the device until you have installed and configured the appropriate driver. Device drivers load automatically (for all enabled devices) when a computer is started, and thereafter run transparently.

Device Manager An administrative tool that you can use to administer the devices on your computer. Using Device Manager, you can view and change device properties, update device drivers, configure device settings, and uninstall devices.

digital signature An attribute of a driver, application, or document that identifies the creator of the file. Microsoft's digital signature is included in all Microsoft-supplied drivers, providing assurance as to the stability and compatibility of the drivers with Windows Server 2003 and Windows 2000 Server.

directory service A means of storing directory data and making it available to network users and administrators. For example, Active Directory stores information about user accounts, such as names, passwords, phone numbers, and so on, and enables other authorized users on the same network to access this information.

disk quota A limitation set by an administrator on the amount of disk space available to a user.

distinguished name (DN) In the context of Active Directory, "distinguished" means the qualities that make the name distinct. The DN identifies the domain that holds the object, as well as the complete path through the container hierarchy used to reach the object.

Distributed file system (Dfs) A file management system in which files can be located on separate computers but are presented to users as a single directory tree.

DNS name servers Servers that contain information about part of the Domain Name System (DNS) database. These servers make computer names available to queries for name resolution across the Internet. Also called domain name servers.

domain A group of computers that share a security policy and a user account database. A Windows Server 2003 domain is not the same as an Internet domain. See also *domain name*.

domain controller A server in a domain that accepts account logons and initiates their authentication. In an Active Directory domain, a domain controller controls access to network resources and participates in replication.

domain functional level The level at which an Active Directory domain operates. As functional levels are raised, more features of Active Directory become available. There are four levels: Windows 2000 mixed, Windows 2000 native, Windows Server 2003 interim, and Windows Server 2003.

domain local group A local group used on ACLs only in its own domain. A domain local group can contain users and global groups from any domain in the forest, universal groups, and other domain local groups in its own domain.

domain name In Active Directory, the name given to a collection of networked computers that share a common directory. On the Internet, the unique text name that identifies a specific host. A machine can have more than one domain name, but a given domain name points to only one machine. Domain names are resolved to IP addresses by DNS name servers.

Domain Name System (DNS)   A service on Transmission Control Protocol/Internet Protocol (TCP/IP) networks (including the Internet) that translates domain names into IP addresses. This allows users to employ friendly names like FinanceServer or Adatum.com when querying a remote system, instead of using an IP address such as 192.168.1.10.

domain naming master   The one domain controller assigned to handle the addition or removal of domains in a forest. See also *Operations Master*.

DWORD   A data type consisting of four bytes in hexadecimal.

Dynamic Data Exchange (DDE)   Communication between processes implemented in the Windows family of operating systems. When programs that support DDE are running at the same time, they can exchange data by means of conversations. Conversations are two-way connections between two applications that transmit data alternately.

dynamic disk   A disk that is configured using volumes. Its configuration is stored in the Logical Disk Manager (LDM) database, and is replicated to other dynamic disks attached to the same computer. Dynamic disks are compatible only with Windows Server 2003, Windows XP, and Windows 2000.

Dynamic Host Configuration Protocol (DHCP)   A Transmission Control Protocol/ Internet Protocol (TCP/IP) protocol used to automatically assign IP addresses and configure TCP/IP for network clients.

dynamic-link library (DLL)   A program module that contains executable code and data that can be used by various programs. A program uses the DLL only when the program is active, and the DLL is unloaded when the program closes.

E

effective permissions   The permissions that result from the evaluation of group and user permissions allowed, denied, inherited, and explicitly defined on a resource. The effective permissions determine the actual access for a security principal.

enterprise   Term used to encompass a business's entire operation, including all remote offices and branches.

environment variable   A string of environment information such as a drive, path, or filename associated with a symbolic name. The System option in Control Panel or the Set command from the command prompt can be used to define environment variables.

Ethernet   A local area network (LAN) protocol. Ethernet supports data transfer rates of 10 Mbps and uses a bus topology and thick or thin coaxial, fiberoptic, or twisted-pair cabling. A newer version of Ethernet called Fast Ethernet supports data transfer rates of 100 Mbps, and an even newer version, Gigabit Ethernet, supports data transfer rates of 1000 Mbps.

extended partition   A nonbootable portion of a hard disk that can be subdivided into logical drives. There can be only a single extended partition per hard disk.

Extensible Authentication Protocol (EAP)   An extension to the Point-to-Point Protocol (PPP) that allows the use of arbitrary authentication methods for validating a PPP Connection.

Extensible Markup Language (XML)   An abbreviated version of the Standard Generalized Markup Language (SGML), it allows the flexible development of user-defined document types and provides a non-proprietary, persistent, and verifiable file format for the storage and transmission of text and data both on and off the Web.

external trust   A one-way or two-way trust for providing access to a Windows NT 4 domain or a domain located in another forest that is not joined by a forest trust.

F

failover   An operation that automatically switches to a standby database, server, or network if the primary system fails or is temporarily shut down for servicing. In server clusters, the process of taking resources off one node in a prescribed order and restoring them on another node.

fault tolerance   The ability of a system to ensure data integrity when an unexpected hardware or software failure occurs. Many fault-tolerant computer systems mirror all operations—that is, all operations are done on two or more duplicate systems, so if one fails the other can take over.

File Replication Service (FRS)   The service responsible for ensuring consistency of the SYSVOL folder on domain controllers. FRS will replicate, or copy, any changes made to a domain controller's SYSVOL to all other domain controllers. FRS can also be used to replicate folders in a Distributed File System (Dfs).

File Transfer Protocol (FTP)   A method of transferring one or more files from one computer to another over a network or telephone line. Because FTP has been implemented on a variety of systems, it's a simple way to transfer information between usually incongruent systems such as a PC and a minicomputer.

firewall   A protective filter for messages and logons. An organization connected directly to the Internet uses a firewall to prevent unauthorized access to its network. See also *proxy server*.

folder redirection   An option in Group Policy to place users' special folders, such as My Documents, on a network server.

forest   A group of one or more Active Directory trees that trust each other through two-way transitive trusts. All trees in a forest share a common schema, configuration, and Global Catalog (GC). When a forest contains multiple trees, the trees do not form a contiguous namespace. Unlike trees, a forest does not need a distinct name.

forest trust   A transitive trust used to share resources between forests. Can be one-way or two-way.

fully qualified domain name (FQDN)   A domain name that includes the names of all network domains leading back to the root to clearly indicate a location in the domain namespace tree. An example of an FQDN is *Accts.finance.adatum.com* or *Sales.europe.microsoft.com*.

G

gateway   A device used to connect networks using dissimilar protocols so that information can be passed from one to another.

Global Catalog (GC)   Contains a full replica of all Active Directory objects in its host domain plus a partial replica of all directory objects in every domain in the forest. A GC contains information about all objects in all domains in the forest, so finding information in the directory does not require unnecessary queries across domains. A single query to the GC produces the information about where the object can be found.

global group   A group that can be used in its own domain and in trusting domains. However, it can contain user accounts and other global groups only from its own domain.

globally unique identifier (GUID)   Part of the identifying mechanism generated by Active Directory for each object in the directory. If a user or computer object is renamed or moved to a different name, the security identifier (SID), relative distinguished name (RDN), and distinguished name (DN) will change, but the GUID will remain the same.

GUID partition table (GPT)   The storage location for disk configuration information for disks used in 64-bit versions of Windows.

Group Policy   Setting of rules for computers and users in Windows Server 2003 and Windows 2000 Server. Group Policy is able to store policies for file deployment, application deployment, logon/logoff scripts, startup/shutdown scripts, domain security, Internet Protocol security (IPSec), and so on.

Group Policy Object (GPO)   A collection of policies stored in two locations: a Group Policy container (GPC) and a Group Policy template (GPT). The GPC is an Active Directory object that stores version information, status information, and other policy information (for example, application objects). The GPT is used for file-based data and stores software policy, script, and deployment information. The GPT is located in the system volume folder of the domain controller.

H

headless server   A server without a monitor, keyboard, mouse, or video card, which is administered remotely.

hive   One of five sections of the registry. Each hive is a discrete body of keys, sub-keys, and values that record configuration information for the computer. Each hive is a file that can be moved from one system to another but can be edited only by using the Registry Editor.

host   Any device on the network that uses TCP/IP. A host is also a computer on the Internet you might be able to log on to. You can use FTP to get files from a host computer and use other protocols (such as Telnet) to make use of the host computer.

hosts file   A local ASCII text file that maps host names to IP addresses. Each line represents one host, starting with the IP address, one or more spaces, and then the host's name.

hypertext   A system of writing and displaying text that enables the text to be linked in multiple ways, available at several levels of detail. Hypertext documents can also contain links to related documents, such as those referred to in footnotes.

Hypertext Markup Language (HTML)   A language used for writing pages for use on the Internet or an intranet. HTML allows text to include codes that define fonts, layout, embedded graphics, and hypertext links.

Hypertext Transfer Protocol (HTTP)   The method by which Web pages are transferred over the network.

I

identity store   A database of security identities, or security principals. Active Directory is the identity store for a Windows Server 2003 domain.

inheritance   The process through which permissions are propagated from a parent object to its children. Inheritance is at work in Active Directory and on disk volumes formatted with NTFS.

instance   The most granular level of performance counter. A performance object, such as LogicalDisk, has counters, such as % Free Space. That counter may have instances, representing specific occurrences of that counter, for example the free space on disk volume C:\ and disk volume D:\.

IntelliMirror   A suite of technologies that allows a complete operating environment to follow the user to other computers, as well as offline. Components include the user's profiles, data, and applications.

Internet Authentication Service (IAS)   The Microsoft implementation of Remote Authentication Dial-In User Service (RADIUS), an authentication and accounting system used by many Internet Service Providers (ISPs). When a user connects to an ISP using a username and password, the information is passed to a RADIUS server, which checks that the information is correct, and then authorizes access to the ISP system.

Internet Control Message Protocol (ICMP)   A protocol used to report problems encountered with the delivery of data, such as unreachable hosts or unavailable ports. ICMP is also used to send a request packet to determine whether a host is available. The receiving host sends back a packet if it is available and functioning. See also *ping*.

Internet Printing Protocol (IPP)   A protocol that allows a client to send a job to a printer over the Internet or an intranet. The communication between the client and the printer is encapsulated in HTTP.

Internet Protocol (IP)   The inter-network layer protocol used as a basis of the Internet. IP enables information to be routed from one network to another in packets and then reassembled when they reach their destination.

Internet Protocol version 6 (IPv6)   A new version of Internet Protocol supported in Windows Server 2003. The current version of IP is version 4, also known as IPv4. IPv6, formerly called IP—The Next Generation (IPng), is an evolutionary upgrade and will coexist with version 4 for some time.

Internetwork Packet Exchange/Sequenced Packet Exchange (IPX/SPX)   Transport protocols used in Novell NetWare networks.

interrupt request (IRQ)   One of a set of possible hardware interrupts, identified by a number. The number of the IRQ determines which interrupt handler will be used.

Internet Protocol security (IPSec)   An Internet Engineering Task Force (IETF) standard that provides authentication and encryption over the Internet. IPSec is widely used with virtual private networks (VPNs).

IP address   A 128-bit number, usually represented as a four-part decimal separated by periods (for example, 192.168.1.10) that uniquely identifies a machine on the Internet. Every machine on the Internet has a unique IP address.

K

Kerberos   An identity-based security system developed at the Massachusetts Institute of Technology (MIT) that authenticates users at logon. It works by assigning a unique key, called a *ticket*, to each user who logs on to the network. The ticket is then embedded in messages to identify the sender of the message. The Kerberos security protocol is the primary authentication mechanism in Windows Server 2003 and Windows 2000 Server.

kernel   The part of the executive (or operating system) that manages the processor. The kernel performs thread scheduling and dispatching, interrupt and exception handling, and multiprocessor synchronization.

L

Layer Two Tunneling Protocol (L2TP)   An extension to the Point-to-Point Protocol (PPP) used in conjunction with IPSec to provide secure VPN connections.

license group   A group of users or devices that shares one or more client access licenses (CALs). License groups are administered using the Licensing tool in the Administrative Tools folder.

Lightweight Data Interchange Format (LDIF)   An ASCII file format used to transfer data between Lightweight Directory Access Protocol (LDAP) directory services.

Lightweight Directory Access Protocol (LDAP)   A protocol used to access a directory service. LDAP is a simplified version of the Directory Access Protocol (DAP), which is used to gain access to X.500 directories. LDAP is the primary access protocol for Active Directory.

LISTSERV   A family of programs that manage Internet mailing lists by distributing messages posted to the list, and adding and deleting members automatically.

Lmhosts   An ASCII text file like Hosts but used to associate IP addresses to host names inside a network. To remember which is which, remember Lmhosts as LAN Manager Hosts.

local area network (LAN)   A group of connected computers, usually located close to one another (such as in the same building or the same floor of the building) so that data can be passed among them.

log on   The act of entering into a computer system; for example, "Log on to the network and read your e-mail."

Logical Disk Manager (LDM)   The service responsible for maintaining configuration information for disks that are configured as dynamic disks.

logical printer   The representation of a physical printer. A logical printer is created on a Windows computer and includes the printer driver, printer settings, print defaults, and other configuration information that controls when and how a print job is sent to the printer.

logon script   Typically a batch file set to run when a user logs on or logs off a system. A logon script is used to configure a user's initial environment. A logoff script is used to return a system to some predetermined condition. Either script can be assigned to multiple users individually or through Group Policy.

M

master boot record (MBR)   The first sector on a hard disk where the computer gets its startup information. The MBR contains the partition table for the computer and a small program called the master boot code.

master file table (MFT)   A special system file on an NT file system (NTFS) volume that consists of a database describing every file and subdirectory on the volume.

media access control (MAC) address   A unique 48-bit number assigned to network interface cards by the manufacturer. MAC addresses are used for mapping in TCP/IP network communication.

media pool   A logical collection of removable media sharing the same management policies.

member server   A server that is part of a domain but is not a domain controller. Member servers can be dedicated to managing files or printer services or other functions. A member server does not verify logons or maintain a security database.

mirror   1. Two partitions on two hard disks (also called RAID-1) configured so that each will contain identical data to the other. If one disk fails, the other contains the data and processing can continue. 2. A File Transfer Protocol (FTP) server that provides copies of the same files as another server. Some FTP servers are so popular that other servers have been set up to mirror them and spread the FTP load to more than one site.

MMC (Microsoft Management Console)   A framework for hosting administrative tools called *snap-ins*. A console might contain tools, folders, or other containers, Web pages, and other administrative items. These items are displayed in the left pane of the console, called a console tree. A console has one or more windows that can provide views of the console tree. See also *snap-in*.

multicasting   Simultaneously sending a message to more than one destination on a network. Multicasting is distinguished from broadcasting in that multicasting sends to only selected recipients.

multilink dialing   Combining two or more physical communication links into a single logical link to increase available bandwidth.

multimaster replication   A feature of Active Directory, multimaster replication automatically propagates every object (such as users, groups, computers, domains, organization units, security policies, and so on) created on any domain controller to each of the other participating domain controllers. All domain controllers contain the same directory data, so the domain does not depend on a single source for directory information.

multitasking   Computer legerdemain by which tasks are switched in and out of the processor so quickly that it appears they are all happening at once. The success of a multitasking system depends on how well the various tasks are isolated from one another.

multithreading   The simultaneous processing of several threads inside the same program. Because several threads can be processed in parallel, one thread does not have to finish before another one can start.

N

name resolution   The process of mapping a name to its corresponding IP address.

namespace   A name or group of names defined according to a naming convention; any bounded area in which a given name can be resolved. Active Directory is primarily a namespace, as is any directory service. The Internet uses a hierarchical namespace that partitions names into categories known as top-level domains, such as .com, .edu, and .gov.

native mode   In Windows 2000 domains, the condition of a domain when all domain controllers have been upgraded to Windows 2000 and the administrator has enabled native mode operation. In Windows Server 2003 domains, where there are no Windows 2000 or Windows NT 4 domain controllers, native mode is simply called Windows Server 2003 mode or functional level. See also *domain functional level*.

Net Logon service   A service that accepts logon requests from any client and provides authentication from the Security Accounts Manager (SAM) database of accounts.

NetBIOS Enhanced User Interface (NetBEUI)   A small and fast protocol that requires little memory but can be routed only by using *token ring* routing. Remote locations linked by routers cannot use NetBEUI to communicate.

network   Two or more computers connected for the purpose of sharing resources.

Network Access Server (NAS)   A server that accepts Point-to-Point Protocol connections and places them on the network served by NAS.

Network Address Translation (NAT)   A technology that enables a local-area network (LAN) to use one set of Internet Protocol (IP) addresses for internal traffic and a second set of addresses for external traffic.

Network Load Balancing (NLB)   A technology that allows for efficient utilization of multiple network cards.

Network News Transfer Protocol (NNTP)   A protocol defined for distribution, inquiry, retrieval, and posting of news articles on the Internet.

newsgroup   On the Internet, a distributed bulletin board system about a particular topic. USENET News (also known as Netnews) is a system that distributes thousands of newsgroups to all parts of the Internet.

node   A location on a tree structure with links to one or more items below it. On a local area network (LAN), a device that can communicate with other devices on the network. In clustering, a computer that is a member of a cluster.

non-authoritative restore   When a domain controller's system state is restored, Active Directory is restored. When the domain controller is restarted, the information in the directory, which is only as recent as the date of the backup set, is brought up to date through normal replication processes between the restored domain controller and its replication partners.

NTFS file system (NTFS)   The native file system for Windows Server 2003, Windows 2000, and Windows NT. Supports long filenames, a variety of permissions for sharing files to manage access to files and folders, and a transaction log that allows the completion of any incomplete file-related tasks if the operating system is interrupted.

O

object   A particular set of attributes that represents something concrete, such as a user, a printer, or an application. The attributes hold data describing the thing that is identified by the object. Attributes of a user might include the user's given name, surname, and e-mail address. The classification of the object defines which types of attributes are used. For example, the objects classified as users might allow the use of attribute types like common name, telephone number, and e-mail address, whereas the object class of organization allows for attribute types like organization name and business category. An attribute can take one or more values, depending on its type.

object identifier (OID)   A globally unique identifier (GUID), which is assigned by the Directory System Agent (DSA) when the object is created. The GUID is stored in an attribute, the object GUID, which is part of every object. The object GUID attribute cannot be modified or deleted. When storing a reference to an Active Directory object in an external store (for example, a database), you should use the object GUID because, unlike a name, it will not change.

Operations Master   A domain controller that has been assigned Active Directory operations that are single master—that is, operations that are not permitted to occur at different places in the network at the same time. Some single-master operations include schema modification, domain naming, and the relative identifier (RID) allocator.

organizational unit (OU)   A container object in Active Directory used to separate computers, users, and other resources into logical units. An organizational unit is the smallest entity to which Group Policy can be linked. It is also the smallest scope to which administration authority can be delegated.

P

packet   The basic unit of information sent over a network. Each packet contains the destination address, the sender's address, error-control information, and data. The size and format of a packet depend on the protocol being used.

page   A document, or collection of information, available over the Web. A page can contain text, graphics, video, and sound files. Also can refer to a portion of memory that the virtual memory manager can swap to and from a hard disk.

paging   A virtual memory operation in which pages are transferred from memory to disk when memory becomes full. When a thread accesses a page that's not in memory, a page fault occurs and the memory manager uses page tables to find the page on disk and then loads the page into memory.

PDC Emulator master   The domain controller that services network clients that do not have Active Directory client software installed and replicates changes to any Windows NT backup controllers. The PDC emulator master also handles authentication requests for accounts with recently changed passwords, if the change has not been replicated yet to the entire domain.

Ping   An Internet Protocol (IP) utility that checks to see whether another computer is available and functioning. It sends a short message to which the other computer automatically responds. If the other computer does not respond to the ping, it is often an indication that communications between the two computers cannot be established at the IP level.

point of presence (POP)   A physical site in a geographic area where a network access provider, such as a telecommunications company, has equipment to which users connect. The local telephone company's central office in a particular area is also sometimes referred to as their POP for that area.

Point-to-Point Tunneling Protocol (PPTP)   A protocol that provides router-to-router and host-to-network connections over a telephone line (or a network link that acts like a telephone line). See also *Serial Line Internet Protocol (SLIP)*.

port   From a computer system perspective, a physical connection point on a computer where you can connect devices that pass data into and out of a computer. For example, a printer is typically connected to a parallel port (also called an LPT port), and a modem is typically connected to a serial port (also called a COM port). From a network perspective, a port is a numbered communication channel through which information passes from one computer system to another. Terminal Services traffic, for example, communicates on port 3389.

Post Office Protocol (POP)   A protocol by which a mail server on the Internet lets you access your mail and download it to a computer. Most people refer to this protocol with its version number (POP2, POP3, and so on) to avoid confusing it with points of presence (POPs).

primary domain controller (PDC) In a Windows NT domain, the server that authenticates domain logons and maintains the security policy and master database for a domain. In a Windows 2000 or Windows Server 2003 domain, running in mixed mode, one of the domain controllers in each domain is identified as the PDC emulator master for compatibility with down-level clients and servers.

primary partition A portion of the hard disk that's been marked as a potentially bootable logical drive by an operating system. MS-DOS can support only a single primary partition. Master boot record disks can support four primary partitions. Computers with the Intel Itanium processor use a GUID partition table that supports up to 128 primary partitions.

profile Loaded by the system when a user logs on, the profile defines a user's environment, including network settings, printer connections, desktop settings, and program items.

proxy server A server that receives Web requests from clients, retrieves Web pages, and forwards them back to clients. Proxy servers can dramatically improve performance for groups of users by caching retrieved pages. Proxy servers also provide security by shielding the IP addresses of internal clients from the Internet.

public-key cryptography A method of secure transmission in which two different keys are used—a public key for encrypting data and a private key for decrypting data.

Q

Quality of Service (QoS) A set of standards for assuring the quality of data transmission on a network.

Queue Length A performance counter that measures the number of instructions that are waiting to be processed by an object such as the Processor or Physical Disk. If the Queue Length is greater than 2 or 3 for an extended period of time, it is a reflection that the system's resources are not sufficient for the demands being placed on that system.

R

realm trust Used to connect between a non-Windows Kerberos realm and a Windows Server 2003 domain. Realm trusts can be transitive or non-transitive, one-way, or two-way.

Recovery Console A command-line interface that provides limited access to the system for troubleshooting purposes. The Recovery Console can be launched by booting with the Windows Server 2003 CD-ROM and, when prompted, pressing R for Repair.

redundant array of independent disks (RAID)   A range of disk management and striping techniques to implement fault tolerance.

relative distinguished name (RDN)   Active Directory uses the concept of a relative distinguished name (RDN), which is the part of the distinguished name that is an attribute of the object itself.

relative identifier (RID)   The part of the security identifier (SID) that is unique to each object.

Remote Access Service (RAS)   Allows users to connect from remote locations and access their networks for file and printer sharing and e-mail. The computer initiating the connection is the RAS client; the answering computer is the RAS server.

Remote Assistance   Allows for a novice user to use Windows Messenger to request personal, interactive help from an expert user. When the help request is accepted and the remote session negotiated, the expert is able to view and, if allowed by the novice, control the desktop.

Remote Authentication Dial-In User Service (RADIUS)   A security authentication system used by many Internet service providers (ISPs). A user connects to the ISP and enters a user name and password. This information is verified by a RADIUS server, which then authorizes access to the ISP system.

Remote Desktop for Administration   A technology based on Terminal Services that allows up to two remote connections to a server for remote administration purposes. In Windows 2000, this was known as Terminal Server in Remote Administration mode.

Remote Installation Services (RIS)   Allows clients to boot from a network server and use special preboot diagnostic tools installed on the server to automatically install a client operating system.

Removable Storage Management (RSM) system   A feature of Windows Server 2003 that interfaces with robotic changers and media libraries, enables multiple applications to share local libraries and tape or disk drives, and controls removable media within a single-server system.

replication   On network computers, enables the contents of a directory, designated as an export directory, to be copied to other directories, called import directories. Active Directory changes are replicated to all domain controllers on a regular schedule.

Requests for Comments (RFCs)   An evolving collection of information that details the functions within the TCP/IP family of protocols. Some RFCs are official documents of the Internet Engineering Task Force (IETF), defining the standards of TCP/IP and the Internet, whereas others are simply proposals trying to become standards, and others fall somewhere in between. Some are tutorial in nature, whereas others are quite technical.

roaming user profile   A profile that is stored in a network-accessible location, thus allowing a user to access their desktop, application data, and settings when they log on to any computer. See also *profile*.

router   A network hardware device (or computer-installed software package) that handles the connection between two or more networks. Routers look at the destination addresses of the packets passing through them and decide which route to use to send them.

S

schema   A set of definitions of the object classes and attributes that can be stored in Active Directory. Like other objects in Active Directory, schema objects have an access control list (ACL) to limit alterations to only authorized users.

schema master   The single domain controller assigned to track all updates to a schema within a forest.

scope   In Dynamic Host Configuration Protocol (DHCP), the range of Internet Protocol (IP) addresses available to be leased to DHCP clients by the DHCP service. In groups, scope describes where in the network permissions can be assigned to the group.

Security Accounts Manager (SAM)   A service used at logon that manages user account information, including group membership.

security descriptor   An attribute of an object that contains ownership and access control information.

Security Identifier (SID)   A unique number assigned to every computer, group, and user account on a Windows Server 2003, Windows 2000, or Windows NT network. Internal processes in the operating system refer to an account's SID, rather than a name. A deleted SID is never reused.

security principal   An identity that can be given permission to a resource. A security principal is an object that includes a security identifier (SID) attribute. Windows Server 2003 supports four security principals: users, groups, computers, and the InetOrgPerson object.

Serial Line Internet Protocol (SLIP)   A protocol used to run Internet Protocol (IP) over serial lines or telephone lines using modems. Rapidly being replaced by Point-to-Point Tunneling Protocol (PPTP). SLIP is part of Windows remote access for compatibility with other remote access software.

server   A computer that provides a service to other computers on a network. A file server, for example, provides files to client machines.

Server Message Block (SMB)   An application-layer protocol that allows a client to access files and printers on remote servers. Clients and servers that are configured to support SMB can communicate using SMB over transport- and network-layer protocols, including Transmission Control Protocol (TCP/IP).

Service locator (SRV) resource record   A record in a DNS zone that specifies the computer (by name) that is hosting a particular service. SRV records allow clients to query DNS for services.

shortcut trust   Used to reduce logon times between two domains in a Windows Server 2003 or Windows 2000 forest. This type of trust is transitive and can be one-way or two-way.

Simple Object Access Protocol (SOAP)   An XML/HTTP–based protocol that pro-vides a way for applications to communicate with each other over the Internet, independent of platform.

site   In Active Directory, an area of one or more well-connected subnets. When users log on to a site, clients use Active Directory servers in the same site. See also *well-connected*.

smart card   A credit card–sized device that securely stores user credentials such as pass-words, certificates, public and private keys, and other types of personal information.

snap-in   A tool that can be added to a console supported by the Microsoft Manage-ment Console (MMC). You can add a snap-in extension to extend the function of a snap-in.

socket   An endpoint to a connection. Two sockets form a complete path for a bidi-rectional pipe for incoming and outgoing data between networked computers. The Windows Sockets API is a networking application programming interface (API) for programmers writing for the Windows family of products.

Software Update Services (SUS)   A server-based technology that centralizes the acquisition and approval of security rollups and critical updates for distribution to network clients running the Automatic Updates client.

subnet   The portion of a Transmission Control Protocol/Internet Protocol (TCP/IP) network in which all devices share a common prefix. For example, all devices with an IP address that starts with 198 are on the same subnet. IP networks are divided using a subnet mask.

superscope   A collection of scopes grouped into a single administrative whole. Grouping scopes together into a superscope makes it possible to have more than one logical subnet on a physical subnet.

SystemRoot   The path and folder where the Windows system files are located. The value *%SystemRoot%* can be used in paths to replace the actual location. To iden-tify the SystemRoot folder on a computer, type **%SystemRoot%** at a command prompt.

System State   The collection of critical system files, such as the registry, COM+ registration database, and startup files that must be backed up regularly to provide for system recoverability.

SYSVOL   The folder on a domain controller that contains group policies and logon scripts. SYSVOL is replicated between domain controllers by the file replication service (FRS).

T

Telnet   The protocol and program used to log on from one Internet site to another. The Telnet protocol/program gets you to the logon prompt of another host.

terminal   A device that allows you to send commands to another computer. At a minimum, this usually means a keyboard, a display screen, and some simple circuitry. You will usually use terminal software in a personal computer—the software pretends to be, or emulates, a physical terminal and allows you to type commands to another computer.

Terminal Services   The underlying technology that enables Remote Desktop for Administration, Remote Assistance, and Terminal Server.

thread   An executable entity that belongs to one (and only one) process. In a multitasking environment, a single program can contain several threads, all running at the same time.

token ring   A type of computer network in which the computers connected in a ring. A *token*, which is a special bit pattern, travels around the ring. To communicate to another computer, a computer catches the token, attaches a message to it, and the token continues around the network, dropping off the message at the designated location.

transitive trust   The standard trust between Windows Server 2003 domains in a domain tree or forest. Transitive trusts are always two-way trusts. When a domain joins a domain tree or forest, a transitive trust relationship is established automatically.

Transmission Control Protocol/Internet Protocol (TCP/IP)   A suite of protocols that networks use to communicate with each other on the Internet.

tree   A tree in Active Directory is just an extension of the idea of a directory tree. It's a hierarchy of objects and containers that demonstrates how objects are connected, or the path from one object to another. Endpoints on the tree are usually objects.

trust relationship   A security term meaning that one workstation or server trusts a domain controller to authenticate a user logon on its behalf. It also means a domain controller trusts a domain controller in another domain to authenticate a logon.

U

Uniform Resource Locator (URL)   The standard way to give the address of any resource on the Internet that is part of the Internet. For example, *http://www.adatum.com*. The most common way to use a URL is to enter it into a Web browser.

universal group   A group that can be used anywhere in a domain tree or forest. Members can come from any domain, and rights and permissions can be assigned at any domain. Universal groups are available only when the domain is in native mode.

Universal Naming Convention (UNC)   A PC format for indicating the location of resources on a network. UNC uses the following format: *Server\Shared_ resource_path*. To identify the Example.txt file in the Sample folder on the server named Ample, the UNC would be *Ample\Sample\Example.txt*.

Universal Plug and Play (UPnP)   A standard that enables a network-attached device such as a PC, peripheral, or wireless device to acquire an Internet Protocol (IP) address and then, using Internet and Web protocols such as Hypertext Transfer Protocol (HTTP), to announce its presence and availability on the network.

universal serial bus (USB)   An interface between a computer and add-on devices that enables simplified connection and Plug-and-Play detection of those devices. USB ports support multiple devices per port and usually allow a device to be added to the computer without powering the computer off.

UNIX   An operating system designed to be used by many computer users at the same time (multiuser) with Transmission Control Protocol/Internet Protocol (TCP/IP) built in. A common operating system for servers on the Internet.

user account   A user's access to a network. Each user account has a unique user name and security ID (SID).

User Principal Name (UPN)   An attribute of every user object in Active Directory that uniquely identifies that user in the entire forest. The UPN includes the user logon name and a suffix, such as *lsmithbates@contoso.com*.

user profile   Information about user accounts. See also *profile*.

user right   A logon right or privilege that allows a user to perform a system task, such as logging on locally or restoring files and folders. Because user rights are system-specific, rather than resource-specific, they will override permissions on an individual resource. For example, users with the user right to Backup Files And Folders can back up a file to tape even if they are denied read permission for that file.

V

Virtual Private Network (VPN)   A network constructed by using public wires to connect nodes. VPNs use encryption, such as Internet Protocol security (IPSec), and other security mechanisms to make sure only authorized users can access the network and that the data cannot be intercepted.

Voice over Internet Protocol (VoIP)   A method for using the Internet as a transmission medium for telephone calls.

Volume Shadow Copy Service (VSS)   A service that creates snapshot backups of files, allowing a backup utility to back up the snapshot regardless of whether the original file is locked or open.

W

Web-Based Enterprise Management (WBEM)   A set of management and Internet standard technologies developed to unify the management of enterprise computing environments. Microsoft's implementation of WBEM is the Windows Management Instrumentation.

well-connected   Being fast and reliable for the needs of Active Directory site communication. The definition of "sufficiently fast and reliable" for a particular network depends on the work being done on the specific network.

wide area network (WAN)   Any Internet or network that covers an area larger than a single building or campus.

Windows Internet Name Service (WINS)   A name resolution service that converts computer NetBIOS names to Internet Protocol (IP) addresses in a routed environment.

Windows Management Instrumentation (WMI)   A programming interface that provides access to the hardware, software, and other components of a computer. WMI is the Microsoft implementation of Web-Based Enterprise Management (WBEM) to establish standards of data in Enterprise Management.

Windows Sockets (Winsock)   Winsock is a standard way for Windows-based programs to work with Transmission Control Protocol/Internet Protocol (TCP/IP). You can use Winsock if you use SLIP to connect to the Internet.

workstation   In Windows NT, a computer running the Windows NT Workstation operating system. In a wider context, used to describe any powerful computer optimized for graphics or computer-aided design (CAD) or any of a number of other functions requiring high performance.

X

X.500   A standard for a directory service established by the International Telecommunications Union (ITU). The same standard is also published by the International Standards Organization/International Electro-technical Commission (ISO/IEC). The X.500 standard defines the information model used in the directory service. All information in the directory is stored in entries, each of which belongs to at least one object class. The actual information in an entry is determined by attributes that are contained in that entry.

Z

zone   A part of the Domain Name System (DNS) namespace that consists of a single domain or a domain and subdomains managed as a single, separate entity.

Index

Numbers and Symbols

@ (at) symbol, 7-25

$ (dollar sign), 6-3, 16-9

64-bit editions of Windows Server 2003, 1-6

A

/A switch, 7-26

access control entries (ACEs), 6-13

Access Control List (ACL) editor, 6-13 to 6-15

access control lists (ACLs), 1-13, 6-13, 16-16

  for groups, 4-3

  for printers, 8-17

  for users, 3-3

account lockout policies, 3-40

account properties, 3-8 to 3-9

Account tab, Properties dialog box, 3-7, 3-8 to 3-9

ACLs. *See* access control lists

activation process, 1-8, 1-17 to 1-18

Active Directory, 1-11 to 1-13

  access control lists (ACLs), 1-13

  authentication, 3-3

  command-line tools, 3-17 to 3-23, 3-26, 4-10

  cross-platform issues, 3-41 to 3-42

  domains, trees, and forests, 1-12, 1-22

  finding objects in, 5-14 to 5-15, 5-16

  Group Policy, 1-13

  objects and organizational units (OUs), 1-12

  overview of, 1-11

  printer integration with, 8-21 to 8-24, 8-26

  recommended readings, 1-13

  restoring objects in, 18-10

  security principles, 15-22, 15-24

  System State and, 13-5

  Windows Address Book, 3-41

Active Directory Client, 3-41 to 3-42

Active Directory Domains And Trusts, 15-14, 15-24

Active Directory Installation Wizard, 1-18

Active Directory Service Interfaces (ADSI), 3-41

Active Directory Users and Computers

  computer object creation, 5-4, 5-9

  group account management, 4-9 to 4-12

  moving user objects, 3-10

  server configuration confirmation, 1-19 to 1-20

  user account management, 3-7 to 3-10, 15-21

  user object creation, 3-3 to 3-6

Add Printer Wizard, 8-4 to 8-6, 8-8

Add Or Remove Programs, A-3 to A-4

Add/Remove Windows Components Wizard, A-3

administrative tools, 2-1 to 2-30

  case scenario exercise, 2-25 to 2-26

  exam highlights, 2-27 to 2-30

  key terms, 2-28

  Microsoft Management Console (MMC), 2-3 to 2-11

  overview of, 2-1

  practice exercises, 2-7 to 2-8, 2-16 to 2-17, 2-24

  Remote Assistance, 2-19 to 2-25

  Remote Desktop For Administration, 2-12 to 2-18

  review questions and answers, 2-8, 2-18, 2-24 to 2-25, 2-29 to 2-30

  summary points, 2-8, 2-18, 2-25, 2-27 to 2-28

  Terminal Server Licensing, A-5

  troubleshooting, 2-26

Administrator group, 18-41

Administrator privileges, 14-7

administrators

  delegation by, 1-12 to 1-13

  device installation by, 10-6

  disk quota for, 11-28

  passwords for, 1-17

  remote management by, 17-1

  resource ownership by, 6-24

ADSI (Active Directory Service Interfaces), 3-41

Advanced Digest authentication, 6-43

Advanced Security Settings dialog box, 6-18, 6-19 to 6-20

  Auditing tab, 6-31

  Effective Permissions tab, 6-21 to 6-22

  Owner tab, 6-24

  Permissions tab, 6-26

Advanced Security Settings For Docs dialog box, 6-14 to 6-15

aliases, Windows Management Interface Command-line (WMIC), 12-27

All Devices and System Summary report, 14-21

Allow permissions, 6-20, 6-21

C

how to:

Make sure your training doesn't end here.

Want to help your Windows Server™ 2003 knowledge stay sharp? Subscribe to TechNet, the definitive resource IT professionals rely on to plan, deploy, manage, and support Microsoft® products. Enhance your career development with monthly technology updates direct from the source — all in a portable package of CDs or DVDs that goes wherever the job takes you.

Subscribe now and get 20% off our yearly rate.*

www.microsoft.com/technet/buynow/keeplearning
or call 1-800-344-2121
Use promotion code: T20001

Microsoft **TechNet know how.**

Microsoft

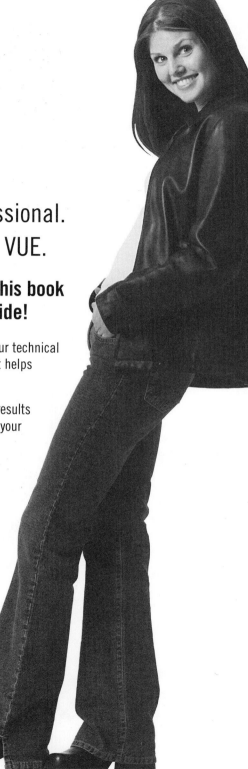

Get a **Free**
e-mail newsletter, updates,
special offers, links to related books,
and more when you

register online!

Register your Microsoft Press® title on our Web site and you'll get a FREE subscription to our e-mail newsletter, *Microsoft Press Book Connections.* You'll find out about newly released and upcoming books and learning tools, online events, software downloads, special offers and coupons for Microsoft Press customers, and information about major Microsoft® product releases. You can also read useful additional information about all the titles we publish, such as detailed book descriptions, tables of contents and indexes, sample chapters, links to related books and book series, author biographies, and reviews by other customers.

Registration is easy. Just visit this Web page and fill in your information:

http://www.microsoft.com/mspress/register

Microsoft®

Proof of Purchase

Use this page as proof of purchase if participating in a promotion or rebate offer on this title. Proof of purchase must be used in conjunction with other proof(s) of payment such as your dated sales receipt—see offer details.

MCSA/MCSE Self-Paced Training Kit (Exam 70-290):
Managing and Maintaining a
Microsoft® Windows Server™ 2003 Environment
0-7356-1437-7

CUSTOMER NAME

Microsoft Press, PO Box 97017, Redmond, WA 98073-9830

Microsoft® Windows® Server 2003
Enterprise Edition 180-Day Evaluation

The software included in this kit is intended for evaluation and deployment planning purposes only. If you plan to install the software on your primary machine, it is recommended that you back up your existing data prior to installation.

System requirements

To use Microsoft Windows Server 2003 Enterprise Edition, you need:

- Computer with 550 MHz or higher processor clock speed recommended; 133 MHz minimum required; Intel Pentium/Celeron family, or AMD K6/Athlon/Duron family, or compatible processor (Windows Server 2003 Enterprise Edition supports up to eight CPUs on one server)
- 256 MB of RAM or higher recommended; 128 MB minimum required (maximum 32 GB of RAM)
- 1.25 to 2 GB of available hard-disk space*
- CD-ROM or DVD-ROM drive
- Super VGA (800 × 600) or higher-resolution monitor recommended; VGA or hardware that supports console redirection required
- Keyboard and Microsoft Mouse or compatible pointing device, or hardware that supports console redirection

Additional items or services required to use certain Windows Server 2003 Enterprise Edition features:

- For Internet access:
  - Some Internet functionality may require Internet access, a Microsoft Passport account, and payment of a separate fee to a service provider; local and/or long-distance telephone toll charges may apply
  - High-speed modem or broadband Internet connection
- For networking:
  - Network adapter appropriate for the type of local-area, wide-area, wireless, or home network to which you wish to connect, and access to an appropriate network infrastructure; access to third-party networks may require additional charges

Note: To ensure that your applications and hardware are Windows Server 2003–ready, be sure to visit **www.microsoft.com/windowsserver2003**.

* Actual requirements will vary based on your system configuration and the applications and features you choose to install. Additional available hard-disk space may be required if you are installing over a network. For more information, please see **www.microsoft.com/windowsserver2003**.

Uninstall instructions

This time-limited release of Microsoft Windows Server 2003 Enterprise Edition will expire 180 days after installation. If you decide to discontinue the use of this software, you will need to reinstall your original operating system. You may need to reformat your drive.

System Requirements

To complete the exercises in Part 1, you need to meet the following minimum system requirements:

- Microsoft Windows Server 2003, Enterprise Edition (A 180-day evaluation edition of Windows Server 2003, Enterprise Edition, is included on the CD-ROM.)

- Microsoft Windows XP Professional—Optional (Not included on the CD-ROM. This software is required in optional hands-on exercises only.)

- Minimum CPU: 133 MHz for x86-based computers and 733 MHz for Itanium-based computers (733 MHz is recommended.)

- Minimum RAM: 128 MB (256 MB is recommended.)

- Disk space for setup: 1.5 GB for x86-based computers and 2.0 GB for Itanium-based computers

- Display monitor capable of 800 x 600 resolution or higher

- CD-ROM drive

- Microsoft Mouse or compatible pointing device

Uninstall Instructions

The time-limited release of Microsoft Windows Server 2003, Enterprise Edition, will expire 180 days after installation. If you decide to discontinue the use of this software, you will need to reinstall your original operating system. You might need to reformat your drive.